I0754504

The English Cart Horse.

The First Prize Animal of the Royal Agricultural Society at Derby, 1843.

EUROPEAN AGRICULTURE

AND

RURAL ECONOMY.

FROM PERSONAL OBSERVATION.

BY

HENRY COLMAN,

HONORARY MEMBER OF THE ROYAL AGRICULTURAL SOCIETY OF ENGLAND, OF THE NATIONAL AGRICULTURAL SOCIETY OF FRANCE, AND OF THE NATIONAL AGRICULTURAL SOCIETY OF THE UNITED STATES.

"For, in all things whatever, the mind is the most valuable and the most important; and in this scale the whole of agriculture is in a natural and just order; the beast is an informing principle to the plough and cart, the laborer is as reason to the beast, and the farmer is as a thinking and presiding principle to the laborer." — BURKE.

VOL. I.

FOURTH EDITION, WITH ADDITIONS.

BOSTON:

PHILLIPS, SAMPSON & COMPANY.

NEW YORK: CHARLES M. SAXTON. PHILADELPHIA: THOMAS, COWPERTHWAIT & CO. BALTIMORE: CUSHING & BROTHER. CHARLESTON, S. C.: M'CARTER & ALLEN. CINCINNATI: H. W. DERBY & CO. BUFFALO: G. H. DERBY & CO.

1851.

STEREOTYPED AT THE
BOSTON TYPE AND STEREOTYPE FOUNDRY.

WRIGHT AND HASTY'S STEAM PRESS.

INDEX,

OR

TABLE OF CONTENTS.

VOL. I.

FIRST REPORT.

SECOND REPORT.

THIRD REPORT.

FOURTH REPORT.

FIFTH REPORT.

STEEL ENGRAVINGS.

WOOD CUTS.

NAMES OF SUBSCRIBERS

TO THE FIRST EDITION.

Name	Place	Copies.
Massachusetts Agricultural Society,	Boston, Mass.	100
New York State Agricultural Society,	Albany, N.Y.	100
Worcester County Agricultural Society,	Worcester, Mass.	40
Philadelphia Agricultural Society,	Philadelphia, Pa.	40
American Institute,	New York, N. Y.	40
Essex County Agricultural Society,	Essex Co., Mass.	25
Massachusetts Horticultural Society,	Boston, Mass.	25
Monroe County Agricultural Society,	Rochester, N. Y.	25
Plymouth Agricultural Society,	Plymouth, Mass.	25
Berkshire County Agricultural Society,	Pittsfield, Mass.	10
Hampshire, Hampden, and Franklin Ag. Society,	Northampton, Mass.	10
Agricultural Society of Newcastle, Delaware,	Wilmington, Del.	10
Livingston County Agricultural Society,	Geneseo, Livingston Co., N. Y.	10
Library of Congress,	Washington, D. C.	10
Rhode Island Society of Domestic Man. and Ag.	Providence, R. I.	5
John P. Cushing,	Watertown, Mass.	100
Hon. T. H. Perkins,	Boston, Mass.	50
Samuel Appleton,	"	25
Joshua Blake,	"	25
Hon. Abbott Lawrence,	"	25
Daniel P. Parker,	"	25
John Bryant,	"	25
William Appleton,	"	25
Henry Codman,	"	25
John A. Lowell,	"	25
Hon. Nathan Appleton,	"	25
B. B. Mussey & Co.	"	13

Name	Place	Copies.
Robert G. Shaw,	Boston, Mass.	12
J. Breck & Co.	"	11
E. B. Swett,	"	10
Hon. William Sturgis,	"	10
Hon. Jonathan Phillips,	"	10
George B. Blake,	"	5
James Jackson, M. D.	"	5
John C. Warren, M. D.	"	5
Hon. Josiah Quincy, Jr.	"	5
Lucius M. Sargent,	"	5
Israel Munson,	"	5
Wm. Prescott, LL. D.	"	5
Hon. Edmund Dwight,	"	5
E. H. Robbins,	"	5
Francis Skinner,	"	5
Henry Oxnard,	"	5
George C. Shattuck, M. D.	"	5
Thomas B. Wales,	"	5
Hon. P. C. Brooks,	"	5
Hon. John Welles,	"	5
Hon. David Sears,	"	5
Hon. Samuel A. Eliot,	"	5
George Parkman, M. D.	"	5
Hon. Martin Brimmer, Mayor of Boston,	"	4
Francis G. Shaw,	"	4
Samuel P. Shaw,	"	4
Hon. John C. Gray,	"	4
Jordan & Wiley,	"	4
Saxton & Kelt,	"	4
Frederic Tudor,	"	3
James Munroe & Co.	"	3
Isaac Winslow,	"	2
J. H. Francis,	"	2
W. D. Ticknor & Co.	"	2
Benjamin Guild,	"	2
Hon. Samuel Dorr,	"	2
R. B. Forbes,	"	2
George B. Emerson,	"	2
William Almy,	"	2
Benjamin T. Reed,	"	2
John Parker,	"	2
George Hayward, M. D.	"	2
John D. Williams,	"	2
Thomas A. Dexter,	"	2
William P. Mason,	"	2
Sidney Bartlett,	"	2

Name	Place	Copies
L. Downer, Jr.	Boston, Mass.	2
Joseph Balch,	"	1
Nathan Rice,	"	1
Benjamin Loring,	"	1
Caleb Eddy,	"	1
Thomas W. Phillips,	"	1
Edward Brooks,	"	1
Hon. Sam'l T. Armstrong, Ex-Lieut. Governor,	"	1
Samuel Greele,	"	1
William Worthington,	"	1
J. W. Paige,	"	1
Andrew T. Hall,	"	1
Benjamin Rich,	"	1
Davis & Blake,	"	1
Edward Renouf,	"	1
John S. Blake,	"	1
Isaac P. Davis,	"	1
Charles H. Mills,	"	1
Frederic H. Bradlee,	"	1
Rev. Samuel Barrett,	"	1
J. M. Smith,	"	1
Jeremiah Mason, LL. D.	"	1
Jacob Bigelow, M. D.	"	1
Benjamin Shurtleff, M. D.	"	1
Rev. Chandler Robbins,	"	1
M. P. Wilder,	"	1
William W. Stone,	"	1
William Lawrence,	"	1
Hon. James M. Robbins	"	1
Hon. William Jackson,	"	1
Ebenezer Wight,	"	1
Robert Waterston,	"	1
Abiel Chandler,	"	1
Edward Tuckerman,	"	1
Charles Sprague,	"	1
John Tappan,	"	1
T. W. Ward,	"	1
Joseph Whitney,	"	1
John Pickering, LL. D.	"	1
Henry W. Dutton,	"	1
James Wentworth,	"	1
Hon. Willard Phillips,	"	1
Samuel E. Sewall,	"	1
P. O. Thacher,	"	1
Benjamin Shurtleff, Jr.	"	1
Ammi C. Lombard,	"	1
Robert G. Shaw, Jr.	"	1
G. H. Shaw,	"	1
William Perkins,	"	1
John Tyler,	"	1
Charles Barnard,	"	1
Joel Nourse,	"	1
William Shimmin,	"	1
Prince Hawes,	"	1
Augustus Aspinwall,	"	1
Ebenezer Francis,	"	1
Hon. B. F. Copeland,	"	1
Isaac Danforth,	"	1
William P. Winchester,	"	1
J. P. Blanchard,	"	1
H. I. Martin, M. D.	"	1
Richard D. Harris,	"	1
Samuel Henshaw,	"	1
Joseph Southwick,	"	1
Rev. John Pierpont,	"	1
George Tyler Bigelow,	"	1
Samuel Frothingham,	"	1
Hon. Thomas Motley,	"	1
Samuel May,	"	1

Name	Place	Copies
George Hallet,	Boston, Mass.	1
Samuel C. Gray,	"	1
Thaddeus Nichols,	"	1
N. G. Snelling,	"	1
Isaac Cook,	"	1
Charles P. Curtis,	"	1
George W. Tyler,	"	1
Fitz Henry Homer,	"	1
Hon. Robert C. Winthrop,	"	1
Hon. Rufus Choate,	"	1
Jonathan French,	"	1
David S. Greenough,	"	1
A. Parris,	"	1
John Deane,	"	1
James L. Baker,	"	1
Rev. Hubbard Winslow,	"	1
C. M. Hovey & Co.	"	1
Hon. Horace Mann,	"	1
Rev. Samuel K. Lothrop,	"	1
Rev. Ezra S. Gannett, D. D.	"	1
Hon. John A. Bolles,	"	1
Hon. Charles F. Adams,	"	1
Prof. George Ticknor,	"	1
Charles T. Jackson, M. D.	"	1
Samuel Hooper,	"	1
Ozias Goodwin,	"	1
Joseph W. Revere,	"	1
Wm. F. Harnden,	"	1
Wm. J. Niles,	"	1
Hon. Jeffrey Richardson,	"	1
Wendell Phillips,	"	1
D. Prouty & Co.	"	1
Rev. C. A. Bartol,	"	1
Alfred A. Andrews,	"	1
Hon. John R. Adan,	"	1
William Stickney,	"	1
Hon. Albert Fearing,	"	1
Cheever Newhall,	"	1
George Newhall,	"	1
Francis C. Lowell,	"	1
Rev. John T. Sargent,	"	1
Charles P. Crane,	"	1
Ebenezer Chadwick,	"	1
P. T. Jackson,	"	1
G. C. Trumbull,	"	1
I. E. Teschemacher,	"	1
George Browne,	"	1
Henry L. Daggett,	"	1
William Foster,	"	1
J. G. Palfrey, LL. D., D. D.	"	1
Ellis Gray Loring,	"	1
Edmund Jackson,	"	1
James Boyd,	"	1
Samuel Cabot,	"	1
J. Baker,	"	1
John Pickens,	"	1
Henry Gassett,	"	1
John Lamson,	"	1
Hon. Stephen Fairbanks,	"	1
Caleb Andrews,	"	1
James Hayward,	"	1
Rev. G. W. Blagden,	"	1
Thomas B. Curtis,	"	1
W. T. Eustis,	"	1
Thomas Lee,	"	1
Rev. Fred. D. Huntington,	"	1
John Collamore,	"	1
Rev. Louis Dwight,	"	1
N. C. Keep, M. D.	"	1
Charles McBurney,	"	1

		Copies.
John Haskins,	Boston, Mass.	1
Otis, Broaders, & Co.	"	1
Edward Chamberlain,	"	1
Richard Soule,	"	1
Henry Burditt,	"	1
William Jennison,	"	1
Miss Clara Crowninshield,	"	1
Henry Jaques,	"	1
Mace Tisdale, Jr.	"	1
Charles C. Mead,	"	1
Wm. R. Deane,	"	1
C. P. Bosson,	"	1
Thomas Davis,	"	1
Dr. A. B. Wheeler,	"	1
Joseph Iasigi,	"	1
A. B. Weston,	"	1
John G. Chandler,	"	1
Henry Rice,	"	1
Hotchkiss & Co.	"	1
Chs. R. Bond & Co.	"	1
Jas. Ellison,	"	1
Hatch & Co.	"	1
Z. Hosmer,	"	1
M. Field Fowler,	"	1
John Preston,	"	1
Wm. A. Davis,	"	1
E. Haskett Derby,	"	1
R. S. Denny,	"	1
Rev. J. I. T. Coolidge,	"	1
Chs. C. Parsons,	"	1
Walter Baker,	"	1
D. P. Simpson,	"	1
E. B. Chase,	"	1
C. M. Hovey,	"	1
Thomas Groom,	"	1
J. S. C. Greene,	"	1
David Paige,	"	1
J. H. Jenks,	"	1
F. J. Oliver,	"	1
S. G. Howe, M. D.,	South Boston, Mass.	1
James Brown,	Watertown, Mass.	1
Wm. A. White,	"	1
Joseph Story, LL. D.,	Cambridge, Mass.	5
Josiah Quincy, LL. D. Pres. of Harv. Univ.	"	5
Rev. Andrews Norton,	"	2
William Pomeroy,	"	2
Prof. James Walker, D. D.	"	1
N. J. Wyeth,	"	1
O. S. Keith,	"	1
Prof. Jared Sparks,	"	1
Rev. R. M. Hodges,	"	1
J. E. Worcester,	"	1
Rev. Wm. Newell,	"	1
Charles C. Little,	"	1
Rev. Daniel Austin,	"	1
Hon. Theodore Lyman,	Brookline, Mass.	5
Benjamin Goddard,	"	2
John Howe,	"	1
Rev. John Pierce, D. D.	"	1
Moses Jones,	"	1
Samuel Philbrick,	"	1
John Hayden,	"	1
Samuel Weld,	Roxbury, Mass.	1
A. D. Williams, Jr.	"	1
Rev. George Putnam,	"	1
Rev. Allen Putnam,	"	1
Hon. Sam'l H. Walley, Jr.	"	1
George R. Russell,	West Roxbury, Mass.	1
Joseph H. Billings,	"	1

		Copies.
Francis Geo. Shaw,	West Roxbury, Mass.	1
Aaron D. Weld,	"	1
George Ripley,	"	1
William Keith,	"	1
John Parkinson,	"	1
Rev. Theodore Parker,	"	1
John Prince,	Jamaica Plains, Roxbury,	1
Francis C. Head,	"	1
Gen. Wm. H. Sumner,	"	1
Charles W. Greene,	"	1
Stephen M. Weld,	"	1
John J. Low,	"	1
M. W. Greene,	"	1
Benjamin D. Emerson,	"	1
John M. Fessenden,	"	1
F. E. Faxon,	"	1
Isaac Parker,	Waltham, Mass.	1
Benj. Wellington,	"	1
Rev. George E. Ellis,	Charlestown, Mass.	2
Samuel Jaques,	"	1
John Fenno,	Chelsea, Mass.	1
Hon. Jno. Quincy Adams, Ex-President of U. S.	Quincy, Mass.	1
Rev. Francis Cunningham,	Milton, Mass.	1
Joseph Rowe,	"	1
Danforth P. Wight, M. D.,	Dedham, Mass.	1
Rev. John White,	"	1
Rev. Alvan Lamson, D. D.	"	1
George Richardson,	Dorchester Mass.	1
Increase S. Smith,	"	1
F. W. Macondray,	"	1
Joseph Peabody,	Salem, Mass.	10
Hon. S. C. Phillips,	"	5
Nathaniel West,	"	5
Hon. Nathaniel Silsbee,	"	3
Francis Peabody,	"	2
Hon. Leverett Saltonstall,	"	2
Wm. H. Neal,	"	2
Hon. D. L. Pickman,	"	2
Robert Stone,	"	2
John H. Silsbee,	"	2
Hon. D. A. White,	"	1
J. H. Ward,	"	1
Asahel Huntington,	"	1
Wm. F. Gardner,	"	1
Jno. Fisk Allen,	"	1
Jno. C. Lee,	"	1
Amos Choate,	"	1
D. A. Neal,	"	1
John G. King,	"	1
Oliver Hubbard, M. D.	"	1
Benjamin Merrill,	"	1
Wm. Deane,	"	1
Charles Saunders,	"	1
David Merritt,	"	1
John Jewett,	"	1
Erastus Ware,	"	1
Nathaniel Frothingham, Jr.	"	1
J. Chadwick,	"	1
John Robinson,	"	1
J. S. Cabot,	"	1
Jno. F. Andrew,	"	1
Nathan Endicott,	"	1
Hon. G. Barstow,	"	1
Joseph S. Leavitt,	"	1
E. Hersey Derby,	"	1
Gideon Tucker,	"	1
D. & J. Pulsifer,	"	1
A. & D. Lord,	"	1
Benjamin F. Browne,	"	1

	Copies.
Robert Brookhouse, Salem, Mass.	1
Rev. Charles W. Upham, "	1
Frederic Howes, "	1
Pickering Dodge, "	1
George Choate, M. D. "	1
Samuel Briggs, "	1
Gen. Wm. Sutton, "	1
Jos. G. Waters, "	1
Hon. Stephen P. Webb, "	1
Charles A. Andrew, "	1
Caleb Foote, "	1
Wm. Ives, "	1
John W. Pepper, "	1
John G. Treadwell, M. D. "	1
Joseph E. Sprague, "	1
N. W. Neal, "	1
Michael Shepard, "	1
James Chamberlain, "	1
B. K. Churchill, "	1
Henry Whipple, "	1
Henry A. Breed, Lynn, Mass.	1
Hon. Marcus Morton, Ex-Gov. of Mass. } Taunton, Mass.	1
Hon. Edward Baylies, "	1
Wm. A. Crocker, "	1
Stephen Salisbury, Worcester, Mass.	2
S. B. Woodward, M. D. "	2
Hon. Levi Lincoln, Ex-Governor of Mass. } "	1
Hon. John Davis, Ex-Governor of Mass. } "	1
Daniel Waldo, "	1
Joseph G. Kendall, "	1
Edwin Conant, "	1
John W. Lincoln, "	1
S. M. Burnside, "	1
William Lincoln, "	1
A. D. Foster, "	1
W. A. Wheeler, "	1
Isaac Davis, "	1
Charles Allen, "	1
Rejoice Newton, "	1
Hon. Pliny Merrick, "	1
L. A. Dowley, "	1
Hon. Thomas Kinnicutt, "	1
Emory Washburn, "	1
H. S. Wheaten, "	1
Oliver Dean, M. D., Framingham, Mass.	1
Wm. A. Lander, Danvers, Mass.	2
Hon. Daniel P. King, "	2
Jno. W. Proctor, "	2
Benjamin Wheeler, "	1
Rev. Andrew Bigelow, "	1
Benjamin Goodridge, "	1
Charles Lawrence, North Danvers, Mass.	1
Enoch Silsby, Bradford, Mass.	1
Rev. Thomas B. Fox, Newburyport, Mass.	1
Edward Tappan, Jr. "	1
Jno. Porter, "	1
Micajah Lunt, "	1
Jeremiah Colman, "	1
Jno. Gray, Jr. "	1
David Wood, "	1
Hon. E. S. Rand, "	1
B. B. Titcomb, "	1
Daniel Adams, 3d, Newbury, Mass.	1
Moses Newell, West Newbury, Mass.	1
Wells Lathrop, South Hadley, Mass.	1
Hon. David Cummins, Springfield, Mass.	2
Hon. W. B. Calhoun, "	1

	Copies
Jas. W. Crooks, Springfield, Mass.	1
Justin Ely, West Springfield, Mass.	1
Hon. Benja. V. French, Braintree, Mass.	1
Hon. James H. Duncan, Haverhill, Mass.	1
Joseph Howe, Methuen, Mass.	1
Hon. D. Webster, LL. D., Marshfield, Mass.	2
Hon. Nath'l B. Borden, Fall River, Mass.	1
A. Robeson, Jr. "	1
Wm. R. Robeson, "	1
John Flint, Andover, Mass.	1
Joseph Kittredge, "	1
Stephen Barker, "	1
Jedediah H. Barker, "	1
Samuel Farrar, "	1
Hon. G. P. Osgood, "	1
J. J. Brown, "	1
Geo. Hodges, North Andover, Mass.	1
N. W. Hazen, South Andover, Mass.	1
D. L. Child, Northampton, Mass.	1
Hon. Joseph Lyman, "	1
Rev. Rufus Ellis, "	1
Edward Clarke, "	1
Wm. Clarke, "	1
Wm. A. Hawley, "	1
Daniel Stebbins, M. D. "	1
Hon. Isaac C. Bates, "	1
Hon. George T. Davis, Greenfield, Mass.	1
Hon. C. K. Grennell, "	1
Alpheus F. Stone, M. D. "	1
Daniel Wells, "	1
Wendell P. Davis, "	1
Henry W. Clapp, "	1
David Willard, "	1
James Deane, M. D. "	1
Rev. Samuel May, Leicester, Mass.	1
W. B. Earle, "	1
J. L. Moffat, Newton, Mass.	1
William Kenrick, "	1
G. B. Slater, Webster, Mass.	1
Hon. F. R. Gourgas, Weston, Mass.	1
Hon. Benjamin Estabrook, Athol, Mass.	1
Hon. Solomon Strong, Leominster, Mass.	1
Hon. George B. Upton, Nantucket, Mass.	1
George W. Wright, "	1
Henry Swift, "	1
Barker Burnell, "	1
John P. Webber, Jr. Beverly, Mass.	1
Rev. C. T. Thayer, "	1
Hon. Jesse Perkins, N. Bridgewater, Mass.	1
Hon. H. W. Cushman, Bernardston, Mass.	1
Horace Williams, Deerfield, Mass.	1
Arthur W. Hoyt, "	1
Theodore G. Huntington, Hadley, Mass.	1
Col. David Wells, Shelburne, Mass.	1
James N. Bates, Barre, Mass.	1
B. D. Whitney, Northboro' Mass.	1
Gen. Josiah Newhall, Lynnfield, Mass.	1
Hiram A. Morse, Holliston, Mass.	1
Wm. R. Rodman, New Bedford, Mass.	1
S. W. Rodman, "	1
Benjamin Rodman, "	1
George Randall, "	1
Charles W. Morgan, "	1
John Henry Clifford, "	1
George Howland, Jr. "	1
William P. Grinnell, "	1
William Rotch, Jr. "	1
William R. Rotch, "	1
Edmund Gardiner, "	1
William C. Whitridge, "	1

	Copies.
William Hathaway, Jr., New Bedford,	1
Matthew Luce, "	1
J. H. W. Page, "	1
John C. Haskell, "	1
Thomas R. Robeson, "	1
Frederic Robeson, "	1
Joseph Ricketson, "	1
Daniel Ricketson, "	1
Abraham Shearman, Jr. "	1
John W. Coggeshall, "	1
Samuel L. Dana, Lowell, Mass.	1
John Avery, "	1
Samuel Lawrence, "	1
William Spencer, "	1
B. F. French, "	1
Alexander Wright, "	1
S. W. Stickney, "	1
John Nesmith, "	1
G. W. Larrabee, "	1
John Clark, "	1
Rev. H. A. Miles, "	1
William Boott, "	1
Daniel Bixby, "	1
Amasa Farrier, Stoneham, Mass.	1
John Abbott, Westford, Mass.	1
H. C. Merriam, North Tewksbury, Mass.	1
N. B. Robbins, Plymouth, Mass.	1
Mrs. Susan Sedgwick, Stockbridge, Mass.	1
Elias M. Stillwell, Lancaster, Mass.	1
Paul Whitin, Whitinsville, Mass.	1
John Page, Hardwick, Mass.	1
S. B. Walcott, Hopkinton, Mass.	1
Johnson Gardner, M. D. Vue de l'Eau, Mass.	1
William Jenkins, Providence, R. I.	5
Alexander Duncan, "	3
Moses B. Ives, "	2
Rev. Samuel Osgood, "	1
Joseph Mauran, M. D. "	1
Samuel B. Wheaton, "	1
William H. Hoppin, "	1
Amory Chapin, "	1
Edward Walcott, "	1
Hartford Tingley, "	1
Robert H. Ives, "	1
Amasa Sprague, "	1
R. W. Greene, "	1
Rev. F. Wayland, D. D., Pres. of Brown Univ. "	1
Henry Anthony, "	1
John I. Stimpson, "	1
Benjamin W. Comstock, "	1
Stephen H. Smith, "	1
Hon. James Fenner, Gov. of Rhode Island, "	1
Owen Mason, "	1
Matthew Watson, "	1
Josiah Chapin, "	1
Adam Anthony, North Providence, R. I.	1
Mark Antony De Wolfe, Bristol, R. I.	1
Wm. Bradford De Wolfe, "	1
Jacob Dunnell, Pawtucket, R. I.	1
James C. Rome, Woonsocket, R. I.	1
Henry Whitney, New Haven, Conn.	25
Prof. B. Silliman, LL. D. "	1
Charles Robinson, "	1
Winthrop Atwill, "	1
Prof. B. Silliman, Jr. "	1
William K. Townsend, "	1

	Copies.
Hon. Wm. H. Boardman, N. Haven, Con.	1
J. T. Norton, Farmington, Conn.	1
Simeon Hart, "	1
E. W. Carrington, "	1
W. Wadsworth, "	1
Timothy Cowles, "	1
S. H. Huntington, Hartford, Conn.	1
Horatio Alden, "	1
A. M. Collins, "	1
D. C. Collins, "	1
Charles F. Pond, "	1
Hon. Jno. M. Niles, "	1
E. W. Bull, "	1
George Tuttle, "	1
T. C. Perkins, "	1
Hon. J. Toucey, "	1
Walter Mitchell, "	1
S. G. Chaffee, "	1
James Dixon, "	1
Isaac Stuart, "	1
George Brimley, "	1
Solomon Porter, "	1
Solomon Olmsted, East Hartford, Conn.	1
Charles H. Olmsted, "	1
S. E. Alden, Enfield, Conn.	1
Henry Thompson, "	1
Levi Durand, Derby, Conn.	1
Charles A. Goodrich, Berlin, Conn.	1
Norman Porter, "	1
Chas. W. Rockwell, Norwich, Conn.	2
Jacob W. Kinney, "	1
Amos H. Hubbard, "	1
William P. Green, "	1
John A. Rockwell, "	1
Ralph H. Avery, "	1
E. B. Brown, Mystic, Conn.	1
Joseph Griswold, Mystic Bridge, Conn.	1
A. Woodward, M. D., Franklin, Conn.	1
H. A. Dyer, Brooklyn, Conn.	1
Wm. G. Johnson, Uncasville, Conn.	1
J. S. Halsey, Preston, Conn.	1
Giles Taintor, Windham, Conn.	1
Hon. C. F. Cleveland, Ex. Gov. of Conn. Hampton, Conn.	1
Daniel Russell, Portland, Conn.	1
Joseph Hall, "	1
Joel Hall, 2d, "	1
E. W. N. Starr, Middletown, Conn.	1
Sam'l D. Hubbard, "	1
Alfred Hubbard, "	1
Charles Hubbard, "	1
Samuel Russell, "	1
Joseph Hurlbut, New London, Conn.	1
Chas. A Lewis, "	1
Wm. P. Cleveland, "	1
Wm. W. Billings, "	1
Lemuel Stoughton, East Windsor, Conn.	1
Azel S. Bowe, "	1
Erastus Ellsworth, "	1
Henry Watson, "	1
Ralph R. Phelps, Manchester, Conn.	1
E. Holcomb, Granby, Conn.	1
D. W. Grant, Bloomfield, Conn.	1
——— Filley, "	1
Hon. G. Merrick, S. Glastenbury, Conn.	1
Daniel Packer, Packersville, Conn.	1
Bethuel Phelps, Warehouse Pt., Conn.	1
Alvah Morrell, "	1
F. W. Wilcox, Salem, Conn.	5
Lucian T. Pearson, Collinsville, Conn.	1

	Copies.
Bangor Mercantile Library Association, Bangor, Me.	1
E. C. Andrews, Portland, Me.	4
H. J. Little, "	2
James Deering, "	1
Joshua Richardson, "	1
William Willis, "	1
Neal Dow, "	1
John Otis, Hallowell, Me.	1
Glazier, Masters, & Smith, "	1
Hon. Reuel Williams, Augusta, Me.	1
Hon. Samuel M. Pond, Bucksport, Me.	1
W. A. Hayes, South Berwick, Me.	1
R. B. Allen, Belfast, Me.	1
E. Seymour, Brattleboro', Vt.	1
John H. Hopkins, Jr., Burlington, Vt.	1
Rev. John Wheeler, D. D. "	1
Prof. Geo. W. Benedict, "	1
E. T. Englesby, "	1
H. B. Stacey, "	1
N. B. Haswell, "	1
Harry Bradley, "	1
Hon. Geo. P. Marsh, "	1
Jno. N. Pomeroy, "	1
Carlos Baxter, "	1
Luther Loomis, "	1
N. A. Tucker, "	1
David Read, "	1
H. S. Morse, Shelburne, Vt.	1
L. S. White, "	1
S. Grout, Bellows Falls, Vt.	1
Charles K. Field, Newfane, Vt.	1
Hon. Wm. Jarvis, Weathersfield, Vt.	1
Jos. P. Fairbanks, St. Johnsbury, Vt.	1
George W. Palmer, Brandon, Vt.	1
Hon. Levi Woodbury, Portsmouth, N. H.	2
Hon. Ichabod Bartlett, "	1
Samuel Lord, "	1
John Rice, "	1
Jno. N. Sherburne, "	1
H. W. Peirce, "	1
Rev. John Parkman, Dover, N. H.	1
R. B. David, Amherst, N. H.	1
Josiah H. Hobbs, Wakefield, N. H.	1
Levi Bartlett, Warner, N. H.	1
W. B. Walton, Schenectady, N. Y.	1
Rev. John Williams, "	1
Jona. Crane, "	1
Prof. Alonzo Potter, D. D. "	1
Prof. J. W. Jackson, "	1
D. & C. H. Tomlinson, "	1
Alexander Walsh, Lansingburgh, N. Y.	1
Maj. Gen. John I. Viele, "	1
Alfred Clarke, East Springfield, N. Y.	1
John B. James, Rhinebeck, N. Y.	1
John H. Walsh, Newburgh, N. Y.	1
Charles Downing, "	1
A. J. Downing, "	1
H. D. Grove, Hoosick, N. Y.	1
Anthony Van Bergen, Coxsackie, N. Y.	1
Tunis J. Van Derveer, Amsterdam, N. Y.	1
Willis Gaylord, Otisco, N. Y.	1
D. D. Campbell, Rotterdam, N. Y.	1
James R. Craig, Niskayuna, N. Y.	1
J. Strachan, Waterford, N. Y.	1
E. D. Windt, Fishkill, Landing, N. Y.	1
Peter C. Dubois, "	1
William S. Ver Planck, "	1
John B. Wakeman, Little Falls, N. Y.	1
John Caldwell, Salisbury, N. Y.	1

	Copies.
Dr. William Bristol, Utica, N. Y.	1
E. W. Teackle, "	1
S. D. Childs, "	1
Capt. William Mervine, "	1
Edmund A. Wetmore, "	1
Theodore P. Ballou, "	1
Hamilton Spencer, "	1
S. V. Aley, "	1
John M. Sherwood, Auburn, N. Y.	5
John B. Dill, "	5
Hon. Wm. H. Seward, Ex-Gov. of New York, "	2
James C. Derby, "	1
E. Rhodes, Manlius, N. Y.	1
L. A. Morrell, Lansing, N. Y.	2
P. V. C. Miller, Shawangunk, N. Y.	1
W. A. S. North, Duanesburgh, N. Y.	1
L. W. Hall & Co., Syracuse, N. Y.	5
P. N. Rust, "	2
Rev. J. P. B. Storer, "	1
Russell Kniffen, Trenton, N. Y.	1
Elon Comstock, Rome, N. Y.	1
Benjamin P. Johnson, "	1
Benjamin N. Huntingdon, "	1
Robert Sandford, Lenox, N. Y.	1
M. R. Patrick, Watertown, N. Y.	1
Henry S. Randall, Cortlandville, N. Y.	1
George I. Pumpelly, Oswego, N. Y.	25
Hon. Gerrit V. Sacket, Seneca Falls, N.Y.	46
William A. Sacket, "	1
Samuel D. Tillman, "	1
C. M. Crittenden, "	1
A. S. & C. W. Dey, "	1
Thomas H. Swaby, "	1
C. L. Hoskins, "	1
William Arnett, "	1
H. C. Silsby, "	1
George B. Daniels, "	1
Edward Myndun, "	1
Thomas C. Magee, Tyre, N. Y.	1
Jason Smith, "	1
David Southwick, "	1
J. W. Bacon, Waterloo, N. Y.	1
Richard P. Hunt, "	1
Aaron D. Lane, "	1
J. Lisk, Junius, N. Y.	1
John Carman, "	1
Orrin Southwick, "	1
William K. Strong, Fayette, N. Y.	7
John Johnstone, "	1
Henry Reeder, Varick, N. Y.	1
John D. Cox, Romulus, N. Y.	1
G. Dickerson, Covert, N. Y.	1
Jeremiah Rappleye, "	1
A. M. Farley, "	1
Abraham Ditmus, "	1
Anson Hopkins, "	1
John L. Eastman, Lodi, N. Y.	1
P. W. Severance, "	1
John De Mott, "	1
Arad Joy, Ovid, N. Y.	1
A. B. Dunlap, "	1
William R. Schuyler, "	1
Andrew Dunlap, Jr. "	1
C. I. Sutton, "	1
Henry Simpson, "	1
Joseph Craven, "	1
Hugh Chapman, "	1
Daniel Scott, "	1

Name	Residence	Copies.
John I. Covert, Ovid, N. Y.		1
Henry M. Ward,	Rochester, N Y.	3
Samuel D. Porter,	"	3
L. B. Langworthy,	"	2
Matthew Brown, M. D.	"	2
C. F. Crossman,	"	1
Henry I. Whitehouse, D. D.	"	1
Ebenezer Watts,	"	1
F. Whittlesey,	"	1
George F. Danforth,	"	1
E. Darwin Smith,	"	1
E. Pomeroy,	"	1
Graham H. Chapin,	"	1
Edward M. Moore, M. D.	"	1
E. G. Munn, M. D.	"	1
W. W. Alcott,	"	1
James H. Watts,	"	1
Nathaniel T. Rochester,	"	1
Henry E. Rochester,	"	1
Thomas H. Rochester,	"	1
William Pitkin,	"	1
Samuel Miller,	"	1
Silas O. Smith,	"	1
Ellwanger & Barry,	"	1
Maltby Strong, M. D.	"	1
Amos Sawyer,	"	1
Strong & Dawson,	"	1
John Hawks,	"	1
John A. Pitts,	"	1
M. B. Bateham,	"	1
Lewis Thies,	"	1
Aristarchus Champion,	"	1
Josiah Snow,	"	1
Alexander Kelsey, M. D.	"	1
John Allen,	"	1
Fletcher M. Haight,	"	1
M. F. Reynolds,	"	1
A. Gardiner,	"	1
I. F. Mack,	"	1
Philander Davis,	"	1
Robert Wilson,	"	1
Moses Chapin,	"	1
Samuel G. Andrews,	"	1
E. F. Smith,	"	1
Hon. Thomas J. Patterson,	"	1
W. E. Lathrop,	"	1
John F. Bush,	"	1
John Haywood,	"	1
Prof. Chester Dewey,	"	1
N. B. Northrop,	"	1
James W. Sawyer,	"	1
John Rolph, M. D.	"	1
James Miller,	"	1
Darius Perrin,	"	1
Rev. Tryon Edwards,	"	1
Charles Hendrix,	"	1
David R. Barton,	"	1
Jasper W. Gilbert,	"	1
Everard Peck,	"	1
Frederick F. Backus, M. D.	"	1
Elias Pond,	"	1
Isaac M. Hall & Co.	"	1
Horatio N. Fenn, M. D.	"	1
Frederick Starr,	"	1
L. A. Ward,	"	1
Stephen Atwater,	"	1
David Hoyt,	"	1
Leander Wetherell,	"	1
George Shelton,	"	1
H. L. Stevens,	"	1

Name	Residence	Copies.
John Briggs,	Rochester, N. Y.	1
R. Haight,	"	1
Hon. Thomas Kempshall,	"	1
Joseph Hall,	"	1
Charles R. Babbett,	"	1
Hiram Smith,	"	1
Lewis Brooks,	"	1
Abelard Reynolds,	"	1
Hiram Blanchard,	"	1
Reuben Sikes,	"	1
George Whitney,	"	1
Samuel B. Chase,	"	1
William W. Mumford,	"	1
W. A. Herrick,	"	1
John Fish,	"	1
John Gifford,	"	1
Aaron Errickson,	"	1
Allen Mason,	"	1
William Kidd,	"	1
William Buell,	"	1
John B. Elwood, M. D.	"	1
Charles O. Shepard,	"	1
Francis Brown,	"	1
Thomas H. Hyatt,	"	1
William Gerry,	"	1
William Brewster,	"	1
School District No. 15,	"	1
William Law,	"	1
Lewis Denny,	"	1
Ephraim Moore,	"	1
Josiah W. Bissell,	"	1
William H. Cheney,	"	1
David Scoville,	"	1
Joseph Strong,	"	1
George A. Wilkins,	"	1
J. George Hodgkins,	"	1
Nathan B. Garnsey,	"	1
Hon. John Greig,	Canandaigua, N. Y.	10
Hon. Francis Granger,	"	5
Henry Howard,	"	2
John Rankin,	"	2
Oliver Phelps,	"	2
Charles B. Meek,	"	2
John A. Granger,	"	2
William R. Macao,	"	1
Henry K. Sanger,	"	1
Hon. Mark H. Sibley,	"	1
Thomas Hall,	"	1
Charles Shepard,	"	1
Francis W. Paul,	"	1
Thaddeus Chapin,	"	1
Walter Hubbell,	"	1
Alvah Worden,	"	1
Charles Seymour,	"	1
Isaac Pierson,	"	1
Thomas H. Johns,	"	1
Samuel H. Andrews,	"	1
Jos. Bull,	"	1
J. L. Stuart Menteath,	"	1
Alexander Murray,	"	1
William Burling,	"	1
Myron H. Clark,	"	1
Henry Howe,	"	1
Jared Wilson,	"	1
Robert Higham,	"	1
G. R. Parbutt,	"	1
R. C. Pratts,	"	1
Oliver Culver, Brighton, N. Y.		1
Daniel P. Bissell, Moscow, N. Y.		1
S. B. Piper, Lewiston, N. Y.		1

Name	Place	Copies.
John S. Shuler, M. D.,	Lockport, N. Y.	1
James D. Shuler,	"	1
Timothy Backus,	"	1
Wm. A. Townsend, M. D.	"	1
F. N. Nelson,	"	1
T. T. Flagler,	"	1
Aaron Parsons,	"	1
Hon. Washington Hunt,	"	1
A. A. Boyce,	"	1
S. Scovill,	"	1
Edward Hardy,	"	1
N. Dayton,	"	1
O. P. Hoag,	"	1
J. Kilbourn,	"	1
Hon. Joel McCollum,	"	1
Trumbull Cary,	Batavia, N. Y.	2
Chipman P. Turner,	"	1
H. M. Soper,	"	1
T. Fitch,	"	1
J. S. Ganson,	"	1
Junius A. Smith,	"	1
Frederick Follett,	"	1
Albert Smith,	"	1
J. L. Brown,	"	1
Ambrose Stevens,	"	1
Rufus Robertson,	"	1
James D. Merrill,	"	1
Shubael Dunham,	"	1
Lucius A. Smith,	"	1
James Brisbane,	"	1
Samuel Heston,	"	1
Byron Densmore,	Kendall, N. Y.	1
Moses B. Gage,	"	1
H. W. Bates,	"	1
N. Whitney,	"	1
Henry Higgins,	"	1
Benjamin Gariss, Jr.,	Bloomfield, N. Y.	1
Ralph Wilcox,	"	1
Rev. Robert W. Hill,	"	1
Frederick F. Rice,	"	1
William H. Hall,	"	1
Myron Adams,	"	1
B. C. Taft,	West Bloomfield, N. Y.	1
Jasper C. Peck,	"	1
John Dickson,	"	1
Joseph Hall,	"	1
O. Thompson,	"	1
William H. Olin,	"	1
Philo Hamlin,	East Bloomfield, N. Y.	1
G. Collins,	"	1
Frederick A. Spalding,	"	1
Sylvanus Emmons,	"	1
M. S. Newton,	Lima, N. Y.	1
M. W. Brown,	"	1
Henry Grout,	"	1
William Arnold, Jr.	"	1
George W. Atwill,	"	1
Erastus Clark,	"	1
Ira Godfrey,	"	1
George E. King,	"	1
Alexander Martin,	"	1
Robert T. Leach,	"	1
Clitus Wolcott,	Oakfield, N. Y.	1
P. M. Smith,	Le Roy, N. Y.	1
Peter Snell,	"	1
John Lent,	"	1
William Sheldon,	"	1
A. B. Murphy,	"	1
J. H. Stanley,	"	1
Ebenezer Mead,	"	1

Name	Place	Copies.
S. W. Olmsted,	Le Roy, N. Y.	1
Noah D. Hart,	"	1
William W. Peck,	"	1
Cyrus Brown,	Pembroke, N. Y.	1
William Cathcart,	"	1
Rawson Harmon, Jr.,	Wheatland, N. Y.	1
John J. Blackmer,	"	1
Joseph Garlinghouse,	Richmond, N. Y.	1
Hiram Pitts,	"	1
J. C. Shelton,	"	1
Elias S. Gilbert,	"	1
Asa Nowlen,	Avon, N. Y.	1
Hon. Henry L. Young,	"	1
Luther Briggs,	Brockport, N. Y.	1
Hon. E. B. Holmes,	"	1
Horace Wheeler,	Honeoye Falls, N. Y.	1
John A. Davis,	"	1
Stephen Barrett,	"	1
John Christopher,	Gates, N. Y.	1
Charles Godfrey,	Geneva, N. Y.	1
Rt. Rev. Wm. H. Delancey,	"	1
Robert C. Nicholas,	"	1
Jos. Fellows,	"	1
James Reese,	"	1
Gideon Lee,	"	1
Thomas D. Burrall,	"	1
Elisha Johnson,	Hornby Lodge, N. Y.	1
George W. Patterson,	Westfield, N. Y.	1
C. Robinson,	Clarendon, N. Y.	1
Charles Lee,	Farmingham, N. Y.	1
Isaac Colvin,	Henrietta, N. Y.	1
M. W. Kirby,	"	1
West Henrietta Library,	"	1
William C. Cornell,	"	1
James S. Wadsworth,	Geneseo, N. Y.	10
W. W. Wadsworth,	"	5
James Wadsworth,	"	5
A. Ayrault,	"	3
E. A. Le Roy,	"	2
Thomas H. Newbold,	"	2
Daniel H. Fitzhugh,	"	1
George T. Olyphant	"	1
C. H. Bryan,	"	1
David Piffard,	"	1
H. A. Wilmerding,	"	1
William H. Spencer,	"	1
Samuel Fitzhugh,	Mount Morris, N. Y.	1
Lucius Southwick,	"	1
J. R. Murray,	"	1
William T. Cuyler,	Cuylerville, N. Y.	1
N. W. Gardner,	Royalton, N. Y.	1
Anson Packard,	Bristol, N. Y.	1
Lewis F. Allen,	Black Rock, N. Y.	1
N. K. Hall,	Buffalo, N. Y.	1
Hon. Millard Fillmore,	"	1
A. & J. McArthur,	"	1
P. Whitney,	Niagara Falls, N. Y.	1
Luther Wilson,	Wilson, N. Y.	1
John Robinson,	Palmyra, N. Y.	1
Micah Brooks,	Brooks Grove, N. Y.	1
Hon. Asher Tyler,	Ellicottville, N. Y	1
Abiel Baldwin,	Clarkson, N. Y.	1
Owen Edmonston,	Phelps, N. Y.	1
E. Willard Frisbie,	"	1
S. Hildreth,	"	1
Carso Crane,	"	1
Elias Cost,	"	1
John Lapham,	Farmington, N. Y.	1
A. Oliver,	Penn Yann, N. Y.	1
Henry Welles,	"	1

	Copies.
S. S. Ellsworth, Penn Yan, N. Y.	1
D. A. Ogden, "	1
George A. Shepard, "	1
H. P. Sartwell, "	1
Abraham Wagener, "	1
Alfred Brown, "	1
Uri Judd, M. D. "	1
Jonathan A. Hall, "	1
Nelson Tunnicliff, "	1
P. S. Oliver, "	1
S. R. Fish, "	1
L. E. Lapham, "	1
John Hatmaker, Milo Centre, N. Y.	1
A. B. Hull, Angelica, N. Y.	1
George Fisher, Oswego, N. Y.	2
George Dean, Westmoreland, N. Y.	1
Henry Chamberlain, York, N. Y.	1
David McDonald, "	1
Edward Brown, "	1
Hollowway Long, "	1
G. O. J. Du Relle, M. D. "	1
Paul Goddard, "	1
John Hollowway, "	1
John P. Root, "	1
F. A. Gray, "	1
Campbell Harris, "	1
J. B. Harris, "	1
James Gilmour, "	1
Roswell Stocking, "	1
Angus McBean, "	1
Artemas Blake, "	1
Reuben Lafever, Reading, N. Y.	1
George Edwards, Bath, N. Y.	1
J. C. Fuller, Skeneateles, N. Y.	1
R. H. Foster, Lyons, N. Y.	1
James Dunn, "	1
John M. Holly, "	1
A. L. Beaumont, "	1
A. Hyde Call, Albion, N. Y.	1
Asa Rowe, Sweden, N. Y.	1
William D. Dickenson, Victor, N. Y.	1
John B. French, "	1
W. W. Marsh, "	1
George J. Jessup, Palmyra, N. Y.	1
Stephen Hyde, "	1
Jonathan Townsend, "	1
Samuel E. Hudson, Newark, N. Y.	1
Cyrus S. Bulton, "	1
Daniel Kenyon, "	1
John B. Crosby, Rush, N. Y.	1
Joseph Sibley, West Rush, N. Y.	1
Daniel H. Burtiss, Chili, N. Y.	1
Elisha Whittlesey, Brooklyn, N. Y.	1
Ledyard Lincklaen, Cazenovia, N. Y.	1
Hon. Leman Gibbs, Livonia, N. Y.	1
Hon. J. Larrowe, Hammondsport, N. Y.	1
Ralph Plumb, Buffalo, N. Y.	1
Abner Bryant, "	1
Albert H. Tracy, "	1
Samuel Hecox, "	1
I. A. Blossom, "	1
Lewis Eaton, "	1
John Craig, Middleport, N. Y.	1
William R. Gwinn, Medina, N. Y.	1
Silas M. Burroughs, "	1
John & George Kirby, "	1
Orrin Scoville, "	1
Hon. R. H Smith, Perry, N. Y.	1
Josiah Andrews, "	1
Mosely Stoddard, "	1

	Copies
Hon. James McNair, Dansville, N. Y.	1
Moses S. Cole, Parma, N. Y.	1
John Sargent, Mendon, N. Y.	1
Joseph Cox, Scottsville, N. Y.	1
Isaac Cox, "	1
W. W. Wilcox, Irondequoit, N. Y.	1
Alexander A. Hooker, "	1
D. H. Buel, Benton Centre, N. Y.	1
Asa Foote, Middlesex, N. Y.	1
Ira Merrill, West Avon, N. Y.	1
Saxton & Miles, New York City,	60
Charles A. Stetson, "	10
D. K. Minor, "	10
J. Prescott Hall, "	5
James G. King, "	5
James Lenox, "	5
I. F. Sheaf, "	5
R. B. Minturn, "	3
Rev. John O. Choules, "	2
S. Verplanck, "	2
Jonathan Goodhue, "	2
M. H. Grinnell, "	2
Robert B. Coleman, "	2
Rev. Joseph Penney, D. D. "	1
George Bird, "	1
H. M. Hayes, "	1
L. N. Fowler, "	1
William H. Aspinwall, "	1
Pelatiah Perit, "	1
Curtis Holmes, "	1
Joseph G. Cogswell, "	1
William Partridge, "	1
David Felt, "	1
William H. Cary, "	1
William Emerson, "	1
Lewis Tappan, "	1
Orsamus Willard, "	1
Rev. Henry W. Bellows, "	1
Greely & McElrath, "	1
Joshua Brookes, "	1
Jacob Harvey, "	1
C. M. Olcott, "	1
A. A. Low, "	1
T. A. Morison, "	1
John Halsey, Jr. "	1
H. T. Chapman, "	1
Isaac H. Frothingham, "	1
Charles G. Carleton, "	1
Lyman Cobb, "	1
J. Atkins, Jr. "	1
Joshua Atkins, "	1
George C. Thorburn, "	1
G. M. Haywood, "	1
Abraham Bell, "	1
J. Smyth Rogers, "	1
George D. H. Gillespie, "	1
J. C. Delano, "	1
John Joyger, "	1
Charles Congdon, "	1
Rollin Sanford, "	1
Jeremiah Brown, "	1
W. J. Cornell, "	1
Isaac R. Cornell, "	1
Charles Richmond, Jr. "	1
N. D. Carlisle, "	1
F. I. Betts, "	1
William T. McCoun, "	1
Daniel Stanton, "	1
Jonathan Sturgis, "	1
Charles M. Leupp, "	1

Name	Place	Copies.
Shepherd Knapp,	New York City,	1
Gilbert K. Lassee,	"	1
Henry Woods,	"	1
F. W. Guiteau,	"	1
E. D. Gillespie,	"	1
Wiley & Putnam,	"	1
J. S. Bartlett,	"	1
Luther Bradish, Ex-Lt. Gov. of N. Y.	New Rochelle, N.Y.	1
Wm. H. Mosely,	Castleton, Staten Island,	1
Nehemiah Denton,	Brooklyn, L. Island,	1
John A. King,	Jamaica, Long Island,	1
E. P. Prentice,	Albany, N. Y.	10
Henry O'Reilly,	"	5
John Townsend,	"	5
A. McIntyre,	"	5
J. McDonald McIntyre,	"	5
Erastus Corning,	"	5
Luther Tucker,	"	5
Hon. Wm. C. Bouck, Gov. of New York,	"	5
Henry L. Webb,	"	2
John N. Wilder,	"	2
Caleb N. Bement,	"	1
Robert E. Temple,	"	1
A. French, Jr.	"	1
James M. French,	"	1
James Kidd,	"	1
Hon. D. D. Barnard,	"	1
James Hall,	"	1
H. Pumpelly,	"	1
Joel Rathbane,	"	1
A. E. Brown,	"	1
James Wilson,	"	1
Prof. E. Emmons,	"	1
Hon. J. Koons,	"	1
C. P. Williams,	"	1
J. P. Beekman, M. D.,	Kinderhook, N. Y.	10
Martin Van Buren, Ex-President of U. S.	Lindenwald, Kinderhook,	1
Joel B. Nott,	Guilderland, N. Y.	2
Edward C. Delavan,	Ballston Centre, N. Y.	1
George Vail,	Troy, N. Y.	1
Hon. John Savage,	Salem, N. Y.	1
Ezra Nye,	Clinton, N. J.	1
Jas. Neilson, M. D.,	New Brunswick, N. J.	1
Hon. John B. Aycrigg,	Pyramus, N. J.	1
J. W. Hayes,	Newark, N. J.	1
John S. Chambers,	Trenton, N. J.	1
Samuel R. Gummere,	"	1
Phil. Dickinson,	"	1
Richard S. Field,	Princeton, N. J.	1
S. A. Hamilton,	"	1
Thomas Hancock,	Burlington, N. J.	1
Ira B. Underhill,	"	1
Bishop G. W. Doane,	"	1
Edward B. Grubb,	"	1
James Thorn,	Bordentown, N. J.	1
Josiah Tatum,	Philadelphia, Pa.	30
Jacob Snider, Jr.	"	5
Peter Hulme,	"	3
Richard Peters,	"	2
James Mease, M. D.	"	1
John Hare Powell,	"	1
William Morrison,	"	1
A. Langdon Elwyn, M. D.	"	1
Henry Zantzinger,	"	1
James Gowen,	"	1
Algernon Sidney Roberts,	"	1
Thomas Nelson,	"	1

Name	Place	Copies
Aaron Clement,	Philadelphia, Pa.	1
E. L. Cary,	"	1
Owen Jones,	"	1
Charles Magargee,	"	1
George W. Carpenter,	"	1
S. Bradford,	"	1
John Farnum,	"	1
George Blight,	"	1
Athenæum,	"	1
Pennsylvania Horticultural Society,	"	1
Frederic Brown,	"	1
Charles Chauncy,	"	1
Dr. George Uhler,	"	1
William G. Malin,	"	1
Charles Roberts,	"	1
Dr. Charles Noble,	"	1
Dr. J. Rhea Barton,	"	1
Samuel Bettle,	"	1
Stephen Colwell,	"	1
Adam Eckfeldt,	"	1
Charles Yarnall,	"	1
William E. Garrett,	"	1
P. A. & S. Small,	York, Pa.	1
John Evans,	"	1
Samuel Willis,	"	1
John Brillinger,	"	1
Samuel Wagner,	"	1
Henry Woods,	Pittsburgh, Pa.	1
John S. Haines,	Germantown, Pa.	3
David George,	Radnor, Pa.	1
Samuel Lippencott,	Mauch Chunck, Pa.	1
Daniel B. Smith,	Haverford, Pa.	1
Ebenezer J. Dickey,	Chester Co., Pa.	1
Pennock Passmore,	Westtown, Pa.	1
Wilson & Heald,	Wilmington, Del.	2
Benjamin Webb,	"	1
James W. Thompson, M. D.	"	1
Samuel Canby,	"	1
Edward Tatnall,	"	1
John Andrews,	"	1
James Webb,	"	1
John Jones,	"	1
Joseph Carr,	"	1
Caleb Churchman,	"	1
Bryan Jackson,	"	1
J. S. H. Boies,	"	1
James T. Bird,	"	1
Henry Dupont,	"	1
Edward C. Hewes,	"	1
Anthony Bidderman,	"	1
C. J. Dupont,	"	1
Chauncy P. Holbomb,	New Castle, Del.	1
John B. Le Fever,	"	1
John W. Andrews,	Stockford, Del.	1
Edward T. Bellah,	Brandywine, Del.	1
William S. Boulden,	Newport, Del.	1
Samuel Sands,	Baltimore, Md.	9
William C. Shaw,	"	1
J. Swan,	"	1
Gideon B. Smith, M. D.	"	1
William Child,	"	1
Henry Mankin,	"	1
William G. Thomas,	"	1
William C Wilson,	"	1
Ramsay McHenry,	"	1
Dr. R. Dorsey,	"	1
W. Cary,	Fork-Meeting Post Office, Md.	1
George Patterson,	Sykesville, Md.	1
Isaac Webster,	Golden Post Office, Md.	1

	Copies.
B. D. Mullikin, Good Luck, Md.	1
Botts & Baldwin, Richmond, Va.	10
Hon. W. C. Rives, Bentivoglio, Va.	2
Thos. S. Pleasants, Bellona Arsenal, Va.	1
Petersburgh Agricultural Society, Petersburgh, Va.	1
Prof. Fred. Hall, M. D., Washington, D. C.	1
Hon. Henry L. Ellsworth, "	1
D. A. Hall, "	1
Rev. S. G. Bulfinch, "	1
K. L. Ellsworth, "	1
J. S. Skinner, "	1
Hon. E. Whittlesey, "	1
J. L. Page, "	1
Darius Lapham, West Liberty, Ohio,	1
Eli Nichols, Lloydsville, Ohio,	1
Charles Anderson, Dayton, Ohio,	1
Cyrus Holt, "	1
Robert W. Steele, "	1
J. W. Smith, Maumee, Ohio,	1
M. L. Sullivant, Columbus, Ohio,	1
J. Sullivant, "	1
Julius Brace, Cincinnati, Ohio,	1
H. Probosco, "	1
Charles Duffield, "	1
Charles Stetson, "	1
E. Brigham, "	1
Ely & Campbell, "	1
Cincinnati Horticultural Society,	1
J. M. Trimble, Hillsboro,' Ohio,	1
Abraham Tappen, Unionville, Ohio,	1
William M. Dawes, Alexandria, Ohio,	1
Hon. John C. Calhoun, Sec'y of State of U. S. Pendleton, S. C.	1
Samuel G. Barker, Charleston, S. C.	3
Sanford W. Barker, M. D. "	1
Charles Alston, "	1
Dr. Benjamin Huger, "	1
C. Cotes, "	1
J. H. Hammond, Silverton, S. C.	1
R. F. W. Allston, Georgetown, S. C.	1
M. C. M. Hammond, Hamburg, S. C.	1
George Cross, Charlotte, S. C.	1
R. F. Davidson, "	1
Dr. William R. Holt, Lexington, N. C.	1
Hon. T. Spalding, Darien, Ga.	1
James H. Couper, "	1
Dr. William C. Daniell, Gainesville, Ga.	1
Dr. Horatio Bowin, Clinton, Ga.	1
Peter L. Clower, "	1
Z. A. Philips, Mount Meigs, Ala.	1
Charles Barrell, Montgomery, Ala.	1
Peter A. Remsen, Mobile, Ala.	1
Benjamin Whitfield, Tuscaloosa, Ala.	1
Samuel D. J. Moore, "	1
Rev. Basil Manly, D. D., Pres. of Univ. of Ala. "	1
Hon. H. W. Collier, "	1
Charles M. Foster, "	1
William D. Marrast, "	1
Hon. J. J. Ormond, "	1
James B. Wallace, "	1
John McCormick, "	1
James M. Crook, Alexandria, Ala.	1
F. W. Siperly, Delavan, W. T.	1
J. S. Rockwell, Milwaukee, W. T.	1
William H. Whiting, Bloomfield, W. T.	2
William Woodbridge, Detroit, Mich.	1
Richard Williams, Jr., & Co. Constantine, Mich.	1
Gen. Calvin Jones, Bolivar, Tenn.	1
Benjamin Litton, Nashville, Tenn.	1
M. Benjamin, Wilmington, Ill.	1
Dendy Sharwood, Ottawa, Ill.	1
J. H. Sherman, Carthage, Ill.	1
Cyrus Bryant, Princeton, Ill.	1
Thomas Affleck, Ingleside, Miss.	1
Dr. M. W. Philips, Edwards Dépôt, Miss.	1
James Brown, Livingston, Miss.	1
Moses Liddell, Woodville, Miss.	1
John R. Liddell, Trinity P. O., La.	1
Dr. John Calderwood, Monroe, La.	1
Branch Tanner, Cheneyville, La.	1
James L. Peacock, Belgrade Plantation, near Clinton, La.	1
George Truit, Kinniconnick, Ky.	1
F. Coolwine, Burlington, Iowa,	1
Robert W. Williams, Tallahassee, Fa.	1
Richard Mendenhall, Richmond, Ind.	1
—— Beadle, M. D., St. Catharine's, U. C.	1
Adam Ferguson, Woodhill, Waterdown, U. C.	1
W. Young, Halifax, N. S.	1
Thomas G. Taylor, Pictou, N. S.	1

☞ *List of English Subscribers on the next page.*

GREAT BRITAIN.

Name	Residence	Copies.
Lady Noel Byron,	Esher,	6
Sir Charles Morgan,	Tredegar, Wales,	6
John Courage, Esq.	Dulwich,	6
Earl of Hardwicke,	Wimpole,	5
Sir George Cayley,	London,	2
Sir John Easthope, M. P.	"	2
E. W. W. Pendarves, M. P.	Pendarves, Cornwall,	2
Henry Morton, Esq.	Chester Le Street,	2
Countess of Hardwicke,	Wimpole,	1
Lord Portman,	London,	1
Lord Ashburton,	"	1
Lord Hatherton,	Teddesley,	1
Rev. Dean of Westminster, Dr. Buckland,	London,	1
Miss Montgomery,	"	1
Thomas Spencer, Esq.	Bransby, Lincolnshire,	1
John Giblett, Esq.	Barnsbury Villas, London,	1
R. J. Thompson, Esq.	Yorkshire,	1
Jonas Webb, Esq.	Babraham,	1
Joseph Joy, Esq.	Boston,	1
Messrs. Drummond & Co.	Stirling, Scotland,	1
Messrs. Lawson & Co.	Edinburgh, "	1

PREFACE.

I HAVE the honor of laying before the public my First Report on European Agriculture and Rural Economy. It is to a considerable degree, miscellaneous, and not so full of that practical information and detail which I design to give hereafter. I trust, however, it will not be found deficient in practical value. Many persons may think that I should particularly point out what is to be learnt from European agriculture; but I understand it to be my province to give an honest account of what I see, premising that there is nothing to be seen from which something may not be learnt, and that it is for others, and not for me, to say what they will learn from that which is placed before them. Where we find ourselves inferior to others, it may be desirable to ascertain how we may reach the excellence to which they have attained; and where the advantage is obviously upon our side, it may be a subject of honest congratulation. In circumstances, even the most different, a sagacious mind will gather instruction from contrast as well as from analogy; and the success of any man, in any trade, pursuit, manufacture, or art, is in itself a powerful stimulus to others to exertion; and, therefore, an instrument of excellence in any and in every other art or pursuit. I know no better way than to record my impressions of what comes under my notice in the field, which I have undertaken to explore, as faithfully as I can, and with as much detail as seems expedient; and to do my best, that every one who reads my pages with candor, will not close the book without finding something agreeable and instructive, something for improvement in the important art to which my labors will be particularly devoted, and something to make him wiser, better, or happier. These latter are the proper ends of knowledge and of life; and this honest aim will in itself sanctify and elevate the humblest efforts.

The objects of my inquiry are, of course, various and extensive, and embrace every thing connected with the cultivation of the earth, the improvements which are now going on in agriculture, and every branch of husbandry and rural and domestic economy.

Among these topics will, of course, be comprehended —

The Soils, and especially in their relation to different crops.

Manures and their application.

The Implements of Husbandry, and various Machines for facilitating and abridging the labors of the Farm.

The different great operations of Agriculture, such as Ploughing, Sowing, Cultivating and Cleaning, Harvesting and preparing the Crops for use or market, with the general application of the Produce of a Farm.

Draining and Irrigation.
Enclosing and Fencing.
Redeeming Moor and Heath Land.
Warping and Diking.
The Crops grown — the Grasses, the Cereal Grains, and Esculent Roots for the food of man or beast, and plants cultivated for clothing, building, and fuel.
Live Stock of every description — Cattle, Horses, Sheep, Swine, Poultry; and their different breeds and classes.
The breeding, rearing, and fattening of Live Stock.
The Dairy.
The cultivation of Silk, Flax, Hemp, Hops, Madder, Woad, Mustard, Chiccory, Olives, Grapes, Figs; the production of Wool and Honey; of Wine, Oil, and Sugar; and various other crops and products which may come under my notice, and the production and growth of which may be possible and useful in any part of the United States.
Markets and Fairs; Farming Accounts.
Agricultural Labor; wages, condition, and service.
The Management of particular Farms — arable, dairy, stock, and wool farms.
Experimental Farms.
Veterinary Establishments.
Agricultural Societies, Museums, and Shows.
Agricultural Schools, Education, and Literature.
The Condition of the Rural Population.
Rural Life — Morals, Manners, and Customs.

These are among the topics which will claim my attention, and upon which, in the course of my tour, I hope to collect and to communicate much useful information. The field, I am aware, is a wide one, and no unaided individual could, under any circumstances, give a full and entire view of these various subjects, so as to satisfy every inquiry; but I will do what I can to glean that which is most valuable, and to direct to more full sources of information the inquiries of those to whom further information may be desirable.

I do not know in what place, rather than here, I can better acknowledge the kindness and hospitality which I have received from gentlemen with whom it has been my happiness to become acquainted; add to this the utmost readiness and courtesy in rendering every assistance in their power to my inquiries. The kindness is sensibly appreciated; and these acknowledgments are due to many noblemen of the highest rank in the empire; and to many gentlemen of more humble condition, who, if they have not the nobility of rank, have even a higher patent — one without which the most brilliant insignia of external distinction become dim — the nobility of intelligence, wisdom, and most active and extensive usefulness. I should be glad here, if it were proper, to illuminate my page with the names of many distinguished individuals, of whose courtesy and kindness the recollection will not fail, while any record remains legible on the tablet of my heart; but this would be contrary to a rule which, with me, has always been absolute in cases of this nature, lest I should be thought even to approach a violation of the confidence of social life. One may wound almost as much by public praise as by censure that delicacy of sentiment which, satisfied with doing good, shrinks from notoriety and ostentation. Nor would I in any way impair or hinder that frankness of communication and manners which constitutes the charm of social intercourse. This would be sure to be checked if we knew that a reporter for the public were constantly present; and, if the humble expression be allowed, it would hide itself in its burrow, as sure as it perceived that one of the feline or the canine race was always at the mouth of its hole waiting its coming out.

My agricultural tour, therefore, must not be expected to have much of personal and private narrative; though I am aware, that, from this very circumstance, it may lack much of that interest which, with a large class of readers, it might otherwise possess. However strong, on these accounts, the temptation, I shall certainly *not* report many interesting conversations to which I have been a party; nor describe the eminent or the more humble individuals to whom I have had the honor of an introduction; nor, after the example of some tourists, tell of the private visits which I have made, and the charming families whose honored guest I have been; nor speak of the "accomplished men, and the delightful women, and the beautiful daughters, and the promising sons," in the houses where, to use the only term by which true English hospitality may be expressed, I have been *domiciliated*, and to do only justice to many of whom, and to a condition of society in the highest degree polished and improved, would not be for me an easy task. I say nothing of the impropriety of stealing for the public the likeness of a friend, without his consent, and without allowing him to choose his position, his dress, or his painter; for, as an agriculturist, this is not the species of live stock which I came to examine, and in which those for whose benefit I travel would be most interested. Yet, while I shall scrupulously avoid all personalities whatever of this description, I shall feel at perfect liberty to give, as far as I am able, a true picture of rural life in England, and of the condition and habits of the rural population; and if, in doing this, I shall, in any ca e, be thought to go beyond the strict line of what may be called the practical and the useful in an agricultural tour, with the candid I shall find an apology in my desire to alleviate the dulness of dry details, by occasional topics more light and imaginative. It is not unreasonable for me to wish to attract to my pages, I hope for their benefit, a class of readers who would be certain to be repelled from a mere skeleton, however accurately and beautifully all the bones were put together, and all the joints and articulations displayed; but who would be delighted to contemplate the same subject covered with flesh, instinct with life, radiant with health, and clothed in the habiliments of elegance and fashion. Every one knows the variety of tastes every where existing. He who caters for the public will be, of course, anxious that each guest at the table should find something which he likes. Though, perhaps, a large portion of mankind might be best satisfied with plain boiled and roast, and content to eat their dinner out of pewter plates, and from a plain and coarse oaken table without a cloth, such as I have seen at Haddon Hall, nearly two centuries old; there are not a few who would prefer the refinements of modern life, a porcelain dish to a wooden trencher, a silver fork to the natural use of the ten digits, the French *entrées* to the more substantial covers; and who, little as it may contribute to the actual support of life, find as high a pleasure in the fittings-out of the banquet, its arrangements, neatness, order, beauty, and in the splendid pyramid of flowers which often crowns its centre, as in any mere gratification of the appetite. Under any circumstances it would be idle in me to presume to spread an elegant and splendid table for my guests; but while I shall be anxious to furnish that which is substantial and nutritious, I shall be equally desirous that at least the dessert shall be made up of the best fruits which I can gather. Though I am not able to present them in vases of gold and silver, or of diamond glass, or Sevrés or porcelain china; yet if the peaches and the strawberries should be seen blushing under a few of the leaves of their own foliage, or if a simple bouquet of the flowers of the sweetbrier and violet, or a handful of the half-unfolded buds of the moss-rose, the queen of flowers, should be sought to relieve the monotony of the table, I hope that my taste will not be condemned, but will be regarded only as in conformity to the rule sanctioned by a high antiquity, that of mingling "the agreeable with the useful."

There are other grounds upon which I claim the indulgence of my readers. We have often heard of the vexation of an artist, who is compelled to paint a picture to order; and, willing or unwilling, well or ill, under the most brilliant spell of poetical excitement, or in an hour of the most sleepy or prosy dulness, he must work at it, and have it completed, and varnished, and framed, and sent home to be criticized, by a certain time. To a degree, similar objections lie to all forced intellectual labor; and in many such cases, a powerfully excited desire to do well, and not to disappoint the wishes and expectations of kind friends, presents, in itself, no small hinderance to success, and, strange as it may seem, is sometimes the cause of failure. It must be obvious to any one what disadvantages I labor under in being obliged to give my reports before I have completed my tour. In this case, I yield of necessity to an impatience of curiosity on the part of my friends, which I would neither condemn nor blame, but which certainly presents a strong claim upon their candor.

I am painfully aware of the greatness of the undertaking, and the sacrifices which, at my time of life, it demands of me, and the difficulties in the case of meeting even my own wishes. But the object being exclusively a public object, and one in respect to the utility of which, however imperfectly accomplished, there can be no dissent, I look confidently for the aid and encouragement, so essential to my success, of the intelligent, disinterested, and public-spirited, among the friends of agricultural improvement. Such aid in any form will be gratefully appreciated.

In whatever light I regard the subject of the improvement of agriculture, my sense of its importance is continually strengthened. In its social, political, and moral bearings — in its connection with the subsistence of mankind, with their general comfort, and with the progress of civilization — no subject, purely secular, more demands the attention of the political economist, the statesman, and the philanthropist. If the familiar experience of half a century in all the labors and details of practical husbandry, a considerable acquaintaince with the agriculture of the United States, and an enthusiastic attachment to rural life and rural pursuits, give me any power to be useful in the advancement of this great cause, that power shall be exerted. I do not know to what object the short remainder of my life can be more rationally devoted.

HENRY COLMAN.

2 Spring Gardens, Charing Cross,
London, 1844.

PREFACE

TO THE SECOND EDITION.

In presenting a second edition of European Agriculture to the public, I take the opportunity to acknowledge gratefully the patronage of my subscribers, and the favorable appreciation of my labors by a liberal and enlightened community.

I hope that the work will do some good by the information which it communicates; and I am happy in the assurance that it has already done, and will continue to do, much good in calling the attention of the public to this great and important subject, this most essential interest of the community. Every, even the most humble, effort to enlighten the public mind on this subject, to interest, if I may so say, their affections in it, and to elevate and ennoble it in the public estimation, is so far a contribution to the best interests of society.

At the present time the world seems mad with the thirst for gold. The unexpected discovery of a large deposit of this precious metal in California seems at once to have carried this passion up to the boiling point, and brilliant dreams of wealth acquired without toil, and gold to be gathered in handfuls at pleasure, seem to have startled many sober minds, and to have moved them from their propriety, and to be drawing them away from the calm pursuits of honest industry and the certain gains of habitual diligence and wholesome economy, into a race to be suddenly rich, in which the competition will be crowded, the dangers to health and life many and great, and, under the best circumstances, the results to possession, enjoyment, and morals altogether uncertain. I firmly believe that, with no more expense than it now demands to reach this golden paradise, with no more toil in tilling the earth, with entire security and peace of mind, and with no danger to health or morals, many a young man might establish himself far nearer home in our beneficent country, on a small farm; and, in the wholesome pursuits of rural industry, would, in the end, become a far richer and happier man than nine out of ten of those who, under a burning sun, in a climate full of danger to life, among a population of the most heterogeneous character, and all burning with unmixed avarice, and entirely out of the protection of law, with the hardest toil, and amidst the most severe privations, seek for riches and happiness in the sands of San Francisco.

My work will be found in this edition considerably enlarged, and all pains have been taken to insure accuracy. There is some miscellaneous matter, but not wholly irrelevant to the subject; and as it has been my constant aim to make it so, the work will, I trust, be found of an eminently practical character; and as full and as exact details are given in regard to every agricultural operation or subject as the nature of the case seemed to demand.

In regard to the plates of animals some distrust has been expressed as to their accuracy. This, in a measure, grows out of an incredulity as to the extraordinary improvements which the British farmers have made in this matter. I have only to say that the drawings have been made from life by some of the best artists which the country affords; that every pains has been taken to render them correct likenesses; that I have seen several of the animals of which cuts are given, and, as far as my judgment goes, know them to be exact; and in respect to those cases in which I have not seen the originals, having seen many animals of the same breeds and families, have not a doubt of their accuracy.

Boston, Mass. *Feb.* 1849.

EUROPEAN AGRICULTURE.

FIRST REPORT.

I. — GENERAL FACTS AND CONSIDERATIONS.

Most of my friends are aware of the circumstances which have induced me to undertake an agricultural tour in Europe. The enterprise was suggested among some friends, at the show of the New York State Agricultural Society, in Albany, in September, 1842; and, upon proposals being issued for its accomplishment, the project met with so much favor as to warrant my sailing for England, in April, 1843.

Ploughing the sea is somewhat different from ploughing the land; but under an experienced pilot, and with favorable winds, we made a broad, a deep, and a comparatively straight furrow, throwing off continually floods of jewels from the mould-board; and in the short space of seventeen days, completed the brilliant line, and unyoked the team in the harbor of Liverpool. Here, for the first time, I set foot in England, the green isle in the ocean, the sight of which had been so long the object of my desire; the brilliant centre of so many youthful imaginations, the home of my fathers, and the advance-guard — if so it may be proper to speak — among the nations of the civilized world in the march of human improvement, in learning and civilization, in science and the useful arts, and in all the elements of social greatness and prosperity.

It would be impossible to describe my emotions on that occasion. If small things may be compared to great, then, if it were not — as with the bold and adventurous Genoese — the discovery of a new and unknown country, yet it was to me an unexplored country; and it was, in truth, almost the first time I had realized the greatness of the enterprise upon which I had embarked.

Some persons may smile at the application of such language to a mere agricultural tour. Things are great or small by comparison; and that work may be considered great to any one, which, in its proper performance, demands the exertion of all the talents which he may possess. I cannot but look upon an agricultural tour in Europe, in the present condition of the art and science, — for in both lights it has now come to be viewed, — as most important; combining a variety of inquiries and observations which would severely tax the highest powers that might be applied to this object. It is for me to assume only the humble office of a pioneer in this great work; and if I can be so happy as to render some essential service to my country, in facilitating the labors of those who shall come after me, in effecting a small clearing that others may more easily bring the field into a state of complete and productive cultivation, I shall be consoled under all the imperfections of my attempt with the conviction that I have not labored in vain.

I cannot help feeling that there is a high responsibleness attached to my undertaking — a responsibleness not merely to the kindness of friends, on both sides of the water, who with an extraordinary liberality and good will have favored the enterprise, but to the great cause itself of agricultural improvement; that the information collected and given might be drawn from authentic sources, selected and combined with judgment, and presented in a condensed, compact, and practical form.

A person who has had no experience in such a matter, who is not accustomed to such investigations, can form no just idea of the difficulties of accomplishing in this case what one would desire to do; and of the impediments, and, I regret to add, in many cases the vexations and disappointments, which, in its prosecution, he will be compelled to meet with. Before I left home, a friend — in many respects highly intelligent, and eminent for his sound judgment, and, withal, a liberal and devoted friend of an improved agriculture — said to me, "that there was nothing to be learned in England; that he himself had travelled much in England, by post, and had occasionally alighted and talked with laborers, whom he saw in the fields by the road-side, but he had learned nothing from them." And another friend, whose eminent position in the community should have saved him from an immature judgment, expressed an opinion that "the climate of England was so different from the United States, and the cost of labor in England was so much less than in America, that the agricultural practice and experience of Great Britain could have no application to the United States." Now, entertaining as I do the high respect for these two gentlemen to which their intelligence and position in society entitle them, I have come, not without some reluctance, to an entirely opposite conclusion — a conclusion which my own observation, in the course of my progress, has daily more and more confirmed.

There is a great deal to be learned in England, which can scarcely be said to be known in the United States. There is a great deal of agricultural practice in England, which may with advantage be transplanted to America; and although, as is most obvious, every agricultural operation must be modified by the climate of a country and various local circumstances, yet, in respect to many facts of a practical nature, the knowledge that under any circumstances a thing is practicable is often of great importance, as it excites to inquiries and experiments which may evolve many other valuable facts; and inquiries and experiments will often suggest modes of operation by which even the difficulties of climate and situation may be counteracted or overcome. Plants and animals are often naturalized to localities very different and distant from their native homes. If the common history of the plant be true, one of the most valuable and nutritious of esculent vegetables, the potato, is an example of a removal from a warm to a temperate, and even a cold climate; and of a conversion from a root very inferior in size and quality, to a vegetable most productive in its yield, universally relished, in the highest degree farinaceous and nutritious, and, under the best cultivation, perhaps yielding per acre as much food for man or beast as any other plant which could occupy the ground. Then, again, to suppose that a knowledge of the agriculture of a country is to be acquired by a transit through it on the box-seat of a coach, or in a railroad carriage, or by a casual conversation with laborers by the road-side, who, especially in England, where labor is so much subdivided that the knowledge of a man in that condition of life seldom extends beyond the particular service to which he has been trained, is a judgment of which, upon further consideration, an enlarged mind would not be tenacious. In respect to any other matter of importance, it would not be the most likely way of obtaining full and authentic information. Why should it be deemed so in respect to agriculture? This art, in its improved condition, combines so many arts and such various subjects of inquiry and observation, that a close scrutiny and long-continued inquiry are as indispensable to a thorough knowledge of it as they are in respect to any of the branches of commerce or manufactures.

After travelling many hundreds of miles over this rich and highly-cultivated country, and seeing many of the landlords, and tenants, and laborers, in their own domiciles and homesteads, in their stables and fields, and enjoying the most free communications, I feel that I have, as it were, only begun to see what is to be seen, and to learn what is to be known, and that every step of my progress is developing new and valuable objects of inquiry and remark.

II. — PARTICULAR OBJECTS OF INQUIRY.

What should an agricultural tour embrace? To this the proper answer is, Every thing connected with the cultivation of the earth, the production of food for man and beast, and the condition of those to whom agriculture is a business and profession. In my preface I have enumerated generally the objects of inquiry. The various operations of husbandry, the implements by which these operations are carried on and facilitated, the plants cultivated, and the live stock produced and maintained, constitute the principal subjects to be observed and treated; but the subdivisions into which these great topics spread themselves are very numerous, and it is as important to consider them in detail as in the gross. It may be expected by some persons that I should merely point out in what respects foreign differs from American agriculture; or, otherwise, that I should only suggest for adoption in the United States such methods of culture as, in my opinion, would constitute an improvement upon American agriculture. This would be assuming too great a responsibility, and would display a confidence in my own judgment with which I would not willingly be chargeable. I design to give, as well as I am able, a full account of subjects which come under my immediate observation. I shall not hesitate to pronounce my opinion whenever I deem it proper so to do, because intelligent minds for whom I write will be no further influenced by it than as it appears reasonable; but I shall, in all cases, endeavor so fully to state any matter in discussion, that they will have the materials before them for making up their own judgment, and with that I shall not any further willingly interfere. Even agriculture, like every other subject not susceptible of mathematical demonstration, is not without its disputed and disputable points, into which, of course, something of the heat of passion may at times infuse itself. Political agriculture is full of such topics, and will be cautiously avoided by me so far as in any way it presents itself as matter of party contention. The different breeds of live stock, neat cattle, and sheep, have each their partisans; often influenced solely by their own honest preferences and convictions, founded — as they at least persuade themselves — upon experience and observation; and in some cases, it will not be denied, by private interests — a stimulus which is too seldom absent from most of the disputes and contentions in life. Now, if a man should pronounce a preference over all others for the short-horns, he must expect to be tossed by the long-horns; if he sides with the Herefords, the Durhams will shake their heads at him; and if he advocates, above all others, the claims of the polled Scotch, the Angus, or the Fife cattle, the West Highlanders will be down upon him with a vengeance. So it is with the South Downs and the Leicesters, — meek, quiet, placable animals themselves, — who may be seen feeding peaceably together out of the same manger, and lying down without passion in the same pen; but not so their owners and breeders. A spirit of rivalry pervades every department of life. Under due restraints and discipline, it is productive of the most useful results; but it too often blinds the judgment, and becomes fierce and vindictive. We are not satisfied with the undoubted good qualities of what belongs to ourselves; but we resolve upon exposing the defects and faults, whether real or

1*

imaginary, of what belongs to our neighbors. It is not enough that our own children are handsome, good-tempered, clever, and accomplished; but we insist upon it that those of our neighbors are ugly, morose, and ill-endowed. Perhaps agriculture presents a more limited field for any ill-natured emulation than almost any other department of life. Here men cannot conceal their discoveries and improvements. Here there cannot be long any monopoly of advantages. Here men perceive how rapidly and widely improvements and discoveries extend themselves. In the present condition of the world, for a man to pretend to keep any distinguished agricultural improvement to himself would be very much like his holding up his umbrella before the sun, so that it might not shine upon other people. All he can be sure of, in this case, is to keep himself in the dark. A liberal and intelligent mind perceives at once, that the light which his knowledge or improvements shed upon others, is always reflected back upon himself.

III. — SCIENCE AND AGRICULTURE.

It must be admitted, however, that although a good deal of selfishness and bigotry might remain, — for, alas! how can it be otherwise as long as human nature is human? — there is a spirit of liberal inquiry abroad in respect to agriculture, blazing in the valleys, and beaming from the hill tops, and every where diffusing an invigorating, a stirring, and a healthful radiance. One of the wisest of our race, who applied his heart, as he says, to understand wisdom, has told us that there is nothing new under the sun; what is, has been; and the human mind is not likely to spring suddenly a mine of truth, which has never before been touched; nor may it expect at once to accomplish the solution of recondite problems, which have baffled the most penetrating and puzzled the most sagacious minds. It would be the grossest injustice to many men of the brightest powers, of profound investigation, and of most liberal and disinterested views, — who, though they have gone out, have left a brilliant track behind them, — to say that agricultural science has never before been prosecuted with zeal, intelligence, and in the spirit of true philosophy.

I am not a believer in the immediate approach of an intellectual millennium; nor can I persuade myself that philosophy has just been born into the world, and that all preceding ages were ages of comparative barbarism. It is true that the natural sciences are now prosecuted with singular advantages and success; that, in a particular manner, chemistry has, in a measure, been created within the last half century; and that it promises to render the most essential aid to agriculture. Excepting, however, the stimulus which it has every where given to inquiry and observation, and the exact experiments which it is prompting farmers — even in the humblest departments of agriculture — to make, it cannot as yet point to very many positive practical triumphs. Sanguine as I am, in common with others, in its application to agriculture, ultimately and perhaps speedily yielding the most beneficial fruits, it has not yet even approached a solution of many of the profound secrets of nature. Whether this triumph is ever to be achieved by human sagacity; whether, with our present faculties, we are capable of entering into these sacred mysteries, and of lifting up even a corner of the veil which Heaven has drawn over them, it would be idle to conjecture; but they are, as yet, a sealed book to us. In the spirit of the Book of books, "Let us wait at Wisdom's gates, let us watch at the posts of her doors;" let us knock, humbly hoping that they may be opened to us. Those who have gone before us have done the same, and were favored with many largesses, which they have bequeathed to their children. Let us do them justice by gratefully acknowledging our debt to them; and not wrap ourselves up, as we are very liable to do, in the vain conceit that they knew nothing, and that we know every thing.

We talk about uniting science with agriculture, as if this were the first time of asking the banns, when we may be sure the marriage was consummated years and years ago. A science, technically speaking, is a particular branch of human knowledge, which has been systematized and drawn up in regular form; its particular principles and rules defined, its department circumscribed, and its peculiar vocabulary arbitrarily established. In this respect, chemistry, botany, and mechanics are sciences; but science, in an enlarged sense, is the observation of nature — the accumulation and comparison of facts, and the deduction of inferences from them, either for the acquisition of more knowledge, or for practical application and use. I venture to assert that, without any knowledge of the particular and technical terms of art, whose utility I am not disposed in the smallest degree to deny, wherever the mind is at work there is science; and many men, who hardly know the letters of a book, are yet profound observers of nature, and may be denominated scientific agriculturists; because they are full of knowledge, which they are constantly applying to practice. Now, without any disparagement of former times, I think it must be admitted that the universal mind of the agricultural world was never so powerfully stirred as it is at this present time. We must do what we can to keep it awake, and to direct the application of its powers. "Practice with science," is the terse and comprehensive motto of the Royal Agricultural Society of England. Philosophy now comes down from her high places, and takes Labor by the hand, that they may walk together among the works of God, and, with an enlightened and commendable curiosity, "search into the causes of things." This is the highest office of the human understanding.

Nature proceeds by fixed laws. She is not a confused jumble of things; to-day one thing, and to-morrow another. All the relations of the different parts of nature are mutual and exact, and every thing moves on in a beautiful agreement with every other thing. The ancients were accustomed to speak of the music of the spheres; this refers to the harmony which prevails throughout the universe, so that no discordant note is ever sounded. There is a reason for every thing; there is a rule by which every thing is directed and controlled. It is not enough for us to say, "This is a mystery; it is in vain for us to inquire;" or, "Here is an arbitrary and miraculous power in nature which we can never understand." There may be many things beyond our comprehension; there is nothing which should be beyond our inquiry. There is a wonderful power at work always in vegetation. The development and progress of vegetable life, the relations of the soil to the plant produced, the effects of light and air, and dew and rain, and frost and electricity, the nature of manures, their uses and their results, may all be considered as mysteries as yet, to a great degree, unresolved; but from what we see in other parts of Nature, which have come under our observation, and where some portion of her laws has been fully revealed, an intelligent mind can have no doubt that all these things rest upon certain determinate principles, and are governed by laws as fixed as any which prevail in other parts of the system of nature. Whoever examines the minutest crystal, will find that in the same classes the laws of aggregation are the same; whoever examines any species of plants, perceives an exact similarity of formation and habit pervading whole classes and tribes. The established principles of gravitation and attraction, and above all that most wonderful discovery of chemical equivalents, all demonstrate the existence, throughout nature, of fixed laws and determinate forces, whose operation is universal and invariable. There is every reason to believe that the laws of vegetable and animal life, and growth and nourishment and decay, are equally well established, and equally universal, and equally invariable. The ascertaining and discovery of any one of these laws is positive knowledge — is, properly speaking, science; and any mind, acute and observing, may, in the daily routine of humble life, become familiar with many of these great laws; and read, at first-hand, on the illuminated pages of external nature, the most useful and the most sublime truths, though it has never been taught to read by the alphabet of science, nor been allowed admission into the schools of philosophy.

It is said of one of the greatest of human intellects, a mind whose sublime discoveries constitute a divine revelation, second only to the written word, that he was led to the discovery of the great principle which binds worlds and systems in one harmonious bond, by the falling of an apple. The cultivator of the earth has before him not merely the fall but the growth of the apple, which, from the germination of the seed to the maturity of the tree, from the opening of the blossom to the ripening of the fruit, is full of lessons of wisdom; and, in every stage of its progress, reveals the power and the skill and the beneficence of that divine agent, who fills all in all.

England presents at this time a more brilliant example, than any age or country has before witnessed, of the application, I will not say of science, for that would not comprehend the idea which I wish to express, but the application of mind to agriculture. The practice of agriculture, and the philosophy of agriculture, are matters of universal interest. Men of all grades and conditions are laboring in this great cause, and are asking for the *how*, and the *why*, and the *wherefore*. The brighter intellects are directing their talents to agricultural inquiries; and the humblest in their humble, but not inefficient way, are seconding their efforts. So many minds concentrating their rays upon the same point, they must be sure to illuminate it with an extraordinary brilliancy.

Agriculture is now getting to be recognized as the commanding interest of the state: so it must ever be as lying at the foundation of all others. Few persons are apprized of their obligations to agriculture; and it is difficult to estimate the extent of these obligations. Every man's daily bread, his meat, his clothing, his shelter, his luxuries, all come from the earth. The foundation, or, as the French would say, the *materiel* of all commerce and manufactures, is agriculture; and its moral influences are innumerable and most powerful. It will be found likewise, upon an observation of the different conditions of different nations or communities, that a laborious agriculture is, in a high degree, a conservator of good morals; and that those countries are, upon the whole, and on this account, most blessed, not where the fruits of the earth are yielded spontaneously without care and without toil, but where its products come only as the reward of industry, and the powers of the mind, as well as the labor of the hand, are severely taxed in a struggle for the means of subsistence and comfort. Every one recognizes labor as the source of wealth. How few things have any value, which have not been either produced or modified by labor! and in what department is labor so productive, so essential, and so important as in that of agriculture?

IV.—ENGLISH AGRICULTURE.

I will not dwell longer upon these considerations, with which every intelligent mind must be impressed; and which must, more or less, constantly present themselves to our notice in that field of observation which we have entered. I shall proceed to present some general views of the agriculture of England, and shall descend, in the course of my reports, to such details as may be deemed useful and practical.

The condition of practical agriculture in Great Britain, as far as I have had opportunity of observing it, must be pronounced highly improved. Many parts of the country present an order, exactness, and neatness of cultivation greatly to be admired; but a sky is seldom without clouds, and there are parts of England where the appearance is any thing but laudable, and where there are few and very equivocal evidences of skill, industry, or thrift. We are often told in America, that England is only a large garden, in which art, and skill, and labor, have smoothed all the rough places, filled up the hollow places, and brought every thing into a beautiful and systematic harmony, and into the highest degree of productiveness. This is not wholly true; indeed, though there are many farms to be altogether admired for the degree of perfection to which their cultivation has been carried, yet there are not a few places where the indications of neglect, and indolence, and unskilfulness are but too apparent; and where, in an obvious contest for victory between the cultivated plant and the weeds, the latter triumph from their superiority both in force and numbers. I shall, however, most cheerfully admit that English farming, taken as a whole, is characterized by a neatness, exactness, thoroughness seldom seen in my own country. An American, landing in Liverpool, is at once struck with the amount of labor every where expended; the docks, and the public buildings, and the lofty and magnificent warehouses astonish him by the substantial and permanent character of their structure. The railways, likewise, with their deep excavations, their bridges of solid masonry, their splendid viaducts, their immense tunnels, extending in some cases more than two miles in length, and their depôts and station-houses, covering acres of ground, with their iron pillars and their roofs, also of iron, exhibiting a sort of tracery or net-work of the strongest as well as most beautiful description, indicate a most profuse expenditure of labor, and are evidently made to endure. He is still more overpowered with amazement when, coming to London, he passes up or down the River Thames, and contemplates the several great bridges, among the most splendid objects which are to be seen in England, two of which are of iron and three of stone, spanning this great thoroughfare of commerce with their beautiful arches, and made as if, as far as human presumption can go, they would bid defiance to the decay and ravages of time. If to this, he adds (as, indeed, how can he help doing it?) a visit to the Thames Tunnel, — a secure, a dry, a brilliant, and even a gay passage under the bed of the stream, where the tides of the ocean daily roll their waves, and the mighty barks of commerce and war float in all their majesty and pride over his head, exhibiting the perfection of engineering, and a strength of construction and finish, which leaves not a doubt of its security and endurance, — he perceives an expense of labor which disdains all the limited calculations of a young and comparatively poor country. He remarks a thoroughness of workmanship which is most admirable, and which indicates a boldness and bravery of enterprise, taking into its calculations not merely years but centuries to come. We have, in America, a common saying in respect to many things which we undertake, that "this will do for the present," which does not seem to me to be known in England; and we have a variety of cheap, insubstantial, slight-o'-hand ways of doing many things, sometimes vulgarly denominated "make-shifts to do," which we ascribe to what we call Yankee cleverness, of which certainly no signs are to be seen here. Agricultural operations and improvements are here in general conducted and finished in the most thorough and substantial manner.

The walls enclosing many of the noblemen's parks in England, which comprehend hundreds, and, in some cases, thousands of acres, are brick walls, of ten and twelve feet in height, running for miles and miles. The walls round many of the farms in Scotland, called there "dikes," made of the stone of the country, and laid in lime, and capped with flat stones resting vertically upon their edges, are finished pieces of masonry. The improvements at the Duke of Portland's, at Welbeck, Nottinghamshire, in his arrangements for draining and irrigating, at his pleasure, from three to five hundred acres of land, — without doubt one of the most skilful and magnificent agricultural improvements ever made, — are executed in the most finished and permanent manner; the embankments, the channels, the sluices, the dams, the gates, being constructed, in all cases where it would be most useful and proper, of stone or iron. These are only samples of the style in which things are done here. The important operations of embanking and of draining, especially under the new system of draining and subsoiling, are executed most thoroughly. The farm houses and farm buildings are of brick or stone, and all calculated to endure.

I cannot recommend, without considerable qualifications, these expensive ways of doing things to my own countrymen. We have not the means — the capital for accomplishing them; but we might gather from them a useful lesson; for, in general, we err by an opposite extreme. We build too slightly — we do not execute our improvements thoroughly — we have little capital to expend, without which, of course, no substantial improvements can be effected; and labor, with us, is with more difficulty obtained, with far more difficulty managed, and requires to be much more highly paid than here. I hope I shall be pardoned for adding, as my deliberate conviction, that we are too shy of investing money in improvements of this nature, however secure, because they do not yield so large a percentage as many other investments somewhat more questionable in a moral view, and vastly more so in respect to the security which they offer.

There are circumstances in the condition of things here, which certainly warrant a much more liberal expenditure in improvements than would be eligible with us. Here exist the right of primogeniture and the law of entail, so that an estate remains in the same family for centuries; and a man is comparatively sure that the improvements which he makes will be enjoyed by his children's children. Things are entirely different with us — houses in our cities are continually changing hands, and are scarcely occupied by one life; and in the country, even in staid New England, few estates are in the hands of the third or fourth generation in the direct line of descent. I shall not at all discuss the comparative advantages, expediency, or propriety of one or the other system. I leave those inferences to others — my business is with the fact as it is; and, like short leases, it has an obvious tendency to hinder or discourage improvements of a substantial and permanent character, involving a large expense.

V. — ENGLISH CAPITAL.

Another marked distinction, already alluded to, between the condition of the proprietors of the soil here and with us, is in the amount of capital existing here. It is absolutely enormous, and almost distances the system of enumeration which we are taught at our common schools. Let me mention some facts which have been stated to me on credible authority; and let me premise that a pound sterling is about equal to five dollars United States currency. Under a law of the present government, here, levying a tax upon every man's income when it exceeds one hundred and fifty pounds sterling a year, persons liable to taxation are required to make a just return of their income under a heavy penalty. A confectioner, in London, returned, as his annual income, the sum of thirty thousand pounds sterling, or one hundred and fifty thousand dollars, or six times as much as the salary of the President of the United States; which showed, at least, how skilful he was in compounding some of the sweets of life. A nobleman, it is said, has contracted with a master builder to erect for him, in London, four thousand — not forty — not four hundred — but four thousand houses of a good size for occupation. In some of the best parts of London, acres of land. vast squares, are occupied with large and elegant dwelling-houses, paying heavy rents, in long rows, blocks, and crescents, and all belonging to some single individual. One nobleman, whose magnificent estate was left to him by his father, encumbered with a debt of some hundred thousand pounds, by *limiting*, as it is termed here, his own annual expenditure to thirty thousand pounds, has well nigh extinguished this debt, and, in all human probability, will soon have his patrimonial estate free of encumbrance. The incomes of some of the rich men in the country, amount to twenty, twenty-five, fifty, one hundred thousand, two hundred thousand pounds sterling — even three hundred thousand pounds annually. It is very difficult for New England men even to conceive of such wealth. A farmer in Lincolnshire told me that the crop of wheat grown upon his farm one year was eighteen thousand bushels. The rent annually paid by one farmer in Northumberland, or the Lothians, exceeded seven thousand pounds, or thirty-five thousand dollars. These facts, which have been stated to me by gentlemen in whose veracity I have entire confidence, and who certainly are incapable of attempting any "tricks upon travellers," show the enormous masses of wealth which are here accumulated. A gentleman of distinguished talents and fine classical attainments, and who adds to them a public spirit in agricultural improvement worthy of his education and his high standing in the community, has recently added to his property, by the purchase of lands, to the amount of two hundred thousand pounds sterling, that is, a million of dollars; and his estate, now in cultivation, and under his own personal inspection, and, with the exception of about four hundred acres lying in one body, amounts to six thousand acres. Another gentleman, of high rank, in respect to whom and to whose amiable family I have a constant struggle to restrain the open expression of my grateful sense of their kindness, and who — an example here not uncommon — to an extraordinary brilliancy of talent and an accomplished education unites the most active spirit of agricultural improvement, has, though not all in his immediate occupation, yet all under his immediate supervision, a tract of more than twelve thousand acres in a course of systematic cultivation or gradual improvement.*

The income of a single nobleman, from his coal mines, exceeds one hundred thousand pounds sterling a year; and I believe this is not the largest of the coal possessions. With such wealth as this, men may make what improvements they please, and attempt what experiments they may deem worth trying; but should such imaginations ever visit a New England or a United States farmer in his dreams, if Æsop's fable of the frog, who attempted to swell himself to the size of the ox, did not cure him, he might be deemed a fit subject for a lunatic asylum. There are other circumstances in the case which are to be added, and those are the cheapness of iron, the abundance of coal, and the admirable facility and skill with which the former material is wrought. Wood, and especially the soft woods, which are so much wrought among us, are here scarce and dear, and, therefore, seldom used for building purposes; bricks, and, in many parts of the country, good building stone, of the best quality, are abundant. Most of the cottages which I have seen have brick or stone floors, though many have only hardly-trodden clay and earth; and the entries of the best houses are generally

---

* I mention these examples — to which, from my own knowledge, I might add many others — *in the form* I *do*, for the purpose, by the way, of showing my American friends that agriculture here takes its proper rank among the liberal professions, and that not merely as a recreation, but as a business; and in all its minute and practical details, it is not deemed incompatible with the highest distinctions of talent, education, and rank, but rather as a pursuit in which they all may most usefully and honorably lend their combined influence.

paved, and the staircases made of stone. A fence of iron, affording a sufficient protection against cattle, is made here at a less expense than many wooden fences are made with us.

VI.—GENERAL APPEARANCE OF THE COUNTRY.

I may be allowed to put down marks of difference in the general appearance of the country, as compared with my own, as they strike my attention. I need not say that England is entirely devoid of a feature which strongly marks the newly-cleared parts of my own country, and that is the stumps of trees, which have been cut down, or the large, naked, and dead standing skeletons of trees, which have been girdled, that the pioneer, in subduing the wilderness, might have a chance of getting bread for himself and his family, while he was endeavoring to tame the wildness of nature and to convert the forest into a fruitful field. England exhibits, of course, nothing of this, for the days of its youth have long since passed, and its agriculture reckons its patriarchal centuries. But there is another thing remarkable: the cultivated fields are entirely free from rocks and stones, excepting the limestone and flint pebbles in the chalk formations. In the clay soils and on the peaty moors, they, of course, are not to be looked for; but, where even they once existed, they have been entirely removed or buried, and there is nothing to interrupt or impede the progress of the plough. This is not so generally the case in my own country as is to be desired. It is, indeed, an affair of very difficult accomplishment in many cases, where, in a granitic region for example, the stones are often within stepping distance of each other all over a farm, and where every fresh ploughing seems to turn up a fresh crop of stones. On the other hand, there are too many cases where, with equal advantage to the purse as pleasure to the eye, such unsightly rubbish might be removed or buried; yet there are fields, within my own knowledge, where I may say, with confidence, the same piles of stones which were collected for removal, full half a century ago, retain their original position until this day; the plough, whenever they are broken up, being always compelled, at no small expense of time and trouble, (as a sailor would say,) to give these heaps a good berth; and only going near enough to them to refresh and invigorate the roots of the briers and bramble bushes, by which they are usually ornamented, and which, to my taste, are quite as offensive in a farmer's field as the "mustachios and imperials" so often seen upon the monkey masque, which passes, by the mere indulgence and good humor of society, for a human face. Throughout those parts of England which I have seen, there are, as I have already remarked, an exactness, a finish, and a cleanness in the cultivation, which impress a stranger most agreeably, and deserve the highest commendation. There are, occasionally, immense tracts of unenclosed commons, and heaths, and moors, where there is no cultivation, where nothing grows, and, in some cases, little can ever be made to grow; or which, otherwise, are abandoned to the growth of furze or gorse for the protection of the game, and for the pleasures of the chase. These are called *preserves*, and are leased to sportsmen occasionally, or, rather, the right to kill game upon them is leased, at a rate which we should deem a high rent, even for purposes of cultivation. An eminent agriculturist has shown that, in England and Scotland, there are full 10,000,000 acres in heath or moor, all susceptible of being brought into productive cultivation. These lands, of course, remain as they are by voluntary neglect or design. But I refer to the cultivated and improved lands; and here there is every where a surprising neatness and finish — every thing is done, as it were, by line and measure; the corners and the head lands are thoroughly cleaned, the open ditches are kept unobstructed, the crops are drilled in straight lines, and a newly-ploughed field resembles a plaited ruffle from the ironing board of a good housewife. Such exactness is exceedingly beautiful, and, though it may appear, at first, to consume a good deal of time, will be found, in the long run, to be more economical than the slovenly way in which things are often done in many places, which I am reluctant to name. There is a pleasure afforded by such neatness which is very great, and which can be properly appreciated only by those who have been largely endowed by nature with the organ of order.

VII.—HEDGES AND ENCLOSURES.

The green fences in England, by which the farms are surrounded and divided, are often a beautiful feature in the landscape. Where they are complete, and neatly trimmed and formed, with here and there a single plant left to rise above the rest, which many deem more beautiful to the eye than a democratic level, and when seen whitened with their blossoms in the spring, or blushing deeply with their fruit in autumn, they are exceedingly pleasing to the eye. In general, they are formed of the white thorn, and sometimes of the holly, and not unfrequently of these two plants intermingled. But I must confess myself somewhat disappointed in the condition of the hedges throughout England. Of course there are many exceptions, and perhaps the cases to which I refer should be considered as exceptions to the general fact; but in frequent instances they are greatly neglected. There are many vacancies in them; they are not well trimmed; they are intermingled with various weeds and rubbish; and, instead of being confined to a width of four or six feet, they are often seen with their pernicious accompaniments occupying more than a rod in width. I inquired why this was permitted; and why, when the rest of the face was so clear and bright, such dirt spots were allowed to remain: the answer was, "that they were left thus for the protection of the game, and that they made excellent covers for partridges and foxes." When so much care and expense are incurred in the protection of this kind of game, it is to be hoped that it may suggest always the higher duty of taking care of the human game, the hungry and ragged children, which in some parts of England are as numerous, and growing up as wild, and many of them as little taught, as the rabbits in a warren.

The enclosures in England are of various extent, from ten to twenty and fifty acres. There are some farms with scarcely a subdivision, and in these cases the stock are soiled. In parts of England, however, they resemble the divisions of New England farms, and are of various sizes, but generally small, and of all shapes, and often not exceeding four or five acres. It is reported of a farmer in Devonshire, that he lately cultivated one hundred acres of wheat in fifty different fields. There must have been here a great waste of land and labor. One of the most competent judges of agricultural improvement in England says, however, that "his tenants never wish to have more than one ploughed field on a farm."

The loss in land by too many fences, the loss of time in cultivating in small fields instead of large, on account of the necessity of more frequent turnings, and ploughing the head lands by themselves, and the actual cost of making and of maintaining the fences, not to add that these fences are a shelter for weeds, and a harbor for vermin, are serious considerations. The statement of an intelligent practical farmer in Staffordshire, on the highly-improved estate of Lord Hatherton, whom I had the pleasure of visiting with Mr. P. Pusey, M. P., as given to Mr. Pusey, is well worth recording. Speaking of the farm called the Yew-Tree Farm, he says, "The turnip field is sixty-five acres; it was, two years back, at the time I entered upon the farm, in eight enclosures. I have taken up 1914 yards of fence, and intend dividing it into three fields; it will take 800 yards of new fence. The field in which I was subsoiling is forty-two acres; it was in six enclosures. I took up 1264 yards of fence; if I divide this field, it will take 300 yards of new fence. The land Lord Hatherton mentioned on my Deanery Farm was originally in twenty-seven enclosures; ninety-one acres. I took up 4427 yards of fences; it will now lie in five fields, and will take 1016 yards of new fence."

"I cannot," he adds, "really say what land is gained by the different operations; but some of the fences were from three to four yards or more wide, that the plough never touched; my new fences are upon the level without ditches. In the whole of the old fences there was a great number of ash-trees, which are all stocked up, as well as a good part of the oak, only leaving a few for ornament and shelter. I think the greatest gain in land will be from getting rid of the trees."*

This is the experience and opinion of a sound practical farmer, and is entitled to great weight. In some of the counties large enclosures prevail. In parts of Lincolnshire the enclosures embrace about fifty acres each; and on the best managed farms which I saw, these fields were mostly laid either in parallelograms or squares. In the fens or redeemed lands of Lincolnshire, the

---

* Journal of Royal Agricultural Society, vol. iv. part 2, p. 306, note.

ditches around and through the land form sufficient and the only fences. In the county of Northumberland, and in the Lothians, the enclosures are very extensive, and, excepting on the outlines, no fences appear. The plough, in such case, when it starts, takes its course, and runs to the end of these long fields without interruption.

Mr. Pusey, in Berkshire, on one of the best managed estates which I have visited, has induced many of his tenants to take away the inner fences and leave the fields open. Sheep are, of course, never suffered to graze or roam at pleasure over these large fields, but are fed in enclosures formed of movable hurdles in different parts of the field, where their manure is required. Cattle never go at large upon them; and the convenience of cultivating where the lands are thus open, to say nothing of the beauty of the appearance, in addition to other advantages already alluded to, is at once obvious and decisive.

VIII.—IRON AND SUNKEN FENCES.

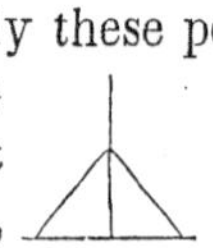

I shall speak in this place of two kinds of fences which are common on gentlemen's seats, and one of which may be safely recommended to my own countrymen. The first is an iron fence, called here an invisible fence. This is made of stout iron wire, about one third of an inch in diameter, and consists of four or five bars or rods, with upright pieces of iron, about an inch and a quarter in width, and about one third of an inch in thickness, placed at about six feet distance from each other. Through these upright and flat pieces of iron the bars or rods are passed, and they serve to keep them secure. Every alternate one of these upright bars has a foot to it, and being sunk in the ground about a foot or more, serves as a post to keep the fence steady; and occasionally these posts, if so they may be called, have side supports, thus; these, of course, increase the strength of the fence, but they are not indispensable. These fences are very cheap, on account of the abundance of iron and the facility with which it is wrought; and being kept painted commonly of a green color, they do not appear until you approach near them; but no animals attempt to pass them, and, when well taken care of, they are durable, and, it is obvious, may be easily removed from place to place.

There is another kind of fence often formed, called a sunken fence; or "ha! ha!" from its generally taking persons by surprise, as it does not appear until you reach it. A trench is dug as deep as it is required that the height of the wall shall be from the bottom of the trench; one side of the trench is perpendicular, and against this side the wall is erected; the other side is made slanting at an angle of about forty-five degrees, and the slanting side is grassed, and may be mowed clear to the bottom, so that no land is lost; but, in truth, a small amount is gained. The object is to conceal the fence, so that when placed round the grounds of a gentleman's house, the prospect of the lawn or field is not interrupted by an unsightly wall; and the grounds within the enclosure may be cultivated or embellished in any way with shrubs, or flowers, or fruit, and yet the cattle feeding beyond it, whom no visible obstruction appears to keep at a distance, are effectually excluded, as no animal attempts ever to leap such a fence.

IX.—THE ENGLISH PARKS.

I will take this occasion to speak of the extensive parks which are to be seen in many parts of the country, and which constitute a truly magnificent feature in English scenery. These are the open grounds, which surround the houses of the rich and noble in the country. By open, I do not mean entirely free from trees, because many of them are exceedingly well stocked with trees, sometimes standing single, at other times in clumps; sometimes in belts, sometimes in rows, and squares, and circular plantations; and more often scattered, as if they were carelessly thrown down broadcast. The ground under them is kept in grass, and depastured by cattle, sheep, and deer; and affords often the richest herbage. With some exceptions, a plough is never suffered to disturb these grounds; and in the neighborhood of the house, which is generally placed in the centre of them, the portion which is separated from the rest, as I have observed, by an invisible or sunken fence just now described, for the cultivation of ornamental trees and shrubs, is kept so closely and evenly shorn, that to walk upon it seems more like treading upon velvet than upon grass. Nothing of the kind can be more beautiful; and I never before knew the force of that striking expression of the prince of poets, Milton, of "walking on the smooth shaven lawn;" for it seems to be cut with a razor rather than with a scythe; and after a gentle shower it really appears as if the field had had its face washed, and its hair combed with a fine-tooth comb. It is brought to this perfection by being kept often mown; and I have stood by with perfect admiration to see a swarth mowed evenly and perfectly, where the grass to be cut was scarcely more than an inch high.

These parks which I have described abound, as observed, with trees of extraordinary age and size. They are not like the trees of our original forests, growing up to a great height, and, on account of the crowded state of the neighborhood, throwing out few lateral branches; but what they want in height, they gain in breadth; and, if I may be excused for a hard word, in umbrageousness. I measured one in Lord Bagot's celebrated park in Staffordshire, and going round the outside of the branches, keeping within the droppings, the circuit was a hundred yards. The circumference of some of the celebrated oaks in the park of the Duke of Portland, which we measured together, when he did me the kindness to accompany me through his grounds, seem worthy of record. The Little Porter Oak measured 27 feet in circumference; the Great Porter Oak is 29 feet in circumference; the Seven Sisters, 33 feet in circumference. The Great Porter Oak was of a very large diameter, 50 feet above the ground; and the opening in the trunk of the Green Dale Oak was at one time large enough to admit the passage of a small carriage through it; by advancing years the space has become somewhat contracted. These indeed are noble trees, though it must be confessed that they were thrown quite into the shade by the magnificent Kentucky Buttonwood or Sycamore, of whose trunk I saw a complete section exhibited at Derby, measuring 25 feet in diameter and 75 feet in circumference. This was brought from the United States, and indeed might well be denominated the mammoth of the forest.

In these ancient parks, oaks and beeches are the predominant trees, with occasional chestnuts and ashes. In very many cases

I saw the beauty and force of that first line in the pastorals of Virgil, where he addresses Tityrus as "playing upon his lute under *the spreading shade of a beech-tree.*" These trees are looked upon with great veneration; in many cases, they are numbered; in some, a label is affixed to them, giving their age; sometimes a stone monument is erected, saying when and by whom this forest or this clump was planted; and commonly some record is kept of them as a part of the family history. I respect this trait in the character of the English, and I sympathize with them in their veneration for old trees. They are the growth often of centuries, and the monuments of years gone by. They were the companions of our fathers, who, it may be, were nourished by their fruit, and reposed under their shade. Perhaps they were planted by the very hands of those from whom we have descended; and whose far-sighted and comprehensive beneficence embraced a distant posterity. How many revolutions and vicissitudes in the fortunes of men have they surveyed and survived! They have been pelted by many a storm; the hoarse and swift wind has often growled and whistled among their branches; the lightnings and tempest have many a time bent their limbs and scathed their trunks. But they, like the good and the truly great in seasons of trial, have stood firm and retained their integrity. They have seen one generation of men treading upon the heels of another, and rapidly passing away; wars have burst forth in volcanic explosions, and have gone out; revolutions have made their changes, and the wheel again returned to its starting point; governments and princes have flourished and faded; and the current of human destiny has flowed at their roots, bearing onwards to the traveller's bourn one family and one people after another; but they still stand, green in their old age, as the mute yet eloquent historians of departed years. Why should we not look upon them with reverence? I cannot quite enter into the enthusiasm of an excellent friend, who used to say that the cutting down of an old tree ought to be made a capital offence at law; yet I deem it almost sacrilegious to destroy them, excepting where necessity demands it; and I would always advise that an old tree, standing in a conspicuous station either for use or ornament, should be at least once more wintered and summered before the sentence of death, which may be passed upon it, is carried into execution.

The trees in the park of the palace of Hampton Court are,

many of them, the horse-chestnut and the lime, of great age and eminent beauty; several straight lines of them forming, for a long distance, the approach to the palace. On a clear, bright day, at the season of their flowering, I passed through this magnificent avenue with inexpressible delight. I passed through them again late in the autumn, when the frost had marred their beauty, and the autumnal gales had stripped off their leaves; but they were still venerable in the simple majesty of their gigantic and spreading forms. I could not help reflecting, with grateful emotion, on that beneficent Power, which shall presently breathe upon these apparently lifeless statues, and clothe them with the glittering foliage of spring, and the rich and splendid glories of summer. So be it with those of us who have got far on into the autumn, or stand shivering in the winter of life!

The extent of these parks, in many cases, filled me with surprise. They embrace hundreds, in some instances thousands, of acres;* and you enter them by gates, where a porter's lodge is always to be found. After entering the park gate, I have rode sometimes several miles before reaching the house. They are in general devoted to the pasturage of sheep, cattle, and deer. In the park at Chatsworth, the herd of deer exceeded sixteen hundred. These deer are kept at no inconsiderable expense, requiring abundant pasturage in summer, and hay and grain in winter. An English pasture is seldom or never ploughed. Many of them have been in grass beyond the memory of any one living. The turf becomes extremely close and hard; and the feeding of sheep and cattle undoubtedly enriches the land, especially under the careful management of one eminent farmer, — and many more, doubtless, are like him, — on whose pasture grounds the manure of the cattle was daily collected and evenly spread.

In speaking of the parks in the country, I surely ought not to pass in silence the magnificent parks of London, as truly magnificent they must be called, including St. James's Park, Green Park, Kensington Gardens, Hyde Park, and Regent's Park.

Kensington Gardens, exclusive of private gardens, within its enclosures contains 227 acres; Hyde Park, 380 acres; Green Park, connected with St. James's Park, 56 acres; St. James's Park, 87 acres; Regent's Park, 372 acres; terraces and canals connected with Regent's Park, 80 acres — making a grand total

* Windsor Great Park contains 3500 acres, and the Little Park 300 acres.

of 1202 acres. To these should be added the large, elegant, and highly-embellished public squares in various parts of London, and even in the most crowded parts of the old city, which, in all, probably exceed 200 acres. These magnificent parks, it must be remembered, are in the midst of a populous town, including upwards of two millions of inhabitants, and are open to the public for exercise, health, and amusement. They are, at the same time, to a degree stocked with sheep and cows.

It is impossible to over-estimate the value to health of these open spaces, and the amount of recreation and rational enjoyment which they afford to this vast population. In each of the large parks — Kensington, Hyde Park, and St. James's — there are extensive bodies of water, artificial lakes, in some places adorned with elegant bridges, and in St. James's Park studded with pretty islands and shrubbery. Here large varieties of aquatic birds are kept, to the great amusement of the thousands of children, who coax them to the shore with crumbs of bread and cake, the birds being so tame as almost to feed out of their hands, and for the instruction of older heads. There is likewise an exceedingly beautiful and tasteful cottage, of Gothic architecture, at the end of the lake in St. James's Park, for the residence of the keeper of the birds. There are always to be found in some parts of the parks, or at the keepers' different lodges, some cows kept, where a glass of milk, unadulterated and fresh from the fountain, can be had for those persons who, for health or pleasure, seek the delicious beverage in its purity. The numbers and tameness of the birds in these pleasure-grounds is a beautiful circumstance, which it might be well to consider in some other quarters. Their safety and lives are held sacred ; and the birds gratefully, and, to a feeling heart, delightfully acknowledge this kindness by the most expressive confidence, alighting fearlessly in the path before you, as though they would invite you to cultivate their acquaintance. Man, in general, is a great savage, and a ferocious and insatiate animal of prey. He makes continual war upon many of the animals below him, not for subsistence merely, but for pleasure. His conduct towards the brute creation shows, too often, how certain he is to abuse unlimited power, and conveys a strong argument against despotic authority. Indeed, his war upon the birds merely as matter of sport, always makes me look upon him with a degree of shuddering, and feel that a man who can find his pleasure in the wanton destruction of little birds, the most humble of all animals in their claims, the most delicate, innocent, and pure in all their tastes and habits, and comparatively useless for food, puts himself beyond the pale of humanity, and could scarcely, with safety, be trusted with a child. It were worth considering always, how many of our pleasures are purchased at a most bitter expense of happiness and life to others! Two or three days' coursing, manly and healthful as the exercise on horseback undoubtedly is, and strongly exciting as the sport is, did not quite reconcile me to it; and the wailings and shriekings of the affrighted and dying hares, in the jaws of the hounds, sounded in my ears, for several days afterwards, like the cries of expiring children.

I shall not be straying from my proper duty if I urge the beneficent example of London strongly upon my own countrymen. In Boston, excepting the Common — containing about forty-five acres of ground, exceedingly beautiful in its location and improvements — and some few openings upon a very limited scale, there is a large and constantly increasing population crowded together in one dense mass, with narrow streets and confined alleys, and basement stories, doomed to a comparative privation of Heaven's freest and greatest blessings — light and air. A Botanical and Pleasure Garden has been laid out, and is maintained by private subscription, accessible to subscribers or upon the payment of a light fee, which it is earnestly to be hoped, for the credit of this city, long distinguished by its liberality and public spirit, may receive every encouragement, so that its improvements and advantages may be greatly extended. New York, with a population of three times the extent of Boston, is scarcely more favored, excepting in the width of its streets; for, with the exception of those delightful grounds, the Battery, at the very extremity of the city, the open space in front of the City Hall, dignified, *par excellence*, by the name of the Park, and the open grounds attached to St. John's Church, and the University, but not accessible to the public, the city has no provision of this kind for public recreation and health. As there is little room in the city proper which can now be obtained, she ought at once, at any expense, to secure the charming grounds at Hoboken, to be devoted forever and exclusively to these objects. Having already, with the most honorable enterprise, achieved one of the most extraordinary undertakings of the age, or indeed of any age, — that of bringing, by a capacious tunnel of forty miles in length, a river of pure water into her city, and dispensing, with an unrestrained munificence, to those who cannot purchase it, this most important element, next to vital air, of human existence; let her go on and make the other provision, to which I have referred, for the health and comfort of a population already great, and destined to increase with an unexampled rapidity beyond any bounds which the imagination would now even dare to prescribe.

Philadelphia has set a better example than most other cities in this respect, in having laid out her streets of a capacious width, in having given to most of her houses yards or gardens of a good size, and in having formed, in different parts of the city, public squares of some extent, which are equally ornamental and useful. But she has done little compared with what she might have done; and it is to be hoped that she will be prompted to add to a city, the most convenient and beautiful in the Union, some public gardens and pleasure-grounds, admission to which shall be freely offered to her inhabitants; and more especially for the benefit of that class of them who can have no such indulgences but as the offerings of public beneficence. Baltimore has nothing that deserves the name of a square or a pleasure-ground, unless we are to rank under that designation the beautiful enclosure which she has recently purchased for a cemetery; a place, indeed, for a melancholy and instructive pleasure, but more properly devoted to silence and seclusion, and not at all of the character to which I refer. Lowell — destined to contain a large and laborious population, and of a character particularly demanding such places of recreation, with an unlimited extent of land at her disposal costing scarcely any thing, and with an investment in her manufacturing establishments of ten or eleven millions of dollars — has not a public square so large as a pocket-handkerchief. This omission has always impressed me with painful surprise. Knowing, as I do, the high character of the gentleman who founded and built this flourishing city, now grown to manhood almost in a day, I can ascribe such an omission only to a want of consideration, and to the fact that the population has already extended far beyond any calculations which they could, with sobriety, have formed at its commencement. It is not too late to supply this omission, which interest, as well as philanthropy, most strongly dictates.

Cleanliness, fresh air, and pure water, and the opportunity and the means of relaxation and innocent recreation, are almost as essential to morals as to health. No one can doubt, in this respect, their direct and beneficial influence. The rich can take care of themselves, and can flee the sources of pestilence, and go after health and recreation where they are to be found. Not so with the poorer and humbler classes in society, to whose labor and service the rich owe all their wealth and many of their pleasures. Whoever goes into the low places in crowded cities, into the subterranean abodes where these wretched beings congregate like rabbits in a warren, or, rather, like swine in their sties, and enters into the melancholy statistics of mortality, in such cases will learn some measure of the suffering which is here endured. In London, and other places of a similar character, the presence of the police and the officers of the peace, always in such places in strong force, will remind him that there is a connection not to be overlooked between condition and character, between destitution and crime, between outward filth and impurity of mind, neglect of person and neglect of morals. The most crowded parts of London are the most vicious parts; and a new should not neglect the experience of an old country. A city without public squares and public gardens should provide them, and on a most liberal scale. In a pecuniary point of view, as rendering a residence in the city the more desirable, and so increasing the value of estates in it, I have no doubt that it would yield ample advantages and profits. But health and morals are not to be measured by any pecuniary standard; and where wholesome water, and fresh air, and light, and sunshine, and cleanliness are concerned, no expense and cost are to be considered as exorbitant. To talk about the value of land in such cases, and to place this in competition with health, comfort, and morals, is equally short-sighted and inhuman.

The public parks and pleasure-grounds in London are highly ornamented with shrubs, plants, and flowers, and accessible to the public for exercise and recreation. In St. James's Park, and in some others, metallic labels are affixed to the foreign plants and shrubs, with the botanical and the vulgar name of the plants upon them, and the class and the country to which they belong. This is a beautiful arrangement, and well deserving imitation; furnishing instruction, as well as satisfaction; inciting to the study of botany, and opening a sealed book to the unaided and curious student of nature. Every one knows the advantage of teaching by example; and what an interest is given to the objects, which the natural and visible world presents, by the associations which science throws around them. This practice, I found, prevailed in other public gardens and pleasure-grounds. It was the case in the beautiful and highly-cultivated botanical garden in the neighborhood of Liverpool, which, though created and supported by private subscriptions, and for scientific purposes, is yet free of access to the public one or more days in the week. The same is the case with the very tasteful garden in Sheffield, a romantic and charming piece of ground, which, though on a small scale, combines many attractions; and likewise with the Arboretum at Derby, embracing, I think, about eleven acres, and formed into a garden and pleasure-ground for the public recreation. This last is the fruit of individual munificence. Mr. Strutt, an eminent manufacturer at Derby, employed Mr. Loudon — the late distinguished horticultural writer — to lay out, plant, and ornament these grounds, at an expense of ten thousand pounds sterling, or fifty thousand dollars; and then, with eminent liberality, gave them to the city of Derby for the public use and enjoyment of its inhabitants. Tens of thousands of pounds expended in the erection of a Corinthian column, or a marble mausoleum, would not have formed so durable or extended a memorial of him; and thousands upon thousands yet unborn, in the enjoyment of this beneficence, will invoke blessings upon his memory.

X. — ORNAMENTAL SHRUBS AND FLOWERS.

The cultivation of flowers and shrubs is a prominent feature in the landscape of England; and a circumstance which has given no little gratification to my national pride, has been the profusion of American plants, azalias and kalmias, magnolias and rhododendrons, and a large variety of pines and firs, which are seen in the shrubberies and plantations and pleasure-grounds, both public and private. A very large establishment in London is exclusively devoted to the sale of American plants; and they are every where admired for the splendor of their foliage and the beauty of their flowers. Greenhouses and conservatories are almost universal in the country, where any thing like a garden exists; and the better class of houses are surrounded and adorned with a great variety of flowering shrubs and plants, presenting, through the season, a charming succession of gay and brilliant ornaments. Even the laborer's humble cottage, ordinarily, I am compelled to admit, any thing but a picturesque object, will occasionally have its flowering shrubs adorning its door-way, and the ivy hanging its beautiful tresses over its window, forming, as it were, a mirror, set in a frame of the richest green. The village of Marr, in Yorkshire, not far from Doncaster, and the village of Edensor, in Derbyshire, near Chatsworth, and the village of Lord Brownlow, in Lincolnshire, the best built and by far the handsomest villages I have yet seen in England, to cottages of an excellent and tasteful construction, monuments of the liberality of their proprietors, add these beautiful rural embellishments of shrubs and flowers, and compel a reflecting mind to admit the moral influence of such arrangements upon the character and manners of their inhabitants. Churches and ruins, likewise, are often seen spread over with the richest mantlings of ivy; and, among many others, the venerable and magnificent remains of Hardwicke Hall, for example, are covered, I may say, in the season of its flowering, with a gorgeous robe of it, matting its sides with indescribable luxuriance, climbing its lofty battlements, and fringing its empty windows and broken arches, as though Nature would make the pall of death exquisitely beautiful and splendid, that she might conceal the hideousness of decay, and shut from the sight of frail mortals these affecting monuments of the vanity of human grandeur and pride.

I have said and written a great deal to my countrymen about the cultivation of flowers, ornamental gardening, and rural embellishments; and I would read them a homily on the subject every day of every remaining year of my life, if I thought it would have the effect which I desire, of inducing them to make this matter of particular attention and care. When any man asks me what is the use of shrubs and flowers, my first impulse always is, to look under his hat and see the length of his ears. I am heartily sick of measuring every thing by a standard of mere utility and profit; and as heartily do I pity the man who can see no good in life but in pecuniary gain, or in the mere animal indulgences of eating and drinking.

The establishment of horticultural societies in Salem, Boston,

Worcester, New Haven, New York, and Philadelphia, — and I speak of these societies in particular because I have attended the exhibitions of most of them, — has rendered an immense benefit to the country, not merely in the introduction of new and valuable fruits and vegetables, and in what they have done to improve and perfect the cultivation of those long known among us, but in the improvement of the public taste, and the powerful stimulus they have given to the cultivation of flowers and the formation of gardens and ornamental grounds throughout the country. Few countries in temperate latitudes are richer in the floral kingdom of nature, and the luxuriance of vegetable growth and the splendors of vegetable beauty, than the United States. Why should not flowers be cultivated? Was the human eye, that wonder of wonders, that matchless organ of our physical constitution, that inexhaustible instrument of exalted and varied pleasures, made in vain? Are the forms of beauty in the natural world, infinitely multiplied as they are around us, made for any other purpose than to be enjoyed? And what better means can we take to strengthen the domestic affections, of all others the most favorable to virtue, than to render our homes as beautiful and as attractive as possible? Who does not see constantly the influence of external circumstances upon character as well as comfort; and perceive how greatly order, exactness, and personal neatness contribute to form and strengthen the sense of moral exactness and propriety?

The horticultural establishments of England, their vegetable gardens, their flower gardens, their shrubberies and plantations, their greenhouses and conservatories, are upon the most extensive scale.

XI. — CLIMATE OF ENGLAND.

Another marked difference in the agricultural condition of England and the northern portion of the United States, is in the climate. I cannot speak with any confidence of Scotland, but the climate of England must be pronounced highly temperate. It is favorable to the growth and the constant vigor and freshness of the grasses. It is not only temperate, but moist. The last season may have been peculiar. I landed in Liverpool near the end of April; and there was more or less rain for forty-six days in succession, until I became quite satisfied that an umbrella was as necessary as a hat. When the clear weather finally set in, we had two months, or more, of as fine weather for harvesting as I ever knew, with scarcely the intervention of a day's rain; yet there was nothing of the parching heat of our summers, and I saw no land burnt up by drought. It is now December, and I have scarcely seen any ice, and not a flake of snow; and there is no frost in the ground. Many persons speak of this as the usual temperature, and say that the cold weather does not commence until after Christmas. The dews appear to me very light, owing, as I suppose, to the mildness of the days; and there have been none of those blowing clouds of dust with which our air is often charged, and which, with us, after long droughts, are very disagreeable. Of thunder and lightning this season I am unable to recall a single instance; and at no time of the day has the heat been in the slightest degree oppressive.*

Their insular situation exposes them to frequent and dense fogs, which interpose to prevent the earth being ever parched by drought; and the rains to which they are subject keep the earth, where it is of a retentive character, much soaked with water, and preserve an almost perpetual greenness of vegetation.

In many parts of England, the crops of turnips are never pulled until they are wanted for feeding in the course of the winter; in other places, they require a very slight covering to protect them from the frost. In most cases, sheep do not require to be housed; and in some cases, neat cattle get their chief living in the fields through a great part of the winter, though I cannot but regard this practice as very bad husbandry. Ploughing appears to be seldom interrupted for any length of time; and wheat is sown

* The annual average depth of rain in England is about two feet. In 1840, for instance, the depth at Aberdeen was 24.627 inches; at Empingham, 18.58; Epping, 20.767; Falmouth, 31.511; Gosport, 25.525; Greenwich, 18.24; York, 24.72 inches. That is perhaps not much below the average of the continent of Europe. Some portions of Western Europe, however, are exceedingly wet; 123 inches have been noted to fall at Coimbra, in Portugal, in a year. The fall of rain is still greater in the West Indies. At St. Domingo, 120 inches; at Cayenne, 116 inches; at Maranham, 277 inches. So that even under the equator, a sufficient supply of rain water can be obtained for the service of the inhabitants. — *Farmer's Almanac.*

from October to April. In parts of New Jersey, Pennsylvania, Delaware, and the states south, the farmers enjoy similar advantages of a mild temperature; but north of these, the despotism of frost and snow commences, and holds undisputed sway for four months in the year. Yet, notwithstanding this, our seasons are quite long enough for the perfect ripening of all the crops grown among us; and, with a little extra labor, even the valuable green crops, which here play so important a part in the feeding of stock and the enriching of the land, might, if deemed expedient, be raised and used among us. Of this, however, I shall speak hereafter. These remarks apply only to what has come under my own personal observation; and I can be said to have seen, as yet, only a small part of England. The winter management of farms here is a matter of as much importance as the summer husbandry, and will claim my particular attention. The disposal of the produce, the fattening of animals, the breeds or kinds of live stock most likely to make a good return to the farmer, and the whole management of the manure yards, are subjects in relation to which much useful instruction is to be obtained.

It would seem as though a country with so rough and severe a climate as New England, and with such long winters as prevail there, which, for more than a third part of the year, interrupt entirely all the out-door operations of husbandry, must be exceedingly unfriendly to agriculture, compared with one where the winters are open and field-labor is practicable through the whole of the year. This is, indeed, the case; yet there are some compensations for these privations and disadvantages, which in New England are duly appreciated, as the winter, when labor is to a great degree suspended, is the special season for the education of the young; for reading and mental improvement, and for the most friendly and social intercourse. If these circumstances may be thought to have no connection with agriculture, strictly so called, yet they are certainly to be considered in reference to the condition of the agricultural population; and in every circumstance which renders their condition more comfortable and happy, and, above all, which advances their intelligence, we may ordinarily look for a corresponding improvement in their cultivation and rural husbandry. A New England village resembles, to a great degree, a united and happy family, where perfect equality prevails; where a friendly sympathy is every where active and strong; and where all seem bound to contribute, according to their power, to the general welfare, comfort, and improvement. Society exists in the United States under circumstances so entirely different from those in which it is found here, that a comparison can hardly be instituted between them. The intercourse to which I have here referred, can scarcely be said to exist in England; the general character of the laboring population being not many removes, as far as intellectual improvement is concerned, above that of the other animals which cultivate their fields.

In several respects, it must be admitted, the mild temperature of the English climate affords singular advantages. The winter season furnishes the best opportunity for draining and ditching; the active operations of the farm being, in a degree, suspended, labor is obtained at a low rate; and as a great portion of field work, in England, is done by the piece instead of the day, the shortness of the days makes no difference of expense to the employer.

XII. — AGRICULTURAL POPULATION.

I have referred to some differences in the condition of society here, and in the United States, and those differences it may be well to understand. The agricultural population in England is divided into three classes — the landlord, the tenant farmer or occupier, and the laborer.

1. The Landlords; Rents; and Taxes. — The landlord is the owner of the soil. Most of the landlords are noblemen or gentlemen, and are looked up to with a deference and veneration, on account of their rank, with which those of us who have been educated in a condition of society where titles and ranks are unknown, find it difficult to sympathize. They own the land. Some few of them keep portions of their vast territories in their own occupation, and under their own management; but, by most of them, their lands are leased in farms of different sizes, seldom less than three or four hundred acres, and in many cases eight hundred, a thousand, and twelve hundred acres. The rent of land varies in different places; in some being as low as five

shillings; in others rising to almost as many pounds. Rents are in general paid in money. Sometimes they are valued in kind; that is, the tenant engaging to pay so many bushels of wheat, or so many bushels of barley, or such amount of other products; but in these cases, also, the landlord usually receives his rent in money according to the current prices of these articles. The rents are paid in semi-annual payments. The fair rent of land is sometimes estimated at a third of its products; by some, a different rule is adopted, which is, after all the expenses of cultivation and the usual assessments are deducted from the gross proceeds, that the balance remaining should be divided equally between the landlord and the tenant. In general, however, as far as my observation has extended, the rate of rent is not determined by any particular rule, other than that which prevails in most commercial transactions, that each party makes the best bargain for himself that he is able. It is only just to add that in all the cases, without exception, which have come under my remark, there has seemed to me, on the part of the landlords, a fair measure of liberality; the rents in general bearing a small proportion to the legal interest of the money at which the lands are valued, and for which they could be sold at once; lands costing £60 sterling, or 300 dollars per acre, being frequently let for 30s. or £2 sterling per acre, that is, less than eight or ten dollars per acre. We are not well satisfied in the United States with a return from our land under five or six per cent. on its cost; but the landlords here seldom obtain more than two and a half per cent. or three per cent. on the price which the land would command, if brought into the market. The low rents which are obtained show the abundance of wealth, and how greatly an investment in land is valued for its security; and the active competition for leases, which appears in almost every part of the country when farms are to be let, seems to imply that the rents are reasonable, and, more than that, liberal. As I shall not hesitate to put down my impressions of the country, of men and things, with the utmost frankness, avoiding all personalities, I must say that there has appeared to me on the part of the landowners, with many of whom, among the largest in the country, I have had the pleasure of becoming acquainted, the most marked liberality in the management of their great estates, both in the terms and continuance of their leases, and in the aid rendered to their tenants in making improvements. The liberality and amount of the expenditures indeed strike an American with astonishment. In the United States, and especially in the northern parts of it, where there is a constant struggle to live, where men have to contend with a severe climate and a stubborn soil, and where money is comparatively scarce, the accumulations small, and the farms extremely limited, and where the first lesson taught to a child, even in his swaddling clothes, is a lesson of self-dependence, it is not surprising that men should be compelled with extreme care to husband their small means, and that a frugality, in itself highly commendable, should sometimes verge within the limits of meanness. This, indeed, is far better than that reckless expenditure, without regard to one's means, which we sometimes see, and which is almost sure to involve the individual who indulges in it in irretrievable debt and ruin. But there cannot be a doubt that in New England we often commit a great error in withholding a reasonable expenditure in the improvement of our lands; and that we are not sufficiently impressed with the obvious truth, that a proper expenditure of capital is as important to a successful and improved agriculture, as to the successful prosecution of any branch of manufactures, trade, or commerce.

Leases may be annual, or at will, or for a term of years. When land is taken by the year, it is understood that the tenant has six months' notice of the intention of the landlord not to renew his lease, if such intention exist. The lands in England are burdened with taxes from which the United States are free. These, in many cases, amount to a sum equal to the rent of the land. The tithes, or tenth of every article produced, are not now taken in kind, but are commuted and paid in money. The poor and parochial rates are often heavy; these all are paid by the tenant, unless a special agreement is made to the contrary.

Some persons are disposed to question the right of individuals to such extensive tracts of land, which, in many instances, they neither cultivate themselves, nor suffer others to cultivate, and which descend undiminished through successive generations in the same family. The legal or constitutional right is determined by statute; upon the moral right, or the right founded upon principles of political justice, I am not disposed to enter, as this would lead me to discuss the foundations of all property — a subject foreign from my purpose. The tithe system, as it exists here, strikes a foreign and unpractised eye as a singular feature in the condition of things. A tithe, or tenth part of the produce of the land, according to the provisions of the Levitical law in respect to the Jewish priesthood, was taken for the support of the established religion ; and the priests and clergy of the different parishes were accustomed to levy it in kind, and to exact it to the extremity of every tenth portion of the honey made by bees in the farmer's hives, every tenth chicken in the good wife's poultry-yard, and every tenth egg laid by her fowls. Indeed, the monks, if reports be true, had always a remarkably keen appetite for honey, and poultry, and eggs. By one of the kings of England, the possessions of the church were seized and confiscated; and the right of claiming tithes, in many parishes or districts, was given to his friends, reserving a very small portion for the support of the clergy. A great portion of the tithes are now, therefore, held by laymen; and in some parishes, for example, where the tithes amount to several thousand pounds, the clergyman gets only as many hundreds; and the tithes of any particular parish or place, or rather the right to enforce and receive them, is as much a matter of sale or traffic as the land itself. It is not for me to quarrel with the institutions of a country of which I am neither citizen nor subject; but it is obvious that every burden upon the land must, to a degree, operate to the prejudice of agriculture; and the matter of levying a tax originally intended exclusively for the support of religious institutions, after it has long since avowedly ceased to be applied in any form to that object, is an affair for those to consider who are especially affected by it. I have not deemed it necessary to inquire into the amount paid in this way, which varies considerably in different places; but the amount stated to me by one farmer, the occupier of 250 acres of land, and whose rent is £370, is at least £60 sterling (or 300 dollars) per year in parochial rates, including all but specific taxes. The poor-rates are in many cases extremely burdensome upon the land, the wages of the laborers being in general so limited as not to admit, but in rare cases, of their laying aside any of their earnings for old age, or seasons of sickness and calamity. The support of the poor formerly rested, in a great measure, upon the religious houses, which were very largely endowed with lands and possessions for this very object; but when these houses were broken up and the property taken by the state, this burden was transferred to the backs of the landholders or occupiers. The individual possessions of the landowners are sometimes enormous,

4

amounting in many cases to scores of thousands of acres, and in one instance within my knowledge, to seventy-five thousand acres; and in another, I believe, to more than a million acres.

2. THE FARMERS. — Next come the farmers, who lease the land of the landowners. These men are not like farmers in the United States, who themselves labor in the field; they rarely do any personal labor whatever. They are, in general, a substantial and well-informed body of men; and many of them live in a style of elegance and fashion. Many of them are persons of considerable property, as indeed they must be in order to manage the farms which they undertake. The capital necessary to manage a stock or an arable farm must be always estimated at double or treble the amount of rent; and, in general, cannot be set down at less than £10 sterling, or 50 dollars, per acre. The stock required for a grazing is, of course, much more than for an arable farm; but in no case can success be looked for without ample means of outlay. In no respect does the agriculture of England differ more from that of the United States, especially from that of the Northern States, than in regard to capital. Our farmers, in general, have little floating capital. They attempt to get along with the least possible expenditure. Under such circumstances, they operate to very great disadvantage. They can never wait for a market. They cannot bring out the capabilities of their farms; and the results of their farming are consequently limited and meagre. The difference between a new country contending, as it were, for existence, and an old country operating with the accumulations of years and centuries, is most sensibly marked; the expenses incurred on some farms in England solely for manures purchased, exceeding thousands of pounds sterling, and the cost merely of grass seeds, are perfectly surprising to an American farmer; yet experience has demonstrated that, in these cases, the most liberal outlay of capital is the most sure to be followed by successful results.

The farmers in England, as far as I have had the pleasure to meet with them, are a well-informed set of men, especially on subjects connected with their particular pursuits. There, of course, is the variety among them which is to be found in other classes; but their manners, without exception, are courteous and agreeable, their hospitality distinguished, and their housekeeping — and I speak with the authority of a connoisseur in these matters — is admirable. Indeed, it has not yet been my misfortune to meet, in England or Scotland, with a single instance of negligence in any private house which I have visited; but, on the other hand, the most exemplary neatness. I cannot say as much of all the hotels or taverns in the country, many of which are far inferior in all respects, and none of them superior in any, to our best hotels. There is one circumstance in English manners so much to the credit of their housekeeping, that I shall, for the best of reasons, venture to remind my American friends of it, although I fear that any reformation in the case is hopeless. In no private house which I have visited have I been smothered or offended with tobacco smoke; and I have seen the offensive and useless habit of chewing tobacco since I came to England in but one solitary instance, and that was on the part of an American. At public dinners, the same reserve is not practised, and the atmosphere becomes as thick as a London fog. I will not interfere with any gentleman's private pleasures; but I will lose no fair opportunity of protesting against a practice which has little to recommend it, and in respect to which I think we have good grounds to ask, What right has any man to indulge in any mere personal or selfish gratification, in-doors or without, at the expense of his neighbor's comfort? I know very well the value to my own country, as a branch of agriculture, of the production of tobacco; but I cannot look upon its cultivation with much complacency. Nor does the exhausted condition of the soil, where tobacco has been some time cultivated, reconcile me to its culture. Indeed, how much were it to be wished that instead of the production of an article useless for subsistence and pernicious to health, there could be substituted the cultivation of plants for the food and comfort of millions now suffering from the want of them!

3. The Agricultural Laborers. — Next to the farmers come the laborers; and these three classes preserve the lines of distinction among them with as much caution and strictness, as they preserve the lines and boundaries of their estates. These distinctions strike a visitor from the United States with much force; but, in England, they have been so long established — are so interwoven in the texture of society — and men are, by education and habit, so trained in them, that their propriety or expediency is never matter of question. The nobleman will sometimes, as an act of courtesy and kindness, invite his tenant-farmer to his table; but such a visit is never expected to be

returned. The farmer would under no circumstances invite the laborer to his table, or visit him as a friend or neighbor. I do not mean to imply that there is, on the part of the higher classes of society in England, any insolence or arrogance in their treatment of their inferiors. Free as my intercourse has been with the highest and the middle classes, I have seen no instance of this, nor any thing approaching it, but the contrary; and the best bred men in the country — the true gentlemen — are distinguished by their courtesy and the absence of all ostentatious pretensions. While they naturally fall into the orbit, in which birth, education, and the political institutions of the country have accustomed them to revolve, the well-principled among them would, I am sure, be the last persons, by any assumptions, voluntarily to mortify one below them with a sense of his inferiority.

The farm laborers are, I will not say in a degraded condition, for that would not, in any sense, apply to them, unless where, by their own bad habits, they may have degraded themselves; but they are in a very low condition, and extremely ignorant and servile. They rarely, as with us, live in the house of their employers, but either in cottages on the farm or in a neighboring village. They are, usually, comfortably clad, in this respect contrasting most favorably with the mechanics and manufacturers in the cities and large towns; but they are, in general, very poorly fed. Their wages, compared with the wages of labor in the United States, are very low. The cash wages paid to them seldom equals the cash wages paid to laborers with us, and our laborers, in addition to their wages in money, have their board; but the English laborers are obliged to subsist themselves, with an occasional allowance, in some instances, of beer, in haying or harvesting. The division of labor among them is quite particular — a ploughman being always a ploughman, and almost inseparable from his horses; a ditcher, a ditcher; a shepherd, a shepherd only; the consequence of this is that what they do, they do extremely well. Their ploughing, sowing, drilling, and ditching or draining, are executed with an admirable neatness and exactness; indeed, the lines of their work could not be more true and straight than they usually are, if they were measured with a marked scale, inch by inch. They speak of ploughing and drilling or ridging by the inch or the half inch; and the width of the furrow slice, or the depth of the furrow, or the distances of the drills from each other, will be found to correspond, with remarkable precision, to the measurement designed. But they appear totally destitute of invention, and have, evidently, little skill or ingenuity when called upon to apply themselves to a work different from that to which they have been accustomed. Their gait is very slow; and they seem, to me, to grow old quite early. The former circumstance explained itself to me when I examined and lifted the shoes which they are accustomed to wear, and which, when, in addition to being well charged with iron, they gather the usual amount of clay which adheres to them in heavy soils, furnish at least some reason why, like an Alexandrine verse, "they drag their slow length along." There are occasional instances of extraordinarily good management where they are enabled to accumulate small sums; but in no case, under the best exertions, can they make, from the wages of labor, any thing like a provision for their old age and decay.

They are little given to change situations, and many of them, both men and women, live and die in the same service. Several instances have come under my observation of thirty, thirty-five, and forty years' reputable service; and many where persons, even upon the most limited means, have brought up large families of children without any parochial assistance. But, in this case, they are all workers; the children are put to some sort of service as soon as they are able to drive the rooks from the corn, and no drones are suffered in the hive. I visited one laborer's cottage, to which I was carried by the farmer himself, who was desirous of showing me, as he said, one of the best examples, within his knowledge, of that condition of life. The house, though very small, was extremely neat and tidy; the Bible lay upon the shelf without an unbroken cobweb over its covers; the dressers were covered with an unusual quantity of crockery, sufficient to furnish a table for a large party — a kind of accumulation which, I was told, was very common; and their pardonable vanity runs in this way, as, in higher conditions of life, we see the same passion exhibiting itself in the accumulation of family plate. The man and woman were laborers, greatly esteemed for their good conduct, and had both of them been in the same service more than forty years. I asked them if, in the course of that time, they had not been able to lay by some small store of money to make them comfortable in their old age. I could not have surprised them more by any question which I could have proposed. They replied, that it had been a constant struggle for them to sustain themselves, but any surplus was beyond their reach. I cannot help thinking that the condition is a hard one in which incessant and faithful labor, for so many years, will not enable the frugal and industrious to make some small provision for the period of helplessness and decay, in a country where the accumulations of wealth in some hands, growing out of this same labor, are enormous.

To the honor of several proprietors, the kindest provision is made for the decayed and superannuated. In some cases, the wages of the laborers are continued to the end of life; and in some, as I saw with great pleasure, comfortable cottages are provided for the old and infirm: they have their rent and fuel without charge, and a regular stipend as long as they live. This was the case at the seat of the late distinguished farmer, the Earl of Leicester, formerly Mr. Coke; and likewise on the estates of the Duke of Devonshire, where even the old schoolmaster of the village is pensioned, and has a house and a liberal allowance provided for him. Several other instances have come under my observation, where the superannuated and decayed laborers were kindly provided for and received a pension adequate to their comfortable support. This is as it should be. In every just community the rights of honest labor ought to be respected and secured. I confess it would be far better for them to be able to provide for themselves than to be dependent upon the precarious bounty either of individuals or the public; but I should be unwilling to overlook any act of justice or honor. It is obvious that the prospect of a supply from the bounty of the landlord can only apply to those who are in the direct employment of the landlord, and not to those who serve the tenant farmer, whose situation and permanency, where the lease of the farm is only for the year, are always, to a degree, doubtful.

It cannot be denied that those who labor with us are altogether a superior class of men to the English laborers; I refer, of course, to the natives of the country. A considerable portion of our labor is now performed by foreigners, who, when they unite sobriety and frugality with faithful industry, are sure of good treatment and success; indeed, I have known several instances of laboring men, and some of them in my own employment, who, by good conduct, have supported themselves, and have accumulated, after a few years' service, their four and five hundred dollars and upwards, that is, their eighty and their hundred pounds — an acquisition which, in England, a laboring man would not dream of as the result of his labor, sooner than he would dream of receiving a pension of the same amount from the government. With us the laborer is vastly better paid than in England. With us the laborer always is, or always may be, the owner of the house in which he lives, and of as much land as he chooses to cultivate. Here the cottager is always a mere tenant, subject to the pleasure of his landlord; and, though there are many cases where allotments of small portions of land are granted them for a garden spot, and for the obtaining of some small supplies for their families, yet there are many where no indulgence of this sort is allowed, not even so much as a cabbage yard. The laborer here is doomed to remain in the condition in which he is born — he cannot rise above it. The provision for the education of the children of the laborers is, in most parts of England, extremely limited and meagre. There are some national schools, and there are, in many places, schools established and supported by the liberality of the landlords, for the benefit of the laborers in their own villages, and on their own farms. Sunday schools are likewise kept up in all the parishes which I have visited; and I should be happy, if it were allowed me, to adorn my page with the names of some noble women, who, with a benevolence truly maternal, take a deep interest in these institutions, and generously support them, and, better than that, personally superintend them. These are bright examples. In one case, at a small country village, on a Sunday, I saw more than four hundred of these children, cleanly and plainly dressed, entering the parish church, and taking their seats together, behaving with the most exemplary propriety. When they lifted up their voices in the solemn chants of the church, and their gentle and shrill tones were heard above all the rest, I could not help lifting up my own heart to God in thanksgiving, that the highest truths of religion can be taken in by the humblest minds; that here was at work an instrument of their elevation, which no human power could forbid; that here they were taught to recognize the dignity of their moral nature; and that there is one place, where all earthly distinctions betray their insignificance, and every human being may, on equal terms and with equal confidence, invoke a common and a universal Father. This school was entirely supported by and under the care of a noble woman, who, to the highest distinctions of rank, education, fashion, and fortune, adds the far higher attributes of a deep sense of religious duty, and an earnest desire to be useful.

The Sunday schools do not, every where, confine themselves to religious instruction, but reading, writing, and the elements of arithmetic, are also taught, because, in many cases, the children of the poor are kept so constantly at labor as to have no other opportunity of getting this instruction. The education given them is of a very limited character, and does not extend beyond reading, writing, and the first principles of arithmetic, exclusive of religious instruction. The British and foreign schools, which are established by aid from the government — which measures its bounty by what may be raised by private subscription in any parish or village — require the catechism of the established church to be taught, and the attendance of the children at the church, under the penalty of exclusion from the school. The National School Society allows the attendance of the children at such church as the parents choose; but the catechism of the established church, and no other, is allowed to be taught in their schools. The schools supported by the liberality of the dissenters are, comparatively, few; and in most of these, without doubt, the same interest is active, and the same influences are at work, to attach their children to the particular sect by whose patronage the school is established and sustained. I speak now of England. I am not yet able to speak of the condition of things in Scotland, although it is constantly boasted of that the education of the Scotch laborer is always provided for, and that the Scotch laborer, in point of instruction, is far superior to the English. This remains for me to see.

The condition of the laborers in this country is a subject of such deep concern to the community, on the ground of pecuniary profit as well as of philanthropy and justice, that I shall, in the course of my inquiries, revert again to it. I do not feel that as yet I am sufficiently well-informed to speak with much confidence on the subject; but I shall not leave it without some further remarks. The common wages of farm labor vary, for men, from six shillings to twelve shillings per week; but I think a fair average would be eight to nine shillings sterling. A shilling may be reckoned at twenty-four cents, so that the monthly wages for a man may be put down at eight dollars and sixty-four cents. This is the whole, where labor is paid for in money, excepting, as a matter of kindness, the farmer generally brings the coals for his laborer. There are cases, too, in which the farmer stipulates to supply his wheat to the laborer at a fixed price, which is to be unaffected by any changes in the market. Six shillings, only, a week are reported to be paid in some places, but I have met with no case less than eight shillings and sixpence a week.

It may be interesting to some of my readers to have a more particular account of the wages and condition of the laborers, and for that reason I will give some statements of their condition in that part of the country where wages are paid in kind.

In the neighborhood of Haddingdon, in East Lothian, I visited a laborer's cottage, being one in a range of six cottages, in a district of country highly cultivated and improved, and presenting some of the finest examples of agricultural improvement which I have ever seen. The wife, a very tidy and civil woman, about forty years of age, was at home; her husband and daughter laboring in the field. This was a very good specimen of a neat cottage, and its inmates had passed the greater part of their lives in it. It had no other floor but the hard ground; and two beds were fixed in the wall, like sailors' berths on board ship. The shelves were covered with crockery; and a Bible, and a few religious and other tracts lay upon the mantel-piece. A cake made of pea-flour and barley-flour was baking over the fire, of which I was asked to eat, but the taste of which did very little towards quickening my appetite. There was, besides the one in which I was, a small room for coal and lumber, where, in case of great emergency, a lodging might be made up. One of her neighbors in the same block, with no larger accommodations, had eight children to provide for. Two grown-up daughters, with one smaller one, occupied one bed; the parents, with one child, occupied the other; the two grown-up sons slept in the lumber-room or coal-house. There is often much closer lodging than this. The husband of the woman, in whose cottage I was, was a ploughman, and likewise a bondager — a species of service or contract which requires him to furnish a female laborer, at tenpence per day in ordinary work, and one shilling per day in harvest, whenever her services are required. If he has not a wife or daughter who will answer this purpose, he must keep a woman in his house to be always in readiness when required. His wages were —

18	bolls of oats, at 4 bushels per boll, . . .	72	bushels.
2	bolls of peas, " " " . . .	8	"
4½	bolls of barley, " " " . . .	18	"

and £1 for "lint" — or shirts.

This payment of wages in kind, if the rate is fairly fixed, is certainly an equitable mode. Its effect upon the laborers, as in this case, as they themselves have grain to sell, is to make them the advocates of high prices, and, consequently, the friends of those restrictive measures by which foreign competition in the grain market is prevented. The employer likewise keeps a cow for the laborer; or if he has no cow, an allowance is made to him of five or six pounds in money. He is likewise allowed 1000 square yards of ground for potatoes, which the farmer ploughs and manures for him; but which he cultivates in extra hours. For the rent of his house he gives twenty-one days' work in harvest, if required; but should it happen that only twelve or fourteen are required, it is accepted as an equivalent.

For the woman's work he receives a fixed amount per day, whenever she is employed; and for her six months' service in the year he pays her three pounds. For the other six months he pays her nothing more than her board and some clothes. The farmer brings his coals for him, which he purchases at a small sum, being small coals, here called *pan-wood.* The value of three shillings and sixpence in coals will serve him through seven weeks in winter. Seven loads (one-horse loads, I suppose) of coals are purchased at the quarries for three shillings and sixpence. The farmer's shoes cost him ten shillings, and one pair will last him eighteen months. His daughter's working shoes last her a year: this is exclusive of her Sunday's shoes. In most parts of Scotland, the women, in the summer season, wear only their natural sandals and hose, which have, indeed, the advantages of being easily washed, and easily repaired; but in this part of Scotland they form the exception of wearing shoes and stockings the whole year. Their living consists of bread made of barley and peas, meal or oaten porridge and milk, and potatoes; and they generally have a pig. They cannot, of course, lay up any money; and she added, in her own pleasant dialect, that "the lassies have muckle sair work in harvest." They depend on the sale of their surplus grain for what little money they need. I will do justice to her modest merit, and say, to the shame of thousands rolling in unstinted luxury, that she spoke of her condition as comfortable, and expressed strongly and religiously her contentment.

The wages paid in the county of Northumberland, where the Scotch system of farming is carried to a high degree of perfection, is as follows, as given by several gentlemen, familiar with the subject, to the parliamentary committee: —

FIRST EXAMPLE.

36 bushels of oats,
24 " " barley,
12 " " peas,
3 " " wheat,
3 " " rye,
36 to 40 " potatoes,
24 lbs. of wool,
A cow's keep for a year,
Cottage and garden,
Coals carrying from the pit,
£4 in cash.

SECOND EXAMPLE.

10 bushels of wheat,
30 " " oats,
10 " " barley,
10 " " rye,
10 " " peas,
A cow's keep for a year,
800 yds. of land for potatoes,
Cottage and garden,
Coals led,
£3 10 s. in cash,
2 bushels of barley in lieu of hens.

THIRD EXAMPLE.

36 bushels of oats,
24 " " barley,
12 " " peas,
6 " " wheat,
1000 yds. of land for potatoes,
A cow's keep,
House and garden,
Coals led,
£5 in cash.

The following, which is a specimen of the half-year's account between a large farmer and one of his laborers in a part of Northumberland, is worthy of observation:—

——— Dr. to ———

	£.	s.	d.
Jane Thompson, (the bondager,) 121½ days at 10d., .	5	1	3
Catherine Thompson, (a child,) 24 harvest days at 1s.	1	4	0
Do., 73½ days at 5d., ...	1	10	7½
Elizabeth Thompson, (a younger child,) 7½ days, . .	0	1	9½
Isabella Thompson, (a dress-maker at other times,) 35¾ days at 1s.,	1	15	9
Do., 20 harvest days at 2s. 3d., ...	2	5	0
Wife, 9 harvest days, ...	1	0	3
His old father, 52 days, ...	3	18	0
John Thompson's half-year's cash, ...	2	10	0
	£19	6	8*

This account, it will be seen, with the exception of the last item, does not include any portion of the laborer's own service, but that of his family only. The difference in the price of harvest work at different periods, as between one shilling and two shillings and threepence, is probably owing to labor becoming more scarce, on account of the general ripeness of the crop, or the hurrying state of the weather.

The Scotch laborers seemed to me, from a very limited observation, strongly attached to their employers. On one farm, where I had the pleasure of visiting, one of the laborers had been in the employment of the same family forty years, and another sixty; to each of whom, although their labor now was of very little value, the farmer continued the same rate of wages, which they had in early life. This indeed would seem to be no more than just, that the honest laborer, whose life had been spent in the service of another man, should not be turned adrift in his old age; but, alas! how rare is jüstice!

Of the extraordinary frugality with which some persons in humble life live, even where prices are high, I may give an

* Parliamentary Report on Employment of Women and Children in Agriculture. 1843. p. 297.

example, which came under my observation. In Arbroath, near the magnificent ruins of the ancient abbey of Arbroath, I heard the movements of a hand-loom, and I took the liberty, with due ceremony, of going in. A middle-aged Scotch woman, of pleasing appearance and neatly dressed, was weaving. I asked her how much she was able to earn. She replied that if she rose early, at five o'clock, and worked all day through the week, after paying for the use of the loom and the cost of winding her spools, her week's work would amount to four shillings. She received no parish assistance. She paid three pounds sixteen shillings for the rent of her house. Her fuel cost her ninepence per week; and out of the remainder — less than two shillings — she had to support and clothe herself and an aged mother, who was very infirm, and incapable of helping herself. What the support that either of the poor creatures could have under such circumstances must be left to conjecture. The woman spoke of her circumstances as being difficult, but she made no complaint, and presented an example of true Christian philosophy, which would have done honor to a superior education and the highest condition in life.

In all parts of the country, women are more or less employed on the farms, and in some parts in large numbers; I have frequently counted thirty, fifty, and many more in a field at a time, both in hoeing turnips and in harvesting. I have found them, likewise, engaged in various other services — in pulling weeds, in picking stones, in unloading and treading grain, in tending threshing-machines, in digging potatoes and pulling and topping turnips, in tending cattle, in leading out dung, and in carrying limestone and coals. Indeed, there is hardly any menial service to which they are not accustomed; and all notions of their sex seem out of the question whenever their labor is wanted or can be applied. The wages of women are commonly sixpence and eightpence, and they seldom exceed tenpence a day, excepting in harvest, when they are as high as a shilling. The hours of labor for the men are usually from six o'clock, A. M., to six, P. M., with an interval of an hour for breakfast and an hour for dinner. The women rarely come before eight o'clock, and quit labor at six, with the usual indulgence for dinner. Many of the laborers walk two and three miles to their work, and return at night. Their meals are taken in the fields, and in the most simple form. The dinner is often nothing more than bread.

In the season of harvest, immense numbers of Irish come over to assist in the labor, and this presents almost the only opportunity which they have, in the course of the year, of earning a little money to pay the rent of their cabins and potato patches. Nothing can exceed the destitution and squalidness in which they are seen; starved, ragged, and dirty beyond all description, with the tatters hanging about them like a few remaining feathers upon a plucked goose. At their first coming, they are comparatively feeble and inefficient; but after a week's comfortable feeding, they recover strength, increasing some pounds in weight, and, if they are allowed to perform their work by the piece, they accomplish a great deal.

I found in one case on two farms — which, though under two tenants, might be considered as a joint concern — more than four hundred laborers employed during the harvests, a large proportion of whom were women, but not exclusively Irish. The average wages paid the men in this case was one shilling sterling (or twenty-four cents) per day and their food, which was estimated at about ninepence (or about eighteen cents) per day. Their living consisted of oatmeal-porridge and a small quantity of sour milk or buttermilk for breakfast; a pound of wheaten bread, and a pint and a half of beer at dinner; and at night, a supper resembling the breakfast, or twopence in money in lieu of it. I was curious to know how so many people were lodged at night. In some cases, they throw themselves down under the stacks, or upon some straw in the sheds, or out-buildings of the farm; but in the case to which I refer above, I was shown into the cattle-stalls and stables, the floors of which were littered with straw; and here the men's coats, and the women's caps and bonnets, upon the walls, indicated that it was occupied by both parties promiscuously. This was indeed the fact. Each person, as far as possible, was supplied with a blanket; and these were the whole accommodations and the whole support. This was not a singular instance. I am unwilling to make any comments upon such facts as these. They speak for themselves. They are matters of general custom, and seemed to excite no attention. I do not refer to them as matter of reproach to the employers, who were persons of respectable character and condition, and whose families were distinguished for their refinement. But it presents one among many instances in which habit and custom reconcile us to many things which would otherwise offend us; and lead us to view some practices, utterly unjustifiable in themselves, with a degree of complacency or indifference; and as unalterable, because they have been so long established. I believe there is only one part of the United States where any thing resembling such a condition of things prevails, or would be permitted; and there only among a class of beings whose claims to humanity seem not very well established in all minds, and whose degradation, on account of their complexion, appears absolutely hopeless. But, even here, this indiscriminate consorting is not common; nor would it be permitted by any respectable planter.

This condition of things should certainly save this country from the reproach, if it be one, which some English tourists are disposed to attribute to American manners — that of treating the sex with too much courtesy and deference. I cannot bring myself, however, to view the subject with any lightness whatever. My confident conviction is, that the virtue of a community depends on nothing more than on the character of the women. In proportion as they are improved, and treated with deference on account of their sex, the women are brought to respect themselves, and the character of the men is directly improved; character itself becomes valuable to both parties. But in proportion as the condition of women is degraded, and they are considered and treated as mere animals, self-respect is not known among them; character is of no value; and the moral condition of such a class, or rather its improvement, is absolutely without hope. Nor is it without its pernicious influences, which must be too obvious to require to be pointed out, upon the classes in the community above them. Much fault as some persons have been pleased to find with the deference paid to the sex in the United States, I should be very sorry to see it in the smallest measure abated. I do not believe, taken as a whole, there is a more virtuous population upon earth, than are the women of New England and the Middle States; and nowhere is there a greater decency and propriety of conversation and manners. I speak of these portions of the country in particular, because with them I am intimately acquainted, and have a right to speak with confidence; but I have no reason to say that the same respectability of character does not prevail in other parts of the United States.

I do not claim for my country any thing like an immaculate condition of society; very far from it: but I do claim for them a highly-improved moral condition; and have no hesitation in saying, that in most of our country villages prostitution is unknown, and an illegitimate child is a comparatively rare occurrence. I add with equal confidence, that under the influence of our free schools and universal education, and the disinterested and philanthropic exertions among all sects for the religious education of the young in Sunday schools, the beneficial and ameliorating results fully equal every reasonable expectation. This comes of the value of character, and the lessons early inculcated upon them to respect themselves as women. I would, if possible, strengthen this sentiment; and therefore would in no department of life render less prominent the distinctive barriers between the sexes. In all my intercourse with society in the United States, and with opportunities as large as any man of observing all classes among them in the various conditions of life, I have never known an instance of a woman going to a public bar for drink, or sitting down in a public bar-room with men, or alone, to regale herself. The ale-houses and gin-shops in England are as much accustomed by women as by men, and the results of such practices are exactly what might be expected — an extreme vulgarity of manners, and a large amount of drunkenness among the lower class of women. What, as a matter of course, comes with it need not be told; but the records of the police courts leave no one at a loss.

My observations in this case must be understood as applying solely to the lowest class: these constitute a very numerous portion. They apply likewise mainly to cities and large towns. In respect to the deportment of the middle and the highest classes — with whom my intercourse, through their kindness, has been familiar and extensive — nothing in manners or conversation can be farther removed from that which is vulgar or offensive; and for propriety and the highest degree of refinement, nothing can be more exemplary and delightful.

In districts strictly agricultural, the low rate of wages does not admit of much expenditure in this way; and, if there are indulgences, they must be at home in the village ale-houses, and only occasional. For a considerable portion of the year, the farm laborers are not allowed any beer; in the haying and harvesting, their allowance seldom exceeds one pint and a half, which, as it is small beer, cannot be considered excessive. I could not learn that any allowance of whisky or spirit is ever given them by their employers, or that it is ever carried by them into the fields. The drinking, in this country, with the lower and laboring classes of people, seems, in a great degree, confined to the licensed houses, of which, certainly, there is nowhere any want. In passing through the village of Glossop, in Derbyshire, a modern and an exceedingly well-built village, in a distance, I should judge, of less than three fourths of a mile, I counted, as I passed along on the box of the coach, thirty-five licensed retail shops, most of which were probably for the sale, among other things, of intoxicating liquors. Indeed, the number of licensed retailers in every village in England is quite remarkable, and would seem, in many cases, to include almost every fourth house.

I am not disposed to object to the employment of women in some kinds of agricultural labor. The employment of them in indiscriminate labor is liable to the most serious objections. Nothing can be more animating, and, in its way, more beautiful, than, on a fine, clear day, when the golden and waving harvest is ready for the sickle, to see, as I have several times seen, a party of more than a hundred women and girls entering the field, cutting the grain, or binding it up after the reapers. In cultivating the turnips, they are likewise extremely expert. In tending and making hay, and in various other agricultural labors, they carry their end of the yoke even; but in loading and leading out dung, and especially, as I have seen them, in carrying broken limestone in baskets on their heads, to be put into the kilns, and in bearing heavy loads of coal from the pits, I have felt that their strength was unnaturally taxed, and that, at least in these cases, they were quite out of "woman's sphere." I confess, likewise, that my gallantry has often been severely tried, when I have seen them at the inns acting as ostlers, bringing out the horses and assisting in changing the coach team, while the coachman went into the inn to try the strength of the ale.

As far as health is concerned, the out-door employment of women is altogether favorable. As far as virtue or moral purity is concerned, out-door employment in itself is not more objectionable than employment within doors. Indeed, from the inquiries which have been made into this matter, and the elaborate reports that have been given to the government, it does not appear that the agricultural districts, where the custom of out-door employment for women prevails, are more immoral than the manufacturing districts. But the natural effect of such employment upon women is to render them negligent of their persons, and squalid and dirty in their appearance; and with this neglect of person, they cease to be treated with any deference by the other sex, and lose all respect for themselves. Personal neglect and uncleanliness are followed by their almost invariable concomitants, mental and moral impurity and degradation. The working likewise promiscuously with men, which is done continually, must expose them to rude jests, and to language and manners which, among the lower class of men, are too often grossly indecent and immoral. In all other respects, many kinds of out-door agricultural employment must be, and is, as it is admitted, favorable to health and vigor. The general health and vigor of such women, so many hours engaged in reasonable exercise in the open air, contrast most favorably with the effeminacy, debility, and early decay of those who are confined in heated and close manufactories, or in sedentary employments within doors. Nor, in point of moral conduct, as far as mere occupation is concerned, is there any reason to suppose that the agricultural classes would suffer in comparison with the manufacturing classes, or with the host of young women in cities, employed in various trades and in-door occupations. We have few instances, in the free states, of women being employed in field labor. The women in Wethersfield, Connecticut, have for years been accustomed to the cultivation of onions, doing every thing for the crop, excepting ploughing and manuring the land; even to preparing it for the market. They certainly have suffered no evil, but, on the contrary, have derived much benefit, from the occupation. Nowhere, it is believed, can men, dependent upon their own exertions for support, find wives better able to manage their household affairs, more frugal, more industrious, or more tidy, than among the industrious young women of Wethersfield. It must seem strange to many persons if I also add, as I know I may with truth, that many of these young women are persons of good education, and to a degree, allowing for the retired condition of society in which they have been brought up, even of refined manners: so totally different, indeed, are the conditions of the laboring classes in England and the United States. In truth, no comparison can properly be instituted between them. In general, among the laboring classes in England, their low condition, their ignorance, and want of education, and the almost absolute impossibility of rising above the estate in which they are born, render them, to a great degree, reckless and improvident. Character becomes consequently of far less importance than it would otherwise be. There are wanting, consequently, the motives to that self-respect, which constitutes the highest security of virtue; and under such a condition of things, it is not surprising to find a laxity of morals, which produces swarms of illegitimate children. This is attended by the usual consequence — an absence, on the part of the parents, of that sense of obligation to support and provide for their offspring, which is to be found in its purity and strength only in legal wedlock.

There are two practices in regard to agricultural labor, not universal, by any means, but prevailing in some parts of England and Scotland, which I may notice. The first is called the "gang system." In some places, owing to the size of farms being greatly extended, cottages being suffered to fall into decay and ruin, laborers have been congregated in villages, where have prevailed all the evils, physical and moral, which are naturally to be expected from a crowded population, shoved into small and inconvenient habitations, and subjected to innumerable privations. In this case, the farmer keeps in permanent and steady employment no more laborers than are absolutely required for the constant and uninterrupted operations of the farm; and relies upon the obtaining of a large number of hands, or a *gang*, as it is termed, whenever any great job is to be accomplished, that he may be enabled to effect it at once and at the smallest expense. Under these circumstances, he applies to a gang-master, as he is termed, who contracts for its execution, and through whom the poor laborers must find employment, if they find it at all; and upon whose terms they must work, or get no work. The gang-master has them then completely in his power, taking care to provide well for himself in his own commissions, which must, of course, be deducted from the wages of the laborers, and subjecting them, at pleasure, to the most despotic and severe conditions. It is not optional with these poor creatures to say whether they will work or not, but whether they will work or die — they have no other resource — change their condition they cannot — contract separately for their labor they cannot, because the farmer confines his contracts to the gang-master; and we may infer from the Reports of the

Commissioners, laid before the government, that the system is one of oppression, cruelty, and plunder, and in every respect leading to gross immoralities. The distance to which these laborers go is often as much as five or six miles, and this usually on foot, and to return at night. Children and girls are compelled to go these distances, and consequently must rise very early in the morning and reach home at a very late hour at night. Girls and boys and young men and women work indiscriminately together. When the distance to which they go for work is ten miles, they are sent in carts. When the distances are great, they occasionally pass the night at the place of work, and then lodge in barns, or any where else, indiscriminately together. To talk of morals in such a case is idle. One of the gang-masters, who has been an overseer seventeen years, gives it as his testimony, under oath, "that seventy out of a hundred of the girls become prostitutes," and the general account given of the operations of the system shows an utter profligacy of mind in their general conversation and manners, when morals must follow of course. If they go in the morning and stay only a little while, on account of rain, or other good cause, they are paid nothing. The day is divided into quarters, but no smaller fractions of time are in any case allowed to them. Then the persons employed are required, in many cases, to deal with the gang-master for the supplies they receive, in payment for their labor. The results of such a system are obvious. The work being taken by the piece, the gang-master presses them to their utmost strength. The fragments of days, in which work is done and not paid for to the laborers, are all to the benefit of the gang-master, who, in such case, gets a large amount of work done at no cost. These poor wretches, being unable to contract for themselves, or to get any work but through him, he of course determines the price of the labor, and, one may be sure, puts it down to the lowest point. But his advantages do not end here, for there is no doubt that he gets a high advance upon the goods which he requires them to purchase of him, and thus their wages are reduced still lower. No just or benevolent mind, it would seem, can look upon any such system in all its details, as given in the Commissioners' Report, but with a profound sense of its injustice, oppression, and immorality.

One of the gang-masters says, "If they go to work two hours

and a half, it is a quarter of a day. If they go a long walk, seven miles or so, and it comes on a wet day, there is the walk all for nothing. Children of the ages of four, five, and six, work in the gangs. They earn 9 d. a day, the big ones; the small, 4 d.; children of seven years old, 3 d. a day." "It is the ruin of a girl," says a parent, one of the laborers, "to be in such a place as that." "My children's hands are so blistered," says another of the parents, "pulling turnips, that I have been obliged to tie them up every night this winter. Pulling turnips blisters the hands very much — they are obliged to pull them up — they must not take turnip crones (a sort of fork) for fear of damaging the turnips."

"The gangsman, or leader," says another witness, "pays the wages of all employed in the gang, and, of course, makes his profit entirely from their labor, as the farmer takes care that the gang system shall not cost him more than the common system of individual laborers. The leader's profit, as I have heard, is sometimes 15 s. per day. The assembling of twenty-five and thirty women and children and lads, of all ages and conditions and characters, together, has a most fatal effect upon their morals and conduct." Another respectable and reverend witness says, "The gang is superintended by a lazy, idle fellow, of profligate manners and a dishonest character — such, at all events, are the characters of two in my own neighborhood."

I will not dwell upon the evils of a management of this kind. It is obvious what a power such a man, the employer of these people, has over them; and it is as easy to infer what is likely to be the character of young persons, more especially, placed under his control. When are men to be just? and when are men, who live upon the hard labor of others, and who hold not merely their physical but their moral destiny in their hands, to feel their responsibleness as Christians and as men?

The most melancholy circumstance in the case is given in the testimony of one witness, a clergyman, who says, "that he fears the gang system will and must increase, especially upon large farms." It would not be unreasonable to fear that God would send blight and mildew upon fields where human life and virtue are thus sacrificed, and decency and morals thrown to the winds; and where the crops are watered with the tears of these wretched victims of injustice and oppression.

There is another system of employment, which prevails in Northumberland and in some parts of Scotland, to which I have already alluded: this is called the *bondage* system, but it does not appear to me liable to the strong objections which the name would seem to imply. In this case, the laborer, when he contracts for his services, makes a condition that he will, as may be required, furnish a woman as an additional laborer; and he receives so much per day for her labor, according to the number of days she may be employed. In such case, if he has not a wife or daughter to supply the place, he engages some young woman who lives in his family, and to whom he pays such a sum by the year as may be agreed upon, in money, clothing, or otherwise, and she lives in his family as one of the family for the whole year. There are few forms of servitude which are not liable to abuses, and the greater the state of dependence and weakness, so much increased is the liability to abuse; but where the employer is a conscientious and just man, such a contract may be mutually advantageous.

In parts of Scotland, what is called the *Bothie* system prevails, and the support of the laborers is a very summary process. The wages are paid in money or kind, as may be agreed upon; and the laborers, if single men, are furnished with a room, fuel, and bedding; with two pecks of oatmeal on Monday morning, and with a daily allowance of new or of sour milk — occasionally they may have beer and bread for dinner instead of the porridge. Nothing more, however, is done for them. They prepare their porridge for themselves in such way as they choose; but this comprehends the whole of their living. It would not be true to say that this diet is insufficient for the support of a laboring man, as it must be admitted that few laborers exhibit firmer health, or more muscular vigor, or really perform more work, than many of these men. This mode of living would, however, I think, be a little too primitive for the New England taste, though on matters of taste we are told there is to be no dispute. Having myself visited a Scotch Bothie, I cannot, how much soever the economy of the arrangements may be praised, much commend the style of the housekeeping. Indeed, it is not difficult to infer that where young men at service are turned into a hovel together, and without any one to look after their lodging or prepare their meals, the style of living cannot have the advantages even of the wigwam of a North American savage; for there, at least, there is a squaw to provide the food and look after the premises.* The wages of a Scotch laborer are about £12 sterling per year, and living as above; and for a woman, as a field laborer, four shillings sterling per week, or about eighty-eight cents, out of which she provides for herself.

The condition of labor forms, as is obvious, a most important element in the agriculture of a country. Human labor, indeed, seems far more essentially concerned in agriculture than in either commerce or manufactures. A few hands may manage a large ship, freighted with immense wealth, and performing voyages which equal the circuit of the globe. A child may superintend a large number of spindles; and a single power wheel sets in motion a vast and complicated machinery. Agriculture has already derived vast benefits from mechanical ingenuity, and may confidently anticipate from this source an immense extension of her power; but there can be no question that she must, at least for a long time to come, continue mainly dependent upon human labor. The cost of labor, therefore, and the general support and condition of this labor, are alike interesting to the agriculturist and the philanthropist.

In an old country like England, where labor is so abundant, it is to be expected that the rules of labor should be exact and stringent; indeed, without this the management of a large farm would be impracticable. The women usually begin work at eight o'clock, and, resting an hour for dinner, they work until five, or, in a pressure of work, until six. The ploughman must feed and clean his horses at four o'clock in the morning, and at six o'clock the plough must be under way. At two o'clock, his horses are put up for the day, and he devotes himself until six o'clock to their cleansing and feeding, and to the care of his plough and harness; eight hours in the field, and the ploughing an acre of

---

* Of the Bothie system, as it is called, or employment of unmarried men, living together in a bothie or hovel attached to the steading, it is hardly necessary to say, that a more effective means of demoralizing and brutalizing a peasantry could not be devised than that of crowding together a parcel of young men, half of them perhaps strangers, Irish, or bad characters, in a hovel by themselves, without even an attempt at moral superintendence. This is one of the worst evils that has attended the introduction of the large farm system.—*Laing's Prize Essay.*

ground, being considered a full day's work. The other laborers begin labor at six o'clock in the morning, and work until six in the afternoon, with the intermission of half an hour for breakfast and an hour for dinner. No laborer leaving his employment before the termination of his engagement, without good and sufficient reason, can recover any portion of his wages; and no employer, without equal reason, can dismiss a laborer before the end of the term for which he is engaged. In general, however, laborers continue for years in the same employment, especially married men; and it is extremely interesting, speaking well both for master and servant, to see men and women who have remained in the same service twenty, thirty, forty, and even fifty years, and their children coming forward to take their places. In such cases, they become, as it were, an integral part of the establishment, and both parties are equally benefited.

In some parts of the country, as in Lincolnshire for example, twice a year, in the spring and autumn, are held, in some principal market towns, statute fairs, vulgarly called "Statties," where young men and women wanting service assemble, and persons wanting laborers or servants go there to supply their wants. Such arrangements have certainly many advantages; but they have also their evils, and the assembling of large numbers of men and women, in such cases, with, not unfrequently, the usual accompaniments of a Fair, are said to lead to much dissoluteness and dissipation. This is to be expected. This arrangement serves to average the rate of wages, and must be to all parties a great saving of time. In the present condition of female labor in the United States, there could be none but the worthless to offer themselves in this way; but with respect to young men seeking employment, there would be great advantages in having a day and place fixed in some principal town, when and where persons wishing for employment might be found by persons wishing to employ them; and such an "Exchange" might be annually held to advantage. An arrangement of this kind has often recommended itself to my mind for its convenience, and I have, before this, urged its adoption.

I have endeavored, with strict regard to truth, to state what I understand to be the condition of the agricultural population in this country. Further inquiries may serve to correct or modify my views on this subject. I am perfectly aware how difficult it is for a foreigner to obtain a correct knowledge or to form a fair judgment of the customs and manners of any country which he visits; and especially where his residence is limited, and his observations necessarily partial. Feeling no prejudices, and having no private interests or partialities in the case, other than those which are inseparable from an education in another condition in society, and under political institutions differing entirely from those which prevail here, I am desirous, above all things, to hold my mind open to the light of further and more exact inquiry.

It does not need any long experience to learn that first impressions are not always the most correct; and every intelligent and candid mind must allow that most men have some reasons which, to their minds, appear sufficient for what they do; that many customs which have prevailed for ages, however objectionable at first sight they may appear to us, have grown out of peculiar circumstances of time and place, which sanction their expediency at the time of their origin, if not the propriety of their continuance; and that, in respect to many acknowledged evils, it is far more easy to deplore the existence than to point out the remedy. While circumstances of this nature prompt to caution and forbearance in our judgments, they do not require us, at the expense of our moral sense, to regard these evils in any other than their true character, to palliate either their nature or extent, or to look upon them, under any circumstances, in utter despair of their removal or alleviation. Nor will they excuse any neglect of all proper and possible exertion to remedy an acknowledged evil.

The condition of the laboring agricultural class is certainly, in many parts of England, exceedingly depressed; and though in frequent instances it may be called comfortable, in few that I have seen can it be considered prosperous. Their labor is not extraordinarily severe; they are by no means treated with unkindness, or, excepting through the misfortune of the ill temper of their employer, with severity; they are decently clad, and there is a great amount of active benevolence every where at work to assist them, and to alleviate their distress in sickness and misfortune. But they are very poorly fed; with many exceptions, they are wretchedly lodged; their wages are inadequate to their comfortable support; and their situation affords little or no hope of improvement, — at least the power of making it better does not rest, where it should, with themselves.

It is a painful, though not an unheard-of anomaly, that, in the midst of the greatest abundance of human food, immense numbers of those by whose labor this food is produced are actually suffering and perishing from hunger; that where ten millions of acres of improvable lands, capable of being made productive lands, lie uncultivated,* millions of hands, which might subdue, enrich, and beautify this waste, from necessity remain unemployed; and that, in a country where the accumulations of wealth surpass the visions of Oriental splendor and magnificence, there exist, on the other hand, such contrasts of want, destitution, privation, and misery, as would surpass belief and defy the power of the imagination, but for the support of incontrovertible and overwhelming evidence. Under the present institutions of the country, a perfect remedy is hopeless, and an alleviation of these evils is all which can be looked for. An entire revolution in the institutions of the country, in the forms of society, and in the condition of property, could only be effected by violence; and the consequences of such a revolution it would be frightful to contemplate. But should a revolution occur, and the framework of society be broken up, and its elements be thrown into a state of chaotic confusion, what sagacity could predict the results, and what security is there that in any re-arrangement these evils would be rectified and the rights of labor any better protected? I say the rights of labor; for who, under any circumstances, will presume to deny that they, by whose labor the earth is made to yield her fruits, and all accumulations of wealth are obtained, have not, indeed, in common justice, a perfect claim to a full share of the products of their own toil? I care not what claims arbitrary and despotic power may set up; nor by what laws and rules she may seek to appropriate to her own use or luxury much the largest portion of these products; but I claim for the laborer an ample share of the fruits of his industry on the obvious grounds of natural right and justice, and the plainest principles of Christianity.

I am not at all disposed to quarrel with any of the institutions of this great and enlightened country — great and enlightened,

* Journal of Royal Agricultural Society, vol. iv. pt. ii. p. 308.

as a whole, beyond almost any precedent. I am not disposed, in any offensive form, to profess my own preferences for institutions to which birth and education may have strongly attached me, founded as they are on the great principles of universal liberty as the birthright of every man, and of social equality as conformable to nature, and the only relation in which men can stand to their Creator, or under which they would dare to approach him. But, to my mind, it is obvious that no great improvement can take place in the character and condition of the laboring population while they remain a distinct and servile class, without any power of rising above their condition. At present, the most imaginative and sanguine see no probability of their rising above their condition, of being any thing but laborers, or of belonging to any other than a servile and dependent class. The low state of their wages absolutely forbids the accumulation of any property. They cannot own any of the soil which they cultivate. The houses which they occupy belong not to themselves, and they may at any time be turned out of them. They must ask leave to live, or they must take it by violence or plunder when they will not be suffered to live. Their only home is the grave.

In a country where labor is superabundant, and the price of land places it utterly beyond the reach of those who have no means to purchase but from the scanty products of their own manual labor, the condition of the laborer is that of absolute dependence. In a condition of society where artificial ranks and classes exist, and where all the wealth and all the power are in the possession of the upper, or, as they are sometimes denominated, the favored classes, the barriers which hem in the lowest class — without property, without power, without education, without even a home which they can call their own — are, of course, impassable. In a country where labor is scarce, where land is cheap and free, and where the advantages of a good education are offered gratuitously to all, where no arbitrary distinctions of rank exist, and every man, by the force of his own talents and character, may occupy that condition in society to which he chooses to aspire, it is obvious how different is the situation of the laboring portion.

I believe it is impossible for a man who lives in a state of entire dependence upon others to have the spirit of a man; and who, in looking out upon the beautiful and productive earth, where God has placed him, is compelled to feel that there is not a foot of soil which, under any circumstances, he can claim for himself; that there is not a tree nor a shelving rock by the road side, where he can shelter himself and gather under his wing the little ones whom God may have cast upon his care, but he is liable to be driven away at the will of another — at the caprice of avarice, selfishness, pride, or unbridled power; that the use of his own hands and limbs is not his own; that he cannot, but at the will of another, find a spot of ground where he can apply them; and that even the gushings from the rock in the wilderness and the manna which descends from heaven are intercepted in their progress to him, and doled out too often in reluctant and scanty measure.

This will not be pronounced an exaggerated or colored portrait of the condition of the agricultural laboring population of England. I suppose that, with the exception of some few rights of common, where some miserable mud-hut has been erected, and the possessor has a kind of allowed claim during his life, few instances can be found of a laborer's owning, in fee simple, a cottage, or so much as a rood of land. I recollect, in passing through a part of Derbyshire, in a region which forms the contiguity of several large estates, the coachman, by whose side I was seated, said to me, that this was the Duke of Devonshire's village, and this the Duke of Rutland's, and this the Duke of Norfolk's, and so on; and I could not help asking myself, with some sinking of heart, Where is the people's own village?

In a part of Lincolnshire, an excellent landlord and friend, distinguished for his integrity and philanthropy, was kind enough to take me to visit several of his cottages, that I might see, as he said, some of the best examples of this kind of life. It was on a Sunday evening. The houses were humble, but they were neat and comfortable. The inhabitants of one house which we entered were advanced in life, and alone; for, although they had children, their children had been under the necessity, as soon as capable of service, of leaving home in search of a livelihood. The appearance of these people was altogether respectable, but there were two incidents, which, though very small in themselves, at least furnished matter for grave reflection. The landlord had given notice, a few days previously, to some of his cottagers to quit, because, with a view to the small profit to be derived from their board, they had taken lodgers into their families, who were not agreeable to him. The old people whom I was visiting, though they had occupied the same place for perhaps more than thirty years, and felt themselves quite too far advanced to seek a new home, were suffering under the apprehension that they too might, in some way, have involuntarily incurred the landlord's displeasure, and might be turned out of their homes likewise; and the woman said that her husband, through fear of such an event, "had had no sleep for several nights." In another house, which we visited, we found the woman of the house had just returned from attending the *accouchement* of a neighbor, the wife of a laboring man; and she told us that when she announced to the father the birth of twins, he received the intelligence with sadness, and replied, that "it would have been a kinder act if Heaven had been pleased to have taken them both away." Where honest and laborious people, in advanced age, feel constantly that they may be turned adrift, at the caprice of their landlord, from the home of their youth, and where a father regards the birth of a child as a curse, the benevolent mind sees evils in the condition, which it must lament if it cannot remedy, and which it must lament the more, in proportion, as all remedy seems hopeless. The landlord in this case, as I am persuaded, was incapable of committing, knowingly, any act of injustice or unkindness; but it is obvious to what abuses such a power is liable, and to what evils a relation of such servile and abject dependence may subject one.

In the present condition of society in England, no material alteration, however, is to be looked for in the position of the laboring classes. Their lot seems to be sealed, and they must remain in this condition of servility and dependence. They cannot rise above it. They are not slaves; but they are not free. Liberty and independence, to them, are words without meaning. They have no chains upon their hands, but the iron enters into their souls. Their limbs may be unshackled, but their spirits are bound.

At the anniversary meeting of the Northamptonshire Agricultural Society, several aged and respectable laborers were called in and advanced to the upper table to receive the premiums for good conduct, "which they had merited," in the terms of the report, "by many years of faithful *servitude*." I confess, as I said on the occasion to the noble president, this term sounded harshly to my ear, and the more, if it expressed their true condition. Go where they will, the same barriers impede their advance; and if the ambition of wealth, or rank, or influence, of which they see such glittering examples continually passing before them, should ever dawn in their minds, it would kindle only to be extinguished under inexorable circumstances.

There are persons who see in this condition no evil nor hardship. I am not about to expatiate upon its evils or hardships, if evils or hardships there be in it. If, in the present condition of society, pecuniary gain is to be the only worthy object of pursuit, and a pecuniary standard the only rule by which the goods of life are to be measured, and the human frame is to be regarded as only so much organized flesh and bone to be worked up at our pleasure into the means of wealth and luxury, then the improvement of the character and condition of the laboring classes is not a subject to attract the attention of the political economist, excepting so far as the perfection of the machine may conduce to the increased amount of the work to be accomplished by it. But, if a better rule is to prevail, and men are to feel their moral responsibility to each other, and the physical comfort of those by whose toil we live, and the moral improvement of those upon whom, as well as upon their more favored brethren, God has equally impressed his own moral image, are to be cared for, the condition of the laboring classes deserves the most serious attention and the most cordial interest of every man who has a spark of patriotism, public spirit, or philanthropy in his bosom.

This attention is now given, in various parts of the country, by many persons of distinguished benevolence and active usefulness, who know no higher pursuit, and find no richer pleasure, than in doing good. They are not willing, while they enjoy the loaf, to put their laborers off with merely the under crust, and not always enough of that.

The census of Great Britain reports the number of laborers employed in agriculture at 887,167, and these, with their families, compose a population of not less than 3,500,000, or one fifth of the whole population of the kingdom. The wages of labor, according to the reports of the committees of Parliament, vary, in different counties, from 7 s. sterling to 12 s. per week; and the rent of their cottages may be said to average about 1 s. 6 d. sterling per week, or £3 18 s. per year.* It may interest some of my American readers to learn the expense of some of the families of the cottagers, as they are given from authentic sources, as below:—

"H. Sopp, laborer, has a wife and four children; earns 9 s. 6 d. a week; spends 7 s. 2 d. in flour and yeast; has been without tea, cheese, butter, soap, firing and candles, clothes and beer, for three months."

"—— Slements, laborer, has a wife and four children; earns 11 s. 6 d. per week; spends 7 s. 3 d. in flour and yeast."

"—— Pullen, laborer, has a wife and six children; wages 11 s. 6 d.; flour and yeast, 9 s. 7 d."

I shall quote, further, the actual expenses of a laboring man with a wife and six children, in March, 1841; and "this will afford an average view of the manner of living of the agricultural population of the southern and midland counties of England."

	s.	d.
6 gallons of flour,	8	0
Yeast,	0	3
1 lb. of meat, and ¼ lb. of suet,	0	8
1 lb. of butter,	1	0
1 lb. of cheese,	0	6
½ lb. of candles,	0	3½
½ lb. of soap,	0	3½
Potatoes,	1	0
Worsted, starch, cotton, and tape,	0	3
Total,	12	3

"This leaves nothing for rent, clothing, education, or any other expenses, the only fund for defraying which consists of the extra earnings during harvest-time, a resource which, in many parts of England, is greatly limited by the periodical influx of Irish laborers. It is obvious, from a glance at this statement, that the bulk of agricultural laborers in the country are, *at the best,* just able to struggle on from hand to mouth, and that any suspension of employment, rise in the price of provisions, or

* One shilling sterling may be reckoned at 24 cents 4 mills; when a sovereign, as now, is estimated at $4.88.

unforeseen casualty, must, of necessity, compel them to resort to charity, or to descend to a coarser diet, and exchange the habits of an English for those of an Irish peasant." *

---

* The condition of living among the poor agricultural laborers may, perhaps, find some strong illustrations in the subjoined note, which is for those only to read who take an interest in so humble a subject:—

" A poor man can seldom afford to purchase even the coarsest joint of mutton; but if he lives near a town, he can often get the *sheap's head and pluck* for less than 1 s. 6 d., indeed very frequently for a shilling; and with these his wife can make up *four* hot meals. These substantial and truly savory meals may be eàten with potatoes only, as bread is not necessary.

"No instruction is *necessary* for the making of pies and puddings," (that is, because the laborer is never expected to have them,) " whether of fruit or meat; but we may just remark that a *meat-pudding* (when a laborer can afford it) is one of the most substantial and savory dishes that can be brought to a hungry man's table; and if, instead of putting pie-crust over the meat, you cover it with mashed potatoes, and put it either into the oven or bake it by the side of the fire, it will answer quite as well as paste. In Cornwall, there is a common practice, among those cottagers who bake at home, of making little pasties for the dinners of those who may be working at a distance in the fields. They will last the whole week, and are made of any kind of meat or fruit, rolled up in a paste made of flour and suet or lard. A couple of ounces of bacon, and ½ lb. of raw potatoes, both thinly sliced and slightly seasoned, will be found sufficient for the meal; the pasty can be carried in the man's pocket, but it costs 4 d., as thus:—

½ lb. of flour, ...	1 d.
Suet or lard, ...	1 d.
Potatoes, ...	0¼ d.
¼ lb. of bacon, ...	1¾ d.

" Oatmeal is a frequent diet of the Scotch and Irish peasantry. The preparation is simply to put a handful at a time gradually into a pot of warm water, and a little salt, simmering it over the fire and keeping it stirred with the other hand, until it becomes as thick as a pudding; or in about ten minutes time. It may then be eaten with a little treacle, or with a piece of butter put into the centre; but the better way is to eat it with cold milk, taking a spoonful of the stirabout with a mouthful of the milk; for if boiled in milk, it is not near so good. Fine meal does not answer the purpose, and the coarse ground '*Scotch oatmeal*' is the best. Now, about half a pound of this, along with three pints of milk, will make a substantial and a very wholesome breakfast or supper for the family. It is indeed a hearty food; and the cottager, who seeks to support his wife and children both frugally and healthfully, should never be without it. The price in London is 4 d. per quart, and the quart weighs nearly 1¾ lb.; so, supposing the milk to be bought at 1 d. the quart, three good meals can thus be got for 8½ d.

"Potatoes will ever be the peasant's standard vegetable; for, if of good mealy quality, they contain more nutriment than any other root; and three or four

The following was given me as the wages paid on a farm in Lincolnshire, where the wages are more liberal than in

---

pounds are equal in point of nourishment to a pound of the best wheaten bread, *besides having the great advantage of better filling the stomach.*

"The liquor in which any meat is boiled should always be saved for the making of soup, *and the bones even of fish should also be preserved; for although quite bare of meat*, yet if stewed down for several hours, they will yield a species of broth, which, along with peas or oatmeal, will make good soup. A lot of bones may always be got from the butchers' for twopence, and they are never scraped so clean as not to have some scraps of meat adhering to them.

"This done, the bones are to be *again boiled* in the same manner, but for a longer time, and the broth may be made the next day into a stew with rice.

"Nor is this all; for the bones, *if again boiled* for a still longer time, will once more yield a nourishing broth, which may be made into pea-soup; and when thus done with (!)" (for, alas! every thing mortal has an end) "may either be sold to the crusher, or pounded by yourself, and used as manure for your garden."

These directions are extracted from a Treatise, of which I do not question the utility, on Cottage Economy, published in the Journal of the Royal Agricultural Society, and which certainly contains many valuable suggestions for the poor cottager. The perfect coolness and calm philosophy, however, with which the writer descants upon a single sheep's head and pluck making four savory dinners for a family; and a pasty made of any kind of meat or fruit rolled up in flour and lard, with a couple of ounces of bacon, and half a pound of raw potatoes thinly sliced, and slightly seasoned, carried in a man's pocket when he goes to work a good distance from home, being *ample* for his dinner; and upon potatoes having the great advantage over bread *of better filling the stomach;* and the advice respecting the cooking of the same bones again and again, three successive days, make one think, to use Burke's expression, "that the Norfolk Squares must have dined" before they could have attained this high degree of philosophy.

The directions for eating the stirabout or oatmeal porridge seem likewise very kindly given to those who appear to have so little use for their mouths as hardly to know the way to them. "The better way is to eat it with cold milk, taking a spoonful of the stirabout with a mouthful of the milk."

The contrasts constantly presenting themselves in human life are often striking and instructive; and it may not be without its moral use if, with the laborer's "savory" viands, his sheep's head and pluck, his cold pasty, and his bones boiled three times over, together with the wholesome advice, given in the same treatise, "to pinch and screw the family even in the commonest necessaries," until he get a week's wages beforehand, that he may not run in debt, (query, what in the name of humanity does "*pinching and screwing*" mean in this case, unless it be to boil the bones again after they are pounded?) we compare the bill of fare at the dinner given to the council of the Royal Agricultural Society, by the mayor in behalf of the city of Derby, at the late agricultural show, holden in July, 1843, in that hospitable town. This bill, as well it may be, is printed on blue satin paper, in letters of gold, in keeping with the banquet.

many places, and the farming of the highest order of excellence:—

ROYAL HOTEL—DERBY

The Mayor's Banquet to the Royal Agricultural Council, July 11, 1843.

Bill of Fare.

FIRST COURSE.

Three turbots and lobster sauce.
Three salmon and shrimp do.
Five dishes of filletted soles.
Five dishes of trout.
Ten tureens of turtle soup.
Eight do. of green pea do.
Eight do. of soup Julian.

SECOND COURSE.

Four haunches of venison.
Four necks of do.
Five couples of boiled chickens.
Four hams.
Three calves' heads, stewed.
Four quarters of lamb.
Four geese.
Four veal fricandeau and ragout.
Four pigeon pies.
Two rumps of beef, stewed.
Four savory pies.
Five turkey poults.
Five tongues.
Three surloins of beef.
Three legs of lamb, and gooseberry sauce.

ENTREES.

Lobster patties.
Stewed kidneys.
Sweetbreads.

ENTREES.

Mutton cutlets with tomatás.
Veal tendons.
Curried lobsters.
Veal cutlets and mushrooms.
Curried rabbits.
Lamb cutlets and cucumber sauce.
Eight leverets.
Eight couples of ducks.
Eight couples of roast chickens.
Eight plumb puddings.
Eighty dishes of Bakewell do.
Eight do. of apricot do.
Twenty do. of cheese cakes.
Thirty do. of maids of honor.
Cherry tarts, and currant do.
Jellies, blanc manger.
Rhenish cream, &c., &c.

DESSERT.

Ices, grapes, peaches, cherries.
Nectarines, strawberries, raspberries, pines.
Almonds and raisins.
Candied fruits.
Damson cheese, Tartarian cheese.
Orange marmalade.
Preserved ginger.
Sponge cakes, pound cakes.
Fruit, brandy, wine, biscuits, ginger cakes, &c., &c., &c.

Wines at pleasure.

In these comparisons most certainly I mean no disrespect to any human being. I myself, with a large party, had the honor to sit down at the hospitable and elegant table of the Mayor of Derby, who, in company with many of the citizens of that ancient town, spared no effort to make the visits of their friends as agree-

The Foreman —

Has a house and garden (about 3 roods) rent free;
He keeps three young men, for which he has £15 a year each, £45;
He has 6 bushels of malt for each man,
— 1 quarter do. for himself,
— the best wheat at 48 s. per quarter,
— seconds do. at 32 s. "
— four pigs kept in the yard with his master's.
He feeds and kills his own bacon,
and has £24 in cash, and two cows kept.

The Shepherd —

Has a house and garden (about 2 roods) rent free,
— 2 quarters of wheat at 48 s. per quarter,
— 2 bushels of malt,
— a cow kept, and
— £22 a year in money.

Four laborers have the following yearly wages, from May-day to May-day: —

2 s. 3 d. per day, from May-day to Michaelmas,
1 s. 9 d. " from Michaelmas to May-day,
2 s. 3 d. per acre for grass and clover mowing,
7 s. " for corn cutting,
16 bushels of wheat, at 6 s. per bushel,
1 bushel of malt, without charge,
1 cow kept, do.

---

able and comfortable as possible; and certainly in this respect no persons could have succeeded better. Nor am I disposed to find fault with the luxuries with which any gentleman or company are disposed to entertain their guests. But the contrast here presented between the condition of the producer and the consumer — between him whose toil creates the food and him who eats it — cannot fail to read a most important and instructive lesson. What its moral uses are, I think, no fair and reflecting mind will be at a loss to perceive. I shall not therefore, as in Æsop's fables, write the moral at the bottom, but I shall leave the whole to my reader, without note or comment; feeling sure that if it leads to no serious reflections, there must be a melancholy obtuseness of intellect; and if it stirs no pity and no humanity within him, there is reason to fear that all the springs are cut off, and the well is utterly dry. Such, alas! are but too often, though not always, the melancholy effects of luxury and prosperity.

Each laborer pays £4 4 s. for a house, and has about 3 roods of garden.

Calculation of what each man receives.

	£	s.	d.
90 days, at 2 s. 3d., ...	£10	2	6
21 acres of grass and clover mowing, at 2 s. 3 d. .	2	7	3
18 " of corn cutting, at 7 s., ...	6	6	0
172 days, at 1 s. 9 d., ...	15	1	0
Cow keeping, ...	8	8	0
	42	4	9
Deduct house-rent, ...	4	4	0
Net yearly wages, ...	38	0	9

"The English laborer," says an assistant poor-law commissioner, "even if he has transcendent abilities, has scarcely any prospect of rising in the world, and becoming a small farmer. He commences his career as a weekly laborer, and the probability is, that, whatever may be his talents and industry, as a weekly laborer he will end his days." "This is the *best* side of the picture: what is the reverse? If he has no chance of rising in the world, how many chances has he of falling? If he is thrown out of employment; if he has a large family of girls or young children; if he yields to temptation, and becomes irregular in his habits; what is to become of him? The answer is obvious: for a time he will be assisted by casual charity, and struggle on against extreme privations; but if the causes of distress continue, one or other of two things will be his final lot — he will either be enrolled among the 1,072,978 paupers receiving parish relief under the new poor law; or he will be starved out of the country into some large town, and absorbed in the floating population who tenant the cellars and lodging-houses, and live by the worst-paid description of manufacturing industry, or by thieving, prostitution, and casual employment." *

As I have before remarked, it is much more easy to point out and deplore an evil, than it is to suggest a remedy. A republican would say that the evil is fundamental, and grows out of a constitution of society establishing different ranks, the appropriation

* Laing's Prize Address.

of the land in a few hands, the high price of land, the depressing sense of dependence, and the hopelessness of competition and of all attempts to acquire influence, respect, or wealth, incidental to, and inseparable from, such a framework of society. Persons born to affluence and distinction, and persons who have never felt their efforts checked or suppressed by a sense of a dependence which they cannot escape, can very imperfectly estimate the effect of these circumstances upon character. But whether desirable or not — and, in this matter, I would leave every man to the enjoyment of his own honest opinion — as all expectation of a change in the constitution of English society seems as vain as to expect to reduce the inequalities of the surface of the country to a common level — it only remains to consider what alleviations of the evils of the condition of the laboring classes can be successfully attempted. The inquiry is one which most deeply concerns religion and humanity. It is only just likewise to remark, — and I do it with the highest pleasure, — that the subject is now interesting innumerable benevolent persons in the highest ranks and in the middle conditions of life, to a degree perhaps never before known; and that many of the brightest minds are now concentrating their energies upon its investigation and cure. It is with equal pleasure that I can say, that I have found among many of the landlords the most watchful attention to the welfare of their laborers, and every kind provision for them in sickness, decay, or misfortune. Alas! that there are so many who do not come within the reach of this provision, and so many who refuse or neglect to make it.

XIII. — ALLOTMENT SYSTEM.

That which seems to be admitted on almost all hands to have operated to the most advantage, is what is termed the allotment system. In this case, the laborer hires of the landlord a small piece of land, — and it is generally limited to one quarter of an acre, and seldom exceeds half an acre, — for which he pays such a rent as may be agreed upon; and he and his family cultivate it in their spare time, either before going to work or after having returned from their day's work. The manner in which this land shall be appropriated is generally determined or prescribed by the landlord; though, in some cases, it remains optional with the laborer. These small lots of land, though generally leased at a moderate rent, — in some cases, as at the Duke of Devonshire's village of Edensor, at a rent merely nominal, — bring at the rate of from one pound to eight pounds an acre, though, in the latter case, the land generally lies contiguous to some large manufacturing town, where the laborer finds an opportunity of disposing of many small products at a high price. In general, the land so taken, exclusive of some few garden vegetables for daily use, is applied to the growing of potatoes and wheat, and alternated with these two crops.

The effect of these allotments upon the character of the occupant is quite remarkable. He becomes himself, for the time being, an owner of the soil; he has a feeling of independence which nothing else can give, and which at once exalts his character. He is able to avail himself to advantage of the labor of his wife and children, who in some cases perform most of the work on the ground in hours which would otherwise be wasted or misappropriated. His ground yields him a large supply of vegetables for his family, and enables him to keep and fatten a pig or two, and likewise some poultry, which very much conduce to his comfort, and that of his family. The cultivation of his ground likewise occupies hours which might otherwise be spent in the drinking-house, where nothing good is to be learned, and where the foundation of the ruin of many a laborer is laid; and the ruin of his family follows generally, as matter of course. Besides these advantages from the allotment system, his youngest children are here early trained to habits of industry and carefulness.

The mere keeping of a pig in such cases is a matter of serious profit, and not of that only, but of pleasure; and I have been so much struck with the remarks of one of the commissioners on this subject, that I transcribe them for the gratification of my readers: —

"Of such a pig, the first product of allotment, garden or potato headland, it is the fashion among political economists to speak disrespectfully. Now, whatever might be the superior profit, to the cottager, of saving the money which he spends on his pigs and buying his bacon in the market, this, as it never has been, and never will be so saved, we may dismiss. In the mean time, his pig, besides its usefulness, is also a real pleasure to him; it is one of his principal interests in life; he makes sacrifices to it; he exercises self-control for its sake; it prevents him living from hand to mouth, stupidly careless of the future. I am persuaded that a greater act of cruelty could hardly be perpetrated, than the discountenancing this practice, or rather amusement and enjoyment, among the poor." *

So much for the moral effects of this simple matter of the poor man's keeping a pig, in which I perfectly agree with the writer, and honor the benevolence which discerns, even in these humble matters, a moral utility. It is difficult to say, why, when the rich man finds his pleasure in his hunters, his dogs, his game, his menageries, and aviaries, the poor man should not have his pleasure in his pig; an animal, indeed, not always of the most agreeable endowments, nor of very refined manners, but yet in temper and manner susceptible of a considerable improvement by education, and entitled to no small respect for his usefulness, since if his master feeds him when living, he returns the kindness, when dead, by feeding his master; a merit which cannot be ascribed to some other domestic pets far more expensively cherished and caressed.

Too much indeed cannot be said in favor of the allotment system, of its justice, its humanity, and its usefulness. Its influence upon the happiness of the poor, and its moral tendencies — its tendency to prevent idleness and dissipation, and to produce sobriety, industry, and frugality, and especially to keep men at home, and attach them to their homes, most strongly recommend it. Many facts prove that the laborers in some instances pay full double the ordinary rent of the land, and find their account in it. In most cases, however, the lease of a farmer forbids his under-letting any portion of his land; and allotments can only be granted under special agreement, or by the particular consent of the landlord. This is not always to be procured; nor is it always without strong opposition from the farmers themselves.

It will perhaps be asked, by some of my readers, why do I

* Sir H. Doyle's Report on Employment of Women and Children, p. 295.

enter so fully into the condition of the rural population in England, when we have nothing which bears a resemblance to it in the United States. This latter is one of the very reasons why I do it; but I hope that others will present themselves, upon reflection, which will at least excuse, if not justify me. I may as well give some of those reasons in this place; then, perhaps, I may be heard with more patience.

I have promised my friends here, and in the United States, that they shall have my honest impressions of whatever comes under my observation connected with agricultural and rural affairs, and the condition of the rural population. In the next place, I see in the list of my subscribers the names of many, who will take a much stronger interest in such views, than in details of crops, accounts of live stock, and the practical operations of husbandry, which I shall go into at large in the course of my reports; certainly I am bound to consult, in some measure, *their* tastes. In the next place, we shall find in the management of small farms and small allotments, examples of successful cultivation, which cannot be without their use and application to farming on a much more extended scale. Lastly, I cannot think it will be without its use to compare the condition of a laborer, where to him land, under the present condition of things, is unattainable, and labor superabundant, with a condition of labor where, as in the free states, every industrious man can have land of the most fertile and productive character almost at his pleasure, and where the price of land places it within reach of his labor; where every man may have his home, and sit down quietly without the apprehension of removal; where it is not a necessary study with him how often he may have meat, or how many days in the week he may have bread; but where, with industry, sobriety, and frugality, he may always have more meat and more bread than he requires, and something for the poor and the stranger.

I shall take the liberty here of inserting an account, sent me by a kind friend, of the working of the allotment system in a village within his neighborhood — I believe in Lincolnshire. It is an interesting and instructive account. His opinions respecting the size of farms must rest upon his own responsibility. I neither endorse nor deny them. On the subject of the size of farms I shall speak at large when my views have become matured by further observation.

"Scampton is the property of a gentleman (Sir George Cayley, Bart.) of liberal views and enlarged benevolence. One of his first movements, upon succeeding to the estate some thirty years ago, was to provide for the comfort of those who, under his superior tenants, were to be the immediate laborers upon his land.

"To fourteen cottages allotments of land were made. A field of sixteen acres was set apart as pasturage, that each cottager might keep a cow; and another field of twenty-six acres was appropriated as mowing ground, that all might be provided with fodder for the winter. Each cottage had an acre of tillage land allotted to it in the field, and something like another half acre as garden ground, around its little homestead.

"A cow club, or insurance, was established, to enable those cottagers who lost a cow by casualty, to replace her immediately, and without loss of time.

"In the spring of the year, the cows are valued by a competent and disinterested person. Each cottager pays sixpence in the pound on the value of his cow. Cows above fourteen years of age are not insurable. If a cow dies within the year, the owner receives *three fourths* of her value. The dead cow is the property of the club.

"Sixpence in the pound, annually, has actually covered, to *three fourths* of the value, all casualties upon a run of twenty years.

"Under the inspection of a shrewd and spirited agent, the whole affair has worked to admiration, and been productive of peace and plenty amidst the little community whose happiness it was designed to promote. No burning of stacks here, because every man has one of his own. No invasion of the rights of property, because every man is a possessor of property, and anxious to guaranty his neighbor's rights, that he may hold his own in the better security.

"The rent that each cottager pays is something less than £10 per annum. The produce that is yielded, much to the credit of the humble cultivators, is abundantly ample to cover the outgoings, and leaves a surplus that makes them comfortable.

"The acre of tillage land is remarkably productive. It is divided into two allotments: half an acre is in wheat, the other half in potatoes; alternating the crops, of course, every year. On this short rotation, the land has not suffered, *but actually increased in fertility.* For the last ten years, the crops of wheat have yielded twenty bushels to the half acre. The twenty years preceding, eighteen bushels was the average. Instances of twenty-seven bushels to the half acre have been known. The half acre of potatoes, with others grown in the garden, are usually fed to pigs, and instances have been known where the cottager has sold twenty pounds worth of pigs and well supplied his own family with bacon. It is common for them to sell from ten to twenty pounds worth of pigs, or pork, per annum, and still keep a good supply for family use. Some of the cottagers, who have been blessed with careful wives and good cows, have sent twelve pounds of butter, per week, to market, during all the flush of the feed.

"It must be understood, that while the cottager's allotment of land is thus multiplying his comforts, he has a constant supply of work, and current wages, from the neighboring farmers. His own farming is done after his master's day's work is completed, with perchance a day now and then, as at seed-time and harvest.

"Happy, comfortable, and superior in condition, as these cottagers appear, yet the system that makes them so has often been called in question. It has been observed, that the children of cottagers, thus happily situated, are not over anxious to go to service, and not over apt to keep their places when they do go. There appears a latent consciousness about them that the house of their parents is well supplied with bread and bacon.

"Perhaps the evil, if it be one, has a deeper origin than at first sight appears. May it not be traceable to our social system, the genius of which delights to keep property in large masses, under great proprietors? These proprietors have a similar predilection for large divisions of their property — large farms, and men of large capital to work them. All this may be well — very well suited to the cast-iron consciences of the political economists; but it creates a chasm between the large farmer — the farmer of two hundred and fifty acres, with a capital of twenty-five hundred pounds, and the mere laboring cottager. The latter can never hope to pass so great a void. There are no intermediate resting-places. There are no farms of twenty, fifty, or a hundred acres, to which the successful and deserving cottager can be promoted. The steps of the ladder are out.

Having obtained the rare blessing of a cottage allotment, the language of his heart is, 'Let us eat, drink, and be merry, for in our present condition we must die.' His highest ambition being achieved, and the family little more to hope for, it is not to be wondered at that some little laxity should be observable. Let the great landlords of the land supply a motive by a more natural division of their property — let them encourage the aspirations of the industrious cottagers by small farms in prospective, and larger beyond them, and the energies of our peasantry will never be found to flag. But this is, perhaps, scarcely to be hoped for."

I shall go still more largely into the subject of allotments, as presenting one of the first and most efficient means of bettering the condition of the agricultural laborer. My own convictions are strong on this point; and they are sustained and strengthened by the testimony of many men of large experience and shrewd observation. The laborer finds, in an allotment, a means of turning his spare hours to advantage, and in a mode of labor which, from its very character, being in the association of his wife and children, under his own control and management, and for his own immediate and personal benefit, becomes a pleasure instead of a toil. He finds in it the means of eking out his scanty wages; of providing, to a degree, for an occasion of sickness, or other suspension of his employment and wages. He is enabled to bring from this source many rare comforts to his own frugal table; and has himself, if he is a man of feeling, — and why should he not be? — an opportunity of enjoying one of the richest of all pleasures, — that of making a small contribution to relieve an unfortunate or a sick neighbor. It presents a good school of industry for his children, under his own immediate inspection. It quickens his own intelligence in making agricultural experiments upon a small and useful scale, and rouses a spirit of wholesome emulation in his crops even with the master farmers. It removes him from strong temptations to gambling, low dissipation, and intemperance. It gives him an interest in the soil; it attaches him to his home; it involves him in all the risks of the public safety; and makes him the friend of public peace and order. It gives him the spirit of a man, raising him above the sense of slavish dependence, and the dread of becoming a pensioner on public charity. In so doing, it at once exalts him in the community; induces a most wholesome self-respect; inspires a just regard for the rights of property; attaches him the more strongly to his superior, who thus shows his willingness that he should walk erect instead of keeping him upon the ground with his foot upon his neck; and presents innumerable, constant, and powerful motives to improvement and good conduct. I wish it were in my power to convey to those, who have been born to affluence, rank, and authority, the force of these sentiments upon minds altogether differently circumstanced from themselves; but I know it would be difficult — I fear it might be impossible. A consciousness of absolute dependence, so extremely difficult to be engrafted in the human mind, seems indispensable to teach us our duty either to man or God.

That the whole of this subject has an important bearing in its economical and moral aspects upon my own country cannot, I think, be overlooked by a reflecting mind; and, in the course of my reports, will, I trust, be made more fully apparent.

A First Prize Short-Horned Bull.

EUROPEAN AGRICULTURE.

SECOND REPORT.

XIII.—ALLOTMENT SYSTEM. (*Continued.*)

My First Report was concluded with the important subject of allotments of land to laborers. This subject, without an explanation, would scarcely be understood by a majority of the farmers in the United States. The agricultural laborers, or, as they are here termed, *the farm-servants*, are seldom or never owners of land. They receive their wages in money or produce, as I have already described; and some of them, living in compact villages, have not even a small piece of ground for a garden, though, in many parts of the country, the cottages have small gardens attached to them. The unmarried laborers sometimes live in the houses of their employers; but this is not now a general nor a frequent practice. The married laborers live in cottages on the estate, or in a neighboring village.

It is obvious how great advantages a poor family in the country may derive from a small piece of land, and how much produce may be obtained from it for their support and comfort by the application of even a small amount of labor, which otherwise, without such opportunity of applying it, would be lost, or rather would not be exerted. Many persons, therefore, have leased to their laborers small portions of land, varying in size from a quarter of an acre, or even less, to an acre, and in some cases more than this, to be cultivated in such crops as the laborer may select, or as may be prescribed by the proprietor. One condition is usually made absolute in these cases — that the land should be cultivated with a spade, and not with a plough. The results therefore become the more interesting.

I shall give here an account of a successful attempt at the improvement of the condition of the poor rural laborers by allotments of land, cultivated by the spade, uniting with these allotments, at the same time, a provision for the education of the poor children by whose labor these grounds are cultivated. The accounts have a twofold value, in showing the practicableness of meeting the expenses of education by the labor of the pupils, and the increased and extraordinary product which may be obtained from land under the spade husbandry.

"A friend to the more general diffusion of a sound education amongst the peasantry of the United Kingdom, who has long witnessed the success with which education may be, *without cost*, combined with instruction, in the best modes of cultivating the soil, begs to submit to those who are impressed with the importance of the effort, the few following facts: —

"A landed proprietor has established what are termed 'Agricultural Schools,' upon the principle of uniting our present national with agricultural instruction, by making the labor of the little scholars, while under tuition in the art of husbandry in the afternoon, to compensate the master, in the way of salary, for the instruction they receive from him, in the usual course of our national education in the morning. Schools have already been established upon this plan at the villages of East Dean and Willingdon, and they are attended with the happiest results. The usual quantity of land required for the purpose does not exceed five acres; and for this the master pays a rent, certainly equal to, and in most cases beyond, that of the adjoining land, occupied by farmers. In the case of the Willingdon school, there is an appropriate house, for which the master pays an additional rent. The only payment in money to the master is the usual penny a week from each scholar.

"Nor can any reasonable objection be made to this plan on the ground of so employing the boys in the afternoon. The girls in our national schools are taught, and for the same number of hours, to work with the needle, the use of which is not more important to them than that of the spade and the hoe to the boys.

"As various questions will naturally suggest themselves to those who read this statement, the following answers, by the schoolmaster, to numerous inquiries already made, are inserted here: —

"Reply of the Master to Inquiries respecting this School.

"'I have twenty scholars, to whom I teach reading, writing, and accounts, the Church Catechism, Collects, and Psalmody on the national plan, with the approbation of the vicar, without any salary, for one penny per week from each boy, from nine to twelve o'clock; and from two till five in the afternoon cultivating the land. I have not lost one from dissatisfaction, but I am glad to say that they willingly assist me.

"'I am satisfied that I can keep two cows on the same quantity of ground, stall-fed, where I could keep but one if I allowed her to graze; and grow more corn.

"'I have no grass land, and all the first winter my cows had only straw, turnips, and mangel-wurzel, till green food came on in the spring; and now my hay is the *clover* I sowed with the grain crop last year.

"'I have experienced a great deal of good from the liquid manure from the two tanks, one from the cows and the other from the pigs.

"'I have just killed a pig weighing twenty-nine stone seven pounds, and one before about the same weight, which I have used in my family. I have a wife and four children.

"'It is allowed that my oats are the best sample in the parish. I tied my oats in sheaves, and set them up the same as wheat, which saves a great deal of scattering: this is the general practice in Cornwall and Scotland, and, I hear, in some parts of Kent, and is particularly useful for barley to malt.

"'I thrash my corn over the cow-house, as in Cornwall, Switzerland, &c., which keeps it perfectly dry, being thus kept from the damp ground.

"'I am entirely supplied with water by the rain which falls on the house, preserved in a tank in the ground.

"'The quantity of land I rent is five acres, on the side of the South Downs, at £3 an acre; this with £5 for my house, makes £20, which I have paid for the year ending Michaelmas last, though I might have taken off my crops, and lived rent-free; but I preferred staying and teaching, though I have no salary; and so, I think, would many others.

"'I have now three cows, a heifer, and a calf, standing opposite to each other, with a road between their mangers for feeding these stall-fed cattle, which have never needed a farrier; and from skim milk I have made cheese like the Dutch cheese.

"'George Cruttenden.

"'Willingdon, near Eastbourne, Sussex, *April*, 1842.'

"'At your request, I send the particulars of my produce last year, which I am perfectly satisfied with, leaving me a balance of £40 after every thing is paid, though the last was an unfavorable, dry summer.

"'I am likewise happy to say, the principal farmers of the parish have taken into their employ six of my scholars, all under twelve years of age, into their service since Christmas, and two of them under nine; and all, after leaving my day school, where they paid me one penny a week in addition to their work, have each paid me fourpence a week out of their wages, for evening instruction; and their master is now using the liquid manure the same as I do, which I have found most beneficial.

"'I have a wife and four children, whom I support in a comfortable way, and wish I could see many of my neighbors do the same; but that is not the case.

"'G. Cruttenden.

"'Willingdon School, *April* 14, 1843.'

"A landed proprietor at Willingdon, seeing the success of this school, recommended the establishment of a similar school in the adjoining parish of East Dean, where, in the spring of 1842, five acres of land were let to John Harris, an infirm man, who, two years before, had been in the Eastbourne Union House, with his wife and seven children, where, at three shillings per head, they cost at the rate, yearly, of £70 4s., which is equal to the rent of three hundred and fifty-one acres of sheep-walk: now he is supporting his family on only five acres, and, when recommended to give up his five acres, said, 'he had rather continue to pay rent, rates, tithes, and taxes, and teach without a salary, than have fourteen shillings a week without the land.'

"Harris, in the Union House, resembled a mouse in a granary devouring the fruits of labor; but does not this same Harris, on his five acres, resemble the mouse in the fable, releasing the famishing lion? for by his rent he is helping to support the owner of the soil, by his rates the poor, by his tithes the church, and by his taxes the state, which surprises those who have long been accustomed to hear it is requisite to let land in *large* farms, for the supply of food for large towns.

"But do not the HIGHER RENTS paid for allotments of land by the spade than the plough, show that, after supporting the cultivators and their families, they *send more to market per acre* than the great farmers?

"It was the eagerness of laborers in Sussex to hire land, that suggested the possibility of some men to obtain as much as five acres, undertaking to teach reading, &c., three hours daily without a salary, without at all anticipating that twelve boys, averaging eight years of age, by their labor for three hours after noon, could well pay for their instruction in school before noon; but a trial of upwards of three years has put this beyond doubt, as dozens of signatures in the visitors' book testify, of clergymen and members of both Houses of Parliament, not only of this neighborhood, but also from Ireland and Scotland, amongst whom was Mr. Townshend Mainwaring, M. P. for Denbigh, who inspected these schools April 29th, 1843, and entered in the East Dean visitors' book, that he was much gratified by the complete success which appeared to attend the simple principle upon which the school was conducted.

"And these self-supporting schools require much less superintendence than where the master has a fixed salary, because, if he neglected or misused the boys before noon, their parents are not likely to send them back to work for him after noon.

"He is interested in cultivating the land well, as it is the only support of his family.

"Landlords are interested in letting land to masters who pay high rents.

"Rate-payers are interested in able-bodied men being enabled to maintain themselves.

"Parents are interested in sending their children where they early learn to earn their livings in that state of life unto which it has pleased God to call them.

"The farmers around, seeing the great produce from stall-feeding and liquid manure, are interested in taking additional hands into their service.

"The more food that is raised from the soil, the more there will be to exchange for clothing, and thus an increased home market be provided for our manufacturers; who, the more they earn, the more they have to lay out in meat, &c.

"And to effect this, there is no deficiency in capital. There is no want of hands, as our Union Houses are overflowing with the able-bodied; nor is there any want of land, as the heaths, commons, and grazing land, even round London, show."

It is stated, likewise,—and it is a fact deserving of all remark,—"that, during a course of twelve years, out of four hundred rents, only three rents have been deficient, though the tenants were taken without reference to character, and told the rent would not be demanded if not tendered; but the desire of keeping the land has secured the annual payment, and only one, during the whole of that time, has been convicted of a misdemeanor." ..... "In fifty parishes in one county in which there are above three thousand allotments, after the most careful inquiry, our agent heard only of one commitment to prison in 1840, and not even one in 1841, out of the whole three thousand families."

The general condition on which allotments are granted being that they shall be cultivated by the spade, the extraordinary product obtained in this way deserves to be remarked. The statements to which I shall refer are drawn from the reports of a committee of Parliament, and seem, therefore, entitled to confidence. I have myself visited several allotment grounds in different parts of the country, and am quite satisfied that the results under this system of management are not overstated. On this subject I shall say more hereafter; but it may not be out of place if I give here some examples which have been referred to.

Jesse Piper, in Sussex, holds an allotment of four acres. He obtained, in 1842, forty-two bushels of wheat from three quarters of an acre of land; he had two hundred and fifty bushels of potatoes from three fourths of an acre; he had ten bushels of barley from the other land, and kept two cows, and three and sometimes four pigs; he considers that there might be an acre of grass, and the cows were kept entirely upon the produce of the four acres; a portion of this was not arable, as some trees were growing upon it. A peculiarity in this man's management is, that he works one of his cows in his cart, and calculates that her labor saves him an expense of five pounds; she is milked in the morning before she is put to work, and, although worked, she makes eight pounds of butter a week, besides furnishing some milk for the family. This is a sort of Robinson Crusoe management, which is well deserving of attention. It would not be easy to find a reason why the female of one class of animals should be exempted from work, rather than of another; and there is no ground to suppose that, with good feeding and careful usage, moderate labor would be injurious to the health of an animal; much more likely is it to be conducive to health, and even, in such case as this, to the more liberal secretions of milk.

Other circumstances in this man's economy are worthy of observation; he saves all his liquid manure in a tank by his own house, and mixes with it a proportion of soot and salt; he throws his land into heaps, and puts the liquid upon the heaps, and then spreads it abroad — "because," as he remarks, "his land is so near the chalk, that if he put his liquid manure upon the land, three fourths of it would be wasted — it would go clean away, so as never to get it again; but when put in a heap of mould it is retained."

Produce of four Acres, held by J. Piper, in 1842.

	£.	s.	d.
42 bushels of wheat, at 7 s. 6 d. per bushel.	15	15	0
250 do. potatoes, at 15 d. per do.	15	12	6
Food for one cow, which gave 4 lbs. butter per week, at 1 s. per lb.	10	0	0
The other cow do. do. do. do. .	10	0	0
Food for three pigs, at 20 st. each, and at 3 s. 6 d. per st.	10	10	0
	£61	17	6

This example shows the extraordinary results of minute and exact cultivation, and the value of economy in husbanding with extreme care all the resources for manure. The cow is an animal I have always looked upon with the greatest respect for her justice and her liberality; in this case she pays for her board by her yield in milk and butter, and adds to it her labor, or, as is said in case of a free passage on board ship, "she works her own passage;" but the good creature's usefulness does not end here. When she has completed her round of beneficence, her benefactions do not close with her life; her hoofs are made into glue; her horns into combs; her bones into knife-handles and cane-tops; her hair worked up into plaster; her skin into shoes; and her meat into food. Who can wonder that the Hindoos always regarded her with a religious veneration?

The next instance presented by the Parliamentary Reports is that of J. Dumbrell. His allotment is six acres, and is managed by himself, his father, (seventy years old,) and a child of nine years old. "The soil is chalk, on a deep soil, in a valley."

His stock consists of two cows and a heifer, and from two to three pigs. His succession of crops is thus described: "First, Italian rye grass, cut four times, watering it each time with liquid manure after cutting it; then tares; then clover; then cabbage comes in, and mangel-wurzel; and second cut clover, and sometimes three; and that carries us all the summer through: then we begin upon the roots in winter, turnips and mangel-wurzel, and straw."

The following is the statement of his produce for 1840:—

	£.	s.	d.
From two cows in nine months and a half, from the 16th of Jan. to the 26th of Oct., made 400¼ lbs. of butter, which at 1 s. per lb.	20	0	3
The cow, all the year stall-fed, yielding a third more than the other, which grazed half an acre; and their two calves sold for	5	18	0
The skim milk, at 3 pints 1 d., or given to the pigs, is estimated at	10	0	0
On one quarter of an acre he grew 18 bushels of oats, which, at 4 s. per bushel, amounts to	3	12	0
On 88 poles (*i. e.*, a little more than half an acre) he grew 32 bushels of wheat, worth, at 8 s. per bushel, (which is equal to the consumption of himself, his wife, and three infant children,)	12	16	0
Besides pigs, potatoes, vegetables, and the butter to be expected to the end of the year, which may fairly be estimated on the whole of the land (including the foregoing, as I understand the account, which is rather imperfectly drawn up) at	60	0	0

Out of this he paid —

Rent, rates, tithes, and taxes of one acre, .		£1 7	
Rent of one acre and a half, ...		7 0	
Rent of half an acre of grass, ...	£2 10		
Lodge in it, ...	1 00		
Rates, tithes, and taxes, ...	15		
		£4 5	
Hired labor, ...	£2 0		
Seed corn, ...	2 0		
		£4 0	
Leaving			£43 8 0

The two pounds paid for labor were paid for threshing. There are two other accounts of the same individual subjoined.

Produce of three and one quarter Acres, in 1841.

	£.	s.	d.
Wheat, 21½ bushels, at 8 s.	8	12	0
Oats, 44 bushels, at 2 s. 9 d.	6	1	0
Potatoes, 80 bushels, at 1 s.	4	0	0
Two calves sold for	5	10	0
Butter, 423¼ lbs., at 1 s.	21	3	3
Milk sold, and given to the pigs, ...	10	0	0
	£55	6	3

Produce of six and one quarter Acres, in 1842.

	£.	s.	d.
Wheat, 40 bushels, at 6 s. 6 d.	13	0	0
Oats, 93 bushels, at 2 s. 6 d.	11	12	6
Peas, 22 bushels, at 4 s. 6 d.	4	19	0
Potatoes, 150 bushels, at 1 s.	7	10	0
Two calves, one fat and one suckled, ...	3	7	0
Butter, 290 lbs., at 1 s.	14	10	0
Milk sold, and given to pigs, ...	8	0	0
	£62	18	6

In 1842, he lost two cows by death, and the additional land was taken in bad condition.

At the same time, he presented a sample of his wheat, on which were eighty-four stalks from one grain. There is another secret of this man's success — he had signed the temperance pledge; he is a tee-totaller, and drinks neither spirituous nor fermented liquor.

An inquiry was made of Mr. Dumbrell, "how it was possible to keep two cows, and maintain a family of five persons, on only three acres of land;" to which this is his answer — "The statement you saw was very true; half an acre of pasture, half an acre and eight rods in wheat, and one quarter of an acre in oats, the other part was green food for the cows, such as rye, tares, cabbages, clover, mangel-wurzel, turnips, and Italian rye-grass. But if you are surprised at my keeping two cows on this quantity of land, I must tell you that one crop a year will not do it: but my plan is to take second crops; that is, rye is the first thing I cut green in the spring; then I dig the land, and manure it with the liquid manure, as far as it will go; then finish with rotten dung, and plant mangel-wurzel and turnips; and the part that I manure with the *liquid* is always the *best.* The next thing I cut is winter barley and turnips, and plant some cabbages for winter: by this time I cut the grass and clover, which grows again in a short time, with a little of the liquid manure as soon as it is cut. Last summer I cut the Italian rye-grass and clover three times; and this year I have nearly cut it twice already, and there were really two good crops of the Italian rye-grass, and I think there will be two more this summer, with a little manuring. My early cabbages I always let stand to grow again all the summer, and they bring a great deal of food. I plant again in November, and put the liquid manure to them as far as it will go; but to the rest I use dung or ashes, which are not so good as the liquid, which any body may tell in the spring by looking at the bed of cabbages; so I hope it now appears how the cows are maintained in winter as well as in summer. During last winter, I had no hay, only turnips, mangel-wurzel, and straw, and they did very well."

I have already apprized my readers that my Reports must be, in a degree, desultory, from the necessity of giving them before the whole ground has been gone over. Compelled at once to begin the erection of my building, I must use such materials as I have; and which, I fear, under such circumstances, may appear incongruous and ill-assorted to an eye accustomed to order and exact arrangement; whereas, if every thing were at hand, I might better succeed in preserving the symmetry and adjusting the architectural proportions of the edifice. I shall therefore make no excuse for saying here something more of spade husbandry, and the extraordinary products of small pieces of land; and it must be admitted that it is by no means disconnected with the subject of cottage allotments.

The utmost productive capacity of an acre of land, in any crop, has not yet been fully determined. The amounts attained frequently surprise us; but we have not yet got to the end of the line.

One of the witnesses before the Parliamentary committee gives an account of a man who supported himself, and wife, and son, from two acres of land, for which he paid a rent for the two of £9 10 s.; and in the course of seven years, he had saved enough from the produce of his two acres to purchase two acres of land, for which he paid about £30 to £40 per acre. He states, likewise, his own personal knowledge of six acres of land, which, under the spade cultivation, produced at the rate of fifty-two bushels of wheat to the acre. Another witness testifies that on the estate of Lord Howard, Barbot Hall, in Yorkshire, a rood of land was dug and planted with wheat by his lordship's direction, and twenty-eight bushels of wheat were obtained from this quarter of an acre, which would be at the extraordinary and unheard-of rate of one hundred and twelve bushels per acre.

The authenticity, or rather accuracy, of such a statement as this may well be considered as questionable; but I have the pleasure of presenting one, exhibiting a most extraordinary yield, on which full reliance may be placed.

In visiting Horsham, (the last summer,) in the county of Sussex, my attention was strongly attracted by two small pieces of wheat in a garden by the road-side. exhibiting an extraordinary luxuriance; and I have been able to obtain a detailed history of its culture and yield, through the politeness of C. S. Dickens, Esq., of Coolhurst, near Horsham.

The seed of this wheat was brought from Australia, being the product of some wheat which had been sent there two or three years before. The quantity of land sown, in one of the pieces, was thirty-four square yards. The wheat was dropped in rows nine inches apart, and in holes six inches apart, and only one grain in a place. The number of corns planted was 682, out of which 33 failed to germinate. The cultivator obtained four gallons of good wheat from the land, exclusive of several of the finest plants, which he saved. The usual number of stems from each seed was 18 to 20; a considerable number gave 30 to 35, and one was counted which had 40 full-sized stems, and three of a smaller size. The straw from the 34 yards weighed 72 pounds, which would be 284 trusses of 36 pounds to the acre. The weight of the 682 corns planted was 17 drachms. This being multiplied by 142, the land being the 1-142d part of an acre, gave about 9¼ pounds as seed for the acre; consequently one bushel of wheat, at 63 pounds per bushel, would plant more than six acres. The produce of 4 gallons, multiplied, as above, by 142, gives the great quantity of 71 bushels, or 17 sacks 3 bushels, to the acre. The ground had borne potatoes the previous year, and had received no top-dressing, nor been in any way manured for the wheat. A sample of the wheat, which has been kindly sent to me, in the straw, and which I have deposited in the museum of the Royal Agricultural Society, was six feet in height.

These are remarkable facts. What has been done can be done. They forbid our resting satisfied with what has been accomplished; and they encourage the hope that the productive powers of the soil are vastly greater than have yet been determined. Onward! is the watchword of the present day, in every department of science and art. Why should agriculture form an exception? Away with the drones! Do not let us mistake a fog-bank for land, nor think that we have reached the end of the voyage until our feet actually press the solid ground.

The allotments referred to above I have myself had the satisfaction of inspecting, and add, with great pleasure, my humble testimony to the skill, industry, and good conduct, with which they are managed. Indeed, in many respects, I do not know where they can be exceeded. The establishments presented striking examples of the most exact economy. Three of the parties had been driven by their necessities into the workhouses, principally, however, owing to accidental injuries and sickness; but now, instead of being dependent upon public support, they were paying punctually a full rent for their land, and were procuring an honest and comfortable living from their own industry. Another of the families, presenting one of the most beautiful and affecting examples of indefatigable industry, of severe economy, and of grateful and religious contentment, which I have ever witnessed, said, with their eyes flooded with tears, that they had been saved from the workhouse — a fate which many of the poor seem to dread almost as much as death itself — only by the kindness of their beneficent proprietor in leasing them the land, and in furnishing them with tools and with cows to commence their operations. Besides supporting themselves and their child, they had also supported an aged father and mother; and had nearly paid a debt of twenty pounds to the physician, incurred by a sickness of three years, of the man himself, before he had the allotment; and the whole of which they were determined fully to discharge. They expressed themselves but too happy in being able to assist and succor their aged parents, who, in time of his illness, took the kindest care of them. In no condition of life have I seen a brighter example, without any pretensions and without ostentation, of some of the highest virtues which can adorn the human character. An inflexible rule with them was, not to incur even the smallest debt for any thing. The matter of medical relief must, of course, form an exception. This same man, living in a poor village, where it would seem that education was never more wanting, had proposed, after the plan of the others, to keep a school, and assist himself by the labor of the children; but a principal farmer in the neighborhood, disconcerted by the extraordinary success of this humble family in sustaining themselves independent of his aid, had threatened his laborers, if they sent their children to this school, they should be dismissed from his employment, and so prevented it. It is to be hoped, for the honor of human nature, that examples of such cold brutality are rare.

Three of these tenants have been kind enough to furnish me with their accounts of the products of the last year, (1843,) which will, I think, not be without interest to my readers.

Mr. Crittenden has five acres of land, of which the following is the produce for the year 1843. He adds, in respect to it, "I have not put in the corn, roots, and hay, which the cows and pigs consume, as they answer to them in their milk and flesh."

"WILLINGDON, *March* 4, 1844.

"The produce of my land, five acres, the last year, (1843,) being the quantity and the price:—

	£.	s.	d.
8 qt. 6 bu. of wheat, at 52 s. per qt.	22	15	0
3 " 0 " of oats, at 21 s. per qt.	3	3	0
1 " 6 " of barley, at 30 s. per qt.	2	12	6
1 " 0 " of peas, at 34 s. per qt.	1	14	0
120 bushels of potatoes, at 1 s. per bushel, ...	6	0	0
1 large hog sold for	4	15	0
1 small do.	1	5	6
1 calf, sold young, ...	1	10	0
1 hog for self, 25 stone, ...	3	15	0
Butter and milk, ...	11	0	0
1 calf, reared for a cow, ...	2	10	0
1 young sow, ...	2	0	0
	£63	0	0
Rent, ...	25	0	0
	38	0	0
1 qt. of tail wheat, worth £2, which we eat, ...	2	0	0
Total,	£40	0	0"

I subjoin the letter with which he has favored me:—

"Sir,

"I send you the rotation of cropping for six years, which I adopt myself; likewise the kinds and quantity which I sow, for two cows and a heifer, on my five acres. First, I sow about one and a half acres of wheat, which I drill in, about nine inches apart between drills. I sow two and a half bushels to the acre. Then I sow one acre with clover in the spring,—about three gallons of seed to the acre,—in order to cut for the cows green, and the rest for hay for the winter; this is the best food that I can get. It may be cut three times. Second, one acre of either oats or barley that I drill in, as every thing drilled is so much best for the boys to work amongst, and likewise a saving of seed. Third, I sow about twenty rods of rye, and sixty rods of winter tares, in September, for the cows in the spring, and they will come off soon enough for potatoes or turnips; after them, then it comes in for wheat. I sow the rye and tares broadcast, as it should be thick on the ground. Fourth, I sow the rest of the ground with swedes, turnips, mangel-wurzel, carrots, and potatoes, for winter food; the mangel-wurzel produces a great deal of food for the cows, if the leaves are taken off properly.

"I leave a piece of ground for spring tares, to come in after the winter tares. I sow these in February.

"This will keep two cows and a heifer all the year round, if they are stall-fed.

"Rotation of Crops.

	First Division.	*Second Division.*
1845.	Wheat.	Rye and tares.
—46.	Clover.	Wheat.
—47.	Wheat.	Clover.
—48.	Turnips and mangel-wurzel.	Wheat.
—49.	Oats or barley.	Turnips, mangel-wurzel, carrots,
—50.	Potatoes.	Oats or barley.

	Third Division.	*Fourth Division.*
1845.	Oats or barley.	Wheat.
—46.	Rye and tares.	Turnips, mangel-wurzel.
—47.	Wheat.	Oats or barley.
—48.	Clover.	Potatoes.
—49.	Wheat.	Wheat.
—50.	Turnips, mangel-wurzel, carrots,	Clover.

	Fifth Division.	*Sixth Division.*
1845.	Spring tares and turnips.	Mangel-wurzel, carrots, swedes, turnips.
—46.	Wheat.	Oats or barley.
—47.	Turnips, mangel, turnips.	Rye and tares.
—48.	Oats or barley.	Wheat.
—49.	Potatoes.	Clover.
—50.	Wheat.	Wheat."

The next account which I shall present is that of Mr. Dumbrell, at the village of Jevington, Sussex county, who occupies six acres and a quarter. The products of the years 1841 and 1842 are already given. The following is for 1843: —

Six Acres and a quarter, 1843.

	£.	s.	d.
Two calves, ...	4	10	0
Peas, 3 bushels 3 gallons, at 4 s. 6 d.	0	15	2
Wheat, 47½ bushels, 5 s. 6 d.	13	1	3
Barley, 10 bushels, at 4 s.	2	0	0
Tares, 6 bushels, at 4 s. 6 d.	1	7	0
Oats, 66 bushels, at 2 s. 3 d.	7	8	6
Butter, 364¾ lbs., at 11 d.	16	14	4¼
Potatoes, 200 bushels, at 1 s.	10	0	0
Milk, sold, ...	8	0	0
Total, ...	£63	16	3¼

He adds, in his letter to me, "You may be surprised at my not making more from six acres and a quarter, than I did, in proportion, from three acres and a quarter; but it is to be understood that, since my farm was made up to six acres and a quarter, the products, as the two last tables show, have not sold so well, and the last three acres, which were added to my farm, were very poor soil."

I give next the report of last year's crop, which has been sent me by John Harris, as the products of the labors of himself and his scholars. He adopts the same system of spade husbandry, and the application of liquid manure to his crops. His allotment comprehends five acres only.

One acre and twelve rods of wheat produced . .	53 bushels.
Half an acre of oats, ...	61 "
Thirty rods of barley, ...	13½ "
Twenty rods of peas, ...	4½ "
One acre of potatoes, ...	404 "
Half an acre of turnips, ...	150 "
Sixteen rods of carrots, ...	3½ tons.
Fifteen rods of mangel-wurzel, ...	3 "

The rest of his land was occupied with green food for his cows; such as cabbages, rye, clover, tares, &c. He kept two cows. He had from eight to twelve pigs all winter, and they consumed all his potatoes, and his turnips, mangel-wurzel, and carrots, were given to his cows. He fatted one hundred and twenty stone, or nine hundred and sixty pounds of pork, which he sold to the butcher. He sold six shotes, at three months old, for stores, and one pig for roasting; and he sold also one sow in pig, for £2 12s. He kept no account of the produce of his cows.

Several things are remarkable in regard to these allotments and modes of management. In the first place, they are all cultivated by the spade. Where labor is abundant, as in England, and the great difficulty is to know how to employ it with advantage, this might be attempted even upon a large scale. The expense of horses upon a farm is always a great consideration; and especially upon small farms, the expense of horses, compared with the amount of product, is very great, and absorbs a large proportion of the income. It is estimated by many intelligent farmers in England, that the horse-teams require for their maintenance full one fourth of the produce of the soil. I propose presently to discuss this whole subject of brute labor upon a farm, and shall therefore go no farther at present than to add my conviction, that the expense of their horse-teams in England, the cost of their horses, which, after a certain age, is always a deteriorating capital, the expense of their maintenance, shoeing, harness, &c. &c., constitute a most serious drawback to the prosperity of English farmers, and that some little of this may be charged to the vanity of display, and the ambition of extraordinary size. Whatever it may be, on these allotments it is all saved; the labor, with the exception of the working of the cow on one allotment, is all human.

The second observation, which occurred to me, was the extraordinary pains taken in saving the manure. Nothing was wasted. The animals were stall-fed, and kept constantly in the stable, and a small brick or stone tank, well cemented with lime, was sunk near the cow stable, and near the pigstye, which received all the liquid manure; and the contents of these tanks, on their becoming full, were pumped into a small cart, with a sprinkling-box attached to it, like that used for the watering of streets in cities, and distributed over the crops, always with the greatest advantage, and with effects immediately perceptible. The tanks in this case were quite small, because the stock was small, and made, with little expense, of common stone laid in lime, and having a wooden cover for security on the top. They were well cemented within, and might be emptied by a pump, or dipped out with a bucket.

An eminent farmer in Yorkshire has lately stated that he has, within the last ten years, made three tanks upon his farm, for the purpose of receiving the liquid manure. The first he made contained forty cubic yards of liquid, but he had enlarged it to one hundred and fifty yards, which was filled three times a year, by the produce of his farm. He is satisfied, from his experience, that thirty cubic yards of this liquid manure would cause it to produce as heavy a crop as any other manure which could be applied to it. With the manure which flowed into the tank, he had manured twelve acres; and this had produced heavy crops of grass, which he had mowed three times, and then there was an abundance, which he mowed late in the season and gave to his horses. This he had found to be the case upon land which had not been pastured for nine years, but always been mown.

I shall not offend any truly sensible person, if I add that the most careful provision is made for the saving of all the human excrements, by a movable tub placed under the seat of the water-closet, and concealed by a door, which is carefully emptied and cleansed daily, and thus saved from being offensive. This is always mixed with soil, and, in the experience of one of the farmers, cannot be safely applied to the land until it is a year old. Of the value of this source of manure, now, in many cases, much worse than thrown away, I shall subjoin some curious calculations in a note, which my reader, being forewarned, may peruse or not, at his pleasure.*

---

* The committee for building a Lunatic Asylum, at Derby, proposed to Mr. Haywood, an agricultural chemist of much talent and experience, the inquiry as to the results which "the manure obtained from a given number of patients is capable of producing, in the growth of crops, supposing the entire drainage of the establishment to be applied to this use."

To this Mr. Haywood replied in a very elaborate and scientific report, with a copy of which he favored me; from which I shall quote a few paragraphs.

"The great object of my inquiry is, to ascertain what quantity of arable land, in the present four-course system of cultivation, can be kept in a constant state of fertility by the application of all the excretions, both liquid and solid, which are produced by a certain number of individuals, together with the minor fertilizing substances which the proper management of a large domestic establishment is capable of producing; also to give, as accurately as possible, the extent of land

The third circumstance remarkable in the case was, that the cows are fed in the stalls, and never turned out. The principal food given them was clover, tares, or rye cut green; the leaves of mangel-wurzel, and, in the winter, turnips, mangel-wurzel, carrots, &c., and straw. The cows were in good condition, and though evidently not of a character to promise much milk, yet the health of the animals was perfect. They were not selected,

---

which can be kept in the same state of fertility by the excrements of a certain number of horses, cows, and sheep.

"The course I have adopted in this inquiry has been, in the first place, to ascertain the average quantity of food, both animal and vegetable, consumed by a certain number of individuals in a given time, and from a knowledge of the composition of such food to deduce the composition of the excrements, and afterwards apply this to the composition of crops; for it is now universally admitted that all those elementary constituents which enter into the composition of plants or animals, are primarily derived from the air or the soil, and that whatever be the quantity of elementary constituents taken in the food of an adult man, in a given time, the same quantity of these constituents will again be eliminated from his system by the lungs, skin, kidneys, and intestines, in the same time. If, therefore, we preserve the whole of the excretions made by an individual in a given time, we preserve the whole of the elements of the food he has consumed in that time, and, by applying these to land, should be able to produce again the same amount of food in the form of corn and potatoes, together with an extra quantity of vegetable matter, which, being consumed by a growing animal, would yield an equivalent amount of flesh; and these changes would be continued *ad infinitum.*

"It fortunately happens that those constituents of food which are eliminated by the lungs are derived solely from the atmosphere, and, as there is an inexhaustible supply of these in the atmosphere, no restoration of them to a soil is required. On the other hand, those eliminated by the kidneys and intestines, are derived exclusively from the soil, and, consequently, require restoring, in order to maintain its fertility."

* * * * * * *

"Thus we export from the fifty acres of wheat and barley, and the fifty acres of green crops, by one hundred young lambs, forty yearlings, four young cows, four calves, and two horses, the following quantity of those constituents of a soil which enter into the composition of plants:—

Potash and soda,	780	lbs.
Lime and magnesia,	948	"
Phosphoric acid,	1549	"
Sulphates and chlorides,	21	"
Silica,	450	"
Metallic oxides,	8	"
Nitrogen,	2681	"

"It will be seen from the tables of the constituents of food, that the ingredients contained in the liquid and solid excrements of one hundred individuals, and the

but chance animals; in one case, the yield had averaged seven pounds of butter each, per week; in another case, nine pounds had been obtained, when another cow, which was grazed in the pasture, yielded a very inferior quantity. The cows stood in well-ventilated stalls, in one case upon a stone pavement, in another upon hard-trodden earth; were well littered, and kept quite clean. The whole of the manure is saved in this way, and

---

bones preserved from their food, *exceed* the above quantity in every substance except *nitrogen* and *silica;* but the deficiency in these substances will be much more than compensated by the atmosphere in the former case, and by the soil in the latter; so that I should not have the least hesitation in saying that the excrements of one hundred inmates of your Asylum, or any other, where the supply of food is similar to the above, would keep one hundred acres of land on the common four-course system of rotation in a constant state of fertility. It appears from the calculations I have made, that for every two hundred and fifty pounds of flesh produced, the elements of one acre of ground are extracted annually on the four-course system, and assimilated by the animals consuming it; from which it follows, that for every *additional* two hundred and fifty pounds of flesh produced, above the quantity here given, the entire excretions of one man will be required. I have purposely omitted the pigs in the above account, as they would live entirely on the grains from the brewhouse and the refuse from the kitchen.

"Should you think it feasible to grow a succession of wheat crops, without any intermission of green food, then the above quantity of ingredients would very well supply sixty acres. The object of growing crops of turnips, clover, &c., is to allow time for those constituents of white crops which exist in the soil, in an insoluble state, to become soluble by the action of the atmosphere in sufficient quantity to supply them. Were the whole of these added annually to a soil in the form of manure, no rest would be required, and a succession of white crops might thus be produced indefinitely. The cause of this not having been profitably accomplished hitherto, is not so much from any difficulty which attends it, as from unwillingness on the part of the farmer, or his ignorance of the mode of proceeding. Had a portion of those liquid manures, which are suffered to run to waste, from every town and farm-yard in the kingdom, been used for this purpose, success would in all cases have attended the experiment; for these contain the *very elements*, which are rendered soluble in every soil by the year's rest, and which, being assimilated by the plant, and afterwards removed in the grain, are allowed to *run to waste* in the following year."

I cannot with entire confidence endorse Mr. Haywood's views, especially on the theory of vegetation, in respect to the cultivation of the same crops in succession, on the same soil. It cannot be said to be yet determined whether a change of crop is rendered necessary by the abstraction of certain ingredients of the soil, which are again supplied to it by the influence of the atmosphere upon it when in a state of rest, or by the excretions of the crop, according to the notions of Decandolle, which are poisonous to a crop of the same kind coming in immediate succession; but the quotations which I have given from his paper show the workings of a laborious and inquisitive mind, upon a homely, and at the same time an important subject.

the amount is much beyond what would be thought, where the experiment had not been made.

There was another economical arrangement here, which attracted my attention. Two or three of the allotments, with their buildings, were on elevated land, where wells could not be sunk but at great expense, and a supply of water would be uncertain. In this case, tanks were formed about eight feet in diameter, by twelve in depth, into which the rain water from the roof of the house and the stable attached to the house was led; and thus, as experience had proved, an ample supply of pure water was obtained for the use of the family and the stock, at a small expense. These tanks were surmounted with a cast-iron frame, which furnished a strong cover and a small windlass by which the water was drawn. These tanks were formed of stone found upon the place, laid in mortar, and carefully cemented by gray lime mortar.

The cows were kept in a stable connected with the house, over which were the school-room and the threshing-floor. The grain, with the hay that was cut, of which there was very little, was stacked out of doors; and the cows were fed, almost exclusively, in winter, upon turnips or mangel-wurzel and straw. I have no doubt a more liberal feeding would have been found profitable, but they were under the necessity of getting along with the most limited and simple resources.

This management showed conclusively, in the fourth place, that, where the resources are all carefully husbanded, and the produce consumed upon the farm, the land is capable of keeping itself in condition. The grain which was grown here was mainly sold in order to pay the rent; but the rest of the produce was used for the animals within doors and without. The crops were certainly good; the wheat yielding about forty bushels per acre, and the potatoes from three to four hundred bushels. The clover was usually mowed three times in a season, and the first mowing was made into hay for winter resource; the lucern was fed green, and was mowed five times. The success of the crop depended much, without doubt, upon the immediate application of the liquid manure. A rotation of crops is made absolute by the conditions of the lease, so that two white crops may not follow each other without the intervention of a green crop. The clover crop of Mr. Cruttenden had suffered a good deal from the wire-worm, which he attributed to keeping the crop two years on the ground. I do not know how far the supposition is well founded, but it deserves attention. A great problem, then, is here solved, if, to any intelligent minds, it has been matter of question, that, where the product is consumed upon a farm, it may be made to furnish an ample supply of the means not only for maintaining but improving its condition. I do not say that manures may not often be purchased to a great advantage ; and undoubtedly a supply from other sources is indispensable where much of the produce is sold from the farm. I have no doubt, likewise, that even these small farmers would find their account in extending their live stock, and purchasing oil-cake, which makes a most enriching manure, or other substances, for their consumption. A farmer in Lincolnshire, of whose successful management I shall presently give a full account, is of an opinion that his profits have regularly increased in proportion to the quantity of oil-cake which he has purchased for the consumption of his stock. There are, undoubtedly, many cases in which the application of mineral manures may be both useful and indispensable, and fully repay any reasonable outlay which may be required for their purchase. It is not certain that even these small farmers had availed themselves of all the resources within their reach. Nor had either of them any advantage from the clearing out of ditches, from bog-mud, or from deposits of marl. Nor had either of them, that I could learn, made any experiments in turning in green crops with a view to enriching the soil. The experiments, therefore, must still be considered as imperfect, and yet conclusive as to the recuperative power of the soil from the economical use and application of the results of its own products. This teaches a lesson to large farmers of the highest importance ; for, while trade and commerce depend, to a considerable degree, upon large investments and successful adventures, the success of agricultural operations depends most essentially upon the limitation of unproductive expenses, and the most careful application and use of the products of the farm. In too many cases it happens, as Scott has described the farming operations of Triptolemus Yellowley, "the carles and the cart-avers make it all, and the carles and cart-avers eat it all."

It was another beautiful circumstance in the case, that three of these individuals, who, with their families, were now subsisting independently upon the fruits of their own labor, had been tenants of an alms-house, where their spirits were broken down, their children separated from them, husband and wife divided, and all power of mending their condition effectually taken away. New life was imparted to them as soon as they were uncaged, and an opportunity afforded of obtaining from the prolific earth, by their own willing labor, that support which Heaven formed it to yield to well-directed industry. Separate from all moral considerations, instead of being a burden and an expense to the community, they now became themselves aids to bear these burdens and to share in these expenses. This was an immense gain; and, regarded by a reflecting mind in all its various bearings upon the community and upon themselves, its value cannot be overstated.

There was another circumstance in the case, to which I cannot help referring with peculiar pleasure; and that is, the provision made by the labor of the boys for their own education. The education, it is true, is of a very limited description. It embraces only reading, writing, the first principles or rules of arithmetic, and instruction in the elements and formularies of the established religion. Even this was a great gain. To be taught even the use of their own minds, in the acquisition of knowledge, is a great gain; to have even a few scattered rays of intellectual light poured into the darkened soul, may call into powerful exercise the desire of knowledge, which will impatiently search for the means of further gratification, and invent resources for itself. Its effect must be to elevate a human being, from a mere senseless implement or machine, into a consciousness of his own intellectual nature, and bring with it a degree of self-respect, which, in its humblest form, cannot but be favorable to good conduct and virtue. But the children found at these schools, in addition to mental instruction, that which many schools of a higher description do not furnish. They were trained to habits of regular and useful industry, instructed in the arts of husbandry, and in the most intelligent and economical application of labor. To what better school could they be sent? Under what better discipline could they be trained? I can fully understand how much in this case, as in all others, must depend upon the character of the teacher; and I can easily suppose that it may be necessary often, especially in a first attempt like this, to work with very imperfect instruments. But while every proper precaution is taken to secure a good moral character in the teacher, and all practicable guards are placed over his conduct by his success being made entirely dependent upon its correctness, a good deal, certainly, is done; and better minds, and persons of higher qualifications, from the success of these experiments, may presently be induced to seek these situations, in a country where the means of subsistence and profitable employment are, from the redundance of the population, becoming every day more difficult.

It is to be regretted that the farmers in general — perhaps it would be more just to say, that many farmers — look with very ill-humor upon the allotment system, and are opposed to granting land for these objects, even when their landlords desire it. I have found no instance of a landlord opposed to it, though I have found with them a prevalent disposition to limit the allotment to a very small size. I am not willing to impute motives where they are not avowed. I have seen too many instances of the highest and best minds acting under very partial and mistaken views, in a manner unworthy of them, to allow me to commit myself by any harsh judgment. The farmers, it is said, are prejudiced against allotments, because the crops obtained under this limited and minute cultivation throw their own inferior crops into the shade, or, by demonstrating what the land is capable of producing, may induce their landlords to raise their rents. It is alleged, further, that the farmers are not willing in any way to diminish the dependence of the laborers upon their favor, as it might give them the power of demanding a higher rate of wages. The farmers, in the next place, it is said, are not willing that their laborers should appear in the public markets as sellers of produce, which, if the competition was not to be regarded as affecting prices, yet it might inspire them with a hurtful sense of their own importance. I report here only the suggestions of others, and presume to hazard no judgment. The motives named are, alas! but too consistent with the weakness and the too often unrestrained selfishness of human nature. Every man, certainly, has a fair right "to live;" and the duty of every just man is "to let him live." Blessed will be the day, if come it ever should, when every man will learn that *his own* true prosperity is essentially concerned in the prosperity of his neighbor, and that no gratification on earth, to a good mind, is more delicious than that which is reflected from the happiness of another, to which he has been himself instrumental. I hope my readers will not consider these reflections misplaced. It is evident that the farmers have no direct pecuniary interest in the success of their laborers, as far as that success might save them from becoming a tax upon the public. This tax, though always assessed by the farmers as guardians of the poor, is yet always paid by the landlord. It is collected from the farmer; but the amount of rent which he pays for his land is always regulated by the amount of taxes by which the land is burdened. If any of the motives which have been assigned do prevail with the farmers, one can scarcely exaggerate the meanness and unworthiness of such motives, and can only desire that these persons may have juster views of what they owe to themselves, and to those whom the dispensations of Providence have made in a degree dependent upon their favor.

I am sorry to add my strong conviction, that the education of the laboring classes is not viewed with favor by some who move in a higher condition of life; at least that they consider it of doubtful value, and are desirous of keeping it within the most restricted limits. There are, indeed, many noble minds, who, properly appreciating its immense value, are willing to impart as liberally as they have themselves received, and heartily aid all efforts to extend its advantages to every individual in the community; but this feeling does not appear to me general. Every allowance is to be made for a condition of society where different ranks are established; where the lines of demarkation are maintained with extreme pertinacity; where there can be no high rank but as there is a low one; and where, according to the depression of the one, the elevation of the other seems increased. Every approach, therefore, in this direction, is likely to be resisted and this feeling of superiority pervades, with an almost equal intensity, every class in society, above the lowest, from the master of the household to the most menial beneath whom there is any lower depth. Education is the great leveller of all artificial distinctions, and may, therefore, well be looked upon with jealousy.

There is wanting, likewise, that just appreciation of the value and benefits of universal education, which can hardly be looked for but among those who have lived in a community where its facilities and advantages are enjoyed by every individual as freely as the sunshine and the rain. While I am writing, a highly-respectable clergyman, not wanting in a benevolent regard for his fellow-men, has said to me that "the most limited education is all that is wanted for these persons, as more would make them discontented with their condition; and if they can read their Bibles and prayer-books, it is quite sufficient;" and this same remark I have heard several times from others. I cannot say that I have not heard the education of the lower classes spoken of, by persons apparently respectable, in very harsh terms, and in terms with which I should be unwilling to stain my pages. I will only add that I deem such views entirely erroneous and unfounded. If, indeed, there are good reasons for the laborers being discontented with their condition, let the evils of it be remedied. But if it be a discontent arising from circumstances of hardship — if so they must be deemed — which no human power can remedy, education, besides furnishing in itself resources to mitigate these evils, will serve to give them more just views of human life, and to reconcile them to a condition which the divine Providence has made inevitable. If education has a tendency to make persons discontented with their condition, is it not equally objectionable in respect to other classes in the community who find others above them? and in truth, as far as my own observation goes, the rich and the elevated are quite as subject to discontent as the poor and restricted, from whom the luring baits of ambition and avarice are absolutely withheld.

That condition of society is of all others most favorable to improvement, and to the development of the best elements of human nature, where every means of improvement is furnished without restraint, and where men become the creators of their own fortune. The favorite maxim of the great French emperor was, "Let the career be open to talents." In New England, this great principle every where prevails; and here, where the advantages of education are freely offered to all, and the highest conditions of influence and honor are equally accessible to all, it may be safely asserted that no evils have grown out of it, and that its moral and social influences have been the best which the most philanthropic could have desired. In New England, where, even among the most humble classes of society, the literary attainments are often respectable, there will be found among those classes the most devoted friends to public order, and the most stanch supporters of her social institutions. I trust I shall not be thought to speak with an undue enthusiasm in saying, that the time has now come when there should be recognized in every human form a moral and an immortal mind; that the ore in this quarry should be brought out and polished; and that the higher conditions of life will be themselves elevated, and the whole community advantaged, by all improvement of the lower classes. The subsoil plough is deemed the great discovery of modern agriculture; and by bringing the lower strata up, and mingling them with the surface soil, and exposing them to the same genial influences of sunshine and air, it will not be denied that the whole, without injury to any, has been rendered the more productive.

The experiments of the public-spirited proprietor of these allotments have been perfectly successful in a pecuniary view. I have seen the accounts. The rents have been paid with punctuality. There has been no distress levied, and, among upwards of four hundred tenants, scarcely an instance of failure to pay. The rents demanded have been fully equal to those received for lands in the vicinity, of the same quality, held in large farms; indeed, they have exceeded them. At starting, she has found it necessary to assist her poor tenants in the purchase of tools and stock; but these obligations are required to be liquidated.

The allotments are held in the following amounts: —

In 4 rod pieces, 3;	in 13 rod pieces, 1;	in ½ acre, 13;
" 6 " " 5;	" 16 " " 1;	" ¾ " 2;
" 7 " " 5;	" 20 " " 75;	" 1 " 22;
" 8 " " 75;	" 24 " " 2;	" 2 acres, 9;
" 9 " " 8;	" 30 " " 5;	" 4 " 2;
" 10 " " 6;	" 40 " " 108;	" 5 " 5;
" 12 " " 71;	" 60 " " 2;	" 9 " 1.

Total, 421 allotments. Amount of rent received, £428 8 s. 5½ d. This is without houses or barns, the rent of which is a separate charge.

Of the occupants, the following are stated to be the number in the families supported from the land, with the exception of the small income from the instruction money.

4 acres,	4 persons in family;				3 acres,	6 persons in family;			
6 "	7	"	"	"	5 "	9	"	"	"
5 "	7	"	"	"	5 "	6	"	"	"

39 persons; 28 acres.

I submit these facts to my American friends as exceedingly curious. With us the land is not locked up by patents, entail, or mortmain. With us land is every where attainable, and at prices which bring it within the reach of every industrious and frugal man. But it will, I think, be interesting to look at these humble instances of domestic economy; and they must stimulate the most useful inquiry into the productive capacities of the land, which seem as yet to be very imperfectly developed. We are, likewise, not without our poor in the United States; and the vast influx of destitute emigrants is constantly augmenting the number. For idleness and profligacy there is no just claim upon public compassion; but I am convinced that a considerable portion of the poor would be glad to earn their own living if they could be put in the way of doing it. Whatever contributes to this object confers a public benefit.

It would be wrong for me to quit this topic without adding, that, since my First Report, I have visited portions of the country where, on the estates of some very large proprietors, (to one of whom the United States and Great Britain are under the highest obligations for adjusting their conflicting claims, and through whose beautiful grounds I rode eight continuous miles,) the cottages of the laborers were of the very best description; and their establishments, both within and without doors, indicated the greatest neatness and comfort. Gardens for fruit, vegetables, and flowers, were attached to all of them; and they were charming pictures of rural taste and embellishment. Many of these persons had likewise small allotments of land. The wages paid to the men were from 10 s. to 12 s. per week, and to the women 8 d. per day while at work. This, of course, however, with the current expenses of living, did not allow them to accumulate any thing for sickness or old age. During the four weeks of harvest, by working by the piece, the laborer would sometimes earn more than 20 s. per week; and the women and children, by gleaning the scattered heads of wheat after the field is cleared of the crop, or, as it is here called, by *leesing*, not infrequently collect four or five bushels of grain. I have met with instances, where even more has been collected. Such are the fruits of the most exact frugality.

XIV. — QUANTITY OF SEED.

The quantity of seed proper to be sown has been a subject of much debate. There may be an excess; and an error may be committed by sowing too small a quantity. An intelligent farmer makes the following calculation of the advantage and saving which would come to the country, if, instead of sowing two and a half bushels of seed to the acre, it should be found, as he maintains from his own practice and experience, it is sufficient to sow one bushel to the acre.

"Allowing," he says, "that, upon a fair calculation, 7,085,370 acres are annually sown in the kingdom, in wheat, at the rate of two and a half bushels per acre, which is the ordinary allowance, there would be required 2,214,178 quarters (eight bushels per quarter) for seed. But to sow one bushel per acre, only 885,671 quarters would be required; so that the annual saving of seed would be 10,628,056 bushels, or 5,901,192 bushels more than the average importation of foreign corn the last fourteen years. Though I merely take the instance of wheat, I am at the same time proving what may be done with all other corn; for the saving of seed, which I practise, is in equal proportions with all other kinds of grain, and with equal success."

The testimony of this farmer is so important that I shall be excused for speaking more at large on this subject. This gentleman has been a practical farmer of more than seven hundred acres of highly-rented, poor land; and what he recommends, he says, he has long and successfully practised — that he grows crops much larger than the general average, and on soils of inferior description, and with less than the ordinary expenditure of labor and manure.

I will allow him to speak for himself; and the results with him, and the account of the proportion of seed for an acre used at Horsham, in the experiment which I have detailed above, afford

10

the strongest reason, if for nothing else, for making further and more exact trials. The subject is clearly one of the first importance.

"The practice throughout England is to sow two and a half and three bushels per acre, and the yield is seldom forty bushels, and more commonly only twenty bushels; and one tenth, at least, of the crop grown, is consumed in seed. These facts, and the knowledge that a single grain of wheat planted where it has room to tiller out, will readily produce four hundred fold, and often very much more, have induced me, in the course of the last eleven years, to make a variety of experiments, the results of which have shown me, that, independent of the waste, *a positive and serious injury is done to the crop from so much seed;* and the result is perfectly analogous to attempting to feed four animals upon a pasture sufficient only for one; and, in consequence, I have gradually reduced my proportion of seed-wheat from three bushels per acre, which was my practice, down to about three pecks, which reduction I have accomplished to the evident improvement of my crops.

"My practice is to drill every thing, (clover seed alone excepted;) to carefully horse-hoe, hand-hoe, and weed, so that the land may be kept perfectly free from weeds, and the soil between the rows may be stirred, and receive the benefit of fine tilth and cultivation, of which gardeners are sensible; but by farmers this is lost sight of, or not sufficiently attended to. My rye and tares for green feeding are sown in rows at nine-inch intervals; all my white corn at twelve inches; my pulse at twenty-seven inches; and my root crops, on the ridge, at twenty-seven inches.

"My proportions of seed per acre are as follows:—

Of rye, 1½ bushel;	Of oats, 8 pecks;
" tares, 1½ do.;	" barley, 7 do.;
" mangel-wurzel, 6 lbs.;	" wheat, 3 do.;
" swedes, 1 quart;	" peas, 8 do.;
" turnips, 1 do.;	" beans, 8 do."
" cabbages, 1 every three feet;	

After detailing his mode of cultivation, to which I shall hereafter refer, he goes on to say, "I have frequently produced above five quarters (forty bushels) to the acre, and have grown above thirteen quarters of oats, (one hundred and four bushels,) and above eight of barley, (forty bushels.) Having shown the success, on an extensive scale, with thin sowing, I will explain why it is that three pecks of seed-wheat must be much nearer the correct quantity than ten or twelve pecks; and that any surplus of seed beyond a bushel must be very injurious to the latter growth of the crop. The produce of one ear of thick-sown wheat yields about forty grains, (I say thick-sown, for thin-sown yields very much more,) and, therefore, the produce of an acre (or twenty bushels, the ordinary average) must be, no matter how much has been sown, the growth of the ears from one fortieth, or two pecks of seed, (and that, too, is allowing only *one* ear to grow from each grain, and forty grains from an ear.) This being the fact, of what use are, I ask, or what becomes of, the remaining eight or ten pecks of seed, which are commonly sown? But, in allowing one ear only to grow from a grain of seed, and each ear to contain only forty grains, I am far from taking what in reality would be the produce; for a single grain, having room, will throw up ten or twelve ears, and these ears will each contain from sixty to eighty grains; and, supposing some of my small allowance to be lost or destroyed, the deficiency of plant is immediately met by the larger size of the ear, and by the tillering which is made, and the additional ears so produced, wherever room admits of the increase.

"Among the many proofs I have had of the advantages from thin sowing, the following is a striking fact: In the autumn of 1840, I had to sow with wheat a field of eight acres, and I gave out seven bushels for the seed; but owing to an error of the drill-man in setting the drill, when he had sown half the field, he found that he had not put on half the seed; but that I might not discover, by the overplus, his error, he altered the drill, so as to sow the rest on the remainder of the field; and in this way one half of the field had little more than two pecks to the acre, while the rest had nearly five pecks. I did not know of the error, and was surprised, in the winter, by finding part of the field so thin, and, had not the rest of the field looked much better, should have ploughed it up; but at harvest the thinnest-sown half proved the best; and I should never have known the error of sowing but for this fact having induced the carter to point it out to me."

"At first, no matter how much seed has been sown, nearly every grain vegetates and finds space to grow; and in the early stages, when the air and soil are moist, and the plants small, there is food for all. But as the plants increase, a struggle for room and nourishment commences, which increases with their growth, and finally terminates by the destruction of the weaker by the stronger plants; but not until after a contest, lasting up to harvest, which leaves the survivors stunted, and the soil exhausted by having had to support three plants instead of one; and producing mischief, which is frequently the cause of blight, mildew, and the falling of the crop.

"It is to this I would principally ascribe the mildew, and blight, and falling, of the crop; for so far my practice proves it, that, since I have taken to sow only a bushel of wheat per acre, — and I have done so now for some years, and on many hundreds of acres of wheat, — I have rarely found any portion affected by any disease." *

This is certainly strong and decisive testimony, and shows how deserving the subject is of the most exact and repeated experiments. Since the foregoing account of the Horsham experiment of the last season, I have received information of the result of a second experiment made this season by the same individual, Mr. Allman, nursery-man of Horsham, Sussex county. He has dug an acre of land with spade or fork, and dibbled it with the same kind of wheat which he sowed the previous year, and the crop is fast advancing to maturity. The amount of seed required for planting the acre, one grain in a hole, at the distance of nine by six inches, was a little more than one and a half gallon; the seed was covered about two inches in depth; the cost of digging the ground ten inches deep was 2½ d. per rod; the cost of planting or dibbling the seed was 10 s. per acre, and the expense of hoeing it was 7 s. per acre. No manure has been applied to the land this year; but of the character of the soil I am not informed. I am assured that it promises to yield as well as it did the last season. A specimen which has been sent to me fully ripe, shows an equal growth both in the size of the stalk, which is more than five feet, and in the number of stems from a single seed. I shall presently have an exact

* Hewitt Davis, on thin sowing.

account of the result, which my readers will receive with great interest. The expense of dibbling by hand has been accurately kept, and, as above, in point of cost, would show a great saving in comparison with even the best machine. The increase from a single seed has been in some cases most extraordinary, and shows the prolificness — may I not properly say the unstinted beneficence? — of nature. I have myself counted, from a single grain of wheat, ninety-five seed-bearing stems; and I shall give the account of another experiment, the product of which I saw.

A farmer, B. King, at Eastbourne, Sussex county, on the 22d July, 1841, planted three grains of wheat; and one of them produced a root with upwards of a hundred ears.

One grain, the shoots of which were divided and transplanted *twice*, yielded, in 1842, three pounds twelve and three quarter ounces of clear grain; and the third grain, the shoots of which were divided *three* times, yielded seven pounds fifteen ounces and a half. The whole product of roots from this grain was 173; of ears, 3272; of grains, 97,028, and the weight as above. Half an ounce of this wheat, carefully weighed, contained 382 grains. This was the product of one grain in one season, which, according to what was required for the Horsham experiment, would be sufficient, in the second year, to plant two thirds of an acre. Of course, it is not to be expected that such an operation as taking up and dividing the plants could be economically practised to any great extent; but it shows how very easily and soon the seed of any valuable variety may be obtained with a little pains-taking. Some of the most esteemed varieties of wheat have been procured from the selection of a single head, which showed in the field an extraordinary predominance over its neighbors. This is understood to be the origin of the celebrated Chevalier barley, which was propagated from a single ear, found by a gentleman of that name in his field, and carefully cultivated. By the methods adopted above, a single head of wheat might be made, in the second year, to furnish a supply for acres; and the means of speedily introducing a new grain into a large district of country, might be transmitted thousands of miles in a letter. Such are the facilities of improvement which a beneficent Providence offers to those who are willing to use them.

An experiment of a similar kind was made, some years ago, by a Mr. Miller, and reported in the Memoirs of the Bath Agricultural Society, in which the result of the cultivation of a single season was even much more extraordinary than the above; but it is well known to the agricultural world, and need not be restated.

XV. — STEEPING SEEDS.

I may as well here as any where recur to an experiment exhibited at the Dundee Show, of the effect of prepared steeps for seed. It excited great attention on that occasion. I visited the grounds of the gentleman who made the experiment; and he has been kind enough to write me, on the subject, a letter, which I subjoin.

"SEMINARIES, DUNDEE, 13th *September*, 1843.

"Sir,

"Since I had the pleasure of meeting you in Edinburgh, I have thought a good deal about the way in which I ought to proceed as to concealing for a time, or at once revealing, my method of preparing seeds, so as to produce superior crops of grain. I have at last determined that the better way is to make the process known to the heads of agricultural societies.

"In accordance with this resolution, I have written to the Duke of Richmond, as president of both the National Agricultural Institutions of Great Britain, and to the president of the Royal Agricultural Improvement Society of Ireland, disclosing the processes which I have used; and I now do the same to you, as agricultural commissioner from the United States.

"I consider this plan better, in every respect, than sending prepared specimens of seeds, as the applications for these might soon become too numerous to be attended to.

"The specimens of growing corn, which I exhibited at the show here, were the produce of seeds steeped in *sulphate*, *nitrate*, and *muriate* of *ammonia*; *nitrates* of *soda* and *potass*, and *combinations* of these. It was objected by some that the tallest specimens of oats were too rank, and would break down before coming to the ripened seed. I should by no means be afraid of such a result, as the stems were strong in proportion to their height; but should there even be some reason in the objection, the result might be modified by a modification of the process. The tallest oats were prepared from sulphate of ammonia, and I am convinced, from experiment, that the addition of a portion, say one half, of sulphate of soda, or sulphate of potass, would so modify the growth as to make the stalks moderately high, and at the same time preserve the superior productiveness of the seed.

"The barley, which, you may perhaps recollect, consisted of an average of ten stems from one seed, and thirty-four grains on each stem, was the produce of seeds steeped in nitrate of ammonia. I may mention that the best illustration of the comparative productiveness of prepared and unprepared seed was exhibited by the contrast of wheat, sown 5th July, which, by the 10th of August, the last day of the show, presented the following results: the prepared seeds had tillered into *nine*, *ten*, and *eleven* stems; the unprepared into only *two*, *three*, and *four;* and both were from the same sample of seed, and sown in the same soil, side by side.

"The various salts above specified were made by me from their carbonates, and were exactly neutralized. I then added from eight to twelve measures of water. The time of steeping varied from fifty to ninety-four hours, at a temperature of about 60° Fahrenheit.

"Barley, I found, does not succeed with more than sixty hours' steeping. Rye-grass, and other cultivated grasses, may do very well with from sixteen to twenty hours; but clovers will not do with more than eight or ten hours, for, being bilobate, the seeds are apt to burst in swelling.

"On the 16th ultimo, I caused four cart-loads of earth, dug from about six feet under the surface, to be laid over tilly ground, and spread there, and in this virgin soil, totally destitute of any organic matter, I sowed seeds of oats and barley prepared in seven different ways; but, having to leave on the 31st, I could not form a correct estimate of the comparative progress of the seeds, as the season is far advanced, and vegetation slow; but, if in health, I shall revisit the place in October, and shall then be able to judge better of the result. Along with the prepared seeds, I sowed also some unprepared, both in the virgin soil and in pure sand. They had all sprung well when I left. I hope soon to have the pleasure of writing you again on the subject. Meantime,

"I remain, sir,

"Your most obedient servant,

"JAS. CAMPBELL.

"HENRY COLMAN, ESQ. *London.*"

There were exhibited, on this occasion, specimens of oats, barley, wheat, and rye-grass, raised from seed chemically prepared. Mr. Campbell adds in another letter as follows: —

"It is now a considerable time since I began to imagine that, if the ultimate principles, of which the proximate constituents of most of the gramineous seeds are composed, could by any means be made so to enter the substance of the seed, and at the same time not to injure its vitality, as thoroughly to imbue its texture with an excess of these principles, the end (viz., of superseding manures) would be accomplished; and it is by doing this to a certain extent that I am certain I have succeeded.

"The specimens of oats prepared from sulphate of ammonia are magnificent, both as to height and strength, being six feet high, and having stems like small canes, and consisted of an average of ten stems from each seed, and 160 grains on each stem. The oats from muriate of ammonia were vigorous and equally prolific, but not so tall; and those from the nitrate of soda and potass were nearly equally prolific, but still less tall. *Big*, or *bear*, from a preparation of nitrate of ammonia, like that in which the barley was steeped, had an average of eleven and a half stems from each seed, and seventy-two grains on each stem."

Mr. Campbell states "that the ground in which his experiments had been made had received no manure for eleven years, and in it there was little organic matter of any kind." It was in a yard, or old garden, next to his house; but unless he had made an analysis of the soil in respect to the amount of organic matter contained in it, I should conclude that his judgment here was at fault. This circumstance, however, is of little consequence, since the experiments were comparative, and made in the same soil, and under the same circumstances. The plants had been principally removed from the ground when I saw it; and I had only to regret that the experiments, of which, from the apparent results, he could hardly, beforehand, have realized the importance, had not been made with more scrupulous exactness. They are, however, sufficiently interesting and decisive to induce other experiments, in which the results may be more defined. Mr. Campbell's disinterested conduct in communicating them to the public does him the highest honor.

Mr. Campbell has since sent the following communication to the Agricultural Society, as to the results of the unfinished experiments noticed in his former letter: —

"The salts were neutralized by adding the carbonates until effervescence completely ceased; and this was done that there might be no excess of acid." Mr. Campbell adds, with respect to his succeeding experiments, which he proposed to examine on the 12th of October, that they were completely successful, showing a decided contrast in favor of the prepared seeds. In the soil dug up from 6 or 8 feet under the surface, the prepared seed showed plants with seven and eight stems, while the unprepared had not more than three.

The preparation of seeds by steeping is not a new process. The preparation of wheat, by soaking in brine or in a preparation of arsenic, has been recommended, and, so far as my own experience and observation go, may be considered as a sure remedy against smut. The steeping of Indian corn in a solution of copperas and of saltpetre has likewise been supposed to stimulate and promote its growth, though this is not so well established as might be desired. But a scientific attempt, like that of Mr. Campbell, to combine, upon chemical principles, the ingredients or salts deemed essential to the growth of the plant, and to furnish them by soaking the seed in them, is a rare, though not wholly an unknown attempt. Its partial success, in this case, affords strong encouragement to further experiments. The steep may be supposed to operate in two ways — either as a stimulant, to cause the seed to develop its powers of germination more rapidly and fully than it otherwise would do, and thus gather more of the nourishment which it needs from the soil or the atmosphere; or as supplying that proportion of saline or inorganic matter which the plant requires. This is indeed very small, "though absolutely essential to the perfect condition of the seed, and to the healthy growth of the plant which springs from it." This is said to be, in wheat and barley, from 1½ to 2 per cent. of the whole weight; and in oats it is said to be 3½ per cent., though much of this is in the husk of the oat. In being applied at once to the seed in a form to enter and saturate the pores of the seed, it may be expected to be taken up by the small roots of the plant as soon as they are developed; and its effects, therefore, must be immediate. But whatever may be the theory in the case, should Mr. Campbell's results be confirmed by further experiments, the fact will be obviously of great importance.

From some pamphlets translated from the German by Professor Johnston, extracts from which have been published in the Edinburgh Journal of Agriculture, it seems that great discoveries have been made in Germany, in the steeping of seeds; and, in the enthusiastic expectations of one of the discoverers, the application of manure may be dispensed with, and the rotation of crops on the same soil, in order to recruit the soil, will no longer be necessary. The confidence with which these experiments are given, and their results proclaimed, would seem to entitle them to attention.

I shall here take leave to quote from a paper of Professor Johnston some of these statements. Franz Heinrich Bickes, of Castel, Mayence, has published An Account of the Discovery of a Method of cultivating the Soil without Manure. He says, "It is twelve years since the discovery was made. The experiments have been made at various seasons of the year, and the same crop has been repeated on the same soil without regard to the usual rotation. The cost is trifling, and the supply of the materials to be substituted for manure is inexhaustible. The testimonies in its favor are said to be from practical men; and they assert that, from examples in the Imperial Garden in Vienna, in general the prepared seeds exhibited a very much stronger growth, were of a deeper green, had thicker stems, finer and fresher leaves, larger grain, and the grain was thinner skinned, and therefore contained more meal.

"The hemp was of a much larger size, and had many side-shoots bearing seed.

"The Indian corn had more ears.

"The buckwheat was upwards of three feet high, and full of seed.

"Wheat, rye, barley, and oats, are thicker, and have more numerous stems, larger ears, and more grains in each.

"The lucern was beyond all comparison stronger, had more shoots, and its roots were as thick again.

"The disks of the sunflower were doubled in diameter; the cabbage had larger heads, the cucumber larger fruit, while the unprepared seed yielded nothing."

Other testimonials are added from persons of respectable standing and condition. Other plants, besides those above mentioned, are said to have been equally benefited. One fourth only of the usual quantity of seed, of wheat and rye, was sown on a poor, unproductive clay; and yet the product was greater than on the newest land of good quality, though aided by manure.

"Ten or twelve potato plants gave, on an average, thirty large potatoes each, and had stems seven feet in height.

"Fifteen stalks of Indian corn had, on an average, five ears each, some having as many as eight or nine ears to a single plant.

"The buckwheat was four and a half to five feet high; the flax had four to five stems from each seed. The white clover was as large in the leaves and stems as the red clover usually is; the red clover and lucern three feet high."

The experiments of Mr. Campbell induced many farmers to try the effects of steeps upon their seeds. One of the most experienced and intelligent cultivators in Scotland informed me that his success had been partial. He had made numerous experiments, and in some instances with remarkable, in others with no effect. I am not yet in possession of the details, which I presently hope to obtain from him, and on which I shall greatly rely. As my Report is going through the press, I have been favored with a reply to a letter written to Mr. Campbell on this subject, which I annex.

"The accounts which I have received from various quarters are conflicting, some exceedingly good, and others equally bad; but this I have learned, that the greatest success has attended the experiments on a great variety of soils.

"I believe — and this is also the opinion of many others — that, where failures have taken place, they are due either to mismanagement or to the drought of the season. The results of my own experiments are highly favorable; and I have a variety of specimens for the exhibition at Glasgow."

He adds, "My nephew writes me as under."

"I have just seen Sir John Ogilvie's overseer, and he states that the steeped oats sold by roup, yesterday, at 1d. per pole more than those which were not steeped on the next rig."

"N. B. The prepared seeds were sown much thinner than the unprepared, at least one quarter.

"Cranch & Co., (Newcastle-upon-Tyne,) 30th July, write, 'We have received some good accounts of the steeps.'

"P. Bruce, (Hull,) 30th July, writes, 'I am glad to inform you that one or two parties tell me that they will buy the steep again, supposing that any falling off is attributable to the drought.' He has himself seen some that looks very well.

"I may add that any that I have hitherto seen looks exceedingly well, better than the unprepared, although sown thinner."

I cannot say that I am sanguine as to those extraordinary results to which, from the quotations which I have made, some persons look forward, when there will be no longer a necessity for a rotation of crops, and even the application of manure to the soil may be dispensed with. But I cannot help thinking that much remains to be achieved, and that much may be hoped for. We are not to be surprised that failures occur; but one well-authenticated experiment, conducted in an exact manner, and in which the extraordinary results may be directly traced to the application, is sufficient to outweigh a hundred failures. The exhibition at Dundee, supposing Mr. Campbell's statements to be true, — and I know no reason to doubt, but, from his manly conduct, the best reason to believe them, — satisfied me that something important had been effected. I rely little upon mere opinion and conjecture, even of parties above suspicion of dishonesty. The mortification of failure, the desire of success, the ambition of notoriety, and especially any degree of personal or private interest, — all may serve to color the vision, to bias the judgment, and present grounds of hesitation, if not of distrust. With a full share of confidence in the virtue of men, I have been too often disappointed not to require the most ample evidence in all cases of moment. I was not a little amused in visiting, with several gentlemen, the farm of an excellent cultivator the last summer, that, when he showed us in his field of swedes, with an air of the most confident triumph, the surprisingly beneficial effects of a certain application upon some marked rows, every one of the party except himself was satisfied that the rows in question had no other distinction than that of absolute inferiority to all the rest. It would have been as useless as it would have been uncivil to avow our convictions to him, for men are seldom convinced against their will, and assaults upon an unduly-excited organ of self-esteem, if they do not arouse combativeness, inflict only needless pain. In agriculture, being eminently a practical art, and as yet, I believe, claiming not a single theoretical principle as established, excepting as first deduced from long-continued practice, experiments are of the highest moment. The careless and slovenly manner in which they are commonly conducted, the haste with which men jump to their conclusions, the variety of circumstances which belong to every case of importance, and the imperfect manner in which these circumstances are observed and detailed, are the just opprobrium of the agricultural profession. A most intelligent and agreeable friend, in speaking of the best modes of fattening poultry, and in expressing her distrust of some which were recommended, said that her venerable grandmother always fed and fattened *her* poultry in a very different way. But upon being asked whether her grandmother's fowls were the best layers, brought up the most chickens, and produced the best poultry for the table of any to be found, she was compelled to answer that on this point she had no information. A learned naturalist, who, in many respects, was justly celebrated for his acquirements, was once asked why black-wooled sheep consumed more food than white, and proceeded gravely to give half a dozen philosophical reasons for it, without having once inquired whether the fact were so.

It is strongly hoped, that, under an enlightened system of agricultural education, for which the auspices now are most encouraging, and by the establishment of experimental farms, many important suggestions, in relation to agricultural practice, as yet only conjectural, may be determined, and much actual progress made in agricultural science, by the only infallible teacher — exact and enlightened experiment.

XVI. — SPADE HUSBANDRY.

The spade husbandry, to which I have already referred, has been undertaken by several gentlemen, in England, on a somewhat extended scale, for the purpose of giving employment to a numerous population in the vicinity of some large towns, suffering for want of the means, or the opportunity, of earning a subsistence. In one case, the extent cultivated by the spade has been fifty acres; in two other cases, over two hundred acres each; and the crops produced have been the same as in other field cultivation with the plough; such as turnips, cabbages, beets, potatoes, barley, clover, and artificial grasses, oats, beans, peas, tares, and wheat. The crops have been cultivated at not an unreasonable expense, and the yield has been fully remunerating. Oats have given at the rate of forty and fifty bushels per acre, and, indeed, very much more; and wheat thirty, thirty-two, and forty bushels. The instrument found by experience best for use has been a three-pronged fork, fourteen inches in depth, and seven and a half inches in width. By this instrument the ground has been stirred to the full depth of the prongs of the fork, but only about nine or ten inches of the soil have been taken out and inverted.*

The principle upon which this practice is recommended is the same with that of subsoil ploughing. The object desired is to loosen the substratum or under soil, so that, in the first place, all superfluous water may be drained off; in the second place, that the soil may be brought into a finer tilth, and rendered more permeable to the roots of the plants, in order that they may find the easier access to the nourishment which they draw from the soil; and in the next place, that it may become enlivened, if the

---

* Mr. Cruttenden has contrived a fork with a sharp blade of about an inch in width, which seemed an improvement on the common form, and which he deemed very useful. The annexed engraving exhibits the shape of the implement. The blade, like a spade, cuts off the roots with which it comes in contact, and the earth, when lifted, becomes broken by falling through the open spaces between the prongs, combining the advantages both of a spade and a fork.

expression be allowable, and enriched by the admission of the air, by which all portions of it are thus visited, and gain from the atmosphere the elements of vegetation which it furnishes. Of the value of this circumstance no intelligent agriculturist can entertain a doubt. There is another advantage attending the spading of land. The tendency of drawing a plough through the land is to render the ground more hard at the bottom of the furrow, where the shoe or bottom of the plough presses upon it, and to make it consequently more impervious to the roots of the plant than it would otherwise be; this is of course avoided in the spading of land. The subsoiling of land is deemed of comparatively little use, unless connected with a system of thorough drainage; and this drainage would seem to be of equal importance upon land cultivated with a spade.

In Flanders, it is said that the cultivation by the spade prevails to a great extent, and is eminently successful. In the United States, where land is abundant and labor comparatively scarce, it would be idle to recommend to any great extent cultivation by the spade. Yet it would be curious to see what might be done in this way on a small scale. One of the most productive farms for its extent in New England, within my knowledge, — if farm it may be called, — consists of seven acres, from which the farmer or cultivator sells annually to the amount of twenty-five hundred dollars, or five hundred pounds sterling. The industrious and frugal owner sustains his family in comfort and independence from this source only, and is actually growing rich. He resides within a few miles of a good market, and by his skill and industry he sometimes obtains five different crops in a season on the same land. The great question of the size of farms will come into discussion as I proceed; but I cannot now enter upon it. Such examples of what may be called cottage economy, are not without instruction to those who hold and manage large possessions. In France, the farms are greatly subdivided, and the holdings are very small. It is estimated by a statistical writer, whose authority is respected, that, among 1,243,200 of small proprietors in France, their possessions do not average over five acres apiece. Political economists strongly object to such small divisions of land, as unfavorable to the production of wealth, and not likely to lead to those improved modes of agriculture, which would be pursued under a system of large proprietorship.

There is undoubtedly a good deal of weight in the latter reason; for implements and fixtures connected with an improved system of husbandry are themselves expensive, and few great and substantial improvements can be made without a considerable outlay of capital. Such improvements likewise demand systematic arrangements, and often extensive combinations, in order to their being effected. I have known numerous instances where lands required draining, and indeed were comparatively worthless without it; but this draining could not be effected, from the obstinacy of a neighbor, through whose land only could the water be made to descend. In other cases, where fields were held in common, the same evil has been suffered from a refusal on the part of the owners of the several pieces to enclose the land, and to unite in accomplishing the common object. It cannot be doubted, likewise, that the minds of men are greatly affected by the nature of their employments; and although there are many cases in which active and strong minds will rise above every barrier, and, in spite of the circumstances by which they are surrounded, will develop their native greatness, yet the constant confinement of the mind to a narrow and very limited sphere of action, will not be without its effect upon all its operations. The successful management of a large farm, like the management of any other large concern, requires a great deal of inquiry, calculation, reflection, and knowledge; and all this, from the necessity of the case, begets more inquiry, calculation, reflection, and knowledge. It is to minds only of this superior cast that we can look with confidence for enterprise and distinguished improvements.

The effect of such small subdivisions of land as those of which I am writing, and those which are said to take place in France, upon the production of national wealth, is another question, and must be put in an exact form before it can be answered. If we could suppose all these small farms to be cultivated in the most improved and perfect manner, the gross produce would be greater than under any other system. This, however, is not to be expected, and, for reasons already assigned, would hardly take place. In a pecuniary result, therefore, the subdivision of land into small farms is likely to fall much short of the product of the land cultivated in large occupations. But in reference to a general competence, and a more equal and just distribution of the products of the land, and in its moral effects upon the character of the laboring population, the system of small farms should doubtless be preferred.* If pecuniary gain alone must be the paramount object of consideration, and the prosperity of a country is to be measured only by dollars and cents, or pounds, shillings, and pence, the cultivation of the land in large parcels would doubtless best effect the purpose; but if the true prosperity of a country is rather to be determined by the general comfort, improvement, and personal independence, of its population, we can hardly doubt that arrangements which most nearly connect an individual's interest with his own exertions and character, and, if the expression be allowed, make him the creator of his own fortune, are those which are most likely to effect these ends. The difference in the condition of an individual laboring always at the will of another, and having no other share in, or control over, the products of his labor, than that which he obtains from the willing consent, or wrings from the reluctant necessities, of his employer, and that of an independent freeholder in the soil, who has a personal stake in the products of his labor, who applies this labor as he chooses, and has the absolute control of its results, can be best understood by those only who have seen mankind in these two different situations.

There are two cases in which the spade husbandry might have an important application in the United States. The English know nothing of, and can scarcely, as far as my own observation goes, be made fully to understand, a condition of things,

* "No one," says the Baron de Stael, "can compare the present state of France with that which prevailed in 1789, without being struck with the great increase of the national riches. Throughout all France, the greater number of laborers and farmers are at the same time proprietors. Nothing is more common than to see a day-laborer proprietor of a cottage, which serves as an asylum to his family; a garden, which feeds his children; a little field, which he cultivates at his leisure hours, and which enables him to sustain, with more chance of success, the terrible struggle between laborious poverty and engrossing opulence." †

"In 1838, the number of separate properties taxed for the *impôt foncier*, in France, amounted to the enormous number of 10,896,000. The population of landed proprietors, with their families, is estimated at 20,000,000, or nearly two thirds of the total population. The average size of each property is about fourteen acres." ‡

† Quoted in Laing's Address. ‡ Porter's Progress of the Nation.

in which every man of common intelligence, industry, frugality, and sobriety, the great and certain elements of success in almost every department of life, may become a freeholder, that is, the possessor in fee-simple of more or less land, according to his desires or wants. Here, in England, land is so dear as to be beyond almost the aspirations of men with small means; still less is it within the reach of those, whose whole wealth consists in the labor of their own hands; or it is held in large masses by men whose active capital corresponds with the extent of their possessions, and who, in such cases, would almost as soon sell their teeth as their land; or it is locked up by the laws of primogeniture and entail, so that even those who hold it have not always the power to alienate it.

It has been said more than once to me, since the publication of my First Report, that it is no evil that a man, and any man, cannot own a house and land, and that the condition of a freeholder is not preferable to that of a tenant. Certainly this must depend, to a great degree, upon the conditions under which the tenancy is held. But, without pronouncing it an evil, and leaving every one to enjoy his own opinion of the case as it is, I deem it a great good where such a blessing as a home of one's own, and a small farm of one's own, subject to no other conditions than such as the common laws of the land extend over it for protection, is within the reach and the early attainment even of the humblest member of the community. Now, we have in New England, and in other parts of the country, a great many instances, in which men and their families, pursuing some handicraft or in-door trade, and professional men, with small incomes, are the owners of houses in the country, with a few acres of land attached, on which they are occupied in their hours of recreation, or at seasons when the calls of their trade or profession do not press too strongly upon them. While these small farms furnish a large proportion of the supplies which they and their families require from the garden or the field, they are alike conducive to their physical, and, I add with equal confidence, to their moral health. To such persons the spade cultivation, and the minute and exact husbandry to which it leads, would be of great importance. Among the Romans, seven acres were regarded as an ample allowance for a family; and it would be extremely desirable to know what are, in fact, the productive powers of an acre. As yet, I believe, they are very far from being ascertained; but, in the course of my agricultural observations, many cases have come under my notice, in which the products from a very few acres, cultivated with all the care and liberality which such cases admit of, have far surpassed those of farms many times as large.

In one instance, which happens to be before me, the following was the result:—

Three men were employed one week in digging an acre with a spade, at 9 s. per week, ...	27 s.
The same amount of land, in ploughing three times, cost 7 s. per acre each ploughing, ...	21
Against the spade, . . .	6 s.

At harvest, however, the spaded land produced fifteen bushels of wheat more than that under the plough. Here, then, was a clear profit, at the current price of wheat at the time, of £ 4 19 s. per acre.

Another example is given of a farmer in Essex, on a farm of one hundred and twenty acres.

"I have annually dug," he says, "from three to five acres, for the last five years. The soil I have operated upon is light, with a substratum of gravel, sand, and tender loam. The expense of the forking is $2\frac{1}{2}$ d. per rod = 33 s. 4 d. per acre; but I always dig under the furrow left by the plough, which adds one ploughing to the expense, viz., 8 s. By adopting this course, I do not bring up the inert subsoil until the second time of digging. The influence of forking on the crops seems to be, that all root crops are much increased in quantity; the cereal crops, which follow, are less injured by drought; and the land becomes much more free from annual weeds, as well as from those which are of a more permanent nature. I had recently a person with me who has made a series of very carefully-conducted experiments, in which digging has been contrasted with ploughing. He thinks the produce of the forked land was nearly double that of the ploughed."

This farmer adds, "First, a man can dig a greater quantity of land, in a given time, with a fork than he can with a spade. My experience shows one sixth; and it strikes me it must be so, because the pointed ends of a three-pronged fork can be more easily pushed into a hard subsoil than the continuous end of a spade; secondly, it does not bring up so much of the subsoil as the spade, but mixes the earth more, a great portion slipping through between the prongs; thirdly, the bottom is left more uneven and broken by the fork, which I consider a great advantage. One great objection to the plough is, the smooth, glazed surface which it leaves below, and which presents a resistance to the delicate fibres of the plant. If it is correct that, in most instances, the present surface soil is nothing more than a portion of the subsoil improved by cultivation, it must be right to increase the quantity of corn-growing earth by subjecting more subsoil to the same operation."

"An instance is given of the spade husbandry of a farmer in Worcestershire, who has cultivated four acres of very stiff clay land, two acres of it for seventeen years, and two acres for twenty-seven years. He grows, annually, wheat and potatoes, with about one quarter of an acre of beans, the crop being shifted alternately from one division to the other. His mode of cultivation is as follows: As soon as the wheat is off, he ploughs his stubble-ground, raking up the stubble to litter his pigs; he then digs it over with a fork, and plants on it potatoes in the following spring; this crop being kept clean, the land needs no further preparation for wheat. He does most of the labor himself; but he estimates it to amount to about £4 6 s. per acre: his average produce has been rather more than forty bushels of wheat and twelve tons of potatoes per acre. The system he follows, as regards the cropping of the land, therefore, is evidently of the most trying description; and this is not all, for he sells all his produce, even his straw, excepting a few potatoes and beans, which he consumes in annually feeding about thirty or forty score of bacon for his own consumption. He litters his pigs with the potato haulm and stubble; and the manure from this source, and from his privy, with some clay out of his ditches, which he gets occasionally and burns, is all that he has to fertilize the land with.

"Leaving out of consideration the small quantity of beans raised and bacon fed, valuing the wheat at 7 s. per bushel, and the rest of his produce at the price he obtains for it, we shall have something like the following account of his farming:—

		£. s. d.
24 tons of potatoes, at 50 s. per ton, ...		60 0 0
80 bushels of wheat, at 7s. per bushel, ...		28 0 0
2 tons of straw, at 50 s. per ton, ...		5 0 0
		93 0 0
Deduct from this, manual wages, at £4 6 s. 1½ d. per acre, ...	17 4 6	
Seed potatoes for two acres, 25 bags of 180 lbs., at 4s., ...	5 0 0	
4 bushels of seed wheat, at 7 s. 6 d., . .	1 10 0	
		23 14 6
Leaves him, subject to rent and parochial payments,		£69 5 6

"This farmer than gives strong and unanswerable evidence in favor of the fork or spade husbandry. He adds that he has pursued this system of cultivation during the period of the last twenty-four years, with the exception of the first three years, when his neighbors *ploughed* his land for him for *nothing;* that they are willing to do the same now, at any time, but *he prefers going to the expense of digging it, to having it ploughed for nothing.*" *

This is certainly an instructive example, and shows what may be done by very limited and small means. We have, in the United States, beyond a question, a large number of farmers, who, if they would cultivate, to the utmost of its capacity, a small extent of land, in the most thorough manner, would find themselves comparatively independent; whereas, now, without capital, spending their deficient labor over a large surface, and doing nothing thoroughly, they lead a life of vexation, toil, and disappointment, without any compensating result.

To these examples I add the subjoined experience of a Scotch farmer, who received a premium from the Agricultural Society for his skill and success.

"In 1831, I determined to ascertain the difference of the expense and produce, between trenching land with the spade, and summer-fallowing with the plough in the usual way. I

* These two instances are quoted by that able and industrious agricultural writer, Cuthbert W. Johnson, F. R. S., in Journal of Agriculture for January, 1844.

therefore trenched thirteen acres of my summer-fallow break, in the months of June and July. I found the soil about fourteen inches deep; and I turned it completely over; thereby putting up a clean, fresh soil in the room of the foul and exhausted mould, which I was careful to put at the bottom of the trench. This operation, I found, cost about £4 10 s. per Scotch acre, paying my laborers with 1 s. 6 d. per day. The rest of the field, consisting of nine acres, I wrought with the plough in the usual way, giving it six furrows, with the suitable harrowing: I manured the field in August: the trench got eight cart-loads per acre, the ploughed land sixteen: the field was sown in the middle of September: the whole turned out a bulky crop as to straw, particularly the trenched portion, which was very much lodged. On threshing them out, I found them to stand as under: —

	£.	s.	d.
To two years' rent, at £2 10 s. per annum, ...	5	0	0
" expense of trenching, ...	4	10	0
" seed, 3 bushels, at 6 s. 9 d., ...	1	0	3
" 8 cart-loads of manure, at 4 s., ...	1	12	0
" expenses of cutting, threshing, and marketing, . . .	1	10	0
Profit, ...	3	18	9
By trenched wheat per acre, 52 bushels, at 6 s. 9 d. . .	£17	11	0

	£.	s.	d.
To two years' rent, at £2 10 s. per acre, ...	5	0	0
" 6 furrows and harrowing, at 10 s., ...	3	0	0
" seed, 3 bushels, at 6 s. 9 d., ...	1	0	3
" 16 cart-loads' manure, at 4 s., ...	3	4	0
" expenses of cutting, threshing, and marketing, . . .	1	10	0
Profit, ...	0	9	3
By ploughed wheat per acre, 42 bushels, at 6 s. 9 d. . .	£14	3	6

"I now saw that, though it might be profitable to trench over my fallow-break during the summer months, it was by no means making the most of the system, as the operation was not only more expensive, owing to the land being hard and dry during the summer, but that it was a useless waste of time to take a whole year to perform an operation that could as well be done in a few weeks, provided laborers could be had; and as, in all agricultural operations, losing time is losing money, — as the rent must be paid whether the land is carrying a crop or not; so that in taking one year to fallow the land, and another to grow the crop, two years' rent must be charged against the crop, or at least there must be a rent charged against the rotation of crops for the year the land was fallowed. As I felt satisfied that, by trenching with the spade, the land would derive all the advantage of a summer fallowing, and avoid all the disadvantages attending it, I determined on trenching thirty-four acres of my fallow-break immediately on the crop being removed from the ground, and had it sown with wheat by the middle of November, 1832. I may here remark that I did not apply any manure, as I thought the former crop was injured by being too bulky. As it is now threshed out and disposed of, the crop per acre stands as follows: —

	£.	s.	d.
To rent of land, per acre, ...	2	10	0
" expense of trenching, ...	4	0	0
" seed, ...	1	1	0
" cutting, threshing, and marketing, ...	1	10	0
Profit, ...	6	7	0
By average of the 34 acres, 44 bushels per acre, at 7s. per bushel, ...	£15	8	0

"The advantages of trenching over summer-fallow are, in my opinion, very decided; as it is not only cheaper, but, as far as I can yet judge, much more effectual. I am so satisfied of this, not only from the experiments above noticed, but from the apparent condition of the land after it has carried the crop, that I have, this autumn, cultivated about a hundred acres with the spade, and the crops at present are very promising."

There are various cases in which the spade husbandry might be most usefully introduced. In New England, especially in Massachusetts, for the support of the poor, several towns have purchased farms, to be connected with their alms-houses and pauper establishments, where there is an opportunity of using to advantage the labor of those persons among the paupers, who are able to do any work, and who are thus made to contribute, in a healthful and unexceptionable occupation, to their own support. This is an excellent arrangement, and the results have in many cases been highly successful. Here, in many cases, the land might be wholly cultivated with a spade, and the expense of a team be saved, which now oftentimes consumes a large portion of the products of a farm, especially where the farm is small, a full or complete team being as much required for the cultivation of a small as of a large farm.

In reference to this subject, though it may not be deemed exactly in place, I may be allowed to remark that, as far as my observation extends, nothing of this sort is done in England; no farm being ever connected with a pauper establishment, and only the smallest avails being had from the labor of the inmates Indeed, it is obviously judged best — a conclusion which I regard with great distrust — to prevent rather than employ the labor of the paupers. At one of the Unions — for the poor-houses in England go by that name, being maintained and managed by several towns or parishes uniting together for this object — I saw a well-dressed and respectable-looking man employed in sweeping the walks, and trimming the grass-plats, in the front yard; and, upon my inquiring whether this man were a pauper, I was answered in the negative, and informed that he was hired as a laborer in the establishment, because it was deemed bad policy to employ any of the paupers in any such work, lest the place should be rendered too comfortable and attractive. I said to myself, — and I hope not to give offence in publishing my thoughts, — "The English certainly have their own ways of doing things." I am not, by any means, prepared to say, they are not the best that could be adopted. Indeed, we perhaps ought to think them the best, if we consider how much experience they have had, and how many means they have possessed for making the most full experiments. But they are certainly, in this respect, very different from what prevail on the other side of the water. It is an extraordinary condition of things, when, in the midst of want and suffering, human labor must be thrown away, or rather the exertion of it forbidden.

XVII. — CONDITION OF THE LABORERS.

I have no disposition to obtrude my opinion, in any form, so as to give offence. Indeed, it has always seemed to me unreasonable in any case, or on any subject, that the honest opinions of any man should be the occasion of offence, as though we had the same control of our opinions as we have of our limbs; as though we should have any other object, in any matter, but the attainment of truth; and as if there were any way of attaining truth but by the utmost freedom of discussion; and, above all, as though men should, under any circumstances, feel at liberty to exercise the same tyranny over the mind which physical force and political stratagem give them over the person.

One cannot help seeing that wealth and prosperity are not always coincident; that wealth is not therefore the infallible index of prosperity. In many cases, — and perhaps it may only be rendered more striking from contrast, — the extraordinary accumulations of wealth on one side are followed by a corresponding depression on the other; while the rich are made richer, in the same proportion the poor are made poorer. As wealth increases, avarice is more powerfully stimulated, and labor more severely taxed. In the richest communities, the price of labor is always the most depressed; and with the increase of luxury the desire of indulgence is quickened with all classes: what might properly be termed luxuries and superfluities become absolute necessaries of life, and the expenses of living are proportionally increased to all. We may deplore such results, and deem it easy to suggest a remedy; but what remedy is of general or of practical application? The more artificial the state of society becomes, the more difficult it becomes to provide the means of living; and yet who would return to the state of nature, or abate one tittle in the actual refinements of life? Communities are growing up among us upon the principles of perfect equality of rank, the equal combination of labor, and an entire community of goods; and there are examples, where such communities, bound together by a strong religious tie, and subject to a most despotic government within themselves, have been maintained, and are still flourishing. But without this religious tie, or some strong personal and pecuniary interest, and without an absolute head, does any sober man dream that such communities can be sustained, excepting within the narrowest limits? or that such principles can be applied, to any great extent, to society at large, without an entire change in the whole structure of society, and, I may almost add, an entire renovation of human nature itself? Far be it from me, however, to suggest that the evils of society are without a remedy, or at least beyond alleviation. Our own country, under a free constitution of government, and with an almost unlimited extent of the most fertile territory, accessible upon the easiest terms, presents, perhaps, the most favorable condition, which has been known, for a security of the rights of labor, and the just fruition of its products; but it would be a great injustice to infer that there are not to be found in England many generous and just persons, devoted to the maintenance of the rights, and the welfare and improvement, of the humble and laborious classes. There cannot be a doubt, that, in a noiseless and unobtrusive way, much is, and infinitely more can be, done for these objects; and the aim of every good man, as far as he has any power, should be to diffuse, to the greatest extent possible, the means of subsistence and comfort to all, and to remove every impediment to the most equal distribution of the products of labor among those whose labor in their production gives them certainly a fair claim upon these products. Now, whether it be by large farms or by small allotments, by plough or by spade husbandry, that mode of husbandry by which the largest amount of product, and at the least expense, can be drawn from the soil, and with the least injury to its productive powers, is to be preferred. This great point is not yet ascertained; and its determination must necessarily be different in different places and conditions. But it is with England a question of tremendous importance, what is to become of the vast accumulations of people, which are continually increasing here at the rate of from seven hundred to a thousand per day. It is impossible to become accurately, though it may be slightly, acquainted with the condition of things in England, the actual suffering for a want of the means of subsistence, which prevails among large portions of the population, especially in some of the agricultural districts, and not to feel that there are powerful elements of disease at work in the social body, whose disastrous effects must presently be felt in all their violence. Men with families dependent upon their labor, earning not more than 7 s., and in some instances even less, per week, and oftentimes with only occasional employment at that rate, present objects of deep interest to a philanthropic mind. Men living themselves upon a single meal per day, and that potatoes only, for the sake of keeping a wife and children from absolute starvation, — and there is ample evidence that such cases exist, — present a sad spectacle. What are the remedies for such a condition of things, if remedies there are to be found, it is not within my province, in this case, to discuss. It is a hard lot, where the most severe and unremitted labor will not avail to procure a subsistence for one's self and family, and where, with immense tracts of uncultivated land, the opportunity even of exerting this labor, however cheerfully it might be rendered, is, for any cause whatever, refused or prevented.*

The subject, it appears to me, — and perhaps wholly from my being unaccustomed to a condition of things in any degree resembling it, — is daily assuming a fearful aspect; I do not mean of danger to the government, — for the government of the country seems never to have been stronger, — but fearful in its bearings upon the public peace, the public morals, the security of property, and the state of crime. I make no apology for touching upon it, because the experience of an old cannot be without its advantages to a new country, and the condition of labor is a subject which materially concerns every just government. Any hopes of a government being founded or administered upon strictly moral principles are contradicted by all past experience.† The

---

* One can scarcely read, without a shudder, the following declaration of a celebrated economical writer: —

"A man born into the world already possessed, if he has no assistance from his parents, upon whom he has a just demand, or from society for his labor, has no claim for the smallest portion of food, and no business where he was. At Nature's mighty board there was no cover for him; she tells him to be gone."

This passage, which appeared in the first edition of his great work, was afterwards suppressed, being, it is said, too strong for the temperature even of the rankest of the economical school.

† "To provide for us in our necessities is not in the power of government. It would be a vain presumption in statesmen to think that they can do it. The people maintain them, and not they the people. It is in the power of government to prevent much evil; it can do very little positive good in this, or perhaps in any thing else. It is not only so of the state and the statesman, but of all the classes

objects of almost all governments seem to be the security of life and property, the prevention of crimes which endanger life and property, and the aggrandizement of those in power. I do not know that more can be expected of them in the way of promoting good morals, excepting in the suppression of the direct instruments of vice, the support of religious institutions, and the provision for the education of the people. A citizen of the United States, from habit, if not from principle, at once resists and abjures any interference whatever with his religion, whether considered as matter of worship, or faith, or feeling, because, under the government of his own country, with which he has every reason to be satisfied, all such interference is absolutely prohibited. All attempts at enforcing moral duties by legal enactments would be futile and hazardous, since, as it is with human rights, many of them are imperfect, so it is with human duties, many of them are so undefined that it would be difficult to prescribe them with any practicable exactness; and laws of this nature are necessarily of a negative character. They may forbid that which shall not be done; but it is much more difficult to enjoin that which shall be done. They may determine by law that provision shall be made that no man actually perish of hunger in the streets; but what degree of provision short of absolute starvation, how much relief, and how much comfort, he shall have, is a matter far more difficult to be thus arranged. The provision for the education of the people is more clearly within the power and the duty of an enlightened government, on the ground, not simply of moral obligation, but of improving the national industry, increasing, consequently, the national wealth, and of elevating generally the character of the people, and so advancing the general improvement, and promoting public happiness and order.

---

and descriptions of the rich. They are the pensioners of the poor, and are maintained by their superfluity. They are under an absolute, hereditary, and indefeasible dependence on those who labor, and are miscalled the *poor*. Nothing can be so base and wicked as the political canting language, 'the laboring *poor*.' Let compassion be shown in action; the more the better, according to every man's ability, but let there be no lamentation of their condition. It is no relief to their miserable circumstances; it is only an insult to their miserable understandings. It arises from a total want of charity, or a total want of thought. Want of one kind was never relieved by want of any other kind. Patience, labor, sobriety, frugality, religion, should be recommended to them; all the rest is downright fraud. It is horrible to call them 'the *once happy* laborers.' "— EDMUND BURKE.

But it is vain to look to any government for any thing like a paternal superintendence of its people. On a large scale it is not practicable. Those who govern can scarcely be expected to have virtue, and disinterestedness, and wisdom, sufficient for such a task; and those who are governed would not willingly submit to their injunctions or regulations. Any compulsory influence would be unavailing. But, then, it is the duty of every just government to afford to every one of its subjects, as far as depends on itself, the means of subsistence; and institutions or regulations, by which the right and opportunity for a man to exert his talents in a way not morally injurious to another, are taken away, or abridged, or in any degree interfered with, seem wholly wrong and unjust. It would be invidious in me, because perhaps out of place, to point out in any way how the institutions of this country so interfere, if interfere they do; but, as I have said before, the condition of a large portion of the population, — I speak of those in the rural districts, — being prevented the opportunity of applying the labor by which they might secure not only a subsistence, but the comforts of life, forebodes nothing but evil, and may, with strong reason, engage the anxious inquiries of those who have any power in the case, either of alleviation or remedy.

The population is increasing throughout the kingdom with amazing rapidity; and, strange as it may seem, the fact is beyond a doubt, that the increase is always greater among the wretched poor, whom extreme misery has made entirely reckless of consequences, than among that class whose circumstances are comparatively comfortable, and who have learnt that their comfort can be secured only by a wholesome and wise providence. The complaint is universal and continual, that the population is too numerous; but this does not prevent their increase. Few will be bold enough to hazard the question, Who is here who has not a right to be here? nor, like a party of shipwrecked sailors in a boat, to propose the decision by lot, as to which of the party shall be thrown overboard. But the great question must be met — not, How are the surplus population to be got rid of? but, How shall they be sustained? The insular character of Great Britain necessarily and absolutely limits its capacity of providing for its population from its own soil, although that capacity is yet far from being reached. Idleness begets idleness; beggary produces and

12*

perpetuates beggary; crime engenders crime. Sickness and neglect — a sad relief, alas! to the benevolent mind — may do something towards checking this rapid accumulation; for it is stated in the commissioners' returns, and has been asserted recently in the House of Peers, by a distinguished nobleman, that, in England and Scotland, fifty thousand individuals perish annually by disease, arising from the wretchedness of their habitations, owing to imperfect ventilation, and the want of sufficient drainage.* This, however, is a small number to be set against the annual increase. Emigration may somewhat alleviate the evil; transportation contributes its small share. It is a curious fact, however, that disease seems scarcely to produce any sensible impression on the population, and that the losses occasioned by severe and wide-spread epidemics are rapidly filled up and obliterated. The effect of the extraordinary improvements already made, and daily being made, in machinery, in the manufacturing districts, is to diminish the amount of human labor employed, and throw more destitute hands into the labor market. What, then, under these circumstances, is to be done, is a question, to the great moment of which I have already alluded. It is not, in such a case, for men to wrap themselves up in their own selfishness and indifference, and say, "Let things take care of themselves."

I was conversing with a friend on this subject, a gentleman of great intelligence, and not wanting in benevolence; and his remark was, that an increase of production would do little for

---

* This same nobleman, in discussing this important subject, stated that, in ten years, a larger number perished, in England, from these causes, than the whole number of slaves emancipated in their colonies; and for which Great Britain paid, by a noble exertion, twenty million pounds sterling, or nearly one hundred million of dollars.

This is a curious fact, and every day's history of public beneficence presents analogous facts — cases in which thousands and millions are lavished upon objects, doubtless deserving of sympathy and kindness, thousands of miles distant from us, where the results are sometimes doubtful, and can never be known, but through the testimony of interested parties, while objects of mercy and kindness, whose claims are not less strong and urgent, and whose condition can be perfectly known, and where the results of our efforts may be watched and ascertained, perish in all their want, ignorance, wretchedness, and profligacy, at the very thresholds of our doors. Certainly, true charity, which extends its wide embrace to afflicted humanity every where, will not *end* at home; and it might often be as well for it to *begin* there.

the lower classes, for *they* would get no more; with the price of bread, their wages, if lower be possible, were likely to be reduced; the advantages of such increased products would, of course, go into the hands of the land-holders and farmers, or the large manufacturers and mill-owners; and that, for his part, he saw no ultimate remedy but starvation; that is, such an actual reduction of the means of living, that multitudes should gradually perish from want, and so thin off the surplus population. He said this, too, with all the coolness and indifference with which he would speak of brushing off the flies from the dinner-table. "Good God!" I said within myself, "has it come to this, that familiarity with want and misery can render the heart of man capable of contemplating such a result with calmness, and that human life on earth should come to be deemed utterly worthless? If there be any humanity, or any religion, left in the world, they must be roused to prevent such a catastrophe."

Whatever anxiety, however, the prospect may excite in a benevolent mind, there is no room for despair. It is not consistent with the nature of my present undertaking, to discuss this subject, in its various bearings and aspects, in this place. If life and health are spared me, I shall do it in another form. The people do not so much demand charity, as work. They do not so much require to be supported, as to be allowed to support themselves. The remarkable experiment, already referred to, of Mrs. Gilbert, a sagacious and benevolent woman, at Eastbourne, in Sussex county, who has four hundred tenants, on small allotments, and of whom not more than three have failed to pay their rent punctually, and who, on these small allotments, do, in many cases, all that is necessary, and in all, much for the support of their families, should command attention. There remains, as I have before stated, an immense amount of land, which might be cultivated and rendered productive. These considerations present the strongest inducements to an improved agriculture. More land should be brought into cultivation; that which is cultivated should be better cultivated. The laborers should have every encouragement and opportunity to help themselves. The interest of the farmers cannot be separated from that of the laborers; the interests of one class from that of another. Embarked in the same vessel, they must succeed or suffer, they must sink or swim, together.

I have been, again and again, told that a material change has taken place in the condition of the farm laborers, within the last fifty years, or even a much less time. The practice of forming large farms, by uniting small ones, has tended to remove the laborer farther from the intercourse and superintendence of his employer. Being engaged in large numbers, individual interest and character have been lost sight of; and, cottages on the estates having been suffered to fall into decay, and not being renewed, the laborers have been driven into villages, with a great restriction of their comforts, and exposed to the temptations incident to such localities. The large establishments have lost that patriarchal character which used to belong to them; men are employed much more by the day, and the week, than by the year, as formerly; and are used, and thrown aside, as occasion may require, like mere implements upon the farm. Those strong personal ties, so favorable in their influence upon the lower classes, and not without most valuable moral effects upon the higher, have almost ceased to exist. It was a delightful circumstance, when, formerly, without any infringement of personal liberty, a laborer was considered as a fixture upon the place, and as having a sort of hereditary connection with the family and the estate of his employer, which only the most imperious reasons could dissolve; so men and women lived in the same service twenty, thirty, fifty years, and often for the whole course of their natural lives; their children and children's children were often born upon the homestead, and the interests of the master and the servants became identical. As they were paid, likewise, in kind, instead of money, they themselves, being, in a small way, sellers of produce, became personally interested in the state of the markets; and ties of familiarity, long vicinity, and connection, mutual dependence, and a mutual stake in the results of their joint labor, served to connect them the more closely together. No one, under these circumstances, can doubt the advantages of such a relation on both sides. There are many cases, which have come under my observation, where a similar connection exists, though in a form very much qualified by modern manners, and where individuals and families have been in the same service for many long years, and the aged among them are provided for, by those in whose service their lives have been passed, in the kindest manner, after all power of useful or active labor has ceased and they are staggering under the heavy burdens of age and decay. I have already, in my First Report, referred to instances of this nature. But the system most prevalent is perfectly heartless: labor is considered merely as labor; human muscles and sinews are regarded like the parts of any other implement; and when their power ceases, or their elasticity is destroyed, they are thrown aside, like worn-out machinery, into those melancholy receptacles of decay and poverty, which have, very properly, ceased to be called *alms-houses*, and which necessity, and not charity, provides. I cannot say that such sentiments are peculiar to England. They are, it is feared, becoming too common in the United States; not merely in the departments of agricultural, and manufacturing, and mechanical labor, but likewise reaching the domestic and household relations, where least of all they should have obtruded themselves. This comes, in some measure, from that narrow and mean utilitarian philosophy, which stimulates avarice into a diseased action, and measures every good in life by a purely pecuniary standard. Whatever tends to divide these different classes, either in interest or feeling, is, to a degree, and ultimately, I fear, it must prove in an equal degree, injurious to both parties. Feelings of indifference, or contempt, or cruel disdain, on the one hand, are likely to be met with a sense of injury, a feeling of hate and revenge, on the other; and one of the greatest curses with which Heaven could have visited mankind, would have been to have made them in any sense independent of each other. There are no circumstances connected with the condition of society more to be regretted than such as separate different classes too strongly from each other, and create hostile or conflicting interests. A perfect equality of condition among men is a chimera; and if, by any conceivable or possible arrangement, it could take place, the earth, in its rapid revolutions, would not pass the half of a degree, but it must be interrupted. But an equality of natural rights is a position which, if I may be allowed to speak for one born and educated in a condition of society where it has been always acknowledged, would not be readily relinquished. Now, if there is any right which should be held sacred, next to that which every man has to his own person, it is the right of honest labor to an ample share of the products of that labor. The rights of the rich man to his possessions, honestly and honorably acquired, are as just as those of the poorest man to the crust which feeds or the coarse garment which covers him; but, in every condition of society, the rights of the rich and the poor are reciprocal, and their dependence mutual and absolute. If the poor are compelled, under the arbitrary institutions of society, — and I use the term *arbitrary* in no offensive sense, — more sensibly to feel their dependence, the upper classes in society, with that spirit of justice and kindness which constitutes the highest grace of power, and wealth, and rank, should be prompt to show their sense of how much they owe even of all this power, and wealth, and rank, to the labors, and services, and fealty, of the poor; and, without losing sight, as far as is consistent with the spirit of Christianity, of what is called their position in society, to endeavor to soften the severity of those distinctions, which, if they mark the elevation of their own condition, equally indicate the depressed condition of others. In that beautiful language, to which every serious mind will listen with profound reverence, "The eye must not say unto the hand, I have no need of thee, nor yet the head to the feet, I have no need of you;" seeing that even those parts of the body which are least "comely," are as essential to the perfect and healthy organization of the machine, as those on which the Creator has impressed the highest attributes of grace, expression, and beauty, and must be equally nourished from the great central reservoir of life and strength, or the whole must suffer from weakness or decay.

I do not mean to imply that there is any greater disregard of these principles than is to be expected in a condition of society so highly artificial as that which exists here, and where the accumulations of individual wealth, and of what, from its hereditary and inalienable character, may be termed *class-property*, are so enormous. I do not mean, as I have already said, to express any apprehension or alarm for the safety of the present institutions of England; for, though the flood of population is rising with a continually accelerated force, and in almost a geometrical ratio, yet wealth here is so strong, and poverty so powerless, and the safety of the whole is so essentially concerned in the maintenance of the integrity of its present form of society, and, above all, the experience of a neighboring nation, on the subject of revolution, is so admonitory and terrific, that almost every thing will be endured before any violence is hazarded or permitted. Still it is obvious to every reflecting mind how important it is to the public peace and the security of property, that the rights of the laborious classes should be fully acknowledged, and maintained in the spirit of kindness and equity, as well as of strict legal justice, and that every philanthropic effort should be stimulated and encouraged to protect and comfort them, and, more than that, by education, moral and intellectual, — for, without moral, intellectual too often proves a curse, — to elevate them in their social condition. Next to the satisfactions of an honest conscience, the highest of all earthly pleasures to a good man, is that of conferring happiness upon others. I have seen, in England, with a gratification which it would be difficult to express, among persons of the most brilliant rank and the most commanding influence, many instances of a conduct which deserved and secured all this felicity. Every where men are to be found feeling their high responsibleness, and, without any offensive assumption of superiority, devoting all their energies to the protection of the houseless, and to the comfort and improvement of those whom divine Providence has cast within the circle of their beneficence, and enjoying all that calm security which such conduct is sure to bring with it. I confess there has been no occasion in my life when I have been so much disposed to envy the possession of wealth and power. On the other hand, I dare say I shall only be compassionated for my simplicity, when I add that the high stone and brick walls, with which houses, and parks, and properties, are here often intrenched and fortified, so high that even the nimblest jail-bird would look at them with despair, and the fences every where bristling with iron spikes and broken glass, and the sullen gates opening "with discordant jar," and the ferocious watch-dogs, to say nothing of other mastiffs, often stationed by them, from whose terrific growl even the honest applicant shrinks back with dread; and then the signs which meet your eye constantly, "All vagrants and beggars forbidden here," "All trespassers here will be prosecuted to the utmost rigor of the law," and "Steel man-traps set here," often bring a cold chill over me, and compel me to feel that property held under such cautions loses somewhat of its value. At the same time, it makes me estimate the more highly a condition of society where the road of acquisition is equally open to all, and where property being more equally distributed, and in almost all cases the fruit of personal industry, its rights are more readily admitted, and its protection becomes matter of equal and universal concern.

I return now to speak of the present actual condition of agriculture in England. I have dwelt largely, but I hope not too largely, upon miscellaneous and incidental considerations. I propose now to consider the actual condition and character of English agriculture; the improvements which it has effected; and those which remain to be devised.

XVIII. — PROGRESS OF AGRICULTURE, COMPARED WITH OTHER PURSUITS.

I have already said that the agriculture of England — and here I include Scotland — is highly improved; but I may say, I think, with confidence, and certainly without censoriousness, that it has not yet reached that degree of excellence to which it is capable of being carried. In parts of the country, not much has been done; in the best cultivated districts, it would be presumptuous to say that the goal of perfection has been reached. Among the highest gifts with which Heaven has endued the human mind is a generous and insatiable ambition after excellence; an avarice of improvement, if so it may be termed, which characterizes a great mind; which knows in no case entire satisfaction; which no sooner mounts one summit than it essays to climb a higher; and which, if in any thing it should reach barriers that are absolutely impassable, would, like the celebrated hero of antiquity, "weep that it had no more worlds to conquer." I am not willing to admit that this ambition, one of the noblest attributes of the human soul, can ever be stimulated to too great a degree. Cobbett, in his terse, energetic, but rather coarse manner, says that "he despises a man who is contented with his condition;" and in the sense in which he obviously designed to be understood, I quite agree with him, that no man should be satisfied with good while better is attainable; and that it would indeed be a sad condition of things, when the capacity, and still more the disposition, for improvement should cease.

It is, and, as long as I can remember, it has been, common to decry the farmers, as a stupid, ignorant, plodding race, satisfied always to jog on in the steps of their fathers, and averse to any improvements, such as are going forward in other departments of industry. I think I may confidently deny the allegation; and I regard the reproach with the disdain which it merits. My own observations, in England and the United States, lead me to the conclusion, that, after making every just allowance for the necessary difference of circumstances in the different cases, there is as much intelligence in regard to their art, and as strong a spirit of improvement, with the agricultural as with any class in the community; and, more than that, the improvements, which have been actually accomplished in the agricultural art, are in no respect inferior to those which have been effected in manufactures and commerce, or in the higher professions, — if so we submit to call them, which I confess I do with great reluctance, — medicine or law; I would add theology, if I dared; but I am afraid I should get into hot water.

In medicine, if under that head we include surgery, one cannot go through the streets of London, and observe, at the shop-windows, the models of wooden legs, and artificial ears, and glass eyes, and mineral teeth, and the promise of a new nose, where the victim of misfortune has been deprived of his proboscis, without acknowledging that the triumphs of the surgical art are as brilliant as they are useful and humane. If one likewise should place any reliance upon the numberless patent medicines and nostrums which decorate the pages of the newspapers, he would be led to infer that the reign of disease was broken up, and the elixir of immortality at length discovered. But whoever looks into the medical reports, and observes the variety of systems and modes of practice which prevail, and which different colleges of physicians seem to bring out as regularly, and in almost equal numbers, as the good housewife's hens bring out their broods in the spring, and especially reads the accounts of the various experiments, to which, for the benefit of science, their patients are unconsciously subjected, and by which, without the credit of inclination or consent, they are made, at their own personal expense, suffering, and peril, to contribute to the most philanthropic discoveries, — it cannot be claimed for medicine, that it is altogether above the charge of empiricism, or that it has yet accomplished all that is to be desired in lessening the number or alleviating the virulence of diseases, or in restoring human life, with any confidence, to even a tithe of that longevity, which is claimed for it in those patriarchal ages when apothecaries' shops, and medical schools, and degrees, do not appear to have been established. It is scarcely better with the law. One of the most distinguished legal gentlemen in England has lately stated, in his place in Parliament, that such is the condition of the criminal law, that even the most learned in the profession cannot, in many cases, determine whether he is, by particular actions, committing an offence or not. The records of the courts daily show that the most momentous decisions often turn upon points the most abstruse, and as yet absolutely unsettled; that even the most learned judges on the bench disagree in matters both of law and equity, involving property and life; and it seems but too often the test of legal eminence and skill to ascertain, not whether it be practicable to get "a camel," but whether the lawyer can get himself or his client, "through the eye of a needle," as being the most brilliant triumph of his art.* In theology, it cannot be said

---

* In a recent trial, a brute in human shape, or rather a demoniac, — for brutes are not capable of actions so malicious, — was indicted for *wounding*, *maiming*, and *injuring*, a horse. He, it seems, in the fury of his passion, had drawn out the tongue of the horse, and, by rubbing it against one of his teeth, had cut off four or five inches of it, which he threw at the horse's head. His counsel opposed the indictment, on the ground that there could, as defined by law, be no *wounding* but where some *instrument* was used; but the tooth was not an *instrument*; — there could be no *maiming* but where some *limb* was injured; but the tongue was not a *limb*; — and that there was no injury, because, though the horse found some difficulty in eating his oats, he was otherwise as useful for labor as before his tongue was cut off. On these grounds the prosecution failed, and the savage escaped. Under such an administration of justice, it would scarcely have been surprising, if the horse, had he not lost his tongue, had himself spoken out; and it would have been only fair if he had been allowed to bite off the ears of the lawyer, and of a magistrate who sanctioned such law.

At a court of assizes which I attended, and where the criminal calendar was heavy, a young married woman, of decent and respectable appearance, having a husband and children, and against whose character, in other respects, nothing was alleged, was sentenced to ten days' solitary imprisonment, for having taken for her fire, on the estate of a countess, near which her cottage stood, a stick of wood, valued at threepence, from a tree that had been felled and partly cut up. If the tree had not been cut down, and she had taken a piece as large, the act

that much progress has been made in determining many questions which have vexed men's minds for centuries. I confess, when I was in the Bodleian library, at Oxford, that immense repository of the labors of so many burning brains and aching hearts, with its five hundred thousand volumes, and considered that, beyond all question, more than three hundred thousand of its thick octavos and ponderous quartos and folios were commentaries upon the Scriptures, or discussions of disputed questions in theology, and yet, in respect to most of them, that we are still at sea, and no land in sight, I could not escape the conviction, that here, too, man is still in leading-strings, and has yet scarcely taken "the first steps of infancy."

In respect to manufactures and commerce, if we compare the common operatives in either of these departments with those of the same class in agriculture, — the laborers in the mills, or the sailors on boardship, with the common laborers on the farm, — we shall find no great advantage, in intellectual progress, which the one has over the other; but, again, if we compare the highest class of farmers with the highest class of merchants and manufacturers, it will certainly be no disparagement to the latter classes to say that they are not in advance of the best-informed agriculturists; and that agriculture is now as much a matter of the mind, as much a matter of intellectual observation and in-

would have been a simple *trespass*, and she would have been mulcted in a fine only: as it was, however, it was a *felony* or *crime*, and she was punished accordingly. I could easily imagine the amazement of the poor unfortunate creature at so subtile and philosophical a distinction. I must add, though it may seem out of place, that a criminal prosecution for an offence of this nature can have no other effect than to engender a bitter malignity on the part of the poor towards the powerful, and that the generally severe administration of penal justice upon the humble and defenceless, (not, I must confess, peculiar to England,) when the large flies so often break through the cobweb of the law, and escape by intrigue or influence, can have little effect in producing reformation; and its main tendency must be to nourish, on the part of the lower classes, a deep resentment of the partiality, and an utter hatred of the power, to which they are subjected. A paternal administration of justice is not, of course, to be expected; but what an infinite amount of guilt and wretchedness would be saved, if the circumstances of the guilty could be more mercifully considered; especially if humanity and public justice could be more exerted in preventing rather than in punishing crime; above all, if society itself, by its omissions or its institutions, were not, in too many cases, the tempter, the minister, and the pander to crime, as well as its terrible avenger!

quiry, as any one of the practical arts of life; and at the present moment, it is occupying as much attention from the highest class of minds as any other of the business pursuits of life.

I hope, viewed in this aspect, I shall not be thought to speak with undue warmth on this subject. I have, I am aware, already alluded to it; but I am anxious to assert the dignity of a pursuit which I regard among the most honorable, as it is among the most innocent and useful, in life; and I would, if possible, soften its aspect, and multiply its attractions, to a large class of persons, who have been accustomed to look upon it with indifference or disdain, but who would be sure to find in it, if ardently and intelligently pursued, health for the body, and peace and satisfaction — nay more, the strongest and most delightful interest — for the mind.

XIX. — ACTUAL IMPROVEMENTS IN ENGLISH AGRICULTURE.

But of what nature are the improvements which agriculture has actually made in Great Britain, which determine the present high condition of the art? A stranger cannot, of course, from personal experience, compare her present condition with what it was; yet the marks of progress are so obvious that the most transient observer recognizes them; and many are now in the process of accomplishment, which fill him with delightful surprise. Many of these improvements are among the noblest triumphs of art, and mark, as strongly as in almost any other cases, the power of mind over matter, the subjugation of physical elements to an intellectual sovereign.

1. Draining, Irrigation, and Warping. — Much of what has been done is entirely out of sight; whole fields, thousands and thousands of acres of land, have been underdrained by pipes and channels, spreading themselves like beautiful net-work under the surface, taking off all the surplus moisture, and converting cold, unfruitful, and unsightly morasses into productive and beautiful fields. It would be curious, if it were possible, to approximate

the amount of this work which has been done; but there are no means even of framing a reasonable conjecture. It undoubtedly embraces hundreds of thousands of acres, and much more is in progress, since, important and indispensable as moisture is to vegetation, nothing can be more prejudicial than a superabundance of water, and especially stagnant water. Of the different modes of draining I shall speak hereafter at large. It is a subject of great importance and utility, and requires to be treated in the fullest and most exact manner. The next great improvement, that I have witnessed in England, is in the fen-country of Lincolnshire and Cambridgeshire, where vast territories, embracing many thousands of acres, have been, it may almost be said, created, that is, redeemed from the sea, fortified by strong and extensive embankments, and now rendered as fertile and productive as any lands which can be found upon the island. These lands, likewise, are kept drained by immense steam engines, which move with an untiring power, and accomplish this mighty work with ease. In other cases, in Lincolnshire, another process is going on, here denominated *warping*, by which, on the banks of the Humber, immense tracts are enclosed, the tide shut in, and compelled to leave its rich deposit, thus forming, likewise, the richest meadows. Still another process is in progress, by which the crooked course of a river is straightened, its channel deepened by its own new current, and rendered navigable, and, by the erection of artificial banks, the soil within them continually raised, and hundreds of acres, where so recently the fish, at high water, sported with impunity, are rescued from the sea, and covered with thriving flocks of cattle and sheep. In Yorkshire, not only are various processes of redeeming and improving land going on, but the curious process of removing, by the aid of steam machinery, the rich deposit from the bed of a river, whose current has been diverted from its natural course; and this deposit, after being taken out, is laid, at not an inordinate expense, on a peat bog hitherto unproductive and worthless. By judicious management, it is spread on the land to the depth of eight inches, and the covering proceeds at the rate of five acres per day. In Nottinghamshire, a most splendid improvement has been effected in turning the course of a small river, so as at pleasure to irrigate several hundred acres of land, which were formerly poor and comparatively unproductive, but now yield the most abundant crops; and in Staffordshire, the same results have been reached, not by a river, but by collecting the springs, and forming a grand reservoir, from which the water is carried over extensive fields, which are thus irrigated at pleasure.

2. Live Stock and Vegetables. — The next great feature in the improved husbandry of England is apparent in its live stock. I do not speak of it as seen at the cattle-shows of the different agricultural societies in the kingdom; for here the animals are all selected, or at a very great expense, and after a long time, fitted for the exhibition; but I speak rather of them as they are seen in Smithfield market, every Monday, and at the other smaller markets and fairs in various parts of the country. Here are the cattle and sheep of several distinct breeds, and all of remarkable excellence of their kind; I do not say perfect, — for that, in almost all cases, is assuming too much, — but leaving very little to be desired beyond what has been attained. Their condition and form, their symmetry, their fatness, are all admirable; and each breed is seen retaining its distinct properties, and, what is most remarkable, showing how much can be done by human art and skill in improving the animal form and condition, and bringing it to a desired model.

From Smithfield market, if he goes to Covent Garden market, in the infinite profusion and variety of fruits, and vegetables, and flowers, which are always to be found here, and in the perfection to which they are carried, and many of the finest fruits, in defiance of an uncongenial climate, he will find evidences of the same admirable skill and art which are displayed in other departments of rural industry.

3. Agricultural Implements. — The next evidences of the improvement of the agricultural art are to be seen in the extraordinary display of agricultural implements at the great shows. The exhibition at the meeting of the Royal Agricultural Society at Derby, in July, 1843, was so remarkable, that I shall be excused for giving a statement of the number, and many of the kinds, of the machines and implements there exhibited.

Of *Tillage Implements*, then, there were, — of ploughs, 148; harrows, 31; scarifiers, 25; clod-crushers, 7; rollers, 12; couch rakes, 4.

Of *Drilling, Sowing, Manuring, and Hoeing Machines.* — Of drills and bessers, and seed-sowing barrows, some designed for sowing manure with the seed, there were 61; of dibblers, for putting in the seed, 4; of horse-hoes, adapted to the cultivation of drilled crops, 20.

Of *Harvesting Machines.* — For hay-making, 4; horse-rakes, 7.

Of *Barn Machinery.* — Horse engines, locomotive or stationary, 7; steam engines for threshing or grinding, 6; threshing machines, 15; winnowing and cleaning machines, 20; crushing and splitting mills, 36; corn and meal mills, 20; chaff-cutters, 51; cake-crushers, for oil cake, 14; corn weighers and measures, 2.

Field, Fold, and Yard Machinery. — Of turnip-cutters, 12; root-graters and cider mill, 3; potato-washers, 2; steaming apparatus, 5; feeding apparatus and fodder preservers, various; weighing machines for carts, cattle, &c., 4; fire and garden engines, 11; machines for stock yard, various; sundries, machines for breaking stones, iron field gates, hurdles, trucks, fences, &c. &c. &c.

Agricultural Carriages, Harness, and Gear. — Wagons and carts for market, for harvest, for manures, (solid and liquid,) for family use, &c. &c., 38; breaks for carriages of all kinds; sets of wheels, axles, &c.; harnesses and horse-gear; drain tiles, and implements for forming tiles, 9.

Dairy Implements. — Churns, 8; cheese presses, 6; curd mills, 4; miscellaneous and various implements, and tools and vessels for domestic and rural purposes.

It cannot be expected that I should characterize these machines, and point out their various properties; though this is what I propose to do hereafter, in respect to such of them as seem to me most desirable to be introduced into my own country; but the number and variety of them which have been produced, and the neatness and care with which they are made, evince great mechanical skill and knowledge, and show that here, as well as in other departments of industry, the mind has been at work, and has produced the natural fruits of intense and well-directed application.

4. Application of Steam to Agriculture.—There is, indeed,

one giant power, of comparatively modern invention, which, it is thought, has not been as successfully or extensively applied in agriculture as in some other departments of the arts. Every one knows, at once, that I refer to the power of steam, which seems, wherever introduced, to defy all competition; and every day's experience appears to demonstrate that its extent is yet hardly conceived, and its application only begun. The experiments, which have been made in the application of steam power to the movement of ploughs, have not, as far as I can learn, been attended with success. It will not be safe to assert that this cannot be done to advantage; but certainly that is not the only application of steam to the purposes of agriculture, which is to be looked for. Indeed, besides the impossibility of an art, so intimately associated as agriculture is with almost all the practical arts of life, escaping its share of the general advantages which the community is enjoying from this mighty agent, it has already received many direct contributions from it. In the Lothians of Scotland, those beautifully cultivated grain districts, which, when seen in the season of their glory, with their green and their golden crops, so rich and delightful as to make the heart of an enthusiastic agriculturist beat as though he himself had a steam engine under his waistcoat, a steam engine is to be found on every principal farm, for threshing out all the grain, and for other economical purposes, to which, on a great farm, these engines are capable of being applied. The average size of these engines for threshing is from a six to an eight horse power, and the cost, which was formerly more than £120, or $600, is now greatly reduced.

The advantage of steam, as a motive power, must be obvious. It is always available, at all seasons, and without reference to the weather. Its movements are uniform, whereas horse power is, to a degree, capricious and unsteady, and horses often suffer a great deal, both from too constant and long-continued pulls, and likewise from frequent stops and starts. The steam power never tires, and its operation may be continued to any length of time or quantity. These are all great advantages, especially when a farmer, from any sudden advance, wishes to bring his grain at once into the market. It is obvious, at the same time, what advantages he has in having his horses saved from the severe work of threshing, and fresh for other farm work. The saving of a pair of horses, on a farm, is estimated at £100 per year, (very much more, indeed, than it would be with us;) and intelligent farmers assert "that, with steam power, they save one fourth of the horse power on large farms."

The usual quantity of grain threshed by a six horse steam power is at the rate of from thirty to forty bushels per hour; though the quantity must vary with the condition of the grain and the straw. The average work of a threshing mill, driven by horse power, is 150 bushels per day, and by steam power may be reckoned at 250 bushels per day, which is certainly a great preponderance in favor of the steam power. The wear and deterioration of the horses, and the expenses of keeping them, are most important considerations to a farmer. Indeed, so far as my observation goes, there is no single source of expense, none which abstracts so much from the profits of farming, and none of which the farmers in general are so little aware, as that of horse teams.

In the great experiment, or rather improvement, going on at Hatfield Chase, in Yorkshire, of emptying the deserted bed of a river, and spreading this rich alluvion over a peat bog, the earth carts are moved on a temporary railway by a steam engine, and carried to their place of deposit, so that, as I have before remarked, five acres can be covered in a day, eight inches deep; and that which it would be perfectly in vain for any inferior power to have attempted, is accomplished with perfect ease by this willing but mighty agent. The fens in Lincolnshire, where the uncertain and capricious power of the wind was formerly depended on, and, of course, with little confidence and uncertain results, are now relieved, at pleasure, of their surplus water, by two steam engines, one of sixty and one of eighty horse power; and the quantity of water removed, the time required, and the expense incurred for doing it, are all matters of exact calculation. The workmanship of these engines — for I have had the pleasure of visiting the spot — is extremely beautiful; and the advantages of the whole arrangement can hardly be overstated. I can easily believe that the same machinery, on a small scale, may be applied in many other similar cases; and a very intelligent and spirited farmer consulted me on the subject of his determination to erect a small steam engine, at his own expense, for the purpose of draining a part of his own premises. At the show at Derby, there was exhibited a movable steam engine, intended to be carried to a farmer's premises as it might be wanted for furnishing a threshing power, and other purposes. I have not yet learnt how it succeeds; but if success is not attained at a first attempt, it is ultimately certain. These machines are made of two, four, and six horse power. The cost of the two horse power is £80, or $400, and a three horse power, £110. This does not include the threshing machine. A fixed steam power must have many advantages over a movable steam machine. It is never safe to calculate upon doing a great many things with any single machine. A self-directing machine would be a great discovery; but, short of man himself, we can hardly look for that, though it seems sometimes to be nearly approached. A great difficulty, in many cases, is, that the machinery must be trusted to the hands of the stupid, careless, and sometimes malignant.

Such a power as this, on a large farm, may be applied to a great many uses; and its advantages, in many cases, will be incalculable. The turning of a grindstone for sharpening scythes and axes, on a large farm, would save, in the United States, a great expense of labor and fatigue; and its application to cutting roots, and chopping long fodder for stock, to breaking and crushing corn and oats, and to grinding grain into flour for the family, as well as for cattle, would be highly useful, especially in those parts of the country where water power is difficult to be procured. This is the case in all flat countries, and particularly on the prairies in the Western States. There, in many cases, coal abounds; and there, if ever it may be expected, where miles almost may be run without occasion to turn the plough, steam may be applied for the purposes of draft.

Agriculture owes, also, a considerable debt to steam, for the advantages it affords in the construction of agricultural implements, in respect to cheapness and uniformity. In cutting, sawing, and planing wood, in grinding and fashioning metals, steam power is applied to great advantage. In one, if not more, extensive establishment, for the manufacture of agricultural implements in New England, steam power is used, so as greatly to reduce the expensiveness of ploughs, and other articles, which are here made. The same thing is done in England; and this application of this wonderful power is every day extending itself to a most extraordinary degree. I may well call it wonderful;

for who could have dreamt, on first seeing a tea-kettle boiling over the fire, that there were the simple elements of a power destined to exert a greater influence in the progress of the arts and sciences, and consequently over the whole condition of society, than any other known; which was to rend rocks, and snap iron asunder, like bands of straw; which was to ride securely and triumphantly over the mountain waves of the sea; which was to drain floods and lakes, and lay open their fertile bottoms to the ploughshare; which should compel the deep places of the earth to disgorge their mineral treasures; and, disdaining time and space, plant distant countries, for all the practical purposes of commerce and friendship, of reciprocal supply and mutual improvement, in the immediate neighborhood of each other?

This brings me to another great benefit which agriculture has derived from steam power, which I should do injustice to pass over. I was in Smithfield market a few weeks since, and, in conversation with a very intelligent salesman, — whom, let me say by the way, I shall never remember but with a grateful sense of his kindness, and a high respect for his character,* — he said to me, "We have the contributions of seven hundred miles brought to market to-day, and without the slightest injury to their condition. We have beasts and sheep here from Sutherland, and from the southern counties of England;" and I believe he might have added, from Ireland and from Belgium. Steam vessels and railroad cars bring them at once to the great places of sale. It was always calculated, by the drovers of cattle from Connecticut River to Brighton market, near Boston, — an

* This gentleman, whose business, in the market, is of the most extensive and responsible character, presents an example so full of wholesome instruction, that I hope I shall be pardoned for enlivening my Report by a reference to it. He spends several days in the week in the most confused, noisy, and busy place in the world, faithful to the interests of his employers, and retires at night, a few miles from the city, to enjoy his cup brimful of domestic pleasures, at his own fireside, in a crowded circle, where mutual love reigns triumphant, where the table is covered with the literary gems of the press, and the walls of his drawing-rooms are adorned with the splendid products of his own pencil, displaying taste and skill. So true it is that men, if they will be but true to their own intellectual and moral natures, need not be utter slaves to the drudgery of business; and, if they will only look for them, may find, at the most moderate expense, within their own reach, in the hours of recreation, too often squandered or abused, sources of the richest and most elevated pleasures.

average distance of about one hundred miles, and which occupied a week in its performance, — that a beef animal so driven lost one hundred pounds in weight; and then he usually came into market foot-sore, sunken, in a state of fever, and looking like the victim of cruelty, and the picture of misery and exhaustion. Where steam power is employed, a journey of excessive fatigue and labor, which formerly occupied seven days, scarcely occupies now as many hours, and the animals are transported without fatigue or labor, or loss of substance.*

A farmer at Ware told me that the driving of a fat beast to Smithfield, about twenty-six miles, occupied, formerly, two days. The animal now goes by railroad in two hours, at a cost, I think, of not more than 2 s., and comes into the market fresh and sleek, like a new bonnet from the band-box. But there is another animal benefited besides the quadruped; and that is the drover himself, who, instead of spending eight or ten days or more upon the road, at a great expense of money, and not a little increased hazard of morals every day he is away from his family, finds his business now accomplished, and his money received, and himself returned to his home in three days. These are considerations of immense importance.†

---

* I cannot say that they have not even some pleasure in the transit. This, perhaps, might be very well ascertained by an inquiry of the passengers in the third class cars, who, through the extraordinary disinterestedness of the railroad directors and corporations, are conveyed with the same advantages of the open air, the refreshing showers, and the full enjoyment of the rural scenery, and, in general, in the same affectionate aggregation, and in precisely the same circumstances of position and comfort, in which the cattle are transported.

† In a recent debate in Parliament, a member, otherwise of considerable cleverness, in referring to the practice of the railroads in rendering the transits of second and third class trains less frequent, and much slower than first class trains, was pleased to say that "it was well enough; for the time of the poorer classes was not of much consequence, and they might as well pass it in the cars as any where else." It would be difficult to say what, to any one but himself, is the value of the time of a man who could make so heartless an assertion. The poor man's time and labor are his only capital. Enable him to do as much again in half the time employed, and you quadruple his power of serving the community, and supporting himself and family. As for the rich man, who made this declaration, I wish him nothing worse than to travel in a third class car attached to a slow night freight train, so that, in one of the long tunnels between Liverpool and London, his pleasant imaginations might be rectified by sober facts, and himself have time for reflection and repentance.

It will not do, then, to say that steam has done nothing for agriculture: perhaps no department of industry has been more essentially benefited. In its equalizing the value of landed estate throughout the country, it has conferred immense benefits. A farm, accessible to the great markets by steam conveyance, though two hundred miles from London, is now of equal value as if it were within twenty miles. The farmer near London may complain of this; but it is proper for the community to remember how many more farms are at a distance from, than how many are near to, London; and how little the interest of a few individuals is to be brought into consideration, compared with the interest of a large community, who are to have the advantages of the extended competition. Singular as the result is, however, and contradictory as it may seem to all theories on the subject, it does not appear, in fact, that any parties are injured by the facilities given to the most distant to reach the market. In respect to all the great interests of society, which are in their nature fluctuating, or at all dependent on external circumstances, so many and such various elements are intermingled and combined, and so many new conditions present themselves, that the calculations of political economists are constantly at fault; and the results are deeply humbling to the pride of human sagacity. Into what a snarl of misery and confusion would every thing in this world be thrown, if man's providence were substituted for the divine providence! and so it constantly proves that, just in proportion as men attempt to interfere with the divine arrangements, to control the great natural laws of Heaven, and to create a perfectly artificial mechanism for the government of society, they find their plans defeated; and the certain result is any thing but unmixed or even general improvement. I remember, a few years since, it was confidently said, that, when the great Erie Canal of New York should be finished, by which the agricultural treasures of the Great West should find an easy transmission to the Atlantic, farms in the neighborhood of New York city would become comparatively worthless. Yet, strange to say, they have much increased in value, and are now certain to hold their own. The vast increase of population throughout the country; the great increase of population in the city of New York, occasioned, to a considerable degree, by the amount of business which this very canal has produced; the multiplication of trades of every variety, and the influx of wealth to which it has contributed; with wealth, the increase of luxury, and the demand for fruits and vegetables, — articles in their nature perishable, and demanding a rapid and certain conveyance, — with various other circumstances, have conspired to keep up the value of farms, and, indeed, to increase their value in the neighborhood of New York, and in every point from which, by these improved facilities of conveyance, this great mart has been rendered the more accessible.

The poorest markets — those which are most poorly supplied — are in general those where the prices are lowest. Competition and abundance create, and, to a certain degree, quicken demand; for the reason that they bring more customers, and create more wants. Peaches are now sent by steam conveyances from New Jersey to Boston, a distance of nearly three hundred miles; and strawberries from Providence, nearly two hundred miles, to New York. What has been the effect? To lessen price in a very small degree in any case, but in many cases not at all; to increase the consumption greatly; and to induce the farmers, directly in the neighborhood of Boston, to go themselves into the cultivation of peaches, to take immense pains to guard against the evils of an uncongenial climate, and to cultivate, as far as possible, fruits of the best quality. Some trades may be overdone; they may be concerned only with articles not of necessity, but of mere fancy, and subject to the caprices of whim and fashion; but in all those for which the demand is necessarily permanent, and in a state of general prosperity in a country, the increased demand, growing out of an increased consumption, will be always likely to afford a remunerating price. But in any event, whatever tends to the improvement of the general condition of the community is to be encouraged. It may often be attended with partial loss or temporary inconvenience; yet, in all cases, unless conscience or morals are involved, individual benefit or advantage should yield to the public good. The farmer near a large town thinks himself injured by a railroad or canal which brings the farm of another man, a hundred miles distant, in competition with his own. Every one sees that the great public is to be benefited by the increased supply which is thus produced. Now, is there any good reason why the distant farmer should not come to the market by any facility which he may create or obtain, as well as his neighbor, provided he does not hinder that neighbor from coming in the best way he can obtain, any more than there is why the distant farmer should be compelled to come on foot, and bring his load upon his back, instead of availing himself of his horse or his carriage?

5. Increased Production. — But in speaking of the advanced and improved state of English agriculture, there are, perhaps, stronger evidences of its progress than any to which I have referred, in the increased productiveness of the fruits of the earth, and in the increased population which are sustained by them.

In the ten years from 1801 to 1810, the average annual import of wheat into the kingdom was such as to allow, if divided among 17,442,911 souls, — the population of the kingdom at that time, — a small fraction over a peck for the annual consumption of each person. The average amount imported between 1811 and 1820, when the mean number of the population had advanced to 19,870,589, would have allowed each person not quite one gallon and a half for the yearly consumption. The average amount of importation for the five years from 1831 to 1835, when the mean number of consumers was over 25,000,000, if fairly divided, would have given to each person one gallon of wheat. Taking the three years 1833, 1834, 1835, the importation would have allowed only one pint and one fifth, or about fifteen ounces, of fine flour to each consumer.*

This is certainly a very small amount, and demonstrates the immense agricultural resources of the country. It shows as strongly the improvements in cultivation, by which, under a fast-increasing population, the dependence on a foreign supply for bread is continually growing less. This can only arise from two causes, the bringing more land into cultivation, and a more improved cultivation. Both causes have probably operated to a degree, and of the latter the evidences are every where numerous and striking.

I was asking a farmer in Berkshire county, England, — venerable as an octogenarian, — whether he had seen any great im-

* See an admirable work, full of information — Porter's Progress of the Nation, Vol. I. p. 147.

provements in agriculture; to which, in spite of the prejudices which too often obscure or pervert the vision at so advanced a period of life, he replied, with perfect candor, "Immense improvements; *we* knew nothing; every thing is now better done; the crops are far more various and more abundant; the product of wheat has almost doubled; the turnip cultivation has been created; the implements are far better; the live stock is beyond all comparison better; every thing, every thing is better." The good old man had lived, like Simeon, in, indeed, a far humbler sense, to see the marked and strong tokens of the divine goodness in the progressive improvement of every thing around him; and he proclaimed it with the glowing enthusiasm of youth, and showed the fire still burning under the snow. Happy old age, when, instead of a mind soured under the accumulated burdens and infirmities of advanced years, and covered with mossy prejudices, it benevolently acknowledges good wherever good is found; progress wherever progress is made; and, instead of growling at the degeneracy of the present times, and sighing over the fading reminiscences of what it deems the superiority of years which are passed, delights in the actual improvements of the present, and sees in them the foreshadowing of far greater improvements in the distant prospect, when the advances now made, great as they may actually be, and still greater as they seem in comparison with those of days gone by, will be found to be only the first lessons of childhood! There is a good deal of this spirit or temper here, called by the gentle name, in England, of *conservatism;* but this man's mind was happily free from it. I have all reasonable respect for antiquity; but, if the presumption may be pardoned, I beg leave to say, with Lord Bacon, I reckon that to be antiquity which is farthest from the beginning. The present times are, therefore, more ancient than those which have preceded them, and are to be reverenced as imbodying the accumulated wisdom and experience of past ages. This spirit of improvement, now so rife and active, is the foundation of all intelligent hopes of further progress; and I am happy in saying that in nothing is it more obvious than in agriculture.

6. Royal Agricultural Society. — In this progress the Royal Agricultural Society of England contributes its full share.

This was established about 1837, and embraces a large array of the highest rank and talent in the kingdom, and a vast body of farmers, landlords, and others interested in agriculture. Its funds are large, arising from donations and an annual subscription of a guinea from each of its members; but it has received no endowment from the government. Its objects comprehend every branch of husbandry and rural economy. It has a central office, or building, in Hanover Square, London, where the secretary of the society resides, and where the council of the society and other members hold weekly and monthly meetings, for the management of the business of the society, and the discussion of agricultural subjects, and the reception of agricultural information. This conduces very much to the interest felt in the projects and operations of the society, and is the means of diffusing a great amount of valuable information.

It has begun here the establishment of an agricultural library and museum, which presently must assume a considerable importance, and become curious and useful. The object of the library is to collect the most useful and valuable publications on subjects connected with agriculture, in all its various and kindred branches, including likewise geology, botany, agricultural chemistry, engineering, and manufacturing, as far as they are connected with the making of agricultural implements, and the great agricultural operations of draining, embanking, irrigation, and other important farming processes. The object of its museum is to exhibit specimens of agricultural productions, which are capable of preservation, seeds, plants, grasses, samples of wool, mineral manures, models and drawings of agricultural implements, and whatever, in any way, may conduce to the advancement of the science or practice of agriculture. It is obvious how very important such an establishment must prove, by giving practical men an opportunity of inspecting, at their leisure, the most improved subjects of cultivation, the best grains, and the best grasses and vegetables, and, at the same time, the best tools and machines, with which to cultivate them. I have often urged the establishment of agricultural museums upon my countrymen, especially in the capitals of the states and of the United States, where the members of the different legislatures assemble. Coming, as they do, from different and distant parts of the country, they will be enabled to carry home information of the utmost importance to the farmers, besides having their own knowledge advanced, and their own zeal quickened in this great cause. The commissioner of patents in Washington, distinguished by his indefatigable exertions for the advancement of agriculture, has already laid the foundation of such a collection, at the metropolis of the country, and in connection with his own department, where models of all patented agricultural machinery are always to be seen. It is to be hoped that the friends of an improved agriculture in the country will encourage and assist him in extending his collection of valuable grains and seeds. There are few ways so little expensive, in which they may render so much service to the country. It would be desirable that the government should enjoin it upon the commanders of all their ships of war, visiting different parts of the globe, that they should collect and bring home such seeds and plants, and such models of implements, as would be likely to be of use. That universal vegetable, the potato, furnishing so much food to man and beast, and scarcely second to any in value, considering the multitudes whom it supplies, and the quantity of food it affords, is said to be an importation from South America. The cotton plant, a source of enormous wealth to the country, is likewise esteemed a foreign plant.

Besides this, the Royal Agricultural Society issues a semi-yearly publication of valuable communications and papers, both on the science and practice of agriculture, which fall in its way, or are made to the society in reply to queries proposed for discussion and for information, upon which it offers premiums of a pecuniary or an honorary nature.

The society, likewise, at some place in the country, easily accessible, hold an annual show or exhibition of animals, implements, and agricultural products, upon the best of which it awards premiums. This occupies, generally, four days. Tuesday is exclusively assigned to the several committees for the inspection of subjects of premium, in the way of implements and agricultural machinery, when no persons whatever, excepting the committees and persons necessarily attendant upon them, are admitted to the yard, so that they have a favorable opportunity of quiet inspection, uninterrupted by any interested or curious parties; Wednesday is devoted, in the same way, to the examination of the animals, and afterwards the yards are open to the public upon payment of a reasonable entrance fee; and on Fridays a public sale, at auction, is held of such animals, or implements, as their owners are willing to dispose of in this way. The collection of people, on such occasions, from all parts of the country, and, I may properly add, from all parts of the world, is immense. Two large public dinners are given on the occasion; the one called the *council dinner*, on Wednesday, and the other, called the *society's dinner*, on Thursday, when provision is made for fifteen hundred guests, in a pavilion erected for the purpose. These dinners are, in general, seasons of great hilarity, and promotive of sympathy in the great cause of agricultural improvement. If no other good comes of them to agriculture, they serve at least the purpose of consumption, and so quicken price and demand.

On these occasions, the prizes are announced to the successful candidates; and these premiums are given either in medals, plate, or money, and are received with no small degree of public and self-congratulation.

The arrangements, in general, are made with great care. The animals are assorted in distinct classes, with separate committees for the examination of each class; and the implements are placed according to their different designs and uses. It would be impossible to convey an accurate or adequate impression of the number and variety of the animals offered, in such cases, for exhibition and premium. I have already given a list and the number of agricultural implements exhibited the last year at the Derby show; but that conveys no idea of the ingenuity and skill evinced in their construction. One is led to conclude, from the inspection, that there is no operation or function, connected with human life and labor, for which mechanical labor does not attempt, and may not presently succeed in furnishing an instrument or machine. In many cases, a machine is any thing but a facility; and not a few of the machines, both in their contrivance and the expensive and showy manner in which they are got up, evince pretty strongly the gauge which the contrivers and makers have taken of the understandings and pockets of the probable purchasers. They are seldom at a loss to put the pail under a full cow.

In many respects, the arrangements are admirable, and well

worthy of imitation.* Every possible effort is made to secure an impartial decision among the competitors; for besides that they are not suffered by their presence to influence the examiners, the examiners themselves are selected from among persons who are as far as possible disinterested, and not likely to be influenced. They are chosen, likewise, with a special reference, in their characters and qualifications, to the nature of the subjects submitted;

---

* The terms on which the premiums for seed wheat are to be awarded are well worth the observation of other agricultural societies, and I therefore subjoin them.

"SEED WHEAT.

"I. Thirty Sovereigns, or a Piece of Plate of that value, will be given to the Exhibiter at the Meeting at Derby of the best 14 bushels of White Wheat, of the harvest of 1842, and grown by himself.

"II. Thirty Sovereigns, or a Piece of Plate of that value, will be given to the Exhibiter at the Meeting at Derby of the best 14 bushels of Red Wheat, of the harvest of 1842, and grown by himself.

"III. Twenty Sovereigns, or a Piece of Plate of that value, will be given to the Exhibiter at the Meeting at Derby of the best 14 bushels of Spring Wheat, of the harvest of 1842, and grown by himself.

"Competitors are requested to send with their Wheat, specimens, fairly taken, of the same in the ear, with the whole of the Straw, in a bundle not less than one foot in diameter, and with the roots attached.

"[12 bushels of the Wheat will be sealed up by the Stewards, and one of the remaining bushels of each variety will be exhibited as a sample to the public; the other being kept for comparison with the produce of the next year. At the General Meeting, in December, 1844, the Prizes will be awarded.]

"The two best samples of each of these three classes of Wheat, without at that time distinguishing, in any of the cases, between the comparative merits of either sample, will be selected by the Judges, appointed for the meeting at Derby; and will be sown, under the direction of the Society, (the Winter Wheats in the autumn of 1843, and the Spring Wheat not earlier than the 1st of March, 1844,) by four farmers, who will make their report, upon which the prizes will be awarded, provided there be sufficient merit in any of the samples. Ten Sovereigns will be given at the Meeting at Derby to each Exhibiter whose wheat has been selected for trial.

"⁂ *No variety of wheat which has been selected for trial at any previous show shall be qualified to compete.*"

The following are the instructions to the Judges on other subjects:—

"As the object of the Society in giving the prizes for neat cattle, sheep, and pigs, is to promote improvement in breeding stock, the Judges, in making their award, are instructed not to take into their consideration the present value to the butcher of animals exhibited, but to decide according to their relative merits for the purpose of breeding."

"In the Class for horses, the Judges, in awarding the prizes, are instructed, in addition to symmetry, to take activity and strength into their consideration."

and every pains is taken in this way to secure the greatest aptness and talents. The name of the competitor is not given where it can be avoided, but only the number of the article presented. The rules of admission and competition are stringent and absolute, and no exceptions are, on any account, allowed. When, last year, a competitor attempted to introduce a machine out of season, or in some way contrary to the published rules, and wrote to one of the agents of the society, that, if a *silver key* should be found necessary to its introduction, he begged him to use it, — this attempt at bribery was rejected with proper indignation by the society, and the individual concerned, though eminent as a machinist and a manufacturer, and offering every apology for his "indiscretion," was forever irrevocably excluded as a competitor for any of the premiums of the society.

The society likewise offers premiums for essays, which are deemed deserving of such reward, upon any given subjects, and for reports on the agricultural condition and habits of different counties and districts. This has been the means of bringing out many valuable papers. Here, too, the decision is sought to be rendered as fair as possible; for the name of the writer is not given with the essay, but under a separate and sealed envelope, which is not opened until the successful essay is announced; and then the seal is broken, and the writer's name declared, in the presence of the society.

The society likewise has a consulting chemist, a consulting engineer, a botanist, and a professor of the veterinary art, of whose services, in any desirable case, it avails itself. Some time since, it numbered on its lists more than 6500 members; and has been, since that time, steadily on the increase. It is impossible to overrate the advantages which such a society brings with it to the agricultural community; for, though it enrols among its members many gentlemen, who are mere amateurs in the profession, and take little interest, and have little knowledge of its practical details, yet, on the other hand, it combines, among the highest men in the kingdom, a very large amount of practical talent and skill — men of the most accurate observation, who carefully enter into the whole subject. There is another great and good influence, which it powerfully exerts, and which must not be overlooked. It gives a high respectability to the agricultural profession, and presents it as a pursuit, not, as has been too often said, for mere dolts and clod-hoppers, but for minds of the highest order, and for men of all conditions, from the prince to the peasant; for "the king himself is served by the field." The prizes are contended for with an ardor little short of that which displays itself in the contests of political life, and received with a high sense of their value. I have seen, at the tables of some of the highest noblemen in the land, the premiums of agricultural success, exhibited in some form of plate, with more triumph than they would display in the brilliant badges of their rank.

7. Agricultural Society of Scotland. — The Highland and Agricultural Society of Scotland is an institution of a similar description, and of a longer standing, than the Royal Society of England. It is richly endowed, and as powerfully patronized, and has long rendered itself illustrious by its Journal, published quarterly, in Edinburgh. This Journal, for the ability with which it is managed, and which has been displayed also in the prize essays of the Highland Society, which are always published in connection with the Journal, has certainly no superior. The Scotch have been long distinguished for their acuteness and excellent management; and the evidences of the justness of their pretensions in these respects, were too obvious and numerous, on my transient visit to the southern portions of Scotland, to leave any doubt of their just claims to the highest reputation. The exhibition of the society at Dundee, the last autumn, was, in the character and condition of its animals, in no respect, in my judgment, inferior to that at Derby, though the Scotch cattle present different varieties from those which are fashionable and most esteemed in England. The short horns and the Leicesters of England would be, as a stock, very poorly adapted to the bleak hills and cold climate of Scotland; while the hardiness and thrift of the Scotch cattle and sheep show how well suited they are to the homes where they are bred, and whence they are sent, in immense droves, in certain seasons of the year, to the southern portions of the country. The general management of the Scotch Agricultural Society does not essentially differ from that of the English Royal Agricultural Society. The general exhibition at Dundee passed off much in the same style as at Derby, excepting that I thought the Scotch drank their toasts with a little more heartiness than the English — a characteristic of the country-

men of Burns. This is not the place for me to describe the different breeds of stock shown at either place, or the various implements exhibited. This I propose to do in another part of my Reports, with all the particularity which my friends can desire. The stock shown at Dundee would bear a comparison with the best stock shown any where; and the fact is too well known to need any confirmation of mine, that in point of intelligence and agricultural skill, and in point of success, — the best test of intelligence and skill, — the Scotch farmers yield the palm to none.

XX. — RELATION OF LANDLORD AND TENANT.

The holdings of many of the Scotch farmers are very large; and their farms are generally held under leases of nineteen and twenty-one years. One would be led to infer that the terms on which the landlords live with their tenants, in Scotland, must be honorable and just to both parties, since renewals are common: the same estates have been, in many instances, in the same families for a century, and the expenses incurred, in some cases, by tenants, in the erection of permanent buildings and other fixtures, are very heavy; showing the confidence of the tenant in his landlord. One farm was pointed out to me where the tenant had recently died, leaving only one child, an infant son. In this case, that the lease might be retained in the family, three of the neighboring farmers had agreed to take the whole management of the estate until the young man came of age. In such cases, there is very little difference between a lease and a freehold in fee-simple. I cannot say, however, that the tenant is raised above all dependence on his landlord, or that removals do not sometimes take place under circumstances of great hardship. In one case, which came under my knowledge, a farm had been withdrawn, or, rather, the renewal of the lease refused, though it had been in the occupation of the same family for many years, on the ground of political opposition and prejudice, the avowed opinions and votes of the tenant not coinciding with those of the landlord. It is easy to believe that this may often happen, though any direct influence of this kind would be likely to meet the reprobation of the public. In one case, in England, to my inquiries whether the tenant was not expected to vote with the landlord, the farmer replied that his own politics were opposed to the politics of his landlord; and that, when taking his lease, to his great regret, he had pledged himself to remain neutral, and withhold his vote — a course by which many overwise and prudent people think that they escape the responsibility of the duty, whereas, in truth, by so doing they virtually give a vote to their opponents. In another case, the reply of two very intelligent and substantial farmers was, that they were at liberty to vote as they pleased; but it was almost the only way in which they could show their respect to, and evince their sense of the kindness of, their landlord, and they felt it therefore a duty of gratitude to vote with him. We are not beyond this influence even in our democratic communities. The voting by ballot may seem to give a perfect security; but this is invaded or destroyed when the candidates of a party are publicly prescribed, and the votes given are in a printed form; so difficult is it, under any circumstances, to maintain a perfect freedom and independence, and in practical life to realize our ideal theories. But politics are not my province; nor should I have thus far ventured upon them, but as connected with the important relation of tenant and landlord, in which I know my countrymen feel the strong interest of curiosity. I shall, perhaps, excite some surprise in stating my belief that the manner in which farms are held here, on hire for a year, or on lease for a term of years, rather than being owned by the occupants, is itself a powerful instrument or incentive to agricultural improvement. In the United States, where farms are owned by the occupant, the farmer seldom keeps any account, and it matters not much to him what is the result of the year's management. The effect of this is to render a man negligent and indifferent to success or loss. But when, at the end of every six months, the rent must be paid, it is not a matter of indifference whether his farming turns out well or ill; for not only the labor employed is to be paid for, but the rent of the farm must be punctually discharged. This consequently compels him to make every exertion by which he may be assisted to meet his obligations. He finds no room for idleness or neglect; and the continuance of his possession depends upon his good management and the punctual payment of the rent. This prompts to watchfulness, skill, experiment, and improvement; and especially it gives to farming a commercial or mercantile character, and obliges the farmer to keep accounts, and so to learn the exact pecuniary result of his operations — a matter in which the farmers of the United States, as far as my observation goes, who are the owners of the farms which they occupy, are almost universally deficient. The strict responsibility to which the farmers are here held by their landlords, is undoubtedly a material element in their success. At the same time, where the occupation is from year to year, and leases are refused on the part of the landlords, as is generally the case in England, — though in Scotland leases are almost universal, — the effect must be to prevent or discourage substantial improvements, as few persons will be inclined to make such improvements with an uncertainty of continuance. It is a fact, however, which may create some surprise, that many farmers are unwilling to take leases when landlords would be willing to grant them. But this happens only when there is a perfect confidence on both sides; the tenant has entire reliance upon the honor and liberality of the landlord, and the landlord is equally confident of the good conduct and management of his tenant. An excellent landlord, in Lincolnshire, says he considers himself bound to continue his old tenants and their children in possession, in preference to any other tenant, as long as they choose to remain, unless some extraordinary contingency presents itself; and virtually admits on their part a property in the soil. The great length of time during which families, on his estates, have held their possessions from father to son, shows that he acts upon the most liberal principles; and the condition of his tenants, and their great improvements, evince that his honorable conduct secures their entire confidence. It cannot be doubted, however, that the uncertainty of continuance, the absolute power of discharge on the part of the landlord, the risk of his caprice, and the possibility of a new one coming in possession, "who might not remember Joseph, but forget him," must have some effect in preventing or discouraging improvements.

A farm which is well managed cannot change tenants without great inconvenience and evil on both sides. On several very large estates, which I have visited, the occupancy had been in the same families for a large portion of a century, and there seemed not the slightest apprehension of any change on either side. A good tenant is evidently almost as important to his landlord as his continuance on the estate can be to himself; and where, under such circumstances, substantial and permanent improvements are to be made, the landlord himself bears a portion of the expense. In draining, for example, the landlord furnishes the tiles, and the farmer makes the drains and lays them. A skilful and intelligent farmer, worth having as a tenant, would hardly be found willing to take a farm for a year, without an expectation of a much longer continuance, and certainly would not, under such an occupation, attempt any improvements but at the risk or expense of the landlord. In Scotland, where leases are, in general, for nineteen or twenty-one years, if the farmer has seven years of unexpended lease, he is expected to pay a third of the expense of any permanent fixtures or improvements; if fourteen years, he is expected to pay two thirds, and the landlord one; if the whole term, the whole expenses are deemed properly chargeable to him.

I confess, under the best circumstances, I should greatly prefer being an owner or freeholder, to being a tenant. There is an excessive caution which characterizes some shrewd calculators, who consider the value of a property diminished, where the lease is limited even to nine hundred and ninety-nine years; but, without any sympathy with such persons, there is, at least, a gratification to a man's self-esteem, to feel that he is "the monarch of what he surveys," and that whatever improvements he makes upon his estate will enure to the lasting benefit of himself or his heirs. In a pecuniary view, however, it is really matter of indifference whether the occupant pays a reasonable rent for the land as tenant, or, as the owner of it, loses the interest of the capital invested in the purchase of the soil. There are few cases, as I have before observed, where the rents paid equal the legal interest of the money which the lands would command, if offered for sale. Certainly, as far as my observation goes, — and I have seen somewhat both of landlords and tenants, — there prevails a disposition, and there are the strongest inducements, to cultivate a mutually-good understanding between the parties. There is, in general, no more reason to fear that landlords will be oppressive and unjust, than that tenants will be wasteful, negligent, and fraudulent. Power is always a hazardous possession, and always liable to abuse, and cannot, therefore, be too much guarded and limited in every condition of life. The abuses of power are not, however, peculiar to persons occupying a high condition in society, but are as often found among the lowest, who seem to have nothing else but the ability to injure and exert it most cruelly when they are most loudly claiming compassion for themselves, as the victims of injustice. I believe there is a great deal more abuse of power on the part of farmers towards their laborers, than on the part of landlords towards their tenants. The farmers can protect themselves; the laborers, in general, are without power. Indeed, the more cultivated and improved is the education of a man, and the higher the condition which he occupies in society, the stronger are the inducements to a just and honorable conduct, not only in his enlarged mind, but in the increased value of character to such a man. In Ireland, the middle-man, who comes between the landlord and the poor tenants, who there are themselves laborers, and especially those middle-men who are themselves subletters of the soil, are always feared for their severity and oppression. How far a man's political independence is affected by his relation to his landlord, is another consideration. A man living under such a constitution of government as that of England, unless he is himself an office-seeker, or dependent upon the emoluments of public office, will not deem this of so much importance as many might consider it; and if he makes up his judgment from the representation which the minority in a republican or elective government always give of the character and measures of the majority, he may be led to conclude that his chance of being protected in his rights, and secured in his person and property, is as good under an hereditary government, or one chosen for him by others, as under one in the choice of which he himself, with others, is permitted to give his suffrage. I would not be thought to undervalue political liberty; and, in my opinion, human wisdom has never devised a constitution of government so just and so favorable to the happiness of its subjects as that of my own country. But I have been too often in the minority not to have learned that a majority composed of thousands may be as despotic as a single tyrant; and I am not unaware that the position occupied by the governments of all civilized countries, is, at the present day, very different from what it was a century ago. As the reformation, under Luther, gave a blow to the doctrine of the infallibility of the church, from which it can never recover, so the successful assertion of the right of revolution against oppression, in 1776, read a lesson to all arbitrary governments, which is not likely soon to be forgotten. Under any form of government, the great security for the subject is, that they who govern shall be equally affected by their own measures as they who are governed; and in countries so free and enlightened as Great Britain and the United States, whoever may rule, no measures of extreme injustice or wrong are likely to be long endured. There is a force in public opinion which can scarcely be resisted, and which is more powerful than any mere legal enactments. What is mainly to be desired is, that education should be so general in its extension, and so elevated and just in its character, that public opinion may be wisely formed, and be not only a commanding, but a safe and worthy guide.

The form or conditions of lease, in England, somewhat differ in different places; but the main terms are every where the same. Leases, generally, are drawn up in an exact form, and become sealed and legal instruments. The farm is entered upon in the spring, and the rent is made payable semi-annually. The mode of cultivation is generally prescribed by the landlord, from which the tenant is not at liberty to depart. Two white crops are seldom permitted to succeed each other without intervention upon the same land. The green produce is required to be fed upon the place; and if hay or straw is sold, an equivalent quantity of manure is required to be brought on. All substantial improvements are the subject of special agreement; and the tenant is never allowed to cut down any tree or timber upon the place, or otherwise to commit any waste. Where a farm is to be quit, or entered upon by a new tenant, the going-out tenant is at liberty to come in to gather the crops which he himself has sown.

There is a class of men, in England, of which we know nothing in the United States; these are called *land surveyors* or *valuers*. These are generally persons of experience and judgment, who examine the condition of the place, and estimate what would be a fair rent to be paid; and by their opinion the parties are usually governed. Such a person is often employed to estimate the value of growing crops, where an allowance is to be made by the incoming to the out-going tenant. This professional man, if well qualified for his office, may be highly useful; and such a course is likely to render the transaction more just than where it partakes more of an accidental or arbitrary character, where one party may be led by his caprice to demand too much, or be betrayed by his ignorance to obtain too little; or the other party may be driven by his necessities, or led by a mistaken judgment of the capacities of the farm, to take it upon very hard terms. The taxes and tithes are usually paid by the tenant; but their amount is always considered in determining the rent, so that, properly speaking, they are paid by the landlord, and not by the tenant. The leasing of farms, in the United States, is quite rare, and but in few cases is it arranged by any established rule. In New England, in such cases, matters are conducted most loosely. Farms are frequently "taken to the halves," which is understood to imply that the farmer returns half of all the produce grown to the owner; but the landlord is almost entirely in the power of the farmer; and, after the farmer has, as is but too common, applied to his own use about half the produce, he divides with the owner the half which remains. If the owner furnishes implements, the farmer returns them as good as he received them; and, if he furnishes stock, as on a breeding or a dairy farm, the tenant pays the legal interest upon the cost, makes good the stock received when he quits the farm, which is generally settled by valuers or appraisers, and divides with his landlord one half the increase. Our practices, in this matter, are various and unsettled; and, as long as the hiring of farms continues with us to be so infrequent, — and it is likely to continue so while land remains as easy to be purchased as it now is, — no exact method will be introduced.

XXI. — GAME AND THE GAME LAWS.

The farmers in the United States are happily free from one evil which presses heavily upon the English farmers; and that is, the nuisance of what is here called *game*, and the curse of the *game laws*. Pheasants, partridges, grouse, hares, and rabbits, are here called *game*, and are protected, by the most severe laws, for the benefit of sportsmen who either own or lease the territory on which they find them, and pay a tax to the government for the privilege of shooting or coursing. The hares and rabbits are extremely destructive to the farmers' crops, and the complaints of them are universal. It is considered that five hares, or seven rabbits, consume as much as one sheep, besides a considerable amount of incidental damage; and it is stated that there were sold, from one farm, in one year, for the benefit of the landlord, no less than two thousand hares and rabbits, which was a tax upon the farmer equal to the support of three hundred sheep. They do great damage to much of the produce which they do not consume, in biting the turnips and in trampling down the grain. A farmer is liable to imprisonment or transportation if he destroys them, even when committing havoc upon his crops. An allowance is undoubtedly made, in some cases, though not in all, for these depredations and injuries. It is obvious, however, that, in most cases, an equivalent can hardly be made, not for the loss merely, but the immeasurable vexation, which they occasion. I entirely accord in the unanimous opinion of the farmers, whom I have met with, that, with the exception of feathered game, the game laws inflict a most serious injury upon the agricultural interest. Of their moral tendency this is not the place for me to speak; but the innumerable convictions for poaching — that is, entrapping or stealing game — with which the judicial calendars are filled, — and some trials for which charges I have attended, — and the several murders of gamekeepers which have occurred even within the last year, present a subject of serious consideration for those who know that one great preventive of crime is to remove the facilities and inducements to it, and that whoever, voluntarily, and without necessity, presents a temptation to crime, necessarily shares in its responsibility. It is a subject which never can be too strongly urged upon just and reflecting minds, how much the manners and pleasures of the upper, the educated, and the influential classes, affect the morals of those beneath them. They inflict, oftentimes, an infinitely deeper injury than any injury to property can be. In the United States, though there are laws to protect from extinction races of birds and of fish, there are none which confer any exclusive privileges for the capture or destruction of that which Heaven has made as free as water and air, though any man would be liable to a penalty if he injured his neighbor in pursuing it.

XXII. — THE ROYAL AGRICULTURAL SOCIETY OF IRELAND.

The Royal Irish Agricultural Society, for the general improvement of agriculture in Ireland, is of more recent origin than the English Royal Agricultural Society, and is established upon the same general plan. It already embraces a large array of numbers, combining men of the highest rank and wealth with others in more humble condition. It is intended to hold its annual shows in different parts of the country; and it bestows large sums in premiums, — thirty sovereigns, or one hundred and fifty dollars, being the prize, for example, in the class of bulls, and other prizes of proportionate value for other objects. It has adopted one very wise provision: in the high prizes for the best live stock, it opens the competition to the whole kingdom, without restriction, so that specimens are brought from England and Scotland, of cattle, sheep, and swine; and thus the Irish are enabled to see, and compare with them, what has been done by others, and in what respects they exceed or fall short of them. This presents the most powerful stimulus to excel; whereas, if the competition were confined wholly to themselves, not knowing what has been done by others, they might be satisfied with inferior attainments. At the agricultural show at Dublin, which I had the pleasure to attend, a good many animals were exhibited from Scotland and England, which were of a superior character, and which gave the Irish farmers a favorable opportunity, not only of seeing the favorite kinds in the sister kingdoms, but the degree of perfection, to which, by careful breeding and keeping, they had been carried.

When I have recommended, as I have repeatedly done, the adoption of the same liberal practice among the county societies of Massachusetts, and with other societies in New York, I have always been met with the argument, that this would be sending the money paid in premiums out of the county, or out of the state, which is an objection unworthy of consideration; for of what consequence is the money, if we can get the improvement? The object of a society, in all its measures and premiums, should be the improvement of agriculture and husbandry. The distribution of money is only an instrument to effect this end. By what means that object is most surely to be attained, is the only matter worth inquiry. Nothing is so likely to serve this end as seeing and ascertaining the degree of improvement to which the art has any where, at any time, or by any persons, been advanced; and how far, and how effectually, in our condition, we may adopt the same means of progress. There is, in my opinion, nothing less worthy of a liberal mind, nor less friendly to advancement in any thing valuable and useful, than a miserable self-conceit, which passes often under the name of patriotism, but which is a spurious metal, and a mere counterfeit of that noble virtue. To value a thing because it is American, or because it is English, or because it is Irish, without regard to its substantial qualities, is worthy only of a child; and a mind bent upon improvement, and capable of any great progress, rises above such mean prejudices; values things according to their intrinsic merit; acknowledges excellence wherever excellence exists, and seeks that which is good, wherever good is to be found. We should dismiss all pride in our own improvements when others have gone beyond us. The advances which others have made, be they who they may, should only be with us an incentive to new exertions; and so far from indulging the slightest regret that they have surpassed us, if we discover that to be the fact, let us rejoice in what has been accomplished, and regard all improvements, of every description, as so much gained for science or for art, for general comfort or advancement, and as the common property of human nature and the world. This is the truest and noblest patriotism, which heartily exults in every good conferred upon its own community, or its own country, and, in the spirit of an enlarged philanthropy, seeks for its universal extension. To a good mind, the good is not diminished by being the more widely diffused.

No benevolent and just man can look upon poor, suffering Ireland, a land full of brilliant minds and generous hearts, and whose eventful history is resplendent with a galaxy of the most noble sacrifices and services of patriotism and philanthropy, without rejoicing in any good which comes to her, or offers itself in prospect. Her Agricultural Society promises to prove of the highest benefit to a country, the soil of which is capable of a most productive cultivation, where labor presents itself in unlimited abundance, and where crowds, almost without number, of the wretched, the half-clothed, and the hungry, demand, in tones which would touch any heart not made of stone, an opportunity of satisfying their own wants by their own labor, and of obtaining from the willing earth that which a beneficent Providence has formed it to yield for the subsistence and comfort of his creatures.

The exhibition at Dublin was, in various respects, creditable to the society. The collection of grasses and grains, dried specimens of which were exhibited by several nursery-men, were extremely beautiful, and highly instructive to the farmers. They were presented in a form which enabled them to compare with each other, and in some measure to determine, their relative qualities. Numerous specimens of flax, and of linen, and lawn which has been long a distinguished product of Ireland, likewise attracted deserved admiration. Specimens of soils, and mineral and artificial manures, and exemplifications of different modes of draining, and models of cottages and farm buildings, were also exhibited, and suggested improved and economical modes of construction. I saw, likewise, an American straw-cutting machine, very slightly varied from the original, and which had been patented in Ireland, of which I could not complain, after many instances of similar plagiarism, which I had seen, in my own country, exhibited as rare specimens of Yankee ingenuity. Of the morality of such tricks, if so they are to be called, I leave my readers to judge; but in other respects, from various things which have come under my notice, the account seems pretty fairly balanced between us.

The exhibition of poultry attracted much attention, and, though an humble object, was not unworthy of observation. It was principally confined to geese, ducks, and dunghill fowls. The Malay and Java fowls, specimens of which are to be found in the United States, were very large, and appeared almost to have some affinity with the ostrich family. It was stated that, when dressed, they would weigh from eight to ten pounds, which is the size of a common turkey. The valuable race of Dorkings was shown in great numbers, as being highly approved; and likewise some crested Spanish birds, which were reputed most abundant layers — a property which, in my opinion, depends as much upon plenty of feed, and houses where a mild temperature is preserved, as upon any peculiarity of constitution. Of game-cocks I saw none. The inhuman sport, which once brought these animals into fashion, is, as far as I can learn, now not permitted nor known. The cause of humanity has certainly accomplished much in the abolition of the cruel games of cock-fighting, dog-fighting, bull-baiting, and bloody boxing-matches. The various military dresses, most brilliant and magnificent as they were in themselves, and which were seen plentifully sprinkled about the show-yard, and in the streets of Dublin, indicated, however, that there were other game-cocks in training, for purposes far more cruel and unchristian, whom, with their glittering swords and bristling bayonets, I seldom pass without a shudder; and to the necessity, if there be any, of whose profession and employment, I can only desire as speedy and as effectual an end may be put. The fights of the lower orders of animals, for which they have been trained, and to which they have been spurred on by the brutality of a higher order of animals, assuming to be rational and moral, are, alas! but a melancholy counterpart of scenes which have covered human history all over with blood, and stained its pages with crimes of a demoniacal malignity and revenge, vulgarly, and by a misnomer which, in a Christian country, makes one's heart ache, called heroism and glory. The native race of cows, principally from the county of Kerry, which were exhibited on the occasion, was quite remarkable. They are much smaller than any thing of the kind which I have ever seen, and can have little value out of the country where they are reared, and to whose scanty pastures and bleak hills they are said to be peculiarly adapted. They are generally black, kept at a very small expense, and are said, for their size, to yield an extraordinary amount of milk. A bull of a year old of this stock, to which a prize of five sovereigns was awarded, was so diminutive, that I could, without difficulty, have lifted my leg over his back. The sight of this animal solved a problem in history which has always puzzled me. It is said of Milo, that, beginning with a calf, and carrying him upon his back every day, the increase of weight was so gradual, that the limit of his personal strength could not be determined, and he continued to lift him after he became an ox. If it were a Kerry ox, the otherwise intrinsic improbability of the story entirely ceases. This Kerry bull was little larger than a goat, and should form a part of the retinue of Tom Thumb, that distinguished American production, who has excited the most extraordinary sensation in England.

XXIII. — MODEL FARM AND AGRICULTURAL SCHOOL.

There is an establishment connected with the agriculture of Ireland, which is in the immediate neighborhood of Dublin, and which I have visited with the greatest pleasure, and that is a Model Farm and an Agricultural School. The national government have determined to appropriate seventy-five thousand pounds annually to the cause of education in Ireland, to be distributed, in proportions corresponding to the subscriptions of individuals for the same objects, in parts of the country where education is most needed. It is considered, and with good reason, that the great want, among the people, is a want of knowledge in applying and using the means of subsistence within their reach; that there is no indisposition on their part to labor; that there is as yet an ample extent of uncultivated land capable of being redeemed and rendered productive; and that a principal source of the wretchedness, and want, and starvation, which prevail in some parts of this country, often to a fearful extent, is attributable to the gross ignorance of the laboring classes of the best modes of agriculture and of rural economy. With this conviction upon their minds, the commissioners have determined to connect with all their rural schools a course of teaching in scientific and practical agriculture, communicating a knowledge of the simple elements of agricultural chemistry; of the best modes and operations of husbandry which have been adopted in any country; of the nature, and character, and uses, of the vegetables and plants necessary or useful to man or beast; of the improved kinds of live stock, and of the construction and use of the most improved and most approved farming implements and machinery. With these views, it is their intention to train their schoolmasters, and to send out such men as are apt and qualified to teach these most useful branches. For this purpose the government have established this model farm, which was begun in

1838, and which has already, in a greater or less measure, qualified and sent out seven hundred teachers. To my mind it seems destined to confer the most important benefits upon Ireland, and I may add upon the world, for so it happens under the benignant arrangements of the Divine Providence, the benefits of every good measure or effort for the improvement of mankind proceed, by a sort of reduplication, to an unlimited extent; these teachers shall instruct their pupils, and these pupils become in their turn the teachers of others; and the good seed, thus sown and widely scattered, go on yielding its constantly-increasing products, to an extent which no human imagination can measure. Three thousand schoolmasters are at this moment demanded for Ireland, and the government are determined to supply them. Happy is it for a country, and honorable to human nature, when, instead of schemes of avarice, and dreams of ambition, and visions of conquest, at the dreadful expense of the comfort, and liberty, and lives, of the powerless and unprotected, the attention of those who hold the destinies of their fellow-beings in their hands is turned to their improvement, their elevation, their comfort, and their substantial welfare.

The Model Farm and Agricultural School is at a place called Glasnevin, about three miles from Dublin, on a good soil. The situation is elevated and salubrious, embracing a wide extent of prospect of sea and land, of plain and mountain, of city and country, combining the busy haunts of men, and the highest improvements of art and science, with what is most picturesque and charming in rural scenery, presenting itself in its bold mountains and deep glens, in its beautiful plantations, its cultivated fields, and its wide and glittering expanse of ocean. The scenery in the neighborhood of Dublin, with its fertile valleys, and the mountains of Wicklow, of singularly grand and beautiful formation, bounding the prospect for a considerable extent, is among the richest which the eye can take in; and at the going down of the sun in a fine summer evening, when the long ridge of the mountains seemed bordered with a fringe of golden fire, it carried my imagination back, with an emotion which those only who feel it can understand, to the most beautiful and picturesque parts of Vermont, in the neighborhood of Lake Champlain. I have a strong conviction of the powerful and beneficial influence of fine natural scenery, where there is a due measure of the endowment of ideality, upon the intellectual and moral character; and I would, if possible, surround a place of education with those objects in nature best suited to elevate and enlarge the mind, and stir the soul of man from its lowest depths. It is at the shrine of nature, in the temple pillared by the lofty mountains, and whose glowing arches are resplendent with inextinguishable fires, that the human heart is most profoundly impressed with the unutterable grandeur of the great object of worship. It is in fields radiant with their golden harvests, and every where offering, in their rich fruits and products, an unstinted compensation to human toil, and the most liberal provision for human subsistence and comfort, and in pastures and groves animated with the expressive tokens of enjoyment, and vocal with the grateful hymns of ecstasy, among the animal creation, that man gathers up those evidences of the faithful, unceasing, and unbounded goodness of the divine Providence, which most deeply touch, and often overwhelm, the heart. The Model Farm and School, at Glasnevin, has connected with it fifty-two English acres of land, the whole of which, with the exception of an acre occupied by the farm buildings, is under cultivation, and a perfect system of rotation of crops. The master of the school pays for this land a rent of five pounds per acre, and taxes and expenses carry the rent to eight pounds per acre. Twelve poor boys, or lads, live constantly with him, for whose education and board, besides their labor, he receives eight shillings sterling per week. They work, as well as I could understand, about six hours a day, and devote the rest of the time to study, or learning. The course of studies is not extensive, but embraces the most common and useful branches of education, such as arithmetic, geography, natural philosophy, and agriculture, in all its scientific and practical details. They have an agricultural examination, or lecture, every day. I had the gratification of listening to an examination of fourteen of these young men, brought out of the field from their labor; and cheerfully admit that it was eminently successful, and in the highest degree creditable both to master and pupil. Besides these young men, who live on the farm, the young men in Dublin, at the normal school, who are preparing themselves for teachers of the national schools, are required to attend at the farm and assist in its labors a portion of the time, that they may become thoroughly acquainted with scientific and practical agriculture in all its branches, and be able to teach it; the government being determined that it shall form an indispensable part of the school instruction throughout the island. The great objects, then, of the establishment, are to qualify these young men for teachers by a thorough and practical education in the science, so far as it has reached that character, and in the most improved methods and operations of agriculture. Besides this, it is intended to furnish an opportunity to the sons of men of wealth, who may be placed here as pupils, to acquire a practical knowledge of, and a familiar insight into, all the details of farming. This must prove of the highest importance to them in the management of their own estates.

The superintendent was pleased to show me his accounts in detail, which evinced, as far as I could ascertain, a successful and profitable management; but as there were several material elements to be taken into the calculation, I shall not speak with any confidence on this subject, without further information, which cannot now be had, but which I shall take pains to give in the fullest manner hereafter.

As the crops were uncommonly fine, and the whole cultivation and management, as far as it appeared, excellent, I shall detail some few particulars in a cursory manner.

The first object was to illustrate the best system of rotation of crops; and three systems of alternate husbandry were going on; one of a course of three crops, one of five, and one of nine; and one especial object pursued in one department of the farm was to show the most eligible course of management of a single acre of land, so as to give an example of the best system of cottage husbandry for the poor man, who might have only a small allotment of land, and whose object would be to feed a cow and a pig, and to get what supplies he could for his family. Such lessons, it is obvious, must appear of the highest importance in Ireland, when we consider the condition of its peasantry, and cannot be without their advantages to every cultivator of land.

Another object aimed at is to show that a farm is capable of being kept in condition from its own resources, and from the consumption of the principal part of the produce upon the land. No manure is ever purchased here; and the manager professed to have an ample supply. Six years' trial, with crops of the highest productiveness, and indicating no diminution, but rather an increase of yield, seems to have satisfactorily established this point. The provisions for saving all the manure, both liquid and solid, for managing the compost heap, and for increasing its quantity by the addition of every species of refuse that can be found, are complete. The stock consists of seventeen cows, one bull, six young stock, two horses, and one pony; and they are all carefully stall-fed, in clean, well-littered, and well-ventilated stables, with ample space before and behind them, and turned out for recreation, in a yard, about two hours in a day. The manure heap is in the rear of the stables; is always carefully made up, and kept well covered with soil, or sods, or weeds, so as to prevent evaporation, retain the effluvia, and increase the quantity. The liquid manure is collected, by spouts, from the stables, into a tank, from which it is, as often as convenient, pumped up, and thrown, by an engine pipe attached to the pump, over the heap; and that portion of it which is not retained, but passes off, is caught again in another tank, and again returned upon the heap by the same process as before. The skilful manager of the farm prefers this method to that of applying the liquid manure directly from a sprinkling machine upon his fields. Either mode may have its peculiar advantages, which I shall not now discuss. The object of each is to save and to use the whole; and I am determined, so important do I deem it, never to lose a fair opportunity of reminding the farmers that the liquid manure of any animal, if properly saved and applied, is of equal value as the solid portions; but in most places this is wholly lost. The manure for his crops he prefers to plough in in the autumn; and the extraordinary crops of potatoes grown by him are powerful testimonies in favor of his management.

His potatoes give an average yield of eighteen tons (gross weight) to an English acre, which, allowing fifty-six pounds to the bushel, would be seven hundred and twenty bushels. He has grown twenty-two tons to an English acre. Either of these quantities, in New England and in Old England, would be considered a magnificent crop. He plants his potatoes either in ridges thirty inches asunder, with the potatoes or sets eighteen inches apart in the drills, or else in what here is called the *lazy-bed fashion*, which is a common practice, but which, as it respects the labor required, is altogether misnamed. In this case, the land is dug or ploughed, and thrown into beds of about three feet wide, first formed by ridging or back-furrowing with the plough, and afterwards covered with earth, thrown from a ditch between the beds about eighteen inches in width, and running between all the beds. After this bed is smoothed off, the potatoes are planted upon it, in rows, crosswise, at the distance of eighteen inches by thirty inches apart, and they are then covered with about four inches of earth taken out of the intermediate ditch with a spade. After the potatoes are fairly above ground, they have a second covering of four inches of earth, as before, and this comprehends the whole of their cultivation in the *lazy-bed fashion.* When they are planted in drills or ridges, the space between the ridges is never suffered to be disturbed by a plough, but is simply dug with a spade, as it is an important object to avoid injuring the young fibrous roots of the plant, upon which the tubers are formed. The potatoes are kept, in this way, with an occasional application of the hand to the weeds, entirely clean; and the luxuriance of their growth throughout a large field, as far as my observation goes, was never surpassed. By his management of his manure, sprinkling the heap with the liquid portions, and so keeping up, through the summer, a slight but constant fermentation, not only all the weeds thrown upon it are rotted, but the seeds of these weeds are effectually destroyed. He says the largest crop of potatoes which he ever produced was had in a field where the sets were placed over the whole field, at a distance of a yard each way from each other. He prefers always planting whole potatoes, of a medium size, to cutting them. He showed me a portion of the field, which had been planted with cuttings of potatoes, sent him by a friend, of a new and valuable kind, and which he cut with a view to planting more land; but the difference in their appearance was most marked, and showed an inferiority of as one to three to those which were planted whole. Ten bushels of seed he considers sufficient for planting an acre.

His turnips promised extremely well. I remarked to him that they were sown in the drills very thickly. He replied that he had never lost his crop by the fly, and he attributed his success to two circumstances — the first, to planting his seed two inches deep, by which means the roots of the plant became extended and strong before the plant showed itself above ground; and the second, by sowing a large quantity of seed; if the flies took a portion of the plants, he would probably have an ample supply left. He suffers them to get somewhat advanced before they are thinned, and then is careful to select the healthiest and strongest plants to remain. I must not be supposed ever to endorse the opinions of another man, simply because I give them; but certainly success is the best test of judgment and skill. However interesting and ingenious a man's speculations may be, his practice is always worth vastly more than his theory.

His crops of mangel-wurzel were magnificent; and he gets a great deal of green feed for his cows, by plucking the under leaves; though, if too severely stripped in the autumn, they are liable to be injured by the frosts.

He sows tares and oats together for green feed for his stock. The oats serve to support the tares, and the mixture seems to be greatly relished by the animals. His great dependence for green feeding of his stock is upon the Italian rye-grass, a most valuable grass, which is very much commended wherever it is cultivated, and which, I hope, will be introduced into the United States. I saw a field of this on the farm, which had already been cut twice in the season, and was nearly ready for another cropping. In Manchester, the last autumn, I saw specimens of three cuttings of Italian rye-grass, all cut from the same field in the same season, the combined length of which was thirteen feet. This was a surprising growth, and indicated the remarkable luxuriance of the plant.

His oats give an average yield of eighty bushels to an English acre; and the oats chiefly preferred here are the Scotch potato and the Hopetoun oat. The weight of the potato oat per bushel is stated to be about forty-four pounds. I have known it in the United States, the first year of its cultivation, to weigh as much, but the second year not to weigh more than thirty-five pounds per bushel. This must be owing to some error or defect in the cultivation; for I can conceive of no natural hinderance, in many localities, to the most successful cultivation of this crop. He sows rye-grass with his oat crop, and gets a good cutting, after the oats are off, from the stubble. It might be thought that this is riding the horse "too hard;" but, as the rye-grass does not ripen its seed in the case, the soil is not exhausted. The next season it gives a full yield. I shall hereafter extend the account of this admirable establishment, if any thing presents itself, upon further inquiry, desirable to be communicated. The institution is one of great importance, and will serve as a model for others; and several, in different parts of the country, through the public-spirited exertions of several gentlemen, who are large landholders, are in the process of being formed. I shall conclude the account with the production, the current year, (1844,) of sixteen and a half acres of land upon this farm, which the manager, in whose established character I have entire confidence, has been pleased to give me. In my experience, the yield has not been surpassed.

From these sixteen and one half English acres, he has fed entirely, from the 4th of April to the 18th of August, seventeen milch cows, one bull, six young stock, two horses, and one pony. Of one acre in vetches, he has used one half the crop; the rest remains. Of one acre in cabbages, he has sold two thirds, and used one third; the two thirds having brought him by the sale £13 sterling; and from the same sixteen and a half acres he has cut and cured, and has in stack, twenty-eight tons of well-made hay, from rye-grass. I took this statement down from his own mouth, with the stack of hay before me, the quantity of which was ascertained by cubic measurement, by a rule which is considered established and accurate.

XXIV. — DUBLIN BOTANICAL GARDEN.

In the neighborhood of Dublin is a Botanical Garden, comprehending twenty-seven acres, enclosed by a high stone wall, with a beautiful rivulet running through it, with ample and elegant conservatories and greenhouses, and in the highest state of cultivation and embellishment. It is supported partly by private subscription, and partly by donations from the government. It is a beautiful retreat, and open to all persons two days in a week, with intelligent and courteous superintendents to show and explain every thing. To my inquiry of the superintendent whether he suffered any injury from the visitors plucking the flowers, or breaking the plants, he replied, very little, if any; none whatever from the highest classes in society, and none whatever from the lowest classes, who visited it in great numbers; and who, coming out of their damp cellars, and their confined streets, and their dark and offensive holes, and fastnesses, and common sewers, no doubt found in it, with their children, almost a transition from earth to heaven; and here breathed the perfumes of the divine beneficence, and contemplated, with a felicity which even princes might envy, the exuberant tokens of God's goodness in the flowers and fruits of the earth, radiant with a celestial beauty. There were other persons, whom he chose to denominate the *vulgar rich*, who were not so abstemious, and who required to be watched. It is to be hoped, as education advances, a higher tone of moral sentiment will prevail, and that every thing of taste or art, designed for general gratification, will be secure against injury or defacement, so that the odious notices and cautions, which are now so constantly seen in such places against depredation, may themselves be deemed a public insult, and the very idea of violating an honorable confidence, and abusing the public beneficence, may so trouble a man's conscience, that he shall desire to run away from himself.

This garden and grounds, and its conservatories, are designed to furnish specimens of all the most valuable and curious native and exotic plants and fruits; and, in addition to their present erections, the proprietors are now about to build a conservatory four hundred feet long, and seventy feet wide, with a height proportioned. The grounds are always open to the studious and scientific, and a course of botanical lectures is given, with the illustrations to be found here.

Botany may here be studied to great advantage, as portions of the ground are allotted to the perfect arrangement of the plants, according to the classification and orders of Linnæus, and in another part, according to the natural order; and for the benefit of agricultural students and farmers, specimens are cultivated and neatly arranged of all the useful vegetables and grasses, with their botanical and their vulgar names affixed to them, with specimens likewise of the most pernicious weeds, that the farmer may see what to choose and what to avoid. The collection is already extensive, and is constantly becoming enlarged. It is difficult to overrate the value of such establishments, both for use and for pleasure, for their pecuniary, their intellectual, and their moral benefit. While penning this account, I hear, with extreme regret, that the Botanical Garden in Boston, a city so eminent for its public spirit and beneficence, is to be strangled in its infancy, and abandoned; and that the ground is likely to be appropriated to buildings, so that the rich prospect of the charming environs of the city is to be shut out, and the fresh and salubrious breezes from the verdant fields and hills of the surrounding country are to be debarred an entrance for the refreshment of the inhabitants of this busy and crowded mart; and even the sight of the glorious western sky, which, with its gilded, and glowing, and gorgeous drapery, I have made, at evening, a pilgrimage, many hundreds of times, to contemplate and adore, is to be excluded by high walls of brick and stone. Should this be done? and how can such an injury, if once committed, be repaired? Surely they will forgive one of their own children, whom no distance of place and no length of absence can estrange from his honored and revered birthplace, in saying that even one half of the expense thrown away upon public dinners and parade, would secure to them permanent provisions for health, instruction, comfort, and delight, whose value no pecuniary standard can measure, and which can never be duly appreciated, but by those who have enjoyed and have then been deprived of them.

A West Highland Ox.

The Property of Mr. Elliott, of East Ham, Essex.

EUROPEAN AGRICULTURE.

THIRD REPORT.

XXV.—AGRICULTURAL EDUCATION.

My Second Report gave an account of the Agricultural School at Glasnevin, near Dublin, Ireland. I propose to add a notice of some other industrial schools, which I have had an opportunity of inspecting. The excellent establishment which I described, and three others, of a similar character, which I have visited, are in Ireland. Ireland, in this respect, has taken the lead of England and Scotland, where we might sooner have expected to find institutions of this nature.

That in a country where the waves of political agitation have for years been tossing all over it like the sea in a storm, and where, certainly in large portions of it, there exist a degradation and state of destitution utterly beyond any power which I possess adequately to describe,—in many parts, a struggle for existence which seems, to an inexperienced spectator, absolutely desperate,—and, in some parts, a ferocity, growing not out of any innate malignity, but out of unfortunate social relations, (for which the remedy is not obvious,) scarcely to be paralleled even among cannibals,—in a condition of society where all the elements of social life appear in a state of violent conflict,—that in the midst of all this there should be growing up institutions of this character, even in advance of places blessed with peace, plenty, quiet, and the highest measure of social improvement which has yet been reached, is not a little remarkable.

But this beautiful and wretched country abounds with intelligent minds, glowing with the warmest philanthropy. They appear, indeed, like stars in a partially-clouded night, pouring, out of their own native fulness, rays of the purest splendor; struggling, as it were, continually, to penetrate the darkness which intercepts them; and appearing to shed a brighter radiance as the mists and black clouds sweep along, and, occasionally breaking open, leave, though only for a time, a way for the transmission of their light. They may, sometimes, seem to serve no other purpose than to render the darkness visible; but they inspire courage, and strengthen the hope of a wider diffusion, and the ultimate dawning of a full day.

These men rightly conceive that education is to be one of the great means of elevating Ireland; and that, an education of a practical character. In an education of a different character, Ireland is not wanting. Strange as it may seem, in some parts of Ireland, even the common people are familiar with the ancient classics; and the household deities of the heathen are enshrined in their cabins among their own numberless saints. When in Killarney, in the vicinity of the lakes of that picturesque and romantic region, I took leave to inquire of the hotel-keeper into the state of education among the people. He immediately called in a ragged, dirty, barefooted boy, — for, indeed, very few of the common people in the rural districts of Ireland are in any other condition, — and told him "to bring his books and show the gentleman what he knew." This boy was only ten years old, and the son of a shoemaker. He brought in his Greek Testament, and in the Gospel of John, in which I pretty thoroughly examined him, he recited with perfect correctness. I then examined him in the declensions and conjugations of nouns, and adjectives, and verbs, in which he was equally expert and correct. I found, likewise, upon inquiry, that this was the general course of education at the school which he attended. The next day, a lad passed me, evidently on his way to school, with his books under his arm. I inquired his age, which he said was fifteen years, and then desired him to allow me to see a book which he had with him, which was Homer in Greek; and he was studying the second book. To my inquiry if there were many in his class, he replied, yes; and to my question whether he was destined for the priesthood, his answer was in the negative. I learned that classical learning was by no means uncommon in Ireland, and among some even of the poorest of the people. Schools, likewise, of a more humble character, abound in Ireland, and benevolent efforts are making to extend and improve them.

It would be wrong, however, to infer, from what I have stated above, that education in Ireland is every where of a high character, or that it is universal. I might do wrong to say even that it is general, though it is certainly much more general than is usually supposed. Many parts of Ireland are wrapped in thick darkness, with its usual concomitant, the grossest superstition. Indeed, without impugning the prevalent religion of Ireland, a fair proportion of the ministers of which are indefatigable in their pastoral labors, and disinterestedly devoted to the welfare of their flocks, it will not be denied that it discourages the general or extended education of the people. I speak of what strikes me as facts in the case, and neither attribute nor insinuate any unworthy motives. Nor would England, as far as my impressions go, gain much by a comparison with Ireland in this respect. In England the higher classes are not without strong, and it may be conscientious prejudices against the education of the lower and laboring classes. The course of education, at the national schools in England which I have visited, — and they are not a few, — is certainly of a meagre and limited description, embracing no more than reading, spelling, writing, and the study of the Bible, the catechism and the creeds, with the committal of hymns to memory. To my inquiry of a noble and enlightened woman, the benevolent patroness and supporter of a large school, and to whom, how much soever I might differ from her in opinion, it would be impossible to ascribe any want of kind regard for her dependants and beneficiaries, whether it would not be useful to teach these children some geography, and induce them to read some books of general knowledge, her reply was, that "she wanted none of the *ologies*, neither geology, mineralogy, nor chronology, taught in her school; and that, in her opinion, it was quite enough of general knowledge for the children to know their prayers and the catechism; and of geography, for them to be able to find their way from their house to their work, to the school, and to the church." If I had not met with repeated instances of the same avowed sentiments, and of a practice conformed to them, I should hesitate in making any general inferences. As it is, however, having stated the case, I prefer to leave it to my readers to form their own conclusions.

I could not help replying to this noble lady, that one of the *ologies* seemed to be pretty assiduously taught in the school, and that was *theology;* for the catechism and creeds were inculcated with peremptory authority, and the Bible was the only reading book in the school. She admitted this, but an exception of this nature needed no apology. I could not help thinking that the course might have been enlarged, and other branches of instruction have been introduced to advantage; that some good for religion itself might be gathered even from the simplest discoveries of geology, and the wonders, and uses, and splendors of the mineral world; that the great and settled truths of physiology, those which are directly practical in their character, might be of service both to the health of the body and the mind, and consequently to the moral health; that a general knowledge of anatomy, both human and comparative, could scarcely be without its use; and that it might be as serviceable, as it would be interesting, if children were taught to understand some of the marvels of their own structure, and led to see how this curious frame of their bodies is knit together and compacted by an all-powerful Architect; and the still more wonderful capacities and faculties of their own minds, where "the inspiration of the Almighty has given them understanding,"—and thus be led to reverence the Divinity, who has made their own souls the temples of his indwelling spirit. I could not think that it would be straying far from the best objects of education, if these children were early accustomed to see every object and operation in nature instinct with lessons of heavenly wisdom. I cannot think that any thing would be lost. Are we not bound to believe that much would be gained by every advance in knowledge of this kind; if children were taught daily to consider the flowers of the field, how they grow; what causes the earth to yield its food for man and beast, and makes the dry seed spring up into a beautiful and fruitful plant, arrayed in a splendor surpassing that of Oriental luxury; and who takes care of the birds of the air, who, though they have neither storehouse nor barn, find their daily and hourly wants supplied by an invisible hand and a paternal and an inexhaustible bounty?

Indeed, I have yet to learn that the acquisition of knowledge can ever be otherwise than favorable to virtue; or that whatever tends to enlarge and improve the mind does not, in an equal degree, tend to render character more valuable, moral obligations more authoritative, and inspire and strengthen that self-respect which is among the most powerful instruments and securities of virtue.

If I should be asked, now, What has all this to do with agriculture? I answer, Much every way. It will be found, with respect to agriculture, — what is true in reference to every other art, — that its proper exercise, and all the improvements which it has received, have been the effects of the application of mind to the subject; in other words, of inquiry, observation, knowledge, and especially the results of intelligent experience. Who does not know the difference between a stupid and an intelligent laborer; between a man scarcely raised above the brute animal which he drives, and a man whose faculties are all awake, and who is constantly upon the alert to discover and adopt the best mode of executing the task which he has undertaken; between a beast altogether the creature of instinct, or a mere machine, moving only as it is impelled, and unable to correct its own errors, and a thinking, knowing, reasoning animal, always searching for the right way, making all his actions subservient to his judgment, and gathering continual accessions of power and facility of action from his own and the experience of others? Every one will admit that the more intelligence, the more skill, the more knowledge, a man has, the better is he qualified, other things being equal, for the management of a farm. It holds equally true that the more intelligence, the more skill, the more knowledge, a laborer has, the better is he qualified to assist in that management, and to perform the part which belongs to him in the working of the whole machinery.

I believe I may safely say, that a New England laborer accomplishes in the same time much more than an English laborer; and this circumstance, in respect to agriculture, and especially in some of the manufacturing and mechanic arts, which more demand the exercise of the mind than the ordinary operations of husbandry, is one among other circumstances which enable us to come in successful competition with the labor of Europe, so very inferior in its cost. I cannot say they always execute their work as well. Certainly, in ploughing and draining, our operations are altogether inferior to what is done in England, where, in the perfection with which these matters are executed, nothing more seems to me either attainable or desirable. But this arises from several causes; — the more we have to do compared with the number of hands we have to accomplish it; the extent to which a system of division of labor is carried in England, so that particular individuals are accustomed to do only particular things, and consequently acquire a precision and facility of operation, which such exact attention and long-continued practice are sure to give, attended with an almost utter disqualification for any other branches of labor. In many departments and operations of husbandry, this exactness is not necessary, though in many I am ready to admit its utility; but in the amount of work which an American laborer will accomplish in a given time, and in the facility with which he turns from one species of labor to another, he is far before an English laborer. This, I believe, is, in a great degree, owing to the difference in their minds; the one being educated, the other uneducated; the one being accustomed to depend upon himself, to inquire, to reflect, to observe, to experiment; the other scarcely exercising his mind at all more than the cattle which he drives, and accustomed to move in the line, and that only, which has been marked out for him. I hold that education, in every condition of life, is a great good. It sometimes gives facilities for particular crimes, of which, otherwise, men would have been incapable; but the viciousness of these men would have shown itself in some other form. It is in no sense attributable to their education. I believe, as much as I live, that every advance in the cultivation and improvement of the mind is an incentive and an auxiliary to good conduct; and although an education purely intellectual falls far short of the beneficial influences which it might yield, when the moral sentiments are cultivated conjointly with the intellectual, yet am I perfectly assured, that every quickening or cultivation of the mental faculties, every thing which contributes, in any measure or degree, to raise man above a mere machine, or a mere animal, is so far positive good — positive good for his efficiency as a laborer, and for his happiness and moral well-being as a man. I am afraid I shall be thought to dwell too long on this subject; but I have felt such a burning indignation when I have heard the cause of popular education spoken of disparagingly, by those who were reaping its richest fruits; I have felt such a deep compassion for the very degraded condition, in this respect, of a large portion of the laboring population of England; I have seen with so much pain, on the part of some of those whose laps were overflowing with these richest blessings of Heaven, so strong a reluctance to communicate of their abundance to these benighted children of ignorance and want, in many cases, undoubtedly, springing from an honest distrust of their utility, — and, at the same time, I have felt my own heart swelling almost to bursting, with gratitude, for the privileges in this respect enjoyed by a large portion of my own countrymen, and the blessed fruits of which are every where seen among them in such rich abundance, — that I cannot refrain from speaking out; and too happy should I be if my feeble voice could do any thing towards commanding that attention to the subject which its importance demands.*

---

* That I do not express myself too strongly on this subject, may appear from the following remarks of a distinguished professor of agriculture, who is much employed in lecturing to the farmers about the country. They were made recently at a large agricultural meeting.

"I put no stress on the spread of knowledge, whether here, in Scotland, in Ireland, or elsewhere. I attach no importance to intellectual improvement amongst the agriculturists. I do not value that instruction which you saw those boys had received to-day, unless that knowledge furnishes you with the means of putting more money into your pockets."

And, indeed, is this all the value which this learned gentleman can see in education? One cannot help feeling that it is greatly to be regretted that he himself should have been put to so much trouble to acquire his own education, for an object in which it is not unlikely, with all his success, many a thimble-rigger, or dog-meat-seller, would beat him.

At the great meeting of the Royal Agricultural Society of Ireland, in Dublin, the last year, a peer of the realm, of high rank, and who (so much better oftentimes are men than the principles which they profess) is esteemed withal a very just and kind landlord, was pleased, after strongly proclaiming his interest in the improvement of the condition of the peasantry and the laboring classes, "to beg of his hearers not to misunderstand him, nor to subject him to the imputation of a desire to raise these people out of their proper condition — the condition which Providence had assigned them."

One would be glad to know, under such an interpretation of the designs of Providence, how any man should ever attempt the improvement of any body, or any thing; and whether he himself could by any compulsory process be induced to exchange his marquisate for a dukedom.

With great personal respect for both these gentlemen, whose publicly-expressed

1. GLASNEVIN AGRICULTURAL SCHOOL.

I promised in my former Report to give some further account of the school at Glasnevin; and since that time the intelligent and obliging superintendent has been kind enough to furnish me with a copy of his farm accounts for two years, which I think must be interesting to my readers. It is obviously a great question whether an institution of this character can be made to support itself; and this question is affirmatively and emphatically answered by the result in this case. It is obviously highly desirable that education should be made as cheap as possible. I very well understand what often comes of making things cheap; that when the price is reduced, the quality of the article is made to correspond. A milkman in New York once told me that he always accommodated his customers as to the price; six and a quarter cents was the standard price for sound and pure milk; but if his customers wished to have it at five or four cents, he took care always to put enough water with it to bring it to the standard price. This *honest* fellow, who was a shrewd Irishman, by the way, (an evidence that all the wooden nutmegs are not made in New England,) was pleased also to tell me that, by straining water through some finely-ground Indian meal or flour, so as to color it, and adding to it a mere dash of skimmed milk, he was able then to afford it at three cents a quart to those who could not give a higher price. Most certainly I cannot recommend, in this sense of the word, a cheap education; but if the advantages of a good, solid, and enlarged education can be made universally acceptable; if they can be purchased by that which most young persons have, and besides which many young men have nothing else which they can give,

---

opinions are certainly just objects of animadversion, I can only express the wish, that they both might be transported, at least for a while, to a land of free institutions, where education is universal, — and learn there, that education, from its high moral influences, may have other uses than that of putting money into men's pockets; and that, where the road of advancement and promotion is freely and equally open to all, even the humblest in the community may ascend to a nobleness of merit, and character, and intellectual elevation, before which the tinsel splendor of coronets, and mitres, and maces, becomes dim, and they are seen in their proper character, as mere baubles for grown-up children.

— their own personal labor, — a great point will be gained; and the price itself will be an efficient instrument of their improvement. I believe this can be done; that is, upon an adequate extent of land favorably situated, by an amount of labor which shall not interfere with their intellectual improvement, but, by conducing to their health, and by demonstrating the practical application of the principles and lessons which they are taught, will most efficiently further this improvement, the pupils themselves may be comfortably sustained, and their instruction paid for. The school at Glasnevin certainly has gone far towards establishing this point. If this is too much to be expected, and the fees for instruction are to be paid in money, yet it will be a great object gained, if the labor of the pupils provides for their subsistence, and pays a fair rent for the land.

I subjoin the following extracts from the letters addressed to me by the intelligent manager of the establishment, Mr. Thomas Skilling.

"I send you copies of my profit and loss account on the transactions of the farm during the last two years, ending the 31st March, 1844. The annual accounts and amount for the previous three years, from 1839, are somewhat similar, with this difference, that, notwithstanding the yearly reduction in the price of farm produce during the said time, there have been increased profits, from the increased products of the land, of course from high cultivation and fertility. The profits of last year would have been very considerable indeed, had I not suffered so much by the fatal disease among my cattle. This year I expect to realize a handsome sum, and you will recollect that these profits are exclusive of the keep of my house and family in all kinds of farm produce."

"From what you will have seen and heard here, you will perceive that my system aims to show what land is capable of producing, when properly cultivated and managed; the greatest quantity of produce from the same quantity and quality of land; and the greatest amount of *profitable* human labor, as opposed to horse labor and expensive machinery. This I believe to be the system suitable for this, or perhaps any part of the United Kingdom, where we have a numerous population within small bounds, and even this small space of land not one third cultivated, nor one half of our people employed as they ought to be. The great evil of this country is *monopoly*, and the most pernicious and extensive is the *land* monopoly. The masses here have no right, property, or interest, in the soil which they inhabit. They are the most wretched of slaves. What we want is a middle class of small landed proprietors — virtuous, *educated*, and industrious. These would be Britain's strength; they are at present her weakness. I want the masses that are idle and starving, or driven into those sinks of vice, the large and crowded towns, spread over the face of the country, holding and cultivating their small farms, leading a comfortable, virtuous, and independent life. But our landlords say, 'The people are poor; they have no capital; they are ignorant; they do not know how to cultivate and manage our land. We will not give it to them. We will keep it for grazing bullocks and sheep. They must look elsewhere for employment and sustenance.' It would be useless here to inquire, who makes these people poor and ignorant. We find the people as represented. This state of things we wish to remove, and take away all excuses on that head. We desire to educate them, and render them competent to manage the land."

"ACCOUNT OF THE AGRICULTURAL ESTABLISHMENT AT GLASNEVIN, IRELAND.

DR. . . . *Profit and Loss.*

1843.		£.	s.	d.
March 31.	To cows lost, ...	47	14	9
	" seeds, ...	2	7	9
	" smith's work, ...	4	9	0
	" servants' meat and wages, ...	44	0	0
	" laborers' wages, ...	2	19	10½
	" coals for the year, ...	9	3	0
	" turnpike " "	1	7	10
	" general charges, ...	22	3	11
	" year's rent, ...	257	7	8
	" profits for the year, ...	120	16	8½
		£512	10	6

Contra . . Cr.

1843.		£.	s.	d.
March 31.	By bulls raised,	15	0	0
	" heifers "	4	0	0
	" pigs,	30	7	3
	" oats,	66	18	7
	" potatoes,	89	16	9¾
	" vegetables,	33	1	4
	" milk,	199	6	5¾
	" butter,	54	12	7½
	" implements sold not required,	19	7	5
		£512	10	6"

"It will be perceived that there is a loss on cows in this year. This always happens, more or less. A large quantity of milk is required for the training establishment,* and when a cow goes nearly dry, she must be sold, and another in milk bought in her place, at a higher price than that at which the former is sold. We have it in contemplation to take another farm, of larger dimensions, in addition to the present one, and of an inferior and different quality of land, in order to show a specimen of the improvement and management of that kind of soil; and in this case the loss on cattle will be obviated, as the second will be more adapted to the raising of young stock and sheep."

"Dr. . . *Profit and Loss.*

1844.		£.	s.	d.
March 31.	To cows lost,	114	0	10
	" horses "	6	2	0
	" general charges,	23	8	7½
	" turnpike,	2	7	4½
	" implements,	6	13	3
	" carpenter's work,	0	8	0
	" smith's work,	3	4	0
	Amount carried over,	£156	4	1

* This is the establishment of the Model School, where young men are trained as schoolmasters at the expense of the government. This place is supplied with milk and other things from the farm, by purchase.

"Dr. . . *Profit and Loss*, . . (continued.)

1844.		£.	s.	d.
March 31.	Amount brought over, . .	156	4	1
	To servants' meat and wages, . . .	31	1	6
	" laborers' wages, ...	5	19	11½
	" coals for farm use, ...	2	10	0
	" rent for the year, ...	257	7	8
	" profits " "	49	4	7
		£502	7	9½

Contra . . Cr.

1844.		£.	s.	d.
March 31.	By bulls raised, ...	8	3	8
	" heifers "	6	8	8
	" potatoes, ...	89	16	3¾
	" milk, ...	183	10	11¾
	" butter, ...	32	5	2½
	" pigs, ...	40	11	10
	" seeds, ...	16	4	6
	" vegetables, ...	90	8	10½
	" grain, ...	34	17	9
		£502	7	9½

"The great loss on cattle, this season, principally arose in consequence of a fatal epidemic, which has prevailed in this neighborhood during the last two years, and carried off a number of mine."

"Besides the real cash profits every year, there is a very important advantage gained from the farm, and which has not been taken into account: I mean, the keep of the family and servants in farm produce, — nine individuals, besides occasional visitors during the year, — in milk, butter, cheese, eggs, poultry, pork, bacon, potatoes, vegetables, &c. &c. This, at a fair computation, may be reckoned at from £80 to £90 more."

"An addition is now being made to the buildings, to accommodate a superior class of twelve pupils, who will pay a moderate annual sum for their board, lodging, and education."

"You will understand that our farm was most injudiciously taken at an enormous rack-rent, double the sum that is paid for much better land in our immediate neighborhood; and when I agreed with the Board to manage it on my own account, and pay all rents, taxes, and other expenses, they agreed to supply me with a certain amount of labor; viz., at the rate of five men in the year; i. e. one ploughman and twelve pupils — the estimated work of twelve boys being equal to four men, or one man to three boys. This I find very near the mark. I would, however, prefer four steady, constant men, to the boys. The boys are difficult to manage; very ignorant at first, and neglectful; and, besides, they work only a part of the day, from ten until two o'clock, and from three until six in summer, and four in winter. This labor, at the present rates, would be equal to about £96, which, deducted from the profits of the year, leaves a remainder of about £24; add to which the keep of my family and servants in farm produce, which, at a low estimate, amounts to £50, with the former makes in all £74 per annum of clear profit, after paying labor and all."

"The accounts of servants' wages and labor which you see, have nothing to do with the pupils. That I pay extra, for servants, cowman, and laborers, occasionally employed in harvest."

"My salary from the Board is merely for scientific and practical instruction rendered to the National School masters and pupils, who are brought up in classes twice a year, (we have one hundred of them here at present.) The profits of the farm are considered an equivalent for its superintendence. This is as much as any farmer gets."

"I am happy to say that, since you were here, the commissioners have made a new arrangement with me, and a liberal one. They have raised my salary to two hundred pounds per year. They pay me for the loss I sustained in my cattle from the epidemic, the last and the present year. They agree to build and make accommodation for a superior class of pay pupils, and give me the benefit of that. They will also encourage me to increase the farm by degrees, according as manure, stock, and capital increase, and some other advantages, which I did not before possess."

"I am paid eight shillings per week, for the board and washing of the pupils, and this is very near what it costs me. If there is a small profit, it arises from my having the farm produce within my power, not having to purchase. They are in general excellent feeders. They are at that time of life, from seventeen to twenty years, when they require most food; and at an employment of all others most likely to create an appetite."

"The dietary is as follows: Every morning, except Sunday, each boy gets one pound of the best bread, and a pint of new milk, cold or hot according to choice; and on Sunday morning they get coffee or tea, with bread and butter. For dinner, four days in the week, viz., Sunday, Tuesday, Thursday, and Saturday, they get meat; two days beef, and two days pork or bacon, three fourths of a pound, each, of good meat, not bone, with soup, and vegetables, and potatoes unlimited. Two days, viz., Mondays and Wednesdays, for dinner, one quarter pound of butter, with plenty of buttermilk and potatoes, and sometimes other vegetables, such as cabbages, &c. One day, Friday, they get fish, with melted butter and potatoes unlimited. For supper, every day, oatmeal stirabout, well made, thick, and of the best meal, with a pint of new milk each; sometimes they choose potatoes for supper, instead of stirabout. By this you will perceive that they are good feeders. I have always been an advocate for good feeding and good working. The one promotes the other. It will perhaps be in your recollection that the boys, during your visit, were the very picture of a sufficient dietary. I had almost forgotten to mention that, on stated occasions, such as Easter, Christmas, Halloween, harvest-home, &c. &c., we give them an extra blow-out; roast beef, plum pudding, &c. &c., with porter and punch for those who are not tee-totallers. The school was formerly under a different regimen; and the doctrine then maintained was, 'Feed them too well here, and they will be discontented with inferior food when they get home.' My answer was this: 'Give them a taste for good feeding while here. Treat them as human beings, and as respectable members of society, and they will not relapse into their former wretched condition, but will work and exert themselves to obtain the comforts of life."

I have laid these details before my readers under the persuasion that they will be deemed both interesting and useful. It is not to be inferred, in any case, because I quote the opinions of another man, that therefore I make them my own. I do not know that it is necessary here, in giving this account, to add a dissertation upon the value of total abstinence; though what my friend here terms a "blow-out," at harvest-home, &c., must be a very gentle explosion, a mere flash in the pan, if we may infer any thing from what he calls, in the other case, a system of high feeding. I wonder what a Vermonter or a Connecticut River boy would think, to be cautioned against excess and indulgence over buttermilk and potatoes for dinner, and oatmeal stirabout, or hasty pudding, for supper; and whether he would not be a little surprised to hear a dinner of roast beef and plum pudding spoken of only as a feast for state occasions, which he feels that he can command every week at his pleasure. I give it, however, as a picture of manners, which, while it conveys a useful lesson in the wholesome example of sobriety which it exhibits, may at the same time impart not an unseasonable admonition of an extravagance with which many of us are justly chargeable, and of which, accompanied as it too often is even by ungrateful complaints, we have good reason to be ashamed. I am neither an advocate for high nor for low feeding, but for that which is plain and sufficient. It is certainly a fault with some of our laboring people, that they expend, in the indulgences of the table, too much of their hard earnings; and it might silence some of the repinings which are occasionally heard, even in the midst of comparative plenty, if they could see, as I have seen, the habitations of thousands and tens of thousands, where the sole and whole diet, for men, women, and children, three hundred and sixty-four days out of the three hundred and sixty-five, is potatoes and water, and by no means always enough of that.

2. TEMPLEMOYLE AGRICULTURAL SCHOOL.

The next agricultural school which I visited was that of Templemoyle, in the north of Ireland, and not very far from Londonderry. In point of situation, it is not easy to find a place more picturesque and beautiful. The soil, however, is of a hard and rather unfertile character, but not the less favorable for agricultural experiments. The farm consists of one hundred and seventy-two acres, and affords opportunities for experiments in draining, in the effects of various manures, and the common operations of ploughing and cultivation, and especially in the adaptation of the crops, and the mode of culture, to the climate, soil, and situation.

The farm is under two different rotations of crops; one part being under the five-course rotation, the other under what is deemed the four-shift. The five-course system of cropping is,

First year; oats after pasture:
Second " turnips, potatoes, vetches, beans, or flax with manure:
Third " wheat, barley, or oats, sown with clover and grasses:
Fourth " clover for soiling, or hay:
Fifth " pasture.

The four-crop rotation is the same, with the exception of the fifth year in pasture.

The department for in-door instruction consists of a head and an assistant teacher; and the course of instruction embraces spelling, reading, grammar, writing, arithmetic, geography, book-keeping, as applicable both to commercial and agricultural accounts, geometry, algebra, trigonometry, with its application to heights and distances, and land-surveying, together with the use of the water-level, the theodolite, and chain.

The agricultural department is intrusted to an experienced and skilful farmer, a native of Scotland, who has under him an assistant, a gardener, and ploughman.

Of the pupils, the one half are at their studies in the house, while the others are pursuing their agricultural instruction out of doors. This is the arrangement for the morning. In the afternoon, the arrangements are such that those in school in the morning are at work in the field in their turn.

The garden and nursery are objects of study and practice, and the lessons received in the house, in surveying and mapping, are applied in the field. Oral instruction and lectures are given in their proper place and time.

The buildings afford the necessary accommodations of school-rooms, dining-hall, and sleeping apartments, and they furnish accommodations for seventy-six pupils. So far as I observed, there was no provision whatever for luxury or indulgence, and the fittings up were of the plainest description. One of the regulations of the school requires the pupils to wash their hands and faces before business in the morning, on returning from labor, and after dinner. I had my doubts whether some of the pupils, whom I saw, did it much oftener than this.

On Sundays, the pupils are required to attend their respective places of worship, accompanied by their instructors or monitors; and it is earnestly recommended to them to employ the remainder of the day in reading the Word of God, and such other devotional exercises as their respective ministers may point out.

This is a very commendable liberality, and rather remarkable in a country, — I speak of England as well as Ireland, — where the first principles of religious liberty are not universally understood, and where men of all parties seem quite as tenacious of their religious differences as of their moral duties. While no reasonable effort should be spared, in places of education, to instil and maintain in the youthful mind a profound and habitual sense of religious duty, nothing can be more unwarrantable than to take advantage of the influence which such places afford, to enforce the principles or peculiar practices of a sect or party.

It may be interesting to learn the general regulations of the school, which the intelligent principal was kind enough to give me in a printed form.

1. As the great object is to make the boys practical farmers, one half of them will be at all times on the farm, where they will be employed in manual labor, and receive from the head farmer such instructions, reasons, and explanations, as will render the mode of proceeding, in all the various operations performed on the farm, sufficiently intelligible to them. Every pupil is to be made a ploughman, and taught, not only how to use, but how to settle the plough-irons for every soil and work, and to be instructed and made acquainted with the purpose and practical management of every other implement generally used. And all are to be kept closely to their work, either by the head farmer or his assistant, or, in their unavoidable absence, by the monitor placed in charge of them.

2. Their attention is to be drawn to stock of all kinds, and to the particular points which denote them to be good, bad, indifferent, hardy, delicate, good feeders, good milkers, &c.

3. At the proper season of the year, the attention of the boys is to be directed to the making and repairing of fences, that they

may know both how to make a new one, and, what is of great advantage, how to repair and make permanent those of many years' standing.*

4. The head farmer will deliver evening lectures to the pupils on the theory and practice of agriculture, explaining his reasons for adopting any crop, or any particular rotation of crops, as well as the most suitable soil and the most approved modes of cultivating for each; the proper management and treatment of working, feeding, and dairy stock; the most approved breeds, and their adaptation to different soils. He will point out the best method of reclaiming, draining, and improving land; and will direct attention to the most recent inventions in agricultural implements, detailing the respective merits of each.

5. After the boys have been taught to look at stock on a farm with a farmer's eye, the committee propose that they should in rotation attend the head farmer to fairs and markets, in order to learn how to buy and sell stock. At the same time, the committee expect the head farmer will make his visits to fairs as few as possible, as his attention to the pupils of the establishment is always required, and he should therefore be as seldom as possible absent from Templemoyle.

An annual examination of the school is held before the committee and subscribers, and conducted by examiners totally independent of the school. The examination is attended by the leading gentlemen in the neighborhood, and many of these take a part in the examination, by either asking or suggesting questions — a practice which is deserving of recommendation, as adapted to give additional value and dignity to the examination.

Such are some of the principal regulations of the school, which I have copied, that its management might be fully understood.

Pupils, in order to be admitted, must be nominated by an annual subscriber, paying two pounds for the first pupil, and one

---

* This, of course, applies principally to live fences, or hedges. It could at present have little pertinency to the United States, where certainly there is very little mystery in making the fences, and as little labor expended in keeping them in repair.

for each additional pupil. The school was established under the auspices of a society in 1827, and the whole number educated, since its foundation, is four hundred and ninety-seven.

The terms for boarding, lodging, tuition, and washing, are ten pounds, or fifty dollars, a year, payable quarterly, in advance. It may be interesting to see the dietary of the school, which I subjoin: —

BREAKFAST. Eleven ounces of oatmeal, made into stirabout, one pint of sweet milk.

DINNER. *Sunday.* Three quarters of a pound of beef stewed with pepper and onions, or one half pound corned beef, with cabbage, and three and one half pounds potatoes.

Monday. One half pound pickled beef, three and one half pounds potatoes, and one pint of buttermilk.

Tuesday. Broth made of one half pound of beef, with leeks, cabbage, and parsley, and three and a half pounds of potatoes.

Wednesday. Two ounces of butter, eight ounces of oatmeal made into bread, three and a half pounds of potatoes, and one pint of sweet milk.

Thursday. Half a pound of pickled beef, with cabbage or turnips, and three and a half pounds of potatoes.

Friday. Two ounces of butter, eight ounces of wheatmeal made into bread, and one pint of sweet milk or fresh buttermilk; three and a half pounds of potatoes.

Saturday. Two ounces of butter, one pound of potatoes mashed, eight ounces of wheatmeal made into bread, two and a half pounds of potatoes, one pint of buttermilk.

SUPPER. In summer, flummery made of one pound of oatmeal, and one pint of sweet milk. In winter, three and a half pounds of potatoes, and one pint of buttermilk or sweet milk.

In lodging, the same system is strictly followed; the beds, bed-clothing, and all other necessary articles, being simple, though clean, and therefore within the reach of any industrious peasant. A proper degree of exercise is provided for by the distribution of hours into field and home occupation, so that each pupil is, in fine weather, half the day in the open air, as explained by the following table: —

"*Work and School Table, from the 20th March to the 23d September.*

Boys divided into two equal divisions, A and B.

Hours.		*At Work.*	*At School.*
5½.	All rise.		
6—8.	. . . .	A, ...	B.
8—9.	Breakfast.		
9—1.	. . . .	A, ...	B.
1—2.	Dinner and play.		
2—6.	. . . .	B, ...	A.
6—7.	Play.		
7—9.	Prepare lessons for next day.		
9.	To bed.		

"On Tuesday, B commences with work in the morning, and A with school, and so on, shifting upon alternate days."

The establishment was purchased for a term of years, and the buildings erected by private subscription, of one hundred and thirty-two shares, at £25 each, and by the liberal donations of several useful societies and associations. The yearly expenditure is nearly met by the pay of the pupils, and the produce of the farm, beyond what goes to the support of the pupils. The annual rent paid for the farm is put down at £80, which would be less than ten shillings per acre for the land, and, as in the case of the school at Glasnevin, no charge is made for interest on the stock invested.

The copy of the accounts of the establishment, for 1841 to 1842, was given me by the superintendent, — some items from which will, I think, afford gratification to my readers.

House, &c.

Salaries and Servants' Wages.

	£.	s.	d.		£.	s.	d.
Head master, . . .	50	0	0	Matron, ...	20	0	0
Second master, . .	20	12	0	Gardener, ...	17	0	0
Head farmer, . . .	81	16	0	Servants, ...	17	5	0

PROVISIONS.

	£.	s.	d.		£.	s.	d.
Groceries, . . .	0	17	10	Fish, ...	5	17	11
Beef, ...	122	4	11½	Salt, ...	0	17	6½
Candles and soap,	16	10	11½	Wine and beer for examination, . .	4	7	6
Potatoes, . . .	46	4	6				

The reason for the salary of the farmer being so much larger than that of the masters, is because, I presume, he provides for himself, whereas they live with the pupils. The charge for groceries is remarkable for its small amount. With us, the expense of tea, coffee, sugar, &c., is considerable, even in the humblest families. I begrudge no man any of the comforts of life; but it is obvious that these must be classed among luxuries, contributing nothing to our strength and subsistence. In this case, it seems well worthy of reflection, how much is to be gained by a rigid economy, and how wise is the example of self-denial, when, by cutting off the superfluities of mere personal indulgence, we secure the enduring and inestimable treasures of the mind.

The farm and garden seemed very well managed, and in good order. Various experiments were being made, in the vicinity of each other, upon different manures; but the results are not yet so fully obtained as to afford grounds for confident practice. The nitrates of soda and of potash upon grass, at the rate of about one hundred weight to an English acre, gave a considerable increase of grass over land which was not manured, but not sufficient to pay the expense of the application. Whether the effects of the application will last more than a year, remains to be determined. The second crop showed no benefit.

Fifty-two different varieties of wheat have been experimented upon by the pupils, besides several varieties of barley and oats. Specimens of the various products, prepared in a form to be partially compared with each other, were exhibited at the annual examination. These are certainly most useful lessons for the pupils. The practice of thorough-draining and subsoiling has been fully tested upon the farm; and it is stated that, on the land thus treated, the crops have been augmented full one third, besides the increased facility given to the cultivation of the land and the harvesting of the crops.

The frugality and excellent economy manifest in all the arrangements at Templemoyle, are much to be commended. "They discourage the admission to the school of lads from England, especially because the diet has not been usually found as well adapted to English as to Irish habits." In my opinion, it is much to the credit of the Irish to be satisfied and contented with a meagre diet. To a large portion of the Irish peasantry, it must be a paradise to get even a sufficiency of food to keep their waistbands from a most melancholy collapse.

This institution has already done much good. In 1843, about sixteen years after its commencement, it was ascertained that most of the young men who had received its benefits were settled in respectable and useful conditions of life. But, according to the present course of studies, the food for the mind is almost as simple and restricted as that for the body. The studies pursued should be greatly extended; and as the principal expenses are already incurred, and the fixtures, both for the school and the farm, are to a great degree complete, the additional cost for providing instruction, more especially in various branches of natural science, would not be large.

3. BROOKFIELD AGRICULTURAL SCHOOL.

This establishment, about twelve miles from Belfast, which I had also the pleasure of visiting, is an eleemosynary establishment, supported by the voluntary subscriptions of the religious society of Friends. It seems that many of this society, in Ireland, from one cause or another, had fallen into poverty and habits of neglect; and their children, many of whom had become orphans, were growing up without the advantage of religious habits, and without that kind superintendence which this remarkable society is accustomed to exercise over those who are connected with it. They took pity upon these stray sheep, which were wandering as it were at large and unprovided for; and, with a spirit of charity, guided by the soundest judgment and wisdom, they determined to gather as many of them together as their means would enable them to support, and, besides giving them a substantial and useful undertaking, to train them in habits of honest and useful labor, intending to make the products of that labor, as far as practicable, conducive to their support. They accordingly purchased the lease of a farm of twenty-four acres; and having erected and fitted up the necessary buildings, they prepared for fifty children; and the number of forty was soon found. The age at which children are admitted is between eleven and thirteen. On account of the condition of the funds, some have been admitted at an earlier age, for whom the friends who placed them there were willing to pay the full cost. In sex they are about equally divided. The establishment is under the direction of a man and his wife, who act as master and matron, and one schoolmaster, with a female assistant, who manage the literary department. The branches taught are "reading, writing, arithmetic, English grammar, geography, the catechism, and Scripture history." The oldest boys are taught likewise geometry and surveying. The children, with the exception of one ploughman, perform all the work on the farm and in the house; and the great object is to qualify them for useful labor and domestic service by a thorough knowledge of husbandry and house-work. An addition, since the first purchase, has been made to the land, so that the whole is now nearly fifty acres. "The boys have levelled about three hundred and forty-two perches of old ditches, which intersected the land, and have thus thrown nearly the whole of the farm into one field, portioned out into suitable sections for a regular four-course rotation of crops. They have also completed four hundred and eighty-eight perches of underground drain filled with stones. The drains are at the distance of from six to eight yards apart, according to circumstances; and in this way it is proposed to go gradually over the farm, as time and opportunity permit."

The average cost of supporting a child at this institution is as under: —

	£.	s.	d.
Provisions, ...	5	19	1¼
Clothing, ...	0	18	6¾
Salaries, ...	1	0	0
Other expenses, ...	1	4	2
	£9	1	10
Deducting the profits on the farm, leaves the average cost of a pupil at . .	£6	6	9

The expenditure for the year in the family I shall give below, as it may be useful to compare it with some similar establishments in the United States.

Expenditure of the Brookfield Agricultural School, *for the Year ending* 31*st of Third Month*, 1844.

	£.	s.	d.			
Butcher's meat, (purchased,)	15	8	0			
Potatoes, meal, groceries, &c., (purchased,)	66	7	9			
				81	15	9
Milk, 10,227 quarts, (supplied by farm,)	63	18	4½			
Potatoes, 1,150 bushels, do.	42	10	0			
Vegetables, do.	6	0	0			
Fowls and eggs, do.	2	18	3			
Oatmeal, do.	31	13	0			
Wheatmeal, do.	9	13	8			
Pigs, &c. do.	23	10	9			
				180	4	0½
Fuel,	13	17	2			
Clothing,	40	17	7			
Salaries,	44	0	0			
Medicine,	5	1	9			
Furniture, for wear and tear,	10	19	0			
Stationery and printing,	16	1	10			
Contingencies,	7	3	8			
				138	1	0
				£400	0	9½

I add likewise the Farm Account, for the year ending 31st March, 1844, with which the superintendent was kind enough to favor me. The result is encouraging, and the good done is certain. The present superintendents and teachers are father and mother, son and daughter, of the same family; and their subsistence is included in the charges against the school.

"*Farm Account for one Year, ending* 31*st of Third Month*, 1844.

Dr.

				£.	s.	d.
To stock, 31st of 3d Month, 1843,				131	2	3
" rent and taxes,				50	2	6
" cattle,				46	4	10
" seeds for sowing,				8	0	9
" smith's work and repairs,				8	7	6
" utensils,				11	19	0
" farm contingencies,				24	2	6
" profit on farm,				121	2	4½
				£401	1	8½

Cr.

By produce sold, viz. —						
" wheat, 15 cwt. 0 qr. 24 lbs.	7	9	7			
" turnips, &c.	1	8	0			
" fowls and eggs,	1	2	2			
" potatoes,	0	11	8			
" cattle,	13	18	0	24	9	5
By produce supplied to house: —						
" wheat, 25 cwt. 0 qrs. 4 lbs.	12	10	2			
" oats, 6 tons, 11 cwt.	43	5	6			
" potatoes, 1,250 bushels,	62	10	0			
" pork,	20	11	3			
" vegetables,	6	0	0			
" fowls and eggs,	2	18	3			
" milk, 10,227 quarts, at 1½*d*.	63	18	4½	211	13	6½
By stock: —						
" hay and straw,	8	0	0			
" oats, £6 : 3 : 6; potatoes, £1 : 8.	7	11	6			
" manure,	20	0	0			
" cattle,	84	0	0			
" utensils,	30	7	0			
" seed in the ground,	9	6	3			
" turnips,	4	10	0			
" fowls,	1	4	0	164	18	9
				£401	1	8½

Value of boys' labor on the farm, £35."

The farming was plain and creditable, the crops good and improving. The strictest economy, as it should be, was studied in every department. The cattle were all soiled — that is, fed in the stalls, as the limits of the farm did not admit of grazing. As an exact account was kept of the milk obtained from the cows, I was curious to ascertain the average amount yielded by each cow. Many circumstances, in such cases, which it is difficult to estimate, ought to be taken into the account; such as the precise number of cows in milk through the year, the length of time any of them may have gone dry, and the number of calves raised. Leaving these matters entirely out of the calculation, the yield was equal to five quarts of milk per day to a cow, for the three hundred and sixty-five days of the year. This is more than an average yield. What is called the Irish cow, the native cow of the country, is a very valuable dairy animal, and of a good character for grazing, but is, I am sorry to say, fast disappearing under the introduction of what are deemed improved breeds, but which may not be better adapted to the wants and condition of the country.

There is no charge in these accounts for what the superintendent at Glasnevin pleasantly calls a "blow-out" at harvest-home and other festivals; and no £4 7s. 7d. for "wine and beer" at the examination, as at Templemoyle, — an omission, in a place of education, which will be looked upon with indulgence by at least one man in Ireland, who bears an infinitely higher title than "very reverend," — I mean the very excellent Father Matthew. I am certain I should be doing a great injustice if my allusions, in this case, implied any immoral excess either in the teachers or pupils of these institutions. There is no ground, within my knowledge, for any such inferences; but the influences of every kind, which bear upon the minds and habits of the young in places of education, are of the highest moment in regard to their welfare. The vinous "blow-outs" which occasionally occur at the anniversaries of some of our own literary institutions might, I think, be very safely dispensed with. But I leave the subject with wiser heads, and with men whose deep interest in the welfare of the young, and in the cause of good morals in the community, cannot be doubted, whatever may be their opinions of the doctrine of total abstinence. Few can have failed to observe that, if a person, who attempts blindfolded to make his way across a room to a particular point, at first setting out turns his feet but very slightly from the direct line, he finds himself, quite unconsciously, brought up at a very different corner from that at which he aimed. In a distance not great, I have seen persons, in this way, without their knowing it, completely turned round, and pursuing an opposite direction from that which they intended. I hope my readers will pardon this homely illustration of a point of infinite moment to the young; I mean, that of setting out right — what the French call "taking the first step." A misdirection, a slight aberration in the beginning, an indulgence in itself wholly venial, may carry them on blindfolded, and consequently without a consciousness of their error, and so without the disposition to correct their mistakes, until they find themselves at a result wholly undesigned, and as deeply as possible to be deplored.

I thought extremely well of this Brookfield School as a charitable institution. The course of literary education was indeed very limited; but how valuable was the training of these children to habits of industry! I think they might add to this institution, with great advantage, some of the useful mechanical trades, — such as tailoring, shoemaking, carpentering, and blacksmithing; and, for the girls, spinning and weaving; knitting and plain sewing they are of course taught. The mere giving of money to the poor is the cheapest of all charities, and in its expediency always the most doubtful. But to give these poor, neglected outcasts a useful education; to put into their hands, beyond the power of its being wrested from them, the means of getting an honest livelihood, and of being useful to the community; to give them, during the exposed period of childhood and youth, a comfortable home, and make them know that they have friends who feel the deepest interest in their character and good conduct; is a benefaction of the highest order, — as creditable to those who bestow as it is useful to those who receive it. "To seek and to save those who were lost" and perishing, was a mission of the divine mercy, which angels came from their celestial spheres to celebrate. How highly is man honored when he is permitted, in his humble measure, to imitate the beneficence of Heaven! When one looks here, daily and hourly, upon the thousands and millions, in Ireland, England, and Scotland, of unprotected, uncared-for, squalid, neglected, half-clad, half-fed, reckless, miserable, suffering children and young persons, growing up in this country of established churches and institutions called Christian, of arts the most polished, of learning the most cultivated, and of a wealth and luxury transcending even the wildest dreams of avarice; and reads in the ever-turning page their certain history, their sure progress from the cradle to the street, from the street to crimes so enormous, so extraordinary, as to make one's head grow dizzy at the recital, and one's hair stand on end with fright; and from these crimes to the prison, and from the prison to the transport-ship or to the gallows; the benevolent heart is ready to burst with grateful joy to see any green spot in the desert, to perceive even one brand plucked from the burning, even one unconscious or struggling victim rescued from the descending and overwhelming current.

4. LARNE SCHOOL.

My next excursion was to the Agricultural School at Larne, where I had the pleasure of witnessing the examination of a class of boys in agricultural chemistry and in practical agriculture. This is not, properly speaking, an agricultural school, but a national school, where the common branches of education are taught; and there is connected with it a department or class of agricultural study, and a small piece of land, which the boys cultivate, and on which, in the way of experiment, the principles of agriculture, and its general practice, are, within a very limited extent, illustrated and tested. The examination was eminently successful, and creditable alike to the teacher and the pupils. It was from this establishment that a detachment of five pupils was sent for examination to the great meeting of the Agricultural Society of Scotland the last autumn, where their attainments created a great sensation, and produced an impression, on the subject of the importance of agricultural education, which is likely to lead to the adoption of some universal system on the subject.

I shall transcribe the account given of the occasion: "Five boys from the school at Larne were introduced to the meeting, headed by their teacher. They seemed to belong to the better class of peasantry, being clad in homely garbs; and they appeared to be from twelve to fifteen years of age. They were examined, in the first instance, by the inspector of schools, in grammar, geography, and arithmetic; and scarcely a single question did they fail to answer correctly. They were then examined, by an agricultural professor, in the scientific branches, and by two practical farmers in the practical departments of agriculture. Their acquaintance with these was alike delightful and astonishing. They detailed the chemical constitution of the soil and the effect of manures, the land best fitted for green crops, the different kinds of grain, the dairy, and the system of rotation of crops. Many of these answers required considerable exercise of reflection; and as previous concert between themselves and the gentlemen who examined them was out of the question, their acquirements seemed to take the meeting by surprise; at the same time they afforded it the utmost satisfaction, as evincing how much could be done by a proper system of training."

I confess the establishment at Larne afforded me, in this respect, very high gratification. The agricultural studies are not made compulsory, but voluntary; and one hour per day is devoted to agricultural labor. The Board of Education in Ireland have now under their control three thousand teachers; and it is proposed, wherever it may be deemed useful, to make agriculture a standard branch of common-school education. They already have seven agricultural training establishments; and it is in contemplation to have twenty-five, with which it is proposed shall be connected small model farms, so that every where, besides furnishing this most valuable instruction to the pupils of the schools, the farmers in the vicinity may be excited and instructed to improve their cultivation. Thus diffusive is the nature of all beneficence. A good deed, like a stone thrown into the water, is sure to agitate the whole mass. Its strongest effects will be felt where the blow is given; but the concentric circles are seen extending themselves on every side, and reach much farther than the eye can follow them. In the moral as well as physical world, the condition of mutual attraction and dependence is universal and indissoluble. We have reason to hope that no good seed is ever sown in vain, but will sooner or later germinate and yield its proper fruits.

These establishments do certainly the highest honor and credit to the intelligence and philanthropy of Ireland, and their beneficent effects must presently be seen in alleviating the indescribable amount of wretchedness under which this beautiful country and fine-spirited people have been so long crushed to the earth — a wretchedness which, to be understood, must be seen.

5. SCHOOL AT EALING.

An establishment of a somewhat similar character exists in England, perhaps many more than one, which I regret that accident merely has prevented my visiting. I refer to the school at Ealing, near London, and I believe there are others, supported by a noble woman, full of benevolence, Lady Noel Byron. At this school, three hours a day are devoted to labor on the farm; and in addition to instruction in cultivating the soil, the boys are taught to perform all the other operations necessary upon it, such as carpenter work, bricklaying, glazing, &c. Each of the boys has a small plot of ground for his own cultivation, from which he derives a certain profit; and some of them had a pound or two in the Savings Bank at the end of the year. Such is the success of this institution, that there are now fifty applicants wishing to be received on the farm as boarders.

The principal objection suggested against the devotion of a portion of the day to agricultural labor at a place of education, is, that it would interfere with the progress of their studies. It is extraordinary to find intelligent minds overlooking the intimate relation between physical and intellectual health. There can be no doubt that a man will perform more intellectual labor, who devotes a portion, and not a small portion, of every day to healthful physical exertion, than the man who, neglecting such exertion, abandons himself in his study exclusively to his books. I am quite aware that many occupations, of a mechanical or a commercial nature, may so exclusively occupy the mind as to unfit it for scientific pursuits; but agricultural labors, quiet in their nature, and carried on in the open air, when pursued with moderation, so far from fatiguing, refresh and invigorate the mind, and prepare it for the more successful application to pursuits exclusively intellectual. The laboratory of nature, open always to the laboring farmer, is itself a school of philosophy to the intelligent, reflecting, and inquiring mind, and presents continually topics of the most healthful, useful, and elevating character.

6. AGRICULTURAL COLLEGE AT CIRENCESTER.

In England, it is now proposed to establish a seminary exclusively agricultural in its character. The preliminary steps have been taken, and the foundation laid for an agricultural college. A considerable sum of money has been subscribed, a farm of about five hundred acres has been taken, and the accommodations for about two hundred pupils are in a course of preparation. It has been felt as a serious want that, while every other profession — law, physic, and divinity — has its exclusive means and institutions for education, and the army and the navy have their schools, — agriculture, the most important and extensive of all the arts, and without which it would be difficult to say where would be the sinews of war or the means of commerce, or what use there would be either for law, physic, or theology, should have no place for the teaching of those arts and sciences, and for the making of those experiments, on which its success so mainly depends. The plans are not fully matured, nor the course of instruction prescribed; but the scientific qualifications of some, and the practical character of others of the gentlemen concerned in its establishment, and standing as its sponsors, warrant the best efforts for its success. The farm is taken at a moderate rent, through the liberality of its noble proprietor; and it is hoped that, aided by the resources of the farm, the expense of a pupil for boarding and tuition may not exceed twenty-five or thirty pounds a year — that is, one hundred and twenty-five, or one hundred and fifty dollars. Twenty thousand pounds, or one hundred thousand dollars, were deemed the necessary capital with which to begin the establishment; and, to the great honor of England, there are few objects of determined public utility, for which, from its abundant resources and public spirit, ample funds may not be obtained. This is a sort of joint stock company, in shares of twenty-five, or thirty pounds each, in which the subscribers will have, as is right, the preference in recommending pupils to the foundation.

XXVI. — GENERAL VIEWS OF AGRICULTURAL EDUCATION.

These details must all be useful to my own countrymen, among whom the subject of agricultural schools has been much discussed, and where a distinct proposition is already before the public for the establishment of an institution of this nature. Under these circumstances, I shall be excused if I extend my remarks on this subject. I shall do this with unfeigned diffidence, and especially from my ignorance of the various establishments for agricultural education upon the Continent. These are often referred to as examples of success, and some of them I hope to have an opportunity of inspecting.

It is quite certain that the course of education pursued at most colleges and universities is quite unsuited to qualify men for the common business and pursuits of life. Indeed, it would seem, in many cases, to operate as a positive disqualification; and men who may have distinguished themselves at our universities for their classical and scholastic attainments, are often thrown upon society as helpless and as incompetent to provide for themselves, or to serve the community, as children. We have small encouragement at present, I confess, to look for any thing better. The system of education at our colleges and universities has undergone little substantial alteration for a century; and what is called classical learning, and the subtleties and puerilities of scholastic divinity, occupy as much attention as formerly, and hold a place in these ancient seats of learning so high in the estimation of those to whom the management of these places is intrusted, that there is little hope of dislodging them. I am no enemy to classical acquirements, as a matter of elegant ornament and taste, as a source of delightful recreation, and as an essential element in a complete education. But to give them a preference in any way to learning more useful, substantial, and practical, is not to estimate things according to their real importance. The time and expense devoted to them might be given to studies infinitely more valuable. As to the time occupied in studying what is called divinity, I am not far from the opinion that the world would be no loser if every commentary upon the Scriptures, and every treatise upon the controversial subjects of religion, since the days of the apostles, were extinguished forever, and men were sent to the New Testament, and to the simple teachings of the Divine Master, only, to learn their duty, and the only elements of true happiness and moral improvement. A college, therefore, of the practical arts, and of those sciences which directly bear upon practice, must be greatly desired by that portion of the community whose education must be to them a means of subsistence, and who have little time to cultivate the arts but with a view to apply them at once to the purposes of practical life.

It must be admitted, likewise, that many of these arts and sciences are, properly speaking, the creations of modern times, and could not be expected to find their place in schemes of education formed in a remote period. Chemistry, mineralogy, geology, and electricity, are all of modern date. There are those living, who may be said to have assisted at their birth, and have rocked the cradle of their infancy. All these are intimately connected with the practical arts, and especially with the advancement of the great art of agriculture; and we may confidently look for the most important benefits to agriculture from the study and application of these sciences. Botany, likewise, and the nature, habits, and uses of plants; comparative anatomy and physiology, the study of which may prove so useful in the improvement of the breeds of domestic animals, and in the treatment of the diseases and injuries to which they are liable; the art of measuring superficies and solids, an art so constantly in demand in practical agriculture; mechanics, and the construction of farming implements and buildings; hydraulics, a science so important in draining, irrigation, and the general management of water, and the uses of steam, that wonderful agent, which seems destined to exert a more powerful influence over the affairs and common business of the world than any or than all other agents besides; the principles of engineering, in the construction of roads and embankments; — all these are matters to be learned and studied, as furnishing direct uses and aid in the practice of agriculture, and bearing immediately upon its advancement. These considerations demonstrate the importance of an institution, where such branches may be taught under the advantages of competent teachers, and means and apparatus adapted to their illustration.

A competent knowledge of these branches should be considered as almost indispensable in those persons who would undertake the cultivation of a farm, or the management of large landed estates, either for themselves or others. It may be said that the style of farming in the United States is so wholly different from that in Great Britain, that, from the necessities of the one, we can make no inferences as to the wants of the other. I know that we have no class of land stewards, or persons employed for the management of the estates of other men; that our farms are comparatively small; and that a class of tenant-farmers is scarcely known among us. It appears to me, however, that it is quite as important that a man should be able himself to manage his own farm well, as that another man should be qualified to manage it for him; and that farms of a moderate size, where the farmers depend upon their returns for their support, have need of the greater appliances to render them productive, and furnish, upon the whole, a better opportunity for a successful agriculture, and for an agriculture of a highly experimental and improved character, than farms of a very large size, where the attention must be greatly divided, and the management — the mere daily routine of operations — requires the most incessant and absorbing care.

But there are considerations, of a more general character, which deserve attention. No one will pretend that agriculture, even in the more improved form in which it is any where to be found, has as yet approximated the perfection of the art. The perfection of the art of agriculture is that in which the largest amount of product is obtained at the least expense of labor and manure, and with the least exhaustion to the land. Indeed, there is reason to hope that we may presently reach a system of cultivation in which, though the crops may be large, the land itself shall not only not be exhausted, but be in a course of continual amelioration. I know well there must be a limit; but that limit no one can yet define. We know already that crops with large leaves, and therefore large powers of absorption, are commonly improving crops; and we know equally well that the growth of a forest upon land, so far from exhausting, is, in fact, an improver of the soil. There is every reason to hope, therefore, that such a system of husbandry may presently be found, when, without any extraneous aid, and from the resources of the farm itself, the largest crops may be obtained, and the powers of production extended. The system of nature every where, if man performs his duty, is a system of amelioration, and not of deterioration; it is every where a system of recuperative compensations, if man does not controvert or pervert its laws.

That our crops, for example, are not what they might be, is universally admitted. Within the last few years, crops of many kinds have increased immensely. A few years since, fifty bushels of Indian corn, to an acre, was deemed a large crop. One hundred have been frequently produced. Thirty bushels of wheat has heretofore been deemed more than an ordinary yield. Fifty is now not uncommon. I have known sixty, and nearly seventy, to have been grown, and, over a large farm, the crop to have averaged fifty-six bushels. Thirty tons of carrots per acre is the ordinary crop of a farmer within my knowledge; and I have on my table before me the authenticated statement of eighty-eight tons of mangel-wurzel to the acre. I am willing to admit that these are rare instances. Some of them may be considered as single instances; but it is obvious that one well-established case is as good as a thousand in demonstrating the practicability of that which is claimed to have been done.

XXVII. — INFLUENCE OF KNOWLEDGE UPON AGRICULTURE.

Here, then, there is an opportunity for the highest degree of intelligence, as applicable to the improvement of agriculture; for who can doubt that these extraordinary results are the consequence of that intelligence and enlightened skill, which are equally the instruments of success in every other art. But it seems idle to argue this point. All the improvements which have been made in agriculture are as much the result of the application of mind and of knowledge to the subject, as any of the improvements made in manufactures or the mechanic arts. Accident has produced nothing. The dull, plodding laborer originates nothing, any more than the beast which he drives. The present advanced state of agriculture as a practical art, all the improvements which have been effected in it, are due to the highly-intelligent minds, the men of science, of learning, of observation, of skill, who have applied their attention, and have devoted their time, talents, and fortunes, to it.

The pioneer in the improved agriculture of the United States was Jared Eliot, of Connecticut — an educated clergyman, whose essays have a permanent value, and may be read with advantage even at the present day. The author of the New England Farmer's Dictionary, a most valuable book, published half a century since, and which has rendered an immense service to agriculture, was the Rev. Samuel Deane, of Maine. John Lowell, who contributed far more than any other individual to the improvement of agriculture in the United States, was an accomplished lawyer, a man of science and of taste, and as much distinguished for his intellectual rank and attainments as he was eminent for the highest virtues which could adorn his character as a man. Aaron Dexter, the beloved physician, an eminent chemist in the very imperfect state of the science, a man whose name was a synonyme for kindness, and to whose memory I shall be pardoned for here recording the humble tribute of my most grateful affection and respect, was an eminent friend and promoter of agricultural improvement. Fessenden, Buel, and Gaylord, were all men of highly-cultivated minds, stored with scientific lore, distinguished for their zeal in the cause of an enlightened agriculture, and honored with the power, which they used with so much zeal and efficiency, of conferring immense benefits upon the agricultural community. While even this Report is in progress, the grave has closed over the remains of a devoted friend to agricultural improvement in Massachusetts — a man of the highest order of intellect, of a mind rich in various knowledge, and of profound legal attainments; and for his personal worth, his public spirit, and private virtues, surpassed by none in his claims upon the affection and respect of his friends and fellow-citizens.* On the English side of the

* William Prescott, Esq., LL. D.

Atlantic, Tull, the author of the improved husbandry; Young, the eminent agriculturist, who kindled so great a zeal, and diffused so great a mass of information, among his countrymen; and Sinclair, as great a benefactor to improved agriculture as England has known, — were all men of liberal education and distinguished scientific attainments. Von Thaer, on the Continent, himself a host in agricultural skill and science, was bred to a learned profession. If I were at liberty to violate a rule which I have made absolute, I might refer to many living examples, on both sides of the water, of men of the finest genius, the most accomplished education, and rare scientific attainments, who have rendered, and are daily rendering, the highest benefits to practical agriculture, and which without their aid and enterprise would never be realized. It is, then, with agriculture as with every other valuable art; — its success and improvement must depend mainly upon the education of those who pursue it, and all hope of its progress must rest upon the science, in the most extended sense of that term, which is brought to bear upon it.

XXVIII. — SCIENCES TO BE TAUGHT.

The Agricultural College at Cirencester proposes a specific education in agriculture, and the cultivation of those sciences which bear directly upon it. Botany, not as a mere catalogue of names and classes of vegetable productions, but as embracing the whole subject of vegetable physiology and the artificial improvement of plants, must of course be highly useful to a farmer. The cultivation of fruit and forest trees is necessarily included in it. The science of mechanics, so useful in the construction and improvement of agricultural implements, must be of constant and valuable application in the management of a farm.

XXIX. — CHEMICAL SCIENCE.

But what seems mainly to be relied on, in this case, is chemical knowledge; and the high value of this knowledge it is at least safe to presume. Confident, however, as some persons seem to be in the discoveries already made, still it must be acknowledged that the application of these discoveries to practical agriculture has been hitherto so limited, imperfect, and doubtful, that we are compelled to consider ourselves as yet only in the infancy of the science. I do not mean in the smallest measure to undervalue the science; nor to disparage what has already been done; nor to discourage the sanguine hopes which some entertain for the future; but in the present state of agricultural chemistry, the extreme confidence of some persons may be at least pronounced premature. The application of sulphuric acid to bones seems as yet to be the only well-established case of the application of chemical science to the improvement of practical agriculture upon scientific principles; and this certainly affords strong grounds to hope for much more. The operations of gypsum are still an insoluble mystery, and the explanations which have been given of its effects do not appear to be confirmed by facts. The application of lime to the soil, and its particular advantages and uses, are still among the vexed questions of agriculture. Its beneficial mechanical effects are often obvious, but its chemical operation is not so well defined. A farmer as eminent as Scotland produces, who has for a long series of years used lime most bountifully upon his farm, told me he remained entirely at a loss to determine whether it was of any service or not. The same uncertainty of explanation is applicable to various manures, in regard to their mode of operation and their precise chemical effects. I do not hold this as a reason for rejecting the aid of chemistry, but only as a ground for moderating a too sanguine confidence in its power. As it offers certainly the most probable means of solving many of the secrets of nature's operations, and as in many of the mechanical arts its triumphs are complete, there are the strongest reasons for pressing our inquiries by means of it, and for the best hopes of as much success as, in the present condition of the human mind, we have any right to expect.

The great value of chemical science is deemed to consist in its facility and power of analysis; but in this respect it seems to have advanced but little farther, excepting in changing the terms, than the ancient doctrine that all matter was resolvable into four elements — earth, air, fire, and water. The composition of albumen, fibrin, caseine, and gluten, and of each of them, is represented, by chemical analysis, as precisely the same in the nature and quantity of their original elements; as, for example, they consist of carbon, 48; hydrogen, 36; nitrogen, 6; oxygen, 15; — but to our senses, and in their uses, they are obviously altogether different. Now, chemistry explains the difficulty, — if explanation it can be called, — by stating that the difference in these substances arises from a different mechanical arrangement of the atoms or particles of which they are composed; but until chemistry can explain how this arrangement differs in the respective cases — until it can take the original elements, and compound or arrange them at its pleasure, so as to produce their different forms or substances — the explanation is certainly very far from complete. It is, indeed, not certain that even these four great principles — the existence of which is so well established and defined — are themselves ultimate elements; but admitting the fact, their precise nature is wholly unexplained, in the present state of human knowledge. Newton, in revealing the operation of a principle of gravitation, and in explaining its wonderful laws, has yet thrown no light upon the nature of the force itself; and, in dissecting the beautiful composition of light into its seven primary elements, has yet not advanced one hair's breadth in defining what light itself is. I know it is now the habit to believe that every thing in nature may be resolved into chemical or electrical agency, the laws of which are determined and explicable, and to discard all notions of what is termed the vital agency. I cannot myself doubt that every thing in nature is governed by determinate and general laws; laws, in respect to whose existence and operation science has already made very great advances, and, for aught that can be foreseen, may presently completely understand them; but as yet the goal is far from being reached; and human reason, with all its illumination, and in the hour of its loftiest pride, must abase itself in the dust, in the presence of that Omniscience before which all human wisdom seems little more than ignorance and folly.

Until Science will explain to me by what force I move my muscles at my pleasure, what mind is, what matter is, what knowledge itself is, and what are the records of memory, — or even afford me some means of conjecture, — I may be permitted to demur to her loud notes of triumph, and to feel that there are still many depths which the line of our philosophy has not yet reached, and innumerable simple processes in nature, of daily occurrence, which are utterly beyond our explanation. That there is at work, in all animal and vegetable life, a vital agency, who can entertain a doubt? I do not know that it is not resolvable into the principles of chemical solution and affinity, or into electrical or galvanic agency; but the assumption, in the present state of science, would be, I think, premature, without stronger grounds on which to rest it.

XXX. — ANALYSIS OF SOILS.

In the chemical analysis of soils, likewise, upon which so much stress is laid, there are difficulties, in the practical application of our knowledge, sufficiently discouraging. The complaint has been constantly and very emphatically made, that the analyses of former chemists, such as Davy, Chaptal, and others, were all too general, and therefore of little or no practical value. It may be said of modern analyses, that they startle one by their precision and minuteness.

I shall be excused, I hope, if I endeavor to lessen somewhat the dryness and dulness of these discussions, to my readers, by a matter of fact, certainly not without its interest to me, and which may bear some analogy to the case before us. Some years since, when suffering under a severe illness for several months, I was sometimes amused, as far as it was possible for me, under such circumstances, to be amused, by the great, and I had almost said, endless variety of articles which entered into the prescriptions of my medical advisers in the customary form of grains, scruples, drams, and mixtures. So much of this article was for this specific purpose, and so much of that for another. This was to qualify that; that was to qualify this. This was to prevent such an article doing too much, and that was to prevent its doing too little. One was to operate upon the bile, another upon the blood; one upon the respiration, and another upon the digestion. And all this was to be going on, and to be accomplished, at the same time. I confess I was often in the situation, in respect to my physician, of the wondering pupils of Goldsmith's village schoolmaster, and marvelled "that one small head could carry all he knew." I had, at least, the consolation in the case of feeling that, as the surgeons often *pleasantly* term it, when amputating a limb, or operating for the extraction of the stone, I was furnishing at least a *beautiful* experiment in the way of medical science; and it must be said to the credit of my physician, whose kindness amidst all this I never can forget, that, although his philosophy and his scientific ardor carried him to the most extreme tests, and he might be said to have suspended me over a precipice by a twine string, confident that, if I dropped, it would at least prove that common twine was not strong enough in such cases, — a most important fact to be ascertained, — I was not quite used up, but was, after a while, enabled to show myself erect again, a perfect monument of the triumph of his skill.

Let us now open at random upon some of the analyses given us in the work of the most distinguished chemist of the day, and inquire who has skill to prescribe for cases so complicated in their nature, or in any event what prescription would suit the case, but one as multiform and mixed as those of my own physician.

SOILS OF HEATHS.

"1. Soil of a heath converted into arable land in the vicinity of Brunswick. It is naturally sterile, but produces good crops when manured with lime, marl, cow-dung, or the ashes of the heaths which grow upon it." [It would be difficult, I think, to find many soils, where the climate did not forbid it, which would *not* produce good crops under such treatment.]

" Silica, and coarse silicious sand,	71.504
Alumina,	0.780
Protoxide, and peroxide of iron, principally combined with humus,	0.420
Peroxide of manganese, *idem*,	0.220
Lime, *idem*,	0.134
Magnesia, *idem*,	0.032
Potash and soda, principally as silicates,	0.058
Phosphoric acid, principally as phosphate of iron,	0.115
Sulphuric acid, (in gypsum,)	0.018
Chlorine, (in common salt,)	0.014
Humus soluble in alkalies,	9.820
Humus with vegetable remains,	14.975
Resinous matters,	1.910
	100.000

"Ashes of the soil of the heath before being converted into arable land: —

" Silica, with silicious sand,	92.641
Alumina,	1.352
Oxides of iron and manganese,	2.324
Lime in combination with sulphuric and phosphoric acids,	0.929
Magnesia combined with sulphuric acid,	0.283
Potash and soda, (principally as sulphates and phosphates,)	0.564
Phosphoric acid, combined with lime,	0.250
Sulphuric acid, with potash, soda, and lime,	1.620
Chlorine in common salt,	0.037
	100.000

" 2. Surface soil of a fine-grained loam, from the vicinity of Brunswick. It is remarkable from the circumstance that not a single year passes in which corn [wheat] plants are cultivated upon it, without the stem of the plants being attacked by rust.

Even the grain is covered with a yellow rust, and is much shrunk. One hundred parts of the soil contain —

" Silica and fine silicious sand, ...	87.859
Alumina, ...	2.652
Peroxide of iron, with a large proportion of protoxide	5.132
Protoxide and peroxide of manganese, ...	0.840
Lime, principally combined with silica, ...	1.459
Magnesia, *idem*, ...	0.280
Potash and soda, *idem*, ...	0.090
Phosphoric acid in combination with iron, . . .	0.505
Sulphuric acid in combination with lime, . . .	0.068
Chlorine in common salt, ...	0.006
Humus, ...	1.109
	100.000."

This analysis must surely be sufficiently close and severe to satisfy even the most fastidious; for here even six hundred thousandth parts of a particular ingredient in the soil, that is, of chlorine in common salt, were ascertained.

" This soil," it is remarked, " does not suffer from want of drainage; it is well exposed to the sun; it is in an elevated situation, and in a good state of cultivation. In order to ascertain whether the rust was due to the constituents of the soil, (phosphate of iron?) or to certain fortuitous circumstances unconnected with their operation, a portion of the land was removed to another locality, and made into an artificial soil of fifteen inches in depth. Then this barley and wheat were sown; but it was found, as in the former case, that the plants were attacked by rust, whilst barley growing on the land surrounding this soil was not at all affected by the disease. From this experiment it follows that certain constituents in the soil favor the development of rust."

But this inference does not appear to me to follow of course. We cannot deny that the rust may have been, in this case, the result of some noxious ingredients in the soil; this appears highly probable. But rust is often the result of influences mainly atmospheric. The fact that the barley grown on soil in the neighborhood of the removed soil was unaffected by rust, while that on the removed soil was affected, is not conclusive. It is believed that plants are subject to rust only in particular stages of their growth. Now, on the supposition that the rust in this case was the effect of atmospheric influences, it is important to know whether the barley (for the wheat is not compared with any other wheat) growing on the removed soil, and that growing in its vicinity, were precisely contemporaneous in their growth, or in the degree of ripeness, or approach to ripeness, which they had attained. Further, it appears that the learned analyst was not himself able to say to what particular ingredient in the soil the rust was owing, nor what manure, if any, was used; and manure always seriously affects the plant to which it is applied.

"3. Soil of a heath which had been brought into cultivation in the vicinity of Brunswick. The analysis was made before any crops had been grown upon it. Corn plants [wheat] were first reared upon the new soil, but were found to be attacked by rust, even on those parts which had been manured respectively with lime, marl, potash, wood-ashes, bone-dust, ashes of the heath plant, common salt, and ammonia. One hundred parts contain—

"Silica with coarse silicious sand,	51.337
Alumina,	0.528
Protoxide and peroxide of iron, in combination with phosphoric and humic acids,	0.398
Protoxide and peroxide of manganese,	0.005
Lime in combination with humus,	0.230
Magnesia, *idem*,	0.040
Potash and soda,	0.010
Phosphoric acid,	0.066
Sulphuric acid,	0.022
Chlorine,	0.014
Humus soluble in alkalies,	13.210
Resinous matters,	2.040
Coal of humus and water,	32.100
	100.000."

Here it will be seen we come again to fractions as minute as hundred thousandths.

"The next analysis represents this soil after being burnt.

One hundred parts by weight of the soil left, after ignition, only fifty parts. One hundred parts of these ashes consisted of—

Silica and silicious sand,	95.204
Alumina,	1.640
Peroxide of iron,	1.344
Peroxide of manganese,	0.080
Lime in combination with sulphuric acid,	0.544
Magnesia combined with silica,	0.465
Potash and soda,	0.052
Phosphoric acid, (principally as phosphate of iron,)	0.330
Sulphuric acid,	0.322
Chlorine,	0.019
	100.000

"By comparing this analysis with the one which has preceded it, an increase in certain of the constituents is observed, particularly with respect to the sulphuric acid, potash, soda, magnesia, oxide of iron, manganese, and alumina. From this it follows, that the humus, or, in other words, the vegetable remains, must have contained a quantity of these substances confined within it in such a manner that they were not exhibited by analysis."

Here it seems, then, admitted, that the most minute chemical analysis, even to hundred thousandths, failed to detect all the latent elements of which the soil was composed.

"Oats and barley were sown on this land the second year after being reclaimed, and both suffered much from rust, although different parts of the soil were manured with marl, lime, and peat-ashes, whilst other portions were left without manure. In the first year, all the different parts of the field produced potatoes; but they succeeded best in those parts which had been manured with peat-ashes, lime, and marl. In the second year, oats, mixed with a little barley, were sown upon the soil; and the straw was found to be strongest on the parts treated with peat-ashes, lime, and marl." [I have never known this to fail to be the case on any soil.] "Red clover was sown in the third year; and it appeared in best condition on those portions of the soil manured with marl and lime. Upon the divisions of the field which had been left without manure, as well as on those manured with bone-dust, potash, ammonia, and common salt, the clover scarcely appeared above ground." [Here, though so much stress is laid upon the infinitesimally minute divisions of the soil, we are left entirely at a loss as to the quantities or forms in which these applications were made.] "The divisions of the field, which had been manured in the first year with peat-ashes, ammonia, and ashes of wood, were sown with buck-wheat after the removal of the first crop of clover. The buck-wheat succeeded very well on all the divisions, yet a marked difference was perceptible in favor of the portion treated with ammonia. These experiments show us, that a dressing of lime did not *completely* remove from the soil its tendency to impart rust to the plants grown upon it." [But if the lime *partially* corrected the evil, is there not reason to infer that the error was in not putting lime enough upon it, and that more would have *completely* removed it?] "Nevertheless," the writer adds, "it is highly probable that, as soon as the protoxide of iron became converted into the peroxide by exposure to the atmosphere, lime would possess more power in decomposing the phosphate of iron."

I shall cite only one more example in this case.

"4. Subsoil of a loamy soil in the vicinity of Brunswick. It is remarkable that sainfoin cannot be cultivated upon it more than two or three years in succession. The portion analyzed was taken from a depth of five feet. One hundred parts contained —

"Silica, with very fine silicious sand,	90.035
Alumina,	1.976
Peroxide of iron,	4.700
Protoxide of iron,	1.115
Protoxide and peroxide of manganese,	0.240
Lime,	0.022
Magnesia,	0.115
Potash and soda,	0.300
Phosphoric acid combined with iron,	0.098
Sulphuric acid, (the greatest part in combination with protoxide of iron,)	1.399
Chlorine,	a trace.
	100.000

"Now, the results of the analysis give a sufficient account of the failure of the sainfoin." [But it seems it can be cultivated upon it two or three years in succession.] "The soil contains one per cent. of sulphate of the protoxide of iron, (green vitriol of commerce,) a salt which exerts a poisonous action upon plants. Lime is not present in quantity sufficient to decompose this salt. Hence it is that sainfoin will not thrive in this soil, nor indeed lucern, or any other of the plants with deep roots. The evil cannot be obviated by any method sufficiently economical for the farmer, because the soil cannot be mixed with lime at a depth of five or six feet." [It requires some courage for a man even to think of such a thing.] "For many years, experiments have been made in vain, in order to adopt this soil for sainfoin and lucern, and much expense incurred, which would all have been saved, had the soil been previously analyzed. This example affords a most convincing proof of the importance of chemical knowledge to an agriculturist." *

Now, I think the strong impression which will be upon every practical man's mind, in looking at these analyses, will be, the utter impossibility of meeting the cases, and of adapting the cultivation and manuring with any very exact reference to the chemical condition of the soil; that is, of prescribing for the patient. I admit that the application of chemical analyses or tests to the soil may be of very great importance in detecting the existence of any substance, as in the latter case for example, which is poisonous to vegetation; though even here, the existence of the evil itself, and the remedy, are left somewhat in uncertainty. I believe it may be of great utility in determining the general and predominant characteristics of a soil; but with great respect for science, and for the labors of those men who, by their distinguished attainments, have conferred the highest benefits upon the community, I can come to no other conclusion than that any expectation of adapting our cultivation, upon any extended scale, to these minute diversities of soil, is illusory; and that the most illustrious chemist living may be challenged in vain to prescribe any practicable culture adapted to meet, with

* These examples of analyses of soils are by Sprengel, and taken from Liebig's Agricultural Chemistry, from the chapter on the Chemical Constituents of Soils, p. 208, 3d American edition.

any degree of exactness, the cases given, or to recognize in his applications or prescriptions, with any peculiar success, the minute diversities of composition which are here presented.

But suppose the application made, and even in the simplest form; what sagacity is acute enough to follow it in all its operations upon the elements, either simple or compounded, with which it comes in contact? or what skill can command the external circumstances of heat or cold, of drought or moisture, which must at the time affect its operation? No human skill has as yet been able to compound a soil, and say, This shall be more fruitful than any other. The habits and nature of different plants require different conditions both of soil and of culture.

The Royal Agricultural Society of England has recently made a liberal grant to aid in the chemical analysis of the different vegetable productions, under the direction of one of the most able chemists of the age; and a good deal of valuable information will undoubtedly be derived from this source. The chemical analysis of different manures has been carried on with eminent zeal and intelligence, and is constantly going on, to the great benefit, without question, of agricultural science; but the extraordinary confidence which some persons indulge in the results of chemical science, in respect to agriculture, seems to me a little too sanguine, and the practical application of this knowledge by no means so easy as has been supposed.

I am quite aware that this may appear like a digression; but, in considering the subject of agricultural education, it was natural to advert to that which seems now to be more prominent in the minds of agriculturists than almost any thing else — the advantages which agriculture is to derive from chemical science, and the consequent importance of making it the prominent subject of instruction. Our expectations in this matter should be in some degree moderated by a remark of Liebig's: in speaking of the analysis of soils, and after having given several examples, "It is unnecessary," he says, "to describe the *modus operandi* used in the analysis of these soils; for this kind of research will never be made by farmers, who must apply to the professional chemists, if they wish for information in regard to the composition of their soils." The science of chemistry has indeed now become of that enlarged character, and is occupied in such profound and difficult investigations and discoveries, that excellence in it can scarcely be looked for but with those persons who, to eminent talents of research, and an extraordinary enthusiasm in the pursuit, devote their time almost exclusively to this object.

A general knowledge of its principles and discoveries, and a facility in making some experiments in it, are all, perhaps, that can be expected to be given in the education at an agricultural college; but it is desirable and most requisite, even for this object, that the institution, in a competent instructor, and all the necessary apparatus, should furnish the means of accomplishing it in the best manner, and to the greatest advantage This undoubtedly will be done.

XXXI. — NATURAL SCIENCE.

Every possible facility should be provided for the study of every branch of natural history, for every branch of natural history may be made subservient to agricultural improvement. There is, in my opinion, nothing which so invigorates and strengthens the mind as earnest and deep inquiries into nature, the study of natural facts, the observation of natural phenomena. There is no knowledge, especially to persons residing in the country, which affords so many practicable uses and such varied and important application. The man who studies books exclusively is always liable to be the slave of other men's opinions; and his mind, losing by such restraints its native elasticity, never travels out of its prescribed limits. The man who goes himself to the original sources of knowledge, and draws water out of the very wells of life, acquires a force of inquiry, maintains a healthful freshness of mind, which grow strong continually by what they feed upon, multiply for themselves the sources of knowledge, turn every object and occurrence which they meet with into an instrument of instruction, and find the world and nature no longer a dull, desolate, inanimate chamber, but its walls all over radiant with lessons of wisdom, and every object with which it is crowded vocal with the teachings of a divine spirit.

I do not overrate the value of natural science to the agriculturist, the resident in the country. For him it is the proper study for use, for ability, for recreation, and for ornament. There is yet much to be done in agriculture. I believe that the quantity of the products of the earth from the same extent of surface may in most cases be quadrupled, and that the number of its productions for the sustenance of man and beast may be multiplied far beyond any present calculation. If we may argue from what has been done to what may be done, the perfection of agriculture is yet very distant, and vast improvements remain to be made. But this can only be effected by bringing vigorous and enlightened minds to bear upon the subject; and the natural sciences are those which of all others best prepare and strengthen the mind for such investigations. The best education which can be given to any man is not that which merely communicates knowledge, but that which enables and induces a man to acquire knowledge for himself. This is what the study of the natural sciences particularly prompt and compel a man to do. These studies, pursued especially in the country, where Nature in such a variety of aspects is continually offering herself for examination, give a vigor and activity of mind which particularly qualify men for practical objects and pursuits.

We are to look, then, to educated men, to men of active and cultivated minds, to men accustomed to study, inquiry, reflection, observation, and experiment, for any great improvement yet to be made in agriculture. These are the men who have always been the pioneers in human progress, and these men are still to lead the onward march. A school, therefore, which trains such minds, not for literary leisure, but for the active and business pursuits of life, must be regarded as one of the most valuable institutions in the community. No branch of art or business will be found to afford greater scope for the application of such an education than agriculture.

XXXII. — MODEL FARM.

To the departments which may be called literary and scientific, the Agricultural College at Cirencester proposes to add those which are strictly practical, by connecting with the institution a farm of five hundred acres. Practical experience is of the highest importance in every practical art. If it be true, that no man can be a thorough sailor who has not served before the mast, and who is not familiar with every rope in the ship, it may be as truly said, that no one should consider himself fully competent to the management of a farm, who is not thoroughly acquainted with every operation to be performed on a farm; and, though he may not always be able to execute it himself, he should know how it is to be done, and be able to determine when it is properly executed.

A model farm is intended to illustrate, as far as the nature of the soil and climate admit, the best practices in husbandry; to show the management of a farm in the details and in the whole; to teach the arts of ploughing, sowing, harrowing, cultivating, reaping, harvesting, stacking, threshing, and preparing the products for market; to explain the management and treatment of all live stock on the place, whether designed for food or labor, for fattoning or working, for beef, mutton, pork, wool, or dairy produce; to teach the whole duty of a shepherd or grazier, and the whole management of the stall and the dairy. These are the objects proposed; and it is intended that the labor of the farm shall be performed by the pupils, and its products go towards the support of the institution, so as to reduce the expenses of education. All this is well, and may be made eminently useful to the pupils.

XXXIII. — EXPERIMENTAL FARM.

It is further intended, besides presenting a model farm, that it shall likewise, in a measure, serve the purpose of an experimental farm. Besides presenting an example of the best management, and the performance of all the customary operations of a farm in the best and most approved manner, it is designed to afford an opportunity of experimenting in various forms upon manures, seeds, plants, cultivation, and the feeding and fattening of animals, and upon every feasible subject, where practical information and exact results are important to be ascertained.

XXXIV. — ECONOMICAL ARRANGEMENTS AT THE AGRICULTURAL COLLEGE.

Such, as I understand, are the outlines of the plan for agricultural education designed to be pursued at the College at Cirencester. Its objects are not to teach its pupils how to labor, but to qualify a class of persons for the management of their own, or the estates of others. The farmers here are not, as with us, workers on their own estates; they are the managers or superintendents of the work; but it is obviously of the highest importance that they should understand how every branch of husbandry should be conducted. For the common laborer here, in the present arrangements of society, I see no hope of his ever rising above that condition in which he is born. There are some extraordinary exceptions; but they are very rare. Besides the impediments which lie in the way from his entire poverty, and the extreme difficulty of his ever acquiring more than six feet of the soil, and that six feet below the surface, and after all power of active improvement of it has ceased, any attempt to alter his condition in this respect, it is to be feared, as I think I have already shown, would be discouraged, certainly not aided, by those above him. I do not know that it is necessary for me to discuss the question whether such a condition of society is preferable to one in which the laborer is first to be served from the produce of his own toil; in which every man, by honest industry, may become the sovereign owner of the acres which he tills, and while he labors he may proudly feel that he is laboring for himself, and not for another. I shall leave all this to the dispassionate judgment of my reader, content even that it should be ascribed to the misfortune of birth, or the perverse prejudices of education, that I immeasurably prefer a condition of society, where the rights of all men are, as far as possible, held equal; where no monopoly of wealth, or education, or rank, or power, limits or impedes the progress even of the humblest members of the community; and where, in a free and equal competition, without injury to his neighbor, every man, for himself and those dependent upon him, becomes the creator of his own fortunes.

No human institution is perfect. Every effort will doubtless be made to adapt the institution at Cirencester to its proper and valuable ends. It is obvious that some practical difficulties will present themselves, which it will require great skill to overcome. The distinctions of rank, which prevail in England, and form a part of its constitution, are as rigorously observed at places of education as in any other departments of society, and are marked there by differences of dress and of privilege. Will these distinctions prevail here? If they prevail here, will they not prove inconvenient in respect to the labors of the farm? or is the institution in no respect intended for the education of persons of rank? I am curious to know how this is to be arranged. Many noblemen in England, of the highest rank, are among the most intelligent practical agriculturists in the kingdom. Will they not desire all the advantages of the institution for their sons? and will they consent to forego all the distinctions and privileges of their rank for the sake of the education? After all, the difficulty may be purely imaginary; for I confess, in my simplicity, educated as I had been in the plain democratic or republican habits of New England, nothing surprised me more than the perfect readiness, with which, in every case, the claims of rank are acknowledged, and in most cases even the pride and pleasure with which this deference is paid, and their rights admitted, on the part of the inferior classes. So far from looking upon this as most of my countrymen are disposed to regard it, and as I should regard it in my own country, as a mark of extreme servility, in a country where such distinctions are established by law, and make a part of the government, it seems to me as much to the credit of their good sense, as it is conducive to their good manners, to conform to them. In any institution of this kind, in my own country, no such difficulties can arise; and it might seem idle for me to allude to them, were it not that an occasional, and I hope not unseasonable, illustration of the manners of England will interest the curiosity of a large portion of my readers.

In the next place, it seems to be designed, and certainly it is very desirable, that the farm shall be managed by the labor of the pupils; and it is proposed that the proceeds of the farm should go towards the payment of the rent, and the reduction of other expenses of the establishment. This is, in my opinion, as it should be; and, with the exception of one or two more experienced laborers, who, in their particular departments of ploughing, &c., should be competent to act as instructors of the pupils, and with a few servants, (and they should be very few, for servants, in almost all places of education, are commonly a great evil, and the best of all training for the young is that which compels them, in a great degree, for all personal services at least, to depend upon themselves,) the whole labor of the farm should be performed by the pupils. This would be, of all others, the most effectual way of making them acquainted with the subject, and the only way, indeed, in which they can become thoroughly acquainted with many of the operations on a farm. I am curious to know how this labor is to be had; whether it is to be voluntary or by compulsion; and how, among two hundred pupils, it is to be apportioned and equalized. If made voluntary, it certainly will not be equally rendered: some will not work at all; and preferences for some kinds of work, and distaste for others, which of course must be expected to exist, will be found inconvenient. If the labor is made compulsory, the enforcing of it will not be easy; and it would be difficult to find the young men, likely to resort to such a place of education, disposed to submit to any arbitrary exactions of this nature. How far it is practicable to make it mercenary, and to reward it by wages, or by a share of the products of such labor, is a subject which will require much consideration; but this mode seems to present the only alternative.

The large number of students — two hundred — to be provided for, seems to me to present another serious difficulty in the case. If any thing like a military discipline could be introduced among them, two thousand might be managed as easily as two hundred. As far as concerns their literary or scholastic improvement, the number presents no impediment in the way of their instruction by lectures or recitations; but when with this is to be combined the management of the farm by the personal labor of the pupils, a number so large, or indeed half that number, must be found exceedingly difficult of management. At the Glasnevin school, the boys are regular apprentices to the farmer, and their work for certain hours of the day is compulsory. The schoolmasters, who come to the farm for instruction, come merely as spectators, and put their hands to the work, or not, as they please. The whole establishment, if indeed it were four times as large as it is, would not, under these circumstances, be beyond the personal superintendence of a single efficient manager. At Templemoyle, the number is limited to seventy, the farm is much more extensive than at Glasnevin, and the labor for half the day is compulsory. As the pupils are almost entirely drawn from the poorest classes, and are persons who must depend for their success in life wholly upon their own efforts, they require no other stimulus to exertion. At Cirencester, the pupils may be divided into two classes — those who work, and are allowed in some form a compensation for their labor; and those who are not required or expected to labor, and pay an extra price for the exemption. Such an arrangement would have many disadvantages, and would be ill adapted to the condition of society in the United States. The number of two hundred seems to me quite too large, and unmanageable with any view to the advantageous application of their labor, if that labor is to be voluntary.

In Scotland, the practical part of farming is learned by young men going to reside one or two years, or for a suitable length of time, with an intelligent and experienced farmer. In such case, the fee paid is about one hundred pounds, or five hundred dollars, a year; and for this the apprentice is received into the family, and provided for at the farmer's table, and every operation on the farm is witnessed by him, and explained to him by the farmer. In such cases, labor with the pupil is wholly optional. Where the farmer is well-skilled and communicative, and the pupil capable and interested in the pursuit, few arrangements are to be preferred — this upon the supposition, however, that in other respects, and previously to his commencing his apprenticeship, he is well grounded in practical science.

The three things of which I have spoken ought to be viewed separately; but I fear, from the manner in which I have treated them, they may appear somewhat confused to my reader's mind.

XXXV. — PLAN OF AN AGRICULTURAL INSTITUTION.

First, then, in every system of agricultural education, there should be an institution for the thorough indoctrination of the pupil in natural science, and in mechanical philosophy, so far as it can be made to bear upon agriculture. I have already treated fully of what, on this topic, should be taught in an institution of this nature.

Secondly, there should be a model farm, which should be accessible to the pupils, and where they might see an example of the best management, and the best practices in husbandry. It is obvious, however, that a single farm can present, excepting on a small scale, only a single kind of farming; and that it would be hardly possible to find a single locality presenting any considerable, or very instructive specimen of the different kinds of farming, such as arable, grazing, stock-breeding, stall-feeding, sheep-raising, and dairying. But the particular and careful observation even of one kind of well-conducted farming would qualify a pupil for understanding and receiving information on every other, whenever it came in his way, or wherever it might be attainable. Stall-feeding is intimately connected and often associated with arable farming, and dairying with grazing. The management of live stock, whether for work, for fatting, or for dairying, might, in a small degree, be exemplified on every well-managed farm. Such an appendage as this to a school of practical instruction, where the pupils might see and have explained to them the very best modes of husbandry, must be of the highest benefit. To these should be added an experimental farm. This need not be extensive, and it might be connected with the model farm; indeed, the model farm might itself be, to a degree, an experimental farm. It may be said that the premiums offered by agricultural societies, for various experiments in husbandry, are sufficient to meet the public wants in this case. I admit that they have in this way rendered immense benefits to the public; but there are still wanted various trials and tests of soils, manures, grasses, plants, implements, modes of cultivation, modes of feeding, breeding, dairying, — and on the effects of temperature, moisture, heat, frost, light, and electricity, — which common farmers can scarcely be expected to undertake, or, if undertaken, to follow out with that exactness which is most desirable, in order to render the results of such experiments worthy of confidence, and lessons for general application.

Connected with the whole should be most extensive gardens, — first, for purposes of botanical instruction, giving the pupils an opportunity of becoming acquainted with all the principal plants, grasses, forest-trees, fruit-trees, and weeds, which enter into their cultivation, to the advantage or injury of the farmer; and next, for making them thoroughly acquainted (a knowledge highly important to them) with the cultivation of all the varieties of vegetables and fruits which may be required for use, profit, or luxury.

Such is the basis on which I should be glad to see an institution for agricultural education rising up in every one of the United States, where the condition of society renders it expedient, and the population is dense enough to sustain it. The expensive plan on which it is proposed here to establish and conduct such institutions, would be quite unsuited to the state of manners and the condition of things in the United States. In their economical arrangements, Ireland has set us an excellent example. With us, they might be made in a great measure self-supporting. The plan proposed for such an institution, some few years since, by the late lamented Judge Buel, who had the subject much at heart, involved an expenditure of one hundred thousand dollars, and might be said to have been crushed by its own weight.

Let us suppose that it were proposed to establish such an institution in the western part of New York. Certainly no location could, in respect to the external circumstances of soil, climate, access, society, and markets, be more favorable. A farm of five hundred acres might be taken, on favorable terms, on a long lease. I would under no circumstances suffer the number of pupils to exceed one hundred, and perhaps it might be expedient to restrict the number much more. Some good-sized hall or building would be requisite for public meetings, lectures, or recitation-rooms, and for a museum, library, and chemical laboratory; but I would erect no college building for the residence of the pupils. They should either lodge in the neighborhood, with such farmers as would be willing to receive them, or other persons who might be disposed to provide for them; or otherwise, I would erect several farm-houses on the place, sufficient to supply the needful accommodations; but in no case should more than fifteen or twenty be lodged in one place; and, whether on the farm or not, the lodging-houses for the pupils should be under the constant inspection or regulation of the governors or instructors of the institution. One or two instructors should be employed constantly for teaching the main branches of education, and a competent farmer should be employed to manage the agricultural department, and to give the necessary practical instruction. Beyond this, no resident instructors would be required, — but regular and full courses of lectures and experiments in geology, mineralogy, botany, comparative anatomy, the veterinary art, and chemistry, by competent professors of these sciences, who might be employed for these objects annually, without the necessity and expense of constant residence, — as is now frequently done at our medical schools. In this way, the best talents in the community might be commanded, and at a reasonable expense.

I would require, in the next place, that the pupils should be placed in a condition of perfect equality, and that a certain amount of labor should be made compulsory on all, at such a rate of wages as should be deemed just, according to the ability of the pupil, and the nature of the work done. An account should be kept for every pupil, and another by every pupil, of the labor performed by him, which should be passed to his credit. The farm account should be kept with faithful exactness, and be always open to the inspection of the pupils; and after the deduction of the rent, and the necessary burdens and expenses, and some small amount kept as a reserve or accumulating fund for the benefit of the institution, the remainder should be divided among the pupils according to the labor performed.

Their board and lodging should be settled for by themselves, without any interference on the part of the directors of the institution, beyond keeping the charges within a stipulated price; and the keepers of the boarding-houses should be required to purchase, at reasonable rates, from the farm, whatever supplies they might require, which the farm would yield. A tax should be levied upon the students for the payment of all the instructors and lecturers, and the use of the library, and chemical and philosophical apparatus; and likewise to meet any extraordinary experiments made upon the farm, with a view to the instruction of the school. Whether it would be advisable for every pupil to have an allotment for himself, either for the purpose of experiment, or for the profit, and in aid of his subsistence, would be worth considering; remembering always how important it is to give to every man an immediate interest in the result of his labors.

Such, in my opinion, is a plan for agricultural education which demands no great advance, and involves no risk. But the project is even much more feasible than I have already stated. Why, for example, should not such an institution be connected with the college at Williamstown, or Amherst, in Massachusetts, or with Dartmouth College in New Hampshire, or Burlington College in Vermont, or the college at Hartford in Connecticut, or Geneva in New York, where all the facilities for scientific instruction are at hand, residences for the students attainable, and suitable farms to be had, either on purchase, or lease, at very reasonable rates? I throw out these hints to my countrymen, not with a view of dictating to their superior judgment, but to show that an institution for a practical and scientific education in agriculture may, without any hazardous expenditure, or any large investment, be made almost immediately attainable, and under every practicable advantage.

A professorship in agriculture is attached to the university in Edinburgh, and the chair filled by an eminent professor, Mr. Low, who has rendered the most useful public services, in the publication of his treatise on agriculture, which is said to contain the substance of his lectures at this institution. He has likewise established an extensive agricultural museum, containing specimens of agricultural productions, and models of the various implements used in improved husbandry. The term required to complete such a course of education, might be matter of after consideration; but I would advise, in every case, that the residence should be absolute, the rules exact and stringent, and the annual or occasional examinations as severe as at the military school at West Point, so that an equal proficiency might be secured.

XXXVI. — ELEVATION OF AGRICULTURE AS A PURSUIT AND A PROFESSION.

Where it is practicable, I would make the education of a high and extended character; and, besides the art of measuring, and surveying, and mapping land, I would have the arts of sketching, and drawing, and landscape gardening, taught in the institution. The pursuit of agriculture is almost universally considered as merely a profession of commerce or trade, the farmer looking wholly to its pecuniary results. In a trading community, pecuniary considerations are always liable to control the judgment, and predominate over every other consideration. Where the means are limited, and the farm must be cultivated as the only source of subsistence, pecuniary returns must, of course, be the main object. Where, as in England, the cultivator is not the owner of the soil, but an annual rent must be paid, and he is liable, as in most cases, to be compelled to quit his occupancy at the pleasure or the caprice of his landlord, farming must be conducted merely as matter of business, and there is no inducement to pursue the profession as matter of taste or sentiment. In many cases in my own country, it must, of necessity, be followed wholly as a means of support and of profit, and in some cases as a struggle for life.

But there are innumerable other cases, in which men have the power, under the most favorable circumstances, and I am most anxious they should have likewise the disposition, to devote themselves to it as an elegant and liberal profession, worthy of a mind gifted even with the finest taste, and enriched by the highest cultivation. The United States present not many examples of very great wealth, at least when estimated by the standard of wealth which prevails in England, where, indeed, are to be found individual accumulations which distance all the dreams of Oriental magnificence. But, on the other hand, no country upon the globe, and no condition of things since the establishment of society, ever presented more favorable opportunities than the United States for any one, by active and wholesome industry, and a proper frugality, to acquire a competence, and that respectable independence, in which, with a full supply for the necessities of life, and an abundant provision for its comforts, there will be found within reach as many of the elegances, and ornaments, and luxuries of life, as a well-disciplined and healthful state of mind can require. I have seen too frequently such beautiful examples in our country villages, and scattered over several parts of a land in many respects favored by Heaven above every other, not to be deeply impressed with a condition of life which, where its blessings are properly and gratefully appreciated, seems to leave little more on earth for a rational and reflecting, a benevolent and truly religious mind to ask. Happy is it where its waters are not poisoned by an insatiate avarice, nor disturbed and thrown into confusion by ambition of political office or distinction, or a feverish thirst for notoriety and excitement; but in a quiet, yet not stagnant repose, they reflect every where the tokens of that divine goodness, which seems in such examples to have poured out its richest earthly treasures. Now, I am anxious that agriculture should occupy that place among the liberal professions, to which it can be raised, and to which, from its importance, it is entitled. But this can only be done by improving the education of farmers as a class, — by multiplying, through the means of a most liberal and extended education, the charms of the country, and the subjects of interest which would be constantly more and more developed to a cultivated and inquisitive mind; and by showing that its successful pursuit, either as matter of business or recreation, where a moderate fortune is possessed or a moderate professional income is secured, is not incompatible with the highest improvement of taste, and even a vigorous and successful pursuit of learning; and that, where so pursued, under favorable circumstances, it affords as fair a chance of rational enjoyment and quiet usefulness as any situation which the most lucrative trade, or the most successful political ambition, or even the highest professional eminence, can command.

But I fear, how much soever I may satisfy the sober and reflecting minds on this point, my opinions and persuasions will scarcely be heard, and far less heeded, in that rush for wealth, for office, and for notoriety, which, like a torrent sweeping over the country, carries every movable object in its course. It seems, however, not less my duty to record my strong convictions, which the experience of a life not short has served only to confirm. I see in my own country every where proffered to an honest industry, a wise frugality, and a wholesome self-government, the most ample rewards: I see a wide extent of rich and beautiful territory waiting the improving hand of skill and labor, to be had in many cases almost for asking, with every man free to choose where he will pitch his tent, not only without injury, but to the advantage of his neighbor: I see the means of education, of competence, and of substantial independence, held out to all who will avail themselves of them. In the midst of all this, I see thousands and thousands of young men, blest with education and fortunes adequate to supply all reasonable wants in the country, rushing into cities, exhausting their small means in the extravagances and dissipations of fashionable life; crowding all the professions to repletion; pressing on, with vexation and disappointment heaped upon vexation and disappointment, into all the avenues of political office and distinction, and into all the bitter strifes of political controversy; forcing their way into the pursuits of trade without talents for their prosecution, and almost sure to involve themselves in bankruptcy and ruin; and, in one form and another, dragging on through life without satisfaction to themselves and without usefulness to others, and too often a ruinous burden upon those whom it is now their turn to succor and relieve. I cannot, therefore, help wishing that the pursuits of agriculture might be made attractive to such persons; and that, with education, and that moderate fortune which would give them the command of the best advantages of rural life, they might find in it, as far as rational happiness and humble usefulness are concerned, that philosopher's stone which in other places they are almost sure to search for in vain.

XXXVII. — RURAL MANNERS IN ENGLAND.

England presents many such examples. The true English gentleman, living, remote from the din of cities, and abstracted from the turmoil of political life, upon his own acres; managing his own estate; seeking the best means for its improvement, and superintending, under his own personal inspection, their application; doing what good he can to all around him; making those dependent upon him comfortable and contented; giving labor, counsel, encouragement, and all needful aid, to his poor neighbors, and causing them, and their wives, and their children, to look up to him as a friend and a parent, to whose kindness their good conduct is always a certain claim; whom when the eye sees, it sparkles with grateful joy, and when the ear hears his footsteps, the sounds go like melody to the heart; who is in his neighborhood the avowed and unostentatious supporter of good morals, temperance, education, peace, and religion; and in whose house you find an open-hearted hospitality, and abundant resources for innocent gratification, and for the improvement of the mind, with a perfect gentleness of manners, and unaffected piety presiding over the whole; — I say, such a man — and it has been my happiness to find many examples — need envy no one save the possessor of more power, and a wider sphere, of doing good; and need not covet the brightest triumphs of political ambition, nor the splendors and luxuries of royal courts.

Whatever contributes, then, in any way, to elevate the agricultural profession, to raise it, from a mere servile or mercenary labor, to the dignity of a liberal profession, and to commend it not merely for its profit and usefulness, but as a delightful resource and recreation for a cultivated mind, will certainly find favor with those who form rational views of life, who wish well to the cause of good morals, and would multiply and strengthen the safeguards of human virtue.

The class of individuals whom I have described — and I assure my readers I have drawn from real life, and deal in no fictions — find often their own efforts seconded and aided by those whose encouragement and sympathy always give new life and vigor to their exertions, and new pleasure to their pleasures, — I mean their own wives and children; and the farming operations, in all their history and details, and all their expediency and fitness, are as much matter of familiar and interested discussion at the fireside, as, in many other circles, the most recent novel, the change in fashion, or the latest triumph of party. Indeed, I have seen, in many cases, the wives and the daughters — and these, too, often persons of the highest rank and refinement — as well acquainted with every field and crop, their management and their yield, and with every implement and animal on the place, as the farmer himself; and I always put it down to the credit of their good sense.

XXXVIII. — A PENCIL SKETCH.

I must claim the indulgence of my readers, if I give them an account of a visit in the country so instructive, so bright, so cheerful, that nothing but the absolute breaking-up of the mind can ever obliterate its record, or dispel the bright vision from my imagination. I know my fair readers — for with some such I am assured my humble Reports are kindly honored — will feel an interest in it; and if I have any unfair readers, I beg them at once to turn over the page. But mind, I shall utter no name, and point to no place; and if I did not know that the example was not altogether singular, and therefore would not be detected, I should not relate it. I know very well, as soon as I return to my native land, if Heaven has that happiness yet in store for me, a dozen of my charming friends, — God bless them ! — with their bright eyes, and their gentle entreaties, will be pressing me for a disclosure ; but I tell them beforehand, I am panoplied in a stern philosophy, and shall remain immovable.

I had no sooner, then, entered the house, where my visit had been expected, than I was met with an unaffected cordiality which at once made me at home. In the midst of gilded halls and hosts of liveried servants, of dazzling lamps, and glittering mirrors, redoubling the highest triumphs of art and taste ; in the midst of books, and statues, and pictures, and all the elegances and refinements of luxury ; in the midst of titles, and dignities, and ranks, allied to regal grandeur, — there was one object which transcended and eclipsed them all, and showed how much the nobility of character surpassed the nobility of rank, the beauty of refined and simple manners all the adornments of art, and the scintillations of the soul, beaming from the eyes, the purest gems that ever glittered in a princely diadem. In person, in education and improvement, in quickness of perception, in facility and elegance of expression, in accomplishments and taste, in a frankness and gentleness of manners tempered by a modesty which courted confidence and inspired respect, and in a high moral tone and sentiment, which, like a bright halo, seemed to encircle the whole person, — I confess the fictions of poetry became substantial, and the *beau idéal* of my youthful imagination was realized.

But who was the person I have described ? A mere statue, to adorn a gallery of sculpture ? a bird of paradise, to be kept in a glass case ? a mere doll, with painted cheeks, to be dressed and undressed with childish fondness ? a mere human toy, to languish over a romance, or to figure in a quadrille ? Far otherwise : she was a woman in all the noble attributes which should dignify that name ; a wife, a mother, a housekeeper, a farmer, a gardener, a dairy-woman, a kind neighbor, a benefactor to the poor, a Christian woman, " full of good works, and alms-deeds which she did."

In the morning, I first met her at prayers ; for, to the honor of England, there is scarcely a family, among the hundreds whose hospitality I have shared, where the duties of the day are not preceded by the services of family worship ; and the master and the servant, the parent and the child, the teacher and the taught, the friend and the stranger, come together to recognize and strengthen the sense of their common equality in the presence of their common Father, and to acknowledge their equal dependence upon his care and mercy. She was then kind enough to tell me, after her morning arrangements, she claimed me for the day. She first showed me her children, whom, like the Roman mother, she deemed her brightest jewels, and arranged their studies and occupations for the day. She then took me two or three miles on foot to visit a sick neighbor, and, while performing this act of kindness, left me to visit some of the cottages upon the estate, whose inmates I found loud in the praises of her kindness and benefactions. Our next excursion was to see some of the finest, and largest, and most aged trees in the park, the size of which was truly magnificent; and I sympathized in the veneration which she expressed for them, which was like that with which one recalls the illustrious memory of a remote progenitor. Our next visit was to the greenhouses and the gardens; and she explained to me the mode adopted there of managing the most delicate plants, and of cultivating, in the most economical and successful manner, the fruits of a warmer region. From the garden we proceeded to the cultivated fields; and she informed me of the system of husbandry pursued on the estate, the rotation of crops, the management and application of manures, the amount of seed sown, the ordinary yield, and the appropriation of the produce, with a perspicuous detail of the expenses and results. She then undertook to show me the yards and offices, the byres, the feeding-stalls, the plans for saving, and increasing, and managing, the manure, the cattle for feeding, for breeding, for raising, the milking stock, the piggery, the poultry-yard, the stables, the harness-rooms, the implement-rooms, the dairy. She explained to me the process of making the different kinds of cheese, and the general management of the milk, and the mode of feeding the stock; and then, conducting me into the bailiff's house, she exhibited to me the Farm Journal, and the whole systematic mode of keeping the accounts and making the returns, with which she seemed as familiar as if they were the accounts of her own wardrobe. This did not finish our grand tour; for, on my return, she admitted me into her boudoir, and showed me the secrets of her own admirable housewifery, in the exact accounts which she kept of every thing connected with the dairy and the market, the table, the drawing-room, and the servants' hall. All this was done with a simplicity and a frankness which showed an absence of all consciousness of any extraordinary merit in her own department, and which evidently sprang solely from a kind desire to gratify a curiosity on my part, which, I hope, under such circumstances, was not unreasonable. A short hour after this brought us into another relation; for the dinner-bell summoned us, and this same lady was found presiding over a brilliant circle of the highest rank and fashion, with an ease, elegance, wit, intelligence, and good-humor, with a kind attention to every one's wants, and an unaffected concern for every one's comfort, which would lead one to suppose that this was her only and her peculiar sphere. Now, I will not say how many mud-puddles we had waded through, and how many dung-heaps we had crossed, and what places we explored, and how every farming topic was discussed; but I will say, that she pursued her object without any of that fastidiousness and affected delicacy which pass with some persons for refinement, but which in many cases indicate a weak if not a corrupt mind. The mind which is occupied with concerns and subjects that are worthy to occupy it, thinks very little of accessories which are of no importance. I will say, to the credit of Englishwomen, — I speak, of course, of the upper classes, — that it seems impossible that there should exist a more delicate sense of propriety than is found universally among them; and yet you will perceive at once that their good sense teaches them that true delicacy is much more an element of the mind, in the person who speaks or observes, than an attribute of the subject which is spoken about or observed. A friend told me that Canova assured him that, in modelling the wonderful statue of the Three Graces, from real life, he was never at any time conscious of an improper emotion or thought; and if any man can look at this splendid production, this affecting imbodiment of a genius almost creative and divine, with any other emotion than that of the most profound and respectful admiration, he may well tremble for the utter corruption, within him, of that moral nature which God designed should elevate him above the brute creation.

Now, I do not say that the lady to whom I have referred was herself the manager of the farm; that rested entirely with her husband; but I have intended simply to show how grateful and gratifying to him must have been the lively interest and sympathy which she took in concerns which necessarily so much engaged his time and attention; and how the country could be divested of that dulness and *ennui*, so often complained of as inseparable from it, when a cordial and practical interest is taken in the concerns which necessarily belong to rural life. I meant also to show — as this and many other examples which have come under my observation emphatically do show — that an interest in, and a familiarity with, even the most humble occupations of agricultural life, are not inconsistent with the highest refinements of taste, the most improved cultivation of the mind, the practice of the polite accomplishments, and a grace, and elegance, and dignity of manners, unsurpassed in the highest circles of society.

XXXIX. — LIFE IN THE COUNTRY.

To live in the country, and enjoy all its pleasures, we should love the country. To love the country is to take an interest in all that belongs to the country — its occupations, its sports, its culture, and its improvements, its fields and its forests, its trees and rocks, its valleys and hills, its lakes and rivers; to gather the flocks around us, and feed them from our own hands; to make the birds our friends, and call them all by their names; to wear a chaplet of roses as if it were a princely diadem; to rove over the verdant fields with a higher pleasure than we should tread the carpeted halls of regal courts; to inhale the fresh air of the morning as if it were the sweet breath of infancy; to brush the dew from the glittering fields as if our path were strewed with diamonds; to hold converse with the trees of the forest, in their youth and in their decay, as if they could tell us the history of their own times, and as if the gnarled bark of the aged among them were all written over with the record of by-gone days, of those who planted them, and those who early gathered their fruits; to find hope and joy bursting like a flood upon our hearts, as the darting rays of light gently break upon the eastern horizon; to see the descending sun robing himself in burnished clouds, as if these were the gathering glories of the divine throne; to find in the clear evening of winter our chamber studded with countless gems of living light; to feel that "we are never less alone than when alone;" to make even the stillness and solitude of the country eloquent; and above all, in the beauty of every object which presents itself to our senses, and in the unbought provision which sustains, and comforts, and fills with joy, the countless multitudes of living existences which people the land, the water, the air, every where to repletion, to see the radiant tokens of an infinite and inexhaustible beneficence, as they roll by us and around us in one ceaseless flood; and in a clear and bright day of summer, to stand out in the midst of this resplendent creation, circled by an horizon which continually retreats from our advances, holding its distance undiminished, and with the broad and deep blue arches of heaven over us, whose depths no human imagination can fathom; to perceive this glorious temple all instinct with the presence of the Divinity, and to feel, amidst all this, the brain growing dizzy with wonder, and the heart swelling with an adoration and a holy joy, absolutely incapable of utterance; — this it is to love the country, and to make it, not the home of the person only, but of the soul.

XL. — VETERINARY COLLEGE.

I must not quit the subject of agricultural education without adverting to some other institutions of great importance. The first of these is the Veterinary College, near London. I believe there is one of a similar character near Edinburgh; but that I have not visited.

The object of this institution was to qualify persons, by the study of comparative anatomy and physiology, and by opportunities for witnessing hospital practice and investigating the symptoms and phenomena of disease in the lower animals, to practise veterinary surgery and medicine; and to do what can be done, by skill and science, for the relief of the sufferings and the cure of the maladies of quadrupeds of all kinds — horses, cattle, sheep, dogs, &c. For this purpose, a number of gentlemen associated, and, by a subscription for life of twenty guineas each, or an annual payment of two guineas, laid the foundation of this excellent and humane establishment. An extensive plot of ground, about three miles from the centre of London, was obtained, and the necessary buildings — consisting of stables and loose boxes; long piazzas for the purpose of giving the patients exercise in bad weather under cover; a room for lectures and dissections, and for a museum of anatomical preparations; and specimens of diseased organization, and a forge for shoeing, together with apartments for the resident professor, and for the accommodation of the servants of the establishment — have been erected; and already nearly or quite a thousand pupils have received diplomas or certificates of their qualifications for practice, and have gone to the business of their profession in different parts of the kingdom, in the army, and in foreign countries.

Subscribers to the establishment have the privilege of sending their horses, or diseased animals, to the institution, without any other expense than the actual cost of their food; but no animal can be admitted which is not the property of either an annual or a permanent subscriber. The horses of subscribers are sometimes prescribed for at their own stables, when it is inconvenient to send them, provided the medicines are compounded at the college. In case the disease of an animal is pronounced desperate, the owner, upon paying the expenses already incurred, may surrender him to the college; and if, by any treatment which they may see fit to adopt, the animal is recovered, the owner may have him again by paying the additional expenses since his surrender, or he will be considered the property of the college. Horses likewise may be shod at the forge of the college at the customary charges. Subscribers likewise, at a distance, have the privilege of procuring any medicines or drugs, which may be required, compounded at the college, and furnished at the actual cost.

A principal and an adjunct professor of veterinary science and practice, men eminent for their knowledge and skill, preside over the institution, and give regular courses of lectures and examinations; and the number of patients in the infirmary is generally such as to afford the students an opportunity of seeing a considerable variety of practice, especially among horses, to which hitherto the practice has been mainly confined. Besides this, through the liberality of the professors of the Medical College, the students at the Veterinary Institution have an opportunity of attending the medical and anatomical lectures gratuitously at these institutions; and, to guard, as far as possible, against ignorance and incompetency, no student can receive the diploma or recommendation of the institution to practise, until he has passed a regular and thorough examination, and has been found qualified for the duty.

This is a most excellent institution. In an economical view, it is highly important; for the amount of property in live stock is every where very great; and here, where, as in several establishments kept by a single individual, there are twenty and thirty, and sometimes forty horses for hunting, and in other cases as many more for racing, — and where, as in several cases within my knowledge, packs of dogs, of very great original cost, are kept at an expense of from fifteen hundred to two thousand pounds, or from seven thousand to ten thousand dollars, a year, and in many cases more than that, — it is easy to see what a large amount of property is at stake, and to what care it is entitled. I have been at one or two establishments where the horses in the stables, exclusive of horses for farm work, amounted to sixty or eighty. The large number of cavalry horses belonging to the army render the services of a veterinary surgeon, in such establishments, of indispensable importance.

Surgery, as an art, has been carried to great perfection; and in some circumstances hardly any thing more seems wanting than actually to breathe into some of the artificial anatomical preparations the Promethean fire, and set the circulations in motion. Medicine, indeed, presents but few infallible remedies, but something has been done; and if comparatively little has been accomplished by physic, yet much has been done by a curative treatment and regimen. I am aware that it is quite customary to say of many novel, and certainly very gentle modes of treatment, of recent date, that the patients are cured by the imagination; and this is as agreeable a mode of cure as bloodletting, or powerful doses of calomel and jalap, or the exciting operation of Spanish flies. It is obvious, however, that, until we make much further progress in phrenological science, we can do little by applications to the imaginations of horses or dogs. But, whatever imperfection attaches itself to medical science, something at least may be gained from it; and it certainly presents the only practicable and probable means of learning the nature of disease, and combating its power. At any rate, medical science, and a thorough medical education, seem to afford the only substantial security against the evils of empiricism or quackery; and, to say nothing of experiments upon the human organism, I have myself seen, under the pretence of remedy or cure, such horrible cruelties practised upon dumb animals, as have filled me with indignation, and have made me indulge the inhuman wish of changing places with the operator — of putting him in the position of his unhappy patient, and of being allowed to try some of his prescriptions upon himself. If they answered, well; but, in many cases, I think he would soon be past answering at all. The public have reason to congratulate themselves that medical practice is now every where assuming the character of prevention rather than of cure; and that the truly respectable part of the profession, dropping that profound air of mystery with which they formerly were accustomed to wrap themselves up, and which made one tremble in their presence almost as much as in the presence of the original professor of the black art, now prefer the more simple to the more artificial practice. They seem to be fast learning that Nature, like others of the sex, may be persuaded, but not forced; may be kindly led, but woe be to the man who attempts to drive her; and that, in truth, the great object of medicine is, not to give health, but to remove disease; to clean and adjust the machinery, and then it will go right of itself, barring accidents, as long as it is intended to go at all.

I have already spoken of the importance of the veterinary art in an economical view. A frightful disease has for some time prevailed among the cattle in England, Ireland, and the Continent. I met with one farmer who assured me that he had lost by it, in one season, ninety-seven cattle, and he feared his whole herd might perish with it, for he could find no remedy. Now, there is no hope of any remedy but from the investigations of medical skill and science. We want men, therefore, who by education are qualified for, and willing to devote themselves to, the inquiry into the causes and means of prevention of such direful calamities. The epidemic still prevails in England and on the Continent; and application has been made to the government to check the importation of foreign cattle, lest they should assist in the spread of the disease. Indeed, numbers of cattle are almost every week, as I have reason to believe, brought to Smithfield in such a state of disease as to be fit for no other purpose — and for this they are actually bought — but to make sausages for the poor Londoners. I hardly dare say that this is not to be complained of; but when one sees the extreme and indescribable misery and destitution of many of these poor wretches, apparently irremediable and hopeless, one almost hesitates, in sad desperation, to lament a mode of disposing of them after the Napoleon example of the treatment of his sick prisoners at Jaffa. I almost tremble while I write upon such a subject as this. It is indispensable to see, in order to believe. I have had the painful, I hope not improper, curiosity to penetrate many of these subterranean hiding-places and dens of misery; and it is my sober conviction that the human imagination cannot exaggerate the physical suffering, and, too commonly consequent upon that, the moral degradation in which many thousands, in this glorious and prosperous country, drag out their wretched existence. But I advocate the establishment of veterinary institutions, and the cultivation of veterinary medicine, on the broad ground of humanity; and I hope many such institutions will grow up in America, and that speedily. It is remarkable that, in the disease of one of our domestic animals, medical science has discovered the only effectual preventive for one of the most dreadful scourges which, in the form of disease, ever afflicted mankind. I refer, of course, to vaccination.

But these animals have bones to ache, and nerves to feel, as well as ourselves. They furnish our support; they perform our labors; they promote our pleasures; they are patient, enduring, and indefatigable, in our service. Has not God cast them upon our care, and put them under our protection? What a responsibility! Shall it be said that those who have no voice to speak for themselves, shall find no one to speak for them? What if they have no moral nature? Then they have not the vices of animals of a superior class, who, dishonoring, perverting, and outraging, that moral nature, degrade themselves far below the class of beings guided only by instinctive impulses. It is said of the great emperor, that his heart was never more touched, if heart indeed he had, than on a certain occasion, when, three days after a sanguinary battle, when human victims were immolated to his dreadful ambition by thousands, riding over a field thickly strewed with the dying and the dead, he found a faithful dog lying by the side and licking the bleeding wounds of his dying master. The noble dog of St. Bernard, dragging the perishing traveller from the snow-drift to the hospitable convent, for warmth and comfort, and the poor spaniel dying with slow starvation upon the grave of his master, and refusing to be led away or to be comforted, are pictures of heroism and fidelity worthy of a place at the side of that of Regulus, deaf to the entreaties of his family, taking leave of the senate on his return to fulfil his pledge, or that of the Grecian daughter nourishing her father in prison.

Humanity calls upon us to alleviate suffering, wherever suffering exists. I wish that veterinary instruction was connected with all our medical schools, and made an indispensable branch of study. We try all kinds of experiments upon these helpless animals for the benefit of science, and science should do something to repay the debt, by attempting, in every practicable form, to alleviate the sufferings of the race. In the country, a medical practitioner, who would add veterinary skill and practice to his other services, would confer immense benefits. It is lamentable that, by a false standard of moral duty, such an office should be thought degrading. In many cases, it might subject him to painful and thankless services; but the life of every benevolent physician is full of such services, and he has only to thank God that he has the power of doing so much good, often at so little cost. So far from such a practice being degrading, the physician who would be willing to render such services would be worthy of double honor; for the more humble, the meaner, the more friendless the sufferer, proportionately is the glory of the kindness enhanced. There is no reason, however, why such services should be gratuitous, and in many situations it would form a profitable branch of practice.

XLI. — MUSEUM OF ECONOMIC GEOLOGY.

This is a most valuable establishment, in the centre of London. Its whole object is utility, and principally in rendering geological discoveries subservient to the promotion of the useful and ornamental arts. It is a most singular, but a well-established fact, that the mineral treasures dug from the mines, in the islands of Great Britain, amount to the enormous sum of twenty million pounds sterling per year, or one hundred million of dollars, — of which eight million pounds, or forty million of dollars, are of iron, and nine million pounds, or forty-five million of dollars, of coal. It is easy to see what a vast interest is at stake in these matters. In another form, I hope to be able to give some account of a visit which I made to one of these immense excavations, where I descended, by a ladder, seven hundred feet, and then groped my way through various crevices, and chambers, and shafts, a distance of perhaps two miles under ground. I am disposed to think it would be misplaced in an agricultural report, where I am afraid my friends will already find too many things out of place. I can only, in this matter, throw myself upon the indulgence of my readers, and remind them of the variety of tastes and appetites which I am compelled to consult. If, in spite of all this, a bill of indictment should be brought against me for making my Reports too miscellaneous, I shall at once allow a plea of guilty to be recorded, and throw myself upon the mercy of the court. I am indeed, in this way, an old offender, and I cannot express the gratitude which I feel for the mercy I have so often experienced.

The Museum of Economic Geology, though not founded principally for the benefit of agricultural science, is yet made subsidiary to this object. The geological structure of any portion of the earth's surface seems intimately related to the nature of the soil which rests upon it; so that, from knowing the structure of the rocky substratum of a country, you can infer strongly its fertility or its infertility, or the adaptation of its soil to various crops. The general opinion is, that all soils are formed from the crumbling or detrition of rocks, mixed with some vegetable or organic matter. This is the received theory, but it is not without its difficulties. I have no disposition to controvert it, for a man who battles with the stones is quite sure to have the worst of it. The original form of the earth is wrapped in impenetrable obscurity. Science is doing every thing she can to unfold the leaves of this wonderful book; but where they have been most successfully separated and expounded, they are found so scratched, and torn, and blurred all over, that the letters are with extreme difficulty made legible. We soon learn that it was a much earlier specimen of printing than has been generally supposed, and some of it in a language that is lost. It does not appear to me more certain that the rocks were first formed, and then portions of them reduced to such a fine state of comminution as to form soils, than that the earth was originally in a state of fine atoms, and then, by the operation of fire, and water, and pressure from within and without, amidst violent terrene convulsions, rocks were formed, and the various strata arranged. It would seem not improbable that, from the earliest period of the reduction of its temperature to a degree that vegetable life could exist upon it, vegetable life appeared; and by successive convulsions this vegetable life itself became overwhelmed, and was transformed into those immense beds of fossil deposits which occupy so large a portion of the surface, or upper portion, of the globe. How afterwards such vast deposits of earth took place over these beds of vegetable remains, can be explained only by some immense and utterly inexplicable convulsion and disruption of portions of the earth. It is admitted that the character of the soil often bears a direct relation to the rocks which it overlays, and evidently a considerable portion of it is formed from the detritus of these subjacent rocks; but the vast amount of drift or diluvium scattered over the earth's surface, and often at immense distances from places where, upon the common theory, it is supposed to have been formed, shows that the geological indications above referred to are not infallible.

The Museum of Economic Geology is intended to exhibit specimens of various soils from the different localities in the country, with illustrations, as far as they can be obtained, of their peculiar adaptation to agricultural purposes; and connected with the museum is a chemical laboratory for the analysis of soils which may have already been obtained, or which may be brought by farmers or land-owners for that purpose. The museum is open to the gratuitous inspection of the public, and is clearly the germ of an institution of great magnitude and importance. The establishment is at present under the management of Mr. Richard Phillips, F. R. S., a man deservedly eminent for his skill in chemistry and natural science, to whose indefatigable kindness I should do great injustice to my own grateful feelings if I did not here record my deep sense of obligation.

XLII. — CHEMICAL AGRICULTURAL ASSOCIATION IN SCOTLAND.

The farmers in Scotland, certainly inferior to none in agricultural enterprise, intelligence, and skill, and demonstrating this by a husbandry most exact and productive, have associated themselves together for the encouragement of the application of chemistry to the improvement of agriculture. Proprietors of land pay a yearly subscription of one pound or upwards to the association, and tenants ten shillings. This sum entitles each of them to two analyses a year at a certain fixed low rate. All above that number are charged half more. The analyst is required to give only such analysis as will answer the desired purpose. Agricultural societies, by a yearly payment of five pounds to the association, are entitled to one lecture from the agricultural professor; for ten pounds, to two lectures, and so on; and the travelling expenses of the lecturer are likewise to be paid by those who employ him.

The society, more than a year since, proceeded to appoint, at a liberal salary, Mr. F. W. S. Johnston, an agricultural lecturer and chemist, to the office of chemist and lecturer to the association; and a chemical laboratory and depository are established and in full operation at Edinburgh. Mr. Johnston is well known to the agricultural community by his valuable works on agricultural chemistry, some of which have been reprinted in the United States, and in both countries have had a very extended circulation. The success of the association, it is reported, has been such as to satisfy the original subscribers of its utility. It has led, through the lectures of the professor, to the establishment of several agricultural periodicals, and has throughout Scotland infused new spirit into the veins of the agricultural body, and quickened its pulse. One of the most substantial benefits as yet resulting from it has been the analytical examination of ninety different specimens of guano imported into Scotland; and that to secure the farmers from impositions, which, in cases before this, have not been infrequent.

After the remarks which I have made in a former part of my Report, it certainly is only just that I should subjoin the analysis made at this place of two soils from Renfrewshire, with the results of the application prescribed for them.

	I. Per cent.	II. Per cent.
"Organic matter,	12.05	10.43
Salts soluble in water; sulphates,	1.23	0.75
Oxide of iron,	5.73	10.78
Manganese,	0.19	0.24
Alumina,	4.69	2.87
Magnesia,	trace.	trace.
Phosphoric acids,	trace.	trace.
Silicious matter and clay,	74.67	73.21
	98.56	98.28

"But a mere trace of magnesia and phosphoric acid was found in either of these soils. It was therefore recommended to add to both of them the magnesia in the state of sulphate, and the phosphoric acid as bone-earth. The effect has been most wonderful and striking." — The letter with which I have been favored adds, "None of the analyses I have given are very elaborate, but they are sufficiently so for practical purposes, and they do not confuse or mystify the farmer with hard names."

I had the pleasure of visiting this institution, and there was certainly no want of the indications of industry. I have only to regret that my friend's account of his two patients above is so short and imperfect. I should be glad to have been able to inform my readers what was the exact condition of the patients before taking the prescription, and their particular state of health after it.

XLIII. — CHEMICAL AGRICULTURAL LECTURES.

During the last winter, a course of ten lectures, illustrated by numerous experiments, was given by Professor Brande, F. R. S., well known in the scientific world, on the chemistry of agriculture, at the rooms of the Royal Institution, — which, through his politeness, I had the pleasure of attending. They might be considered as almost wholly scientific, and were exceedingly interesting and instructive. Mr. Brande spoke of himself as having been a pupil or associate of the distinguished Sir Humphry Davy, who lectured on the same subjects in this same institution, and who may be said to have taken the first step in the great movement, which is now so widely felt, of the application of science, properly so called, to agriculture.

Professor Brande's lectures were numerously attended, by ladies as well as gentlemen. Several of the ladies were always busy in taking notes of the lectures. I felt the highest respect for them on this account; and if I had been, as is said among the clergy, "a candidate for settlement," with my strong predilections for agricultural pursuits, I might have been tempted to inquire about some of them, whose high and capacious foreheads gave a noble indication of what was within, whether they also were in the transition state. Certainly here, as well as any where, I may claim for an American woman the honor of presenting from her own pen an excellent translation, from the French, of Chaptal's Agricultural Chemistry, to the American public. Her name is modestly withheld from the title-page, and therefore I have no right to give it.

I shall give below a syllabus of Professor Brande's lectures on these occasions, because I so strongly wish the example should be followed in my own country.

Ist. Lecture. The Soil. — Its components; whence derived. — *Inorganic Constituents of the Soil.* Silica; alumina; lime; magnesia; oxide of iron; alkalies; phosphorus; sulphur; salts; water; decay of rocks; sand; clay; marl; chalk; other simple soils. — *Organic Constituents.* Humus or humic acid; their influences and uses. Absorptive power in regard to air, water, and gases. Radiating and receptive powers in respect to solar rays. Various physical conditions of the soil.

II. The Atmosphere. — Its composition; invariable and variable constituents. Influence of the moisture, carbonic acid, and ammonia, of the atmosphere.

III. The Vegetable. — Its *Ultimate Constituents*, and their sources; carbon; oxygen; hydrogen; nitrogen. The sources and importance of the so-called inorganic constituents of the vegetable; acids; alkalies; oxides; salts. — *Proximate Constituents* of the vegetable; sap; wood; starch; sugar; gum. Their metamorphoses; gluten; albumen; fibrine; caseine; legumine; *proteine;* resins; oils; acids; alkalies; fermentation; eremacausis; putrefaction.

IV. Functions and Growth of Vegetables. — Germination; general organization of vegetables; roots; trunk; branches; leaves; flowers; buds; functions of the roots and of the leaves.

V. Principles of the Improvement of Soils. — Mechanical, as influencing texture; chemical, as influencing *composition manures*, of inorganic, organic, and mixed origin. . Draining; ploughing; burning; irrigation; green crops; interchange of crops; fallows.

I make no apology for giving to my readers this instructive syllabus in full. It is said of Queen Elizabeth that, being asked by one of her maids of honor for a book to read, she gave her an English dictionary. The lady presently returned it to her majesty with many thanks, and stated "that she had been much interested in the perusal." There was more wisdom in this reply than at first appears. To say nothing of its convenience, yet I have often found a copious index, or a well-digested table of contents, an interesting and instructive portion of a book.

XLIV. — EMPLOYMENT OF AGRICULTURISTS.

In the technical sense of the term, *agriculturist* means a teacher of agriculture. Under the excellent management of

William Blacker, Esq., on the estate of Lord Gosford, in the county of Armagh, Ireland, an experienced and intelligent man, well skilled in communicating his ideas, is employed to visit the tenants on the property, to advise them in regard to the management and cultivation of their small farms, and to encourage them by some small premiums, and by reporting their condition and success to the principal manager. The occupations in these cases are very small, often not exceeding three, four, and six acres. As I understood Mr. Blacker, he has the care of twenty-five hundred tenants on the property of this nobleman. This number, I confess, seems very extraordinary; but the subdivisions on the place are quite small and numerous. I shall, on another occasion, give a particular account of Mr. Blacker's excellent management of small farms, because it is full of useful instruction, and does the highest honor to his judgment, perseverance, and benevolence. At present, I speak only of the employment of an agriculturist, which has been attended with the best effects. This person lives on the estate, and has a small amount of land in the neighborhood of his own house, which he is expected to keep in the best possible order, according to the system which he lays down for others, — so that he is called upon to teach by example as well as precept.

The same arrangement has been made, at the suggestion of Mr. Blacker, on the farm of Lady Bassett, near Camborne, in Cornwall, which I had the pleasure to visit. Here, too, it works well. The farmers in Cornwall hold larger farms than in Armagh, and therefore have a higher idea of their own importance. They were at first very jealous of the direct approaches of the agriculturist to advise and instruct them. But by a little address, and by especially avoiding any thing like dogmatism or self-conceit, and by a frank manner convincing the farmers that he was disinterestedly seeking their good, his success is becoming remarkable, and he is every day gaining upon their esteem and confidence. A horse, loose in a pasture, can rarely be caught if you approach him swinging the bridle, the emblem of his subjugation, before his eyes; but if you go to him shaking only the measure of oats before him, and concealing the bridle under your coat, you can generally take him without difficulty. I am no advocate for treachery under any form; but where the object aimed at is unexceptionable and excellent, I see no occasion for unnecessarily alarming the prejudices of those whom we wish to serve, or for awakening resistance by command, when we can easily enforce acquiescence by persuasion.

That the plan is sure to work well where the class of tenants, as in Armagh, are very small tenants, and ignorant withal, is quite plain; but farmers on a large scale would be likely to reject any direct interference. Yet these men often need instruction. The knowledge of improvements, in some cases, extends itself by slow degrees; oral instruction, coupled with familiar illustrations, is always more interesting than books; and the employment of an agricultural missionary, of unobtrusive and kind manners, and perfectly competent to impart instruction, to visit a district of country, that he might point out errors and defects of cultivation, and explain the best modes of husbandry adapted to the climate and locality, would prove a most powerful means of awakening attention to the subject, of reforming errors, and introducing desirable and substantial improvements.

XLV. — GUANO.

Having now completed what I designed to say upon the provision for agricultural education in Great Britain, I shall beg the indulgence of my readers in reverting to a topic of a different character, and which, in a more methodical arrangement, would have had a place in a different part of my work. A strong and impatient desire has been expressed that I should give what information I possess on the subject of the recently-introduced and most extraordinary manure called *guano;* and I therefore speak of it in this place.

I do not deem it necessary to go into the history of a substance which has been made so familiar by the public discussions which have taken place in relation to it. That it is an animal deposit, is well established. It is the excrement of sea-birds accustomed to frequent certain islands in the Pacific Ocean and other places in the tropical latitudes. Its use as a manure is not new in those countries where it has been found. In Peru, the birds who caused the deposit were protected by severe laws, and the value of the manure was fully understood. The amount of the accumulations, considering the nature of the deposit, is immense, being represented, by travellers, as from three to seven hundred feet in depth. The number of birds is stated to be almost beyond calculation; and any person who will take the trouble to read, in that delightful book, Wilson's Ornithology, the accounts of the roosting-places of the passenger-pigeon in some of the Western States of America, will readily confide in well-authenticated accounts of the number of these birds, which would otherwise be deemed egregious exaggerations. To the gentlemen in England who are fond of what is termed a *battue*, a voyage to the Pacific to shoot the guano birds would afford excellent sport; and if in such case they would bring back loads of this valuable manure, it might not prove an unprofitable enterprise, and they would perform a double work of conciliation to the farmers. Their accounts of one or two days' shooting, or knocking down the birds with the butt-ends of their guns, would be read here with the greatest avidity, and eclipse all their former exploits of killing hundreds of game in a single day where the beaters were employed to drive them directly under the muzzles of their guns, and where occasionally they are obliged to knock down a poacher instead of a penguin.

These deposits are made in a climate where, for a considerable part of the year, little rain falls, and where the intense heat of the sun forms such a crust over the deposit, that it becomes almost insoluble. Supposing a deposit to be made of two inches a year, for three thousand years, this would give a depth of five hundred feet; and therefore the report of the depth of these deposits, though surprising, is by no means intrinsically incredible. The extraordinary effect of this manure is another remarkable circumstance. The dung of the domestic pigeon or fowl is among the strongest used, but it is not so powerful as guano. In the excrements of birds, the solid and liquid portions are combined. This is one secret of their strength. In the case of the guano birds, their food is wholly fish, and not, as with our domestic birds, mainly farinaceous; and therefore it abounds in nitrogen, and in bony substances, or phosphates.

The secret of the extraordinary success of this manure is not yet solved, however nearly a solution may have been approximated. This is evident from the fact that, after the most exact and minute analysis of this manure, conducted with all the skill and science which can be brought to bear upon it, no one has been able to form an artificial guano with any degree of its efficacy. Chemistry determines with wonderful accuracy its inorganic properties; but fifty per cent. of it is organic matter, and this being dissipated or lost in the process of analysis, nothing is known of it but its absolute quantity. Every common farmer knows that horse manure, cow manure, hog manure, sheep manure, are all specifically different, and their effects and uses are different; and I believe this depends not more upon a difference in their inorganic elements, than upon some specific effects of their organic elements; and though horses, and cows, and sheep, should be fed upon precisely the same food, their excrementitious matter would be specifically different, and the effects upon vegetation different. I pretend not to say in what this difference consists; this, chemistry has not yet reached, though I can but hope the goal will presently be attained. I am not therefore entirely satisfied with any account which chemistry has given of guano, so far as its operation is concerned. It has done much, and is clearly able to determine the different specific values of different samples. This is of great importance to the farmer, and not less so to the honest dealer. But the specific qualities of this extraordinary manure, as proved by its effects, are, I presume to believe, with all possible respect for science, yet to be discovered. I know the consequences of questioning the infallibility of the pope, but I am no Catholic.

One, indeed, may well speak of its effects as extraordinary, from what I myself have seen. In Scotland, last autumn, two shrubs were shown to me, sweet-briers, growing in front of a two-story house, and trained upon its sides; one at one, the other at the other end. The soil in which they grew, the aspect, and other circumstances, were the same. One, in the season, had grown six or seven feet; the other, nearly thirty feet! It had actually climbed to the roof of the house, and turned and hung down, reaching half the distance down from the roof to the ground. I judged this could not have been less than thirty feet. This had been repeatedly watered with liquid guano, by the hands of its fair cultivator; for this was another experiment by a lady, (which I hope my American friends will bear in mind.) The other had received no special care or manuring. This charming woman, surrounded by her lovely children, was equally engaged in teaching the young idea as the sweet-brier how to shoot, and they too showed the beautiful results of devoted and assiduous culture.

I have seen the extraordinary effects of the application of guano all over the country, and I have met with very few instances of disappointment. I have been favored with a great many reports of its application; but my readers will, I think, be better satisfied with general results than with a long list of particular examples.

When I speak of its extraordinary effects, I yet do not consider them as so surprising as the effects of gypsum in many parts of the United States, whose operation, I venture to say, remains wholly unexplained. I do not, of course, mean to imply that one can be substituted for the other. The effects of half a bushel of finely-powdered gypsum, scattered over an acre of land, in some places, in increasing the crop of grass, and in respect to some other crops, is amazing; yet in all England, I have not been able to find a single well-attested example of its being applied with any benefit whatever. The application of guano has been made, in England and Scotland, to all kinds of plants, and in some instances with great success; indeed with rarely a failure.

It has been used for turnips, barley, wheat, oats, grass, garden vegetables, onions, asparagus, potatoes, flowers, and trees. I have seen its application in all these cases, excepting asparagus and trees; but the testimony which certifies its success in these cases is unquestionable. Comparisons made between guano and other manures, are not quite satisfactory in respect to quantities, because it is obviously very difficult to institute any instructive comparison between so many pounds of guano, and so many loads of manure; manure is so various in its nature, quality, bulk, &c.; but it will be quite easy to compare the two in respect to the ease or difficulty of their transportation, and of their application to the plant or soil. Comparisons, likewise, in respect to the cost of different applications, as made here, would be of little use in the United States, as prices of manure and of labor are totally different; and the one can afford no rule for the other. In this matter, the farmers of the United States must judge for themselves.

The quantity which it is deemed best to apply varies from two hundred weight to four hundred weight, or five hundred weight. Frequent cases have occurred of the application of five hundred weight and eight hundred weight, to a statute acre, with great advantage. Cases are on record of twenty-nine and thirty hundred weight being applied to grass-land with a great, but not, most certainly, a remunerating increase of crop. I met one farmer in Lincolnshire, who thought more than one hundred weight applied to turnips was unnecessary; but the almost universal testimony is in favor of three hundred weight. A bushel of sifted guano weighs from fifty-two to fifty-four pounds.

In regard to the mode of application, it is well settled that it should seldom be applied alone. To garden vegetables, or greenhouse plants, it may be applied in a state of solution in water. In field cultivation, it may be applied by being mixed with four or six times its quantity of dry earth or mould. In this way, it may be sown broadcast over the field, and then lightly harrowed or turned in; or it may be sown first in the same drill where the seed is to be dropped; great care must be taken, however, that it does not come in contact with the seed, or it will destroy its vegetative powers. It is desirable that it should be covered as soon as may be after being sown. The best farmers give a caution against mixing it with lime, or bones, or wood-ashes, as these substances, coming in contact with it, will drive off its ammonia.

Where a portion of barn manure has been applied in conjunction with guano, the mixture has been found much more efficacious than the manure when applied alone. In an application which I saw, guano gave seven tons of turnips increase to an acre over an artificial manure which had been much praised, and was applied at the same time.

A good mode of preparing it for application is to mix it with fine earth, on the headlands of the field where it is to be used, forming it, with the earth, into alternate layers, in the proportion of earth to the guano of three to one; and after it has remained two or three days, thoroughly incorporating them together by turning over the heap.

With potatoes, it should be placed in the drill or hole, but not in contact with the set or seed; and for Indian corn — a case in which I have had no experience — it would seem advisable to adopt a similar method.

The experiments of Mr. John Dudgeon have been given to the public at large. As I had the pleasure of visiting his farm, one of the best-managed in the kingdom, and saw some of the experiments going on, I feel at liberty to give them, and it may be interesting to my readers to have them in his own words.

"The following results, communicated by John Dudgeon, Esq., of Spylaw, to the Highland and Agricultural Society, in April, 1843, show, first, the relative produce of turnips from *guano* applied at the rate of three hundred weight, four hundred weight, and five hundred weight, per acre, in competition with the produce from the farm-yard manure, applied at the rate of eighteen yards per acre; secondly, the trial of *bone-dust* with coal-ashes against *guano alone*, and guano mixed with a portion of *sulphate of soda;* thirdly, the trial of *guano alone* against *bone-dust alone.*

"'The first experiment was in a field lying upon a slope, with a southern exposure, the soil consisting of a good loam upon a retentive sub-soil; the upper part of the field, for about a fourth of its length, gradually becoming shallower in soil, and resting upon a hard muirland pan, so that the value of the lower portion of the field, as compared with the upper, may be estimated as three to one. This field has been but imperfectly drained. It was dunged in the usual way, immediately before sowing, with well-prepared farm-yard manure, at the rate of about eighteen cubic yards to the acre, with the exception of that portion to which guano was applied. Two ordinary drills for the latter were selected at random, and the guano distributed in them by the hand, without any mixture, at the rate of three hundred weight per acre. Leaving an interval of three drills, which were manured like the rest of the field, two other drills were treated with guano, at the rate of four hundred weight per acre; and finally, with a similar space intervening, two drills with guano at the rate of fully more than five hundred weight per acre. No difference appeared in the turnips (which were the variety named Dale's hybrid) previous to singling or thinning the plants with the hoe; after that, however, the superiority of the drills with the guano became manifest, and continued to increase with the growth of the turnips, particularly in those drills which received the greatest quantity, till the whole were carted off in October, when the produce (topped and rooted) of the whole six drills were weighed, each two as differing in the quantity of guano applied, compared with two drills immediately adjoining, on which the farm-yard manure had been used. The following was the result: —

Kinds of Manure.	*Quantities applied.*	*Produce per Acre.*
Two drills with GUANO, . .	5 cwt. per acre, . .	25 cwt. 5 st.
" " " dung, . .	18 yds. " " . .	18 " 7 "
" " " GUANO, . .	4 cwt. " " . .	22 " 6 "
" " " dung, . .	18 yds. " " . .	19 " 7 "
" " " GUANO, . .	3 cwt. " " . .	20 " 6 "
" " " dung, . .	18 yds. " " . .	19 " 2 "

"'In the second experiment, a comparative trial was made between guano and *bone-dust mixed with coal-ashes.* The ashes were sifted, and intimately mixed with the bones, some days before being applied, in the proportion of sixteen bushels of bones and eight of ashes, per acre. The quantity of guano applied was at the rate of three hundred weight per acre upon four drills, two and two together, at an interval of eight drills manured with bones and ashes. Then, at a similar interval, followed two drills, operated upon with guano together with *sulphate of soda,* (Glauber salts,) at the rate of four hundred weight per acre — being the only instance, in the course of these experiments, in which any foreign substance was used with the guano. The turnips were drawn about the end of November; and on a comparison of the weight of the crop on two of the four drills done with *guano alone,* with the produce of the average of four drills, nearly immediately adjoining, manured with *bone-dust and ashes,* the result stood thus (the plants being topped and rooted): —

Manures.	*Produce per Acre.*
GUANO, alone, ...	23 cwt. 2 st.
Guano and sulphate of soda, ...	23 " 0 "
Bone-dust, ...	19 " 2 "

"'In the third experiment, guano was used against *bone-dust alone*, applied, as is usual in that district, at the rate of sixteen bushels per acre. The guano was used at the rate of two hundred weight only per acre. The drills manured with the latter showed a very early superiority, and were ready for the hoe fully eight days earlier than the rest of the field. This more vigorous growth they maintained throughout; and when the turnips (the white stone globe variety) were weighed, on the 22d March, after standing throughout the winter, the result was as follows (the roots and tops being in this instance retained):—

"'Two drills guano, ... 31 cwt. 4 st.
Two " bone-dust, ... 24 cwt. 7 st.'"

"The following table, extracted from the *Scotsman*, is the result of an experiment on a field which had, till the present crop, been in grass from time immemorial. The soil was a dry, friable loam. The turnips were sown on the 20th of May, and lifted and weighed on the 27th of November, 1843.

Kinds and Quantities of Manures used per Acre.	*Price of Manure per Acre.*		*Weight of Turnips without Roots or Tops.*			*Weight of Roots and Tops.*			*Weight of rotten Turnips.*			*Weight of total Produce per Acre.*		
	£	s.	T.	C.	lb.	T.	C.	lb.	T.	C.	lb.	T.	C.	lb.
GUANO, 5 cwts.	2	15	29	17	13	6	12½	11	1	13	17	38	2¾	13
Farm dung, 12 carts, . .	3	12	25	7	8	6	15	6	2	12	13	34	14	27
Bones, 26½ bushels, . .	3	3	25	12½	12	5	1¾	14	0	14	22	31	8½	20
Rape-dust, 12 cwts. . .	3	0	22	19½	22	5	9	0	2	8½	6	30	17¼	0."

Guano has been applied to winter wheat, both in drills and broadcast, and with signal success. It has been applied, likewise, with great success, to grass and pasture land, as the following statement will show:—

"On an eight-acre field, sown with three hundred weight of guano, and three bushels of Italian rye-grass per acre, on the 29th of April, cut on the 3d of August, the produce weighed, when cut, eighteen tons, and when dry and ready for stack, four tons, per acre. Much of this crop was upwards of five feet long. So rapid was the growth, that, fifty hours after cutting, it had again sprung up to the height of three and one eighth inches. With such grass, and such manure, so easily convertible into liquid, I see no reason to doubt that the cottager, with his five roods of land, could supply his house with vegetables, and cow with winter and summer food, thereby providing for his family an almost entire subsistence."

It has been questioned whether its effects will be permanent. I can only answer, that I have seen its obviously beneficial effects three years after its application upon grass. How much longer its efficacy may be expected to continue, experience only can determine.

Several kinds of guano have been brought into Great Britain; but the great distinction is between that from the Island of Ichaboe, on the coast of Africa, and that from the islands in the Pacific. The former seems entirely deficient in uric acid, and consequently lacks what is deemed a valuable element in vegetation. The comparative value of the two in public estimation, and in the opinion of a distinguished chemist, is supposed to be as four to five. The supply from Ichaboe is said to be exhausted, the enormous quantity of five to six hundred thousand tons having been taken, as is stated, from that single island.

I should do wrong to say that guano is always successful. There were many complaints this year of its failure, attributed to the excessive droughts which prevailed at the beginning of the season. A farmer likewise, in Cambridgeshire, communicates to the Royal Agricultural Society, in their last journal, his failure in two successive applications of it to crops of barley. In neither instance does any advantage appear to have been gained. He attributes this to something in the nature or character of the soil; but this, without further trials, must be set down as wholly conjectural.

It is quite proper, likewise, that I should urge upon the farmers of the United States, that, however auspicious and brilliant may be the promises which guano holds out to them, they must not overlook the resources for enriching their own lands within their own reach. The following statement will strengthen this advice.

Philip Pusey, Esq., M. P., than whom, I believe, wherever his character for intelligent, accurate, and philosophical observation is known, it will be universally admitted, there is no higher agricultural authority in England, informed me that, the last season, he carted to the headlands of one of his fields a quantity of loam, mixed with coal-ashes and rubbish, and, having formed it into a bed, heaped upon it a quantity of barn manure, from the drippings of which the loam, &c., became completely saturated. Upon the application of this to the land for a crop of turnips, by the side of the same crop manured with three hundred weight of guano, the advantage was very greatly in favor of the former.

Mr. James Smith, of Deanston, states that a friend of his manured three acres; the first with fifteen tons of stable-dung, cost £4; the second acre with three hundred weight of guano, cost £1, 6s.; the third acre with eight tons of liquid manure, cost 2s. 6d.; and the crop on the last was far the best. Dr. Playfair was kind enough to communicate to me this statement.

In an admirable lecture, delivered by the last-named active and intelligent friend of an improved agriculture, at the meeting of the Royal Agricultural Society, that gentleman saw fit to state that one pound of urine contained materials for producing one pound of wheat; and that the effete matter which runs into the Thames, annually, from the city of London, amounts to

1,095,000,000 pounds in one year,

and contains nitrogen sufficient to produce

1,600,000,000 pounds of wheat,
1,800,000,000 pounds of barley;

and, calculating this waste at a moderate value, for agricultural purposes, London suffers a loss of £1,000,000 sterling, or 5,000,000 dollars per year.

These curious statistics will, I know, give no offence to any sensible person; and they may suggest considerations of the very highest moment to the rising cities of the United States, where the sanatary and economical arrangements are not completed, and in many cases not begun. They especially enforce upon every individual farmer the duty of examining and husbanding, with a miserly frugality, all the resources of his own farm, even the most inconsiderable and humble. They have, I may be allowed to say, a far higher use by leading the reflecting and serious mind to admire and adore the never-ending circles of the divine beneficence; the mixed and wonderful compensations and mutual subserviences which pervade the whole system of nature; and, above all, that constant miracle of miracles, going on continually in the vegetable world, by which the most worthless and the most offensive substances are returned again to bless the animal creation, in those substantial products by which life is sustained, and comfort every where diffused, in fruits most delicious to the senses, and in plants, and flowers, which, in their variety, and beauty, and wonderful glory and splendor, infinitely surpass the highest triumphs of human art and luxury.

I think proper here to subjoin several analyses of guano with which I have been favored by a most accurate chemist, Mr. E. F. Teschemacher, to whose unremitted kindness, in various forms, I am most deeply obliged. Indeed, when I think of the debts which I have incurred, in this way, and which have been forced upon me, on this side of the water, I fear nothing is left for me but to take advantage of the act of general bankruptcy, with the mortification of feeling, from the number of my creditors, how very small a dividend can be made.

"Dear Sir:

"I have taken the first moment I had to spare, to fulfil my promise of giving you some details relative to guanoes — especially the analyses of the various kinds imported within the last eighteen months into this country, which have come under my cognizance. The analyses were performed by me during the course of my business, and are so arranged that a comparison may be easily made between them. Upon comparing these analyses with those of other analysts, I find them generally to agree in all their essential characters.

"*No.* 1. *Peruvian.*

"100 parts consist of 9 parts of ammonia, combined with phosphoric, carbonic, uric, and organic acids, forming, of

Ammoniacal salts, . . .	40
Animal organic matter, .	6½
Sulphate and muriate of potash and soda, . . .	11½
Phosphate of lime and magnesia, ...	29½
Sand, ...	1
Water, ...	11½
	100

"The Peruvian contains 11½ parts of uric acid.

"*No.* 2. *Bolivian.*

"100 parts contain 10½ parts ammonia, combined as in No. 1, forming, of

Ammoniacal salts, . . .	36
Animal organic matter, .	5
Sulphate and muriate of potash and soda, . . .	15¾
Phosphate of lime and magnesia, ...	27¾
Sand, ...	1½
Water, ...	14
	100

"The Bolivian contains 3 per cent. of uric acid.

"The uric acid is considered to furnish the crops with additional ammonia, which, after application, is given out by degrees.

"*No.* 3. *Chilian.*

"100 parts containing 3 parts ammonia, combined with phosphoric, oxalic, carbonic, humic, and organic acids, forming, of

Ammoniacal salts, . . .	12½
Animal organic matter, .	2½
Sulphate and muriate of potash and soda, . . .	7½
Phosphate of lime and magnesia, and oxalate lime, .	53
Sand, ...	2
Water, ...	22½
	100

"This guano contains no uric acid.

"*No.* 4. *Ichaboe Guano.*

"100 parts containing 7½ parts ammonia, combined with phosphoric, oxalic, carbonic, and humic acids, forming, of

Ammoniacal salts, . . .	26½
Animal organic matter, .	7½
Sulphate and muriate of potash, and phosphate potash, ...	10
Phosphate lime, and magnesia, and oxalate lime,	30
Sand, ...	1
Water, ...	25
	100

"Contains no uric acid.

"*No.* 5. *Angra de Pequena.*

"100 parts contain 5 parts ammonia, combined as in No. 4, forming, of

Ammoniacal salts, . . .	20
Animal organic matter, . .	5
Sulphate and muriate of potash, and phosphate potash, ...	11
Phosphate of lime and magnesia, and oxalate lime, .	32
Sand, ...	2
Water, ...	30
	100

"No uric acid.

"*No.* 6. *Possession Island.*

"Very like that from Angra de Pequena, but very lumpy.

"No uric acid.

"*No.* 7. *Pedestal Point.*

"100 parts contain 4½ parts ammonia, combined as in No. 4, forming, of

Ammoniacal salts, . . .	14
Animal organic matter, .	6
Sulphate and muriate of potash, and phosphate potash, ...	6½
Phosphate of lime and magnesia, and oxalate lime,	37
Sand, ...	7
Water, ...	29½
	100

"No uric acid.

"*No.* 8. *Bird Islands; Algoa Bay.*

" 100 parts contain 2½ parts ammonia, combined as in No. 4, forming, of

Ammoniacal salts,	10½
Animal organic matter,	8½
Sulphate and muriate of potash,	2½
Phosphate of lime and magnesia, (no oxalate lime,)	62
Sand,	1½
Water,	15
	100

"No. 8 contains no uric acid.

"No. 1 to 3 are South American guanoes.

"No. 4 to 8 are African guanoes.

"I have examined guano from other localities, but as I do not know those localities, I have omitted them in the list.

"*Guano Testing.*

" 1. A small portion, about 100 grains, mixed and rubbed with 10 parts of chalk to 1 part of quick-lime, should give out a strong smell of ammonia; and on holding over the mixture a glass rod moistened with muriatic acid, a dense white vapor should be given off. If this effect does not take place, the guano will contain very little ammoniacal salts.

"2. 100 grains guano, heated to redness in a Hessian crucible, should leave a white ash. This white ash should be nearly soluble in dilute muriatic acid. The residue should not exceed 10 grains; in good guano, the residue would be only 1 or 2 grains.

" The quantity of white ash will vary from 30 to 60 per cent., according to the nature of the guano.

"Yours truly,

"E. F. Teschemacher.

"No. 2 *Park Terrace*, Highbury,
24 *January*, 1845."

I add to these some analyses forwarded to me from the Edinburgh Agricultural Chemical Association, by my esteemed friend, Mr. John P. Norton.

"*Two Guanoes from Ichaboe.*

	No. I.	No. II.
Water,	20.46	18 00
Organic matter and ammoniacal salts,	44.96	52.60
Sulphate of soda and potash, with common salt,	4.49	4.89
Phosphates of lime and magnesia,	27.31	19.22
Carbonate of lime,	0.07	4.83
Silicious matter,	2.15	
3 per cent. free ammonia in No. I.	99.44	99.54

"These are fair samples of the Ichaboe guanoes. Their only defect is too much water.

"*Two South American Guanoes.*

	Peruvian.	Bolivian.
Water and free ammonia,	3.14	5.34
Organic matter and ammoniacal salts,	63.52	58.00
Sulphate and muriate of soda,	5.02	6.37
Phosphate of lime, and a little phosphate of magnesia,	22.20	25.27
Carbonates of lime and magnesia,	4.96	3.95
Insoluble silicious matter,	1.16	1.07
	100.00	100.00.

"These are both most excellent guanoes. The small proportion of water is remarkable, and the large quantity of organic matter and ammoniacal salts. This first, and then the phosphates, are the criteria of value. Carbonate of lime, sulphate and muriate of soda, &c., are valuable manures, but may be bought lower than £6 or £8 per ton.

"*Artificial Guano, (Potter's.)*

Water, ...	14.55
Organic matter, ...	17.32
Salts soluble in water, consisting of common salt and gypsum, with a small quantity of potash and ammoniacal salts, ...	40.43
Phosphate and carbonate of lime, ...	11.61
Coarse sand, with bits of gypsum, ...	16.06
	99.97

"This, therefore, contains 30 per cent. of water and sand. One by the same maker, previously examined, had about 30 per cent. of sand alone."

The following is from a chemist of the highest scientific character, Dr. Ure:—

"Reserving, for the present, the more particular analyses, the following may be offered as the average result of those I have made of genuine guano, in reference to its agricultural value:—

"Azotized organic matter, including urate of ammonia, and capable of affording from 8 to 17 per cent. of ammonia by slow decomposition in the soil, . . .	50.0
Water, ...	11.0
Phosphate of lime, ...	25.0
Ammonia, phosphate of magnesia, phosphate of ammonia, and oxalate of ammonia, containing from 4 to 9 per cent. of ammonia, ...	13.0
Silicious matter from the crops of the birds, ...	1.0
	100.0."

A North Devon Steer.

The Property of Mr. Thos. Umbers, of Wappenbury, near Royal Leamington Spa, for which the First Prize and Silver Medal were awarded in Class Three at the Smithfield Cattle Show, Decr. 1843.

EUROPEAN AGRICULTURE.

FOURTH REPORT.

XLVI.—GENERAL CONSIDERATIONS.

The great incentive to all agricultural improvement is profit. The man who is satisfied with a bare subsistence will do little towards making his condition better. It is one of the prominent blessings of civilization, that it multiplies human wants and desires to such a degree as to call out all the powers of the body and mind to supply them. In proportion as civilization is advanced, human wants increase. From necessities we proceed to indulgences, from indulgences to luxuries; until what were at first indulgences and luxuries become themselves transformed into necessities. Out of these spring other indulgences and other luxuries, which go on by a sort of reduplication or spontaneous generation, to which as yet no limits have been reached, and we have reason to think that none are very near. When one class or species fails, or passes away, others come into its place, like sprouts springing from the living stump of a tree which has been cut down; or like the countless plants which come up where a single plant has been suffered to ripen and tc shed its seed.

Besides this effect of use or indulgence in increasing, and in giving an insatiableness to, human wants, there is an original and native element of the human mind, which the phrenologists designate as acquisitiveness, or a desire to obtain. This, when joined with secretiveness, becomes a desire to keep or to accumulate as well as to obtain, which, though liable to abuse, yet, like all other original tendencies of our nature, is designed for good. This operates as a continual stimulus to exertion, and rouses energies, and awakens an ambition, and strengthens and produces a perseverance and tenacity of purpose, which, in the creation and accumulation of wealth, lie at the foundation of most of the great improvements of society, and again in its turn creates a power or instrument of influence, which itself commands thousands of minds, and thousands of hands, to unite with an energy similar to its own in the accomplishment of its own objects.

All this does good; prevents the waters of society from becoming stagnant and unwholesome, and keeps them in a state of continued and healthful agitation. If human wants, having a sort of polypus vitality, are constantly increased by being supplied, it is no less true that the powers of the human mind and body are always increased and strengthened by being properly exerted. As the mind becomes enlightened and expanded, it is tempted to extend its dominion over matter and over other minds. In the spirit of an ambition never knowing enough, it goes out "conquering and to conquer." It invades other dominions of nature, and makes every where the elements of the material world subservient to its purposes.

It is said that an Indian, when, on a certain occasion, he was brought from the solitude and destitution of his forest-home into a busy manufacturing town, and saw windmills with their sails inflated by the air, and water-wheels driven by the running stream, and steam-engines impelled by an agent of which before he had scarcely conceived, and the furnaces where, by the applications of fire, the iron-stones were made to flow in liquid streams, and to take the forms which the workman's pleasure dictated, exclaimed, in his amazement, that the white man made every thing work for him — the fire, the air, the water. Nothing could have been more natural than his surprise. Thus it is that human genius devotes itself to science; and every step in science imparts a disposition and capacity to advance farther. It invents language and signs, that it may transfix, and hold fast, thoughts, and facts, and discoveries, for further use. It employs the powers of nature to increase, and multiply, and strengthen, other powers, and thus is constantly extending its sovereignty over mind and matter, and assuming more and more to itself, in its humble capacities, the character of a creator. Thus it is that the fruitful powers of nature are called forth; the means of animal life and subsistence extended; the productions of the earth increased, diversified, and improved. Under an improved cultivation, ten men find ample and luxurious support, where, before, one would have starved. New vegetables and new fruits are brought into existence and use, or others rendered more abundant; and with the increase of vegetable, the increase of animal life is immeasurably extended. Thus it is that new forms of comfort, luxury, and ornament appear with corresponding wants on the part of those who are to enjoy them; new means of subsistence are supplied; new forms of habitation are demanded; new articles of clothing are provided. All the wonders of art spring up; the multiplied embellishments of refined life present themselves; and the progress of society is in all respects advanced and continually advancing.

All this grows out of that original element of the human mind to which I early alluded, — acquisitiveness, the desire of gain, or advance, or betterment, or profit, — which thus stimulates men to the continual improvement of their condition. But all this, we are told by some men, springs from selfishness, and they denounce it as criminal. Their denunciations are without reason, and they make no just discrimination between the different conditions of a principle which in its original nature is wholesome and useful, and becomes wrong and pernicious only by its extravagance and abuse.

What would man be without any regard to his own interest? It is an instinctive impulse which prompts us to take care of our lives. Self-preservation is the first law of our nature. But the same law implies the most diligent care of our health, and all that varied and extended provision for health and comfort, necessary to the continuance of life, and to its continuance under circumstances most favorable to its activity, usefulness, and reasonable enjoyment. But who is to take care of us, if we do not take care of ourselves? If every man, instead of providing for his own wants, gave himself up to the care of his neighbor it is not easy to see that any advantage would be gained by it. Every one would find that, besides multiplied inconveniences, the provision for himself would be far less complete and satisfactory than when under his own immediate superintendence and control. The evils of selfishness do not lie in a man's appropriating to himself that to which he has a just claim, and which he may enjoy without injury to his neighbor, but in the appropriation of that to which he has no fair title, and which he cannot so appropriate without injury to his neighbor, and without an invasion of the just rights of other men. That meanness of selfishness, which some men exhibit, and which seeks the exclusive enjoyment of whatever it can accumulate, irrespective of the comfort, and at the expense of the toil, of others, — that dog-in-the-manger selfishness, which accumulates without imparting, and seems to experience its highest zest in contrasting its own fulness with the destitution and misery of others, — is as odious as it is criminal. On the other hand, that rational regard to one's own interest which prompts a man continually to take the best possible care of his body and mind; to secure his health, that his physical activity and vigor may be increased, and to cultivate and improve his mind, that it may resemble, in its fruitfulness, a well-tilled and enriched field; to increase likewise his estate, and embellish and adorn it; and to accumulate wealth that he may multiply the sources of good to others, stimulate others to exertion, and lead to those generous improvements which wealth is capable of producing, and to which it may be beneficially applied, — this is a sentiment, which, so far from being to be condemned, is to be commended and cherished as the great instrument and spring, as much of social and public, as of personal and individual good.

Improvement of every kind lies in action. The happiness which never satiates or wearies is to be found in the consciousness of progress. Who that has experienced a dead calm at sea, — not a breath of wind to ruffle the waves, the vessel tossing from one side to the other like a cork upon the water, the rigging shaking, the sails flapping, the crew idle and listless, no progress reported, and the whole company wearied, impatient, desponding, ill-humored, — and compares this with a brisk gale blowing, — every rope straightened, every sail spread and filled, the planks of the ship creaking as it were with intense exertion, the masts bending almost to breaking under their burden, the crew awake, the passengers all animated with hope and delighted with the certainty of progress, and the noble ship, with her priceless cargo of human life and fortune, moving like a thing of life over the billows, and, as she ploughs her proud path through, as it were, a flood of liquid silver, throwing the glittering and brilliant tresses of jewels from her neck, — who has had this experience, and will not feel how little to be desired, either for the body or the mind, for health or enjoyment, for the animal or the moral man, is a state of inanity and sluggish repose?

The poets — those ethereal beings, who deal in fiction, and whose imagination becomes a sort of *ignis fatuus*, a "Will-of-the-wisp," leading them they know not where — love to descant upon the Golden Ages or the Paradisiacal state, when men, without care for food or clothing, had nothing to do, but, under a calm sky and a soft air, to lie down on banks of fragrant flowers, by the side of gurgling streams, under the shade of spreading aromatic trees, and let the richest fruits fall into their laps, and listen to the Æolian strains of the winds whispering among the branches, and the melodious songs of birds of the gayest plumage fluttering around them, and abandon themselves to the charms of a purely animal and sensual existence. But what reflecting man would desire such a life as this for himself, and would not feel an intolerable restlessness, and especially a mortifying consciousness that it falls, one may almost say, infinitely below the capacities of his nature and the purposes of his being?

I cannot look out of my window, where I am now writing, in Trafalgar Square at Charing Cross, without seeing a world of indescribable life, and bustle, and activity. The night in London is seldom longer than from half past two o'clock until four o'clock in the morning, when the flood-gates begin gently to open, and gradually the rushing torrent of life pours through in a turbid and boisterous flood. After the waters begin to move with force, there is perhaps not a minute in the day when more than a thousand, or rather thousands, of people cannot be counted from my window. Here are carriages without number, from the splendid chariot with its noble horses, its gorgeous equipage, its liveried servants, and its precious cargo of figured porcelain, down to the humble gig, the dray-horse, the wheelbarrow, and the donkey-cart with its precious load of garbage or of dog's-meat. Here are shops without number, replete with all the most exquisite productions of science, genius, art, and mechanical contrivance, and full of buyers and sellers. Here are crowds of men, women, and children, passing and repassing, sauntering, walking, running, and jostling each other, waiting upon and being waited upon, entertaining and being entertained, carrying and being carried, laboring and enjoying. Here are caravansaries for the travellers, banks for merchants, monuments to heroes and princes, schools of science, galleries of art, and temples to God, adorned with the finest embellishments of architectural skill, and lifting their beautiful spires to the skies, as if, from the glittering vane upon the top, they would emulate the brilliancy of a fixed star, and as if, like the star which stood over the sacred spot of a divine nativity, they would present Heaven's brilliant emblem of mercy to encourage man's faith and piety. Here, too, are fountains of water throwing up their liquid treasures over their heads, and coming down in constant showers of brilliants. Here are men, and the busy and exciting concerns of men, under all the varying aspects of human life and activity. Here are the magnificent triumphs of human art and skill; here are the fruits of centuries of toil and labor; and here is one continued intensity of action, as if it were the very heart of the great world beating with violent emotion. But none of this, properly speaking, is mechanical; it is all intellectual; it is all under the dominion of mind to excite, to urge, to direct, to control it. There is a far mightier power at work within than appears without. If you could take off the roof of some of these moving tabernacles; if you could see what is there lying beneath, the burning thoughts, the anxious desires, the resolute purposes, the beating affections, and the fiery passions, which are there at work, and as it were mingling in one common flame, you would indeed see objects more curious and wonderful, an exhibition far more extraordinary, than any thing ever before presented to your senses, or even to your imagination. But what is the secret spring, the great power-wheel which sets all these things in motion, which excites and quickens all this activity? It is acquisition, the desire to acquire subsistence, pleasure, profit, wealth, or power.

Would it be better that all this should cease, and society become a mere stagnant pool? Would it be better that all the necessity of labor should be taken away, and men should have no other destiny than to repose in quiet, with all their wants supplied, and all their senses gratified; and that down couches should be spread round these gushing fountains, and instead of water they should send forth the delicious juices of the grape, — though perhaps, to suit the English taste, it should be ale or beer, or what is vulgarly called "half and half," for that is the Englishman's nectar, — and that men should have only to drink it in at pleasure, or, in common parlance, to enjoy themselves? I think not. I believe Heaven could send no greater curse than to exempt mankind from all necessity of labor.

If we look at the condition of the inhabitants of tropical countries, where the richest fruits of the earth grow spontaneously, where clothing and shelter are scarcely required, and where men are exempted from the necessity of labor, we shall find them sunk in sensuality, abandoned to animal indulgences, and in intellectual and moral condition at the lowest scale. If we compare them with the inhabitants of temperate regions, the disparity will be seen to be great, but vastly in favor of the latter. The intellect is sharpened, as well as the muscular vigor increased, in proportion to the difficulties with which it has to struggle, and the labor by which it is taxed, provided that labor is not excessive and unnatural. Though there may be a severity of toil wholly discouraging, and difficulties which are perfectly hopeless and insurmountable, — which cases we must of course except, — yet, in point of actual enjoyment, there cannot be a doubt on which side the advantage lies; and that the necessity of exertion, and every wholesome stimulus to useful and honest labor, is a blessing from Heaven.

The condition of the Irish peasantry likewise strongly illustrates and confirms these truths. Nothing can exceed the destitution and wretchedness in which millions of these people live. I have been into many of their cabins, and have seen the habitations of thousands and thousands of these miserable people; and, in regard to external accommodations, I can scarcely think that there is upon earth a lower condition of human existence. Certainly the wigwam of an American savage may often be regarded with envy for its comforts, compared with many an Irish cabin. I have been into those which were mere holes dug into the side of a peat bog, and have put my hand upon the wet and velvety walls, that I might be certain my senses did not deceive me. In these caves, covered with sticks, and straw, and sods; without chimney, window, or floor; with a fire of turf slowly burning upon the ground and filling the place with smoke; without bed, table, chair, or plate, or knife, or fork; with, indeed, no article of furniture save a kettle in which to boil their potatoes, and a basket in which to take them up; with no other seat but a bit of dried turf or peat, and no bed to lie down upon but a flock of straw, which was frequently shared in common by the children and the pig, — I have found a crowded family, with rags for clothing that scarcely hid their nakedness, living from one year's end to the other upon potatoes and water, and never more than once a year tasting either bread or meat.

This is not the place for me to enter into the political considerations connected with this condition of things in a country which, in respect to its climate and soil, and resources for useful industry, and means not only of comfortable subsistence to a population quadruple of that which exists there, but in means of abundance and wealth, is eminently favored of Heaven. But I refer to the example of Ireland to show that where persons can remain satisfied under privation and extreme penury; where they are content to live upon the meanest fare, and to occupy habitations scarcely fit for the shelter of the lowest of the brute creation; where, with only a mud-cabin and a potato patch, without even money enough to pay the wedding-fee, (for this is made out by the contributions of friends on the occasion,) they are willing to take upon themselves the responsibilities of marriage, and become the founders of families to be born only to inherit a similar destitution and wretchedness, it is difficult to find motives to rouse them to exertion and industry. Until a revolution can be effected in their feelings, and a set of wants created within them, any strong hopes of the improvement of their condition seem idle.

The wants of men, then, are the great incentives to exertion; and the stimulus of profit, the desire of gain and of accumulation, is that which induces enterprise and effort, which excites inquiry and leads to knowledge, which prompts to labor, and thus urges men on to new acquisitions and continual progress. We may appeal to higher motives than self-interest, where there are minds capable of appreciating a higher class of motives; but it is absurd to consider inferior motives as wrong, where better cannot be had; and self-interest and the desire of gain are not only innocent, but commendable, where we do not seek gain or pursue our own interests to the injury and loss of others.

I fear I may be thought to have gone out of my way by such a preface as this; yet I hope I may have the indulgence of my readers for an honest endeavor to enliven a subject of dry details with matter which, though it may seem distant from, is certainly not irrelevant to my purpose. I have not always found it a hinderance, though it may appear like an interruption, in making a tour of business, sometimes to dismount, and, throwing the reins over the neck of my horse, that he too might regale himself by the roadside, lie down on a green bank, under a quiet shade, by some sparkling stream, and abandon myself for a while to the charming thoughts which then come fluttering round the mind, like fireflies upon a meadow in a quiet evening of summer; or at other times to leap the fence, and rush into the fields or the neighboring forest, and return with a handful of golden grain, or a bouquet of wild flowers gathered fresh from the bosom of nature, and showing the exuberant bounty of Heaven, or the triumphs of artificial culture. I could then mount my horse, refreshed by the indulgence, and pursue my journey with new speed, with senses more alive to the beauties of the country through which I was passing, and with a more grateful sense of the goodness of the great Author of nature, who, by this varied mixture, by alternations of light and shade, of labor and rest, of toil and indulgence, and by an endless succession and diversity of objects, makes life, which would be otherwise deplorably monotonous and tedious, not merely agreeable, but delightful.

I should be happy, in my humble way, in any degree to accomplish so desirable a purpose in respect to my kind readers, and render the journey which we have undertaken to travel together as pleasant as I could wish to make it useful and instructive.

Some men, very much addicted to great refinements in casuistry, and especially in respect to the motives of human actions, would condemn every motive, but such as are purely disinterested, as criminal. I agree with them that the highest of human actions must have its origin in the highest and purest of all motives; but I cannot deny the innocence, and, more than that, the positive virtue and worth of many actions and pursuits, that are prompted by motives which some persons would designate as inferior, but which, nevertheless, have their origin in our own nature and constitution. Self-interest, profit, accumulation, are all of them reasonable and commendable objects, when they do not lead us to invade or infringe upon the rights of others, and when our accumulations are used foı useful ends.

I am anxious to vindicate the profession of agriculture from every aspersion which may be cast upon it, and to contribute my mite to place it in that rank, in the scale of human pursuits, which it may justly claim for itself. I may say, with Bacon, "that it has the divine sanction," for in the beginning God placed man upon the earth to cultivate and make it fruitful. I may claim for it, further, that it is an innocent pursuit; that it can do no injury to any one; and that it invades no man's just rights, and prejudices no man's safety, health, peace, or reasonable enjoyment. I will add to this, that it is a beneficent employment. Whoever cultivates the earth, and covers it with rich and golden crops, renders it more beautiful; whoever causes the earth to yield its fruits, increases the means of human comfort and subsistence; and in proportion as this cultivation is improved and skilful, and by such improvement, and such skill, the products of the earth are many times increased, so the means of human subsistence and comfort, and of subsistence and comfort to a very large portion of the brute creation, are correspondingly extended.

I will make no invidious comparisons between agriculture and other professions and pursuits of life; but certainly none is more innocent, more honest, more useful, or more rational. That happens, in respect to agriculture, which does not equally appear in many professions, that its improvements cannot be monopolized; they are of necessity exposed. Emulation or competition, so often productive of the worst results in many pursuits of life, in the improvement of agriculture can produce nothing but good.

XLVII.—AGRICULTURE AS A COMMERCIAL PURSUIT.

Men, then, may lawfully pursue agriculture under the stimulus of profit. In many cases, the gains of one man are made at the expense or loss of another. The celebrated Madame Roland used to say "she was always sorry to hear that a man had made a good bargain, because she knew, in that case, that some person must have made a poor one." It is not so in agriculture. The more a man increases his wealth by increasing the products of the earth by a skilful cultivation, so much the more is the whole community benefited, excepting only where human laws interpose to intercept the widest possible diffusion of the bounties of Heaven.

Agriculture, in order to excellence, requires as much the stimulus of profit as any other pursuit in life. In England and Scotland, it has had that stimulus. It has had governmental protection and indulgence, the propriety and justice of which are questionable with many men of distinguished wisdom, observation, and patriotism, and the expediency of which is capricious, being dependent upon circumstances ever liable to fluctuation and change. The protection which it has received has been in laws prohibiting, under heavy duties, the importation of agricultural produce from foreign countries, and affording relief from various forms of specific taxation, to which other professions or conditions are subjected. The horses, dogs, servants, and carriages, of all other classes of the community here are taxed; but those of the farmer are exempted from taxation. In the tax upon income, the farmer's income is fairly assumed from the rent which he pays; but in levying the assessment, only half his rent is reckoned, so that a farmer paying in fact £400 rent, would be considered, for the purpose of taxation, as paying only £200. In some respects, it must be confessed that what is called "protection" is of a suicidal character. A duty is laid, for example, upon imported clover-seed, whereas the amount produced in the country, or likely to be produced under all the encouragement which its cultivation receives, bears a very small proportion to the amount used by the farmers, and used in fact by no other persons; so that the duty paid upon this article is a heavy tax upon the many farmers, for the exclusive benefit of the few. Great complaint is likewise made, by the farmers, of the introduction of fat cattle from abroad, which come into injurious competition with their own stock, and of the admission of foreign salted provisions. At the same time, the very provision upon which these cattle might, if imported lean, be fatted at home, is prohibited. The Indian corn from the United States can be admitted only by the payment of a duty which is almost prohibitory. It cannot be grown in England, though, under some extraordinary circumstances in accidental localities, it has occasionally ripened. If, instead of importing fat cattle from the Continent, to supply their markets, they would import lean cattle, and at the same time import Indian corn under a low or nominal duty, to fatten them with, (and it would be difficult to find a substance which, in proportion to its cost, is more nutritious,) it is obvious that, besides the profit upon the labor of fattening these cattle, they would have the great advantages of their manure — certainly a most serious consideration.*

Agriculture in England appears altogether as a commercial pursuit. Where heavy amounts of rent are to be periodically and punctually paid, men are compelled to look carefully at their expenditures, purchases, and contracts, and their pecuniary results. It is by no means so with us in the United States, where most farmers are their own landlords and the owners of the estates on which they live, and where, if their sales from their farms are sufficient to meet the expenses of labor, the light taxes of the government, and those supplies for their families which the farm itself does not yield, they feel themselves at least secure, if they are not satisfied. I design presently to give some example of the manner in which farm accounts are kept here by the most careful farmers, and which show all the exactness of mercantile transactions. Indeed, it must be so, or they would become involved in inextricable confusion, which would surely terminate in bankruptcy and ruin. I know farmers here who pay their two hundred, four hundred, six hundred, and one thousand pounds' rent; I have been credibly informed of a farmer in Scotland, or on the borders of Scotland and England,

---

* The alteration of the tariff, allowing the admission of fat cattle, and foreign cheese, &c., under a reduced duty, does not appear, at present, to have produced so great results as was expected, whatever may be the case hereafter.

The report made to Parliament this present session, (1845,) returns, as imported into the country from abroad the last year, of cattle, 2,241, (which, if we suppose them to average 800 pounds per head, would give only about three fourths of a pound of meat to each individual;) of sheep, 1,063, (which, at 80 pounds per head, — a large average, — would give half an ounce of mutton to each individual;) of cheese, 11,000 tons, (which would give about one pound per individual.) At the same time, the minister in Parliament states that, during the last year, the population of the kingdom has increased by 380,000!!

whose annual rent, at one time, was seven thousand pounds, or thirty-five thousand dollars; and it is quite obvious how disastrous must be the consequences, if such properties are managed otherwise than with the most scrupulous commercial exactness.

It cannot be denied that our habits in this respect are altogether different from what they should be; that perhaps a majority of our farmers keep no accounts whatever, and many who keep accounts exhibit only imperfect and slovenly examples. It is said, — and it is certainly much to his honor, — that a distinguished individual here, possessing immense estates, but who had become somewhat perplexed, not to say embarrassed, in his pecuniary affairs, and whose education had not been, in this matter, of a character to enable him to manage his affairs to advantage, employed an accurate accountant in his house for some time, for the sole purpose of learning from him the science of book-keeping by double entry. With a natural love of order, and a firm resolution, having acquired this knowledge, he was soon enabled to bring order out of confusion, and rescue himself from embarrassment, and its attendant and inevitable mortifications. Such an example as this is certainly worth recording.

Many farmers, more systematic than others, keep not only an account of cost and expenditure, and the amount of sales and profits, in the form of a cash account, but likewise a regular account with every field and every crop, and I had almost said with every animal, taking, as every careful trader or merchant will do, a yearly account of stock at a fair valuation. Every thing is accounted for; not so much as a quart of milk is used in the family, but it is charged at the current price. I should be doing great injustice not to say that I know many examples of such carefulness in my own country. Besides the great satisfaction springing from this exactness, the sense of security and integrity, which it brings with it, is invaluable.

XLVIII. — MARKETS. CATTLE MARKETS.

The English farmers have great advantages in their markets and exchanges; and in this matter, to a certain extent, we ought to follow them. I do not say these markets are an unmixed good; but the benefits arising from them, I am convinced, greatly preponderate over the evils; and, taking advantage of the long experience of others, some of these evils we may either remedy or avoid. It would prove highly beneficial to our farmers if they could have certain established markets for the sale of their produce when it is ready for sale; if prices could be fairly adjusted and equalized; and especially if the markets could be for cash; and that credit, in all cases excepting for very short periods, could be abolished. It would be equally useful to them to know where they could buy as well as where they could sell; for they often want lean or store stock for fattening, a change of seed for sowing, horses for farm service, young stock for grazing, and cows for dairy use.

With the exception of three or four of our large towns, — as Boston, New York, and Philadelphia, — we have no established cattle market in the country; and markets such as Brighton near Boston, and the Bull's Head near New York, are almost exclusively for the sale of fat cattle, sheep, and swine. Our farmers sell, as they can, to agents or purchasers travelling through the country, and buy as they can, and where, by chance, after taking, in many cases, long and expensive journeys, they may find the stock which they need. In frequent cases, stock, both cattle and swine, are driven through the country and sold to those who wish to purchase, as accident may direct. A wool fair or market, is not, within my knowledge, held in the country; nor a corn or grain market.* In the purchase of wool, agents scour the country, and in general the farmers are quite at their mercy. In respect to grain, the farmer carries his wheat, or other grain, to the miller or the trader, and must make the best bargain that he can. In such case, in the first place, there is no competition; and no possibility of calculating the quantities on hand for sale; and no mode of fixing any general or equal price; and, indeed, no

* Howard Street, in Baltimore, affords the only place in the United States resembling an exclusive market for the sale of grain or flour; and this is only attended by individual purchasers, and is not a meeting of farmers, grain-dealers, and millers, coming together on particular days in the week, and at a particular hour in the day, to exhibit samples, to collect and impart information respecting the grain prospects of the year, to discuss prices, and to afford to all parties the advantages of comparison and competition.

certainty to the farmer of finding any market at all. These evils might be remedied, and a change effected, to the great advantage of buyers and sellers, by the adoption of the system of weekly or periodical markets, which prevails throughout England and Scotland. Here are wool fairs, for the sale of wool, of which samples are exhibited; and corn and grain markets, where wheat, barley, oats, rye, beans, and peas, samples of which are exhibited, are sold; and markets for the sale of fat cattle, and markets for the sale of lean cattle, and markets for the sale of horses, and markets for the sale of sheep and lambs, and markets for the sale of cheese and butter; these markets sometimes uniting several objects, or otherwise limited to some single object.

I have attended several of these markets, and some general account of them may have an interest with my readers.

XLIX. — FALKIRK TRYST.

The largest cattle market in the kingdom, uniting sheep and cattle, takes place three times a year, — on the second Tuesday in August, September, and October, — at Falkirk in Scotland, about equidistant from Edinburgh and Glasgow. This is called the Falkirk Tryst, and is held on an extensive plain about three or four miles from the town. Here are congregated a vast number of horses, cattle, and sheep, and of buyers and sellers. It was estimated, when I was there, that the number of cattle then on the ground exceeded fifty thousand head, and of sheep seventy thousand; and the banker informed me that the money employed in the negotiation would exceed £300,000, or one million and a half of dollars. The cattle and sheep exhibited at this tryst are almost altogether of the Scotch breeds, and many come from the remote Highlands. They are purchased to be distributed, in the neighborhood and the southern provinces, for wintering, or for fatting for the winter and spring markets. Besides cattle and sheep, a large number of horses are brought for sale at the same time; as many as three thousand horses are sometimes offered for sale, and the field presents the appearance of a grand military display; indeed, I have seldom seen a sight more imposing. For a week or more before the tryst, the roads leading to Falkirk will be found crowded with successive droves of cattle and sheep, proceeding to this central point; and it is extremely curious, on the field, to see with what skill and care the different parties and herds are kept together by themselves. In this matter, the shepherds are greatly assisted by their dogs, who appear endowed with a sagacity almost human, and almost to know every individual belonging to their charge. They are sure, with an inflexible pertinacity, to follow and bring back a deserter to the flock. Purchasers come in great numbers from various parts of the kingdom. Some cattle are bought to be re-sold at other and smaller markets. The larger number are bought in order to be fed or fatted on the arable farms at the south. Cattle which have thus been driven from the extreme north are afterwards to be found even in Cornwall, at the Land's End.

The sales in these cases are, of course, for cash. Bankers are always present, or near at hand, to facilitate the transactions. Here, at a distance little less than four hundred miles from London, bankers go down from London, carrying their funds with them, and occupying, during the time of the market, (which continues at least four days,) a temporary stand or office in the field.

L.—THE BALLINASLOE FAIR.

At Ballinasloe, in Ireland, a similar fair is held; though here the fair is usually confined to the sale of sheep, and they sometimes number as many as eighty thousand sheep. A very large fair is held in the southern portions of Scotland, for the sale of lambs, where the collection is immense.

LI.—THE GALWAY FAIR.

A very large fair is held at Galway, Ireland, in the county of Galway, called the Fair of Rose Mount, at which I was present. This was chiefly for the sale of ponies, or horses of a small breed, with some few cattle. On this occasion, the collection of people was surprisingly great; and I could then well understand what was intended by the public meetings in Ireland, called "monster meetings," in respect to which, until I saw this collection of people, I had always supposed the account of the numbers assembled had been much exaggerated. There were here, on this occasion, some cattle and sheep; but there were, also, four thousand ponies, the catching of which, for examination or sale, as they had, in general, neither bridle nor halter, was sufficiently amusing, and I was about to add, sufficiently Irish. The fair was held on the sea-shore, where the receding tide left a large bed of mud. The ponies, when required to be caught, were surrounded and driven into this mud; and here, in a very ignoble way, they were secured, though it was not always without some difficulty they were extracted after being caught.

1. Temperance in Ireland. — There were two circumstances connected with this fair at Rose Mount, a reference to which, though not having an immediate connection with the principal object of my Reports, yet having a direct bearing upon rural manners and customs, may not be considered wholly out of place. Here, as well as at the fair at Donnybrook, where immense numbers of people were congregated, I could observe most distinctly the beneficent effects of that powerful reformatory movement, which, under the ministry of a good man, worthy of the name of an apostle, has effected a glorious moral triumph throughout Ireland, such as the pages of history scarcely record. I cannot say that at either place there was no drinking and no quarrelling; but there was comparatively little; and knowing, from report and from the natural excitableness of the Irish temper, what had been usual on such occasions, I could not but feel how much had been accomplished, when a foreigner might truly say, of such vast and mixed assemblages, they were quiet, orderly, and kind; and a well-behaved man, disposed to keep his elbows

to his own sides, might feel an almost equal security as he would feel in church.

2. The Galway Women. — There was another circumstance, perfectly unique in its character, to which I shall be pardoned for alluding. There was another species of live stock exhibited at the fair, which I cannot say is never seen at such places, but which does not always present itself under the same frank circumstances. The kind nobleman who accompanied me, and who, like many others, noble and simple, whom it has been my good fortune to meet with on this side of the water, left no effort unessayed for my gratification, after looking at the various objects of the fair, asked me, at last, "if I would like to see the girls." I confess my natural diffidence at once took the alarm; and my imagination cast a few furtive glances over the sea at some precious objects I had left behind. However, upon a voyage of curiosity, why should I not see what was to be seen? and, confident that my good friend could have no sinister design, I gave him an affirmative reply. Upon inquiring of one of the trustees, or masters of the fair, "if the girls had come," we were informed they would be there at twelve o'clock. At twelve o'clock we went, as directed, to a part of the ground higher than the rest of the field, where we found from sixty to a hundred young women, well dressed, with good looks and good manners, and presenting a spectacle quite worth any civil man's looking at, and in which, I can assure my readers, there was nothing to offend any civil or modest man's feelings. These were the marriageable girls of the country, who had come to show themselves, on the occasion, to the young men and others who wanted wives; and this was the plain and simple custom of the fair. I am free to say that I saw in the custom no very great impropriety. It certainly did not imply that, though they were ready to be had, any body could have them. It was not a Circassian slave-market, where the richest purchaser could make his selection. They were in no sense of the term on sale; nor did they abandon their own right of choice; but that which is done constantly in more refined society, under various covers and pretences, — at theatres, balls, and public exhibitions; I will say nothing about churches, — was done by these humble and unpretending people in this straightforward manner. Between

the noble duchess, who presents a long train of daughters, rustling in silk, and glittering with diamonds, at the queen's drawing-room, or the ladies of rank and fashion, who appear at public places with all the beauty and splendor of dress and ornament which wealth, and taste, and art, and skill, can supply, meaning nothing else but "Admire me!" and these honest Galway nymphs with their fair complexions and their bright eyes, with their white frilled caps, and their red cloaks and petticoats, — for this is the picturesque costume of that part of the country, — all willing to endow some good man with the richest of all the gifts of Heaven, a good and faithful wife, I can see no essential difference.

> "Let not ambition mock their useful toil,
> Their homely joys, and destiny obscure."

I hope I shall be excused, if I say something more of these Galway women. I never saw a more handsome race of people. I have always been a great admirer of beauty — natural beauty, personal beauty, mental beauty, moral beauty. For what did the Creator make things so beautiful as they are made, but to be admired? For what has he endowed man with an exquisite sense of beauty, but that he may cultivate it, and find in it a source of pleasure and delight? As I have grown older, this sense of beauty — and I deem it a great blessing from Heaven — has become more acute; and every day of my life, the world and nature, nature and art, the animal, the vegetable, and the mineral creation, the heavens and the earth, the fields and flowers, men, women, and children, wit, genius, learning, moral purity and moral loveliness, deeds of humanity, fortitude, patience, heroism, disinterestedness, have seemed to me continually more and more beautiful, as, at the setting of the sun, man looks out upon a world made richer and more glorious by his lingering radiance, and skies lit up with an unwonted gorgeousness and splendor. But the human countenance seems in many cases to concentrate all of physical, of intellectual, and of moral beauty, which can be combined in one bright point. Why should it not, therefore, be admired? In the commingled beams of kindness and good-humor brightening up the whole face, like heat-lightning in summer on the western sky; or in the flashes of genius sparkling in the eyes with a splendor which the fires of no diamond can rival; or in the whole soul of intelligence, and noble thoughts, and heroic resolution, and strong and lofty passion glowing in the countenance, — there is a manifestation of creative power, of divine skill, unrivalled in any spot or portion of the works of God.

The extraordinary personal beauty of these Galway women was not mere imagination on my part, nor the result of any undue susceptibility. I said to the coachman, as we passed through this part of the country, that I never saw a handsomer people. "That," said he, "travellers always remark;" and when I left the country, in casting my eye over a recent book of Travels in Ireland, I found the author's impressions corresponded with my own. Tradition says that a colony of Milesians formerly settled in this part of the country, and that the remains of this race, or the offspring of the intermixture of them with the native tribes, present these results. This is a remarkable fact, and not without its bearing upon one great branch of agricultural improvement.

LII. — SMITHFIELD, LONDON.

The great market for cattle, in England, perhaps the greatest in the world, is at Smithfield, in London. This market is principally for fat cattle and sheep, and for cows. It is held weekly, in the centre, and in one of the most crowded parts, of this great metropolis. Monday is the day of general sale for fat cattle and sheep; Tuesday for hay and straw; Thursday is again a day of sale for hay and straw; and Friday for cattle, sheep, swine, and particularly for the sale of milch cows, and at 2 o'clock for scrub horses and asses. This day is not so large a market as Monday, and embraces the cattle that were left over on the Monday's market.

The market opens at daylight, at all seasons of the year, and closes at 3 o'clock in the afternoon, at which time every thing, sold or unsold, must be removed. The sheep and swine are enclosed in pens, railed in with wood, and containing seldom more than fifteen sheep in a pen. The cattle, as far as the accommodations will admit, are tied, by the horns or neck, to long railings, which extend on the outside of the market-place, and likewise down the centre of the area. Between the rows of animals tied to these rails and facing each other, there is a passage-way; and there are, likewise, open spaces behind them and between them, so as to enable the purchasers to see the stock. In respect to the supernumerary animals, or those for which, for want of room, no tying-place is to be had, they are often driven into small circles, and, by a great deal of severity and cruelty, they are made, after being dreadfully beaten over the head and eyes, to stand with their heads turned in towards the centre of the circle. The poor animals, finding themselves in so novel a situation, stunned with a din and noise which no language can describe, and exhausted by fatigue and terror, are often glad to be let alone, and to remain quiet in situations, into which they may be forced, which would otherwise be scarcely endurable. Man is almost sure to be a tyrant, when possessed with absolute power; and there is good reason to believe that he will have a heavy account to settle hereafter with the brute animals which he has most cruelly abused.*

It is obvious that it would be difficult to make any exact assortment, or classification, of the animals in the case, according to their different breeds. The sheep are placed in one part of the market. The cattle occupy another. The cows, and calves, and swine, occupy other separate positions. But no classification of the beasts into the different breeds of Short-Horns, Herefords, Devons, or West Highlanders, or Scots, is attempted, although, from the fact that individual farmers generally limit themselves to one species of stock, the contributions of different individuals, standing by themselves, present a sort of classification; and so give a better opportunity to an intelligent observer to compare the different breeds with each other.

* It is said that much of the cruelty, which was formerly practised in these cases is now prevented by the influence of the Animal's Friend Society, an association quite numerous, whose exclusive object is to prevent cruelty to dumb beasts, and thus to protect those who are unable to protect themselves. They have numerous agents, and prosecute, without fear or favor, every case of inhumanity, — for it is a great misnomer to call such cases brutality, — which comes under their notice, deserving censure or punishment. It is, undoubtedly, greatly owing to their exertions, that the odious practices of cock-fighting and dog-fighting are now not practised; or, if practised, conducted in the most secret manner.

1. Forms of Business in Smithfield. — It is not here, as it is with us, that a drover goes through the country collecting, on his route, cattle from the different farmers, as he may chance to find them; but usually the farmer himself sends them to Smithfield, where they are put for sale into the hands of an accredited agent, whose commission for sale is established and understood. This commission is not a percentage upon the amount of sale, but so much per head. These, of course, are persons well known, and whose shrewdness and skill are undoubted. In the most extensive transactions of buying and selling, no paper is passed; but the price of the stock on sale being inquired, if the bargain is struck, the buyer and seller merely touch each other's hand, and there is no retraction. It is highly creditable to the commercial character of the country, and to the general integrity which prevails among the persons concerned in this great market, that, as I am informed by an individual familiar for years with the most extensive transactions in this place, a failure to fulfil these engagements, though no paper is passed between the parties, is of very rare occurrence.

In the sale of sheep and cattle, the business is always transacted through an accredited and established salesman, who has his regular commissions upon every animal sold. The sales are always for cash, unless the salesman himself chooses to assume the responsibility of giving credit, and there are always banking houses in the vicinity to render the usual facilities for business.

The customary commission for the sale of an ox of any value is four shillings, or about ninety-six cents; of a sheep eight pence or sixteen cents. The city receives a toll, upon every beast exposed to sale in Smithfield, of one penny per head, and upon sheep at the rate of one shilling or twenty-four cents per score.

The value of the services of an intelligent, experienced, and honest salesman, is very great to the farmer, and much beyond the compensation ordinarily demanded. He is familiar with the state of the market, with the supply to be expected, with the prices generally taken, and with the characters of the persons with whom he has to deal, who know him as well. The farmer, going into the market to sell his cattle for himself, is liable to various impositions, of the extraordinary ingenuity and coolness of which, many experiments will not be necessary to convince him. It might happen, that, instead of returning home with bank notes and sovereigns in his pocket, he might, like Moses in the Vicar of Wakefield, bring back only a quantity of green spectacles.

The state of the market, the current demand, the supply to be expected, together with the state of the dead-meat market, and what supplies of meat already killed are to be expected, are all matters to be taken into calculation. These are all inquired into, and well known to a thoroughly intelligent and experienced salesman, but are very imperfectly understood by any other persons than those who make it their constant business to become acquainted with them. The division of labor is carried to a great extent in all the business pursuits of this great country, and, while it seems unfriendly to that general tact with which persons among us apply themselves to a great variety and diversity of pursuits, must obviously contribute to a high degree of skill or improvement in the particular art or profession where it is applied.

2. Weights and Measures. — Animals in Smithfield are almost always sold on the hoof; yet an estimate is formed of their weight, and the price given is calculated upon the number of pounds the animal is computed to yield after being slaughtered. The gross hundred weight of one hundred and twelve pounds is still used in England; but the calculations are generally made in stones of eight pounds. By an act of Parliament, the stone of fourteen pounds is required to be adopted in the reckoning in the market; but custom in this, as in many other cases, defies the authority of the government, and eight pounds continue to be reckoned as the Smithfield stone.

The different measures and weights used in different parts of the kingdom are extremely inconvenient, and sadly perplexing to a stranger. The English, the Scotch, and the Irish acre are each different from each other. Grain is, in different places, sold by the bushel, by the quarter, by the comb, by the boll, and by the load; and a load is in some places four, in others three bushels. A Scotch pint is two English quarts. In Covent Garden market, two pottles of strawberries, containing little more than a pint each, are called a gallon. Potatoes are sometimes sold by weight, and sometimes by the barrel; in some *places by the stone of* fourteen pounds, in some by the stone of sixteen pounds. A dozen of eggs is in some places fifteen. I may perhaps be asked, if this is not in Ireland; but I shall not say, excepting to add, as far as my experience goes, fifteen to a dozen would be a very proper index of Irish hospitality and kindness. In one market, in Yorkshire, a pound of butter is twenty ounces avoirdupois; in Staffordshire, eighteen ounces. In Norwich, butter is sold by the pint; in Cambridge, it is literally sold by the yard, being made into rolls of a certain size, and measured off in feet and inches. In one of our hot days in July, with the glass at 95°, our market-men, at this rate, would have little difficulty in giving full measure. I have already alluded to the force of custom. It has many advantages, but why should it stand in the way of improvement? The prevalence of an unmeaning or a useless custom has nothing to recommend it. Yet I believe I shall be doing no injustice to the English, — the last thing certainly which I should wish to do to a people whom I so highly respect and love, — if I were to say, many of them greatly prefer antiquity to utility, and will hold on to an ancient custom with the pertinacity of a drowning man, though its meaning has entirely ceased, and its observance is on every account inconvenient and burdensome. With such persons, all argument on the subject of improvement is idle; the conception has never yet dawned upon them.

Such a varying standard of weight, or measure, or value, renders many statements quite unintelligible to a stranger or one ignorant of local customs, and comparisons and calculations all but impossible.

3. Weight of Animals, Mode of ascertaining. — The weight of an animal in Smithfield is reckoned by the weight of the four quarters. The hide, rough tallow, and offal, are not taken into the account. There are rules given by which to determine the weight of animals, when slaughtered, by external measurement of them when alive. The salesmen in Smithfield do not rely upon these rules, but estimate the weight of cattle by the eye; and mere judgment, founded upon long practice, evinces most extraordinary approaches to exactness, seldom varying but few pounds. The rules, however, to which I refer, have a value to persons who are not accustomed to estimate by the

eye; and a series of tables have been constructed upon these rules, which, if they could be relied upon, would be of considerable use in private practice.* The girth of the ox (for it does not apply to cows as well as to oxen, as their shape is much less regular) is to be taken directly behind the shoulder, and the length is to be measured from the front of the shoulder-bone to the end of the bone on the rump, where a line dropping down at right angles with the line on the back would just clear the thigh, or buttock. Then, according to a rule given me by Lord Spencer, "Reduce the feet into inches; multiply the girth by the length, and that product by the fraction .001944, which will give the weight in pounds;" or, in another form, as the rule is quoted by Mr. Hillyard, "Estimating the weight of a cubic inch of meat at 171 grains, then girth 7 feet 6 inches, and length 5 feet 4 inches, gives $41{,}235\frac{84}{100}$ cubic inches, which, multiplied by 171, gives 7,051,328 grains, equal to 125 stones, 7 pounds, of 8 pounds to the stone." Another mode of estimating the weight of cattle is to ascertain their live weight upon a platform balance, common enough in the United States. Then, according to some authorities, every 112 pounds live weight will produce 72 pounds of beef; but a coarse, large-boned ox will not produce so much. Another way is to deduct one third of the live weight, which is commonly deemed a fair allowance; and also, if the beast is not quite fat, from $2\frac{1}{2}$ to 5 per cent. in addition. Another able authority states, "that the proportion which the dead weight bears to the live weight of animals was reckoned at one half the live weight; but subsequent experiments in the more improved breed of animals show that this is much too small a proportion, it being more correctly represented by the fractional quantity .605, the weight of the animal being assumed as 1. This would be about three fifths for the dead weight. The gross weight of the animal being then multiplied by .605, will give the result in the same denomination in which the gross weight is given." It is obvious, however, that such rules can be little more than an approximation to exactness, since the circumstances under which the animal is weighed,

* These tables are to be found at large in Mr. Hillyard's useful and sensible book, entitled "Practical Farming and Grazing," a fourth edition of which appeared in London in 1844.

whether upon a full or an empty stomach, must essentially affect the result. It will be interesting, I am persuaded, to many of my readers, if I give an account of the weights of some of the most remarkable animals which, within a few years past, have been exhibited at the show of the Smithfield Club, which takes place annually in December; and the account, besides giving the weight of the animals, will show, at the same time, how nearly the weight calculated by rule, and the weight estimated by the judgment of experienced men, corresponded with the actual weight, ascertained upon the animals' being slaughtered.

	YEAR.	GIRTH.		LENGTH		STONE OF EIGHT POUNDS		
		Ft.	In.	Ft.	In.	*Computed Weight.*	*Estimated Weight.*	*Butcher's Weight.*
Lord Spencer's Durham ox,. . .	1828	9.	2	6.	0	211	210	210
The Scotch heifer,.	1830	7.	8	5.	7	138	140	138
Mr. Townsend's Durham heifer,	1833	8.	3	5.	9	164	175	176¼
Mr. Baker's Durham ox,.	1833	8.	9½	6.	0	195	205	206½
Mr. Buckley's Hereford ox,. . .	1833	7.	11	5.	5	143	150	144
Lord Spencer's Durham ox, . . .	1834	9.	7	6.	1	236	240	236
Lord Oxford's Hereford ox,. . .	1834	9.	4	5.	10	214	222	
Mr. Hillyard's do. heifer, .	1834	8.	7	5.	7	175	184	192
Lord Brownlow's do. do. . .	1834	8.	0	5.	9	155	164	
Marquis of Exeter's do. do. . .	1835	7.	11	5.	0	134	138	142½
Lord Spencer's do. do. . .	1835	7.	8	5.	3	130	138	
Lord Spencer's Durham ox,. . .	1835	9.	2	6.	0	211	218	210
Lord Spencer's do. do.. . .	1836	9.	2	6.	1	215	222	218
Marquis of Tavistock's do. do.	1836	8.	10	5.	8	187	196	
Lord Leicester's Devon ox,. . .	1837	8.	1	5.	2	142	145	152
Mr. Giblet's one year old Devon,	1837	8.	4	5.	5	158	162	166.4
Mr. Baker's heifer,.	1837	7.	11	5.	6	148	152	152.3
Mr. Hillyard's Devon ox, ...	1838	8.	1	5.	2	142	142	139.6
Marquis of Exeter's Durham ox,	1841	8.	9	5.	9	185	185	185
Duke of Bedford's Hereford ox,	1841	8.	9	5.	9	185	185	180

The practice at Brighton, Massachusetts, is to sell the animal at a certain rate per pound, or per hundred pounds. The animal is then slaughtered, and the return of his weight made to the owner or drover. The owner or drover does not see his animal killed or weighed. The market takes place on Monday, but he is commonly detained until Thursday, before the weight of the animal is ascertained, and he receives his pay. This, besides its expense, is on every account a serious evil. It cannot be denied, likewise, that the temptations to a fraudulent return of the weight are very strong, and that much dissatisfaction, very often without question groundless, frequently arises. It is surprising how near to exactness the judgment of an intelligent and experienced man approaches; but as this method is liable to the objection of a man's being judge in his own case, it would seem very desirable that some less exceptionable method should be adopted. I can think of no one more eligible than that of ascertaining the live weight on a platform balance, and then adopting some general rule as to the allowance to be made for the difference between the live and the dead weight. A rate of discount or allowance, founded upon repeated and exact experiments, would be equally fair for both parties. The adoption of such a rule would be of the greatest service in enabling the drover or owner to close his business in one day, and would, in general, be much more satisfactory to the farmer, who sends his cattle to market, and is not always without his suspicions of an imperfect return. I offer these suggestions with great diffidence, especially when I read, in a letter addressed to me by a practical man, "that there is no mathematical rule upon which he places any reliance; that he has often been invited to test the correctness of measuring beasts, and also to determine their dead, from ascertaining their live weight, but has found that no confidence can be placed upon such rules." He adds, "that after handling beasts to ascertain their fatness, the mind, by practice, is intuitively impressed with about the weight of the four quarters, exclusive of any offal; and that experienced men can tell the weight of beasts, on an average, within three stone of eight pounds, and of sheep within two pounds." I believe all this; and it presents a beautiful example of what the mind is capable of, and of what it may be brought to under careful training and long practice. We certainly know that the mind is a very good clock, and measures the time with wonderful exactness, both sleeping and waking. I have been often struck with the extraordinary precision with which the poor blind horses, which move the ferry-boat between Troy and the Albany side of the river, measure the distance which they have come, and after making a pause just before they touch the opposite shore, seem to know exactly how many more strokes or turns to give to the paddles, in order to reach it. I hope I shall not offend the pride of any of my readers, by this comparison of the brute with the human mind. Man is very apt to think himself the only knowing animal upon the earth; and I have no doubt that some of the lower animals have the same self-conceit. It is interesting to see reason and moral sentiment, the noblest gift of Heaven, any where diffused, and even in the most humble forms. Such indications strengthen the claims which all sentient beings have upon our kindness and respect; and several of the lower animals — if any being is to be considered inferior who accomplishes the true purposes of his creation — read many striking moral lessons to mankind.

The character of a salesman in Smithfield Market, for judgment and integrity, is of immense importance to him. He is forbidden by law to purchase on his own account; and it is clearly most important that his private interest should not conflict with that of his employer. But it is easy to see the futility of all laws to make men honest, where evasions in a variety of forms are so practicable. Personal character, and a healthful state of public opinion, form, in such cases, the great security.

4. Amount of Business. — The amount of business transacted in Smithfield is enormous. It is estimated at not less than £100,000, or half a million of dollars, every week. The Smithfield Market is certainly one of the great sights of London. The returns of the market on the Christmas week of 1844, when I was present, gave 5000 beasts and 47,000 sheep. This was considered the largest market ever remembered; and the extraordinary quantity of stock was doubtless, in some measure, to be attributed to the severe drought of the preceding summer, and the consequent scarcity of fodder, which compelled the farmers to lessen their stock. The largest return of stock ascertained for any year, between the years 1821 and 1842, was in the year 1838, and was,

Of cattle,	183,362
Of sheep,	1,403,400

In the year 1830, there were sold in Smithfield,

Beasts,	159,907
Sheep,	1,287,071
Pigs,	254,672
Calves,	22,500

In the year 1842,

Of cattle, ...	175,347
Of sheep, ...	1,468,960

The supplies since that have not diminished. But this by no means comprehends the whole supply of provision to London, as immense amounts of slaughtered meat are brought constantly to the dead market, from distant parts of the kingdom, by the innumerable steam conveyances, which have so much increased the facilities of access to the metropolis. We need scarcely be surprised at any distance from which it may be brought, since I have seen Leicester or Southdown mutton, killed and dressed in England, for sale in the market at Boston. In spite of the doctrines of restricted or free trade, the benevolent mind cannot help rejoicing in a facility of intercourse, which renders the mutual interchange of the respective advantages and blessings of different countries and climates so convenient, and thus does away forever with all that fear of want or famine which, in former times, so often followed any extraordinary contingency of the seasons. The quantity of meat, and that principally mutton, brought from six different ports in Scotland to London, was ascertained, in one case, to be about 2364 tons in six months; besides a very large amount of live stock. It has probably greatly increased with the opening of every new means of conveyance.

The friend to whom I am indebted for much of the above information, in regard to Smithfield, states the average weekly sale of beasts in Smithfield at about 3000, and of sheep, about 30,000; of calves, about 300; of pigs, about 500. At the dead market, about 3000 sheep are sold weekly. Of the live stock, the beasts average from £15 to £18 per head, and sheep 30 shillings. A pound in this case may be most conveniently reckoned at five dollars, and a shilling, therefore, at a quarter of a dollar. The average age of beasts sold in Smithfield is from two to three years, and of sheep from fifteen months to two years. It is not to be supposed that these returns by any means embrace all the beasts slaughtered, or the meat consumed in the metropolis and its vicinity; for great numbers are sold before they reach the market, and are therefore not reported. Vast amounts, likewise, are imported from Ireland; and the cotters of this fertile but wretched country, where a large portion of the inhabitants are, for a considerable part of the year, upon the borders of starvation, are obliged to see their only pig — the companion and pet of their children — and their only calf or steer, sent off to other markets to fill other mouths. Smithfield, though much the largest, is only one of the markets of the country; but the immense supplies which are here furnished must give some idea of the improvement and degree of perfection of the agriculture of a country from which they are drawn.

The poultry markets, and the markets for game, are also most extensive. The fish markets in London seem to me unsurpassed for their excellence, and certainly embrace a great variety of the very best kinds. These, of course, furnish their full proportion of the supplies of London.

5. Character and Quality of Stock. — The quality of the cattle exhibited in Smithfield market, of sheep in particular, is extraordinary for its fatness. The show of the Smithfield Club, which is held in December, under the patronage of some of the first noblemen in the kingdom, may very properly be denominated a show of monstrosities in the way of fatness. They are moving elephantine masses of flesh, and if, as according to modern chemical philosophy, all fat is the result of disease, they are far from being attractive to any but the grossest epicure. No advantage can come from rearing animals to such an inordinate degree of fatness, save in the matter of showing what the art of man can accomplish in respect to the animal economy, and also that of testing the nutritious and fattening qualities of different kinds of food.

In respect to the weight of the animals in Smithfield, an individual familiar with the subject, and in whom I have great confidence, states that the beasts from two to three years old will average from 85 to 100 stone of 8 pounds, or from 680 to 800 pounds, when dressed — that is, the four quarters. Others place it not higher than 82 stone, or 656 pounds; of calves, 150 pounds; of pigs, 100 pounds; of sheep, 90 pounds. Calves are seldom sent to market under six or eight weeks old; and large hogs are never seen in the market. If we may rely upon ancient authorities, within a century past the weight of animals in Smithfield Market has nearly doubled; perhaps more than doubled. It is said that, in 1710, the average weight of beasts was 370 pounds; of calves, 50 pounds; of sheep and lambs, 28 pounds. This increase of size is probably attributable in the main to two great causes, which deserve serious consideration. The first is, the improvement of the breeds of cattle. A person has only to go into Smithfield Market to remark the perfection to which the art of breeding has been carried, and the distinctness of the lines by which the different breeds are separated from each other. Three great points seem to have been gained. The first is, great size and weight have been attained; the second is, the tendency to fatten, and to keep in fat condition, has been greatly cultivated; the third is, that the animal arrives early at maturity. All these are most important points; the last certainly not least; for if an animal can be brought to the same size and weight, without doubling the expense, at eighteen months old, that he could formerly be made to reach not sooner than at three years of age, the quick returns, so essential in all commercial transactions, are secured, and as the expenses are lessened, the profits are greatly increased. Nothing strikes one with more surprise than to see what, in the improvement of the appearance and constitution of the stock, intelligence, skill, and perseverance can effect. I may here with propriety quote what my friend, before referred to, says in relation to the quality of the stock in Smithfield. "I fear many of our breeds of beasts and sheep are becoming worse than they were, from an excessive attention to neatness and symmetry of form, so that bulk and quantity of good flesh have been too much overlooked. Our Hereford beasts are much inferior to what they were; also other breeds of beasts; and particularly some breeds of sheep. Some persons are so very particular about purity of blood, that they often run into great error; their stock losing flesh, constitution, and size. This is particularly observable in Leicester sheep. So wedded are some persons to this breed, and to what they call purity of blood, that their sheep keep dwindling into very insignificant stock. I am satisfied that we cannot go on breeding in and in, without losing size, quality, and worth." I give these opinions of a very practical man, as familiar with the Smithfield Market as any man in England, without endorsing them, and leave them to speak for themselves.

The second great cause of the improvement of the stock in

Smithfield Market is, the improvement of the husbandry of the country, particularly by the introduction of what is called the alternate husbandry, and the cultivation of green crops. The cultivation of turnips and swedes is comparatively modern; and perhaps no single circumstance has effected so great an improvement in the agricultural condition of the country. Formerly, cattle were fatted, if fatted at all, upon grass and hay, and these of inferior kinds; the store stock were wintered upon straw, and came to the spring in such a condition that the greater part of the summer was required, in order to recover what they had lost in the winter. Now, the introduction of the artificial grasses, clover, and rye-grass, the growing of vetches, rape, turnips, swedes, carrots, and mangel-wurzel, and the use of oil-cake, have multiplied in an extraordinary manner the resources of the farmer; and the practice of folding his sheep, and stall-feeding his fatting beasts, give him a command of feed, and, if I may so say, such a control over the season, that the results are most remarkable in the supply of the market, at all times of the year, with animals of the finest description.

I may be inquired of, what I think of the English meats. The fatness of the beef and mutton is most remarkable. I have seen single beasts in the United States as fat as any I have seen here; but these are comparatively rare exceptions; and here the general character of the beasts and sheep is, in this respect, most striking. It would, however, I fear, be hopeless to attempt to persuade an Englishman of that which is my honest conviction — that our meats are sweeter to the taste than those which I have eaten here. Our poultry is incomparably better. An Englishman will be likely to set this down as mere prejudice, which possibly it may be, for who can escape such prejudices, or be fully conscious of them when they exist? — but I believe it is not prejudice, but Indian corn, (the grain upon which our animals are fatted,) which gives to their meat a peculiar sweetness, which is not produced by other feed. Our beef animals are not killed until from five to seven years old, and our sheep seldom until three years old. Here sheep are killed at about fifteen months, and beasts at two years and upwards. The flesh of these young animals is wanting in that consistency which more age would give, though an extreme on the other side, and the hard-working of our oxen until eight and ten years old, is liable to give a toughness to the meat, which would not be found if fatted at an earlier, though not a very early, period. If price is to be taken as a correct index of quality, then it will be found that the beef of the small West Highland cattle, and the mutton of the Welsh sheep, are decidedly superior to any other, the prices which they command being always higher than others. The smaller size, and the better intermixture of lean and fat meat which they present, render them more convenient for family dishes, and more attractive than those immense rumps of beef, and saddles and legs of mutton, covered with an inordinate thickness of fat, which, by their grossness, repel any but the most inveterate epicure — the animal who seems to live only to eat.

My conviction is, that there is no agricultural improvement in England so great and striking as that which has been effected in their live stock: I refer particularly to its size, aptitude to fatten, early maturity, symmetry, and beauty. Of the milking and dairy properties of their stock, I shall speak hereafter. I must include, likewise, in my commendation, their horses — working, carriage, pleasure, and race horses. It could scarcely be expected to be otherwise. The highest degree of skill has been concentrated upon these objects; and this skill has been stimulated by premiums of the most honorable and liberal character, and by expenditures absolutely enormous. The splendid and magnificent premiums of gold and silver plate for successful competition, which one sees on the tables and sideboards of the fortunate winners all over the country, and which are exhibited with an honest pride, while they display the highest triumphs of artistical skill and taste, serve only to fan the flame which they enkindle, and to quicken an ambition, which never can be quiet while a more distant point remains to be attained. How happy would it be for the world, if human ambition were always directed to objects so innocent and commendable; to purposes which benefit, instead of those which curse, the world; to the triumphs of genius, industry, and science, over the elements of nature, instead of the bloody conquests of power, avarice, and despotism, over human comfort, liberty, and life!

6. Smithfield by Night. — Smithfield by night, and in a dark night, presents a most extraordinary scene, which, though I have witnessed it, it would be very difficult for me adequately

to describe. A large proportion of the stock arrive in the neighborhood of London either on Saturday or early on Sunday, where they are fed in the fields, or the extensive lairs prepared for their reception. These lairs, especially Laycock's at Islington, are well worth a visit, being composed of open yards and most extensive sheds, covering fourteen acres of ground, furnished with watering troughs and mangers, and divided into different compartments. Here the farmer or drover is supplied with hay or straw for his stock, not by the day or night, but by the truss, the hay which is sold in London being always put up and tied in bundles of 56 pounds each — certainly an excellent arrangement, which, while it prevents all temptations to waste, requires a purchaser to pay only for that which he has. The cattle here get a little rest and refreshment in these stalls after their long journeys; and here they are visited by the salesmen preparatory to their appearance in the market on Monday. It would not be surprising, likewise, and not altogether unlike some occurrences on the other side of the water, if some purchasers, with an acquisitiveness not disturbed by religious scruples, should occasionally make their way there and anticipate the bargains of the ensuing day.* About midnight the different detachments, almost treading upon the heels of each other, begin to make their way to the place of rendezvous through the winding streets of this wilderness of houses, and enter the great market-place by different and opposite avenues, and, like hostile parties, often meet each other in the very centre. Then comes the conflict: the driving of so many thousand of sheep into their several pens; the assorting and tying up, or arranging, so many thousand of cattle, driven into a state of terror and frenzy by the men and dogs; the struggles of the different owners or drovers to keep their own and prevent their intermingling with others; the occasional leaping the barriers, and the escape of some straggler, who is to be brought back by violence; the sounds of the heavy blows over the heads, and horns, and sides, of the poor crazed animals; the shrieks of the men; the yelling and barking of hundreds of dogs, who look after the sheep and

* I will say, however, by the way, and as an act of simple justice, that London, as well as every other part of England which I have visited, is remarkable for its sober and decorous observance of the Lord's Day.

cattle with a ferocity perfectly terrific, and a sagacity almost human; the bellowing of the cattle, and the bleating of the calves; forming, if the expression is allowable, a concert of discordant sounds utterly indescribable and hideous; and in the midst of all this confusion, the darting about of hundreds of torches, carried in the hand by men looking for their cattle and sheep, and seeking to identify their marks, — all together present an exhibition for which it certainly would be difficult to find a parallel, and sufficiently gratifying to the lovers of the picturesque in human affairs. The calves and pigs enter the market in a more aristocratic style, in carriages and vans, with the regular attendance of out-riders and footmen; but in spite of this luxury, after the example of some of their betters, these indulgences do not appear to lessen or quiet all their complaints, and they add their portion to the general harmony. Their owners are quite wise to carry, instead of attempting to drive, them; for I think no human power would be sufficient to drive and assort a herd of pigs, coming into a scene of this description. When the day dawns, however, every thing is found in order; all the different parties at their respective posts; and the immense business is transacted with a despatch, an efficiency, and precision, which are quite remarkable.

7. Attempted Removal of the Market from the City. — It certainly is not a little surprising that a market of this description should be held in the midst of such a city as this. Its name implies that, in former times, it was held in the outskirts of the town; but that time must have long since passed away, and the "field," so called, is now surrounded with miles of houses in every direction, and in the very centre of a most densely-packed population. It would seem, at first sight, that the obvious and innumerable discomforts of such an arrangement, and the danger to human person and life from driving so many beasts through the crowded streets, were sufficient reasons for transferring the whole business to a more retired and convenient situation in the neighborhood of London. A wealthy individual by the name of Perkins, under the influence of the best of motives, made an attempt to do this, and erected an establishment for a market at Islington, about two miles from the centre of London, which is well worth looking at for the completeness and excellence of its

arrangements. The cost of the establishment is said to have been £100,000, or half a million of dollars. It forms a hollow square, and embraces a space of more than twenty acres, com pletely enclosed by high brick walls, which form the backs of deep sheds, slated, and open in front, furnished with mangers and with water troughs supplied from two very large tanks in the centre of the yard, which are kept constantly filled by machinery from wells sunk in the neighborhood. The sheds are capable of accommodating 4000 beasts; and here they might remain from day to day until sold, without inconvenience. In the centre of this immense quadrangle are four extensive squares, all neatly paved with flat stones, and divided into several compartments, railed in with neat iron railings, and capable of accommodating 40,000 sheep. Other pens are constructed for calves, pigs, and other animals usually brought to market; and all are arranged in the most simple and convenient method, with ample passages furnishing easy access to every part of the enclosure. Besides these, there are convenient and ample offices for all the various clerks, salesmen, bankers, &c., connected with the business; and it was designed to erect commodious hotels for the acommoda-tion of persons attending the market, and extensive slaughter-houses for the killing of the cattle, directly in the neighborhood. The whole space is entered under a handsome archway; and for its particular purposes, it would be difficult to conceive of any thing more commodious or better arranged.

In spite of all these obvious advantages, the market could not be removed from Smithfield. The persons in the neighborhood of the old market whose business and profits were intimately connected with it, opposed its removal. There was fear of a rival market being got up on the other side of the city. The city would lose the tolls, which are now received at Smithfield, and which, in the course of the year, make up no inconsiderable revenue. The meat, if the animals were slaughtered out of the town, would, of necessity, have to be conveyed to the city in carts, whereas, now, much of it is killed directly in the neighborhood of the market. These and many other reasons were urged, but, perhaps, would not have availed, excepting for the fact that Smithfield was discovered to be a chartered market, for the sale of cattle; and the twelve judges of the high courts decided, upon consultation, that this charter could not be abrogated; and even in spite of an act of Parliament, which was obtained in the case, this great public nuisance must be continued.

8. Chartered Rights. — When the vast amounts of property, which are here locked up, by the disposal of generations long since departed, for the most frivolous, useless, and obsolete purposes, and under the most absurd tenures, are considered, and that even public and acknowledged nuisances cannot be abated, while maintained under the plea of chartered rights, it is quite well worth considering whether this doctrine does not admit of some qualifications, which would render its operation less burdensome and offensive. Many cases, which are constantly occurring, would do much towards reconciling one to an occasional and general revolution, under which, freed from the rusty fetters of ancient prejudices, superstitions, follies, and crimes, society might take a new start, and avail itself of the improved experience and enlightenment of modern times. The right of a man to dispose of property, after his death, other than that which is the direct fruit of his own skill and industry, is, in my mind, quite questionable on moral and economical, however well established it may be upon legal grounds; and I hope I shall not give offence by an opinion, however erroneous, yet very honestly held, that no man, under any circumstances, has a right to appropriate property to any object which the state may not annul when that object becomes either pernicious or useless; above all, that no man, under any circumstances, has any right in the soil, which is not entirely at the disposal of the state, always premising that the state make adequate compensation for individual cases of hardship or injury, and for any substantial improvement, which may have been effected in the property by the labor or skill, or at the personal expense, of the occupier. Let us suppose, for example, that Smithfield had been, by some ancient charter, appropriated exclusively for public executions, — as it was indeed the melancholy site of the martyrdom of Rogers, and other heroic victims to bigotry, — and that the government determined that executions should cease to be public, or should take place in the prison-yard; or, what is infinitely to be desired, that, under the mild influences of Christianity, the punishment of death should be abolished; must this field therefore forever remain

useless and unoccupied? The English, as I have before had occasion to remark, — and I do it certainly as far as possible removed from any spirit of censoriousness or ill-humor, — are excessively conservative. Their judges still swelter under their full-bottomed wigs; and their courtiers and civilians, in the midst of crowds of gentle ladies, wear swords on state occasions, when there is reason to think that some of them, if called upon to draw and defend themselves, would scarcely know which end to seize upon. I am not for indiscriminate changes; but I go for universal improvement, wherever the improvement to be made is obvious, decided, practicable, and remunerative. If otherwise, what is the value of experience and of education? and how idle it is to talk of the progress of society! Even in this matter of chartered rights, the government, with an inconsistency not uncommon, does not hesitate to take private property for public uses, and to invade the property even of charitable trusts for the passage of railroads, which, whatever may be said of their public uses, can scarcely be considered in any other light than as private corporations. I should be glad to know what business has a dead man with the affairs of the living; and what has a man to do with the earth after he has left it? He has had his day, and is of no further use in it, excepting in the good example which he may have left behind him. Indeed, as Goldsmith remarks, he takes care to rob it of what little he might return for its benefit, by ordering himself to be buried six feet below the surface. The earth belongs exclusively to those who occupy it. It seems to me to behoove us much more to take care for the good of those who are to come after us, and may be essentially affected by what we do, than for the wills of those who have gone before us — whom what we do, or are, cannot affect at all; and who themselves, if they were now living, would see, in a change of circumstances, the absurdity, or uselessness, or inconvenience, or hardship, of the arrangements which they propose, and be among the foremost to condemn and alter them. If public faith requires that the wills of those who have departed should be observed, it should take care that the objects for which those wills provide should be in themselves just, reasonable, and useful, as long as that provision may continue; but the locking up of land *in perpetuum*, for private or public uses, seems of very questionable right and expediency.

It is quite obvious that I am no lawyer; and I give my opinions with the more freedom, knowing that they will not be quoted as authority.*

Besides Smithfield, markets for the sale of live stock, botn lean and fatted, are held in various parts of the country. These being held in determined places, and at established and well-known times, the farmers and others have always an opportunity of disposing of cattle, for which they wish to find purchasers, and of obtaining such as they require for keep or fattening.

LIII. — GRAIN MARKETS.

Next to the cattle markets, in England, the grain markets deserve attention. They perhaps should have a higher place, as the value of the grain crop of the country must very much exceed that of its live stock. The amount of grain produced in

* I might get upon forbidden ground if I ventured to speak of chartered opinions, and of the variety of artificial and stringent contrivances to regulate what men shall think in all times to come. I have my own notions on these subjects, with which I shall not trouble my readers, further than to say that I hold mental slavery as the most ignominious of all kinds of bondage, and thank God, every day of my life, that attempts to inthral the mind are, in the end, as idle as to attempt to chain the wind, convinced as I am that all hopes of human improvement, and the moral advancement of society, must depend upon the utterly free, unrestricted, and independent inquiries of the human mind after what is good, and useful, and true.

I trust I shall be pardoned these reflections, which otherwise might seem inopportune, when it is considered that, in some respects, Smithfield is classical and consecrated ground. I think it was one of the Oxford martyrs, who said to his heroic companion at the stake, that "they should kindle such a fire that day in England, as he trusted in God would never be extinguished." Such were the fires kindled in Smithfield, which, as they were reflected from the surrounding objects, showed the grim, and hideous, and bloody features of bigotry and intolerance, in all their deformity and hatefulness, and still send up their light to Heaven, as the signal of that liberty of judgment, opinion, and conscience, which constitutes the glory of the human mind, and which every true man should claim, at any and every peril, as his independent and inalienable birthright.

England is immense, as is quite evident from the great population which is fed.

KINDS OF BREAD. MAIZE, OR INDIAN CORN. — In Scotland, a considerable portion of the bread is made of oatmeal. In Ireland, a large portion of the poorer classes live upon potatoes; and many scarcely taste bread from one year's end to another. In some parts of the country, meal from pease, and barley meal, are mixed with a portion of wheat meal, and used for bread. But the vast majority of the people use wheat bread exclusively. There is very little or no rye consumed for bread. Indeed, I have not known it used in a single instance. The poor are extremely tenacious of the kind of bread which they eat; and I have seen, in more instances than a few, where the farmer was under an obligation to supply his laborers with wheat at a certain rate, and was using wheat of an inferior quality for his own table, and sending the best to market, the laborer insisted upon that of the best quality, though he might have had an inferior quality at less than the stipulated price. I certainly do not deny their right to do this; and I begrudge the poor none of their small round of comforts and luxuries. I wish they whose toil, under the blessing of Heaven, produces the bread, may never want an ample supply, and that of the finest kind. As a general rule, likewise, I believe it sound economy to use the best of every thing. But I refer to this fact, as showing to a degree, in my opinion, the hopelessness of introducing our Indian corn as bread for the English poor — a scheme which many persons have advocated on both sides of the water, as reciprocally advantageous to both countries. They will not eat it. If the rich should adopt it as a luxury, (and, if they understood its proper use, they would with reason deem it so,) their example or estimation of it might have its usual effect; but to commend it to the exclusive use of the poorer classes as a cheap kind of bread, acknowledged inferior, though it were as sweet as the ancient manna, would be met with that pride of resentment, which any thing short of absolute starvation would scarcely be able to overcome. With Arthur Young, I deem Indian corn, or maize, as among the best and most useful crops ever yielded by the earth. Nothing within my knowledge is grown at so little comparative expense.

Nothing furnishes by the acre more nutritious food for man or beast. Nothing, as grain or grass, is capable of more varied and useful application. No plant cultivated returns more to the land, in manure, by way of compensation for what it takes from it. The dampness of the English climate, the deficiency of sunshine, and in general the coldness and heaviness of the English soil, forbid its production here.* If it were introduced here without duty, with a view to fatting swine and cattle, there would be, in my belief, a clear gain, on the part of the farmers, of the manure. I am not conscious of any interested views to bias my judgment in this matter; for, besides an absence of all commercial interests, from which my pursuits in life are entirely foreign, I think there is reason to believe that, if its admission into England were free, the supplies of this article from the shores of the Mediterranean would nearly preclude the competition of the United States.

LIV. — GRAIN MARKETS OUT OF LONDON.

Grain markets are established in all the principal towns of the country, and are generally held weekly. In almost every town where a regular market is held, there is held a corn market,

* In some few cases, where the locality and the season have been peculiarly favorable, the earliest kinds have ripened; but it cannot be depended on, and any attempt to cultivate it on an extensive scale would doubtless prove a failure. I am not certain that it may not succeed as a green crop for fodder. If so, it would be found that no crop would yield more, or more nutritious feed for stock: or make more milk, beef, or mutton; or furnish a better feed for horses. It is confidently stated, upon authority which I cannot doubt, that it has yielded, in New England, at the rate of thirty-nine tons of green feed to an acre; and some persons have assumed that double this quantity can be grown. A distinguished agricultural friend here is now making the experiment of growing it for green feed. We must wait for the result. I imported the seed for him; but the various expenses attending it almost forbid a repetition. The unfortunate man, who has to run the gantlet through salesmen, and freighting agents, and commission agents, and wharf agents, and carriers, and above all custom-houses, finds himself, at the end, much in the situation of the man who went down from Jerusalem to Jericho; but without even a kind Samaritan to pity his destitution, or assuage his wounds.

although the grain market is always distinct from the general market, sometimes in the same place but at a different hour, but, in most cases, on the same day but in a different place. All grain here goes under the general denomination of *corn*. In a great many towns, large and elegant halls are erected for what is called the Corn Exchange, where the farmers, millers, corn-factors, and grain-merchants, assemble for this particular object exclusively. In some cases, these buildings have considerable pretensions to architectural elegance; and many of them larger pretensions to utility and convenience, as there are connected with them extensive rooms and chambers for the storage of grain.

1. Forms of Business. — The general standard of measure is a quarter, which consists of eight imperial bushels, though still, in some markets, the reckoning is by loads of three bushels. The markets are of two kinds, one by sample — the grain to be delivered on a future day; the others are in some parts of the country called *pitch markets*, where the grain is brought into the market, and sold and delivered at the same time. In these market-houses, the factors, or sellers of grain, have their respective stands, with the necessary appurtenances of counting desk and writing implements, and with the various samples of grain exhibited in boxes or bags before them. In some markets, I have found many of the factors and farmers bringing their samples of grain, in small bags, in their hands and pockets. In most cases, the markets are opened and closed at fixed hours, and this is notified by the ringing of a bell, to which there is universal submission. Such habits of punctuality, in the transaction of business, are of the highest importance; and should there be occasion, I beg leave strongly to commend them to my own countrymen. The rules of commercial transactions cannot, in my opinion, be too stringent and absolute; yet certainly nothing is more loose and slovenly than the ordinary modes of transacting business in my own country; and the necessary consequence is, a great want of punctuality, and that dreadful curse of the community, angry and interminable litigation. A fixed time to begin and to close the market quickens both buyer and seller; but how often have I seen, especially in the country, men wasting the whole day, and chaffering, hour after hour, with all the

necessary amount of trickery and prevarication, about that which might be much better determined in fifteen minutes!

2. Advantages and Convenience of such Markets in the United States. — The convenience of these markets, scattered all over the country, is very great. They would be very useful with us, and I think cannot be too soon established, especially in our grain-growing districts, such, for example, as Western New York. The farmers in this part of the country would certainly derive great advantages from regular and quick sales, and from the extended competition to which such established markets would certainly lead. Once a week, however, in the same district, would be too often, as they would be likely to take the farmers too much from home; and at the breaking up of the winter, when the state of the roads renders travelling difficult, or during the busiest season of summer, it might be advisable to suspend them. In any event, the hour of opening and of closing them should be fixed and absolute. Mutual agreement might determine this; and the custom, once established, would be as imperative as any laws on the subject. If it should be asked how these markets might be established, I think the agricultural societies in the different counties could easily arrange the matter; and that it would be a very useful object of their attention. I would advise, further, that a grain market, and a cattle market, should be always a cash market; and that all giving or taking credit in such cases should be considered disgraceful both to buyer and seller, and entirely out of the question. If bread should not be paid for in cash, what should be? I am afraid my advice may be deemed a work of supererogation, but it is well intended; and whoever contributes in any way to limit (I am sensible the abolition is hopeless) that system of private credit and long accounts, which prevails to so great an extent all over the country, does a public benefaction. With honest men who mean to pay their debts, nothing, in the end, is ever gained by it; and the frequency with which a man's own integrity is undermined by it is not the least of its evils. I am strongly of the opinion that it would be better for the community if there were no laws for the recovery of debts, excepting cases involving fraud either in the act or the representation; and all such instances should be punished as other crimes. The value of

integrity would then be better appreciated; economy in the modes of living would prevail much more; and industry and frugality would be greatly stimulated.

3. Modes of Selling. — The sale by sample seems, on many accounts, more eligible than by bringing the whole quantity at once to the market. The sample, in such cases, is divided between buyer and seller, for there should be a guarantee of fair dealing on both sides, as, in case of a fall in price, the purchaser might substitute a better sample than that which he had received, and in this way evade his engagement. In all cases, the selling by sample is liable, however, to objections of this kind, and more especially as the seller himself is likely to separate from a small sample what might injure its appearance; and a small sample is always likely to be cleaner, and appear better, than a large quantity. One cannot say of wheat what the shopkeepers say of their silks and calicoes, "They appear better in the piece than the pattern." While it is very desirable, in all commercial transactions, to avoid, as much as possible, occasions of misunderstanding, much must, after all, be left to personal integrity, and that sense of honor and right which commercial men would find it for their interest to guard with as much tenacity as they would their lives. But alas! if commercial transactions were so exact and explicit as to be incapable of misconstruction or evasion, and men were always under the influence of a strict principle of integrity and justice, what would become of the lawyers, the paid moral police and the strict guardians of justice always on one side? Many of them would make very good farmers, — a transmutation from which, in some cases, the community might suffer no inconvenience.

Where grain is sold in quantity, or by the load, and delivered at the time of sale, these occasions of misunderstanding are avoided, and the whole business is concluded at once. The farmer leaves his corn and takes home his money; and any anxiety respecting the rise or fall of the market, and the fulfilment of the engagement, coupled as it may be with the usual contingencies of the future, is prevented. But the farmer or seller is placed somewhat at the mercy of the buyer, when, as the close of the market approaches, he finds himself with a load of grain, which he must either sell, or carry back, or store, if it be practicable, at considerable trouble and expense. In large markets, however, where the sellers are numerous, and competition is in proportion, the prices become soon settled by common consent; and the seller may calculate, if he does not, through timidity or greediness, overstay his time, upon getting the current price, if the quality of his grain justifies it. "The tide, if taken at the flood," to borrow the simile of a great authority, "leads on to fortune;" but with those who neglect the opportunity, the ebbing tide often leaves the vessel stranded, high and dry upon the shore.

4. Multiplication of Markets in England. — There are circumstances of difference, in the condition of things here, and in the United States, which it may not be uninteresting to remark upon, as a special reason why the grain markets prevail all over the country. Here there is an immense population to be fed, scattered every where; and there are many more, in proportion to the whole number, who are buyers of bread than with us. The manufacturing villages are crowded with a population who are to be fed by other hands than their own. The villages and small towns are full of tradespeople, mechanics, and professional men, who are to be supplied with bread. The laboring agricultural population, too, are buyers of bread. With us, every farmer raises his own bread, and feeds his laborers in his own house. With us, there are comparatively few married laborers employed at all, and of those, there are scarcely any who have not small farms of their own, on which they raise their own bread, and commonly much more. Here the laboring population, excepting in the case of some small allotments, grow no bread for themselves; and the expense of fuel is so great, likewise, that they depend upon public bakers, rather than bake their own bread. In consequence of this, markets are held at all the principal towns, where the millers and bakers supply themselves. Purchases are made, likewise, in these markets, for the supply of London, where the facility of carriage allows its being sent.

LV.—THE CORN EXCHANGE IN MARK LANE, LONDON.

The supply of London itself is an immense affair. The ordinary population of this mammoth city is estimated at about 1,800,000; and during the session of Parliament, in what is technically called "the season," when the legislature may be said to be in full blast, all the places of public amusement opened, and the court in the plenitude of its luxuries, it is supposed that the population of London does not fall much short of 2,500,000. Nothing impresses a reflecting mind with more force, than the consideration how such vast numbers of people, all of whom are consumers, are to be fed. Yet they are fed, and the cases of want and starvation do not arise from any deficiency in the supply of bread, of which there seems always enough and to spare.

"The total importation of corn and grain of all kinds into London averages, at the present time, about 28,000,000 bushels annually, besides about 50,000 tons of flour and meal—the weight being at least 530,000 tons." The Corn Exchange, in Mark Lane, is the great place of trade in corn and flour, and in all kinds of grain and pulse. There are two spacious buildings adjoining each other for the transaction of business and the exhibition of samples, and the market is holden three times a week,—on Monday, Wednesday, and Friday,—Monday being the principal market-day. The business done here is immense in home-grown and in foreign grain.

LVI.—CORN DUTIES.

Grain is not admitted into England from foreign ports, Canada excepted, free of duty, excepting when the price reaches its maximum. The highest duty, of 20 shillings per quarter, is paid when the price is 50 shillings per quarter, and the scale of duties is a descending scale, in certain determinate proportions, until the price reaches 80 shillings per quarter, when it is admitted free of duty. In consequence of these regulations, large amounts of foreign grain are stored in warehouses, waiting for admission, when, by the variations of the market, the duties are at the lowest. The amount of duty payable on the introduction of foreign wheat being regulated by the current price of wheat, it becomes obviously of the highest consequence to determine what is the current price of wheat, since this price has no reference to the cost of the wheat, and, as is plain, the price may vary in different parts of the kingdom. With a view to determine this, returns are received weekly, at one of the government offices in London, from the different counties in England and Wales, comprising reports of the sales in two hundred and ninety-two market-towns, designated by law, upon which the price is averaged, and by this the duty is regulated for six weeks at a time; the current price, with the duty payable, being announced in the public papers, by authority of the government. This variation of the duties is called the "sliding scale," and has been the cause of much warm political controversy.

The whole subject of restrictive duties is now constantly before the public mind; and while it will not be denied that there are interested partisans on both sides, who have only some private and personal ends in view, it can as little be doubted that there is a fair proportion, on both sides, of men of intelligence, honor, and integrity, who, in the measures which they advocate, are governed wholly by their convictions of what is due to great and valuable interests, concerned in the question, and of what they deem best for the country. I know how difficult it is to acknowledge this; how easy it is to impute corrupt motives to even the purest minds; and how our own views may be affected by circumstances, of whose influence we are not aware, but which are certain seriously to bias our judgment. Men who think that the corn laws should be abrogated, and those who think that they should be maintained, may be equally honest and equally patriotic; but nothing can be more disgraceful and unworthy of an intelligent and honorable mind than that bigotry and intolerance, which would stifle inquiry on any subject of public interest; which would prevent the free utterance of an honest judgment, and impute sinister intentions or interests for any difference of opinion. It is to be regretted that examples of this intolerance, both in respect to politics and religion, are not wanting on both sides of the water. One is almost discouraged to perceive, in many cases, that the only advance made upon the intolerant and ferocious spirit of the dark ages, is the immunity from personal violence and suffering. Men are not now, for their religious or political convictions, burned at the stake; but to a sensitive mind, a penalty scarcely less bitter is often administered, in the opprobrium which follows the profession of unpopular opinions. The tiger, though muzzled, still growls, and beats the bars of his cage with his tail, showing what he would do if he could. It is a singular and instructive fact, that formerly it was the great aim of the municipal and the national government to keep down the price of bread, but that the present policy of the government is to keep it up. Two centuries and a half ago, the city itself provided large stores of grain, imported from the Continent, and even established and maintained several public ovens, in order to prevent a scarcity of wheat, and to save the poor from suffering by a high price, consequent upon a deficient supply. The several livery companies of London were required by law to have several thousand quarters of grain always on hand, for the same object. It contrasts strongly with such provisions, that, a few years ago, two thousand quarters of wheat, that is, sixteen thousand bushels, were thrown into the river, because the owners would not pay the duties or keep it longer, subject to expenses of storage and port charges. Whether the policy of the present day is an improvement upon the wisdom and good government of former times, I shall leave to the calm judgment of my readers; but such a fact as that detailed above, occurring where so many thousands are constantly suffering, and many dying by slow degrees, from a deficiency of food, can hardly fail to bring a cold chill over a man of common sensibility, though he be cased in the triple brass of the most orthodox school of political economy, and seems such a resentment and defiance of the goodness of Heaven, that one can scarcely trust himself to speak of it.

1. Arguments for Protection. — The protectionists, who are opposed to the introduction of foreign grain, maintain that a free competition in their own market by supplies from abroad would so reduce the price of grain as to render its cultivation not

merely profitless, but ruinous; and that the result would be to throw much land out of cultivation, and consequently deprive the laborer of his present resources; and though the price of bread were reduced, yet such would be the scarcity of employment, and the reduction of his wages, that he would be without the means of paying even a reduced price.

2. Arguments against Protection. — The opponents of restrictions in the introduction of foreign grain maintain, on the other hand, that, from the necessities of the case, the land will continue to be cultivated; that the introduction of foreign grain will induce the farmer to cultivate more land, to introduce improvements in cultivation, to bring into a productive condition much land which is now waste and profitless, and thus increasing the amount of his crops by a more skilful cultivation, this excess will be very much more than an equivalent for any diminution of price. The saving of the expenses of transportation, incident to the importation of grain from abroad, must be considered, in its very nature, as virtually a considerable protection to the English farmer.

I do not deem it necessary further to discuss this great question. It does not appear probable to me that, even if the ports were thrown open, much larger amounts would come in than what are now brought; and one effect is certain — that of increasing the price of wheat in the exporting countries. If more wheat is cultivated in foreign countries for exportation, then it must be obtained from territories more distant than those from which it is now brought, and the expense of transportation would be proportionately increased. The production of wheat would be in no case, as many persons seem to imagine, without limit. The United States have vast markets growing up among themselves for the consumption of their surplus products; and in a free trade, the wheat from the United States must come into severe competition with the continental wheats. Every one must see that the financial bearings of the question are quite complicated; and under such a change in the policy of the country as the abrogation of all duties or restrictions, many new circumstances would spring up to affect the results, little thought of by even the shrewdest calculators. How limited is human prescience! and what countless and complex influences are continually intermingling themselves in the affairs of nations, as well as of individuals, which defy equally man's sagacity to understand, and his power to control!

3. Moral Views of the Question. — Having stated, with what impartiality I am able, the principal commercial and financial arguments in the case, on both sides, I feel that there are views of this subject, of a moral character, to which I may without impropriety refer. The question is considered by many as a great question of humanity, which I shall endeavor to look at in the light of a calm philosophy, if I may make any pretensions — and I am certain they must be of the most humble character — to such a lofty gift. I hope my readers, even among the parties most deeply interested, will approach it in the same spirit. I believe, from my personal knowledge of many of them, that there is as ample a share of real benevolence for the poor, among the advocates of the corn laws, as among their opponents; and men of this high character will listen with patience and with eagerness to any discussions of the subject which may serve to correct wrong impressions, if wrong impressions exist, or to make the path of duty more plain, if at present it is in any degree misunderstood or overshadowed.

4. Patriotism and Philanthropy. — It may be supposed that, as the citizen of a comparatively young and growing country, anxious to extend its profitable commercial relations in all directions, and spurred on with an eager and breathless avarice, — stimulated, by an enterprise every where left free to be exerted, and by natural and social advantages of an extraordinary character, to enrich itself by the wide disposal of the products of its industry and its virgin soil, — I should be most anxious for the admission of these products into England under the most favorable circumstances, and should be the strenuous advocate of free trade, certainly on the English side of the water, which is about as far as any man's impartiality may be expected to go. I plead guilty to a strong attachment to my own country, and a most ardent desire for her prosperity; neither of which sentiments has suffered the slightest abatement by my protracted absence, and my familiarity with other countries and other institutions. But I am not conscious of any interested views

which should unduly bias my judgment in this case; and I will assert, in all the strength of the most heartfelt conviction, that I regard patriotism as a very mean virtue compared with philanthropy, and that the mere interests of trade are to be trampled under foot with scorn and disdain whenever they conflict with the interests of humanity. I know very well that they are oftentimes coincident. Some time ago, in the United States, at a public celebration, where I am aware that sentiments occasionally get a little colored by the wine in which they are drank, a distinguished public character gave, as a toast, "Our country!" which would have been very well had he stopped there, and I should have had no objection to emptying my glass, if that had been necessary to sanction it; but when he added, "Our country, right or wrong!" I regarded the sentiment with inexpressible detestation, to which the wine, if I had drank it, would only have added intensity. Some apology may be made for him as a military man; for what has a military man to do with right or wrong? His duty is only to obey orders; and, as a facetious divine said in another case, he has neither the trouble nor expense of keeping a conscience.

5. Proper Ends of National Policy. — When, under the blessing of Heaven, will mankind cease to estimate the prosperity of individuals or nations by a mere pecuniary standard? When will they learn that the true glory of a nation is the glory of justice and humanity, and that the only legitimate and worthy objects of a good government are, — not the mere accumulation of wealth, the triumphs of military ambition, the extension of territory, the multiplication of pageants and of luxuries, the intrenching of power already too arbitrary and despotic in its exactions, the higher elevation of ranks already too high for sympathy with the wants, and sufferings, and privations, of the depressed and low, — but the far nobler purposes of giving to all the opportunity and the means of exerting an honest industry, and an ample share, and a perfect security in the enjoyment, of the fruits of that industry; allowing no individual to be above the reach of that law which inflicts its penalties upon the most humble and down-trodden, and suffering no person to pine in obscurity, uncared for and unpitied; but, in the exercise of an exact and impartial justice, seeking to protect the defenceless, to

succor the oppressed, to raise the fallen; by a wise education, and a paternal care, to inspire even the lowliest with the ennobling consciousness of his own moral and immortal nature; and, in the spirit of true Christianity, to regard all men as one family, and to seek to impart to every man, without stint or abatement, his full share of all the advantages and all the goods which God, when he made men for each other, and endowed them with human sympathies, designed that they should find in the social state? — When, indeed, are these celestial visions of philanthropy to be realized? when is the bleeding victim to be plucked from the jaws of an unrelenting avarice? when is the imprisoned bird to be let free to breathe the clear air of heaven, and pour out his songs of ecstasy upon the floating breeze? when is humanity — in too many cases oppressed, degraded, plundered — to be allowed to stand erect in the conscious dignity of freedom and of manhood?

6. Bread regarded in a peculiar Light. — In civilized states, bread has always been considered in a different light from almost any thing else, and has been the subject of special regulations. For many years, speculators in grain were looked upon with peculiar suspicion and odium, and were the subjects of particular legal restrictions. They were considered as the creators of scarcity, by their hoarding up large stores of corn; whereas, in fact, it was through their providence that these times of suffering were anticipated and mitigated, or avoided. They are not disinterested, but are as useful and important as any class of persons, employed as agents in any branch of trade. They are most useful in enabling the grower of grain to dispose of it to the best advantage; and it would be difficult to say how a large community could be supplied without them; as if, for example, London itself were left to the precarious supply of individual farmers. They perform, indeed, a most essential and important service, and are entitled to a fair remuneration. The indispensable importance of a character for fair dealing, and the competition to which they are exposed, are securities against that compensation being excessive. As speculators in grain were regarded with peculiar vigilance, so were bakers, and so are they still, held to a strict responsibility, and the weight of their loaves subjected to an assize. In Turkey, a baker giving light weight is nailed by the

ear to his shop door — a most awkward position, certainly, to be placed in, and sufficiently admonitory.

The corn laws are regarded by some persons with a sentiment of similar distrust or dislike. They are considered as a tax upon the bread of the poor, or a reduction of the size of their loaf, to which they ought not to be subjected. The effect of the duty upon corn is obviously to increase the price of bread, as the abrogation of the duty would be to lessen its price, or otherwise it would be of no importance whatever. In two respects, bread differs from other articles which man wants or desires. In the first place, its supply is indispensable to human subsistence; in the second place, though to a degree the product of human industry, its production is not controllable at human pleasure. Of other articles, in regard to which man's only province is to work up the raw materials, he may manufacture a large or small quantity, at his will. In respect to bread, man can only sow the seed, and then wait with humble hope for that blessing, "which shall give the increase." These circumstances have undoubtedly had their influence on the exertions which have been made every where to prevent a monopoly of bread, and to keep it, as far as possible, within the reach of the most destitute.

7. Peculiar Condition of the English laboring Population. — But there are circumstances, connected with the condition of English society, which give peculiar severity to these laws. A large portion of the laboring population depend wholly upon their labor from day to day, for a supply. If wages were paid in kind, the price of bread would not so much affect the laborer. If wages rose or fell with the price of bread, the case would be different from what it is. But this is not the case; labor is superabundant; the competition for employment is severe; and constant employment difficult to be procured. Land, for the purpose of growing bread for themselves, is a matter wholly beyond the reach of the greater part of the laboring population. They might as well think of getting possessions in the moon. The soil is locked up in comparatively few hands. It is stated confidently that, from the year 1775 to the year 1815, the number of landed proprietors in England was reduced from 240,000 to 30,000, and that the process of absorp-

tion has been continually going on from that to the present time. Labor here, then, is wholly dependent upon capital. Emigration, from the insular character of the country, is extremely difficult, and not as in the United States, where a man has only to take his axe upon his shoulder, and find for himself a home. Though the price of bread, therefore, should increase, the rate of wages would not be affected; the laborer would get no more; and, from the advance in the price of that which is indispensable to his subsistence, his wages would virtually become of less value, though the nominal amount remained the same. Add to this, that the increase of the population of Great Britain is going on at a rapid rate, the increase for the last year, as stated upon the highest authority, being no less than 380,000. These considerations, as connected with this subject, cannot fail to have their weight upon reflecting and benevolent minds. Whether any restraint, therefore, should be put upon the supply of food to the people, is a matter which I submit to the opinion of those whom it concerns.

If "property has its rights, it has also its duties," and those of a most responsible character. The condition of the laborer is sufficiently striking. His labor creates the product, but this product passes immediately into other hands; sometimes into the hands of those whose skill, and care, and enterprise, combined with his labor, did their full share in the creation of this product, but often into the hands of persons who produce nothing, and live only to consume and to enjoy. He must be satisfied if a very small portion of it is returned to him by way of compensation for his toil; but it would seem at first blush a hard case, if even a portion of this must be abstracted in its progress to him, or otherwise he will not be allowed the opportunity of laboring at all. Our horses and oxen are well fed and cared for, in proportion to the labor which they are compelled to perform. What should we say of the man who refused them this? But alas for the poor men! I have seen hundreds and hundreds of the laborers, who, after a most scanty breakfast, in the midst of their labors, sometimes severe and always unremitting, had nothing for their dinner but a bit of dry bread and a draught of water, and who would return at night, when the toil of the day was over, to a supper as scanty. Even the inferior butter is not suffered to reach them, but is mixed with tar at the custom-house, that it may be destroyed as human food. What an extraordinary fact this is! In one of the great breweries in London, where, I think, forty of the magnificent London horses are kept, they are worked but six years, and are then sent into the country to enjoy rest and comfort the remainder of their lives. What an enviable condition is this compared with that of many of the human laborers, in a country enriched by their toil, and flooded with a wealth unknown before in the history of the world. I should do the greatest wrong if I did not say, however, that there are many bright examples of a justice and humanity towards those by whose toil they live, of the noblest character — a conduct which is sure to be followed by its appropriate reward; and that the evils are deplored by many more, who have not the sagacity to discern, nor the power to apply, a remedy. But the condition which I have described is but too common, and must afford a most instructive lesson to the laboring portion of the people of the United States.

8. Excess of Population. — The constant complaint here is, that there are too many people. This is an extraordinary complaint, while there are several millions of acres of productive lands lying waste and uncultivated. But what is "the preventive check"? Poverty and hunger are not found effectual. It is an extraordinary remedy adopted at Manchester, where, according to the returns, seventy-six out of every hundred of the children born die before the usual age of weaning, a large proportion of whom are dosed out of existence by the excessive use of opiates. Such a mode of disposing of a surplus population is certainly as little to be commended as Defoe's *Short Method with the Dissenters*, advising to hang them all! A valued friend of mine, a celibate, and so likely to continue, whose great passion is statistical science, very gravely asserts, that if men and women would not marry until they were twenty-seven years old, there would be no surplus population. The only reply to be made to such practical theories, is in the words of the old proverb, "When the sky falls, we shall catch larks;" and it would not be surprising to find such a man as gravely recommending the old method of catching birds, by putting salt upon their tails. I was one day, in London, importuned for charity, by a healthy-looking woman with a young infant upon her arms;

and it is not at all uncommon to find them with two, often, no doubt, hired for the occasion. "Why," said I, "do you beg? Why do you not work?" "Because," said she, "I can get no employment." "But," said I, "if you have no means of supporting them, why do you have children?" "Sir," said she, with a simplicity which was irresistible, "Providence sends them." It would have been much more true had she said, improvidence; but it was evident she was no adept in the Malthusian school. Children, then, will be born into the world. The improvement of the lower classes by education, the general elevation of the standard of living, the increase of what may be termed the artificial wants of life, and the influence of the higher class of religious and moral considerations, giving a deeper conviction of responsibility, and rendering the domestic affections more elevated, and the social interests and the parental relations more sacred, as far as they can be brought to bear upon the mind, are among the only certain remedies for this improvidence. These considerations, however, can only be expected to have their proper influence where the mind is in some measure prepared for them by a rational and virtuous education. But it is in no case a sufficient reason for subjecting the poorer classes to any new hardship or privation, to say that there are too many people; because there are other questions, which inevitably arise in the case, to which a reply might not be very easy; — namely, Who is here who has no right to be here? and, Whose duty is it to retire? or, Who should be put out? I do not say that society is bound to support gratuitously any man, other than such as by the providence of God are made incapable of providing for themselves. Here the obligation is imperative. I hold the obligation on society to be equally imperative to afford to every man, as far as possible, the opportunity, by his own honest labor, of providing for himself and those whom the divine Providence has cast upon his care. Now, wherever the appropriation of the soil, or the institutions of society, are such as to deprive a man of this power, or to prevent him the opportunity of its exertion where otherwise he would use it, it would seem, without the most cogent reasons, a measure of great severity to live upon his labor, and to take even from the small pittance which enables him to render that labor; to see him reduced to the borders of starvation, and then to demand a piece of his last crust. I do not speak of motives in this case at all, but only of what seems to some minds to be the tendency or character of certain measures. I do not believe there is any prevalent want of compassion among the strongest advocates of restriction, or any disposition to drive the laborers to the wall. Indeed, I shall utter only my honest conviction, founded upon the closest personal observation, that the laborers of England have no warmer friend than in the public-spirited nobleman * who has taken the lead in the protection societies; and this likewise applies, as I well know, to many associated with him. No man in England is surrounded with more contented and attached laborers. But we cannot all see the same subject in the same light; and while nothing is easier or more congenial to a mean temper, nothing is more foreign from a generous and honorable mind, than the imputation of mean or unworthy motives to those whose opinions or measures differ from our own.

I have spoken thus at large, and given, as well as I am able, the opinions prevalent with different persons on the great subject of the corn laws — first, because it is intimately connected with the agricultural condition of England; and next, because I know the strong interest which is taken in the subject in the United States. It certainly is not for us to complain of the restrictive laws of England. I give no opinion as to the policy or impolicy of such restrictions on either side; but, while we barricade our own doors, we cannot, with a very good grace, require of others to leave theirs open.

LVII. — MODE OF ADJUSTING LABOR AND WAGES.

Every circumstance, which tends to widen the distinction or separation between the rich and the poor, the employer and the employed, and to create opposing interests between them, is alike unfriendly to both parties. The rich and the poor, the employer and the employed, are equally essential to each other.

* The Duke of Richmond, president of the Agricultural Protection Society.

Formerly, the laborer lived in the family of the employer, and sat at the same table. This custom is now almost entirely done away with; and laborers, instead of being members of the same family, live wholly by themselves. It used to be much more the custom than now to pay the laborers in kind; and then the laborer had a special interest in the crop, and high prices were quite as much for his advantage as for that of his master. This practice still prevails to a degree in Scotland, but nowhere, that I have found, in England. Under present arrangements, however, where wages are paid in money, the two interests, as in all other cases of commercial trading, become distinct, and, I may add, opposed to each other. What one receives, lessens, of course, the gains of the other. The employer gives as little as possible; and where labor is abundant, and competition severe, it is obvious he has the laborer very much at his mercy. The laborer, on the other hand, will not be likely to return any more than the strictest interpretation of his obligation requires. This may be the occasion of a matter to which I have before alluded — that, in my opinion, an English laborer does not accomplish nearly so much in the same time as an American laborer. I speak of cases in which the American is working for himself, the Englishman for another. In cases where work is taken by the piece or job, as in harvest for example, there seems to be no want of application or success, on the part of the English laborer.

Philanthropic minds are now every where anxiously at work devising means or schemes for the benefit of the laborers, and to mitigate the evils of their condition, which otherwise are likely to be increased rather than diminished, as the population increases. In Austrian Poland, where the peasants are themselves occupiers of land, the landlord or proprietor of the soil claims from them a certain number of days' work, each week, exclusively for himself; but no such arrangement would be possible in England; nor would it obviate the difficulty to which I have referred.

1. Experiment in Germany. — A German baron, with whom I have the pleasure of a friendly acquaintance, has given me an outline of his arrangement with his laborers, which, as far as it is practicable, deserves much consideration, as, according to his

own account, it secures their industry, fidelity, and contentment. No human arrangements are perfect, and no human laws can be framed which the ingenuity of men will not contrive to evade; but as there appears in this plan every motive to good faith, good faith on both sides would seem to be all that is necessary to its successful operation.

First, from the products of the place, the customary rent is paid, and the wages of the labor employed. The surplus remaining is then divided into five equal parts. Two of these parts are claimed by the proprietor for his skill, intelligence, and care, in the superintendence and management of the property; one part is retained as an insurance upon that part of the property which is liable to loss or destruction; one part is devoted to actual improvements upon the place; and one is divided among the laborers themselves, according to the rate of wages which they receive for their work. Whether these proportions are properly adjusted or not, I shall leave to the judgment of my readers. It is obvious that any others might be adopted which should be deemed more just. It is certainly an approach to an equitable arrangement; and my friend assures me that it works well. He says, he leaves his estate at any time with a perfect confidence that his interests will be cared for and protected, and that there will be no waste of time, and no squandering of property, and no neglect of duty. Success is, in proportion, as much the interest of the laborers as of the proprietor.

2. Claims of Labor, and Duties of Wealth. — This has always impressed my mind as only an equitable adjustment, and must be equally as soothing to a good man's conscience as to a poor man's stomach. Contradicted, as I have often, and severely reproached, as I have sometimes, been for the assertion, I nevertheless maintain as my sober conviction, that in all business where success depends on labor, — whether it be in the case of manufacturing industry, in agricultural labor, or in the toils and hardships of a seafaring life, — the person who does the work, who endures the hardships, who encounters the exposures, has the first claim upon the proceeds, and should come in for an equitable share of the profits. I admit that there is much labor and anxiety in mental application, and in the active enterprise and care on the part of the manager of such concerns, which are

often as severe as any bodily toil, and which deserve to be fully compensated. In general, this enterprise is perfectly competent, however, to take care of its own interests, and seldom fails to provide for itself. But it is said, these people take no risks; they are sure, in any event, of their stipulated wages; they have no right to any more. I know they have no legal right. But I do not understand that they take no risks. There is always a risk of losing their wages, which is something; but in all employments there is a risk of health, and in many a constant exposure to disease, to accidents of various kinds, to loss of sight, or loss of limbs, or loss of life. There are many trades and professions where health is almost certain to be impaired, and life to be prematurely cut off. There are peculiar dangers in mines, among complicated machinery, in unhealthy climates, on the open seas, and on the ice-bound and rock-bound shores, bristled with pointed cliffs and ruffled with foaming waves.

I know very well the great rules of trade, as they are called — "Buy as cheaply as you can; sell as dearly as you can; get your labor performed for the least possible wages; and accumulate, accumulate, accumulate, as your great end and aim." This men call Christianity; I think, to give it such a name is a libel upon a religion which teaches us to do justly and to love mercy, and which enjoins it upon us, as the highest law of social duty, to do to others as we would that others should do to us. I admit that, if men could enter into a perfectly free and equal competition, unmixed self-interest, though an inferior, might yet not be so objectionable a rule as in other circumstances; but how seldom is the competition equal between capital and labor, wealth and poverty, skill and ignorance; and especially in a country like England, where wealth is enormous; labor superabundant; the professions, and trades, and occupations crowded to repletion; the lower classes extremely ignorant and dependent; and the population increasing with a rapidity perfectly astounding. I complain of no man's wealth, if that wealth be the fruit of honest industry and enterprise. I envy no man's power, if that power be justly acquired. But I do envy — with no desire, however, to pluck a single jewel from his crown — that man's honor and felicity, and equally his wisdom and goodness, who, in the possession of ample power, whether of wealth, or learning, or talents, finds his highest honor in being just, and his purest happiness in using this power in doing good; in succoring those who need succor; in helping those who are trying to help themselves; in encouraging and stimulating self-respect, and a virtuous ambition to make their condition better, even in the most humble; in proving himself the friend of the friendless; in protecting and rewarding industry, sobriety, and frugality, not in a niggardly, but a generous manner; in sharing some liberal measure of his abundance with those by whose labor, under the blessing of Heaven, this abundance has been created; and in sending light, and comfort, and plenty, into the cottages and hearts of those who have sowed his fields, and brought on their toil-worn shoulders the fruits of their cultivation to his stores. The golden harvests of such a man in every wave reflect Heaven's purest sunshine; his dew-bespangled fields glitter with a radiance brighter than ever shone in a regal diadem; and the happiness and joy, which he sends into the homes and hearts of others, return in gushing streams to flood his own home and his own heart.

I know my poor words will find a warm response in many a kind bosom, and, by Heaven's blessing, may throw a spark into that smoking flax, which too much of what is called prosperity may not yet have quenched. There are many such hearts; but in general we see "who gets the lion's share." To reason with avarice, is well nigh desperate. If it were an iceberg, we might hope that, under the rays of a clear sun, it might be made to trickle; but it is a mass of granite, which, like the monumental column in Trafalgar Square, stands wholly unmoved by the forlorn and pitiable objects of destitution and wretchedness, whom I have often seen, in a winter's day, sunning themselves at its base; and remains alike impervious to heat or cold, to calm or storm, to summer's fires or winter's frosts.

3. Results of the German Experiment. — The friend, to whom I have referred, has three hundred laborers in his employment. He says, the system works well; and that every year's experience gives him stronger confidence in its justice and advantages. First, his work is done; secondly, it is done in the best manner in which his laborers are able to execute it, because it is the interest of all that it should be done, and well done. The laborers have a system of rules and fines among

themselves, always subject to his approbation, and, after once approved, always rigidly enforced. They inquire, of their own accord, into the best methods of doing what is to be done; they point out mistakes which have been committed, and improvements which may be made, subject always to his judgment. If men are found unskilful or incompetent in the particular branch of duty assigned them, he is advised of it, and persons more suitable are selected by their judgment who best understand the capacities of their fellow-laborers for the work. They are held jointly responsible for any injury to the property, unless the offending person is found. An individual guilty of any neglect of duty, or any improper conduct, or any violation of the established rules, is mulcted in a pecuniary fine. The names of the offenders are always announced at the close of the year; and these fines go towards a general entertainment and festivity. The proprietor himself hears all complaints, and a laborer, whose bad habits are judged incorrigible, is discharged.

I have been somewhat amused by his telling me that the great evil which he has to contend with is the use of tobacco. Smoking upon his premises he absolutely forbids, for three good reasons — first, the danger of fire; secondly, for the time which it occupies, and the lazy habits which it induces; and thirdly, because he deems its effects upon the stomach extremely pernicious to health, and incapacitating men in a degree for labor. In other words, he views it as a poison. So do I. I wish it was as quick and fatal in its operation as arsenic, or prussic acid, always premising, however, that those who now use it in any form should be fully and reasonably forewarned.

4. Scotch Customs — a Digression. — My readers will, I hope, be indulgent to my infirmity, which has been, even in this country, sometimes put to a severe test. In Scotland, for example, they take snuff with a spoon. A small silver spoon, or one made of bone, is filled from the horn, and then thrust up the nose. To complete the refinement, there is also a small brush to clean the upper lip, and edges of the nostrils. The reader may judge of my sensations when the spoon and the horn were both actually offered to me in church. There may, however, in this case be some claims to indulgence, for in one of the Scotch meetings which I attended, the extempore prayer was actually

one hour, and the sermon which followed, two hours in length; both, I admit, excellent in their way. But then, although the argument and the doctrine were sufficiently stimulating to a stranger, yet veterans accustomed to such engagements might get to sleep, from pure exhaustion, under the discharges even of musketry and cannon, and might require extraordinary applications to keep their sensibility alive. I will say, however, in justice to the Scotch, that I never witnessed more decorum, and more wakeful attention, in time of service, than in the Scotch meetings; and they bore these inflictions or penances, as less serious minds would consider them, with a philosophic submission, worthy of the pillar saints in the dark ages.

While speaking of the manners of the rural population, I may allude to another practice prevailing in some of the rural districts in Scotland, which some persons in the rural districts in the United States may feel an interest in knowing. I attended worship, in Scotland, in a most quiet and delightful district of country, and among green fields cultivated with the highest skill, and loaded with the richest crops, where, when the first regular service was through, and all done, after an interval of about ten minutes, during which the minister never left his pulpit, nor the congregation their seats, the minister began and went through another whole service, and gave a second sermon on a different subject, as long as the former. This finished for the day, and, as I was informed, was so arranged that the farmers, and farmers' wives and daughters, who lived at some distance, might get home in season to milk their cows, and tend their cattle. I had likewise a slight impression come over my mind, that they meant to have their money's worth of instruction, and did not choose to let their spiritual laborer off with half a day's work for full wages. It required, however, a healthy intellectual digestion to dispose of two full meals at once.

LVIII.—THE DEAD-MEAT MARKETS.

Besides the cattle and grain markets, there are other markets, to which I have already alluded, connected with agriculture, which are sometimes called by the startling designation, *the dead markets*, by which is only intended markets for the sale of slaughtered animals, beef, mutton, pork, lamb, veal, &c. &c., and which in London are quite worth a visit. The largest of these, in this great metropolis, are Newgate and Leadenhall Markets; and it is a curious fact, that the former occupies a building (the magnificent entrance of which still remains, with its high and ornamented archway, and its aisles, with the old columns, form the meat-stalls) which was formerly a literary institution, or college. Instead of food for the mind, it now furnishes food for the body; and instead of the purveyors of intellectual provisions, — poetry, philosophy, eloquence, and science, — here stand the purveyors of mutton, pork, and beef — a very ignoble office, and a very humiliating descent, as some refined and sensitive persons would deem it: but alas! what would become of science, philosophy, eloquence, or even poetry itself, without mutton, pork, and beef? The philosophical Edward Search, in his most admirable work, "The Light of Nature," says, "that he has found a draught of Daffy's Elixir, on getting up in the morning, a powerful means of grace, dispelling doubts and despondencies, and strengthening and brightening his faith;" and though, through a foolish pride, we may be disposed to deny or not to recognize our relations in humble life, as citizens sometimes "cut" their country cousins when they meet them in town, yet the stomach and understanding are near neighbors, and the one absolutely dependent on the other. What nature hath joined no man can put asunder.

The markets in London display their meats to considerable advantage; and besides the great markets, meat shops prevail all over the town, and are found in some of the best streets intermingled with other kinds of shops of the most splendid description. Even Bond Street, the very emporium of fashion, elegance, and taste, has its meat shops, where whole carcasses of mutton are suspended before the doors in long rows, as, under the bloody code of former years, prisoners at the close of the sessions used to be suspended at the Old Bailey, — except in this case in an inverse order, the heads of the sheep being downwards, as mutton-heads are apt to get inverted. A fine lady, in passing from one milliner's or jeweller's shop to another, must take very good care, lest, instead of encountering a fine beau, to which she might not object, she encounters a fine quarter of beef, or a fine sheep, which certainly, if taste only were consulted, she would prefer to meet in another form and place. The incongruity is at first offensive to a stranger, and seems in very bad taste; but an amateur finds some compensation in the beauty of the objects thus exhibited. I do not mean the ladies, of whom possibly I may speak in another place, but the meats. Mutton is always the prevailing meat, for this seems to be the favorite dish on English tables. It is a remarkable fact, that mutton is the prevalent dish at the public schools and colleges. At the Blue Coat School in London, for example, it is the sole meat for the eight hundred boys, four or five days out of seven. The same is the case, I am told, at Eton; and this not, as I supposed, from its comparative cheapness, but from experience, and the opinion of medical men, that it is the most wholesome diet, and least likely to interfere with intellectual application and health.

The Southdown and the Leicester sheep are generally preferred, though the small Welsh mutton, for its exquisite flavor, is most esteemed; and the fatness of the beef, and mutton, and lamb, is every where most striking. Indeed, in the English markets, lean meat is hardly to be seen. If it is sold, it is certainly seldom displayed. The meat-shops are eminently clean; this, indeed, is the universal characteristic of the English people above the lowest classes, who in London are eminently dirty. The salesmen, however, with their blue woollen frocks and aprons, in tidyness of appearance would hardly bear a comparison with the salesmen and women in the Philadelphia markets, with their white linen frocks and aprons. Indeed, in this respect, Philadelphia, as far as my observation goes, stands preëminent. Cleanliness, it is often said, and with a good deal of reason, is next to godliness. I confess to this creed. I think it should be inculcated as a religious duty, and for its useful moral influences. The sect of Friends regard it as such; and it is doubtless much owing to their influence and example, that Philadelphia is so proverbially neat. Many of the English butchers and salesmen are distinguished for their intelligence, and the great extent of their concerns.

1. Slaughter-Houses in London. — I have already said that a great deal of the meat which is exposed for sale in London is

killed in the country, and at some seasons of the year brought even from remote parts of Scotland. But I shall perhaps surprise some of my readers by informing them that London is full of slaughtering-houses. The police of London is so exemplary, and many of these places are kept with such perfect neatness, that even the nearest neighbors are not apprized of their existence.* This fact may be recommended to the attention of the butchers in the vicinity of Boston, and some other of our large towns. Their neighbors certainly will join in this recommendation, for most of these slaughtering establishments are an intolerable nuisance. In some of the best streets in London, where the meat-shops are found, will be found behind these shops the slaughter-houses, where this meat is killed. You will sometimes see cattle and sheep brought in by the front door of very respectable looking houses, (for the yards of the houses are otherwise inaccessible,) like acquaintances of the family. Back of these shops, I have been introduced into elegantly furnished drawing-rooms, and did not discover that the slaughtering establishment was immediately adjoining, until I looked out of the window. There is not the slightest odor perceptible, to offend the senses. The animals come out in a very different form from what they go in. The blood goes at once into the common sewers, and the offal is carefully removed. In the neighborhood of the

* One great means of the extraordinary cleanliness of London is, that no swine are ever allowed to be kept in it. The lower class of Irish, who migrate to London in vast numbers, (for where, indeed, do not these laborious creatures migrate?) are thus obliged to abandon the tender familiarities of their early years, which have "grown with their growth, and strengthened with their strength." As the ruling passion, however, is always strong, and the Irish heart, even in the humblest condition, is distinguished by warm affections, they contrive, as some of the gentlemen of the health commission have informed me, many times in a very adroit manner to evade the law, and the pig and the donkey are often regularly installed lodgers in their rooms, and free sharers at their humble board. It is said that when the terror of the Asiatic cholera prevailed, and a health committee visited the premises of the poorer classes in Edinburgh, with a view to remove the incitements of disease, they found in one of the upper chambers of one of the very high-storied houses of that city, inhabited by an Irish family, a large hog among the children. Upon inquiry how he could have been got up there, the owner replied with genuine Hibernian simplicity, "Plaze yer honor, he was never got up here at all at all; but he was barn here." I do not know why an Irishman should not be attached to his pig, as well as a nobleman to his dog. In substantial usefulness, the pig would not suffer by the comparison. I cannot say as much of his moral developments.

great markets, however, the slaughter-houses are in cellars under ground, and are not managed with equal neatness. It requires some courage to enter these places. In the extensive market at White Chapel, the slaughtering establishments are above ground in the rear of the stalls, and the gutters of the streets literally flow with blood.

2. CUSTOMS OF THE JEWS. — The market at White Chapel is in the immediate neighborhood of the quarter of the city where most of the Jews reside. The Jews will never eat or buy any meat, which is not killed by some one of their community deputed or appointed for that express purpose. He comes at the time fixed and kills the animal; and after the meat is dressed, if he finds upon it the slightest blemish or indication of disease, the meat is condemned, and no Jew will buy it, though the Christians betray no scruples of this sort.* If the meat is found perfectly sound and healthy, a clasp or token is put upon the leg, and the Jews are at liberty to purchase it.

Any person who has the curiosity to go into the Jews' quarter, and see how they live, behold the filth of their streets, the wretchedness of their habitations, remark a squalidness which no description can exaggerate, and inhale the odors of which the place is redolent, which seem to be the very compound of

---

* The subjoined note is of a nature scarcely to be read by any person of a very sensitive and delicate mind. I advise such persons, therefore, by all means to pass it over. I give it in self-defence, and to show that I do not intend to make statements without authority.

In my Third Report, page 261, I said that "numbers of cattle are almost every week, as I have reason to believe, brought to Smithfield in such a state of disease as to be fit for no other purpose — and for this they are actually bought — but to make sausages for the poor Londoners." This statement a kind and intelligent friend complained of as unwarrantable, and not well founded. The form of expression might, I admit, have been better chosen; but the *reason I had to believe* the fact, was the direct assertion of some respectable salesmen in Smithfield Market, who spoke of the practice as undoubted. This was particularly applicable to the time when an epidemic prevailed among the cattle. I do not believe any city officer would permit or connive at it, if known; but cases of a strongly suspicious character are yet established with so much difficulty by what would be deemed legal evidence, that parties notoriously criminal often escape with impunity.

But the following statement, given under oath to Dr. Playfair and Sir Henry de la Beche, of the Health of Towns Commission, during their inquiry into the

corruption and pestilence, and of all that is odious and disgusting, will feel no little surprise at their particularity and fastidiousness in regard to their meats. But these are among the inconsistencies and anomalies of human nature, which are to be found among persons in almost every condition. The same inconsistency is seen, for example, among the lower class of Irishwomen in their own country, however humble in condition, with whom it seems to be the ruling, and an indomitable passion, to have a clean and handsome cap, though in most other respects one would be half inclined to think they were laboring under a species of hydrophobia. You will see them, the head surmounted with an elegant frilled cap, emulating the whiteness of the drifted snow, while the lower parts of the person, in a state of nudity, (for the drapery of the statue of an Irishwoman seldom extends below the knee,) though, as pieces of sculpture, exhibiting originally the highest artistical skill, are yet so rough, and torn, and begrimed and stuccoed with mud and dirt, that you can hardly believe that both ends belong to the same person, and that the head has not by some awkward mistake got upon the wrong shoulders.

3. Mode of slaughtering Animals. — I have felt it a duty of humanity to inquire into the mode of slaughtering animals,

---

state of Bristol, may serve to clear up some of my friend's doubts on the subject. *Report on Lancashire*, p. 30.

"Have you resided some time in this house?" "Yes, for several years."

"What occupation does your neighbor pursue?" "He kills pigs, which he gets over from Ireland. Often the pigs, in coming over in the packet, die, and I have seen as many as thirty dead pigs at a time brought into the yard. They are thrown into the shed there until there is time to cut them up; and by that time I have seen the maggots fairly dropping out of them. Then they are cut up, and, I believe, are made into salt bacon, or sold for sausages." * * * *

"Have you not complained of this nuisance?" "Yes, we have; but we were told it was of no use complaining, for doctors agreed that these smells were very healthy. Besides, the owner of the yard is a very good neighbor, and tries to keep things as clean as he can; but his occupation beats him in that."

What can go beyond this? But why, it may be asked, refer to such cases? Because, in order to correct an abuse, and to guard against it, that abuse should be exposed. Nor is it without a melancholy instruction, to see to what extremes avarice will hurry its votaries; nor without a moral use, to hold up the perpetrators of such wickedness towards the poor and ignorant to the execration which they deserve.

with a view to discover if there be any way of lessening the suffering necessarily inflicted. When it is considered that from thirty to forty thousand animals, poultry and game not included, are put to death weekly, for the supply of the city of London alone, it becomes a grave question of humanity whether any, and if any, what amount, of the physical suffering necessarily incident to such operations, can be saved.

> "The poor beetle, that we tread upon,
> In corporal sufferance finds a pang as great
> As when a giant dies."

The moral influences of the employment, in this case, are certainly deserving of consideration. The notions of former times were such, that a butcher was not allowed to sit as juror in a trial of life and death. I cannot sympathize in these prejudices; but any practice, which tends in any degree to render us indifferent to the infliction of pain, even in the case of a dumb animal, — any practice bordering upon cruelty, — cannot be without its pernicious effects upon the temper and character of persons accustomed to it. It may seem to some persons a ridiculous squeamishness, but I confess that I never see cooked animals brought upon table as near as possible in the form of life, whether it be game or any thing else, without a painful disgust, which I find it impossible to overcome. It is a mysterious law of nature that animals should feed upon each other; and certainly, as we cannot doubt, like all the laws of nature, a beneficent law; but it is the ferocity of a tiger, and not becoming a man, which delights to regale itself with the warm blood of his victim; and though I am no Bramin, I wish always that the food which I eat should be as far as possible separated from al associations of life.

Sheep are slaughtered by thrusting a straight knife through the neck, between its bone and the windpipe, "severing the carotid artery and jugular vein on both sides," by which they bleed freely, and life soon becomes extinct. They are kept fasting twenty-four hours before death, as it is said that, if killed upon a full stomach, the meat is not so agreeable to the taste, and sooner passes into a putrid state. Sheep are placed here upon a cradle or stool, to be killed, as with us. I am not very well able to describe the mode of cutting up and dressing, further than to say, that it exhibits a remarkable neatness; that the

30 *

meat, as far as I can observe, is never blown; and that the carcass is not, as with us, slit down by the back-bone, and so divided into four quarters; but a piece nearly square is cut from the loins, termed here a saddle of mutton, which is esteemed a more choice part for roasting than the leg, and is always a favorite dish upon an elegant table. The butchers, or cooks, have likewise a habit, not certainly general with us, but much to be commended — that of separating the joints before the meat is cooked, which greatly alleviates the difficulty of carving.

The mode of slaughtering cattle differs from that of slaughtering sheep. Some gentlemen, a few years ago, interested themselves much on this subject, on the sole ground of humanity, and experiments were made of killing the animal, by driving a sharp instrument directly into the spinal cord, back of the horns; but, although the animal fell instantly, yet the convulsions continued much longer than when he was killed by being stunned, by the former method, and it was reasonably inferred that the suffering, therefore, was much greater. This is said to be the mode adopted in the great slaughtering establishments in the neighborhood of Paris, "where a sharp-pointed chisel is driven, with a smart stroke, between the second and third vertebræ of the spine; insensibility immediately ensues, and the blood is let out by opening the blood-vessels of the neck." Besides the objection made above to this mode of slaughtering, it is said the animal does not bleed so freely and entirely as when stunned on the forehead, as by the former method. The present mode of killing is by bringing, by means of a ring on the floor and a rope passed round the foot of the horns, the ox's head to the ground; and he is then struck on the forehead, not, as with us, by an axe with a flat head, but with a similar instrument, with a pointed end, two or three inches long, of the size of the small finger, this point being hollow, and with sharp edges, — and this is driven directly into the upper forehead. The animal falls at once: this point is immediately extracted, and a wooden pin, of about the same diameter, is driven into the wound, and forced into the brain or spinal marrow, and the animal dies at once. I am not certain, that this is an improvement upon the mode of killing which prevails with us; though the killing of an ox, with us, requires great adroitness and great strength; otherwise, the blows require to be repeated, and much suffering is inflicted, which, it would seem, might be avoided. The English method might be tried; and if it has any advantages to the sufferer or the executioner, I cannot doubt it would be adopted.

Calves, as I have observed, are not killed under six or eight weeks old, and they are bled daily for a week before they are slaughtered. I do not know that this is a very painful operation, but very little seems to be gained by it. They are killed, as with us, by cutting the throats across. The manner, however, in which they are often conveyed through the streets, piled into a cart, lengthwise, by dozens, with their heads hanging down as they are jolted over the pavements, is perfectly shocking to humanity, and deserves the interference of the benevolent society for the prevention of cruelty to animals. It is sufficiently humiliating to feel, that in nothing does man more need watching and restraint, than in his treatment of the helpless and defenceless.

It is a subject certainly worthy of concern. It is no affectation of sensibility, though by some it may be deemed a morbid sensibility, to say, that the subject is a painful one. The passion which one sometimes sees excited in the killing of animals, and the utter callousness and indifference with which some persons go about it, to whom the work is familiar, are very far from being agreeable features, either in temper or conduct. The sight and smell of blood excite an instinctive horror even among the inferior animals; and any man, who contributes, in any way, to alleviate pain and suffering, even among the lowest of sensitive existences, and to prevent cruelty, more especially to the dumb and defenceless, need not feel that he has lived wholly in vain.

LIX. — VEGETABLE AND FRUIT MARKETS.

England may with reason boast of the fineness of her fruits, especially as, in this matter, she has to contend with the adverse influences of temperature and climate. The country abounds in greenhouses, hothouses, conservatories, and forcing-beds. All the appliances of art, and the highest measure of horticultural skill, are exerted to counteract the unfavorable circumstances under which their cultivation is carried on; to protect plants whose frail nature requires protection; and by every possible means to stimulate and bring to perfection those plants and fruits which seem to demand the same assiduous and parental care as the young of the animal creation.*

Few of the country houses belonging to persons whose means allow of such indulgences, are without forcing-beds, green-houses, and conservatories. Many persons, whose means are restricted, with a high refinement of taste, sacrificing the common pleasures of a frivolous and inferior character, prefer this far higher class of enjoyments and luxuries. In these green-houses and conservatories, the gayest flowers, the most precious exotic plants, and the richest fruits, are cultivated. Many of these conservatories, filled with the choicest varieties of flowering

---

* I wish we knew more of vegetable life. Indeed, what branch of science is there, of which we have not reason to wish we knew more? The microscope, under those modern improvements which have increased its power, and consequently extended the field of its triumphs in a most astonishing degree, is constantly bringing new wonders to light; disclosing the curious and complex structure of the vegetable world; and enabling us to watch in some plants, in their wonderful frame-work, the rapid circulation of the streams of life. Such discoveries almost make us feel that the man who would wantonly pluck a lily from its stem, and scatter its leaves to the winds, or would trample a damask rose upon the ground, offers an offence to conscious life, and casts an indignity upon some of the most beautiful expressions of the divine skill and beneficence.

I have recently had the pleasure of looking through as powerful an instrument, of this kind, as human art has perhaps as yet been able to produce. Leaves, woods of different kinds, and different insects, were presented upon the field of vision, and exhibited a structure so various, complicated, and exquisitely finished, that one seemed endued with a new sense, and almost born into a new world.

I often hear it said that divine revelation is complete and full, and that we must look for nothing more. It may be so with a written word; though I know of no right which any human mind has to limit the dispensations of Infinite Wisdom; and with the most reverential gratitude for what has been given, I confess there are many more things, than have been revealed, which my impatient curiosity is thirsting to know. But the revelations of the natural world seem only just now begun. The telescope and the microscope are unfolding many a book hitherto closed and sealed, and pouring a flood of light upon fields of wonders which have not before been brought within the reach of human vision, and disclosing objects, forms, structures, contrivances, modes of being, of activity, of life, and of enjoyment, which force upon the mind a sense of the Creator's skill, goodness, and power, absolutely oppressive, and awaken a feeling of reverence and adoration wholly incapable of utterance. We may presently come to understand the organization, for respiration and digestion, of the vegetable as we do of the animal world; and one is scarcely less mysterious than the other.

shrubs and plants, are at the side of, and immediately accessible to, the drawing-rooms of the houses, furnishing, besides the most beautiful objects of sight, an attractive recreation and delight to the female members of the household, and a refreshing retreat from the dissipations of society, or the harassing cares of domestic life.*

The hothouse or greenhouse productions of England (such as pine-apples and grapes, the natives of climates of a higher temperature) are not surpassed by any which I have ever tasted. The pines, or pine-apples, appear to me in size quite equal, and in

---

* In one of the most beautiful parts of England, endeared to me by the hospitalities of friends whose kindness I cannot too highly appreciate, I found even a right reverend bishop, a man eminent for his intellectual powers and his literary attainments, entering, with all the enthusiasm of Bacon, into the cultivation of his garden, as "one of the purest of human delights." He was then considered as among the warmest patrons of a religious party, whose eminent piety no one questions, who have, at least for a while, converted the Established Church into the church militant, broken up the dead calm in which it had for years reposed, and lashed its waves into a tempestuous foam. When I visited him, he was anxious to show the friend who accompanied me, and myself, his *rosary*, as he termed it, where, in a separate and extensive enclosure, he was cultivating a great variety of roses, with something of the enthusiasm which is said to have characterized the cultivation of tulips some years gone by. I could not resist the inclination to tell him, without any intentional discourtesy, that he had been for some time *suspected* of certain heresies, but I hardly supposed matters had gone so far with him that he would openly show his friends his *rosary*. He was then in the midst of a religious war, if it be not an abuse of language to call any sort of war, or any angry contest whatever, "religious," and in the very heat of the fight. I could not avoid thinking, at the same time, what a refreshment to the soul, as well as to the body, must it be thus to retire from the field of theological controversy, bristling with points of angry dispute, like the bayonets of an opposing column on a field of battle, to the charming quiet and delightful occupations of rural life. Soothing it must have been, to cease for a while a well-nigh hopeless struggle for a perfect unity of opinion, form, and faith, to contemplate the infinite and harmonious variety which pervades creation, and reflect, at the same time, what an abatement of utility and enjoyment it would have been, had God comprehended all this infinite diversity in one, and made all animals of one form, all vegetables of the same kind, and all flowers of the same color and fragrance. Though I was far from being willing to censure this venerable man for anxiously and devoutly turning to the east, when he recited the articles of his creed, if he deemed it important so to do, I could not help thinking that he must sometimes turn his face to the west, to offer his evening sacrifice, when, standing upon the threshold of his door, he saw before him the wide-spread ocean glittering with matchless splendor, and the setting sun bathing in a flood of glory, and throwing his slanting beams over, a landscape as diversified and as beautiful as, within my observation, the pencil of nature has delineated.

flavor superior, to any which I have seen brought directly from their own native region, — for the reason, perhaps, that the latter, as is understood, are gathered in a green state, and are left to ripen on the passage, usually crowded in bulk in the hold of a vessel. The grapes are magnificent in size, and delicious in taste. I cannot say that there are no native grapes, and none growing in the open air; but I do not recollect meeting with any. It seems to me to be the humidity of the climate of England, rather than its low temperature, which prevents the ripening of many fruits and plants, which can be grown in an equally high latitude on the western continent. It remains to be seen what will be the result of that remarkable system of drainage, which is here prosecuted in different parts of the country with great spirit and resolution, and which bids fair, as soon as any such great operation can be expected to be effected, to become general, if not universal. Its sanatary effects upon the human, as well as the brute animal, are said to be already in some places determined.

The smaller fruits — such as strawberries, raspberries, gooseberries, and currants — are cultivated with great success. Of a kind of strawberries, called the Alpine Pine, and more properly the Elton Pine, the size is most remarkable, ten of them, as I saw in the market of Dundee, where they are cultivated in perfection, actually weighing a pound avoirdupois. I saw others as large at the horticultural exhibitions, called by a different name; but those were forced in pots in greenhouses.

The gooseberries which I have seen on private tables, and in the markets, are of a very extraordinary size, the purple varieties being preferred. I cannot learn that they are as much subject, as in New England, to a species of mildew, or bluish mould, which soon becomes black, and ruins the fruit. Here they are always cultivated upon a single stem, in the form of a small tree, kept trimmed high, and entirely clear of all rubbish or weeds at the bottom. The disease, or blight, to which I refer, is not unknown here, but it is not common; and the fruit is grown in the highest perfection. This disease may come from an unhealthy condition of the soil, or the application of improper manure; but the general and most probable conclusion is, that it is atmospherical. It has appeared to me, that the climate of England, where they have far less sunshine, and much more dampness, than in the Northern United States, does not produce mould in the houses upon plate, furniture, and books, so soon as it does with us, and provisions, both raw and cooked, appear "to keep sweet" longer. I do not undertake to give any scientific reason for this; but it seems probable, that it arises from a more even temperature, and the absence of that intense heat which, with us, often follows rain and dampness. The black currant is almost as much cultivated as the red and white, and quite commonly eaten. Raspberries are cultivated; but I have seen none to be compared with the fine kinds common in the United States. Blackberries I have not seen cultivated. I have met with them in the southern parts of England, but ripening so late in the season that they have no richness of flavor.*

Of plums there are several kinds: damsons are common; the Orleans plum, the large egg-plum, resembling what I think is called, with us, Bolmar's Washington, are the most esteemed; but they are not abundant, and I cannot say that those which I have seen are equal to those seen in the best markets of the United States, and especially, of all other places, at Albany, in New York, where this fruit is found in a degree of perfection and abundance which I have seen nowhere else. Cherries are

---

* I am quite aware of the old proverb, "that there should be no dispute about matters of taste," and that it is perhaps quite *too late in the season with myself*, for me to discuss these matters. I remember very well when a half-grown, green, hard, sour apple, was as much relished by me as now a delicious Muscat grape; but, alas! "the times change, and we change with them." I will not complain. To complain would be ungrateful. There are tastes for all ages, as there are fruits and flowers for all seasons. I thank God every day of my life for the beautiful world in which he has placed me; but I would not wish to be always young, any more than I would desire to be always old. I cannot say that I ever sighed for a perpetual summer; for nature every where abounds in compensations. I exchanged the bright, sunshiny days of my own country for the foggy and humid climate, and the cloudy and weeping skies, of England, where sometimes I have scarcely seen the moon and stars for a month, and where, when the sun shows himself, one seems to recognize an acquaintance of former times. But what of that? Habit and use reconcile us to various and ever-changing circumstances. I have become amphibious, like a true Englishman, and take a good wetting quite naturally. The moderate temperature of the climate has become agreeable; and even the cloudy skies seem better for my eyes than the bright and dazzling snows of New England, in the clear days of winter. Age itself, if it has not the vivacity of youth, and is sometimes oppressed with the consciousness of having not even half accomplished our duties and desires, brings with it many delicious treasures of memory, which, like good wine, lose nothing of their sweetness by time; and hopes, which we would not exchange for all the pleasures of the whole of life's brightest summer, are daily approximating their fruition.

plenty in the market, and in great perfection; the Tartarian, the bigarreau, and the large black-heart and mazard, predominate.

Peaches, nectarines, and apricots, are seen occasionally at private tables; and in great perfection, though in very small quantities, at the great market, and at some of the splendid fruit shops in London. Peaches are grown in favorable situations on open walls, but in general under glass, and early in the season are forced by an artificial climate. They are brought to great perfection in appearance, and command, when first they appear in the market, two guineas, or about ten dollars and a half per dozen, as pine-apples cultivated here, at some times of the year, bring a guinea or thirty shillings sterling apiece, — that is, from five and a quarter to seven and a half dollars each!

One, in such cases, ceases to have any solicitude to know where the peaches or the pines come from, but is curious to learn where the guineas come from. To most of us, however, unindoctrinated in the financial contrivances and complex labor-saving machinery of society, this inquiry seems hopeless, and generally ends in the conviction that wealth is very unequally distributed in this world, without any possibility of devising any practicable scheme for a more even and impartial adjustment. Suppose we could at once level all the waves of the sea, and produce a dead calm, and a perfectly even surface; still it would seem that, while the drops on the top are glittering and radiating in the sunshine, a vast proportion of the drops must be underneath, or near the bottom, sustaining those at the top. The only hope in such case is that, in the continual fluctuations of the whole mass, amid the conflicts of under-currents and upper-currents, the spontaneous effervescence, and the turbulence of winds and storms, the lowest may often be brought to the surface, and the uppermost descend, and this continual change of place and position may give to all, in the long run, an equal chance.* This analogy, perhaps,

* It is by no means the case, I am aware, that the low position is always to be commiserated. The place of humble obscurity is, in general at least, the place of safety, and is quiet and peaceful, while the surface is swept and disturbed by the violence of every storm. There is a measure of selfishness and narrowness in the conception of a charming poet, which is not to be approved, when, in the tones of pity and complaint, he says, —

"Full many a flower is born to blush unseen,
And waste its sweetness on the desert air;"

as if the beauties of nature were made only for man's eyes, and as if the hum-

can scarcely be said to apply to a country, where the masses of wealth are the accumulations of centuries, and are fortified and hedged in by the strong iron fences and the bristling *chevaux-de-frise* of laws of entail and rights of primogeniture. It may serve better to illustrate a condition of society like that in the United States, where the paths of competition in the various departments of life are equally open to all — the condition of the laws and the habits of the country favor the more equal distribution of wealth, and seem to forbid any extraordinary permanency to any large accumulations. Which condition is to be preferred, my reader must determine for himself.

The luxury in which the higher and wealthier classes in England live is, probably, unequalled in any country, and is, perhaps, not surpassed in the history of Roman grandeur or Oriental magnificence. They expend, whether willing or unwilling, with a profusion which it is difficult for those of us brought up in the school of restricted and humble means to understand; and in respect to true liberality, there is probably the same diversity of disposition and character to be found as among those, who, instead of dispensing guineas, are obliged to keep their reckoning in pence and farthings. I do not forget that excessive wealth, as well as extreme penury, have each their peculiar moral dangers. But the liberal expenditures of the rich, even upon many articles of pure luxury, are a great public benefit. Certainly, no immoral indulgence is ever to be justified or excused. I do not say that it is the best appropriation of the money; that point I shall not now discuss; but certainly the person, who gives his two guineas for his dozen of peaches, encourages industry, rewards horticultural skill, stimulates improvement, excites a wholesome competition, and would, surely, be doing much worse with them if he kept them parsimoniously and uselessly hoarded in his coffers.

The apples, in England, are in general inferior, excepting for cooking purposes. The superiority of our Newton pippin is every where admitted and proclaimed. Of other of our fine apples, — such as the golden russet, the Baldwin, the blue pearmain, and many others, — I have seen none, though it is not to be confi-

blest flower did not perform its proper part in purifying the air, the great element of life to all animated existence, and regale many a sentient being by its fragrance, and feed myriads upon its leaves, and yield to many a busy insect the precious honey from its expanded bosom.

dently inferred, from that circumstance, that none are imported. Large quantities of apples are sent from the United States to England, and sold to advantage.*

The English have not yet learned the value of apples as food for stock. Many of the farmers in the United States, after repeated trials, both for fatting swine, for neat stock, and even for milch cows, rate them in value in the proportion of three bushels of apples as equal to two of potatoes. There are many parts of England, where apples might be cultivated to advantage for this very purpose, where the finest kinds might not ripen, but where the inferior sorts would be likely to yield abundantly. There are many hedgerows where they would grow to advantage; and they certainly might be substituted, without loss to beauty, and with a clear gain to utility, for many thorn-trees, ash-trees, and others, which now stand in the parks and open grounds of the country.

Of pears I have seen several good kinds, but none comparable to the Seckle or the Bartlett. This, however, may be mere matter of personal taste. Melons are grown only under glass, and by artificial heat. The English walnut grows abundantly, and is used both dried and for pickling; and chestnuts are plentiful. The common shagbark, or hickory nut, I have not met with, though it is sometimes imported. Filberts are cultivated in the county of Kent for the market, on a gravelly soil, where they are raised on small bushes, or trees with one stem, and suffered to grow not more than five or six feet high. They grow together on the same ground with hops, and pear or apple-trees; and the proportionate number of each to an acre, is stated at 800 hills of hops, 200 filberts, and 40 apple or pear-trees. "The

* Small adventures sent in this way, as presents from friends to friends, are often so badly packed at home, and so adroitly unpacked on the passage, and withal, are taxed with such a variety of charges in the transit, that one is compelled, from bitter experience, to give up a much greater pleasure than that of eating the fine fruit — the pleasure of enabling one's friends to eat it. The Christians, as we are called, have, at least many of them, very little honesty, and, one would be half inclined to think, live upon a system of piracy, or privateering, or reprisals, among themselves. The Turks have more; for all travellers assert that what is intrusted to their keeping, under a pledge of fidelity, is sure to be held sacred. The violator of such a trust, upon conviction, would be likely to find himself a head shorter. But then the Christians have a great deal more, and a truer, faith; and after all, common honesty is a very homely virtue, which any body can practise if he would.

hops are said to last twelve years, the filberts thirty, and after that, the apples and pears require the whole ground."

The vegetables grown for table use are many of them in appearance of the finest kinds. The potatoes grown in England are in general of a superior quality, though I think them inferior to the potatoes grown in Nova Scotia. In Nova Scotia, they have not only the advantage of a climate as cool as that of England, but likewise of a virgin soil, which circumstances seem particularly favorable both to the growth and the quality of the potato; and nothing of the kind, which I have ever eaten, is equal to a fine Nova Scotia potato. In our old soils, surcharged with manure, the potatoes are always inferior in quality. In Ireland, deemed of all other countries the adopted home of the potato, I was seldom able to find one that was even eatable. This arose, however, not from the quality of the root, but from the mode of cooking — the Irish always desiring, to use their own expression, "to have a stone in the middle;" so that the aim of the cook was only to boil, or rather scald, the outside of the potato, and leave the inside as hard as when it went into the pot. The advantage of this, as gravely stated to me, was that they were longer in digestion, and therefore gave more support. This may be sound philosophy in Ireland, where the stomachs of the poor find an equal difficulty in getting, as they do in keeping what they get. It would be inhuman to treat the extreme destitution of these poor wretches with any levity; but I found this mode of cooking prevailing also at the tables of the rich and noble; and after seeing such an abuse of one of the most useful and nutritious plants which come out of the earth, I was half inclined to advise them to try a few granite pebbles of a size to pass through a McAdam ring, and see whether they would not serve the digestive organs still longer. It was a curiosity to me in London, likewise, to see them selling in the market, by the quart, the small, not half-grown, not quarter-grown potatoes, not even so large as cherries, and many not larger than peas; and these were bought up as luxuries. I should quite as soon think of sitting down to a dish of boiled bullets, or duck-shot; and I should suppose with almost equal chance of nourishment. If it were such potatoes only, at which Cobbett launched his anathemas, one would not be surprised at his indignation.

It is a very great point to bring the earliest potatoes into the market, and I have seen them offered in Covent Garden Market as early as March. Indeed, by a method which I will presently explain, there would be little difficulty in having them at the coming in of the new year. In Penzance, in Cornwall, at the very south of England, where there are some parcels of most excellent soil, and great skill in its cultivation, where the winter is open and the climate very mild, and where, for this purpose, land is let at twenty pounds, or one hundred dollars per acre, large supplies of early vegetables, potatoes especially, are raised for the London markets. In this case, they are sprouted under and upon warm horse-dung, or under glass; and are planted as early as February, and carefully attended, pains being taken to select the earliest kinds. The mode of sprouting them in this case is similar to that adopted by the excellent and spirited cultivators at West Cambridge, near Boston, where the sets are started, under a bed of fresh horse-dung, on the sunny and protected side of a hill.

I will here quote the directions of the celebrated Mr. Knight, president of the Horticultural Society, for raising early potatoes; which, it is obvious, can be applicable only to our mild and southern latitudes, where the winters are open.

"Drills may be formed in a warm and sheltered situation, and in the direction of north and south, during any of the winter months, two feet apart, and seven or eight inches deep. Stable-dung, half decomposed, should be laid in the drills, and combined with the earth four inches downwards, and covered with some of the mould which had been thrown out in forming the drills, by the rake, to within four inches of the surface. The sets uncut are then to be placed, with the crown-eye uppermost, in the centre of the furrow, four inches from each other, and to be covered with only an inch of mould at first, and afterwards with an occasional quantity of sifted ashes, until the plants are so vigorous and advanced as to require the usual earthing, of which, however, very little is necessary." Mr. Knight also used leaves as a lining at the side of the drills, in the early periods, to preserve as much warmth as possible, and better to guard against the effects of frost. The soil in this case should be light and dry, and not tenacious of water. It is recommended by some gardeners, early in the season, to lay the sets upon a floor in a warm room, and occasionally sprinkle them with water, which will cause them to germinate. As soon as they have sprouted, cover them with some finely-sifted mould; and the sets will be ready for transplanting at the earliest period.

Another mode of obtaining early potatoes, not *new* potatoes, which is, I am told, sometimes practised, is to plant potatoes only so early in the season, as that they shall be about half-grown at the usual time of taking them up. These may be taken up in the autumn, and replaced in earth; and early in the succeeding spring they may be sold as new potatoes. I should be sorry, by any account of the deceptions and tricks practised in this old country, to be in any degree instrumental in corrupting the simplicity and true-heartedness of any of my own countrymen, who, good souls, may possibly never have heard of any such thing as trick or deception! but excepting the lie in this case, the potatoes would be quite as good as the half-grown, waxy, new potatoes usually brought to market.*

Potatoes are sold in the market by weight, fourteen pounds constituting a stone weight; in Ireland, a stone of potatoes weighs sixteen pounds. In Ireland, the crop is measured by barrels, and an acre of ground is stated to have yielded so many barrels. Then the Irish acre differs very much from the English statute acre, being, I think, the former compared with the latter, as 196 to 121, or nearly 5 to 3. A barrel of potatoes in Ireland may contain five, or only three bushels, and the weight of the bushel of potatoes is not determined, though customarily estimated at 56 pounds. Few beans are cultivated for the table, excepting the Windsor bean, which is a coarse vegetable; and a small bean, used like our string beans, and called the French bean. Our Lima bean, and other rich pole-beans, I have not met with. Peas are abundant in market, are brought in early, and continued late, and are of several different kinds, the Charlton pea (so called from the town where the earliest peas are

---

* Nor, if they should be tempted to practise any such fraud, will I go so far as to recommend them, by way of encouragement or consolation, to read the chapter on Lying, in Paley's Moral Philosophy; nor, above all, that celebrated treatise of the same exquisite master in casuistry, that perfect anodyne for weak consciences, the Letter on Subscription, in which he shows, with admirable skill, in how many different ways an honest man may subscribe the thirty-nine articles of the church without believing one of them.

grown) being preferred as an early pea. In order to bring peas to early maturity, or rather to a state for sale, a ridge of land or high furrow is thrown up in a direction from east to west, and the peas are planted on the south side of this ridge at the bottom of the furrow. In this way the young plants are protected from the cold winds on one side, and enjoy the warm rays of the sun reflected on the other. This is a simple and excellent arrangement, especially in a climate where we may say, with some truth, that a handful of sunshine is worth much more than its weight in gold.

Carrots and turnips are of the finest quality, and always sold in bunches. The orange carrot seems preferred for the table; the Belgian white for stock. Onions are generally eaten small. They are planted early in the autumn, and gathered in July and August. Spinach, endive, cresses, lettuces, are always in the market, either forced or grown in the open ground. Blood-beets I have scarcely seen, either in the markets or on table, unless pickled in vinegar. The fine egg-plant, so common in the New York and Philadelphia markets, does not appear to be known here. That most luscious vegetable, the sweet potato, of course cannot be grown. I have once seen some for sale at a shop window, and, thinking I would indulge in a reminiscence of home, I found, on weighing, at the price asked, a single potato would be 1*s.* 6*d.* or 37½ cents. Of course it ended in inquiry; and I was obliged to be satisfied with other forms of remembrance. Of squashes, they can scarcely be said to have any. They have a very inferior kind, which they dignify with the name of vegetable marrow; but of our fine crook-neck and Canada squashes, or our autumnal vegetable marrow, nothing is seen, and their excellence cannot be appreciated without being tasted. Of our delicious green Indian corn, of course they have none. Cucumbers are always in the market. In the early part of the season, they are forced; in the latter part of the season, they grow out of doors. Every possible pains is taken to protect their plants, as may be seen by the hundreds of hand-glass frames and bass mattings which are to be found in every extensive vegetable garden.

There are four species of plants, or edible vegetables, in which, it must be admitted, the English markets cannot be surpassed, at least in the size of their products. They are asparagus, rhubarb, cauliflowers, and cabbages. The asparagus and rhubarb are gigantic, the rhubarb more especially, which is often brought to market three and four feet in length, and of the size of a woman's arm — some women of course excepted. The early asparagus is forced under glass; the later is forced in the open ground by all the appliances of manure. The quantity of rhubarb consumed is enormous, for it comes not in baskets, but piled up in four-horse wagons in bulk. The asparagus shows the want of sun, and appears as if grown in a cellar, the mere head of the early kinds being the only part eatable. I think Cobbett somewhere says, that "the English do not know how to eat asparagus, for they always begin at the white end." I have not myself observed among them any remarkable deficiency of gastronomical science; but certainly, in this case, they have not far to go to find a white end. Sea-kale or Scotch kale is very much eaten early in the season. It is blanched under cover, and is a delicious vegetable, that is, for those whose taste agrees with mine. The Jerusalem artichoke seems a favorite vegetable with most persons.*

One of the principal vegetables found in the market, and this at all seasons, is cauliflower; and it is certainly grown here in perfection. They are sown, for the next year's use, some time in August, in hotbeds, and are transplanted into the open ground in February. They, of course, before being transplanted, are cultivated under glass, and for some time after they require protection. They are a frequent, and almost an invariable dish at well-furnished tables. Cabbages likewise are brought into the market with a profusion absolutely astounding, which itself

* In this case I am in the minority. I have not studied under Mrs. Briggs, or Dr. Kitchener, or I would inform my readers how they are cooked. Under modern refinements, meats, and vegetables, and fruits, come to table as much disguised, as were men and women at the late *bal-costume* of the queen, when nothing nearer than *engagés* or *attachés* knew each other, — and that, either by magnetic *clairvoyance* or previous arrangement; and it is said, (I do not vouch for its truth,) some nobleman addressed his valet as "my lord;" and some gentlemen, like the Smithfield drovers in penning their cattle at night, as I have described, had to look carefully for some private mark, to be sure that they had got their own wives to carry home with them. I would not insinuate that the English wives, exemplary as they are for their fidelity, were not as anxious to be found, as their husbands were to find them. Sometimes I agree in a remark, often quoted by persons who are not very abstemious in the use of strong language, that "Heaven sends us meats, but" —— I had rather not say who —— "sends us cooks."

shows how much they are eaten. One would be disposed to consider them as the favorite vegetable of the English. The early ones of course are forced in hotbeds and transplanted; and a constant succession is kept up. I have sometimes seen in the market, at one time, very early in the morning, many large four-horse wagon-loads of cabbages, lettuces, and rhubarb, all distinct, and piled up in the most beautiful manner, with a precision which is admirable; and when I have had the curiosity to inquire how many heads of cabbage were on a single load, the answer has been, two hundred and twenty-five dozen.

The celery brought into market is, like the rhubarb, gigantic. The solid-stalked is greatly preferred. It is finely blanched. It is not so agreeable for eating as a smaller-sized plant, but it shows the perfection of cultivation. The celery, like the rhubarb and the lettuce, is brought into market in the neatest manner. Nothing is tumbled into the carts, or thrown out upon the ground topsy-turvy, or indiscriminately. Even the heads of lettuce are every one of them tied with a string of bass matting; and when presented in the stalls, the various articles are arranged with great care — I may add, with taste, and a view to effect.

In looking down from the high bridge, in Edinburgh, upon the vegetable and fruit market below, and observing the arrangement of the different articles in the stalls, the intermingling of the white cauliflowers with the purple cabbages, the orange carrots, the yellow turnips, and the red beets, and other articles of various hues, like the colors in a Turkey carpet, the effect is really picturesque and beautiful. I have gazed at them repeatedly with much pleasure. The same remarks apply to the arrangements in the London markets. I know some will say, What is the use of all this? I have just given the answer. It gave me, and it gives others, pleasure. That is reason enough, if there were no other. I think in this respect we have a good deal to learn. There is a natural concord or harmony among all the senses, and the stomach seems better satisfied when that which enters it gives pleasure to the eye. Suppose that our fine rare-ripe peaches were a dingy black, instead of presenting, as they now do, a sample of that most lovely and perfect intermingling of colors to be found in nature — such as the soft blending of red and white in the leaf of the damask rose, or, in a still more radiant form, on the cheek of virgin beauty and innocence;

I think in such case we should eat them with a far inferior relish.

Grapes of the very finest description are produced in England, but wholly, as I have already remarked, by artificial culture. This, of course, places them beyond the reach of the great mass of the people; but they are always found on the tables of the wealthy and noble. In the stalls of Covent Garden Market, they present themselves in such a rich and luscious display, as to tempt a visitor to break at least one of the commandments; and, if it were not for the plate glass, which protects them, it might be, another also. This interposition is certainly humane, as a violation of the latter commandment referred to, under the lynx-eyed system of espionage necessarily practised here, might place one in an awkward position. The violation of the commandment of not coveting what we cannot possess, must be settled in another court. I can only hope that human weakness will be considered; for, in passing from one part of London to the other, and among the shops crowded with the splendid productions of nature, refined and embellished by the highest art and skill, with all the means of sensual gratification, with every thing to minister to luxurious indulgence, to feed the animal appetite, and the often more hungry intellect, and to delight and gratify the fastidious and cultivated taste, it requires a most rigid self-control, so far as our desires are concerned, to keep the peace, from day to day, with one's own conscience.

One of the best gardeners in England has given me some instructions on the management of grapes, which some of my readers may be glad to receive: —

"With regard to the best way to manage the vine, when fruiting, I invariably stop the shoot *one* eye above the bunch; and it is the practice of the best gardeners in England. I generally leave one shoot not stopped without fruit, and to fruit next season, and cut the shoots out that have borne fruit this year. On the short-spur system, every shoot is stopped an eye above the bunch, except the top one, and then it must be managed like the rest; all the lateral shoots *must be stopped one eye* above another, until they cease growing, as, the more leaves you get, the fruit will swell larger."

I should add more on the cultivation of this delicious fruit, but I know it is very well understood in the United States, where the best grapes grown are not, within my knowledge, surpassed for size, abundance, and flavor. So, at least, I thought them before I left home; but in my long exile, in order to keep down a dreadful homesickness that sometimes makes sleep almost as much a stranger to my pillow as though it was stuffed with McAdam's angular stones, I try to think, like the fox in the fable, that the American grapes are sour. But I cannot do it. Affections, which no time nor distance can quench or abate, defy every such idle effort; and memory returns, with all its sensibilities quickened, and all its delicious colorings heightened and embellished, to triumph over the impotence of the resolution.

There is another article abounding in the markets here, which, though by no means unknown in the markets of the United States, is not common; and therefore, from the same intelligent gardener, I shall give the best account I could obtain of the mode of cultivating them. I mean, mushrooms. There are few extensive gardens without a mushroom-house, which is a dark room fitted up with shelves, and with the means of producing the desired temperature.

"The cultivation of mushrooms in the winter months, in order to have a daily supply, requires a house for the purpose. The house at Welbeck is divided into four tiers of shelves, three shelves in each tier. The shelves are ten inches deep, [that is, a sort of boxes, like the berths on board ship. —H. C.]

"The first three shelves are generally filled about the beginning of September, as the field mushrooms begin to go out then. The material used to fill the shelves is pure horse-dung droppings, without any straw. It is suffered to ferment a little before being put in, and beaten quite hard with a wooden mallet. As soon as the heat decreases to 65° by the thermometer, or ascertained by a piece of wood thrust in, to see that the burning heat is gone off, the bed may be spawned, by opening holes two inches deep in the dung, and putting in bits of spawn about the size of a walnut, nine inches each way, all over the bed. It is then covered with two or three inches of good fresh loam from a pasture field. If a little road-scrapings is added to the loam, it helps to bind it, which is important, as a great deal of the success of the crop depends on the soil and dung being incorporated into one solid mass, not liable to crack, or get too dry. The soil must be beaten with the mallet, like the dung, quite smooth and hard all over. In eight days after spawning, the bed will be covered with a whitish substance, which shows that the spawn is running all through it, and that the heat is right.

"Mushrooms generally appear in six weeks after making the bed, if the temperature of the house is kept from 55° to 60°. They are very impatient of too much water; and water is required to be put on them only with a fine watering-pot rose; and that when the bed gets dry; and it should be always of the same temperature as the house, or it chills all the young ones, and the crop never lasts so long. If hot-water pipes are used to heat the house, there is no occasion for watering. We generally make fresh beds every month, to keep up a succession all through the year, excepting the months they come naturally in the open fields.

"Mushrooms may be grown in winter in a dark cellar, where there is no artificial heat, by covering the top of the ridges, or box, with good dry hay, at least ten inches thick. They will not come in so quickly as in a house kept at a steady temperature, but will keep in bearing a great deal longer, so that one good bed will last all through. As a good deal of the success of growing mushrooms depends on the goodness of the spawn, it is necessary to get it from some respectable nurserymen, who generally sell it in the shape of bricks. Its quality may easily be ascertained, if good, by breaking it, and seeing it full of white threads, and the smell is exactly like a mushroom. If it smells musty, it has lost its vegetative powers. It will keep good for a year or two, if kept dry, and out of the power of frost. The best is made in London about Battersea, where many cows and horses are pastured in the fields. The old droppings are taken from the surface where the natural mushrooms grow, and mixed with fresh horse-dung, and cut into the shape of bricks. There is always good spawn in the old beds, which may be preserved to put into new ones."

I have gone thus fully into this, as it may appear to some, unimportant subject, because, as a vegetable, this plant is esteemed a great delicacy; and next, because of the great quantities of ketchup which are used, and which may be manufactured in the country, and of which mushrooms are the principal material.

Pines, or pine-apples, are, as I have remarked, cultivated to a large extent, and with the greatest success, in the hot-houses of the affluent, where fire heat is employed; but in Cambridgeshire I found them cultivated, with great success, in common hotbeds. The beds were formed in the usual way; and in order to keep up the heat, or renew it when it declined, additional supplies of fresh stable manure were applied, from time to time, to the sides of the bed. The plants were healthy, and fruited well; and so far as the quality of the fruit goes to approve the mode of growing, I will say, on my own knowledge, better need not be desired.

I have one remark to make in regard to English vegetables and fruits, that will not, I hope, be deemed ill-humored, — which is, that, though cultivated with extraordinary skill, with the exceptions I have above named, they are tasteless, and without that fine relish which one would like to find. I think it is Voltaire who says "that the only ripe fruit to be found in England is a baked apple." I cannot accede to a censure so sweeping; but it is plain that their fruits and vegetables want ripeness and flavor. This may arise partly from a deficiency of heat from the sun, and partly from the excessive forcing of their vegetables, in the vicinity of large markets, by unlimited quantities of manure. I know how difficult it must be to make an Englishman believe this statement; for under the national peculiarity of a large endowment of self-esteem, which their Anglo-Saxon descendants over the water seem to have inherited, (and sometimes, I think, with a considerable enlargement of the organ, from long cultivation,) a genuine Englishman thinks that nothing out of his own country can possibly be so good as what is to be found in it. Now, in intellectual fruits, and the products of art and science, I will not dispute their preëminence — only hoping that, while they are reposing upon their laurels, a young and ambitious rival, in a fair and generous competition, may be up with them as soon as possible, and distance them, if he can. But climates and sunshine are not under human control; and the fact which I have stated is in my mind established, and not the result of mere prejudice, of which, on any subject, if I were conscious of it, I should be ashamed.

LX. — MARKET GARDENS.

My remarks above have chiefly referred to the supply of vegetables in London. There are large markets in all the principal towns; but it is difficult to conceive the amount required for the supply of this mammoth city, with its two million hungry mouths, not one of whom, scarcely, in any direct form, produces a single mouthful for himself.

The extent of the vegetable gardens in the neighborhood of this great city is enormous, and the multiplied facilities of conveyance make even remote places, now, in many articles the suppliers of London. Fifty years ago, it was calculated that there were two thousand acres cultivated by the spade, and eight thousand by the spade and plough conjointly. The extent of cultivation must, of course, be at present much greater. It is said of one individual that he had eighty acres in asparagus, and of another that he had sixty, and that the forming of the beds was estimated at £100 per acre. This undoubtedly was under the old system of growing asparagus, when the soil was to be taken out to a depth of some feet, and a bed of stones placed at the bottom, and other expensive arrangements. Now, asparagus is grown almost as easily as carrots or celery, it only requiring to be first grown in a nursery or seed bed, and then transplanted in the bottom of deep furrows or trenches, made two feet distance from each other, well bedded with manure, and the bed itself kept constantly clean, and annually covered with a loading of manure in the autumn, which must be dug in with a fork in the spring. This, in three years from the seed, gives as good and abundant a plant as under the old method of trenching and bottoming with stones, and laying a foot of manure on the stones.

The amount of vegetables sent by some individual salesmen is enormous. The principal market-days are three times in a week, but Saturday is the principal day; and it is confidently stated — though in relating it I fear that some persons may think the credulity of their too-confiding countryman has been practised upon — that a single grower has been known to send, in one day, more than nineteen hundred bushels of peas in the pod, and seven or eight loads of cabbages, averaging eighteen hundred cabbages each; and at another season, from the same farm, fourteen or fifteen hundred baskets of sprouts will be sent in one day, and in the course of the year from five to six thousand tons of potatoes. In his account of the agriculture of Middlesex, Middleton says, that in 1795, in the height of the fruit season, each acre of the gardens cultivated in small fruits gave employment to thirty-five persons, among whom were many women, who were employed in carrying the fruit to market on their heads; and that the gathering of a crop of peas required forty persons for every ten acres. The account given of the sum of money received from the produce of a single acre is quite worthy of remark, it being the statement of a market-gardener. Radishes, £10; cauliflower, £60; cabbages, £30; celery, first crop, £50; second crop, £40; endive, £30,—making a total of £220, or 1100 dollars, for the gross produce of an acre in twelve months.*

Besides the market which London presents for the disposal of the products of these immense gardens, it is to be remembered that labor may be procured at an hour's notice, at any season and for any term, and at a low rate of wages. The farmer or gardener is therefore saved the burden of keeping up an expensive establishment for any longer time than their services are needed; with this addition, that he makes no provision whatever, at any time, for housing or feeding them. Any person, who has had the management of a large farm in the United States, knows quite well, that the sum of all its difficulties is in the feeding

* What some persons may deem the intrinsic improbability of such accounts, will disappear, when one considers that, in London, every thing, and any thing, may be sold, and may find purchasers, excepting only, I believe, children. These are to be given away; for it is a sober truth, that in the streets of London I have been repeatedly offered the present of children, and that from the breast too, though none the better for that, if I would take them. Whether it is, by a sort of natural phrenological skill, they discover my philoprogenitiveness to be large, or from a destitution, the bitterness of which extinguishes the maternal affections, or from a profligacy even more bitter, and more deeply to be deplored, (in too many cases the pitiable consequence of this destitution,) this is not the place for me to consider. But it is for my own countrymen to consider, with the deepest religious gratitude, the difference between a condition of things in which children are felt to be a burden, and almost a curse, and that in which a healthy and perfect child may be looked upon always as a choice blessing from Heaven; and the more hungry mouths, and sparkling eyes, gather round the well-filled board of the humblest cottager, morning, noon, and night, so much the more, in fact, are the means of supply increased, and the parental heart filled to overflowing with joy and love

and management of the human machinery. In the next place, here there is no want of capital with persons who undertake such occupations; and it is applied with liberality wherever there is a chance of using it to profit. This is a great consideration, wherever capital may be safely and advantageously applied to land. We often hear the counsel given to cultivate a little land well, rather than a large extent of land imperfectly. In the main, this is sound advice on the score of profit. But in agriculture, viewed as a commercial transaction, the profits will correspond with the amount of capital invested or employed. Large returns are to be expected only from cultivating a large extent of land; or, in other words, pursuing agriculture as a man, who would command success, pursues any other branch of trade, by devoting his time, talents, and zeal to it, and applying all the means within his reach to its advancement. While

> "Little boats should keep near shore,
> Vessels large may venture more."

The man who, as above, can cultivate one acre of ground with such eminent success, may cultivate one hundred with similar profit, provided he can give to it the same requisite attention, provided a sufficiency of labor and manure are equally attainable, and provided, likewise, the market is equally sure and favorable for the disposal of his products. Whether capital can in any particular case be profitably applied to agriculture, must depend upon a great variety of local and temporary circumstances. It is so with commerce, and with most other branches of business. No human power or skill can control the vicissitudes of the climate and the weather; but the contingencies on which the success of agriculture depends are perhaps not so great as those on which the success of mercantile transactions depends. It is idle to expect reward without labor, fruit without seed, profit without risk, success without effort, — unless in those games of mere chance, of which sober men will beware, and in which there are always vastly more losers than winners, and many more blanks than prizes. The great want with most of our farmers is clearly want of capital, to apply to the land in labor, or manure, or in the way of permanent improvements of drainage and irrigation, which change at once the whole face of a country. The main elements of success in agriculture are the same as in any other profession, — skill, judgment, application, industry, and capital, either in the form of education, money, oi credit; the risks are not greater; the road to a reasonable competence, which is all to which a good mind should anxiously aspire, is as certain as is common in human affairs; extraordinary success — which I do not say it is criminal to desire, but even lawful to aim at — is not unfrequently attainable: but, what is better than all, the gains of agriculture, where the labor by which those gains are secured is honorably and justly provided for, and its products disposed of without any betrayal of conscience, are so unalloyed, so untainted by corruption, so clearly in themselves not the occasions of privation, but the very instruments of good to others, that one reposes on them with entire and grateful complacency, and their value to the winner is more than quadrupled. My friends, I know, will pardon my enthusiasm, which, like a half-smothered fire, is continually bursting out in this way. If it sometimes sheds a flickering light by its blaze, it never burns to destroy; and if, in respect to that noble pursuit which Heaven first ordained for man, it awakens in any pure and honest minds, not crazed with speculation nor hardened and corrupted by the too common tricks of trade, any gentle vibrations of sympathy, I shall feel that my two mites have found their way into the great treasury of public good.

The eminent success of the market-gardeners near London depends on several circumstances in their management, which I will point out. In the first place, the land is thoroughly drained, so as not only to cut off the springs which might render the wetness of the land permanent, but likewise to carry off speedily the rain which falls. In the next place, the land is completely trenched, to the depth of from two to three feet, with the spade. This serves two purposes; first, to assist in the drainage by giving a free passage into the principal conduits of the rain as it comes down; and next, to enable the roots of the plants freely to extend themselves in search of food. In trenching, it is necessary to keep the top soil at the top, and not to bring the lower stratum to the surface, or to suffer a large portion of the cold earth to be mingled with the rich mould. This requires some little calculation. The soil of the first trench made across the field must be completely thrown out; and so likewise the top soil of the second trench. The bottom soil of the second trenching is then to be thrown into the vacant space of the first, and the top soil of the third line upon that. Things will then come rightly into their places, the bottom soil being always thrown upon the bottom, the top soil upon the top, while at the end of the piece trenched, that which was first thrown out must be brought and replaced. The third point particularly attended to, is ample manuring. For this object they have always plentiful stores on hand, to be applied as may be desired; the old hotbeds, when broken up, furnishing large quantities in that decomposed state, in which only is its application safe in respect to many kinds of plants. Manure is sometimes applied in a solid and sometimes in a liquid form. Sometimes, when the ground is dug, the manure is dug in with it; sometimes it is laid on the surface; sometimes it is used with every successive crop, at other times with the first crop only: but all these are matters directly dependent upon experience and practice, and which it would be impossible, in such a report as this, particularly to define. Manure, in its coarsest state, is seldom applied to garden vegetables; and it is found expedient, in respect to liquid manures, to apply them in a diluted and mixed form. The next point aimed at, is to avoid the immediate repetition of the same crop on the same ground; for, though manure may be had in abundance, yet the second and third crops gradually become deteriorated. Chemistry has not yet determined with precision how this evil, if so it is to be regarded, is to be counteracted. It is strongly hoped that this may be one of its first achievements. Most of what it has yet given us in the case is theory. What we want is practical and efficient rules by which the health and strength of the declining patient may be at once and with certainty recovered. The next object is, to have a succession of crops, one crop often growing between the rows of another, and prepared to take its place as soon as it is removed, so that there is no respite of the cultivation, while the season allows of it; and near London, with the help of straw covering, and mats, and glasses, some plants are on the ground all the year. For this object, and to counteract the effect of the seasons, the most extensive preparation is made; articles are prepared of brush, of matting and straw, and hand-glasses, or boxes with glass tops, and, to guard against insects, boxes with coarse gauze tops are prepared in the greatest abundance, and changes of the temperature and weather are watched with the most sedulous care. Hot and forcing beds, likewise, and conservatories, and hothouses, are made ready in the most extensive forms, for the purpose of forwarding plants to be set out at proper seasons, and for the growing of those plants which require artificial heat. Lastly, irrigation is as much as practicable attended to, and engines, and watering-pots, and other contrivances, are in constant requisition for these purposes, and as far as they can be applied. The science of gardening is here a substantial science; and young men are as carefully educated in its various departments as in any of the learned professions, and receive a patronage according to their skill and merit. Under such circumstances, the market gardens near London are managed with a skill and enterprise worthy of all praise, and sure of rewards much more substantial.

LXI. — COVENT GARDEN MARKET.

The great market in England for vegetables, fruits, and flowers, is the market of *Covent* Garden, without question a corruption for *Convent*, as this place is understood to have been formerly the garden of the convent, and connected with the establishment of Westminster Abbey. The whole square included in the market-place is said to embrace five acres; but this, I think, must take in the buildings, dwelling-houses, hotels, shops, &c., forming the exterior boundary of the square. In the centre of this square is the market-house, of which no verbal description can convey a very exact idea to the reader. It combines open stalls and close shops, sellers within and on the outsides, with a long hall or arcade, running through the centre, sixteen feet in width, and fitted up with shops on each side, and with shelves projecting into the passage, which are spread out with all the fruits and flowers of the season.

1. Fruits and Vegetables. — The outer stalls are for the coarser vegetables, potatoes, cabbages, &c., and for the common foreign fruits. This is by no means the only vegetable and fruit market in London, but it is the principal one; and some of the other markets, and many of the fruit-shops, scattered over Lon-

don, receive their supplies from Covent Garden. There is hardly any season of the year when every variety of fruit and vegetables, which can be forced, is not to be found in this market; and in the proper seasons a great variety is to be found, the product of natural and artificial culture, in the highest perfection. The sale of dried foreign fruits is here likewise immense. England can scarcely be considered as a fruit country, and the high prices charged for the finest fruits place them beyond the reach of all but the most wealthy classes. Two shillings, or half a dollar, for a single peach, — and at no season are they much less than half that sum, and many other fruits in proportion, — render them forbidden fruit to the great multitude. In quantity, Covent Garden is limited compared with the city of London, which it is intended to supply; but it is high tide here on a market-day, at daylight in the morning, when the wholesale market-men supply the retailers, and the streams from this fountain flow into and permeate every part of the city and its neighborhood. The market in Farringdon Street occupies as much ground as Covent Garden, but this embraces butchers' stalls as well as fruits and vegetables.

Covent Garden presents an interesting spectacle on a great market-day, at 4 o'clock in the morning, when the wholesale business commences, and the retailers, seeking supplies for their different stalls, and the occupants of stalls in other markets, and the keepers of vegetable shops in the town, and the various itinerant dealers, who penetrate all the by-places and streets in different parts of the town and the vicinity, come to make their purchases. This occupies two or three hours; and a busier scene is hardly to be witnessed. All the smaller articles — gooseberries, currants, peas, beans, new potatoes, apples, &c. — are brought in baskets; cabbages, lettuces, rhubarb, celery, &c., in bulk, as I have described. Peas, in Covent Garden Market, are shelled before they are sold, and after they come out of the hands of the wholesale dealer. These come frequently in sacks. It is an interesting sight to see the poor and squalid women and young girls, who come to earn a few pence by shelling the peas, sitting about in different squads, (and I have counted at one time as many as eighty in one party,) all busily engaged in this occupation at about one penny, or two cents, per quart. Raspberries and strawberries are brought in small cone-shaped baskets, containing little more than a pint; and these are usually brought long distances on the heads of women. It is said that these women, who carry such heavy loads upon their heads, are principally from Wales, and that many of them, for example, come into market twice a day from Brentford, where great quantities of strawberries are raised, and return; and this is a distance of more than seven miles, making at least thirty miles in a day. To such endurance may even a woman's frame be trained. Many of the milk-women in London, who carry their milk in large tin cans slung from their shoulders, and containing from six to eight gallons each, travel long distances in the course of the day. But the most remarkable instance of strength and endurance is perhaps to be found in the fish-women of Edinburgh, who attend the market from New Haven and Musselboro'. Their load, which is in two baskets, one over the other, containing different kinds of fish, slung upon their backs, often weighs 150 lbs., and has been known to weigh 200 lbs. The distance from New Haven to Edinburgh is more than two miles, and in this distance they stop to rest but once only; and after their arrival they are to be found crying their fish in all parts of the town. How many of the Chestnut Street, or Washington Street, or Broadway belles would it require to lift even one of these loads from the ground? Yet these market and milk-women, and the fish-women of Edinburgh, are perfect models of health and strength. The latter — with their elephantine arms and legs, their bright, clean caps, and fair complexions, their firm tread, and their stentorian lungs, with their gay costume of various colors, and their five petticoats, so arranged in different lengths that a portion of each may be displayed — are among the most picturesque, and not unpleasing, objects of that beautiful city.

The advantage of bringing the finer fruits to the market in this way is, that they come in the best possible condition. The wholesale business being completed, the growers of the produce return home, and the marketing goes at once into the hands of the shopmen and retail dealers, who are, in general, residents in the city.

2. Flowers. — Having said so much of the vegetables and fruits, I must not omit another article in Covent Garden Market, of which the sale is immense, — that is, flowers. In the winter

they are sent here from the greenhouses; at more genial seasons, from various gardens and conservatories in the neighborhood. They are displayed in the greatest profusion and perfection, and are, undoubtedly, a large source of income to the cultivators. The English appear to me to have a strong passion for flowers, and I commend their taste. A country house, without its plantation of flowers and flowering shrubs, would be quite an anomaly; and many of the humble and moss-grown cottages have their small gardens of flowers, their doors trellised with woodbines and honeysuckles, and their outer walls covered with a thick mantling of ivy, and made gay with the sweetbrier and the monthly rose. The door-yards of the English, in the country, their windows, their halls, their palaces, are all decorated with flowers; they are among the most beautiful ornaments at their festivals; and even the highest charms of female loveliness are studiously augmented by these innocent and splendid adornments.

Looking out of my window a short time since, I saw that the laborer wheeling his barrow before the door had his button-hole decorated with a beautiful geranium. I went into the street, and the driver of the omnibus, whom I first met, wore a handsome nosegay. I met a bridal party, and, besides the white favors worn by all the servants in attendance, each one had a bunch of flowers at his breast. I met the crowd of magnificent equipages hastening to a drawing-room to pay their courtly homage to a sovereign queen, whose virtues and most exemplary demeanor render her worthy of the homage of true affection and respect; and every lady bears in her hand a magnificent bouquet; and the coachmen and the footmen seem to emulate each other in the gayety and beauty of the flowers which they all wear. At St. Paul's, at the opening of the term of courts, the long procession of grave and learned judges, who then go in state to church, appears, each one, with an elegant nosegay in his hand. At the opera, upon the breathless and successful competitors for public favor, in the midst of a tempest of applause, descends a perfect shower of floral wreaths and rich bouquets.

I sympathize heartily in this taste of the English for flowers, which thus pervades all ranks, and, flowers being accessible to all, and among the most innocent and the cheapest of all pleasures, diffuses a vast amount of enjoyment. They are, indeed, among the richest adornments of God's beautiful creation, and every where, in the tangled forest, in the most secluded thicket, on the ocean prairies, and even upon the desolate heaths, are scattered about in such an endless variety and profusion as cannot fail to impress a reflecting and devout mind with the most grateful veneration and delight.

As for those persons who can see no good and no utility in any thing beyond that which fills the belly, or covers the back, or puts money into the pocket, they are of the earth, earthy. Such grovelling selfishness and animalism I trample under foot with ineffable scorn. But the cultivation of flowers does much for the benefit of the mind. A taste for objects so pure expels a taste for others, which are unworthy. A passion for what is beautiful and refined in nature often secures the mind from the intrusion of passions low and hurtful. Every advance, which is made in any direction for the improvement of the taste or the refinement of manners, is so much done for the general comfort of social life and for good morals.

LXII. — GENERAL MARKETS.

Besides the markets to which I have referred, there is a market in London exclusively for the sale of raw hides and leather; and in various parts of the country markets are held, at fixed times and places, for the sale of wool, and of butter and cheese. These generally go under the name of *fairs;* and I do not think they can be too soon established in the most populous districts of our country. There may be evils, but there are great and overbalancing advantages, attending them. The large dealers attend in numbers to make their purchases, and both sides have equal benefits from an extended competition. Prices assume an equal and a fair rate. The farmer may feel, ordinarily, quite sure of a market for his produce at a fixed time, and to receive his money, instead, as now, of depending almost upon accident for a purchaser. Last, but not among the least of the benefits of the markets in question, is the wholesome emulation which is created by bringing different articles of produce into comparison with each other. The producer of an inferior article is stimulated by the success of his neighbor to produce a better; agricultural information becomes generally diffused; and thus agricultural improvement is essentially advanced. Should such markets be established, the most stringent rules should be adopted for their management; but, above all things, all trickery and fraud should be eschewed and denounced. A man guilty of it should be so branded with infamy, that he should never presume to show himself there a second time. Men, under such circumstances, would be sure to discover that "honesty is the best policy."

In London, there are markets for the exclusive sale of poultry and game, and in Dublin, I found one wholly devoted to the sale of eggs. The amounts here collected and disposed of almost surpass belief. The statement of a respectable witness and custom-house agent, recently, before a parliamentary committee, is quite remarkable. He said that there were five vessels annually engaged in that trade between Normandy, on the coast of France, and London, which brought about 3700 tons of eggs in the year. Ten cases went to a ton, and from 1000 to 1200 were in each case. This trade was between Cherbourg, Harfleur, Caen, and Portsmouth. Forty millions of eggs were annually imported through this channel alone. Some one asks very emphatically, "Why should they not be produced at home?"*

* "The value in money of one seemingly unimportant article, eggs, taken, in the course of the year, from Ireland to the ports of Liverpool and Bristol, amounts to at least £100,000. The progress of this trade affords a curious illustration of the advantages of commercial facilities in stimulating production and equalizing prices. Before the establishment of steam-vessels, the market at Cork was most irregularly supplied with eggs from the surrounding district; at certain seasons they were exceedingly abundant and cheap, but these seasons were sure to be followed by seasons of scarcity and high prices; and at times, it is said to have been difficult to purchase eggs in the market at any price. At the first opening of the improved channel for conveyance to England, the residents at Cork had to complain of the constant high price of this and other articles of farm produce; but as a more extensive market was now permanently open to them, the farmers gave their attention to the rearing and keeping of poultry; and at the present time, eggs are procurable at all seasons in the market at Cork; not, it is true, at the extremely low rate at which they could, formerly, be sometimes bought, but still at much less than the average price of the year. A like result has followed the introduction of this great improvement in regard to the supply and cost of various other articles of produce. In the apparently unimportant article feathers, it may be stated, on the respectable authority above quoted, that the yearly importation into England, from Ireland, reaches the amount of £500,000 sterling." — *Porter's Progress of the Nation*, vol. iii. 83.

Markets of a general character are held once or twice a week in all the principal towns; and in those cases where the farms are small, the farmers' wives and daughters will be seen going six or eight miles on foot, or in vans, (i. e. lumber and freight coaches or wagons,) to sell the week's product of their dairy or their poultry-yard. In this case, they are always found, with their neat baskets upon their arms, in a particular part of the market assigned to them. Their neatness of dress and person commend them to attention. It requires some courage to elbow your way among them, if you do not design to be a purchaser; and their chaffering and courteous solicitations to buy, with the emphatical recommendations of the articles for sale, together with the usual chatter and gossip to be expected among such a collection of gude wives and bonnie lasses, are sufficiently amusing.

W.H. Davies. H. Beckwith

An Aberdeenshire Polled Bull.

The Property of Mr. Isaac Machray, Torie Farm, Kincardineshire, which received the first prize at the Highland Society's Show, at Aberdeen, October, 1840.

EUROPEAN AGRICULTURE.

FIFTH REPORT.

LXII. — GENERAL MARKETS. (*Continued.*)

1. MARKET AT DERBY. — NOTHING can be more miscellaneous than an English country market; and my readers may be gratified with the partial account which I took of one of them as I went through it. This may be considered as a fair sample of others. Many of the goods are spread upon the ground, or under temporary stalls or booths erected for the purpose. Every seller pays a certain tax to the town for permission to sell, or for the load of goods brought into market. This toll is generally collected at the entrance of the town, as it is to this day in London, from every loaded vehicle which enters the city.

This market was held in the open square at Derby, and the stalls were chiefly attended by women. 1. Nails and tacks. 2. Old iron, chains, &c. 3. Cutlery of various sorts. 4. Shoes and boots. 5. Hats and caps. 6. Hosiery. 7. Millinery. 8. Iron ware. 9. Tin and copper ware. 10. Various kinds of female dress, caps, laces, &c. 11. Household furniture, old and new. 12. Brushes, mops, &c. 13. Bread. 14. Bacon and salted pork. 15. Muslins and caps in upturned umbrellas on the ground. 16. Children's toys. 17. Combs and paste. 18. Flour. 19. Butter and cheese. 20. Fish of various kinds. 21. Baskets. 22. Old books. 23. Sofas, bureaus, and tables. 24. Crockery ware and glass ware of various kinds on the ground — a great many sellers. 25. Glass ware in abundance.

26. Rabbits and game. 27. Poultry. 28. Meats of various kinds. 29. Vegetables and fruits. 30. Straw bonnets. 31. Refreshments, gingerbread and ginger beer. 32. Wool in large packs. 33. Oranges, &c. 34. Sieves, wire-baskets, and bird-cages. 35. Bandboxes and trunks. 36. Dolls. 37. New books and stationery. 38. Live birds. 39. Confectionary of various kinds. 40. Shoes, combs, &c. &c. 41. Saddles, bridles, collars, &c. 42. Rakes and agricultural tools. 43. Ginger pop, as usual. 44. Garden seeds. 45. Patent medicines, and especially worm lozenges, with about fifty bottles of worms preserved in spirit to evince the efficacy of the medicine — a terrific exhibition. 46. Meats of various kinds. This comprehends but a small portion, and by no means all the varieties of stalls. The whole are dispersed by 3 o'clock in the afternoon. The population of Derby is about 37,000, and is chiefly a manufacturing population.

LXIII. — GENERAL REMARKS AND DIVISIONS OF THE SUBJECT OF ENGLISH FARMING.

The agriculture of England presents itself under three great divisions — that of arable farming; breeding and grazing, or feeding; and dairying. I propose, in a great degree, to arrange my observations conformably to these three parts.

There may be, with some of my readers, a misconception as to my plan, and, in consequence, expectations which will fail to be met. I do not undertake to give a complete system of farming, and specific and exact directions in detail for the cultivation of every crop, and for every department of farm management. This would oblige me to execute a work vastly more extensive than that which I have undertaken. With respect to many of my readers, it could prove only a work of supererogation, for much of these details must be as familiar to them as the roads over their farms. I have always found, likewise, in respect to such directions, with which many books are crowded, extending, as they frequently do, to circumstances the most minute and insignificant, that they are often inapplicable, from the infinite diversity of circumstances which different cases present. Most men have their peculiar methods of accomplishing an object, which are in truth the best for them, because the most natural; they would be hampered and embarrassed by other modes, less familiar, which might be prescribed. Unless, therefore, there is some striking originality, or some obvious and peculiar convenience, in the method suggested, it is only necessary to say in general what is to be done, and leave it to every man's own ingenuity to find out the best method of effecting it.

My principal object is to point out, in European agriculture, such circumstances of difference between it and our own as may serve for the improvement of the agriculture of the United States, and to give such an account of the modes of management which prevail abroad, and which have been sanctioned by long practice and experience, as may facilitate their adoption, as far as the circumstances existing among us would render their adoption eligible. Every country, differing from other countries in its climate and temperature, in its soil, in its facility for procuring manures, in the character and supply of its labor, in its commercial and political relations, must be expected to have an agriculture in some respects peculiar to itself; and the practices of another country can only be partially adapted to its own. At the same time, the general principles of agricultural practice are every where the same; and these, with the various modifications, which they may be expected to assume under different degrees of civilization, or different degrees of improvement in science and the arts, and their general and special application, cannot be too fully discussed and illustrated. We may learn much from others, who do things which we are never called to do; who cultivate crops which we never cultivate, and never can cultivate; and we may learn much from persons who do the same things which we do, but in a different way from ourselves — who cultivate the same crops, but by their own peculiar methods. We may learn much from those who cultivate better, and from those who do not cultivate so well as ourselves. There is little hope in any thing, so far as any great improvement is concerned, for the man who implicitly follows any guide whatever. He must exercise his own reason, experience, observation, and judgment, in the application of rules which may be laid down for his direction.

The celebrated Bakewell, whose name occupies a distinguished place in the annals of agricultural improvement, advised farmers, who would improve their cultivation and management, "to go abroad and see what other people were about." Every observing man, who acts upon this advice, will find its advantages. I have often heard it said, and, if I thought it of any value in the case, I should say that my own experience confirmed it, that one of the best modes of understanding a book written in a foreign language is to read different versions or translations of it. The different forms of expressing the same thought adopted by different persons, or the different conceptions which different minds gather from the same expressions, whether in themselves right or wrong, may give us a clew to the true meaning, and correct many a misconstruction, or reveal and make light many a hidden or obscure passage. This analogy suggests the true mode in which an inquisitive mind may gather instruction and knowledge from the practices of other men.

Three things seem to me absolutely essential to human progress in any and every art, in any and every science. The first is a profound conviction of the imperfection of all human knowledge; the second, an entire distrust of all human infallibility; the third, a perfect docility of mind, and a readiness to receive light and instruction from any and every quarter where it may be gathered, or by which it may approach us. Self-esteem, which, when combined with a good measure of benevolence and conscientiousness, and so leading men to admit and respect the just claims of others, is a useful and harmless sentiment, and prompts to many valuable enterprises, — when found excessive, and in a great degree unqualified, becomes an almost hopeless impediment to improvement.

I was told, before I left the country, by some American friends, that there was nothing in the way of agriculture to be learned in England, and that American agriculture was as improved as English agriculture. I had been but a short time in England before I heard, from various quarters, that in no country on the globe had agriculture reached that degree of improvement which it had attained in England; and really in some cases, at public dinners, when, in the language of modern agricultural chemistry, the gases of the wine began to stimulate the brain, one would be almost led to infer that agriculture itself was a recent invention of British genius; and England presented herself to the enchanted imagination leaning upon the handles of a plough, with piles of scientific books spread open at her feet, weeping, like the Macedonian hero, that she had no more worlds to conquer. A Flemish gentleman informs me that the agriculture of the Low Countries is altogether superior to that of any other part of the world. The Chinaman puts forth his claims to superiority, and shows pretty conclusively how much justice he has upon his side, when he points to the extraordinary and unquestionable fact, in his own country, of the largest amount of population supported upon the smallest extent of land. In the midst of all this comes a German, of wide possessions, of long practical experience, and of much intelligence, and says to me, "The English are the most arrogant and conceited people under the sun; and, in respect to agricultural improvement, they are far inferior to the Germans." Now, I do not feel it necessary to buckle on my armor and defend my good friends the English against language which, it must be admitted, is sufficiently peremptory and harsh. Nor do I deem it necessary to enter the lists with either of these parties, and endeavor to force him from his position. A diseased or inordinate self-esteem brooks no argument, and, in contending with national prejudices, the result can only be as it is, to use the rather coarse metaphor of Dr. Franklin, with a man who spits against the wind — that he spits in his own face. The first conclusion to be drawn from these confident assumptions is, to distrust them all; and the second is, by looking calmly and impartially at the improvements in which each claims a superiority, to gather instruction from the results of each one's experience, and new facilities and motives to enterprise, inquiry, and exertion.

LXIV. — THE SOIL.

Agriculture rests, first of all things, upon the nature of the soil which is to be cultivated. The soil is the basis on which the plant is to be supported, and the medium through which it is to receive the food by which its life is to be sustained, its growth promoted, and its progress advanced to maturity. Some scientific persons assert that the principal, if not the only, use of the soil is for the support of the plant, and that the food of the plant is derived wholly from the atmosphere. In the heat of their imaginations, they have even asserted that a man's fields may be enriched, or rather his growing crops may be fed, by the exhalations from his neighbor's manure-heap in an adjoining field. This would be very much like a man's being fed by standing over the grating of a hotel, or a cook's shop kitchen, in London, and inhaling the odors from the savory viands which are there in the process of preparation. How much flesh might be gained, and how long life might be sustained, in this way, we shall know when the experiment is once successfully tested. That plants receive a large proportion of their nourishment from the air, does not admit of a doubt. But the calculations of the philosophical chemists as to the amount of carbon which the atmosphere, taking it at its estimated height of forty-five miles, is capable of supplying, (equal, according to some calculators, to the sum of seven tons to an acre;) and the discussion of the great question how the atmosphere was first supplied with this great element in vegetable life; and the apprehension which some persons express, on account of the supposed actual diminution of carbon, — though there appears to be enough, according to the most rigid calculations, to last several thousand years longer, — are, to say the least of them, sufficiently amusing; but of what practical use they can be to the common farmer, is not so easy to determine. If the animal creation is to be starved out some thousands of years hence, it need not give the present generation, whose average of life does not much exceed thirty-five years, any great personal concern. It will not be a harder fate than that which certain of what are called the higher order of animals seem disposed to anticipate for some of their fellow-beings now living. But, whatever may be the part which the atmosphere performs in the food or nourishment of vegetables, it is beyond human power to affect or control it, unless we can grow our crops under bell-glasses or in greenhouses. The duke of Devonshire, in his magnificent conservatory at Chatsworth, three hundred feet long, seventy-five feet wide, and sixty-four feet in height, heated by seven miles of pipes, and covering, with its appurtenances, a full acre of ground, might manage to charge the atmosphere in which his plants respire with gases exactly suited to their wants, and of the most nutritious character; but, beyond this gigantic experiment, to which few can aspire, nothing certainly is to be hoped for. The farmer's whole business, as far as cultivation is concerned, lies with the soil; and upon the soil, and the skill and intelligence with which he manages it, must depend entirely his success. The notion, that plants receive a large portion of their nourishment through their leaves, — although some experiments, in my opinion not sufficiently decisive to determine the question, seem to favor it, — appears to me about as probable as that animals receive a large portion of their nourishment through their lungs. If they absorb carbon and discharge oxygen by day, they reverse the process, and absorb the oxygen of the atmosphere, and discharge the carbon, by night; and what portion of the latter in this way is assimilated, and made to form a part of the plant, (as far as I can understand the experiments which have been made,) does not as yet seem to be determined. I know the confidence with which this is affirmed, and, as a philosophical fact, I admit that it is of great interest and extremely worthy of inquiry. A friend, a few days since, said to me that he was conscious, when immersed in water, of absorbing considerable water by means of the pores of the skin, and wished me to believe it. With great respect both for his intelligence and honesty, I still remain skeptical. What may be the case after death, when decomposition has commenced, is an entirely different matter. At present, I believe that the only way in which the food, by which the body is nourished, is received, is by the mouth; always excepting the case of the soldier at Washington, so fully reported in the medical journals, who had a hole in his stomach, by which, in order to watch the process of digestion, food was supplied, as a servant puts away cold meat in a cupboard. The fact is undoubted that plants by day absorb carbonic acid and exhale oxygen, and that by night the process is reversed, and they inhale oxygen and expel carbonic acid; but it does not seem so well established that in this way they obtain the carbon which is assimilated in their organism. At least, the supposition is so little favored by analogy, that I hope it may be lawful still to doubt.

That the atmosphere contributes essentially to vegetation — that plants derive much of their nourishment and substance from the air, as I have already remarked, does not admit of a question;

but, so far as any practical use whatever is to be made of this fact, we must consider this nourishment as received through the roots, and consequently through the medium of the soil in which these roots spread themselves, and the manures by which it is enriched. The soil therefore, as the basis of all vegetation, is the great object of the farmer's consideration.

LXV. — THEORIES OF THE OPERATION OF THE SOIL.

Soils may be considered in two points of view; first, in reference to their intrinsic or absolute character, and next, in reference to the plants to the growth of which they are adapted. In a preceding number, in speaking of the chemical analysis of different soils, I think it appeared how little practical advantage had as yet been derived from any experiments in this way which had been made. The common properties of soil may be distinguished by the eye or the feel with persons of experience and practical observation; but chemical examination may often be of the highest importance in detecting the presence of some mineral ingredient by which the cultivation of particular crops may be hindered or wholly prevented. A friend, eminent for his agricultural knowledge, pointed out to me a particular field, in which all attempts to grow wheat had been unsuccessful, while no such incapacity existed in the adjoining fields. In such a case as this, one would look to the chemical analysis of the soil to determine what ingredient was deficient, or what unfriendly element existed or predominated in the soil to prevent the growth of the plant; and, this being ascertained, perhaps a remedy might be found. But the extraordinary and minute exactness to which the chemical analysis of the soil is sometimes carried, and upon which many scientific persons insist, it would seem, can serve little other purpose than that of producing despair of adapting our cultivation to such diversified and minute variations.

What portion of the soil is abstracted for vegetable food is not yet determined; and it is a singular fact, that, though analytical chemistry has demonstrated that certain mineral substances are taken up in the organism of plants and are essential in composing its structure, and has proceeded to calculate the actual amount in pounds' weight abstracted by the growth of crops of a particular quantity, it has never yet, by an analysis of the soil before the planting, and as exact an examination after the crop has been removed, determined the loss in such case. Why this has not been done, or whether it be beyond the present power of chemical analysis to accomplish, — extraordinary as is the degree of perfection to which the science has been advanced, — must be left to others to answer. I am perfectly aware, of course, that the same identical soil cannot be subjected to the process of analysis, and then employed for the purposes of vegetation, with a view of ascertaining what has been lost or abstracted; but an equal weight taken from the same place with that employed for growing the plants might be examined, and afterwards that in which the plants were grown, so that, by this kind of comparison, the truth might be to a degree approximated. I am quite aware that it may be said, in this case, that the amount of mineral ingredients found in the produce would show the exact amount abstracted; but it would be extremely interesting to know, by an examination of the soil, that these results exactly or nearly corresponded. But it is found that land left to itself for a length of time recovers its fertility, and, after a lapse of two, three, or more years, the same crop, which failed when grown in immediate succession to another of the same kind, can be advantageously cultivated again. It would be highly curious, then, by retaining a portion of the land in which the plant had been grown, and leaving it exposed to the ordinary influences of light and heat, and rain and frost, to ascertain in what length of time the soil would recover its exhausted elements of fertility. This has not, within my knowledge, been attempted.

The ingenious theory of Decandolle, that the exudations or excrementitious matter from one kind of crop unfitted the ground for an immediate repetition of the same species of plant, seems now to be generally abandoned. It is a well-established principle, which practical men understand quite as well as the scientific, that a rotation of crops is indispensable to a successful agriculture; and the theory is altogether probable that a particular crop exhausts the soil of certain elements essential to its production, which must be somehow supplied before a second crop of the same kind can be grown on the same land; but it would be extremely interesting if the fact of such exhaustion, and its extent, could be more particularly determined by a chemical examination of the soil which has been cultivated. The beautiful theory of the great agricultural oracle of the day, that certain mineral ingredients which are always found in the ashes of plants, and which are carried off when these products are removed, and, being essential to vegetation, require to be either artificially replaced or supplied by a natural process, — and that, the land being suffered to rest, or applied to a different production, the ordinary influences of air and moisture in decomposing the rocks of the soil will renew the supply of these mineral elements which have been removed, — seems to offer the desired explanation; and the experiments to which this theory has led, and which, under its influence, are now going on in various parts of the country, must presently determine it, and, what is better, show its proper application, and greatly simplify the processes of agriculture, reducing its expenses and giving comparative certainty to its results.

The operation of air and moisture upon the soil, the effects of light, and electricity, and frost, upon vegetation, all admit to be powerful; but they are as yet only partially understood, and present subjects of the most interesting inquiry. In the progress of science, technically so called, we have much to hope for; but in what it has already accomplished, enough has been gained to quicken, but very far from enough to satisfy, the appetite. One of the most eminent agricultural chemists of the present day, Boussingault, second perhaps to no other, has said,* "A great deal has been written since Bergman's time upon the chemical composition of soils. Chemists of great talent have made many complete analyses of soils noted for their fertility; still, practical agriculture has hitherto derived very slender benefits from labors of this kind. The reason of this is very simple; the qualities which we esteem in a workable soil depend almost exclusively upon the mechanical mixture of its elements; we are much less interested in its chemical composition than in this; so that simple washing, which shows the relations between the sand and the clay, tells, of itself, much more that is important to us than

* Rural Economy, Law's edition, p. 266.

an elaborate chemical analysis." This is certainly a great confession for an eminent chemist to make.

To exemplify the different results to which the most scientific men arrive in these cases, I will refer both to Boussingault and Von Thaer in respect to a simple point, the presence of the carbonate of lime in the soil as essential to the growth of a crop of wheat, on which subject the public mind has been so long, so generally, and so confidently made up.

Von Thaer says,* "The richest argillaceous soil that I ever analyzed, the fertility of which was regarded as of the very richest quality, was taken from the right bank of the Elbe, some few miles from its mouth; it contained eleven and a half parts in a hundred of humus, four and a half of lime, a great quantity of clay, a little coarse silica, and a considerable portion of very fine silica, which could only be separated from it by ebullition. It certainly possessed a great degree of cohesion, but, when moderately moistened, it was not very tenacious. It was made to bear the richest crops, as cabbages, wheat, autumnal corn, beans, &c.; but every sixth year it was necessary to manure it thoroughly, and to give it a fallow."

On the preceding page, he says, "The richest land I ever analyzed, and which was taken from the marshes of the Oder, contained 19¾ parts in 100 of humus, 70 of clay, a little fine sand, and *an almost imperceptible* quantity of lime; but the situation of this land was too low, and it was too damp, to admit of a correct estimate being formed of its fertility."

Boussingault says,† "I may remark generally, that, from the whole of the analyses of good wheat lands which have hitherto been made, it appears that carbonate of lime enters in considerable quantity into their composition; and theory, in harmony with practice, tends to show that it is advantageous to have this earthy salt as a constituent in the manures which are put upon soils that contain little or no lime."

On the next page,‡ he says, "M. Berthier's analysis is still far from proving that the presence of lime in a soil is indispensable, inasmuch as beautiful wheat crops are grown in the neighborhood of Lisle without lime. In proof of this fact, I shall here cite the analysis of one of the most fertile soils in the world,

* Vol. i. pp. 355, 354. † Rural Economy, p. 294. ‡ p. 295.

the black soil of Tchornoizem, which Mr. Murchison informs us constitutes the superficies of the arable lands comprised between the 54th and 57th degrees of north latitude, along the left bank of the Volga as far as Tcheboksar, from Nijni to Kasan, and stretching over a still more extensive district upon the Asiatic side of the Ural Mountains. Mr. Murchison is of opinion that this land is a submarine deposit formed by the accumulation of sands rich in organic matters. The Tchornoizem is composed of black particles, mixed with grains of sand; it is the best soil in Russia for wheat and pasturage; a year or two of fallow will suffice to restore it to its former fertility after it has been exhausted by cropping; it is never manured.

"M. Payen found in this black and fertile soil,

"Organic matter, .	6.95	(containing 2.45 per cent. of azote.)
Silica, ...	71.56	
Alumina, . . .	11.40	
Oxide of iron, . .	5.62	
Lime, ...	0.80	
Magnesia, . . .	1.22	
Alkaline chlorides,	1.21	
Phosphoric acid, .	a trace.	
Loss, ...	1.24	
	100.00"	

It is a little remarkable, judging from the analysis here given, that not only is the quantity of lime extremely minute, but even the phosphates, deemed so essential and indispensable to success, are also absent.

Such are the diversified results to which even the most scientific are led; and they are well adapted to admonish us of the imperfection of human knowledge, and the limitation of human powers. In Lincolnshire, where some of the best farming in England, as is universally admitted, is to be found, on a soil where the whole substratum was chalk, or the carbonate of lime, and where the mould or loam was not more than three or four inches deep, I found the farmers manuring the land, from pits dug in the field, with the very chalk by which the whole soil was underlaid. Upon my proposing the question to an eminent geological professor, then with me, much interested in agriculure, why this was done, he replied that the lime in the surface soil had probably become exhausted by sinking down, through its greater specific gravity; but I could not see that there could be any difficulty in the plants reaching it, where the whole body of lime lay within so short a distance of the surface. My own belief is, that, in this case, its operation is chiefly mechanical, and that its use was merely to consolidate the upper surface, and make it more adhesive for the roots of the plant, and that any other substance or marl, equally firm and consistent, would have served the same end.

One of the most eminent chemists of the present day, distinguished for the splendor of his attainments, seems to entertain, with no small confidence, the opinion that chemistry, including probably electricity and galvanism, is destined to solve all the secrets of vegetable and animal life; that the various processes going on in nature are mere chemical processes; and that any thing like a vital power above or beyond them all, and incapable of being solved by scientific investigation, is an hypothesis unworthy of an enlightened mind. It is certainly not for the human mind, as yet, to say what cannot be done; and it would be quite premature for Science to assume that she has reached the ultimate boundaries of investigation, as it would be impious for her to claim the prerogatives of omniscience. But if I may in the case adventure the remark, — admiring as much as any one can the actual and wonderful achievements of science, — there still remains beyond even the farthest advances an impassable barrier, a *terra incognita*, which the most adventurous have not yet penetrated. It is easy to ascertain that certain substances have an affinity for each other, and science, with wonderful ingenuity, has determined the forms of combination under which they become united. The action or force by which they are brought together and there held may hereafter be explained, and may be ranked under some unknown chemical force; but as yet any attempts to define, or even conjecture, its nature, have been wholly abortive. The simple and familiar fact, that the muscles are obedient to the will in moving the limbs, every one admits; but in what this will consists, and how it is exerted, and how it effects its purpose, seems as yet as far from being reached, as on the day that the first child was born into the world.

We are very apt to exclaim, in the ecstasy of the Grecian philosopher in the successful investigation of an interesting problem, "I have found out! I have found out!" when, with all the apparent and flattering loosening of the strings, the Gordian knot remains as firm as ever. The processes of nature must be all simple enough to the great Mind which established them, but that is not the human mind. To compare a rushlight to the sun would fall infinitely short of expressing the difference between them. But it is obvious that so many circumstances must combine to accomplish even the simplest and most familiar results in nature, that, to a finite understanding, the simplest processes must be complicated. Any person of common observation, who will go into a meadow or pasture, and observe the different varieties of plants which cover the ground, and remark how every one preserves its own peculiar distinctive character and form, and, though all growing upon the same soil and under the same external influences, each one extracts for itself, and for itself alone, that which its own peculiar character and constitution require, — and that in size, and form, and color, and odor, and stem, and leaf, and fruit, and seed, there are essential, and inviolable, and invariable distinctions, — and that each one appropriates to itself that which is required to form the stem, and to expand the leaves, and to throw in the coloring, and to mature the fruit, preserving always the perfect identity of the species, and furnishing in some cases a nutritious, and in others a poisonous compound for animal life, — will, I think, be very far from considering the phenomena of vegetable life as simple, or resolvable into those few chemical laws which have been established in what must at least be still considered as only the infancy of the science.

LXVI. A MODERN DISCOVERY.

It is lately stated, as one of the great discoveries of the age, that an eminent agricultural chemist has invented (or rather determined how they should be compounded) a variety of manures specially adapted to the particular crop to be cultivated, furnishing in exact measure and kind the food which is required. The professed object is to supply those mineral and alkaline substances to the soil of which it has been exhausted in the process of cropping, and to furnish them in such form, and so combined, as that they may be best taken up by the plant, and presented to the plant only so gradually as the habits of the plant may require. This eminent chemist claims, to use his own words, "to have found means to give to every soluble ingredient of manure, by its combination with others, any degree of solubility without altering its effect on vegetation. I give, for instance, the alkalies in such a state as not to be more soluble than gypsum, which, as is well known, acts through many years, even as long as a particle of it remains in the soil. The mixture of manures has been adapted to the mean quantity of rain in this country, (England;) the manure which is used in summer has a greater degree of solubility than that used in winter. Experience must lead to further results, and in future the farmer will be able to calculate the amount of produce of his fields, if temperature, want of rain, &c., do not oppose the manure coming fairly into action. I must, however, observe that the artificial manures in no way alter the mechanical condition of the fields; that they do not render a heavy soil more accessible to air and moisture; for such fields the porous stable manure will always have its great value; it can be given together with the artificial manure." *

With the highest respect for this eminent man, whose scientific labors have given a spur to agricultural inquiry and experiment unknown in any former time, one cannot but remark the convenient reservation afforded by the qualification "if temperature, want of rain, &c., do not oppose the manures coming fairly into action;" and the recommendation to apply the stable manure together with the artificial manure, and the statement, in another place, that certain manures "act far more favorably on the production of grain crops, especially if they are added to the animal excrements, and are given to the fields at the same time," present sagacious and certainly very safe advice. They slightly remind one of a custom formerly prevalent in some Catholic countries on the Continent, when, at the opening of the spring, the priest was accustomed to go over the fields of his parishioners to give them his blessing; but when he came to fields which were exhausted and sterile, he was very careful to add, "This needs manure." The doctrine of the occasional and temporary

* Liebig on Artificial Manures.

exhaustion of the soil, by the continued repetition of the same crop, of ingredients or elements important to its growth and maturity, certainly seems reasonable and well established; but the dread which seems to possess some minds of an exhaustion which would doom the soil to perpetual barrenness, without some extraordinary supply of the materials of which it has been deprived, may have more ground to rest upon, when the birds in any country or locality are unable to find lime to form the shells of their eggs, and animals become mere lumps of gum-elastic for want of material to form their bones.*

There is a recuperative power in nature by which it would seem that any soil, originally adapted to the growth of any particular plant, by rest, or by the growth of other and different plants, becomes again fitted for the original cultivation. That this may be hastened by artificial manures, there can be no doubt. That science may at last achieve the great discovery of a way by which the same plant may be cultivated uninterruptedly year after year on the same soil, is certainly to be hoped for. Whether this object is already accomplished by this distinguished philosopher, is now to be submitted to actual experiment by those who can afford to purchase this artificial manure.

---

* The fears which seem to haunt some minds, lest, by cultivation, the exhaustion of the soil should proceed so far as ultimately to put even the existence of the human race in peril, from famine, may be useful enough in exciting men to frugality in the saving of manures, and enterprise and industry in their application; but seem as little warranted as the sanguine expectations of the Millerites, who looked for the end of the world in April, 1843, and some of whom, having got their white robes fitted, and their wings spread, seemed to be rather out of temper that their predictions failed, and that Heaven in its mercy granted the "poor dogs," the unbelievers, a short reprieve. Voltaire, when admonished that coffee was a slow poison, remarked that it must be very slow indeed, for he had drunk it constantly for seventy years. Mr. Lyell, in his late Tour in the United States, (which, let me remark by the way, is written in the calm spirit of a philosophical observer, and does honor to his candor and sense of justice, as well as to his scientific attainments,) is of opinion that the time occupied in the recession of Niagara Falls from the shores of Lake Ontario, where they once were, to their present position, could not have been less than 35,000 years; and that the fossil remains, both vegetable and animal, now found there, show that even this period, startling as it may seem, belongs to a modern and not a primeval era. How idle in respect to these matters, seem, then, the calculations of beings, who

"——— are such stuff
As dreams are made of, and whose little life
Is rounded with a sleep!"

These compounds are advertised for sale at £10 sterling, or $50, per ton, and a ton, it is said, will be sufficient for manuring four acres. Some agricultural friends, who have applied them, have promised me the results of their experiments. My readers shall have them when they are received. Such a discovery would certainly constitute a great advance in agricultural improvement. I shall not venture to predict, but patiently wait the issue, not deeming it necessary to caution those, whose funds are limited, against large investments. It seems, from some examples already given, that, with time, the soil itself, by its own inherent energies, for which we cannot be sufficiently grateful, will recover its exhausted fertility. In the mean time, its use is never to be abandoned; for the improved agriculture of modern times has certainly made one great advance in utterly condemning a naked fallow, and the soil may be occupied with equal advantage, both to itself and its cultivators, by a succession of tenants.

LXVII. — SOILS OF GREAT BRITAIN.

The soils of Great Britain, in two or three respects, differ essentially from the soils of the United States. In Great Britain, or rather in England, — for I believe the formation does not extend into Scotland or Ireland, — there is a vast amount of chalk, coming, in some cases, directly to the surface, and turned up by the plough; in other cases, formed a few inches below a surface of mould or loam, interspersed, in some cases, with an infinite number of small or broken flint-stones. We have much calcareous soil in the United States, much of the primitive and secondary limestone formation, but I know of no deposits of chalk. I have not seen in Great Britain any soils of pure sand, such as we find on Cape Cod, in Massachusetts, on the eastern shores of New Jersey, and in the South Atlantic States. Nor do I know in the United States of any such mountain peat, or bog, as is to be found in parts of England, and in vast tracts of Ireland. In the latter country there are many hills, of very considerable elevation, and in Scotland and England likewise, covered with pure bog-peat to the depth, I have seen in some instances, of ten or twelve feet, and holding water like a sponge. Of course, these must have formed, in some distant period, valleys, or level surfaces, where vast forests once stood, and, falling down, passed into decay, succeeded by those plants which constitute the principal substance of which these beds are composed; and then afterwards have been elevated above the surrounding country by some great convulsion of nature. These hills are entirely destitute of trees, and covered only with furze, or heather, or moss. I know of no examples in the United States of deep deposits of peat being found upon elevated summits; but there are likewise in Ireland, as in the United States, very extensive tracts of level peat-bog shut in by high grounds, saturated by water, and of unascertained depth. There are likewise in England some extensive peat-bog meadows, of the improvement of which I shall presently treat; but such tracts, within my observation, are not common.

There are likewise in England immense extents of alluvial soil. The valley of the Thames, for a great part of its extent, is clearly alluvial; so are the flat lands upon the Humber and its various branches; so are the immense tracts, denominated *fen lands*, in Lincolnshire, Bedfordshire, and Cambridgeshire; so is the beautiful valley of the Trent, and the valley in which York is situated; so likewise is the rich White Horse Valley, as it is termed, in the county of Berkshire. Some of these are a stiff, adhesive clay, of the most tenacious character; others a deep, rich loam; and some of them have been redeemed from the sea by a process called *warping*, which I shall presently describe. These are composed of what is here called *silt*, which consists of a very fine sand, and muddy or aluminous matters, held in suspension by the water of the tides, and brought down likewise by the waters of rivers coming from the interior and swollen with rains, which have swept down the cultivated hills, and robbed them of some portion of their riches. These lands are justly deemed some of the most fertile in the kingdom.

There are likewise extensive tracts of soil resting upon the red sandstone, like some of the soils in New Jersey, producing large crops of the richest herbage in pasture, and fine crops under tillage; but of the common granitic soils of New England I have met with few examples. There are, however, I believe, extensive tracts of them, especially in the north. A geological survey of the Island of Great Britain has been executed with great skill, and the various geological formations distinctly indicated on a map; but such have been the extraordinary convulsions on the earth's surface, that the geological lines are not an infallible guide to the character of the soil. It may be safe, in general, to infer the character of the soil from the nature of the rocks prevalent in any particular locality; but the diluvial and alluvial deposits often differ entirely from the character of the rocks which lie beneath them. No knowledge of the geological formation of a country, therefore, — so far as its cultivation, and the general character of the crops to be raised, are concerned, — will supply the place of personal observation and experience.

If the nature of the soil were the only circumstance to be taken into consideration in determining the character of the agriculture to which it is adapted, the mode of cultivation, and the crops to be grown upon it, the whole subject would evidently be greatly simplified; but the climate, including heat and moisture, and the aspect and elevation of the land, are quite as much concerned in every question connected with this subject.

LXVIII. — CLASSIFICATION OF SOILS.

For all practical purposes, soils may be ranked under five different heads — sandy, clayey, calcareous, peaty, and loamy. I purposely avoid all scientific distinctions, and use such terms as even the commonest farmer will understand. A sandy soil is that in which sand abounds; clayey, in which clay; calcareous, in which lime in some form prevails; peaty, in which peat; loamy, in which a rich loam abounds. These soils are sometimes found so combined, that it might be difficult to designate their character by any one of these general terms. In some places, they are found in almost a pure state. In general, where there is found in a soil 80 per cent. of sand, it must be pronounced a sandy soil; and so the clay, the peat, or the lime; but it is not always easy to class a soil which is of a mixed character, and say what kind of element predominates. By sight and feeling, however, practical men are able to form an opinion of a soil upon which it may be safe to act. Besides the principal elements, to which I have referred, there is often found some mineral ingredient, which may seriously affect the character of the soil, and the degree of the presence of which can only be determined by scientific examination. Iron, copper, or mineral coal, is in general sufficiently indicated to the eye, or shows itself in the water which percolates the soil. The different forms, too, in which lime presents itself in the soil, whether as chalk, or gypsum, or magnesian limestone, are all to be considered in determining the character of a soil.

LXIX. — PHYSICAL PROPERTIES OF THE SOIL.

In addition to the characteristics of a soil of which I have spoken, there are other circumstances, usually denominated the physical properties of a soil, by which its fertility, or the kind of cultivation to which it may be proper to subject it, are to be in a great degree determined. These are its wetness or dryness, its power to absorb or retain moisture, its consistency or friability, and its temperature. All these matters are essentially connected with the fertility of a soil, and the kind of crops to which it is to be applied.

1. Wetness of a Soil. — Wet soils, or soils a considerable part of the time under water, produce a coarse herbage of little value to stock — in many cases scarcely sufficient to support life, and rendering scarcely any nourishment. The manure of animals fed upon the produce of such soils is comparatively worthless. It has been found, likewise, by repeated experiments, that water allowed to remain upon land for any length of time is injurious to vegetation, when the rapid transition of water over the land might be highly beneficial. An exception, of course, is to be made where the passage of a turbid stream or flood is arrested long enough to afford opportunity for the depo-

sition of the enriching matter with which its waters are charged. The effect of too much water is to reduce the temperature of the soil, to obstruct the access of the external air to the roots of the plants, and, in fact, to macerate and destroy the texture of the finest kinds of herbage. Perhaps it would be a more simple statement, and equally just, to say that the aquatic plants are, with some exceptions, not adapted to the nourishment of animal life, and that those which are most suited for the food of man or beast, are not suited to be grown under water. Water is of great importance to their sustenance and growth. They cannot live without it; but they cannot live in it. As to the human being, it may be of the highest benefit, both as an internal and external application; but there is soon an end to the matter when man is plunged into water, and kept under it.

All hope of cultivation or improvement must be abandoned, where land is under water any considerable portion of the time, or where it is fully saturated with water, like a sponge.

2. Power to absorb Moisture in a Soil. — I may remark, in the next place, that the fertility of a soil very greatly depends upon the power of the soil to absorb and to retain moisture. Some very distinguished men have maintained that the fertility of a soil may be measured by this power, an opinion which, it may be said, (without meaning a pun,) has much ground to rest upon, but which cannot be admitted without considerable qualifications. Moisture and wetness are in this case to be carefully distinguished. A soil consisting almost wholly of sand possesses no retentive powers; and though of all other soils the most absorbent, yet the water passes through it as through a sieve. Clay, on the other hand, is extremely retentive of water, often to the prejudice of the vegetation which grows upon it. Liebig, in a recent treatise upon artificial manures, to which I have already referred, seems to be of opinion that the system of drainage now prosecuted with so much enterprise in England may be carried to an injurious extent, so as to induce the too rapid passage of the soluble manures which are applied, and before they can be taken up by, or have performed their proper office to, the growing plants. As every thing which this distinguished gentleman asserts is now deemed oracular in the agricultural world, I will quote his observations at large.

"The reason why, in certain years, the influence of the best and most plentiful manuring is scarcely perceptible, is that, during the moist and rainy springs and summers, the *phosphates and other salts with the alkaline bases*, as also the *soluble ammoniacal salts*, are entirely or partially removed. A great amount of rain and moisture removes, in the greatest quantity, the very substances which are most indispensable to the plants at the time they begin to mature and form seeds. The system of draining which of late has been so extensively followed in England brings the land into the state of a great filter, through which the soluble alkalies are *drawn off* in consequence of the percolation of rain, and it must, therefore, become more deficient in its *soluble* efficacious elements. Attentive farmers must have observed that, after a certain time, the quality of the grain on land laid dry according to this principle deteriorates; that the produce of grain bears no due proportion to the produce of straw."

"What is more evident, after these remarks, than that intelligent farmers must strive to give to the soil the manuring substances in such a state as to render possible their acting favorably on the plants the whole time of their growth. Art must find out the means of reducing the solubility of the manuring substances to a certain limit, — in a word, of bringing them into the same state in which they exist in a most fertile virgin soil, and in which they can be best assimilated by the virgin plants."

"The attention which I have paid to this subject has been crowned with success. I have succeeded in combining the efficacious elements of manure in such a manner as that they will not be washed away; and thus their efficacy will be doubled. Owing to this, the injurious consequences of the present system of draining are removed; agriculture is placed upon as certain principles as well arranged manufactories; and, instead of the uncertainty of mere empiricism, the operations of agriculture may be carried on with security; and, in place of waiting the results of our labors with anxiety and doubt, our minds will be filled with patience and confidence."

Such are the brilliant visions which are held up before the mind of the farmer; and such is the distrust which this great man would throw over the enterprising practice of draining. It is not quite easy to understand how the plants are to take up their food but in a condition of the most minute solution; nor how, if they are dissolved, they are to be kept from being washed away. It is not for any finite mind, in cases which admit of any doubt, to say what is possible or what is impossible; and it would be premature to condemn that which comes recommended upon such high authority, and is yet to be made the subject of experiment. After the extraordinary and most beneficial results which have been effected by the thorough draining of all superfluous wet from the soil, the agriculturists may, however, pursue the system with a good degree of confidence, especially if a mode has been discovered of combining the alkalies and the phosphates, that they shall not be so dissolved by rain and wet as to be washed away, and yet that they shall be so dissolved that they may be taken up by the plant as its wants may require. Within the last month of writing this, I have seen, on a thin, dry, and light soil, in which sand abounded, the beneficial effects of thorough drainage, where, on a field of turnips, the crop of the drained portion, with no other difference than the drainage, was evidently better, by one half, than that on the undrained part. If it be the fact that soils of a friable or porous nature are, in this way, liable to lose these beneficial elements by rains and wet, it would seem extraordinary that the fact had not been sooner discovered, and their deficiency and destitution made evident. I would not express these doubts in any captious spirit, knowing how much agriculture must, in the end, owe to science, and being ready to hail with the highest satisfaction any triumph it may achieve.

3. Consistency and Friability of Soils. — The next point to be considered, in the character of a soil, is its consistency or friability. A soil, if too closely packed, — which soils of almost pure clay are liable to be, — not only forbids the passage of water, which it holds stagnant upon its surface, but is impervious to the roots of plants, especially of those plants which send their roots downwards in search of nourishment. It is likewise extremely difficult to be worked in wet weather, being not easy to move upon, adhering to the feet of the workmen and the horses, and to the implements, and in dry weather being sunburnt and hard, and, when turned up, remaining in large and unmanageable clods. In the northern parts of the United States, where the frosts are severe, plants are always liable to be thrown out, and

their roots torn asunder, by the violent disruption of the clods. On the other hand, soils may be too fine, powdery, and friable, being subject to be blown by the winds, being too little retentive of moisture, and therefore liable to be severely affected by drought, and failing to furnish a sufficiently strong hold for the roots of those plants which spread themselves upon the surface. A soil neither excessively consistent and close, nor excessively friable, is undoubtedly to be preferred. All pent-up or stagnant water, either on the surface or within the ground, is unquestionably prejudicial to a healthy vegetation; and a freedom or porosity of soil, so as to admit the free access of the air, is an important and valuable feature. It seems to be a well-established fact, that a newly turned up surface attracts moisture from the atmosphere; and the more friable a soil is, the more surface it exposes to the external air. In condensing the aqueous particles floating near the surface, it thus procures for the plants growing upon it some of the most important elements of vegetation. This is undoubtedly the secret of the success in forwarding vegetation by frequent stirring of the earth around plants even in time of drought, especially plants with broad leaves, such as cabbages and lettuces, which, by means of their expansive foliage, protect the earth underneath them from the direct rays of the sun.

4. Temperature of Soils. — It is not my intention to give a treatise on this subject, nor to extend my remarks beyond such notices as will best explain the great improvements in cultivation, or the management of soils, which have been undertaken and accomplished here, and which may properly be said to constitute the glory of English husbandry. I proceed, then, to observe, that another important property of soils may be said to be their temperature. This is a matter of great importance in respect to vegetation. Heat, as well as moisture, are both equally essential to vegetable life and growth. The temperature of a soil would seem to be very little under human control; yet undoubtedly much may be done in some ways for this object. At certain seasons of the year, on the approach of frost, vegetation is arrested, and at all seasons, in certain altitudes, cultivation is hopeless. In Great Britain, this limit is reckoned at fifteen hundred feet above the level of the sea; but the cultivation of wheat cannot be recommended above six hundred feet. The main source of heat to

the soil is the rays of the sun. Whatever may be thought of that immense internal fire of liquid matter supposed to exist within the centre of the globe, and occupying a large portion of it, while we are resting only upon a thin outward crust, yet little of this heat is felt at the surface; and animal and vegetable life is dependent upon that magnificent orb which the Creator seems to have placed in the firmament as the emblem of his own inexhaustible, impartial, and widely expansive goodness, which bids the sleeping earth, in the spring time, arise as it were from the dead, and put on the habiliments of vegetable splendor and beauty, which fills the luscious vine of summer with its rich clusters, and gilds the autumnal harvest with a beneficent and matchless glory.

The temperature of the soil is then dependent upon external influences, — upon the sun primarily, and the atmosphere as affected by the heat of the sun. This temperature is, of course, affected by the condition of the soil as to wetness or dryness, and somewhat by its inclination and aspect.

The more direct are the rays of the sun, the stronger the heat produced by them; and the lighter or brighter the surface on which they fall, the less strongly are they absorbed, and the more strongly reflected. In judging of the fertility of a soil, with some persons its color is always matter of consideration; black soils absorbing heat much more strongly than white or light-colored soils. A rich garden black mould is a great absorber of heat. A sandy soil, or soil composed mainly of silex, becomes soon heated, first, from its dryness, the water passing directly through it, and, second, from the smooth surface and crystalline form of the particles of which it is composed; the heat is increased by being reflected from one side to the other, as in a tin oven. The temperature of a soil is materially affected by its condition as to moisture or dryness. This is obvious to every one. But there is another curious fact in this case, not so generally observed — that water is a non-conductor of heat downwards. It would be difficult to make a kettle of water boil by making a fire over it. So the sun's heat upon a wet surface is repelled, and not transmitted; and while evaporation may be going on at the surface, the lower strata remain cold. The temperature of a soil is materially affected by its aspect. Hence soils lying to the south, receiving as they do the more direct rays of the sun, are much warmer than those to the north, and, in both cases, the temperature is affected by the angle of inclination at which the land presents itself towards, or recedes from, the rays of the sun; the steeper it is towards the south the warmer — the steeper it is towards the north, for obvious reasons, the colder the temperature. It is well known, in respect to the tenderer fruits — such as peaches, for example — in high northern latitudes, that the crop is generally more certain on the northern than on the southern side of a hill, for the reason that, the frost continuing longer and more constantly, they come into flower at a later period, and therefore are less liable to the dangers of being repeatedly frozen and thawed, and to be cut off by the late frosts in the spring.*

LXX. — PEATY SOIL.

There are two other varieties of soil to which I have referred, upon which I shall take leave to make some passing remarks. The first is the peaty soil, which is composed wholly of vegetable matter, and is sometimes found of a great depth. It is evidently formed of the deposit and decay of vegetables, and in different stages of decomposition, — some being reduced to a fine and compact pulp, which cuts like butter, other being only partially decayed, and retaining the original forms of its leaves and stems. If vegetable matter were, as is often reckoned, the best food of plants, it would seem as though no soil could be so fertile as that of peat. This is not found to be the case, however, but for reasons not so well established as the fact. The plants of which peat land is composed have perished under water. It may be said, therefore, that they are rather in a state of preservation than decay, and this is quite obvious from the fact, that the water is required only to be drained out, or dried up in them, and they furnish a fuel equal to wood. "From the

* "In the country in which I reside, it has been remarked, that those portions of land which receive the first rays of the morning sun are more apt to suffer from the effects of white frosts than others, because the sudden transition from cold to heat sensibly affects delicate plants." — *French Trans. of Von Thaer.*

nature of its formation under the surface of water, it acquires a portion of tannin, which has the property of preserving animal and vegetable matter from decomposition." It may be, likewise, that the species of plants of which, in general, these preserved plants are composed, being of an aquatic nature, they do not form the most suitable nourishment to plants of a different description. I speak in this case according to the vulgar apprehension of the manner in which plants are fed, well knowing that the received doctrine is, that the organic portions of plants are obtained wholly from the atmosphere, and that the soil supplies only their mineral ingredients. Yet it must be admitted that, in ordinary cases, the fertility of a soil essentially corresponds to the amount of vegetable matter found in it, whether it supplies, in any degree, the actual substance of the plant, or, by its gradual decay, be merely the vehicle of transmitting for its nourishment the gases out of which its substance is to be composed. It is certain, however, whatever may be the philosophical reason in the case, that pure unmanufactured peat does not form a nourishing soil or substance for plants, other than those to which a wet soil is particularly congenial, and that it cannot be made so, but under a particular management, which I shall presently describe. The vegetable matter of which peat consists, being once thoroughly reduced, and mixed with other substances of an alkaline character, is rendered a most enriching manure for most kinds of land, though a much less substantial one than is generally supposed. One of its great uses is that of an absorbent, taking up the liquid matters which would otherwise be lost.

Immense bogs have been redeemed, and brought into a state of productive cultivation, in England; and, of late, these improvements have been going on with greater success than usual. In Ireland, such improvements have proceeded to a great extent, and the Waste-Land Improvement Company have at this time, in one place, five thousand acres of bog in the process of improvement. This place I had the pleasure to visit, and shall presently speak of what has been, and what is proposed to be, accomplished. The peat-bog, under favorable circumstances, as I have seen in the United States, as well as in England, may be rendered in the highest degree productive and profitable. The bog of salt marshes is of a different character from the fresh water peat-bog. This, however, is composed of vegetable matter in the main, being altogether marine plants, which have served as a kind of net-work to collect the earthy matter brought among them by the tide. The quantity of salt intermixed with these deposits gives them a peculiar character. They are favorable to the production of plants congenial to them; but other plants cannot be made to grow upon them until they become thoroughly decomposed; and, in that case, no soils yield a more luxuriant or richer vegetation. In truth, they require to be reduced to the state of fine mould, and the greater portion of the saltness exhausted, which time itself will effect where they are kept from the access of the tide, in order to be in a condition favorable to the growth of other than marine or saline plants.

LXXI. — LOAMY SOILS.

Next to peaty soils, I have to speak of what are called loamy soils. These are not very well defined. There has been much debate as to what constitutes loam or mould; but if it be difficult to define it with exactness, there is no great difficulty with practical men in understanding what is intended by it. I suppose the proper definition of *mould* to be decayed vegetable matter, and of *loam* to be that portion of the soil in which this mould, or decayed vegetable matter, (or *humus*, as it is technically called,) is mixed up with other common mineral elements, such as sand, clay, and lime, and in a state of fineness and equal or diffusive commixture. I do not know that any great error would be committed by considering *mould* and *loam* as synonymous, and by saying that mould or loam is a rich, unctuous, dark-colored matter, abounding in vegetable as well as mineral substances, found usually on the surface of fields, especially of those which have been cultivated, or those which are entirely in a state of nature; and of various depths, from inches to feet. In the rich valley of the Mississippi, I have seen it extending to a depth of twelve and eighteen feet, and of extraordinary richness. In cases of pure sand or clay, little or nothing of this is to be found. In chalk soils, its depth is usually very small. It constitutes the rich and fertile upper stratum of a soil which is usually cultivated by the plough; and it becomes gradually deepened as the land is cultivated and manured. The depth of this loam or mould may be considered, in general, as the best test of the goodness of the soil, or its productive character. I know that this is sometimes denied. The dark-colored condition of the upper stratum is not always an indication of mould, for occasionally there is met with an upper stratum of deep sand, colored with some mineral substance, which is almost utterly barren, and very difficult of improvement; but ordinarily, other circumstances being equal, the surest test of the fertility of a soil is the depth of the vegetable mould or loam on the surface.

Loamy soils receive their particular designation from the mineral substance with which they abound; thus we speak of sandy loams, or clayey loams, from the predominance of either of these substances in the soil; and undoubtedly the richest of all soils is that in which there is an intermixture of various elements — some one says, where lime, clay, and sand, are mixed in equal proportions with mould, or decayed vegetable matter; but it is not certain that the exact proportions are ascertained.

LXXII. — HUMUS, OR VEGETABLE MOULD.

The substance designated as vegetable mould, or humus, in its pure or unmixed state, is not an infallible indication of the fertility of a soil, as I have already stated in respect to peat formations. Liebig refers to the soils in the neighborhood of Mount Vesuvius, composed wholly of matter thrown from the crater, as highly fertile. "The land in the vicinity of Vesuvius may be considered as the type of a fertile soil, and its fertility is greater or less, in different parts, according to the proportion of clay or sand which it contains. The soil which is formed by the disintegration of lava cannot possibly, on account of its origin, contain the smallest trace of vegetable matter; and yet

35 *

it is well known that, when the volcanic ashes have been exposed for some time to the influence of air and moisture, a soil is gradually formed in which all kinds of plants grow with the greatest luxuriance. This fertility is owing to the alkalies which are contained in the lava, and which, by exposure to the weather, are rendered capable of being absorbed by plants. Thousands of years have been necessary to convert stones and rocks into the soil of arable land; and thousands of years more will be requisite for their perfect reduction — that is, for the complete exhaustion of their alkalies."

This is a very extraordinary statement, and, without implying any distrust of the authority on which it is made, is certainly not consonant to general experience. General experience would seem to show that soils without any vegetable mould are not productive, and most practical farmers would prefer, of all others, a soil where the vegetable matter, well compounded, existed in abundance, forming, as it is termed, a deep and rich *loam*. But it would seem that, in the case to which Liebig refers, thousands of years are necessary to render a mass of lava fertile, and in such a case it might be fairly presumed that some vegetable matter might accumulate and produce the desired mixture. I do not presume to call in question an authority so distinguished, and for which no man has more respect than myself; but I could wish that we had more facts in the case, or that they were more definitely stated.

Until recently, almost all agriculturists, both the scientific and practical, have considered the quantity of vegetable matter contained in a soil as the test of its fertility. A prejudice so universal, and so long established, would seem, on those grounds, strongly entitled to respect. It has been as well understood that vegetable matter alone, as in the case of peat, and this but partially decomposed, was not fertile. But the opinion of the connection of vegetable mould with fertility applied to vegetable matter in a state of comminution and intermixture with other elements of a soil, and here the fertility of the land has been understood to bear a very close relation to its predominance or deficiency. Peat itself, when thoroughly decomposed, has been found a most efficient manure. The effects constantly accruing from the application of decayed vegetable matter to the soil, from the application of the dung of cattle, which is in the main decomposed vegetable matter, and the extraordinarily luxuriant vegetation always appearing upon dung-heaps left on the field, or upon places where dung-heaps have been formed, seemed to speak the same language. The supposition has been, that this vegetable matter constituted, in fact, a part of the food of plants, and went to assist in forming their substance.

The doctrine of Liebig denies directly the supposition that this humus, or vegetable matter, is taken up as the food of plants, because, where a forest grows, the vegetable matter in and upon the soil actually increases, instead of diminishing; but then, although, in the case above referred to, of the volcanic soils near Mount Vesuvius, one might be led to infer that he considered it of no moment, yet this I think would be doing him an injustice. He does consider the humus of the soil as furnishing, in its decay, a necessary supply of carbonic acid to the plant in the process of germination, though of no use after the plant gets above ground; and he supposes that the manures of animals fed upon the product of the land return to the land those mineral elements which they took from it, and which are indispensable to their perfect formation. This may be so; and in this view he does not deny the value of vegetable mould, or humus. But certainly there was nothing improbable in the supposition that plants might have found some portion of their food in those decayed substances which once constituted a part of the substance of their predecessors. Indeed, I see as yet no sufficient grounds to conclude that their office in supplying carbon to the growing plant ceases as soon as the plant is above ground, and able, as he supposes, to gain its own supplies for itself from the atmosphere. It is quite certain that the growth of a forest would be checked, and the amount of humus in the soil be diminished, if all the decayed leaves and limbs, which fall from the trees, were constantly removed; and it is as certain that the continual cultivation of land, without supplies of manure, exhausts its vegetable mould; and that the application of vegetable manures to crops in a growing state is often as efficacious as when applied, or ploughed in, with the seed.

LXXIII. — PECULIARITIES OF SOIL.

There are some characteristics of different soils which seem to be generally admitted by practical men, but not very well defined. Thus some soils are deemed much better than others for the production of beef, others for that of butter, others for that of cheese; and I found farmers, in some of the dairy districts, going so far as to assert that cheese could not be made on some soils, or rather, as I inferred from their remarks, could not be made to so much advantage as on others. But this, it seemed to me, could only be an indirect inference. That these products, both in quality and quantity, depend much upon the nature of the plants upon which the animals are fed, is an obvious fact; and that some soils may be more favorable than others to the production of such kinds of plants as are particularly suited to particular uses or objects, I could easily understand; but any other connection of the products with the nature of the soil seemed to me far from being established. To speak, therefore, of a cheesy soil, as I heard in some dairy districts, seemed to me of questionable propriety, as, under an intelligent agriculture, I could hardly doubt that a different species of herbage might be cultivated upon the same soil which now produced that which was unfavorable.

I have given these brief notices of the general character of soils in England, of which the counterparts may be found in the United States. I have given them in terms which will, I think, be understood by the commonest farmer. I could without any difficulty have borrowed learning enough for the occasion, and have talked philosophically in the case; but in all I have read on the subject, I have as yet discovered no practical advantage to the general mass of readers, from so viewing it, beyond what is secured by more simple statements. The importance of the nature of the soil to the husbandman, who spends his labor upon it, is very great. Some of the mineral ingredients, which are found in the soil, are indispensable to vegetation. Those which are found in the plants can only be received from the soil; but it is a singular fact that, in case of a deficiency, one may sometimes be substituted for another. "Potash is not the only substance necessary for the existence of most plants; indeed, it has been already shown that the potash may be replaced, in many cases, by soda, magnesia, or lime."*

LXXIV. — APPLICATION OF CHEMISTRY TO AGRICULTURE.

It must not be inferred, from any remark which has fallen from me, that I overlook the value of chemical science and inquiry in respect to agriculture. An inference of that nature would do me a great injustice. Our obligations in this matter are already very great, and more and wider triumphs are to be looked for. But two or three things, in this case, appear to me deserving of consideration, and likely to moderate an excessive confidence. The first is, that vegetation, and consequently cultivation, in the most scientific sense of the term, is not so simple a matter as some persons would have us imagine. How, for example, particular plants from the same soil are capable of extracting entirely different substances, according to their own peculiar and individual characters, each one preserving its own identity in form, taste, odor, color, fruit, and use, is not yet explained. The explanation is not even approached. In the second place, it seems assuming quite too much to suppose that all the processes of vegetation are to be resolved into mere chemical processes — understanding by chemical processes those laws or operations of which chemistry has attained a knowledge. The remarks which I have just made seem to demonstrate this. In the next place, the knowledge which chemistry has already furnished, either of the nature of soils or manures, or of the phenomena of vegetation, has not as yet been of so practical a character as is to be hoped for; and it would seem extremely difficult, not to say impossible, to meet on any extended scale the diversities of soil which it has illustrated. The newly-invented manure, to which I have above referred, should it be found to equal what it seems to promise, may fully meet this objection, and thus effect an important stride in agricultural improvement.

* Liebig.

LXXV. — THEORY OF AGRICULTURE.

The present theory of agriculture assumes that plants consist of two species of matter — vegetable and mineral; that the former is derived wholly from water and the air, and the latter from the soil. The plant is not perfected without the conjoint aid of both. The former consists of oxygen, hydrogen, carbon, and nitrogen; and the latter of at least eight different kinds of mineral substances. The latter are found in the ashes of plants, and are indestructible. They consist usually of four acids and four alkalies; — silicic acid, phosphoric acid, sulphuric acid, and muriatic acid; and, of the alkalies, potash, soda, lime, and magnesia. Other mineral substances are found; but these which I have enumerated are the principal. Boussingault thus designates them: "The residue left by the combustion is commonly composed of salts; alkaline chlorides, with bases of potash and soda; earthy and metallic phosphates; caustic or carbonated lime and magnesia; silica; and oxides of iron and of manganese. Several other substances are also met with there, but in quantities so small that they may be neglected." *

The mineral substances found in the ashes of plants may be supplied by art; yet whether to be applied to the land in a direct and simple, or in a combined or mixed form, and, if so, how combined and mixed, are points not as yet determined. It is certain that there is only one form in which they can be taken up by the plants, and that is, in as extreme a degree of solubility as they are capable of being reduced to. Whether they shall be so reduced before they are applied, — whether, for example, they shall be presented to the plants in a solid or a liquid form, or whether they shall be by any art prepared, or it shall be left to the vital operations of the plant to prepare them, — are points yet to be determined. These questions will naturally present themselves again when the subject of manures is considered.

In respect to the organic parts of vegetables, — those which form their largest portion, and consisting of oxygen, hydrogen, carbon, and nitrogen, — the two former are understood to be supplied by water, the carbon by the atmosphere, and the nitrogen, consti-

* Boussingault, p. 54.

tuting the nutritious part of the vegetable, from ammonia, which is itself a compound of nitrogen and hydrogen, and supplied partially by rain, by the decay or putrefaction of animal matter, and in the excrements of animals. In the escape of ammonia from our dung heaps, it is supposed a great portion of their most valuable material passes off; and attempts have been made to fix this volatile substance, so as to secure it for the service of the plants, to be taken up by them as required. For this purpose, gypsum has been strongly recommended to be sprinkled in stables, and to be spread upon manure heaps. It is quite doubtful whether its effect has met the sanguine expectations which were formed of it. In the report given by Professor Henslow, which he has been kind enough to send me, of fifteen attempts to fix ammonia by the application of gypsum to dung, the result seems to leave the question wholly undetermined. His conclusions from these experiments are given in this result: "It will be seen that, with turnips, the effect has been uniformly in favor of gypsumed dung. With the straw of wheat, the result is twice in favor of the gypsumed dung, once against it, and in one case there is no difference. In respect to the wheat itself, it is six times in favor of the gypsumed dung, and six times against it. The practical inference to be deduced from this part of the inquiry favors the idea of using gypsumed dung for a turnip crop, but shows that it produces no better effect than ungypsumed dung upon a wheat crop." Such results certainly lead to no very strong conclusions. But the beneficial effects of covering manure heaps with mould, in order, in the first place, to prevent the escape of the volatile parts of the manure, and, in the next place, to absorb the gases, — so that the soil used for a covering becomes itself a valuable manure, — are points long ago determined by the practice of many enlightened farmers.

Whatever may be the success or the ill success of dealing with the mineral qualities of the soil, or with those subtile gases of which vegetables are composed, there are processes of a practical nature to be applied, the propriety and utility of which are established. The practice of agriculture is still very much in advance of the theory of agriculture. I do not undervalue scientific agriculture. Science may do as much for agriculture as for any other department of business, or art, or health, or comfort, or enjoyment. In no department is success more desirable, or would it prove more extensively beneficial. The human mind finds the greatest of all delights in the acquisition of knowledge, and is impelled by an instinctive impulse "to search into the causes of things." A man, if familiar with the place and route, may find his way, if the lamps were not lighted, even of a dark night, in the labyrinthine streets of London; but he must proceed slowly and doubtingly, and may tumble into an open sewer, or run against a post, or encounter other obstructions more yielding than the post, yet twice as dangerous. But since science has kindled the beautiful and far-reaching silver flame of gas, and converted night into day, he walks in security and confidence; he escapes, if he has wisdom so to choose, all perilous obstructions; and he reaches his destination by the most direct, the most expeditious, and a certain route.

LXXVI. — ACTUAL IMPROVEMENTS.

The soil must be the great object of the farmer's attention; and here he may accomplish much. I mean much relatively, and with a due consideration of the limitations by which human power is always hemmed in. Light and heat, sunshine and rain, wind and frost, and many other influences most important to vegetation, of which as yet the human imagination has not, in all probability, taken cognizance or conceived, are wholly beyond his control or dictate. Arrogant and presumptuous as he is, the earth could not contain him, if he were not chained down by the fact of his absolute dependence. There is a beautiful moral in the mythological fable of Jove's having given the reins to Phaeton, and the disastrous consequences which followed. But the ameliorations which an improved agriculture may effect are great, and sufficiently encouraging to the loftiest self-esteem. A wet soil may be drained; a dry soil may be irrigated. A barren soil may be enriched; a rich soil may be made more fertile and productive. A thin soil may be deepened; a heavy soil may be made lighter; a loose soil may be made more compact. A bleak soil may be sheltered; and an unfavorable aspect may be alleviated. Waste lands may be converted into fertile fields, and a growth of nauseous or unnutritious weeds supplanted by bending sheaves of golden grain. Rivers may be diverted from their tortuous courses, now rendering vast tracts of land inaccessible, and made to flow in straight lines, leaving their recovered banks open to the plough; and immense extents of the richest alluvial lands may be rescued from the sea — the feeble arm of human art and industry drive back the spoiler, and stay even his proudest waves. All these noble triumphs English agriculture has achieved; and I shall take pains to lay them before my readers. What I propose to do then further, in this number, is, to detail their various improvements, and then to speak of the adaptation of particular soils to those purposes for which experience has shown them best fitted.

LXXVII. — PLOUGHING.

The first and most general operation, to which the soil is subjected, is ploughing. Man must have been early taught that, in order to render the earth productive, it must be tilled; and it would be extremely curious, if the materials of such history were attainable, to trace the progress of improvement from the first instrument employed to stir the earth to the present beautiful and ingenious implement, by which acres, and miles of acres, are at pleasure inverted. It would be interesting to know how the North American Indians cultivated their corn (maize) when the country was discovered; tradition has not preserved the traces of the method which they adopted. Their implements must have been few, and of the most simple description. The smooth stones, some of which I have myself found in places known as their favorite haunts, of a wedge shape, may have been used for digging the ground for the deposit of the seed, and perhaps for keeping the soil loose round the plants: near the sea-shore a clam-shell may have answered the same purpose. Of weeds, probably they had few to contend with, as the land was new and not surcharged with manure, of which perhaps they did not know the use, since, within the memory of persons now living, farmers in the vicinity of Albany were accustomed to cart the manure from their barns on to the Hudson when frozen, and in the neighborhood of Montreal on to the St. Lawrence, that, at the breaking of the ice in the spring, it might be carried away by the stream. Even much more recently, in some parts of the country, farmers, when they have found the piles of manure round their barns accumulated to an inconvenient size, have preferred to desert them, and build other barns, rather than be at the trouble and expense of removing these heaps. One is often amused at hearing people boast of "the wisdom of our ancestors;" and, to be consistent, we should expect to see such persons adjusting the equilibrium of a bag of grain upon the horse's back by putting the corn in one end and a stone in the other.

When I come to treat of the implements of husbandry, I shall describe an English plough; at present I have to deal only with the operation itself.

I think I may say that, in England and Scotland, the art of ploughing has reached perfection, and that it is unrivalled and unsurpassable. This at least is my opinion, which must be taken at what it is worth. I cannot conceive how it can be improved; and this not in rare instances, and at ploughing matches, but I may say universally. In some cases, the work has been done better than in others; but I have not seen an example of bad ploughing in the country; I have not seen one which, in the United States, would not be pronounced superior.

LXXVIII. — THE ENGLISH CHARACTER — A DIGRESSION.

It may be thought a little out of the way, but I will take this occasion to say, that the English know what right lines are. It is but just to say of them that of which I am convinced, after a familiar and close observation, — that they are an upright people; that they have, with as few exceptions as are ordinarily to be expected in a commercial community, none of that slyness which some men chuckle over as a commendable quality, but which, though it may mount a fine beaver and wear the best Saxony broadcloth, is only a soft name for villany; that their habits, like their ploughing, are direct and straight-forward, and are opposed to all balks and all tortuous windings. I thank God that the blood of such a people flows in my veins; for I look upon honesty as the true nobility of man, and the only aristocracy to which my heart burns to pay always its spontaneous and unclaimed homage. "An honest man is the noblest work of God;" a passage, of which a facetious divine, a man as true as he was witty, once said, "If it were not in the Scriptures, it ought to be."

LXXIX. — THE PERFECTION OF PLOUGHING.

The perfection of any art consists in its accomplishment of its particular object in the best manner, and by the simplest means. The perfection of ploughing consists in its performing its work exactly as you wish or require to have it done. You wish the surface soil of your field completely inverted. You wish this to be done at a particular depth, and the furrow-slice to be cut in perfectly direct lines. You desire it to be of a certain width and certain thickness, and the same in every part of the field. You require that it should be raised without breaking, and either laid completely flat upon its back, or made to recline upon its neighbor at a particular angle of inclination; and you wish it so done that, if it be greensward, every portion of the herbage shall be completely shut in, and not a spire shall dare show its head between the furrows, any more than a straggling Frenchman on the field after the battle of Waterloo. And you want this performed at the rate of about an acre a day of eight hours' work, with your team moving at the rate of two miles or two miles and a quarter per hour, so that they may work comfortably every day in the week. You desire your ploughman to follow his team, and execute his part with entire attention to what he is about, without perturbation, without sweating, without fretting, and especially without swearing, which some men whom I have known, both at ploughing matches and in their own fields, have deemed indispensable to the proper performance of their work; in which matter I beg leave to say I always entirely differed from them in opinion, having never yet discovered any reason why men, who assume to belong to the order of rational animals, should, by their passion and the indecency and profaneness of their language, degrade themselves below the brute animals which they undertake to govern. Now, in all the particulars which I have pointed out, the ploughing here will be done exactly according to a prescribed form. I said, in my first report, that the ploughed land resembled a ruffle just come from under the crimping iron. The representation is perfect.

LXXX. — PLOUGHING MATCH AT SAFFRON WALDEN.

I attended, among several others, a ploughing match at Saffron Walden, where there were at least ten competitors, with lots of an eighth of an acre; and, as well as I can remember, the furrow-slices were to be seven inches in width and five inches in depth. It was not a match against time, although the work was required to be completed within a certain time. I do not misstate when I say that I do not believe there was the variation of an inch, in the whole field, in the width or depth of the furrow, or a single crooked line, or even one solitary balk. The fields or lands were struck out before beginning. Two horses composed a team, and the ploughman was his own driver. Some boys under eighteen were allowed to enter as competitors for boys' premiums. I went over the field in an ecstasy of admiration at its uniformity, neatness, exactness, and beauty.

There were some peculiar regulations adopted on this occasion, to which I may properly refer. Ploughmen who had obtained a first-prize premium on any former occasion, for ploughing, were disqualified, by the rules of the society, from entering into the general competition. But, with a view "of giving such meritorious ploughmen another opportunity of showing that their skill and energies remain unimpaired," a special competition was offered to them, and seven prizes were proposed — the first amounting, in money and clothing, to £8 10s., or about $43, the lowest to £2 10s., or more than $12, and the unsuccessful competitors, to the number of seven, were to receive £1 each. This was putting them through a fine sieve, so as to come at the best quality. A premium of five guineas was likewise offered to the farmer who had employed the greatest number of ploughboys on his occupation, in proportion to acreage, for the preceding year, provided one of the boys in his employ should have obtained a prize for ploughing at the Annual Meeting. Such a premium as this seemed well suited to induce the farmers to give particular attention to the improvement of the lads in their service. Two circumstances contribute strongly to the perfecting of this most essential art. The first is, that boys are trained to it as early as they can possibly be employed with safety. The second is, the division of labor which generally prevails, so that individuals devote themselves, to a degree exclusively, to one particular object; a ploughman is constantly employed at the plough, and a herdsman in the pastures, or stalls.

There are two points, which have seemed to me always particularly to test the skill of a ploughman. The one is the mode in which he lays out his land, and strikes the first furrow; and the second, that in which he finishes the last furrow. In the case to which I have referred, the last land remained, at the close, a single unbroken strip of equal width, from one end of the field to the other, lying like a stretched-out ribbon, which, as the ploughman came down the course, he turned without breaking, and with perfect precision, from one end to the other. In this instance, the horses seemed almost as well trained as the driver, and inspired with an equal emulation. The finishing of the ends of the lands is always a work of great care; they are cross-ploughed, and the whole affair is completed with an equal neatness throughout.

I have seen very good ploughing in the United States, and perhaps in no department of agriculture has greater improvement taken place than in ploughing, and in the construction of ploughs. Formerly, nothing could be more slovenly executed. A straight line was not to be seen. The land was not half turned over. The furrows were of such depth or thickness as they might chance to be; and the plough itself, when in action, resembled very much a live animal, with a sort of grasshopper motion, which one man at the stilts, and often two men riding upon the beam, were struggling to keep down, and, like police officers, to prevent its escape. A man was always required, likewise, with a hoe, to assist in turning the furrow-slice at the end of the share, or in the discouraging duty of raising again, and turning over by main force, those furrow-slices which, notwithstanding they had been raised by the plough, like a reluctant boy pulled out of bed in the morning, with his eyes half open, insist upon getting back again as soon as the master's back is turned. I remember many a thump on the breast from the handles of the plough, and many a sudden jerk, which has thrown me upon the furrow, when I have been riding on the beam, and many a splitting of a beam, and many a breaking of a share; and have looked back with dismay upon a long furrow-slice obstinately turning back into the furrow, after I had supposed it securely laid over. Somewhat of this experience may have been necessary, to enable me to estimate properly the excellence of English ploughing, when the implement seemed to move through the ground with as much quietness, directness, ease, — I may almost add grace, — as a boat through the water, with its sails spread to a favoring breeze, and an accomplished steersman at the helm. Some allowance is to be made for the condition of our fields, compared with the English fields. Here there are no stumps of trees, and no stones, to impede or derange the plough. With us, alas! in many cases, the stumps and stones remain in resolute opposition, to dispute our entrance, and, like bad tenants, can be dispossessed only by main force.

I know that some may ask, What is the use of doing things with so much care? I answer, in particular, that, the field being more thoroughly worked, the advantages to the crops, both in the suppression of weeds and in furnishing a more favorable bed for the extension of the roots of the plants, and its after cultivation and management, are quite sufficient to recommend it. But I answer, in general, that the labor in the end is less, and more easy, in doing things well and regularly than in half doing them, and that in a slovenly manner; and that habits of order, neatness, and regularity, in one branch of labor, lead to the same habits in other branches, and are of eminent advantage; and, according to an excellent proverb, a thing which is well done is twice done.

LXXXI. — GENERAL RULES FOR PLOUGHING.

The depth of ploughing, the width of the furrow-slice, the number of ploughings which should be given to land, and the season at which it should be executed, depend on such a variety of circumstances, that it would be difficult to prescribe any universal rules.

The objects of ploughing are, to loosen the soil, and to render it permeable to the roots of plants, that they may extend themselves for nourishment and support; to make it accessible to the air and rain, from which, according to modern theories, it gathers both oxygen and ammonia, for the food of plants; and, lastly, to give an opportunity of incorporating manures with the soil, for their support and growth. It has another object, of course, where greensward is turned over, which is, to bury the herbage then on the ground, and substitute other plants.

The depth of ploughing varies in different soils, and for different purposes. The average depth may be considered as five inches, but no direction on this subject will be found universally applicable. Three of the most eminent practical farmers with whom I am acquainted here plough not more than three inches; but the surface mould, in these cases, is very thin, and the understratum is a cold, clammy chalk. One farmer, whose cultivation is successful, and who cultivates "a light, poor, thin, moory soil, with a subsoil of either blue or white clay, peat, or white gravel," carefully avoids breaking up the cold subsoil, and cuts up the sward with a breast-plough, which is a kind of paring spade; and, after burning the turf, and spreading the ashes with a due application of artificial manure, consisting of equal quantities of lime, wood and turf ashes, at the rate of sixty bushels to the acre, and sowing turnip-seed, cultivates between the rows with a single horse-plough, which cannot, of course, take a deep furrow. The second year of the course, when he sows wheat. he ploughs it very lightly with a horse, after having first breast-ploughed it, so as thoroughly to cover in the manure which the sheep who have been folded upon the land have left upon it. The third year it is breast-ploughed, sown in turnips, and cultivated between the rows with a horse, as before described. The fourth year it is simply breast-ploughed for barley. The fifth and sixth years it is in grass. Thus, in the whole course of a six years' rotation, this land is only ploughed four times by men, and three times with a single horse-plough. Another farmer in the same neighborhood says that, upon this description of land, any other than the breast-plough would not leave the ground sufficiently firm for wheat. Mr. Pusey, M. P., whose excellently managed farm I have had the pleasure of repeatedly going over, in remarking on the above accounts, says, "Occupying similar land, I may add that I never plough it deeply, but I repent of so doing; and am falling more and more each year, by the advice of neighboring farmers, into the use of the breast-plough, instead of the horse-plough. This manual labor is quite as cheap, for a good workman can pare such hollow tender land at 4 s., or even at 3 s. per acre. It is possible that the drought of our climate in Gloucestershire and Berkshire may be one cause of the success of this practice in those counties, and that the same soil, if transferred to Westmoreland, would require deeper working. Therefore, without recommending shallow cultivation in districts where deep ploughing has been hitherto practised, I would merely warn beginners against plunging recklessly into the subsoil." These examples are certainly well worth considering. I do not understand that these practices at all militate against the doctrine of the advantages to be obtained from subsoiling. In cases where subsoiling and thorough draining are not applied, this shallow ploughing may be preferred, as the mingling of the cold and inert subsoil with so thin a surface of vegetable mould would doubtless be prejudicial, at least for a length of time; but the improvement of such land by a system of thorough draining and subsoiling is another matter, to which I shall refer in its proper place. There are considerable tracts of this moorish land — that is, a thin, black, coarse peat, not half decomposed, resting upon a cold and hard pan of gravel or clay, or what some persons have mistaken for marl, in Massachusetts, and other parts of the country, the improvement of which, so far as my experience has gone, has been almost hopeless.

While upon this subject, I may as well give the results of the management of the first farmer referred to, and therefore subjoin them. "By this mode of management, an economical system is followed up through the whole course, by being nearly all performed by manual labor, by which means a remunerating crop will be produced, and the land always kept firm, which is the only difficulty to be overcome on this description of soil. The farm, when first taken by me, was wet; as much out of condition, and as light and weak, as it well could be — parts of it being merely held together by the roots of grass and weeds, natural to moory land, but which must be very prejudicial to the production of those crops that are to benefit the farmer. I commenced by draining, and then pursued the foregoing system of cultivation, by which my most sanguine expectations have been realized, though I was told that the land would be too light and too poor to plant wheat after turnips. I have never found any ill effects from paring and burning, experience having taught me that it produces a manure particularly beneficial to the growth of turnips; thereby enabling me to firm the land by sheep."* This farmer speaks of performing a great portion of his work with manual labor. I think some part of it might rather be called pedestrian than manual; for, if he ploughs his land by men, he treads it out by women. He says, "Before the horse-roll can be used, I send women to tread it, and, if occasion require, tread it again; after which, I have it twice hoed. I have found more benefit from this mode of pressing than any other, being done at a time when wheat, on this description of soil, requires assistance." †

I have found other farmers, who, with their wheat crops on light, chalky soils, ploughed in a very shallow manner, and then were accustomed to tread their land with sheep, in order to give the wheat plant a firmer footing; as, otherwise, in a very light soil, it might be thrown out by the wind. These cases, how-

---

* Journal of the Royal Agricultural Society, vol. vi. p. 1.

† This is a use to which women have not as yet been put in our "half-civilized" country. I dare say, however, many persons think that it is very well to make such clever animals serviceable; their "keep," agriculturally speaking, is somewhat expensive; and, as they have their share in the pleasure of consuming, they may as well take their part in the labor of producing. Whatever any persons may think, however, I will say no such uncivil thing; but, since the celebrated *danseuse*, Fanny Ellsler, returned from the United States, after a two years' tour, with a gain of twenty thousand pounds, or one hundred thousand dollars, it cannot be denied that the Americans are quite willing to pay for the use of women's feet — in a way, we admit, more elegant, tasteful, and classical, but certainly not more respectable, and not half as useful, as that of treading the wheat-ground.

ever, must all be deemed exceptions; and the general rule in England, where the soil admits of it, and manure is abundant, is that of rather deep ploughing. Five or six inches is the average depth; in many cases, much more than this. The loam, or vegetable mould, is, without question, the great source or medium of nourishment to the plants. Be it more or less deep, it is always safe to go to the bottom of this, and, by gradually loosening a portion of the subsoil, or lower stratum, and incorporating it with the mould, and rendering it accessible to the air and light, it acquires the nature of mould, and the whole arable surface is enriched. The deeper the soil, the more deeply the roots are permitted to descend, and the more widely they are enabled to spread themselves,—unless they penetrate a substratum unhealthy from wet or the too great prevalence of some unfavorable mineral substance,—so much the more luxuriant and productive is the vegetation likely to prove. The depth to which the roots of plants will go down in search of food or moisture, where the soil is in a condition to be penetrated by them, is much greater than a superficial observation would induce us to suppose. It is confidently asserted that the roots of some plants — such, for example, as lucern and sainfoin — go to a depth of fifteen, twenty, and even thirty feet. This seems scarcely credible. Red clover is known to extend its roots to the depth of three feet, and wheat to the depth of two or three feet, where the condition of the soil is favorable to their extension. Von Thaer, the distinguished agriculturist, says, "he has pulled carrots two and a half feet long, the tap-root of which was probably another foot in length." The tap-root of a Swedish turnip has been known to extend thirty-nine inches; the roots of Indian corn full six feet. These statements may appear extraordinary; but, by the free and loose texture of the soil, it is obvious a good husbandman will give every opportunity for the roots and their extremely fine fibres to extend themselves as far as their instincts may prompt them.

Next to the depth of ploughing, the width of the furrow-slice is to be considered. This, of course, depends mainly upon the construction of the plough. A plough with a wide sole or base, in the hands of a skilful ploughman, may be made to cut a narrow furrow-slice; but a narrow-soled plough cannot be made to cut a wide furrow-slice, though it may sometimes appear to do so by leaving a part of the ground unturned, which the furrow-slice is made to cover. Where, as in old ploughed land, the object is solely to leave the ground loose and light, it is advisable to take a very narrow furrow. Where, otherwise, the object is to move greensward or stubble ground, and to cover in the vegetable matter, such a width of furrow must be taken as will cause the slice, as it is raised by the share, to turn over easily. This width may generally be reckoned at nearly twice the depth, though less will answer; but a furrow-slice of equal sides would not turn, but stand on end. The manner in which the furrow-slice will be turned depends somewhat upon the form of the mould-board, but more, in general, upon the skill of the ploughman. Two modes are adopted; the one to lay the furrow-slice entirely flat, shutting its edge exactly in by the edge of its neighbor; the other, to lay it at an inclination of 45 degrees, lapping the one upon the other. The former mode, where land is to be sown with grass-seed, and, as the phrase is with us, laid down, is, undoubtedly, to be preferred. Perhaps, in any case where a grain crop is to be cultivated, it should be preferred, as its beneficial effects have been well tested in the United States. In the United States, however, from a higher temperature, the vegetable matter thus pressed down may be expected sooner to be decomposed, and thus sooner furnish a pabulum for the growing plants, than in a climate where, in a much lower and more even temperature, the decomposition cannot be expected to take place so rapidly. In other cases, and for vegetable crops, — I mean in contradistinction to grain crops, — a different mode of ploughing, that is, laying the furrow-slices one upon the other at an angle of 45 degrees, or half turned over, would leave the ground more loose, as well as expose a larger surface of the inverted soil to be enriched by the air. In this way, by harrowing and rolling, the vegetable matter will be completely buried. This mode of ploughing is evidently preferred throughout the country, as I have seldom seen the sward completely inverted and laid flat, though I know the practice prevails in some counties. To avoid having any of the grass protrude itself between the furrow-slices, they have here, what I have never seen in the United States, a skim-colter, that is, a miniature ploughshare, or blade, placed under the beam, and so adjusted as to cut an edge from the furrow-slice as it is turned over; this piece, so cut off, at once dropping down, and being buried under the furrow-slice as it goes over. The consequence is, that there is no grass on the edge of the furrow-slice to show itself, and great neatness is therefore given to the whole work. There is another mode of ploughing, which I have sometimes seen practised, by which the furrow-slice is not merely lifted, but may be said to be rolled over, or twisted in a sort of bag-fashion. This seemed to me to be principally owing to the concave form of the mould-board, for no workman could have done it with a straight or convex form of mould-board. It would seem to render the soil more friable and loose; but every departure from a straight line, or wedge form of the mould-board, evidently much increases the draught. The skim-colter, to which I have referred above, somewhat increases the draught, but in a very small degree.

The great object of the English farmers, in ploughing, seems to be the thorough pulverization of the soil; and they are therefore very seldom satisfied with one ploughing, but their land is repeatedly ploughed, scarified, and harrowed. They cross-plough their land, and think it desirable to reduce the sward land to a fine tilth, tearing it to pieces, and bringing all the grass, and roots, and rubbish, to the surface, that they may be raked up and burned, or carried to the manure heaps. The propriety of this practice is, in my mind, quite questionable. It would seem to me much better to turn the sward completely over, and then cultivate on the top of it, without disturbing the grass surface, leaving that, when thus turned over, to a gradual decomposition, that it might in this way supply food to the growing crop, whereas the abstraction of so much vegetable matter must greatly diminish the resources of the soil. Where, however, the field is infested with twitch grass, (*triticum repens,*) — in which, indeed, many of the fields in England abound to a most extraordinary extent, — there may be no getting rid of it but by actually loosening and tearing it out; but where it is a mere clover ley, or an old grass pasture or meadow, the taking out and removing the vegetable matter seems to be a serious waste. Even the twitch might be managed where the crop is to be hoed, though, in grain crops, its presence is extremely prejudicial.

Having thus described the general style of ploughing, as it prevails in England, I come to speak of particular processes which are occasionally practised.

1. Lapping in Ploughing. — A field of greensward, or stubble, is often, in the autumn, only half ploughed; that is, a furrow-slice is turned over directly upon an unploughed surface; and then another furrow is turned upon another unploughed surface, until the whole field, being thus ploughed, presents a succession of open furrows and of lapped lands, and only half of it is in fact stirred. In the spring, these intermediate places are broken up by the process being directly reversed. Some advantage may come, in this case, from the decomposition or rotting of the vegetable matter placed between the two surfaces thus brought together, although this can hardly be expected to proceed at a rapid rate, if at all, during the winter season, and the furrows may serve as drains to carry off the water from the land; but, excepting the saving in time by half doing instead of wholly doing the work, I see no advantage in this process over the regular mode of ploughing the whole field at once. It is advised, however, in performing this operation, that the part of the sward which is laid over should be wider than that upon which it is laid, that, by its weight, it may be broken, and the whole rendered more friable.*

2. Ribbing, or Raftering. — There is another mode of ploughing called *ribbing*, or *raftering*, differing scarcely from the method just described, excepting that two furrow-slices are laid upon one, instead of one upon one. In this case, an open furrow and an alternate ridge present themselves over the whole field; the furrows serve to keep the land from stagnant water, and the turned-up land is exposed to the ameliorating processes of

* "When land has become very full of twitch, it is a good plan to half-plough it — that is, turning over one furrow and then another opposite, to meet it. If this is done in November, it will check the growth of the twitch during the winter. The land, when ploughed in a contrary direction early in the spring, will lie in heaps, and thus become quite dry, when the twitch may easily be got out, and a good turnip fallow be made. Scufflers are now made, which will answer the purpose of stirring land that has been ploughed, and thus save the labor and expense of a ploughing: Finlayson's harrow is a most useful implement." — *Hillyard's Practical Farmer*, 4th edition, p. 36.

the air and the frost. The field, when done in the best possible manner, as it often is, presents a beautiful example of artistical skill. In the springing, preparatory to after cultivation, the whole is broken up and levelled, by reversing the operation. I am not able to see any decided advantage which this mode has over the regular ploughing of the whole field at once, except in the saving of time, and this saving is at the expense of only two thirds of the land being ploughed.

3. Laying in Beds, or Stitches. — There is another mode of ploughing, or rather of laying the land, which prevails in England and Scotland to a great extent, and is nearly universal upon low and wet soils; that is, the practice of laying the land in beds, or what are here commonly called *stetches.* In this case, a ridge is formed in the centre, by laying two furrows back to back, and then ploughing up to them on each side, until a sufficient land is gone over to form a bed. These beds vary much in width, from five to eighteen and thirty-six feet. In some cases, under a system of ploughing which is called *two in and two out*, four beds are formed into one bed, of perhaps sixty feet in breadth. In Essex county, on the lowlands, they are only five feet in width. An open furrow is of course left for the water to flow off, which runs down the sides of the beds. The object is to lay the land dry; but it is obvious there is a loss of land in the furrows, and, while there is a constant accumulation of rich soil on the centre of the bed, the mould must gradually become thinner as you approach the furrow, and the furrow is always indicated by an absence of product, or the growth of coarse and worthless grasses.

These ridges, in English cultivation, are seldom altered, but (though often, far from being bounded by a straight, are bounded by a winding or crooked furrow) remain the same as they have been doubtless for a century. Indeed, they are in many places regarded with a kind of superstition, as though the land would lose its fertility if they were broken in upon; and some writers on English husbandry assert that water flows better in these winding gutters than it would in straight furrows, which is certainly a new philosophy. Though, where they are not properly ploughed, there is liable to be a continual accumulation towards the centre, yet I cannot say that I have ever seen so great an increase of them as is described in Von Thaer's Agriculture, which has been recently translated into English, and published in two volumes in London. "In places," says this author, "where, as is frequently the case, there have been no ditches between the lands of different proprietors, or where these ditches have been filled up for the sake of gaining additional surface, all the ploughmen have avoided throwing the earth to the outside, from fear that, if they did so, their neighbor might carry off that which was thus placed within his reach. *In this manner, ridges of considerable breadths have become elevated in the middle to such a degree, that two men, walking in the parallel furrows which bound them, will not be able to see each other.*" * This seems to be a regular piece of Munchausen; and if all book agriculture were of this description, one could hardly be surprised at some little incredulity and distaste on the part of common practical farmers.

The advantages of laying land in this form, in cases where land is wet and heavy, or where the rain does not pass off readily, are obvious. Where the ridges or beds, likewise, are made equal, and with care, the ridges and furrows furnish a convenient measurement of land in sowing, reaping, or harvesting. There is a considerable loss of land in the furrows, where the beds are, as in some cases, made very narrow, as for example when formed of ten furrow-slices, and two furrow-slices are taken for the drain, the amount of land taken for the drains will be equal to one sixth of the whole, or one acre in six — a very considerable loss, it must be admitted; but then, in every system of ploughing, there must be open furrows left at the sides, if not in the centre, of the fields; and where the beds are large, as described above, throwing, for example, four common beds of fifteen feet each, so as to form one of sixty feet, the loss by open furrows would be greatly reduced. In countries subject to much snow, and severe frosts, it is objected that, the snow being naturally blown from the elevated into the lower parts of the field, the ridge, or highest part of the bed, is more exposed to the alternations of freezing and thawing, and so the grain plants on the ridge are liable to be

* Principles of Agriculture, by Von Thaer, vol. ii. p. 84, as translated from the French by those two most intelligent and industrious agricultural writers, William Shaw and Cuthbert W. Johnson, Esquires.

thrown out and destroyed. I do not know that this objection is entitled to much consideration. Where the furrows are made from east to west, instead of from north to south, — and the latter ought always to be the direction, — there will be a considerable difference in the temperature of the two sides of the ridge, as the difference in the effect produced by the sun's rays, when falling directly upon a surface inclined towards the sun, or upon one directly the reverse of this, must be considerable. It is urged, likewise, as an objection to these ridges, that the rain, as it falls, passes too rapidly into the furrows, and is carried off without gradually soaking into the land, as on a flat surface, and giving the whole its full advantage. These are some of the objections urged against this system of laying the land in ridges; and, since the introduction of the system of subsoiling and thorough-draining, Mr. Smith, the introducer of this immense and extraordinary improvement, and in general those persons who follow out his notions in other respects, disapprove altogether the plan of laying out the ground in ridges or beds, and leave an even and unbroken surface. In cross-ploughing fields laid in beds, there is likewise an inconvenience arising from the furrows; and the same difficulty likewise applies to the harrowing of such fields, especially if it is attempted to be done across the furrows. Harrows formed with a concave under-side, to adapt them to the shape of the bed, are sometimes used lengthwise with the ridge; but they are ill adapted to cross-harrowing these ridges, or to be used upon land with a flat and even surface.

The beauty which is given to the cultivation, where such ridges prevail and are well formed over extensive fields, is certainly some recommendation of them; but this supposes them to be made evenly and with care. Upon as fair a view of the subject as I can take, I should recommend them, not for their beauty, but for their utility and convenience. But in this case, excepting where the land is very wet and low, I should insist upon a width certainly not less than forty feet; and I should avoid by all means too much accumulation of earth in the centre of the ridge, which an expert ploughman is very capable of doing.

4. Lazy-bed Cultivation. — There prevails in Ireland a mode of ridging land, different from what I have described, and called

— with what propriety I am unable to see — the *lazy-bed* system. It is done, in general, only in wet and low lands, though I have seen it upon other lands. In this case, the whole land may be either ploughed or dug over by the spade, before the formation of the beds, or it may be left in grass, and the process proceed in this way: Beds of four feet wide are marked out, and divided by a furrow-drain about one foot wide. The potato sets or seed are laid upon the ground or bed, at such distances as are deemed best, generally in lines across the bed, and the earth in the furrow is cut down to the hard pan, even a foot and a half in depth, by a spade, and taken out and thrown upon the seed which has been deposited on the bed, and the whole is carefully smoothed off with the shovel. The fresh earth thus taken from the furrow-drain brings no seeds of weeds with it, and the after cultivation is easy. The potatoes in the autumn being dug with a spade, the whole ground is pretty thoroughly forked, or dug over, and, when it is used the next year for a crop, — it may be of potatoes again, or of oats, — the furrow-drain is filled up, and one made in another place, or in the centre of that which was the bed, so that, in truth, the whole field becomes pretty thoroughly cultivated.

A very intelligent farmer, whom I had the pleasure of meeting in Ireland, was kind enough to give me an account of his management of some of his land on this plan, a system which he considers as extremely well adapted to a cold, wet soil, not yet carefully drained, or to a dry soil which may have become exhausted by constant cropping and shallow ploughing.

"I lined out the ground to be tilled, in ridges four feet wide, and furrows two feet wide. I then dug out of the parts lined off for the furrows, and put on the ridges, all the active soil which could be taken up by the spade. The sets were then planted, and covered by the earth which had remained in the furrows, and which was for this purpose cleanly shovelled. By this mode I obtained a *dry* seed-bed in *moist* ground — a *fresh*, *active* soil in *exhausted* ground, and *a depth* of surface in *light land*.

"In one instance, on a cold, retentive soil not *drained*, where there had been a very poor crop of potatoes the previous year, and the soil not stirred from the time the potatoes had been dug out until the oats were sown, a good crop of oats was obtained. In the other case, a second crop of oats was taken off the same field, the stubbles having been ploughed in October. This crop was much superior to the former. It produced fine grain, and was so luxuriant that the greater part of it was lodged previous to reaping on the 9th of August. Should the surface or active soil be very shallow, the breadth of the ridge may be narrowed, or the breadth of the furrow increased. The wide furrows allow of loosening the subsoil, either with crow-bars, picks, or spades, and I carefully reserve all stones which appear, for drains, where draining is necessary; and where it is, I now drain wherever I find the stones at hand — sometimes before tilling. I make the drains at forty or sixty feet apart at first, and put in my intermediate drains in each succeeding year, as I obtain stones in loosening the subsoil.

"I lay out my ridges for potatoes, the breadth as for oats, putting the sets in rows across the ridges, five sets in each row, and the rows varying from eighteen to twenty-two inches apart; — thus saving seed, being enabled to keep the plants free from weeds, to dig out the potatoes at less cost without injury, and increasing the produce, over the old lazy-bed system, in the proportion of one sixth."

The object of this farmer is to till his low land, in a way to avoid the evil of excessive wet, by this simple method, before he can go to the expense of completely furrow-draining. The method of managing land by complete drainage, which I shall presently describe, would undoubtedly be to be preferred, where there is a sufficiency of time and capital; but in the mean time the other system may be adopted as a temporary substitute.

This gentleman gave me, at the same time, an account of an experiment made as to the distance at which potatoes should be planted, which seems worth recording, and which I will insert here, though not exactly in place.

The potatoes were cultivated in the lazy-bed fashion described. Six ridges were laid out four feet wide, with two feet furrows; an equal quantity of manure laid down for each. Two ridges were planted, the cuttings being laid thick, without any regularity; two ridges had the cuts placed in rows across the bed, fourteen inches apart, five sets in a row; and two ridges, seventeen inches asunder, five sets in each row. The manure was spread over the entire of the ridges tilled in the old lazy-bed way, and immediately over the sets planted. The quantity of seed required by the first mode of planting was six and a half stone, or 91 pounds; by the second method, 77 pounds; and by the third method, 70 pounds. The quantity of ground, in each case, was seven square perches. The produce was as subjoined: —

In the first method, ...	1218 pounds.
In rows at 14 inches, ...	1358 "
In rows at 17 inches, ...	1442 "

He adds that the advantage of the latter method is not only a considerable increase of produce by the acre, amounting to 5152 pounds over the first method, but there is a decided advantage in every operation which takes place, from the planting to the digging. The ridges take less seed; require less labor; can be freed from weeds with greater ease and less danger to the tender stalk, and dug with greater facility, and without injury from the spade. Another advantage is, in those places where there is but a light surface, they may be "moulded up," or the dirt brought to the plants, with much benefit.

I give this as an example of spade husbandry. As such, it will have its value with many of my readers. It is not adapted to cultivation upon any extended scale; but there are small pieces of low, wet land throughout the country, which the owners cannot afford at once to drain thoroughly, but from which, in this way, good crops may be obtained, and the land brought into a condition of productive improvement. The experiment, in regard to quantity of seed, is certainly worth considering. Potatoes are never cultivated in England or Ireland, as with us, in hills. I have known as large a production from a field cultivated in hills three and a half feet apart each way, as in almost any other mode; but the expense of gathering them is more than upon one planted in drills, so as to be easily turned out by the plough. A distinguished farmer in England has invented what he calls a hog's-head plough, for the purpose of turning out potatoes which are planted in drills, without injuring them. It resembles a hog's snout attached to the front part of a plough, without a colter, by which the potatoes are raised and turned out of their bed. This may be said to be copying nature, for it is clearly the way that profound race of investigators, the swine, would turn out the crop, if they were sent into an undug potato field; but it has no great advantages, in this matter, over a double mould-board plough.

5. Correct Ploughing. — The proper and best mode of ploughing is so exactly and well described by a recent and eminent Scotch agricultural writer, that I think I cannot do better than to give it in full to my readers.

"Whatever mode of ploughing the land is subjected to, you should take special care that it be ploughed for a winter furrow in the best manner. The furrow-slice should be of the requisite depth, whether of five inches on the oldest lea, or seven inches on the most friable ground; and it should also be of the requisite breadth of nine inches in the former case, and of ten in the latter; but as ploughmen incline to hold a shallower furrow than it should be, to make the labor easier to themselves, there is less likelihood of their making a narrower furrow than it should be, a shallow and a broad furrow conferring both ease on themselves, and getting over the ground quickly. A proper furrow-slice in land not in grass, or, as it is termed, in red land, should never be less than nine inches in breadth and six inches in depth on the strongest soil, and ten inches in breadth and seven inches in depth on lighter soils. On grass land of strong soil, or on land of any texture that has lain long in grass, nine inches of breadth, and five inches of depth, is as large a furrow-slice as may possibly be obtained; but on lighter soil, with comparatively young grass, a furrow-slice of ten inches by six, and even seven, is easily turned over. At all seasons, but especially for a winter furrow, you should endeavor to establish for yourself a character for deep and correct ploughing."

"Correct ploughing possesses these characteristics: The furrow-slices should be quite straight, for a ploughman that cannot hold a straight furrow is unworthy of his charge. The furrow-slices should be quite parallel in length; and this property shows that they have been turned over of a uniform thickness, for thick and thin slices, lying together, present irregularly horizontal lines. The furrow-slices should be of the same height, which shows that they have been cut of the same breadth; for slices of different breadths, laid together at whatever angle, present unequal vertical lines. The furrow-slices should present to the eye a similar form of crest and equal surface; because, where one furrow-slice exhibits a narrower surface than it should have, it has been covered with a broader slice than it should be; and where it displays a broader surface than it should, it is so exposed by a narrower slice than it should be, lying upon it. The furrow-slices should have their back and face parallel; and to discover this property requires rather minute examination after the land has been ploughed; but it is easily ascertained at the time of ploughing. The ground, on being ploughed, should feel equally firm under the foot at all places; for slices in a more upright position than they should be not only feel hard and unsteady, but will allow the seed corn to fall down between them and become buried. Furrow-slices in too flat a state always yield considerably to the pressure of the foot; and they are then too much drawn, and afford insufficient mould for the seed. Furrow-slices should lie over at the same angle; and it is demonstrable that the largest extent of surface exposed to the action of the air is when they are laid over at an angle of 45°, thus presenting crests in the best possible position for the action of the harrows. Crowns of ridges, formed by the meeting of opposite furrow-slices, should neither be elevated nor depressed, in regard to the rest of the ridge, although ploughmen often commit the error of raising the crowns too high into a crest — the fault being easily committed by not giving the feered" (that is, the first, or marking-out slices) "furrow-slices sufficient room to meet, and thereby pressing them upon one another. The furrow-brows should have slices uniform with the rest of the ridge; but ploughmen are very apt to miscalculate the width of the slices near the sides of the ridges; for if the specific number of furrow-slices into which the whole ridge should be ploughed are too narrow, the last slice of the furrow-brow will be too broad, and will therefore lie over too flat; and should this too broad space be divided into two furrows, each slice will be too narrow, and stand too upright. When the furrow-brows are ill made, the mould-furrows cannot be proportionately ploughed out; because, if the space between the furrow-brows is too wide, the mould-furrows must be made too deep, to fill up all the space, and *vice versa*. If the furrow-brow slices are laid too flat, the mould-furrows will be apt to throw too much earth upon their edges next the open furrow, and there make them too high. When the furrow-brows of adjoining ridges are not ploughed alike, one side of the open furrow will require a deeper mould-furrow than the other." *

There is no more accuracy and exactness prescribed in these directions, in the execution of this first great operation of husbandry, than what is actually attained and practised both in England and Scotland. The Lothians, in the vicinity of Edinburgh, — and which may indeed be considered as the garden of Scotland, — the counties of Northumberland, Lincoln, and Norfolk, in England, exhibit this perfection of cultivation. It may be seen in many other places, but in these on a more extended scale than in others. But such excellence, however, is not attained without very great pains, and, with expert ploughmen, a long course of practice. I shall be asked, perhaps, what advantage comes from this exact mode of performing the work. It might be enough to answer, that, in every species of labor, and in every practical art, what is done should be well done, and perfection, how far soever he may fall short of it, should be every man's great aim. It might be enough to say, that the moral influences upon a man's own character, and life, of habits of exactness, order, care, and neatness, are always great, and of very serious value; but I may confidently add, that the perfection with which land is tilled is of great importance to the crops, and directly conducive to their perfection and abundance. The man, too, who studies to plough and cultivate his lands in the best manner, will be anxious to have his implements of the best kind, and to keep his team in the best order and condition. Indeed, multiply as we will the excuses for slovenliness, irregularity, and carelessness, there cannot be a doubt that habits of order, exactness, and carefulness, in all respects, are directly conducive to, nay, are the true foundations of, all profitable arrangement. I may add, likewise, that where every thing is kept in order, and all work proceeds by rule and system, though these rules may sometimes appear extreme or severe, affairs are managed at less expense of labor and time than in a more negligent and reckless mode.

The great object of ploughing is to pulverize the soil, to open it to the admission of those great enrichers of the land, and those great instruments of vegetation, heat, light, air, and moisture; to furnish a penetrable bed in which the roots of the plants may

* Stephen's Book of the Farm, vol. i. p. 633.

establish themselves, and stretch themselves out in search of food; and, by bringing the stony portions of the soil under the influence of external agents, to produce a chemical decomposition, and supply of those mineral ingredients, a portion of which is indispensable to the healthy growth and productiveness of the plants which are cultivated. It is important, therefore, to reduce the soil to as fine a tilth as possible. It is important to do this, likewise, that the manures which are applied may be thoroughly intermixed with the soil. In gardens, and in small plats, this is done by the spade, which in fields is attempted by the plough; the object in both cases being to render the soil loose, fine, and friable. The more care is exercised in the ploughing, the more certainly will these ends be accomplished.

6. Trench-Ploughing. — I come next to speak of what is called *trench-ploughing*. This term is applied to a deeper ploughing than usual, or to a double ploughing, where one plough follows directly in the furrow left by a preceding plough. In trenching land with the spade, which I have before described, the object is completely to invert the soil, laying the surface soil underneath, and covering it with that stratum of soil upon which it had previously rested. The object obviously is, to deepen the cultivatable soil, — if I may coin a word which will be very well understood, — and, by bringing the lower stratum to the surface, expose it to influences by which it may gradually become enriched. Soil taken from almost any depth, after lying upon the surface for a length of time, will ordinarily of itself acquire a productive power, and may be cultivated with success. I have known this to be the case with earth taken from the bottom of a deep well, which, after a length of time, became productive. There is always, in such cases, an accumulation or accession of extraneous matters, which come one hardly knows whence, how, or when. The surface of the coral reefs, of which the islands in the Pacific are examples, after being raised above the water, are gradually decomposed and enriched; seeds of plants, floating in the air, or brought by birds, or cast ashore by the waves, gradually establish themselves. The lichens, or mosses, and an humble class of vegetation, present themselves, until presently, from their decay, and the deposits of animal life in various forms, a rich mould is formed, and this barren rock becomes, in

time, the fertile abode of animal and vegetable life. The recuperative power of nature is every where seen most active. Lands exhausted by cultivation are restored by the skill and labor of the faithful and enlightened cultivator. Even left to themselves, to the spontaneous efforts of nature, they recover their exhausted fertility; and soils, which have never yet seen the sun, by being brought to the light and warmth of day, and to the refreshing and renovating influences of sun, and air, and rain, become productive, and stand ready to perform their part in supplying the wants of the vegetable, and through them of the animal creation. Trench-ploughing, which aims wholly to assist this operation of nature, and take advantage of its ready benevolence, is done by a single plough, which goes to a depth of at least fourteen inches, completely inverting this quantity of soil; or the land is first ploughed in the ordinary mode, and a second plough follows in the same furrow, at a depth determined at the pleasure of the ploughman. In the former case, it is obvious that the surface soil is completely inverted and buried; in the latter, the substratum is rather mixed with the upper soil. In the former case, it is clearly a very bold operation. On the Island of Jersey, famous for its cultivation of esculent roots, parsnips, and the white carrot, and other crops, they have what is called a *trench-plough*, which, going to the depth of fourteen inches, and throwing out a wide furrow, requires a heavy team. In this case, the neighbors club together, uniting their teams so as to assist each other.* The subsoil, unless there is a super-

* I will give here the account of this operation, from Colonel Le Couteur, whose high reputation is well established in the agricultural community.

"In most cases, in the month of October or November, a skim-ploughing is given to an old, or two years' lea, which is left exposed to the winter frosts. It is well harrowed and cross-harrowed previous to carting out the manure, which is spread on the ground at a rate ranging between 12 and 20 tons per acre. In some cases, the above previous skim-ploughing is deferred until January or February, in order to allow the cattle to feed off any herbage that may be left on the land, so that the two ploughings now to be described take place in the same month.

"A short time (the shorter the better) previous to putting in the crop, the land receives its second, and generally last ploughing. The trench-plough then comes into play, preceded by its pioneer, the two-horse-plough. A trench is opened through the middle, or length of the field, in this manner. The two-horse-plough is made to cast off a furrow up and down, so as to assist in forming the trench; the trench is then neatly sunk 18 inches deep, more or less, according to

abundance of manure to be applied and mixed with it, cannot be brought at once into a state of active productiveness. Where there is a sufficiency of manure, however, there is, no doubt, some advantage gained, to what extent it is not easy to say, from the freshness of the virgin soil which is brought up. Otherwise, time and cultivation will be required to bring this fresh and comparatively inert soil into a condition of productiveness. In this case, however, the farmer must exercise his own judgment, and consider his own means. He may be sure that the deeper and the richer is the soil, or mould, which he has to cultivate, so much the more abundant will be his crops. To create a soil, however, is not a sudden operation; and, in cases where the

---

the depth of the soil, and squared off two feet with spades, the earth being thrown off to a distance on each side.

"A man with a spade should then be placed at each end of the furrow, to dig and square it out half the length of the trench-plough, as wide as the furrow intended to be taken, in order to enable it to plunge into its depth at once, on turning in to work; this is made at the left-hand side of either furrow, after the small two-horse-plough has made its start.

"This two-horse-plough (one that will take a width of furrow one inch wider than the trench-plough) then precedes and turns in the manure and turf, together with three inches of soil, into the bottom of the furrow, or prepared trench. The trench-plough, drawn by four, six, or eight horses, according to the depth desired, then turns over from ten to eighteen inches of clean soil on the turf, which is so completely buried as to destroy all vegetation, even in the freshly-broken sod. When the sod is quite fresh, as little soil as possible should be taken up by the small plough, so that the couch or weeds may be more completely covered by a great mass of clean soil. When the ploughed land becomes so wide as to render it inconvenient for one man, at *each end*, to open the furrow for the plough on one side, and square up the other side neatly, one man is placed at *each corner* to perform this work, so that two additional men at each end of the land, or four in all, are now digging, levelling, and squaring up the corners. Two acres or more may thus be turned up in a day, as the trench-plough takes a wide furrow from eleven to thirteen inches, and, by its excellent construction, moves and turns the whole soil.

"This operation is performed by joint-stock labor by all the farmers in Jersey, who bring their teams to assist each other. It is appropriately denominated, not a great ploughing, but a GREAT DIGGING; indeed, no spade husbandry is so efficient, as most men, in digging, merely turn the secondspit upon the under, or trench-slice, whereas the whole soil is shaken and broken by the trench-plough."

Certainly the soil, in this case, must be very rich to bear being inverted at this depth. I give the whole account, rather as matter of agricultural curiosity, than with any notion of its being adapted to our husbandry. These very great operations, in which so many men and so many horses are employed at one time, I have always found of doubtful expediency, and should deem it prudent to seek more simple means of accomplishing the end, if more simple could be found.

surface is completely inverted, the rich soil is buried, and the undersoil brought to the top, he may labor in a sure hope of an ultimate compensation; yet he must in such case wait with a manly patience; and it may be advisable in some instances to have some regard to the length of his purse, and the time of his life; perhaps, in England, it would be as well to add the terms of his lease, which may not always be such as to encourage substantial improvements. Such improvements, being intended to be permanent, can hardly be otherwise than expensive.

I do not know where I can better introduce to my readers an experiment upon soils, which I witnessed in progress in that admirable establishment, the Agricultural Museum and Nursery-Grounds of the Messrs. Drummond, in Stirling, Scotland, which I strongly recommend to the notice of every intelligent traveller in that picturesque and most interesting locality, whether his objects of pursuit be of an agricultural nature, or otherwise. If the experiment leads to no practical results, it is deserving of attention, as matter of philosophical curiosity. I give it from their own written communication to me.

" *Notice of a Comparative Trial of the Qualities of various pure Earths for supporting Vegetation, made in the Nursery-Grounds of W. Drummond and Sons, Stirling.*

" Garden pots eight inches in diameter were filled each with a pure earth, reduced, by pounding, to the consistency of gravelly sand, where it had previously existed in the indurated or rocky state. Oats were then sown about the middle of April, three plants being allowed to remain in each pot. The pots were plunged to the rim in an open border, cinders of coal being put under them, and care otherwise taken that the roots of the oats should obtain no extraneous nourishment. The plants were watered with common spring water, a few times, in very dry weather.

" The stalks attained, in general, to the height of two and a half to three feet. The grain fully ripened about the beginning of September.

" PRODUCE.

Earths.	*Ears.*	*Grains.*
" Granite, (Aberdeen,)	13 .	220
Clay slate, (primitive,)	11 .	241

Earths.	*Ears.*	*Grains.*
Greenstone, (secondary trap,)	10	245
Limestone,	9	251
Chalk,	13	355
Gypsum, (very sickly plants,)	6	40
Sandstone, (silicious,)	12	230
Pit-sand, (brown,)	12	210
Blue clay, (taken ten feet under the surface,)	10	242
Mixture of all the above kinds,	9	190
Common light loamy soil,	18	453

"Experiments of this nature seem worthy of further prosecution, particularly relative to the respective influence of the atmosphere and soil in the nourishment of plants. When the oats were sown, scientific as well as practical men predicted, that in most of these earths they would not grow; and when they saw them growing, predicted that they would not ripen seed. The results have proved otherwise."

A single experiment, in such case, can hardly be considered as decisive, excepting as to the possibility of plants living and maturing in an unmixed soil. The fact of their not succeeding, with one exception, so well in a soil composed of the several varieties as in a simple soil, is likewise noticeable. The superior success of the plants in loam is also to be observed, to show that their growth was not wholly dependent upon the atmosphere, as some would have us believe, and that the soil furnishes something more than a mere support for the plants. The growth, in each case, must be considered as inferior; and, without deducing any general conclusions, which might be premature, or endeavoring to fit the facts to any received theory, I submit it to the further inquiries of those who have the curiosity and talent to pursue these interesting investigations. If it prompts to other well-conducted experiments, my object will be answered.

The bringing of any considerable quantity of inert soil to the surface is obviously attended with uncertain results, so much depends upon the nature and condition of the soil so brought up. At the Duke of Portland's, at Welbeck, places were pointed out to me where the surface mould had been removed, a portion of the subsoil taken away, and the mould, or top soil, returned to its place; but in no instance was its previous fertility restored. Deep cultivation will undoubtedly in the end recover such places, but time and patience are indispensable.

7. Subsoil-Ploughing. — The next great operation, performed with the plough, is here called *subsoiling*. The object of this is similar to that of trench-ploughing — that of loosening the substratum, and deepening the soil to be cultivated. But it differs in this respect: trenching, either by the spade or the plough, buries the surface soil, and covers it with that which is turned up; but subsoil-ploughing aims to loosen the substratum to the depth required, without bringing it to the surface or covering the mould, and, by the gradual intermixture of the lower stratum with the upper soil, to enrich it, and ultimately convert the whole into an equally arable and fertile condition. Subsoiling is performed by a plough of a peculiar construction, following in the furrow of a common plough. If we suppose the first plough to have turned up the land to the depth of seven inches, the next plough loosens it to the depth of nine inches more, so that the whole land ploughed is in this case equal to sixteen inches. The great objection to trenching land, either by the plough or spade, is, that it brings the inert soil to the surface in a condition unsuited to the purposes of vegetation, and that thus much time is necessarily lost before it can, without great expense, be restored to its former fertility. The advantage of subsoiling is, that it so gradually raises the substratum to mingle with the top soil, that the cultivation of the latter is not interrupted, but the soil is benefited by the slight intermixture. Another and very great advantage derived from subsoiling, is in the admission of air and heat to the loosened soil, by which it is improved, and better subserves the purposes of vegetation, and at the same time opportunity is given for the free expansion of the roots of the plant. On many descriptions of soil, the surface, or vegetable mould, rests upon a hard pan at greater or less depth, and which is impervious to the roots of the plant, and does not suffer even the water to pass off freely. However long this may have existed, as the plough has usually gone only to a certain depth, this substratum has become the more indurated by the treading of the horses in the ploughed furrow, and the constant sliding of the sole of the plough over it. It is the object of the subsoil-

plough always to break up this pan, which, after being broken up and exposed to the air, gradually crumbles and becomes mingled with the upper soil.

This is subsoiling, as it is here termed, of which every modern treatise of English husbandry is full. It can scarcely be said to be an absolutely new practice,* for passing a second plough in an open furrow may be considered as a species of subsoiling; yet the credit of introducing the practice, and establishing it upon just principles, as connected with draining the land, must be fully accorded to Mr. James Smith, of Deanston, in Scotland, a man of whose sound understanding and practical skill I might speak in the highest terms, if my humble voice would add any thing to the distinguished and substantial reputation which he enjoys throughout the kingdom. I have been over the estate in Scotland which was under his care; and, though the land may be considered as inferior, yet its fine appearance, the regular arrangement of his fields, the condition of his fences, and the perfect cleanness and productiveness of his grounds, present an eminent and beautiful example of the most improved husbandry. A great portion of his labors are indeed under ground, and out of sight; but the results of them are obvious.

Mr. Smith was the active manager of an extensive cloth or cotton factory, in the neighborhood of which was the farm on which he effected such improvements. The condition of the factory in all its departments, the buildings for the persons who are employed in the factory, the whole arrangement of the factory village, the condition and reputable conduct of the operatives, and the measures taken for their educational improvement, are very much in advance of what is to be found in many places both in England and the United States, and, while they do Mr. Smith himself the highest honor, present a beautiful example for imitation. Mr. Smith is entitled to the high merit, not of applying

---

* Worledge, in his Mystery of Husbandry, describes (A. D. 1677) very clearly the first rude attempt to construct a subsoil-plough. He tells us of "an ingenious young man of Kent, who had two ploughs fastened together very firmly, by which he ploughed two furrows at once, one under another, and so stirred the land twelve or fourteen inches deep. It only looseneth or lighteneth the land to that depth, but doth not bury the upper crust of the ground so deep as is usually done by digging." Quoted in Ransome's excellent work on the Implements of Agriculture, p. 12.

the subsoil-plough to the land merely, (by which the most valuable improvements have been effected,) but to the interesting community of several hundreds, over which, as the agent of the Deanston works or factory, he presided. By education, and by paternal care and interest in their welfare, he has done what he could for the improvement of their condition. He may be said to have broken up and elevated the lower strata, that, by bringing them from a degraded condition to the light and air, and by degrees preparing them to intermingle with the higher strata, he might alike benefit both parties, and substantially improve the character of the whole.

Mr. Smith invented a plough for the express purpose of subsoiling, of which I design presently to give a plate. It is without a mould-board, but it has a feather on the share. Several other ploughs have been invented for the same purpose — one made under the direction of Mr. Pusey, called the Charlbury plough, which proposed to perform both the operation of ploughing the land and subsoiling at the same time. It was therefore a common plough, and, several inches below the sole of the plough, and behind it, there was attached a turned-up or crooked tine or foot, calculated to descend into the soil in the furrow to the prescribed depth. The draught of this plough must be of course, by such an arrangement, considerably increased, and the instrument would appear rather clumsy in its operation. If it did its work well, this is all that could be required. One of its great merits is stated to be a considerable superiority over the Deanston plough, in lightness of draught. I have never seen it employed. Another subsoil-plough, which has been recommended, is a single iron tine or foot, attached to a proper frame with handles, and which, being drawn through the furrow after the other plough, loosens the soil in a single line. It would seem to be an instrument of small expense, as well as simple construction; but it executes the work very imperfectly, not stirring the whole ground, but dividing it only in single lines. Mr. Smith's plough, having a small feather on the share, not only moves the whole bottom of the furrow, but it raises a small portion of the subsoil, and lays it against the side of the furrow already turned over, thus mingling the subsoil and the upper soil in some small portions together. This may be considered as a decided advantage. But, to describe the practice of subsoiling land without that of thorough-draining, which forms a part of the same system, would be unjust to Mr. Smith. This, however, I shall do most fully under the subject of draining, which will come as matter of course.

To subsoil without draining is not to be indiscriminately recommended. In heavy and clay soils, it would be of little use, as they would soon settle down into their former compactness. In some soils it would only serve to increase their wetness, as the water, sinking deeper into the ground, without any provision for its escape, would pass off less quickly by evaporation than if nearer the surface. In lighter soils, where its only effect would be to loosen the soil, it would undoubtedly be beneficial.

8. Experiment in Subsoiling Heath Land. — An example of success in the application of the subsoil to heath land, which is within my knowledge, is so remarkable, that I will give it to my readers at large. The gentleman to whom I shall refer, Sir Edward Stracey, is himself the inventor of a subsoil-plough, known as the Rackheath plough, after the name of the property which he occupies, and which is much lighter of draught than the Deanston plough.

"On my coming to reside on my estate at Rackheath, about six years since, I found 500 acres of heath land, composing two farms, without tenants, — the gorse, heather, and fern shooting up in all parts. In short, the land was in such a condition that the crops did not return the seed sown. The soil was a loose, loamy soil, and had been broken up by the plough to a depth not exceeding four inches, beneath which was a substratum (provincially called an *iron-pan*) so hard, that with difficulty could a pickaxe be made to enter in many places; and my bailiff, who had looked after the lands for 35 years, told me that the lands were not worth cultivating; that all the neighboring farmers said the same thing; and that there was but one thing to be done, viz., to plant with fir and forest-trees. To this I paid little attention, as I had the year preceding allotted some parcels of ground, taken out of the adjoining lands, to some cottagers, to each cottage about one third of an acre. The crops on all these allotments looked fine, healthy, and good, producing excellent wheat, carrots, peas, cabbages, potatoes, and other vegetables, in abundance. The question then was, How was this to be done?

On the outside of the cottage allotments, all was barren. It could not be by the manure that had been laid on, for the cottagers had none but that which they had scraped from the roads. The magic of all this I could ascribe to nothing else but the spade; they had broken up the land eighteen inches deep. As to digging up 500 acres with the spade, to the depth of eighteen inches, at an expense of six pounds an acre, I would not attempt it. I considered that a plough might be constructed so as to loosen the soil to the depth of eighteen inches, keeping the best soil to the depth of four inches, and near the surface, thus admitting air and moisture to the roots of the plants, and enabling them to extend their spongioles in search of food, — for air, moisture, and extent of pasture, are as necessary to the thriving and increase of vegetables as of animals. In this attempt I succeeded, as the result will show. I have now broken up all these 500 acres eighteen inches deep. The process was by sending a common plough drawn by two horses to precede, which turned over the ground to the depth of four inches. My subsoil-plough immediately followed in the furrow made, drawn by four horses, stirring and breaking the soil twelve or fourteen inches deeper, but not turning it over. Sometimes the iron-pan was so hard that the horses were set fast, and it became necessary to use the pickaxe, to release them, before they could proceed. After the first year, the land produced double the former crops, many of the carrots being 16 inches in length, and of proportionate thickness. This amendment could have arisen only from the deep ploughing. Manure I had scarcely any, the land not producing then stover sufficient to keep any stock worth mentioning, and it was not possible to procure sufficient quantity from the town. The plough tore up by the roots all the old gorse, heather, and fern, so that the land lost all the distinctive character of heath land, the first year after the deep ploughing, which it had retained, notwithstanding the ploughing with the common ploughs for thirty-five years. Immediately after this subsoil-ploughing, the crop of wheat was strong and long in the straw, and the grain close-bosomed and heavy, weighing 64 pounds to the bushel; the quantity, as might be expected, not large, (about 26 bushels to the acre,) but great in comparison to what it produced before. The millers were desirous of purchasing it, and could scarcely believe it was grown upon the heath land, as in former years it was difficult to get a miller to look at a sample. Let this be borne in mind, that this land then had had no manure for years, was run out, and could only have been meliorated by the admission of air and moisture, from deep ploughing. This year the wheat on this land has looked most promising; the ears large and heavy, the straw long, and I expect the produce will be from 34 to 36 bushels per acre. My Swedish turnips on this land this year are very good; my pudding and sugar-loaf turnips failing in many parts, sharing the fate of those of my neighbors, having been greatly injured by the torrents of rain which fell after they had shown themselves above the ground. Turnips must have a deep and well-pulverized soil, in order to enable them to swell, and the tap-roots to penetrate in search of food. The tap-root of a Swedish turnip has been known to penetrate 39 inches into the ground. I will add only two or three general observations.

"1st. The work done by the plough far exceeds trenching with the spade, as the plough only breaks and loosens the land all around, without turning the subsoil to the top, which in some cases (where the subsoil is bad) would be injurious to the early and tender plants; and if the subsoil is good, it would be rendered more fit for vegetation after the air and moisture had been permitted to enter. The ploughing is also far preferable to trenching by the spade, even for planting, (i. e. trees,) as it may be done at one fourth the expense.

"2dly. It were very preferable, if possible, to work the horses abreast, pair and pair; but, in using this plough, the horses *must* work in a line, for, if abreast, the horse on the land ploughed would soon be fatigued, by sinking up to his hocks; and, to render the draught more easy, the second horse from the plough should not be fastened to the chains of the horse next the plough; but the chains of the second horse should be made long enough to be hooked about two feet behind the back-band of the chains of the horse next the plough, so that the second horse will draw at an angle of about 33 degrees; otherwise, were the chains of the second horse hooked in front of the back-chain, he would pull the whole weight of his draught, together with that of the horses preceding him, on the back of the horse next the plough; and the strength of the horse would be lost in the draught, as his whole powers would be exerted in his endeavors to prevent being brought down upon his knees. By so arranging the chains, the power of three horses would be equal to that of four."

Such were the favorable results of this bold experiment. In many other cases, however, the result has not been so successful; and when the state or character of the land is such as to retain the water, as (to use the expression of one highly intelligent farmer, who subsoiled his land without first draining it) "it sometimes does like a sponge," the subsoiling is as likely, and perhaps more likely, to be injurious than beneficial. The Deanston system, as it is here called, of subsoil-ploughing and furrow-draining will presently be fully stated to my readers.

9. Subturf-Plough. — The same gentleman last referred to, Sir Edward Stracey, is the inventor of what is called a *subturf-plough*, which is fitted for use in lands where it is desirable to stir the soil beneath without breaking the turf. It does not differ much from the subsoil-plough; and, being once inserted into the ground, breaks it up to the depth of about ten inches, leaving no other marks of its operation than the lines cut in the turf, which very soon, by the natural growth of the grass, become obliterated. The lines are at the distance of about fourteen inches from one another. It loosens the soil underneath, admits the air and rain, and permits the roots to spread themselves. He says, "after a trial of it, that the quantity of the aftermath, and the thickness of the bottom, have been the subject of general admiration. Another advantage from this subturf-ploughing is that, before that took place, water was lying stagnant on many parts, (after heavy rains,) especially in the lower grounds, to a great depth; now, no water is to be seen lying on any part, the whole being absorbed by the earth." This supposes that the lower strata, below where the plough has reached, are porous, and easily transmit the water, or, otherwise, it might be liable to the objections to which I have referred above.

10. Perfection of English Ploughing. — I have spoken of the various modes of ploughing, and of the extraordinary exactness with which it is executed. It would be curious to trace

SMITH'S SUBSOIL-PLOUGH.

(See p. 450.)

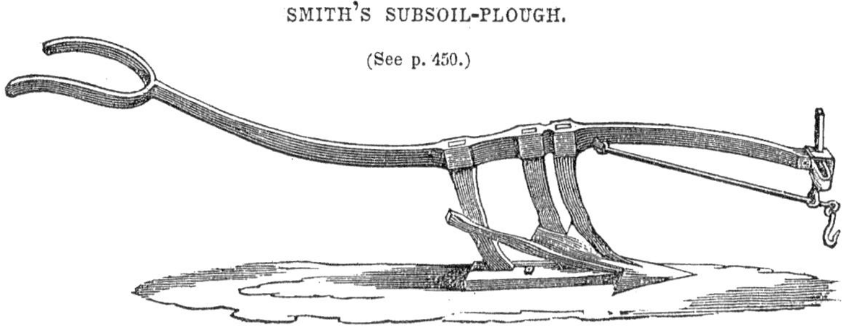

RACKHEATH SUBSOIL-PLOUGH.

(See pp. 451, 452.)

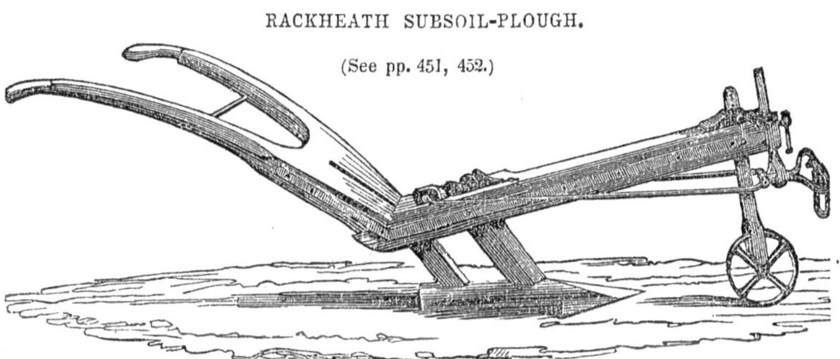

"This performs the operation of subsoil ploughing, to the depth of from ten to sixteen inches below the surface, and, when preceded by the common plough, which is the plan recommended, the depth reached below the surface ground is just so much the more than the first plough effects."

RACKHEATH SUBTURF-PLOUGH.

(See p. 454.)

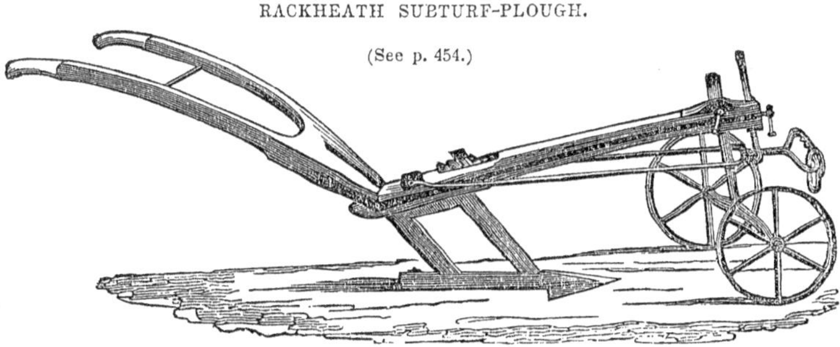

"This plough answers admirably for under-ploughing grass lands, and is made into a subturf-plough by changing the wheel gear in front to that of a carriage and two wheels."

the progress of this art, from its rudest stages, to the beautiful and facile manner which distinguishes its performance in the best cultivated districts of England and Scotland. I do not like to say that no further improvements can be made. No reflecting man, who has witnessed the extraordinary changes, and inventions, and improvements, of half a century, and seen the continually-shifting scenes, and the new actors presenting themselves on the stage, and bringing the treasures of their wisdom and skill to the vast accumulations which genius and science have already heaped up, will assert this of any human art; but it is safe for me to say, that I do not know how, in the best cases, the execution of the work can be improved. Under the direction of an experienced and well-skilled ploughman, and an efficient and well-trained team, the implement itself moves like a thing of life, and performs its office with the precision of the highest intelligence.

This is not the effect of accident; it is the work of severe and careful training. Boys are early accustomed to stand behind the plough, and stimulated by the strongest motives which can be addressed to their cupidity, their love of approbation, or their ambition of excellence. Under the prevalent subdivision of labor, to which I have before alluded, the advantages arising from practice, and a fixed attention to one particular object, are obviously secured. The man who ploughs, and does little else except ploughing, is far more likely to execute his work thoroughly and well than the man whose attention is divided among a multitude and diversity of pursuits.

11. Ploughing-Matches. — The ploughing-matches, likewise, in which most intelligent and severe judges are appointed, the rules of competition are stringent and absolute, and the golden rewards most liberal, have contributed essentially to the improvement of this art.

We have witnessed the same results in the United States. I recollect the first ploughing-match at Brighton, under the auspices of the Massachusetts Society for promoting Agriculture. The gradual proficiency, from these early and comparatively rude trials, to the triumphant and beautiful results which, more than a quarter of a century afterwards, with honest pride, I have witnessed at Worcester, shows that there is no deficiency of talent and skill, and no lack of an honorable ambition of improvement, and that in the various departments of the arts, and in spheres of improvement and progress higher than those of the mechanical arts, all that is wanted among us, to the development of power and skill, is "a fair field and no favor."

The regulations of the English ploughing-matches differ in some respects from those in the United States. The judges in the English ploughing-matches never come on to the field until the work is done and every team withdrawn. With us, they are present from the commencement to the close of the work. Our practice is, in my opinion, to be preferred. In the former case, no party is known, and impartiality, therefore, may be said to be perfectly secured. So far it is well. The work is accurately surveyed and measured ; the depth of the ploughing, the width of the furrow-slice, the mode of laying it over, the straightness of the lines, the manner in which the first furrow-slices are brought together if it is ploughed back to back, or the finishing of the last and middle furrow if the piece is ploughed from the outside to the centre, the freedom from balks and breaks, are all carefully considered in the verdict rendered. In the United States, every effort is made to secure impartiality, consistently with other arrangements, inasmuch as that no names, but only numbers, are given to the judges, and the different plats of ground to be ploughed are drawn for by lot. Then the judges on the field observe the whole progress of the operation ; measure the different portions, as the work goes on ; and watch the temper and conduct of the ploughman and the training of his team, the manner in which he treats his team, and the condition in which they come off from the work. These circumstances all deserve consideration, and should come in as elements on which a judgment is to be made up. In both cases, it is understood, as it should be, that no party having any personal or pecuniary interest in the result shall have a place on the bench. The English are exact and positive in prescribing the depth of the ploughing, and the width of the furrow-slice even to a half-inch, and insist upon a uniform width throughout the whole. I have urged this same thing often upon committees, in my own country, on which I have had the honor of being placed, and have been met with the objection, that this was requiring too much, and would operate as a discouragement. In my opinion, you

39

cannot require too much, provided you make your premiums in proportion liberal. Excellence is never attained by presenting an inferior standard. Let your rewards be as liberal as possible; require the work to be done as well as possible; and make your rules reasonable, but as stringent as possible; and hold conformity absolute and inevitable. In every such competition, there are minds in which the superior value and splendor of a triumph under such circumstances will rouse a powerful and noble ambition; fire will be brought out of stone, and, as in some beautiful chemical experiments, you will see the blaze burning under the ice. But if you must have a scrub race, have it in another part of the field, and after the noble-spirited horses are withdrawn, and the donkeys and the Rosinantes are brought forward. I have never known a case, in which this loose system of accommodation and indulgence prevailed, and where the rules were narrowed or expanded to fit the occasion, that the decision of the judges gave general satisfaction, or ought to give satisfaction.

It is very mortifying to fail in an object for which one has had a hard struggle. Many a noble fellow, after having reached the upper limbs of the tree, as he was upon the point of putting his hand on the fruit, has found himself, with every effort and strain, not quite high enough to reach it, and perhaps has come tumbling down, with his clothes torn, and his face scratched, to the ground. Upon such a mind, the only effect was to rouse his ambition to a stronger pitch, to give new vigor to his muscles and new energy to his determination. This was as it should be.

I have been told of an Irishman, — an Irishman he was, of course, for none but this clever people ever do such pleasant things, — that he called to demand the payment of the highest prize in the lottery, which he said he had drawn. Upon presenting his ticket, he was told that it was the number next above his to which the prize had fallen. He said "he knew that very well; but he did not suppose that such great folks would stand out for a single number." In all cases of competition, the prize should only be paid to the number which has actually drawn it. It may, in many cases, be expedient to give prizes for effort, and for partial excellence; but if the premium is announced for accomplishment, to accomplishment only should it be paid.

12. Horses used for Ploughing. — Ploughing here is almost universally done with horses. I saw some oxen ploughing at Holkham, with leather harnesses and breastplates, instead of yokes and bows, as employed in New England, and I have found oxen used in some few other cases, but, within my observation, these cases are very rare. The question of the comparative expediency of employing horses or oxen in farm work will come up for discussion presently.

The horses are extremely well trained, and usually groomed with the greatest care. I have found one remarkable exception to this practice, and that of a very large farmer of high repute. He never suffered his horses to be curried or sheared, or confined in stables. When brought home from their work, they were turned into open yards, with capacious sheds, and the stable doors, without any division of stalls, were always left open. The mangers were plentifully supplied with food, and the troughs with water, and they ate and drank, stood or reclined, or walked about, as they pleased. The yards and stalls were always most abundantly littered. I should have scarcely thought proper to mention a case of management, which some might pronounce careless and slovenly, and of which, in riding through some parts of New England, one would hardly be at a loss to find examples, were it not that this was the practice of a very large farmer, extremely skilful and intelligent, and the favorite tenant and model of one of the largest proprietors, and one of the greatest agricultural improvers in the country, (the late Lord Leicester,) and that he pursued this practice from choice, and because he deemed it most conducive to the health and comfort of the animals. He maintained that the animals, not being kept in warm stables, but familiar with the changes of the weather, bore them with less inconvenience and suffering than they otherwise would have done; that a great deal of time and trouble was saved in the care of them; that, being at liberty to lie down when they pleased, their rest was more refreshing than if confined and tied in a stall; that, the hair being given them for a covering, it was wrong to strip them of their flannels at a season when they most needed them; and that the dirt itself, matted among their hair, assisted in retaining the warmth. These were all philosophical reasons, which did not quite convince me of the wisdom and expediency of this mode of managing. The last argument, in respect to the dirt keeping the animals warmer, seems well understood, and practically exemplified, by many of the lower classes in London, Edinburgh, and Dublin, and, if well founded, might do something towards lessening the compassion which one must otherwise feel for their suffering from the want of fuel. The horses in possession of the farmer spoken of appeared in good condition, and were strong for labor; and the practice pursued was of several years' standing.

The usual practice is for the ploughman to be at the stables at four o'clock in the morning; to clean, water, and feed his horses, and to be in the field at work at six o'clock. With a short time to rest occasionally, he continues his ploughing until two o'clock, when he returns to the homestead, the horses are thoroughly cleaned, and rubbed, and watered, and fed, and at last littered for the night — eight hours being considered as a day's work; and, in ordinary cases, an English statute acre, of the same size as an American acre, is his allotted stint. There are cases of heavy land, in which only three quarters of an acre are considered a day's work; and others, of lighter land, in which upwards of an acre and a quarter are accomplished. In Scotland, a pair of horses are ordinarily considered sufficient for any kind of land, and they are worked side by side. If three are employed, two walk upon the land, and one in the furrow. The practice of employing only two horses to a plough is beginning to prevail in England; but, in many instances, three and four horses are used, drawing at length. This practice is not so entirely without reason as some travellers represent it, for in some land it is desirable and necessary to avoid trampling it, and consolidating it the more, by the horses' tread; but when, as it has occasionally happened, I have seen five horses harnessed lengthwise to a single plough, with two men at the plough, and three men or boys with the horses, my own admiration has sometimes bordered upon the ridiculous. The affair of turning at the end, in such a case, is somewhat like wheeling a battalion of undisciplined militia at a country muster, and, unless the field be very long, a large portion of the day must be occupied by these evolutions. The Scotch ploughman, with only two horses, and the reins over his neck, turns a corner like an officer's charger, and requires no aid.

In some cases, ploughs with double mould-boards are used,

which regularly turn two furrows at the same time. In light land, and where the ploughing is shallow, they save time and expense. In stronger lands, where three horses are sufficient, it is obvious that the expense of one horse is saved. In heavy lands, where four horses would be required on account of the double mould-board, it is obvious nothing would be gained. In parts of Lincolnshire, on the chalk formation, where the ploughing for wheat was not more than three inches, these ploughs were much approved. I give below a cut of a double furrow-

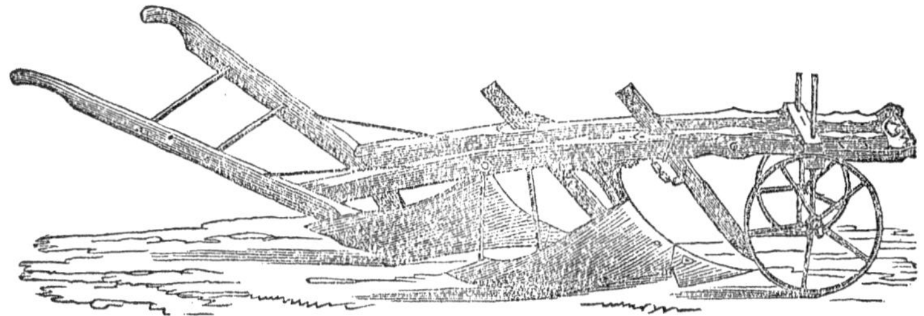

plough. The invention of this plough is by Lord Somerville; and it is certainly creditable for the ingenuity of its construction.

LXXXII. — A DIGRESSION.

Progress of Improvement. — I have gone thus at large into the operation of ploughing, because it is the great operation of husbandry; and having finished the field, let us stand aside, and, looking at the work, indulge a moment the reflections which suggest themselves.

A ruffle from under a crimping iron does not present a more beautiful object than a well-ploughed field from under the hands of an English or a Scotch artist. The lines are all straight; the furrows well turned; the headlands cross-ploughed; the corners finished. A well-disciplined mind enjoys the highest pleasure from seeing an operation of any kind, even the most humble, well performed, and perfected according to its proper measure.

There is something, likewise, extremely gratifying in witnessing the progress and advancement of human skill and art. From digging the ground with a stick, that a hole might be made for the deposit of the seed, to the perfect inversion of it by the plough, what an immense stride! That is now done in a day, which, in the rude ages referred to, could scarcely have been accomplished in a year; and that is now performed with ease, and without any unkind tax upon the health of man or beast, which could not otherwise have been effected without the most severe exactions of human toil, and often at the expense of the premature shortening of human life.

LXXXIII. — IMPROVED MACHINERY.

There are persons continually complaining of the introduction and use of machinery in the place of human labor, and as therefore prejudicial to the interests of the poor. At an agricultural dinner, I listened with a good deal of interest to a distinguished nobleman, who was defending machinery against this charge, by endeavoring to show that, so far from machinery lessening the demand for labor, it was the ordinary result of it to cause the employment of more persons than were occupied before its introduction. This may be the fact; but if this were the only result, or if this result stood alone, it would not be a very strong recommendation, and should be classed with the kind of argument used not long since in Parliament, in commendation of the corn laws, that they encouraged labor by rendering agricultural produce dear, when it is obvious that, just in proportion as the price of agricultural produce increases, the value of the wages of the laborer decrease, his supplies are diminished, and, though labor is more in demand, it is worse paid.

1. Machinery lightens Labor. — The value of improved machinery rests upon different grounds. Its first effect is to lessen the severity of human toil. Through the ingenious application of the mechanical powers, that is effected by the hand of a child, which the united force of hundreds of men, strained

to an intensity most painful and injurious, could scarcely accomplish. The wheel, and the lever, and the pulley, and the indefinite multiplication and curious combination of powers which art invents, execute works of a magnitude, before which the armies of an ancient or a modern Alexander might sit down in despair. Instead, according to the fashion of ancient monarchs, of throwing golden fetters into the torrent, to stem its force, modern science puts an iron bit into its mouth, and rides triumphantly upon its crested waves. The victories which human art has achieved over the elements of nature, once deemed untamable, adorn with matchless splendor the annals of our times; and yet, like the crepuscular light, like the first darting up of the morning rays upon the eastern horizon, they only presage the full light of day. Fire, water, air, in various forms, stand ready to do man's bidding; and, as the miracle of modern art, the winged lightning presents itself to his service, and becomes the instantaneous bearer of intelligence between places the most distant — between places whose distance, be it what it may, will make no perceptible difference in time or certainty, where once the means of an uninterrupted continuity of communication shall have been discovered. These are great achievements, and their effects are felt in every department of labor. In agricultural operations, if the mechanic arts have not yet done as much as in many other branches of industry, yet they have rendered no small contributions; and it is not to be forgotten, that the agricultural interest, if not specifically served, shares as largely as any other class in the general benefits which the improvements of the mechanic arts confer upon society. The plough is an immense advance upon the spade; the cultivator, upon the hoe; the horse-rake and hay-tedder, upon the hand-rake and the common fork. The steam-engine performs the work of many men and many horses in the threshing of grain, and the pumping of water, and various other operations to which it is applied. In the fens of Lincolnshire, two immense steam-engines, one of eighty, and one of sixty horse power, under the care of one or two individuals, completely drain an extent of surface of many thousands of acres. They bring these hitherto waste tracts of country under the dominion of productive cultivation, and, by its magical influence, bid these unsightly and barren sands adorn themselves with the glittering tresses of a golden harvest. These are among the miracles of machinery, under the guidance of an intelligence which is an emanation from the Divine Spirit. One hundred and fifty thousand acres, in the neighboring fens, are now in the process of being redeemed from the sea, and completely drained, by a similar machinery. The courtiers of the king may now safely challenge him to place his chair upon the beach, and bid the waves retire. What could human labor effect in such cases without the aid of machinery? For all the men, and women, and children, in England, to have attempted to accomplish such a work, without such help, would have been as wise as to undertake to dip out Lake Superior with a table-spoon.*

2. Machinery increases Production. — The second effect of machinery is, to multiply production to an unlimited extent. A cotton manufactory at Manchester turns out in a day as much cotton cloth as, under the old system of household spinning and weaving, could have been made in all Lancashire in a fortnight, perhaps a month. With improved machinery, twenty acres — may I not say fifty? — can be ploughed, harrowed, manured, drilled, cultivated, and the produce harvested, and threshed, and

---

* "If reference is made to the evidence given before the House of Commons, to which the numerous petitions complaining of agricultural distress were referred in 1821, it will be seen that, at that time, almost the only grain produced in the fens of Cambridgeshire consisted of oats. Since then, by draining and manuring, the capability of the soil has been so changed, that these fens now produce some of the finest wheat that is grown in England; and this more costly grain now constitutes the main dependence of the farmers in a district where, fourteen years ago, its production was scarcely attempted."

"It has been found that an engine of the power of ten horses is sufficient for draining 1000 acres of land, and that, on the average of years, this work may be performed by setting the engine in motion for periods amounting in the aggregate to 20 days of 12 hours each, or 240 hours in all. Several engines have been erected for this purpose within the last three or four years, some of them having the power of 60 or 70 horses: each of these large engines is employed in draining from 6000 to 7000 acres of land. The cost of the first establishment of these engines is stated to be £1 per acre, and the expense of keeping them at work 2 s. 6 d. per acre. This plan is found to bring with it the further advantage that, in the event of long-continued drought, the farmer can, without apprehension, admit the water required for his cattle, and for the purpose of irrigation, secure in the means he possesses of regulating the degree of moisture, if the drought, as is frequently the case, should be followed by an excess of rain." — *Porter's Progress of the Nation.*

prepared for food, where, under the rude system of the aborigines of the country, the cultivation of only one could be carried on, and its produce secured. Indeed, all such comparisons seem idle, because, without machinery of some kind, no cultivation whatever could take place. The human hand is itself a machine, and one of the most perfect description. If there is any advantage in having two hands rather than one, then there must be a correspondent advantage in any contrivance by which one hand can be made to do the work of two, or two hands of four, and still more when one can be empowered to do the work of thousands.

From the manner in which some men speak of machinery, one would suppose that the world would be better and happier if men and women were to go back to simple fig-leaves for aprons, and undressed sheep-skins for coverings, and find shelter and repose at night under some overhanging rock, or on a bed of hemlock boughs, in a wigwam of birch-bark. I have no sympathy with such "simple and primitive" notions. I will say nothing of the charms and blessedness of a state of perfect innocence, because I would not offend any honest man's prejudices, nor thrust my face and hands against the porcupine armor of controversial theology; but I confess I have always had some misgivings as to the happiness of what poets describe as the golden age, and theologians depict as the paradisiacal state, when the human race had nothing to do but to enjoy themselves, and to enjoy themselves in doing nothing — an experiment which, whenever I have tried it, I have always found extremely monotonous and wearisome. Strength is to be found only in the exertion of the muscles; food yields its nourishment only when the machinery of digestion is in full operation; and health, and power, and happiness, are compatible only with the highest activity of the physical and the intellectual faculties.

When the ignorant and vulgar, whose views do not extend beyond the first immediate effects, burn factories, and break threshing-mills to pieces, an enlightened and generous mind would feel compassion for their ignorance and infirmity; but when minds of a different order, professing to be enlightened, become, as we sometimes see them, the cavillers against improved machinery, and prate about the "simplicity of the good old times," when men used clam-shells for spoons, and thorns for pins, and goat-skins for glass bottles, and wooden bowls instead of china, — and, in some instances, do far worse by fostering the vindictive prejudices of the vulgar against those inventions of art and genius which relieve the severity, facilitate the exertion, and immensely increase the productive power of labor, — I hold them as without excuse, and could wish them no worse lot than to be exiled for a season to some parts of Ireland, where these prejudices against improved machinery are as fierce as theirs can be, and where they may find millions living in a state of destitution as complete and absolute as seems compatible with the continuance of life.

3. General Effects on Labor. — I confess, however, there is one view of this subject which I must not pass over, and which I cannot take with equal complacency. The effects of improved machinery should be to alleviate and to shorten human toil, and, in multiplying production, to extend more widely the supply of food, and the common comforts of life. The laboring man should, on every principle, be the first to share in these benefits; but far too often he is the last. Food is greatly multiplied both in quantity and variety; but, in a country where labor is superabundant, the wages of labor become proportionately reduced, and the power to purchase restricted. There can be no doubt that, in respect to clothing and furniture, the condition of the laboring population is greatly improved above what it formerly was. An American clock, for example, made in Connecticut, — that home of industry and the useful arts, — an article both useful and ornamental, and in which the "gude" housewife is sure to take an honest pride, may be purchased in London for a pound. A century ago, this would have been an article of furniture which a nobleman might covet.

But it is too true that improved machinery scarcely diminishes — in many cases it increases — the demand for human and brute labor. Two men only are required to thresh grain with a flail; from five to eight, besides the horses, or the attendants upon the steam-engine, are employed at the threshing-machine. Much more is threshed, and, in consequence of these increased facilities, much more is grown, and therefore requires to be threshed. "But for the invention of the steam-engine, a large proportion of the coal mines now profitably worked could not have been opened, or must have been abandoned. It is well known that, by the consumption of one bushel of coals in the furnace of a steam-boiler, a power is produced which, in a few minutes, will raise 20,000 gallons of water from a depth of 350 feet — an effect which could not be produced in a shorter time than a whole day through the continuous labor of twenty men, working with the common pump. By thus expending a few pence, an amount of human labor is set free, to employ which would have cost fifty shillings; and yet this circumstance, so far from having diminished the demand for human labor, even in the actual trade where the economy is produced, has certainly caused a much greater number of persons to be employed in coal-mining than could otherwise have been set to work." *

It certainly is matter of congratulation, rather than of complaint, that more food is produced to be eaten, more clothing to wear, and more fuel with which to warm our habitations and to apply to other purposes of utility, necessity, or enjoyment; but, in looking at the severity and long continuance of toil to which a large part of the laboring portion of the community are subjected, and how, in many of the arts and operations of manufactures and trade, human health and comfort are wholly disregarded, and human life is used up with as much indifference as fuel is thrown into the furnace of the steam-engine, one cannot help deeply lamenting that the burden cannot be lightened on the back of the hard-driven animal, and that they whose toil produces every thing are put off with the smallest and meanest portion of the fruits of their own industry. How far government should interfere, in such a case, between the employer and the employed, is a question not without great practical difficulties. Human society is such a complicated web, that the extreme tension of any single thread disorders the whole piece. Every provision should be made for the protection of the young and helpless; opportunity should be afforded for the full development of their physical powers, and for the education of their minds. No pains should be spared to protect good morals and decency, and to secure human life against any extraordinary perils. The hours of labor should not be too long extended, nor the hours of seasonable rest encroached upon; and, in any case

* Progress of the Nation, vol. i. p. 335.

where they are wholly dependent upon others for the provision which they require, that provision should be at least as kind and liberal for the human bipeds as for the domestic quadrupeds. It might be extremely difficult to effect this; but, until this is done, our condition is not half Christian. Avarice, by force, or cunning, or art, — openly sometimes, but more often covertly, — is constantly triumphing over humanity and justice; and it may be regarded as the Juggernaut of civilization, crushing with indifference all who come in its way.

LXXXIV. — MORAL CONSIDERATIONS.

Before we turn from the ploughed field which we have been contemplating, I have but one or two more remarks to make, which will not, I hope, be deemed out of place. The ordinary operations of nature are so familiar, that we cease to look at them with surprise. We choose to wrap ourselves up in our own conceit, and, certain facts regularly occurring under certain conditions and circumstances, we satisfy ourselves with saying that it is according to the laws of nature, and think therefore that we understand it. I do not perceive that we understand it any the better because it is according to the laws of nature; since these laws themselves, in their ultimate causes and operations, are utterly insoluble to the human understanding, and the frequency and uniformity of their results, so far from lessening, actually increase the miracle. I say *miracle*, for in no other light than as miraculous can we regard the changing scene which is now to pass before our eyes. The field, as we now look at it, presents but a naked surface of inert dust; but there are powers and influences at work, within and around it, of the most subtle and amazing character. The earth has opened its bosom, and the children of men are to receive nourishment and life from the bounty of their common mother. Man casts the dry seeds upon these naked furrows, and they are at once quickened into life. The earth, the air, the sun, the rain, all lend their combined aid, in exactly such measure, and at such time, as is needed for the perfection of the work. The plants rise out of the ground with a spirit and beauty which no human art can rival. The hand of an invisible artist is at work to expand the roots, to train the stem, to mould the leaves, to protect all with a net-work of the finest web, to throw in colors of exquisite beauty, and to fill the pendent seed-vessels with bread, for the sustenance and nourishment of animal life. In a few weeks, or months, the field so lately naked and desolate is laden with treasures far richer than gold, and for which all the glittering diamonds of Peru, and all the shining pearls of Orient climes, would be no substitute. Man gathers what, with strange presumption, he calls the products of *his* skill and labor, and fills his garner with the golden treasures of the fields. Now, because this happens so regularly and so frequently, shall it cease to excite his surprise, and touch his heart? In my humble opinion, its frequency, and its comparative certainty, vastly expand the miracle; and if the rich fruits of a beneficence, so entirely beyond his command and control, yet withal so constant, so faithful, so liberal, call out no aspirations of piety, if "harvest home" awakens no anthem of thanksgiving and reverence in his soul, he must not claim an equality even with the animals which he drives, for "the ox knoweth his owner, and the ass his master's crib."

LXXXV. — HARROWING.

There are various operations to be gone through with, after the ploughing. The first object in English cultivation is to reduce the soil to as fine a tilth as possible. Tull, who is sometimes called the father of English arable cultivation, deemed the loosening, and stirring, and reducing the soil, as all that was necessary to its productiveness, and that manure might be dispensed with. The first position was the foundation of great improvements; but the latter was soon discovered to be an error. His practice, which was tried by many persons, laid the foundation of what is called the New Husbandry, and may be considered as constituting an era in English agriculture. It is curious to observe, that oftentimes, in human history, great mistakes lead to great improvements and discoveries; and in the complicated course of human affairs, a divine Providence, in comparison with which human sagacity can scarcely be considered other than as arrant folly, converts the errors of man into instruments of truth and knowledge. Experiment is the highway to science, and it is as desirable, in many cases, to know what will not, as to know what will succeed. Men are always ready, through self-esteem and the love of approbation, to detail and magnify any fortunate results; but he is a brave man, and more entitled to respect, who, by way of caution, will expose his failures, and guard the sanguine and adventurous against the errors in which he himself became involved. This is a noble disinterestedness; but many men, like the fox who lost his brush in a steel trap, wish nothing so much as to see their neighbors subjected to the same mortification.

The Romans, in their husbandry, prescribed four distinct processes of arable culture. The first was to break the land; the second to turn it over; the third was to break it again; the fourth was to turn it again.* They understood perfectly the use and advantages of thorough and deep tillage. The English farmers are fully aware of this, and follow repeated ploughings, with various other processes.

The first is that of harrowing. This is done lengthwise with the furrow always in the first instance, and then crosswise, until the surface is completely mellowed and pulverized. With us, in general, harrows are made single, and the teeth set in wooden frames, and, though they are usually made square, yet the chain is generally attached to one of the corners, which gives them a diamond shape, and is supposed to lessen the draught. We seldom take a breadth, in such case, of more than four and a half or five feet. Here the best harrows are made, both frames and teeth, of iron. The teeth, or tines, work to a depth of five to eight inches, and follow each other in lines about four inches apart. Seed harrows, or harrows for covering the seed, have tines about four inches in length, and are made proportionately light.

* 1. Fringere. 2. Vertere. 3. Refringere. 4. Revertere.

I do not know that I can do better for my readers, than to subjoin the remarks and illustrations of one of the most eminent implement makers in Great Britain, Mr. J. Allen Ransome, in his valuable treatise on the "Implements of Husbandry."

"It is admitted, by all acquainted with the subject, that harrowing, especially on heavy soils, is the most laborious operation on the farm, — not so much, perhaps, on account of the quantum of power requisite for the draught, (though this is sometimes considerable,) as for the speed with which the operation is, or ought to be, accompanied; and yet it is frequently left to the charge of mere boys, and sometimes performed by the worst horses on the farm.

"If we examine a field, one half of which has been harrowed with weak, inefficient horses, and whose pace was consequently sluggish, the other half with an adequate strength and swiftness of animal power, we shall find the former will be rough and unfinished, the latter comparatively firm and level, and completed in what would be called a husbandry-like manner. Scarcely any thing in farming is more unsightly than the wavy, serpentine traces of inefficient harrowing. The generality of harrows appear too heavy and clumsy to admit of that despatch without which the work cannot be well done; and though it is evident that different soils demand implements of proportionate weight and power, yet, for the most part, harrows have been rather over than under weighted, particularly when employed after a drill, or to bury seeds of any kind.

"Harrowing has been so long regarded as an operation which must be attended with considerable horse-labor, that attention does not appear to have been sufficiently turned to the inquiry whether this labor might not be greatly reduced, by lightening the instruments with which it is performed. Many would be surprised at the amount of reduction of which seed-harrows, at least, are capable, and, where land is clean, to see how effectively a gang of very light small-toothed harrows may be used.

"Having noticed, in some parts of Norfolk, the perfect manner in which seed corn is covered by a common rake with wooden teeth, a friend of mine constructed a gang of harrows on the following plan, and he states that it proved the most popular and useful implement of the kind to the farm.

Gang of Light Seed-Harrows.

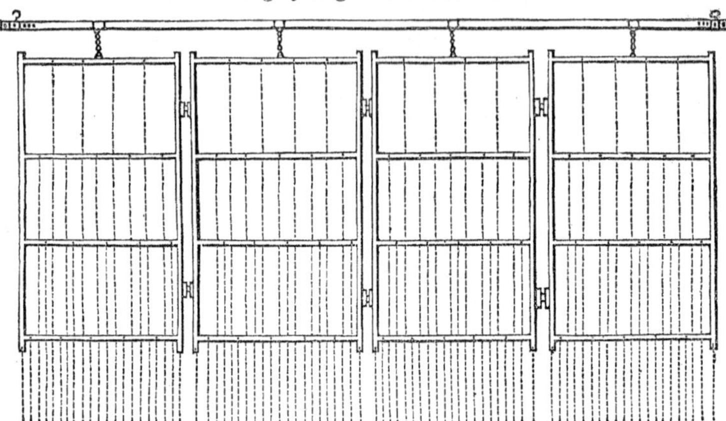

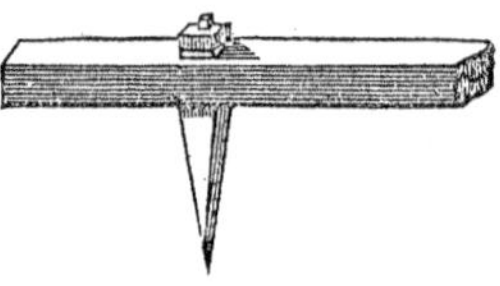

"The frames are of ash, and as light as possible, with iron teeth, being but three inches long, exclusive of the part which enters the wood-work. They screw into the balks in the manner shown in the annexed figure.

"It should be observed that the above four harrows are amply sufficient to cover a twelve-furrow stetch or ridge, of 108 inches, but three will be wide enough for a three-furrow stetch of 90 inches, exclusive of a small portion of the furrows. If for some purposes the teeth be found too thick, every alternate tooth may be taken out; but for general purposes this will hardly be necessary. The two horses require, on this plan, to be kept quite level; for, if one be suffered to go in advance of the other, a diagonal line is produced, by which the teeth will be made to follow each other, instead of cutting fresh ground. I am aware that, by the usual construction of harrows, a diagonal line of draught is required, in order to throw the teeth into a proper working position; but I am strongly inclined to the opinion, that the correct working of the implement ought to depend on its construction, and not on any particular mode of working it. Besides, the system of keeping one horse in advance of his partner is bad in principle; it is an unequal division of labor, the fore-horse being compelled to do more than his share of the work, which, under any circumstances, is always heavy enough.

The balks of the above set of harrows were made of wood, in order to insure extraordinary lightness; but, for general purposes, I prefer those made of iron, the weight of which can be increased to any reasonable degree, without adding much to their substance. This is important in working tenacious clays, which, by adhering to the common clumsy wooden balks, considerably increase the labor, and at the same time impede the proper execution."

Sometimes harrows are made in two parts, that is, two small and complete harrows, placed side and side, and united by flexible hinges. In such case, the harrow can be reduced to half its width, by one part being doubled over on the back of the other; or, when the land is in ridges, and the harrow travels on the summit of the ridge, the two parts, by the flexible junction in the centre, are able to accommodate themselves to the curvature of the ground upon which they travel. Sometimes three or four harrows are attached first to each other, by these hinges, side and side, and then to a single beam, to the ends of which the traces of the horses are appended, and in this case they sweep a breadth of nine feet. This carries on the work with great rapidity. A pair of good horses might carry such a breadth without difficulty, upon light land; but upon a heavy and tenacious soil, the labor would be too great for them.

"*Gang of Heavy Iron Harrows.*

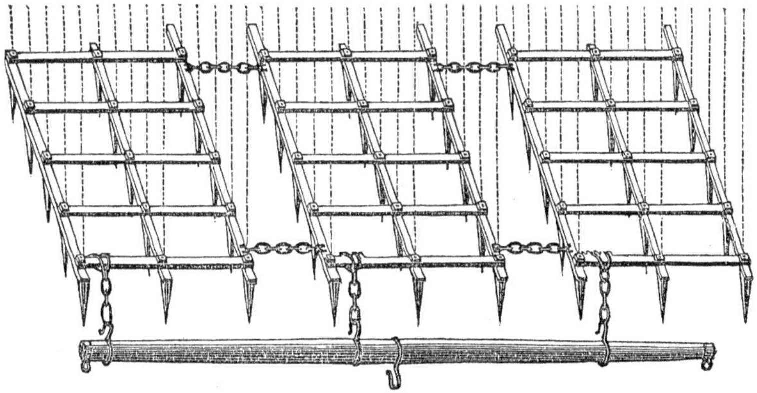

"The above engraving of iron harrows is introduced to show the form in which they are usually made; they are used in gangs of three, four, or five, as may be required to suit the lands on which they are used, and may be made to any weight required."* No intelligent farmer, however, will ever think of harrowing his land, unless it be of the lightest description, in a wet state. It has been by some persons deemed an improvement to make the front tines of a harrow shorter than the back ones; but no advantage comes from this. By many the practice — and in my opinion with reason — is condemned, as the instrument, in such case, unless brought too near the horses, will be found to dip in front, by which means the draught is considerably increased. Teeth of a uniform length throughout are to be preferred. The flexibility given to a harrow, by a hinge in the centre, is a great improvement. In many cases, one harrow is attached to another so as to follow it, but so far removed to one side or the other, that the teeth follow in different lines. In such case, it is obvious that the draught must be very much increased, both from the distance of the last harrow from the moving power, and from its lying flat and dead upon the ground, and having no advantage of the lift which is given to the forward harrow by the chain which attaches it to the horses, and which it would have, if it were set in the same frame.

There are several varieties of harrows, but, excepting the frame being made of iron instead of wood, and their being connected by hinges, so as that the frame becomes, so to speak, flexible, I see no prominent excellence to be pointed out. "In an experiment made between a pair of wooden harrows and a pair of iron ones constructed on the same plan, and having the same number, and precisely the same disposition, of the teeth and frames, although those of iron were found to be 20 pounds lighter than those of wood, yet the former worked decidedly better and steadier than the latter; in fact, the iron harrows cut into the land, while those made of wood rode, or rather danced, upon the surface."

A harrow, called a web or chain brush harrow, invented by Mr. Smith, of Deanston, I have seen, but not in operation; and its effect must be to reduce the surface to a very fine tilth, but it is not its object to penetrate the soil. If we take a number of small iron circular plates, perhaps three inches in diameter, with

* Ransome.

thin or sharpened edges, and string them upon iron rods, upon which they will revolve freely, and arrange them in squares like the panes of a window or sash, and with enough of them to form the desired size of a harrow, we shall have formed the instrument to which I refer. As they revolve vertically, and are drawn over the surface, their tendency is to cut all the lumps into fine pieces, and to leave the surface well reduced and pulverized.

At Lord Hatherton's well-managed farm, at Teddesley Park, Staffordshire, I saw a revolving harrow, somewhat resembling a hay-spreading machine, the long and curved teeth of which penetrated the ground deeply, thoroughly stirred it, and brought the weeds and rubbish to the surface. It was moved upon low wheels, and performed its work most effectually.

I shall borrow, for the benefit of my readers, an account of Biddell's extirpating harrow from Mr. Ransome's valuable book, before quoted. I have not seen the instrument at work, but its efficiency will be understood from the account.

"Biddell's Extirpating Harrow.—This is a new implement, invented by Arthur Biddell, of Playford, and similar to the scar-

ifier which bears his name. It is intended for breaking up land when it is too hard for the heaviest harrows, and for bringing winter fallows into a state of fine tillage. In working summerlands, it is calculated, by the shape of its teeth, to bring to the surface all grass and rubbish. The teeth are placed in three rows, in order to allow sufficient distance from each other to prevent choking, and the implement is so constructed as that, by means of levers, the teeth may be elevated or depressed at pleasure. According to the form of the lands it may be required to operate upon, it may either be used perfectly parallel, or the fore teeth may be made to penetrate deeper than the hinder ones, whilst those at either side may, when one wheel is required to run in the furrow, be instantly adjusted to the level of the land, so that every tine shall penetrate to a uniform depth of six inches, if required; and they will work equally well at any less depth.

"I have frequently seen this implement at work on very foul land and on stubbles, when it has been too hard to allow the use of the plough. As the interval between the lines formed by its teeth does not exceed four inches, the soil has been completely stirred. The tines may be either used with points or with steel hoes; and with the latter the skimming, or, as it is frequently called, the 'broadshare' process, may be quickly accomplished. The weight is not found to be a disadvantage, but, from the stability it gives, the contrary; and, being borne on high wheels, it does not require so much horse-labor as might be supposed, two horses, on most soils, being generally sufficient."

LXXXVI. — SCARIFYING, OR GRUBBING.

What is called, in England, the scarifying or grubbing of land, is little else than harrowing it with a deeper and stronger instrument than a common harrow, with a view to reduce it to fine tilth, and to bring up the roots and weeds which may infest the land. The English and Scotch aim, in their husbandry, at an extreme cleanness of cultivation. There are — as it would be strange if there were not — examples among them of slovenly cultivation; but cleanness is the prominent and almost universal characteristic of their husbandry. The late Lord Leicester, (Mr.

Coke, of Holkham) used to make it his boast, that not a weed could be found in extensive fields of his cultivation, and offered a high reward for the discovery of one. The couch grass, (*triticum repens,*) and the common charlock, (wild mustard,) and the poppy, abound, in some districts, to a most extraordinary degree; and in cleaning the fields, in the autumn, of couch grass, the piles of it which are sometimes seen would lead one to suppose that it was the only crop grown on such places. In some cases, where the land is very dirty, and the cleansing very thorough, the heaps of weeds have been as numerous as cocks of hay in a mown field.

The general practice is, to burn these heaps upon the field, to the expediency of which I strongly demur. The amount of ashes obtained in such case is altogether inconsiderable. The couch grass being extremely vivacious, and propagated from every joint, it is not easy to bury it so deep as to extirpate it. Some of the Scotch farmers pile it up at the outside of their fields, and mingle with it quicklime, which of course soon consumes it. I cannot help thinking it would be much better to use it as litter in the cattle-sheds or stalls, and fold-yards, where, by the trampling of the stock, it would soon become decomposed, and, without danger of starting again into life, it would go to essentially increase the compost heap.

The operation of scarifiers, or grubbers, will be seen at once by a reference to the plate. Many of them are certainly very efficient instruments, and, when the team is sufficiently powerful, stir the land most thoroughly to a great depth. There is a considerable variety of them; and the peculiar excellences of each of them are always fully set forth by the inventor or maker, — in doing which, there seems to be no want of talent or address among the English, and some of them may fairly challenge competition with Peter Pindar's razor-seller, or with any of the vivacious and voluble tribe of Connecticut pedlers.

The infinite variety of machines and mechanical contrivances exhibited at the great agricultural shows in this country, covering literally acres and acres of ground, strikes a visitor with astonishment. As, in reading the accounts of patent medicines in the public newspapers, one is led to think that the reign of disease is abolished, and the victory of health, life, and perpetual youth, on earth, secured, so, in looking at the number and variety of agricultural implements presented on such occasions, and the diversity of purposes which they are most *certainly* and *effectually* to accomplish, one is almost persuaded that human labor and superintendence may be dispensed with; and that the farmer, as he would wind up his clock on Monday morning so that it may run all the week, so he has only to set his agricultural machinery in motion, and may then leave the field with a quiet confidence that every thing will proceed as he desires it should. After having visited, likewise, the establishments of many large proprietors, and seen the broken and condemned implements, and the piled-up, useless lumber of this description, in their implement-rooms and sheds, I cannot help thinking that there is, among a great many men well informed in other matters, a fair share of susceptibility to imposition; that "razors made to sell" meet with no want of purchasers in England; and that the manufacturers perfectly understand themselves, when they have got their pail under a full cow. The human tongue is certainly an extraordinary piece of machinery, and its flexibility cannot be sufficiently admired. I see, in the papers of the week when I am writing, an advertisement of a potato-powder, recommended to families to be put into the pot with the potatoes to be boiled, so as to correct the evils of the diseased potato, and not only to neutralize its pernicious influences, but actually to convert the diseased portions into useful nourishment. The price and place of sale are both given. There will be many to buy, beyond all question. When will the reign of empiricism cease on earth? When the last man has left it; and not sooner.

The operation of scarifying will be better understood from a picture of some of the principal instruments in use than from any verbal description.

The first to which I shall refer is called, after the name of its inventor,

Biddell's Scarifier — and I shall allow the manufacturer to speak for himself.

"This implement is for the purpose of cultivating land under a variety of circumstances, and bringing it into a proper state of tilth much more effectually, and at less expense, than can be done by the means generally employed for that purpose.

"It may be successfully used to clean wheat, bean, and pea stubbles, directly after harvest;

"To break up such parts of clover layers as may have failed in the plant, and to break up land after green crops, in May or June, in preparation for turnips, coleworts, &c.; thus accomplishing fine and deep tillage, without bringing fresh earth to the surface-land, in preparation for barley and oats.

"*Its Advantages are — Saving, in Tillage*, of half the labor, both manual and horse, over the ordinary method of cleaning land.

"*Saving of Time.* Lands may be broken and stirred, with this implement, in much less time than with the plough.

"*Improved Cultivation.* The operation of this scarifier is much more effective for spring crops on strong lands than ploughing, as it occasions less treading by horses, produces more mould, and allows the moisture to be more advantageously retained; and the seed will be deposited in the soil which has been exposed to the winter frosts.

"*Less harrowing is required*, as the land is broken up, and left much finer than after the plough.

"*The couch grass* (*if any*) is brought to the surface without breaking it.

"The land is left by this implement in a state to be immediately harrowed, which may be done in time to break the clods before they become too hard.

"In all cases, where it is desirable to give tillage to the land without turning down the surface, this implement may be used with great advantage.

"*Directions for using the Scarifier.* — In using the scarifier, attention should be paid to set it level, and the depth of scarifying may be varied from one to ten inches, which is done by means of the two levers.

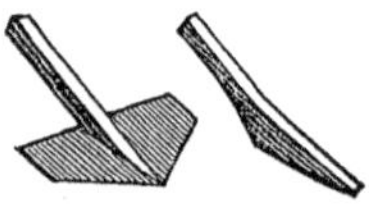

"When the land is very hard, and required to be cut clean, first use the chisel points, and then follow with the wide hoes.

"The chisel points only should be used on clover leys; the roots of the clover being too tough for the hoes, and are not required to be cut up.

"The horses should be kept in a direct line, and *the implement not suffered to turn without taking the fore part out of the ground by means of the long lever.* Particular attention should be paid to this; for, although the slanting direction in which the tines are set will bear the draught required while the horses go straight forward, they cannot stand against the twist, if the scarifier be turned round before the front tines are taken out of their work. It is also needful to observe, that the draught iron from the fore wheels, upon which the whippletrees hang, should be suspended by the draught chain higher than where the three draught irons (when in work) go upon the upright part of the fore axletree; otherwise, this may bend or give way.

"The wheels, on either side, may be made to go higher or lower by shifting the coupling irons, where holes are made for that purpose, where one wheel has to work in the furrow; which may be the case when a stetch is scarified by going on one side of it, and coming back on the other.

"It is essential to have whippletrees adapted to the implement; if otherwise, it will fail to scarify up the foot-marks of the horses."

The next implement for the purposes described, and which has been a long time in use, is called

Finlayson's Self-Cleaning Harrow. — "This is an efficient implement for cleaning lands under tillage from couch grass and other weeds; the curvature of its teeth being so formed as to bring to the surface all weeds and vegetable rubbish."

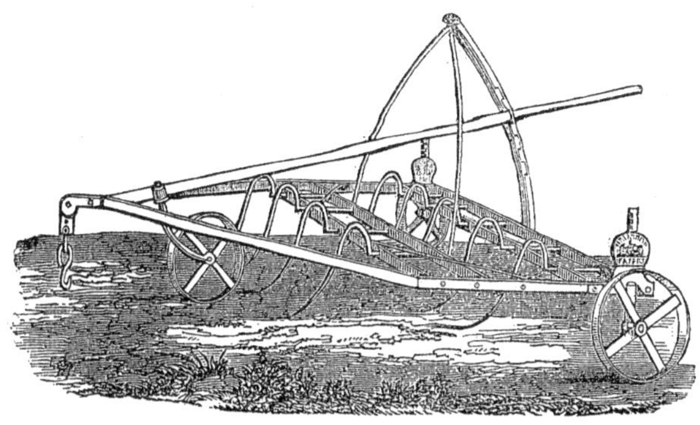

This was among the first improvements of the kind, and has been followed by a great many other inventions, of which I shall offer only two other examples. The first is,

Kirkwood's Grubber. — "The leverage that is obtained by pressing on the handles or stilts of this machine, whether in action

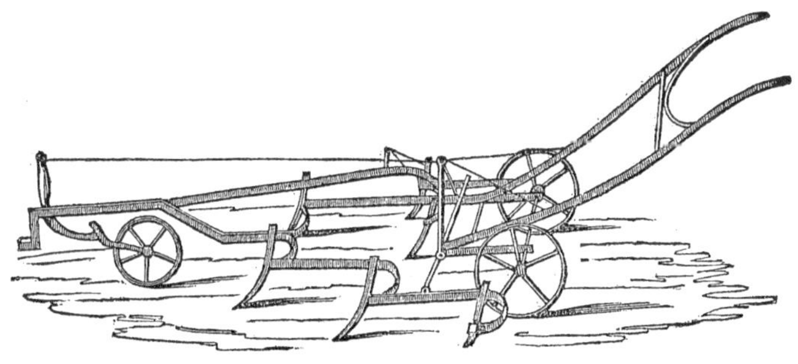

or at rest, is so simple, and yet so powerful in its effect, as to regulate the depth of the tines to the greatest nicety; or, in cases of obstruction, to throw them out altogether. It is an admirable implement, and well deserving the high commendation generally bestowed on it." Objections have been made, however, to the form of its teeth.

The next instrument which I shall notice is called the *Uley cultivator,* and made at the iron and agricultural implement works of the Earl of Ducie, at Uley, in Gloucestershire, and under the direction and management of a highly intelligent and practical machinist, Mr. Richard Clyburn, a visit to whose establishment afforded me the highest gratification.

THE ULEY CULTIVATOR. — "No. 1 size, with 5 tines, covering a space of 40 inches.

"No. 2 size, with 7 tines, covering a space of 56 inches.

"The improvements consist, first, in a new method of fastening the tine into the frame, so as to insure a sufficiency of strength to the upper end of the tine, where the greatest strength is required; secondly, in making the scarifiers and grubbers concave on the under side, which causes them to wear to a sharp edge, and enter the ground better, where it is very hard; thirdly, in constructing them in such a way, they can be made of wrought iron.

"The frame is of cast-iron, made to receive five or seven tines, each tine covering a space of eight inches, and so arranged that, although drawing lines only eight inches apart, they are two feet from each other; this, with their curved shape, and length, prevents its clogging in the foulest land. There are three sorts of points; one, two inches wide, for grubbing up or breaking land; another, nine inches wide, for working stubble; the third set has steel blades, and are used for paring, instead of the breast-plough: these points all fit the tines without pins to hold them. The tines are fastened into the frame with a split key and cotter; and, in case of breaking, they can be taken out and others put in, as easy as the colter of a plough. The height of the frame from the ground is about two feet; the wheels are of cast-iron, the front ones 1 foot 6 inches diameter, and the back ones 3 feet 4 inches diameter. The machine is raised and lowered by turning a handle, the axle of which has a worm fixed on it, working into a wheel fixed in the crank-axle of the back wheels. This wheel has a projecting arm, in which a stud is fixed: to this stud is attached a connecting-rod, the upper end of which is connected to the long lever which has its fulcrum in the centre, and is connected with the frame by a joint; the other end of the lever is connected to the top of the T axle, on which the front wheels work. It will be seen by this arrangement that, if the handle is turned to the right, the machine is lifted up; and if to the left, let down: this is indicated by the dial-plate on the right-hand side of the machine, marked in inches, in and out of the ground; one rotation of the handle raises or lowers the machine one inch."

This instrument, wherever it has been used, has been highly approved.

It will be obvious to my readers, that the object of these several inventions is to put the ground into a fine and deep cultivation; and, in many cases, the scarifier will be substituted with great advantage for the plough. In the spring of the year, especially, where land has been ploughed in the autumn, it would be most injudicious, in many cases, to reverse the sward with a plough, and at the same time, as the wetness of the land may require that it should be cultivated lightly, a harrow or scarifier presents the most proper implement.

As a matter of curiosity, a Table of ingenious, exact, and somewhat useful calculations, in regard to the business of ploughing or scarifying land, will be inserted on the last page of this Report.

LXXXVII. — GENERAL REMARKS ON THE USE OF AGRICULTURAL MACHINERY.

In presenting these different examples to my readers, they will not expect me to recommend them, nor to mark a preference of one over the other. That I must leave wholly to their judgment. I have only to say that the best results are to be expected only from the most careful and thorough cultivation; but with the best feelings towards those ingenious mechanics and artisans who have done so much to alleviate and facilitate labor, my own experience, and that of many friends, would lead me to advise to caution in the purchase of any machines whose utility has not been thoroughly tested, and especially those of a complicated or expensive character. A machine which promises much may greatly disappoint us in the results. Some of the most complex machines perform only that which the most simple would accomplish with half the trouble, and it is often quite as difficult to manage the machine as to perform the labor. A machine constructed upon the most sound and philosophical principles requires, many times, a philosopher to guide it. Agricultural machines of a complicated nature are constantly liable to get out of repair, and at times when the inconvenience and loss, occasioned by the stoppage of the work from such accidents, are excessive. Then the conduct and management of the machine must go into the hands of persons who are ignorant and stupid; who have a prejudice against the success of machinery, because they erroneously suppose that it interferes with their labor; who generally resist all innovations, and who but too often find a malicious gratification in the failure of all attempts at improvement. The remedies for this very common evil, it is not easy to determine. The first is, if possible, to give the laborer a direct personal interest in the success of the machine in use. The second is less direct, and can only be looked for in the future; that is, the better education of the laboring classes, which shall enable them to take more just views of their own private interests, and understand their inseparable identity with all measures of general improvement, with the progress of the mechanic arts, by which, if labor is not abridged, production is greatly increased, and with the interests and welfare of every other class in the community. Happy will it be for the world, when the true principles of political economy — so well illustrated in the well-known Latin fable of the revolt of the limbs against the stomach, and as clearly in the sacred writings, when the apostle reminds us that "we are members one of another, and if one member suffer, all the members suffer with it, and if one member rejoices, all the members rejoice with it" — shall be every where understood, and, if we may dare hope for such a result, conscientiously applied and practised upon.

LXXXVIII. — PARTICULAR EXAMPLES OF IMPROVEMENT.

I have spoken of the preparation of the land, by culture, for the deposit of the seed, under the heads of ploughing, subsoiling, paring, deep-stirring, scarifying, and harrowing; but there were two processes going on, in Cornwall, of so peculiar a character that I deem it proper to detail them.

1. Tehidy. — The first was at Tehidy, the residence of Lady Bassett, under the direction of an intelligent and accomplished agriculturist, a gentleman well established in the principles, and familiar with the practices, of agriculture, in the best cultivated districts of Scotland, and who was employed not merely to put the home-estate under a proper course of management, but, by example, counsel, advice, encouragement, and rewards, to assist and induce the tenants on the property to abandon the objectionable and profitless modes of husbandry which they had long followed, and introduce a better system, which the experience of the most improving and best farmers in the country had sanctioned.

An extensive tract of land on the sea-coast was underlaid, about three inches below the surface, with a compact bed of flint stones, of four and six inches in depth, and might indeed be very properly called macadamized. Vegetation on such land was almost hopeless, for the mould, or vegetable matter, on the surface, had little depth, and no plough or cultivator could penetrate this obstinate mass of stones. But this farmer undertook to remove with pickaxes this entire mass of stones, and had accomplished a considerable tract when I had the pleasure to visit it. The piles of stones lay as thick, as and very much larger, than cocks of hay, upon the field, preparatory to their being carted away, for the making or repairing of roads. Under this layer of stones was found a soil which could be brought into, and, under proper manuring, would liberally reward, good cultivation. The Cornish men, who, in the capacity of miners, are accustomed to face difficulties of no ordinary magnitude, and will march up against the brazen walls of a copper mine, where they may pick and hammer away for weeks and months without reward, with as much indifference as they would cut away upon a loaf of stale bread, performed this service with a labor and perseverance worthy of all praise. Under this layer of stones was a soil capable of productive cultivation, and the reward was found in the crops which were growing on a portion of the recovered land. After the stones were removed, the land was subsoiled, and a crop of turnips, manured with guano, was taken. The effects of guano, when the land manured by it was compared with a part of the field manured only with the ashes of the furze, were here most remarkable. The experiment was a brave, and, though labor was at a low rate, it was an expensive one; but as the land was comparatively without value in its former state, the only question in the case was, whether the land, after being redeemed in this way, would be worth the expense of the recovery. Heavy as this expense was, the land became worth a great deal more than it cost. In fact, it was so much land literally created by the process; and its situation, where it was easily accessible, greatly enhanced the value.

2. Scobell's Farm. — The other experiment to which I referred was going on between Penzance and Land's End, on the farm of Colonel Scobell — a farm, in respect to parts of which the culture would seem like going upon a forlorn hope, the land presenting a most forbidding aspect; and yet in its results exhibiting a conclusive test of the best husbandry, by its permanent improvements, and its ample returns for the labor and expense bestowed upon it.

Some parts of Cornwall — where the hospitality of the inhabitants is in an inverse ratio to the quality of the soil — reminded me of a tract of country very well known to many persons in the United States, through which the turnpike-road passes between Lynn and Salem, in Massachusetts, which some one facetiously called the "abomination of desolation," and of which the British prisoners, in passing over it on their way to Boston, in the last war, demanded, with considerable emphasis, "whether that was the ——— " (here using a theological phrase, which it would be quite improper to repeat out of the pulpit) "country for which the Americans were fighting." There is this remarkable difference, however, in favor of Cornwall, that, like some old miser, who seeks to conceal his riches under an appearance of extreme squalidness and destitution, it is underlaid with inexhaustible mineral treasures, as I myself, in a dress befitting the infernal regions, with a lighted torch in my hand, descending by the slippery rounds of a ladder seven hundred feet, and traversing two miles under ground, had the gratification — for so I may call it, since I am once more on the surface — to witness. In this part of the country there is little wood, and no coal, and, for fuel, the inhabitants pare the surface of the land, which seems covered with a thick matted moss and heather, and which, when taken off, leaves under it a mixture of white gravel, and black, peaty mould. This being taken off in spots, the country resembles the face of a man reduced to a skeleton, with his skin pitted and blotched all over with the small-pox. It will be understood that I am speaking only of a part of Cornwall, and, in particular, the mining districts; for in some parts there are spots of eminent fertility, of which the culture is singularly skilful, and the productiveness nowhere exceeded.

Some of the land owned by Colonel Scobell is of the description of which I have spoken. He sells the moss and heather, taken off by, what a native American may properly call, this *scalping* process, at twenty-four pounds per acre; and then, by deep and brave cultivation, and by most ample manuring, at an expense of ten pounds an acre, he brings this very land into productive cultivation. This is what, in New England, we should call adroitly, and, certainly, most honestly and creditably, " turning a penny; " here it is evident it might be designated by a denomination two hundred and forty times larger. After this land is in this way brought to, it would readily let at thirty or forty shillings per acre. After the land has been pared, his process is to drain, subsoil, and manure it, and then he gets excellent crops of turnips, barley, and wheat.

All circumstances considered, the whole management of this farm seemed to me excellent, and it will not be deemed out of place if I now speak of it, since the subject is before me.

The farm embraces an extent of some hundreds of acres, of a gravelly soil, and much of it composed of rotten and decomposed granite rock. It required no small resolution and courage to take such a tract of country in hand, with a determination to make its cultivation profitable; for, though I have referred to some cases in which the returns from the sale of the furze and heather upon it were very large, it could scarcely be expected that such a process of profit was applicable to a large extent.

The farm is not in what would be called "pink style," and nothing is done for show. The fixtures, though very convenient, are of a plain and inexpensive character. He keeps 150 head of neat stock; he raises all his calves; he fats a large number of swine, of which he has an excellent breed, being a mixture and cross of the Essex, the Neapolitan, and a boar procured from the United States, which appeared to be a chance animal with excellent points. His cattle are of the improved Durham, which seemed not the kind best adapted to the short pastures of the country, and were not in good condition, having, as he said, suffered from the extreme drought which had prevailed during the summer, and of which it was quite evident the stock in all that country had felt the severity.

His stock are kept in the house the greater part of the year, and fed upon steamed food. His swine are generally killed at one year old, and weigh from fifteen to seventeen scores of pounds; and when kept until two years old, he calculates them to weigh about thirty-five scores of pounds. He has killed those which weighed thirty-six score. They run in the pasture upon grass only, "with no meat," — that is, no grain or meal, — from April until October. They are then put up and fed with steamed potatoes, mixed with barley meal, and given to them while warm; and twelve gallons of barley meal are deemed sufficient for the fattening of a hog. His swine, when put up for fattening, are fed several times a day. Indeed, the hind watches them constantly, and supplies them with food as often as their troughs are emptied.

The cattle are tied in stalls with chains. Provision is made, by a movable trough, to let in water to them, so that they are not turned out except for occasional airing. The stable and barns are upon the side of a hill, and the cattle are kept upon a lower story.

The upper part of the barn is devoted to the washing and steaming of the food; for all of it, the chaff as well as the vegetables, are steamed for the stock. The turnips and potatoes are placed in a large trough or tub, directly under a full current of water, coming from a drained field, which falls some short distance directly upon them, and immediately passes off, carrying the dirt with it. The potatoes are steamed in barrels. The barrels are suspended in an iron half hoop, and are swung back and forward by a crane. They turn upon a pivot, and have but one head in. They are easily swung round to the trough, where the potatoes are washed, and then filled. A movable bottom, full of holes, is then placed in the open head, to prevent the potatoes from falling out, and they are again swung round and dropped upon a platform, and a steam-pipe, opened by a cock, introduced under the bottom, which effectually steams them in fifteen minutes. They are then again attached to the lever, swung round, inverted, the movable head taken out, again inverted, and the cooked contents poured into a trough, and the barrel again filled and cooked as before; so that, from the beginning to the end of the process, they can scarcely be said to be touched with the hand.

The turnips, with their tops on, are dropped from the cart into the washing trough, and, when washed, are shoved along, and thrown into steaming boxes level with the floor, on which they are washed. These boxes have a false bottom, or grating of iron, under which the steam is introduced by a pipe, and, after being sufficiently cooked, the end of the box is dropped, and they are easily shovelled into a cooling box, set still lower than the other, for their reception. The chaff is steamed in a large closet. All the hay for the cattle is cut by a machine, on an upper floor, and easily shovelled into this closet, where it is steamed by a pipe introduced from the common steam machine. Every thing is contrived to simplify and relieve labor. The food is then put into barrows, and wheeled, through the passages, to the different stock to be fed. The water, which comes from the turnips when steamed, is always saved, and, being mixed with a small quantity of barley meal, is given to the store hogs. It will ferment if left to stand, and is deemed quite nutritious. Oatmeal is used for the stock, when barley meal cannot be obtained, and is deemed much better.

The potatoes and turnips are all washed, and shovelled, and steamed, by a single young woman, stout, healthy, active, and energetic, not in appearance much to my taste, as "a fine gentleman," but entitled to respect for her cheerfulness and good-humor, and for the spirit and fidelity with which she performed her humble duty. Her master spoke of her in the kindest manner, and, in looking at her in her laborious service, I could not help thinking of that noble line, —

"Act well your part; there all the honor lies."

The manure of the stock is thrown into the yards. Different kinds are mixed, and some hogs are kept among it, who, by stirring it constantly, prevent its fermentation. The liquid manure is all saved in tanks, and, in some cases, is, with great success, led over the fields.

With the water obtained from the drainage of the land, Mr. Scobell has created a mill-power, which turns a wheel twenty-eight feet in diameter. With this is connected a threshing machine, a winnowing machine, and a flour and grain mill, for the purposes of the establishment; and the same power is applied to a mill for crushing and sifting bones, to a chaff-cutter, and to a grindstone.

From the situation of the ground, likewise, on the side-hill, Mr. Scobell is enabled to irrigate portions of his land, which he does with great advantage. From the rocky character of the country, the fences on the farm are stone walls, a very desirable mode of disposing of the surplus stone in the fields; and his gates upon the farm are of iron, at the moderate cost of 7s. 6d. per gate. They appeared, however, quite too light and frail for endurance.

The fixtures on the farm are of the rudest description, and no pretensions are made to neatness or exactness; but every thing seemed well cared for; and for economical arrangements, for effecting the purposes intended, for a management combining the lowest scale of expenditure with the highest scale of profit, few more successful examples have ever come under my observation. The courageous enterprise, which could boldly face the obstacles to be encountered in this most inauspicious tract of country, would qualify a man for a much higher military commission than that which its proprietor had borne, and the sound judgment and skill which suggested and planned the improvements, and carried them out with such a creditable economy of labor, are well worthy of commendation.

LXXXIX. — CORNWALL AND THE LAND'S END.

Many of the practices prevailing in Cornwall, with the modes of speaking, and forms of expression among the people, are so nearly allied to those of New England, as to satisfy me that we must have imported them from this part of the world, and that scions from Cornwall are thickly ingrafted in our pilgrim land. I wish we might inherit, in the fullest measure, the spirit of full-souled hospitality which I found among them. I have only to regret that the rules which I have prescribed to myself forbid my saying what I would. But the feelings of grateful and affectionate respect are not the less strong for being suppressed; and my Cornwall friends, from their own generous natures, may be assured that my sense of their constant and disinterested kindness is all which they themselves would desire it should be.

On this excursion into Cornwall, I went to the Land's End, and planted my foot on the very last rocky point, extending into the sea, which I was able to reach. I had but a few moments before passed a traveller's home, with the significant sign, "The First and the Last House in England." Nothing can be more picturesque than this rude and rock-bound shore, with its white-fringed ruffle of surf, as far as the eye can reach, and a few scattered rocks at a distance, over which the swelling waves were profusely pouring their showers of diamonds, so treacherous to the home-bound mariner, so picturesque and beautiful to the landsman, as he suns himself upon the grassy shore, watching the distant sails scattered upon the wide expanse, full-freighted with human life and hopes, glittering in the sunlight, and floating like water-fowl in their native element.

As I stood upon the far-jutting point of the promontory, and felt that no intervening country separated me from the land of my birth, and the home of what is most dear to me, I found my head growing dizzy, my heart beating as though it were struggling to get out, and my cheeks quite wet, perhaps with the spray; and I could only find relief in sending a thousand unspoken messages of affection, and in more earnest prayers for the prosperity of the land, and the loved ones whom I had left behind. May the winds waft the former to their objects, and the last find a response in heaven!

TABLE,

By John Morton,

Showing the Distance travelled by a Horse, in ploughing or scarifying an Acre of Land; also the Quantity of Land worked in a Day, at the Rate of sixteen and eighteen Miles per Day of nine Hours. —(*Johnson and Shaw's Farmer's Almanac*, vol. i. p. 191.)

Breadth of Furrow-slice or Scarifier.	Space travelled in ploughing an Acre.	Extent ploughed per Day, at the Rate of		Breadth of Furrow-slice or Scarifier.	Space travelled in ploughing an Acre.	Extent ploughed per Day, at the Rate of	
Inches.	*Miles.*	18 *Miles.* *Acres.*	16 *Miles.* *Acres.*	*Inches.*	*Miles.*	18 *Miles.* *Acres.*	16 *Miles.* *Acres.*
7	$14\frac{1}{8}$	$1\frac{1}{4}$	$1\frac{1}{8}$	34	$2\frac{9}{10}$	$6\frac{1}{5}$	$5\frac{1}{2}$
8	$12\frac{1}{4}$	$1\frac{1}{2}$	$1\frac{1}{4}$	35	$2\frac{4}{5}$	$6\frac{1}{3}$	$5\frac{3}{5}$
9	11	$1\frac{3}{5}$	$1\frac{1}{2}$	36	$2\frac{3}{4}$	$6\frac{1}{2}$	$5\frac{4}{5}$
10	$9\frac{9}{10}$	$1\frac{4}{5}$	$1\frac{3}{5}$	37	$2\frac{2}{3}$	$6\frac{2}{3}$	6
11	9	2	$1\frac{3}{4}$	38	$2\frac{3}{5}$	$6\frac{9}{10}$	$6\frac{1}{8}$
12	$8\frac{1}{4}$	$2\frac{1}{5}$	$1\frac{9}{10}$	39	$2\frac{1}{2}$	$7\frac{1}{8}$	$6\frac{1}{3}$
13	$7\frac{1}{2}$	$2\frac{1}{3}$	$2\frac{1}{10}$	40	$2\frac{1}{2}$	$7\frac{1}{3}$	$6\frac{1}{2}$
14	7	$2\frac{1}{2}$	$2\frac{1}{4}$	41	$2\frac{2}{5}$	$7\frac{1}{2}$	$6\frac{2}{3}$
15	$6\frac{1}{2}$	$2\frac{3}{4}$	$2\frac{2}{5}$	42	$2\frac{1}{3}$	$7\frac{2}{3}$	$6\frac{3}{4}$
16	$6\frac{1}{6}$	$2\frac{9}{10}$	$2\frac{3}{5}$	43	$2\frac{6}{20}$	$7\frac{4}{5}$	7
17	$5\frac{3}{4}$	$3\frac{1}{10}$	$2\frac{3}{4}$	44	$2\frac{1}{4}$	8	$7\frac{1}{10}$
18	$5\frac{1}{2}$	$3\frac{1}{4}$	$2\frac{9}{10}$	45	$2\frac{1}{5}$	$8\frac{1}{6}$	$7\frac{1}{4}$
19	$5\frac{1}{4}$	$3\frac{1}{2}$	$3\frac{1}{10}$	46	$2\frac{1}{6}$	$8\frac{1}{3}$	$7\frac{2}{5}$
20	$4\frac{9}{10}$	$3\frac{3}{5}$	$3\frac{1}{4}$	47	$2\frac{1}{10}$	$8\frac{2}{3}$	$7\frac{3}{5}$
21	$4\frac{7}{10}$	$3\frac{4}{5}$	$3\frac{1}{3}$	48	$2\frac{1}{12}$	$8\frac{3}{4}$	$7\frac{3}{4}$
22	$4\frac{1}{2}$	4	$3\frac{1}{2}$	49	2	$8\frac{9}{10}$	$7\frac{9}{10}$
23	$4\frac{1}{4}$	$4\frac{1}{5}$	$3\frac{7}{10}$	50	2	$9\frac{1}{10}$	$8\frac{1}{10}$
24	$4\frac{1}{8}$	$4\frac{1}{3}$	$3\frac{9}{10}$	51	$1\frac{9}{10}$	$9\frac{2}{5}$	$8\frac{1}{4}$
25	4	$4\frac{1}{2}$	4	52	$1\frac{9}{10}$	$9\frac{1}{2}$	$8\frac{2}{5}$
26	$3\frac{4}{5}$	$4\frac{3}{4}$	$4\frac{1}{5}$	53	$1\frac{9}{10}$	$9\frac{3}{4}$	$8\frac{1}{2}$
27	$3\frac{3}{5}$	$4\frac{9}{10}$	$4\frac{1}{3}$	54	$1\frac{4}{5}$	$9\frac{4}{5}$	$8\frac{9}{10}$
28	$3\frac{1}{2}$	$5\frac{1}{8}$	$4\frac{1}{2}$	55	$1\frac{4}{5}$	10	9
29	$3\frac{1}{2}$	$5\frac{1}{4}$	$4\frac{3}{5}$	56	$1\frac{3}{4}$	$10\frac{1}{4}$	9
30	$3\frac{1}{3}$	$5\frac{3}{5}$	$4\frac{4}{5}$	57	$1\frac{3}{4}$	$10\frac{2}{5}$	$9\frac{1}{5}$
31	$3\frac{1}{5}$	$5\frac{3}{5}$	5	58	$1\frac{7}{10}$	$10\frac{3}{5}$	$9\frac{1}{3}$
32	$3\frac{1}{10}$	$5\frac{4}{5}$	$5\frac{1}{4}$	59	$1\frac{7}{10}$	$10\frac{3}{4}$	$9\frac{1}{2}$
33	3	6	$5\frac{1}{3}$	60	$1\frac{3}{5}$	$10\frac{9}{10}$	$9\frac{7}{10}$

END OF THE FIRST VOLUME.

www.ingramcontent.com/pod-product-compliance
Lightning Source LLC
LaVergne TN
LVHW021307110826
845150LV00003B/504

* 9 7 8 1 4 2 5 5 5 8 6 3 5 *